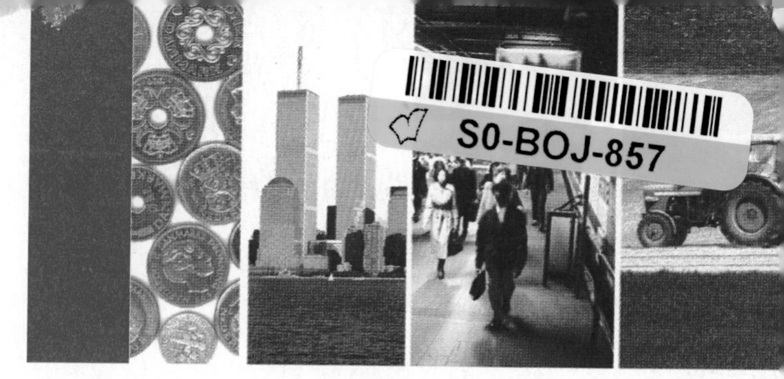

PRINCIPLES OF MICROECONOMICS

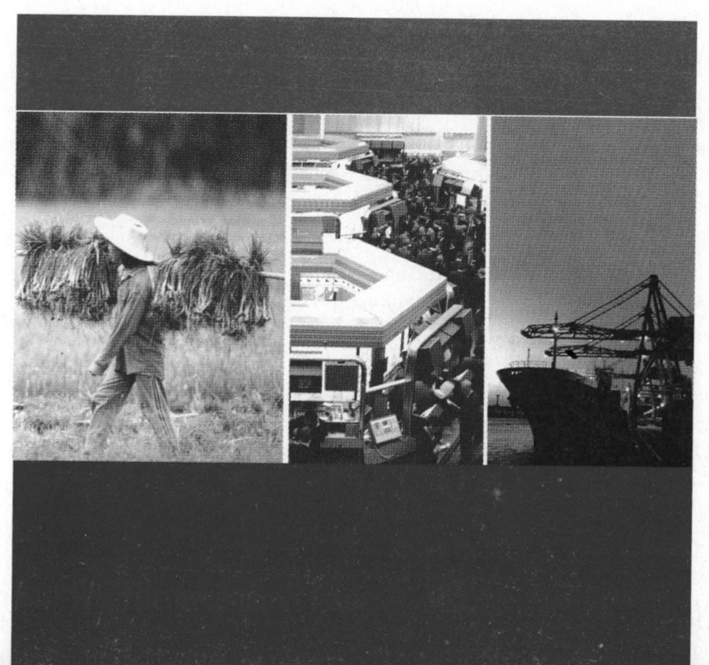

The Addison-Wesley Series in Economics

Abel/Bernanke
Macroeconomics

Berndt
The Practice of Econometrics

Bierman/Fernandez
Game Theory with Economic Applications

Binger/Hoffman
Microeconomics with Calculus

Boyer
Principles of Transportation Economics

Branson
Macroeconomic Theory and Policy

Bruce
Public Finance and the American Economy

Burgess
The Economics of Regulation and Antitrust

Byrns/Stone
Economics

Carlton/Perloff
Modern Industrial Organization

Caves/Frankel/Jones
World Trade and Payments: An Introduction

Chapman
Environmental Economics: Theory, Application, and Policy

Cooter/Ulen
Law and Economics

Downs
An Economic Theory of Democracy

Eaton/Mishkin
Online Readings to Accompany The Economics of Money, Banking, and Financial Markets

Ehrenberg/Smith
Modern Labor Economics

Ekelund/Tollison
Economics: Private Markets and Public Choice

Fusfeld
The Age of the Economist

Gerber
International Economics

Ghiara
Learning Economics: A Practical Workbook

Gordon
Macroeconomics

Gregory
Essentials of Economics

Gregory/Stuart
Russian and Soviet Economic Performance and Structure

Hartwick/Olewiler
The Economics of Natural Resource Use

Hubbard
Money, the Financial System, and the Economy

Hughes/Cain
American Economic History

Husted/Melvin
International Economics

Jehle/Reny
Advanced Microeconomic Theory

Klein
Mathematical Methods for Economics

Krugman/Obstfeld
International Economics: Theory and Policy

Laidler
The Demand for Money: Theories, Evidence, and Problems

Lesser/Dodds/Zerbe
Environmental Economics and Policy

Lipsey/Courant/Ragan
Economics

McCarty
Dollars and Sense: An Introduction to Economics

Melvin
International Money and Finance

Miller
Economics Today

Miller/Benjamin/North
The Economics of Public Issues

Mills/Hamilton
Urban Economics

Mishkin
The Economics of Money, Banking, and Financial Markets

Parkin
Economics

Parkin/Bade
Economics in Action Software

Perloff
Microeconomics

Phelps
Health Economics

Riddell/Shackelford/Stamos
Economics: A Tool for Critically Understanding Society

Ritter/Silber/Udell
Principles of Money, Banking, and Financial Markets

Rohlf
Introduction to Economic Reasoning

Ruffin/Gregory
Principles of Economics

Sargent
Rational Expectations and Inflation

Scherer
Industry Structure, Strategy, and Public Policy

Schotter
Microeconomics: A Modern Approach

Sherman/Kolk
Business Cycles and Forecasting

Smith
Case Studies in Economic Development

Studenmund
Using Econometrics: A Practical Guide

Su
Economic Fluctuations and Forecasting

Tietenberg
Environmental and Natural Resource Economics

Tietenberg
Environmental Economics and Policy

Todaro
Economic Development

Waldman/Jensen
Industrial Organization: Theory and Practice

PRINCIPLES OF MICROECONOMICS

SEVENTH EDITION

ROY J. RUFFIN — UNIVERSITY OF HOUSTON
RESEARCH ASSOCIATE
FEDERAL RESERVE BANK OF DALLAS

PAUL R. GREGORY — UNIVERSITY OF HOUSTON

Boston San Francisco New York
London Toronto Sydney Tokyo Singapore Madrid
Mexico City Munich Paris Cape Town Hong Kong Montreal

Sponsoring Editor: Victoria Warneck
Project Manager: Rebecca Ferris
Developmental Editor: Barbara A. Conover
Senior Production Supervisor: Juliet Silveri
Supplements Editor: Meredith Gertz
Design Supervisor: Regina Hagen
Text Designer: Leslie Haimes
Cover Designer: Joyce Cosentino
Photo Researcher: Sara Owen
Manufacturing Manager: Hugh Crawford
Production Services: Lachina Publishing Services, Inc.
Printer and Binder: Quebecor World, Taunton

Library of Congress Cataloging-in-Publication Data

Ruffin, Roy, 1938–
Principles of microeconomics / Roy J. Ruffin, Paul R. Gregory.—7th ed.
p. cm.
Includes bibliographical references and indexes.
ISBN 0-321-07731-8
1. Microeconomics. I. Gregory, Paul R. II. Title.
HB172. R75 2000
338.5—dc21 00-063935
CIP

3 4 5 6 7 8 9 10—QWT—04 03

to our wives
Barbara Ann Ruffin and Annemarie Gregory

Brief Contents

In this volume, Chapter 22 is followed by Chapter 35.

Detailed Contents

In this volume, Chapter 22 is followed by Chapter 35.

PREFACE

The seventh edition of *Principles of Microeconomics* is being written in the first year of a new millennium booming with interest in economics. Whether the stock market had a good day or a bad day is reported in major news broadcasts before the latest news on the presidential campaign or a famine in Africa. Alan Greenspan, just a few years ago a figure recognized by only a few people, has become a household name. Meetings of the Federal Reserve, under his direction, are awaited with bated breath by taxi drivers and waitresses as well as corporate executives. We have become a nation of millions of owners of stock. The value of the shares of stock owned by families has replaced the family home, for the first time, as our major source of personal wealth. We must choose between investing in high-tech companies that have yet to earn a profit and traditional blue-chip companies—Coca-Cola, ExxonMobil—that have been the stalwarts of the economy in the past. Young men and women in spectacles and blue jeans—not the distinguished gray haired board members of the past—now call the shots of industry and commerce. Bill Gates's image appears more often on the covers of weekly news magazines than does that of the president of the United States.

We are told by pundits and economists that we have entered a new era of economics—the New Economy—thanks largely to these young blue-jeans-clad entrepreneurs, who began their businesses in garages, creating the hardware, software, computer games, voice-recognizing equipment, and other new means of distributing information and entertainment that characterize everyday life early in the twenty-first century. We are told that we no longer have to fear economic decline because nothing can halt our technological advance in a world in which information is becoming cheaper day by day. Our economy can grow at a fast pace, with low unemployment, and with little or no inflation. The economic rules have changed. Our last economic downturn ended in mid-1991; thus, the economic expansion continuing at the end of 2000 is the longest in post–World War II history.

Change has been the major constant throughout the two-decade existence of *Principles of Microeconomics*. Economics must evaluate evidence as it unfolds: Are we really in a New Economy dictated by technological advances that cannot be halted? Or are we going through a rather fortunate, but short-run, period of good fortune, which, like all good parties, must end? Past editions of this book related the ideas of great economists who sought to explain the major economic events that changed our lives. We now turn to those, such as Austrian economist Joseph Schumpeter, who sought to explain how a New Economy could be created.

We are strong believers in the scientific method. We must confront competing theories with the facts and declare which facts are consistent with the theories. An economic theory that is not supported by the facts has a short life in this book. We do not hesitate to tell readers which theories are not working.

We regard economics as the root discipline of the social sciences. It has a century of tradition. Economic science was formed by major events and by the major scholars who explained these events. To attempt to explain the state of economic knowledge without discussing its Defining Moments and the great thinkers who explained these defining moments would be like viewing a great play by starting with the final act. We are prosperous today because almost 250 years ago an *Industrial Revolution* began in Great Britain and quickly spread to the European continent and to North America. The Industrial Revolution combined new economic institutions with the fruits of the beginnings of modern science and technology. The *rise of socialism* in Russia in 1917 and its final collapse in 1991 had a profound effect on the way one-third of the world's population lived at the peak of the socialist experiment. The way in which we eradicate its effects will influence the shape of our new century. The *Great Depression* of the 1930s, which saw a collapse of the American economy, left a profound impact on those who lived through it, prompting a great fear of an eventual replay. We live in a world of economic *globalization.* Our major industrial concerns operate without national boundaries. Our employer is as likely to be a multinational concern as the local department store. Most of the products we buy were made or assembled, in whole or in part, in other countries. The Volkswagen or Toyota you have just purchased was probably assembled in the United States by U.S. workers. Blockbuster films, such as *Titanic,* earn more revenues in other countries than in the United States.

It is easier to understand and explain the defining moments of economics in retrospect. We usually need a considerable amount of time to confirm that an event is of sufficient importance to be a Defining Moment, and it also takes time for economists to agree on its causes. The final—and new—Defining Moment in this book is the *information revolution,* an event of the past two to three decades associated with the increasing power and falling costs of personal computers, linked to new forms of communication in such a way as to allow the cheap and effective transfer of information. The information revolution allows one employee to do the work previously done by twenty skilled employees; it allows consumers to buy airline tickets, CDs, clothing, and even stocks by computer; it allows large manufacturing concerns to search the Internet for the lowest priced materials. In a word, the information revolution has significantly lowered the cost of doing business on a worldwide basis. It will make it possible for more of us to work at home and for software specialists in India to telecommunicate to work in Germany or Spain. We cannot judge the ultimate effects of the information revolution—in particular what its limits are—but we do know enough to conclude that this is a new Defining Moment of economics.

In addition to offering the same spirit of freshness, the same cutting-edge philosophy of the first edition of *Principles of Microeconomics,* the seventh edition carefully consolidates the economic theories and policies of the past and present as we prepare for the economic changes of the future.

New to This Edition

With the publication of the seventh edition of *Principles of Microeconomics,* we remain the most modern and up-to-date economics text on the market. We discuss both traditional and new topics at a level accessible to the reader. New to this edition are the following updates and refinements:

- The popular Defining Moments of economics have been retained and are used throughout. A fifth (and new) Defining Moment—the information revolution—has been added and is used in connection with the role of the Internet and as an explanation for the New Economy.
- This is the first edition of *Principles of Microeconomics* written with the Internet. Most data tables and charts are provided with an Internet reference to guide students in finding economic data. Many examples are drawn from the Internet as well, again instructing students on how to apply the Internet to the study of economics. The use of the Internet means that the data are more up-to-date than was possible in previous editions. Much of the data go through the year 2000.
- The text has always been praised for its many examples, which make clear and give real-world relevance to economic concepts and theories. Classic examples, such as the Pin Factory and the Demand for M&Ms, have been retained. However, three-quarters of the examples are new, relating to current issues such as third-party payment and medical costs, scalping, the Microsoft case, organization of the Internet through fees or advertising, and intraindustry trade. A large number of examples relate to the Internet and to a globalized service economy, rather than to the bricks-and-mortar economy of yesterday.
- Chapter 5, Unintended Consequences, introduces students to the unintended consequences of economic actions, marginal analysis, and to strategic behavior. These topics are introduced early because they have become an integral part of the study of microeconomics. In addition, a new section on Third-Party Payments uses as its example the important topic of health care.
- In Chapter 10, Perfect Competition, a new section on buffet pricing and its application to the Internet emphasizes the importance of the technological revolution.
- The topic of dynamic competition is introduced in Chapter 12, Competition, Efficiency, and Innovation.
- Streamlined Chapter 13, The Game of Oligopoly, contains a new section on Measurement and continues to include its unique summary comparison of the four market forms.
- Chapter 14, Regulation and Antitrust, has been heavily updated to discuss the very latest merger and antitrust information.
- Chapter 19, Inequality, Income Distribution, and Poverty, contains an up-to-date discussion of the economic impact of welfare reform.

Pedagogy. As in the sixth edition, each chapter opens with an Insight, a real-world anecdote alluding to a major concept in the chapter; text terms and concepts are highlighted by simple color screens; and the end-of-chapter summary, key term list, and questions and problems aid students as they review the chapter. A number of pedagogical tools are new to this edition:

- Chapter Learning Objectives: Each chapter begins with a list of learning objectives that offers students a guide to major concepts as they proceed through the chapter.
- Chapter Puzzle/Puzzle Answered: A puzzle related to a major concept of each chapter is posed at the beginning of the chapter; the answer is given within the end-of-chapter pedagogy.

- Internet-related Questions and Problems: Each end-of-chapter Questions and Problems section now includes several questions related to an Internet site that students must investigate in order to compute the answers.

Each chapter continues to include timely and relevant examples for understanding the economy of the new millenium. Among the many new topics are:

- Should We Organize the Internet by Market or by Plan? (1)
- Trading on the NASDAQ Stock Market (4)
- Third-Party Payments and Medical Costs (5)
- The Importance of Substitutes: The Importance of Call Forwarding (6)
- The Tulip Market—A Classic Market Bubble (8)
- Entry Is Easy on the Internet—Changed Conditions in Retailing (10)
- America Online—A Dominant Firm (11)
- Standard Oil vs. Microsoft (14)
- Scalping and the Theory of Supply and Demand (15)
- How to Deal with Trash (20)
- The Importance of Intraindustry Trade (35)

Organization

Principles of Microeconomics, Seventh Edition, is divided into six parts. Part I (Chapters 1–5) introduces the basic concepts of economics that provide a firm foundation for both microeconomics and macroeconomics. In addition to introducing the basic economic methodology, Chapter 1 describes five Defining Moments of economics—the Industrial Revolution, the rise and collapse of socialism, the Great Depression, globalization, and the information revolution—each of which has had a major influence on both economic theory and economic policy. An appendix to Chapter 1 explains how to read graphs and avoid distortion pitfalls. Chapters 2–4 contain the standard topics of scarcity, opportunity costs, the production possibilities frontier, the law of diminishing returns, the law of comparative advantage, the workings of the price system, and the laws of demand and supply. Discussing the means and the ends to economic decision making, Chapter 5 introduces the topics of marginal analysis, incentives, games, and unintended consequences—tools and themes that are used throughout the text.

Part II begins the microeconomics core of the text, with ten chapters on product markets (Chapters 6–15). Chapter 6 covers price elasticities of demand and supply as well as income and cross-price elasticities of demand. Chapter 7 deals with demand and utility and includes an appendix on indifference curves. Business organization, corporate finance, and financial markets are discussed in Chapter 8, and short-run and long-run costs are explained in Chapter 9, which includes an appendix on the least-cost method of production. The standard market models of perfect competition, monopoly and monopolistic competition, and oligopoly are covered in Chapters 10–13; Chapter 13 includes both a section devoted to game theory and a summary comparison of all four market models. Chapter 14 discusses antitrust law and regulation, and Chapter 15 introduces the role of information costs.

Factor markets are presented in the four-chapter Part III (Chapters 16–19). Chapter 16 gives a theoretical overview of the workings of factor markets, and Chapters 17 and 18 focus on specific factor markets of labor, and interest, rent, and profit. Chapter 19 examines the determinants of income distribution and poverty.

Microeconomic issues are the focus of Part IV (Chapter 20–22). Chapter 20 explains the economics of natural resources and of market failure (public goods and externalities). Chapter 21 focuses on the issue of taxation and Chapter 22 discusses public choice. Final Chapter 35 shows how the law of comparative advantage applies on an international scale.

Suggestions for Course Planning

Principles of Microeconomics is intended for a one-semester sequence in microeconomics that is traditionally taught as a first- or second-year college course. The book is available as part of a combined hardbound volume and as a separate softbound volume. This softbound volume can also be used for an intensive one-quarter course, building around the 19 core chapters listed below as time and interest allow.

1. Economics and the World Around Us: Defining Moments
2. Unlimited Wants, Scarce Resources
3. The Price System and the Economic Problem
4. Demand and Supply
5. Unintended Consequences
6. Elasticity of Demand and Supply
7. Demand and Utility
8. Economic Organization: Property Rights and the Firm
9. Productivity and Costs
10. Perfect Competition
11. Monopoly and Monopolistic Competition
13. The Game of Oligopoly
14. Regulation and Antitrust
15. The Economics of Information
16. Factor Markets
17. Labor: The Human Factor
18. Interest, Rent, and Profit
19. Inequality, Income Distribution, and Poverty
20. Market Failure, the Environment, and Natural Resources

Supplements

This book has a complete package of supplements, which includes an *Instructor's Manual, Study Guide, Test Bank,* companion Web site, and an Instructor's Resource CD-ROM.

The *Instructor's Manual* was revised by Henry Thompson of Auburn University. It supplies the instructor with many teaching tools, including additional numerical examples and real-world illustrations not contained in the text. A chapter outline gives a brief overview of the material in the chapter to assist the instructor in preparing lecture outlines and in seeing the logical development of the chapter. Special-approaches sections tell the instructor how this chapter is different from corresponding chapters in other textbooks and explain why a topic was treated differently in this text or why an entirely new topic not covered by other texts was introduced in this chapter. Optional-material sections give the instructor a ranking of priorities for the topics in the chapter and enable the instructor to trim the size of each chapter (if necessary). Each chapter also includes key points to learn, teaching hints, special projects, bad habits to unlearn, additional essay questions, and answers to the end-of-chapter "Questions and Problems."

The *Study Guide* was written by Jeffrey Parker of Reed College. The analytical nature of the *Study Guide* should challenge students and help them to better prepare for exams. The *Study Guide* supplements the text by providing summaries of critical concepts and by taking students step by step through a review of each key graph and equation presented in the text. It contains multiple-choice and true/false questions and, unlike other study guides, not only lists the answers but also gives *explanations for the answers*. In addition to objective questions, each chapter of the *Study Guide* also contains analytical problems and essay questions. Again, the *Study Guide* provides not only the answers to the questions, but also the step-by-step process for arriving at the answers.

The *Test Bank,* prepared by Brandt Stevens of the California State Energy Commission, contains 3000 multiple-choice questions, most of which have already been class tested. For each chapter in the text, the *Test Bank* contains four different tests (coded A, B, C, or D).

Fully compatible with Windows NT, 95, and 98 and Macintosh computers, the Instructor's Resource CD-ROM contains PowerPoint slides of all the figures and select tables, word processing files for the entire contents of the *Instructor's Manual,* and computerized *Test Bank* files. The easy-to-use testing software (TestGen-EQ with QuizMaster-EQ for Windows and Macintosh) is a valuable test preparation tool that allows professors to view, edit, and add questions.

The text's companion Web site is available at http://www.awl.com/ruffin_gregory. The site offers self-administered multiple-choice quizzes and numerous Web links for each chapter. For easy navigation, the Internet Connection questions from the text are also on the Web site. The companion Web site system provides an online syllabus builder that allows instructors to create a calendar of assignments for each class and to track student activity with an electronic gradebook. For added convenience, many of the instructor supplements are available for downloading from the site, including the PowerPoint lecture presentation, computerized *Test Bank* files, and *Instructor's Manual.* Please contact your sales representative for the instructor resources password and information on obtaining the Web content in WebCT and BlackBoard versions.

To the Student

Albert Einstein, perhaps the greatest scientist of the twentieth century, began his study of relativity by imagining what it would be like to be sitting on a ray of light shooting out into the universe at the speed of light. Few scientists would have had Einstein's brilliance even to imagine what it would be like, and it is clear that Einstein would never personally be able to sit on a ray of light traveling through the universe. As a student of economics, you find yourself in a much more favorable position than Einstein. You are an immediate participant in the universe of economics in several capacities. You have a budget, probably limited, that you must spend on a limited number of things. You already know how you will behave when the price of that leather jacket, which you could not afford, goes on sale at 40 percent off. You know that when the price of gas rises to above $2 per gallon, you'll drive less. As many of you have jobs, you know what it is like to look for a job, what is required for you to change your job or quit, perhaps what it is like to be fired. A rare few of you who have started a business know the importance of profits and the ever-present existence of competition for customers. Those of you who have bought a home or a car on credit know that the interest rate clearly affects your cost of ownership. In your own buying, you cannot avoid noticing that more and more of the things you buy were produced in another country. Even if you buy a Toyota or a Volkswagen, you cannot be sure if it was produced at home or abroad.

You also know that what goes on at a macro level affects you and the way you conduct your lives. Young readers, who may be concerned that they will not receive social security payments when they retire, may decide that they need to save more. Many of you own stock or are contemplating buying stock when you have some extra money. You know that these stocks will rise if general economic performance is good and fall if general economic performance is bad. You know, as well, that chances of getting a good job upon graduation depend on whether the economy is booming or busting.

Unlike the authors of this book, you have probably grown up with computers and computer games. You are accustomed to finding information not in the library but on the World Wide Web. You are accustomed to buying airline tickets or the latest CDs through a virtual shopping site. You chat with your friends not by phone but online. On your job, you most likely begin your day by turning on your computer, not by opening the cash register. When you check out groceries, the checker scans each item rather than entering the price by hand. With such personal experience with computers, the Internet, and other technological advances, you can well understand that the information superhighway has changed the way in which our economy works, perhaps so much so that we should call it, as some do, the New Economy.

Textbook authors must adapt to change as well. This seventh edition is the first true "Internet" version. Not only is the book about the effect of the information revolution on the economy; it also makes active use of the Internet. Most data sources are drawn directly from such Web sites as Economagic; many of the examples are drawn from articles discovered on the Web. You are asked at the end of each chapter to do several Web-based exercises. The WWW makes this edition better for students in a number of ways: First, the Web provides much more up-to-date data. Most of text's data go through the year 2000, the year in which this book is being written. Second, the book gives you valuable Web sites for gathering data or information for subsequent courses in economics. Third, the text itself delves specifically into the issue of how we are to organize the economics of the Web by discussing matters such as the proposed breakup of Microsoft and whether the Web will be paid for by advertising or by user fees.

Economics is valuable only if it explains the real world. Economics should be able to answer specific questions such as Why are there three major domestic producers of automobiles and hundreds or even thousands of producers of textiles? Why is there a positive association between the growth of the money supply and inflation? Why does the United States export computer software and corn to the rest of the world? Why do restaurants rope off space during less busy hours? If Iowa corn land is the best land for growing corn, why is corn also grown in Texas while some land stands idle in Iowa? Why do interest rates rise when people expect the inflation rate to increase? Why does a rise in interest rates in Germany affect employment in the United States?

Economics cannot be mastered through memorization. Economics relies on economic theories to explain real-world occurrences—for instance, why people tend to buy less when prices rise or why increased government spending may reduce unemployment. An economic theory is a logical explanation of why the facts fit together in a particular way. If the theory were not logical, or if the theory failed to be confirmed by real-world facts, it would be readily discarded by economists.

What we call the modern developments of economics are simply new attempts to explain in a logical manner how the facts bind together. Modern developments have occurred because of the realization that established theories were not doing a good job of explaining the world around us. Fortunately, the major building blocks of modern theory—that people attempt to anticipate the future, that rising prices motivate wealth holders to spend less, that people and businesses gather information and make decisions in a rational manner—rely on commonsense logic.

As you finish the chapters of this text, you should be able to apply the knowledge you have gained of real-world economic behavior to explain any number of events that have already occurred or are yet to occur.

We have also included a number of carefully planned learning aids that should help you master the text.

1. The *Chapter Insight* that opens each chapter provides an economic anecdote related to the important points to be learned in that chapter.
2. *Chapter Learning Objectives* that begin each chapter offer students a guide to major concepts as they proceed through the chapter.
3. A *Chapter Puzzle* related to a major concept of each chapter is posed at the beginning of the chapter; the answer is given at the end of the chapter.

4. *Terms* and their *definitions* are set off in the page design.
5. *Key Ideas*—important economic principles or conclusions—are set off in a blue box.
6. *Boxed examples* allow the student to appreciate how economic concepts apply in real-world settings without disrupting the flow of the text. They supplement the numerous examples already found in the text discussions.
7. A *Summary* of the main points of each chapter is found at the end of each chapter.
8. *Key Terms* that were defined in the chapter are listed at the end of each chapter.
9. *Questions and Problems* that test the reader's understanding of the chapter follow each chapter.
10. *Internet Connection questions* in the end-of-chapter Questions and Problems section direct students to an Internet site in order to compute the answers.
11. A *Glossary*—containing definitions of all key terms defined in the blue shaded boxes in chapters and listed in chapter "Key Terms" sections—appears at the end of the book. Each entry contains the complete economic definition as well as the number of the chapter where the term was first defined.
12. A thorough *Index* catalogs the names, concepts, terms, and topics covered in the book.
13. Statistical data on the major economic variables are found on the front and back inside covers for easy reference.

The *Study Guide* provides extensive review of key concepts and an abundance of drill questions and challenging problems.

Acknowledgments

We are deeply indebted to our colleagues at the University of Houston who had to bear with us in the writing of this book. John Antel, Richard Bean, Michael Ben-Gad, Joel Sailors, Thomas DeGregori, Thomas Mayor, Janet Kohlhase, David Papell, and Roger Sherman gave their time freely on an incredible number of pedagogical points in the teaching of elementary economics. Thanks are also extended to Daniel Y. Lee of Shippensburg University, Steven Rappaport of DeAnza College, Bill Reid of the University of Richmond, and Ed Coen (the Director of Undergraduate Studies at the University of Minnesota) for their valuable comments. To Gary Smith of Pomona College, Calvin Siebert of the University of Iowa, and Allan Meltzer of Carnegie-Mellon University, we are particularly grateful for sharing with us their vast knowledge of macroeconomic issues.

It is impossible to express the depth of our appreciation for the suggestions and contributions of numerous colleagues across the country who reviewed this edition: Nader Asgary, SUNY, Geneseo; Antonio Bos, Tusculum College; Robert Carlsson, University of South Carolina; Marc Chopin, Louisiana Tech University; John Dorsey, University of Maryland, College Park; Erick Elder, University of Arkansas, Little Rock; Scott Fausti, South Dakota State University; Steven Francis, Holy Cross College; Rajeev Goel, Illinois State University; Richard Hergenrather, Whitworth College; Philip King, San Francisco State University; Malcolm Robinson, Thomas More College; and Mark Strazicich, University of Central Florida.

In addition, we acknowledge the suggestions of reviewers of earlier editions. Their contribution to the ongoing evolution of the text is invaluable:

David Abel, Mankato State University; Jack Adams, University of Arkansas, Little Rock; Mark Aldrich, Smith College; Ken Alexander, Michigan Technical University; Susan Alexander, College of St. Thomas; Richard G. Anderson, Ohio State University; Richard K. Anderson, Texas A&M University; Ian Bain, University of Minnesota; King Banaian, St. Cloud State University; A. K. Barakeh, University of South Alabama; Daniel Biederman, University of North Dakota; Geoffrey Black, Bates College; George Bittlingmayer, University of Michigan; Robert Borengasser, St. Mary's College; Ronald Brandolini, Valencia Community College; Wallace Broome, Rhode Island Junior College; Pamela J. Brown, California State University, Northridge; William Brown, California State University, Northridge; Dale Bumpass, Sam Houston State University; James Burnell, College of Wooster; Louis Cain, Loyola University of Chicago; Anthony Campolo, Columbus Technical Institute; Than Van Cao, Eastern Montana College; Kathleen A. Carroll, University of Maryland, Baltimore County; Shirley Cassing, University of Pittsburgh; Harold Christenson, Centenary College of Louisiana; Robert E. Christiansen, Colby College; Richard Clarke, University of Wisconsin, Madison; M. O. Clement, Dartmouth College; John Conant, Indiana State University; Barbara J. Craig, Oberlin College; Jim Davis, Golden Gate University; Larry De Brock, University of Illinois, Urbana; David Denslow, University of Florida; John Devereux, University of Miami (Florida); Tim Deyak, Louisiana State University, Baton Rouge; Michael Dowd, University of Toledo; James Dunlevy, University of Miami (of Ohio); Mary E. Edwards, St. Cloud State University; Anne Eicke, Illinois State University, Normal; Charles J. Ellard, The University of Texas, Pan American; Herb Elliott, Allan Hancock College; Michael Ellis, Kent State University; Randy Ellis, Boston University; Sharon Erenburg, Michigan State University; Gisella Escoe, University of Cincinnati; Andrew W. Foshee, McNeese State University; Ralph Fowler, Diablo Valley College; Dan Friedman, University of California, Los Angeles; Joe Fuhrig, Golden Gate University; Janet Furman, Tulane University; Charles Gallagher, Virginia Commonwealth University; Dan Gallagher, St. Cloud State University; Charles Geiss, University of Missouri; Eugene Gendel, Lafayette College; Kathie Gilbert, Mississippi State University; Lynn Gillette, Northeast Missouri State University; J. Robert Gillette, University of Kentucky; Debra Glassman, University of Washington; Glen Graham, State University of New York at Oswego; Philip Grossman, Wayne State University; Ronald Gunderson, Northern Arizona University; David R. Hakes, University of Missouri, St. Louis; Charles E. Hegji, Auburn University at Montgomery; Ann Hendricks, Tufts University; David J. Hoaas, Centenary College of Louisiana; Thomas K. Holmstrom, Northern Michigan University; Richard Holway, College of Notre Dame (California); Edward Howe, Siena College; Todd L. Idson, University of Miami (Florida); S. Hussain Ali Jafri, Tarleton State University; James Johannes, Michigan State University; James Kahn, State University of New York, Binghamton; Yoonbai Kim, Southern Illinois University; Chris Klisz, Wayne State University; Byung Lee, Howard University; Daniel Y. Lee, Shippensburg University; Jim Lee, Fort Hays State University; Richard Lotspeich, Indiana State University; Robert Lucas, University of Chicago; Ron Luchessi, American River College; James F. McCarley, Albion College; Jerome L. McElroy, St. Mary's College; Roger Mack, DeAnza College; Jim McKinsey, Northeastern University; Larry T. McRae, Appalachian State University; Michael Magura, University of Toledo; Allan Mandelstamm, Virginia Polytechnic Institute; Don Mar, San Francisco State University; Jay Marchand, University of Mississippi; Barbara Haney Martinez, University of Alaska, Fairbanks; William Mason, San Francisco State University; Ben Matta, New Mexico State University; Michael Meurer, Duke University; Robert Milbrath, Catholic University of America; Jon Miller, University of Idaho; Masoud Moghaddam, St. Cloud State University; W. Douglas Morgan, University of California, Santa Barbara; Kathryn A. Nantz, Fairfield University; Clark Nardinelli, Clemson University; Norman Obst, Michigan State University; Patrick O'Neill, University of North Dakota; Anthony Ostrovsky, Illinois State University; C. Barry Pfitzner, Randolph Macon College; John Pisciotta, Baylor University; Dennis Placone, Clemson University; John Pomery, Purdue University; Marin Pond, Purdue University; Hollis F. Price, Jr., University of Miami (Florida); Henry J. Raimondo, University of Massachusetts, Boston; Betsy Rankin, Centenary College of Louisiana; Stanley S. Reynolds, University of Arizona; Dan Richards, Tufts University; Jennifer Roback, Yale University; Malcolm Robinson, University of Cincinnati; Robert Rosenman, Washington State University, Pullman; Mark Rush, University of Florida; Dorothy Sanford, College of Notre Dame (California); Elizabeth Savoca, Smith College; Robert Schmitz, Indiana University; Ruth Shen, San Francisco State University; Earl Shinn, University of Montevallo (California); Steven Soderlind, St. Olaf College; David Spencer, Washington State University; Mark A. Stephens, Tennessee Technological University; Brandt K. Stevens, Illinois State University; Alan Stockman, University of Rochester; Don Tailby, University of New Mexico; Michael Tannen, University of the District of Columbia; Helen Tauchen, University of North Carolina; Robert Thomas, Iowa State University; Roger Trenary, Kansas State University; George Uhimchuk, Clemson University; James M. Walker, Indiana University; Richard J. Ward, Southeastern Massachusetts University; John Wells, Auburn University; M. Daniel Westbrook, Georgetown University; John B. White, Old Dominion University; Roberton Williams, Williams College; Douglas Wills, Sweet Briar College; F. Scott Wilson, Canisius College; Laura Wolff, Southern Illinois University, Edwardsville; Gary Young, Delta State University (Mississippi).

We also appreciate the work of Jeffrey Parker, Henry Thompson, and Brandt Stevens in preparing the supplementary materials.

At Addison-Wesley, we are grateful for the editorial support of Rebecca Ferris. The eagle eyes of Barbara Conover and Grace Davidson saved us from innumerable errors of style and content. It has been a great pleasure to work with these professionals.

Roy J. Ruffin
Paul R. Gregory

Introduction

part I

Chapter 1

Economics and the World Around Us: Defining Moments

Chapter Insight

In 1900, 11 million people worked on farms in the United States. Today, a hundred years later, fewer than 1 million people are employed on farms. A century ago there were no airline pilots, truck drivers, medical technicians, or radio and television announcers, and engineering was considered a new profession. Fifty years ago only 70 percent of U.S. households had indoor plumbing; now over 99 percent have this necessity of modern life. In the 1950s, only the richest families in town had air-conditioned homes; today air conditioners are so common that we have them in our automobiles. Just 10 years ago, only the defense department and major corporations had the facilities to transmit computer messages over telephone lines. Now, school children routinely exchange e-mail messages and spend hours surfing the 'Net. Life has changed so much that a time-traveler from a century ago would be lost in a technological wonderland.

The enormous improvement in our standard of living is the most important economic fact of this century. Indeed, many of the poor in the United States, because they enjoy a number of things that were unheard-of luxuries in the 1930s and 1940s, live or could live like the middle class of just 50 years ago.

Yesterday's luxuries become today's necessities. With the rising multitude of new products and inventions, we wonder whether our children and their children will see such monumental changes in their lifetimes as we have seen in our own or whether economies are subject to "limits of growth." There are always skeptics. Two of our most famous economists (David Ricardo and Thomas Malthus) argued 150 years ago at the beginnings of the Industrial Revolution that standards of living cannot rise further. Computer specialists from a major Ivy League university concluded less than 30 years ago that current living standards cannot be sustained more than a decade with our limited resources. Other skeptics prophesy overpopulation, famine, and human disaster. Optimists see no reason why the next century should not see as much progress as the twentieth century. The respected chairman of the Federal Reserve System declares that "information technology has begun to alter, fundamentally, the manner in which we do business and create economic value."[1] Scientists and corporations foresee a future of ever more powerful computers, human gene therapy, molecular medicine, the marriage of biology and engineering to produce brand-new materials, and hybrid cars that use advanced fuel cells built with ultralight polymers and ceramics.

A fact of economic life is that not all of us share in economic progress. Less than 20 percent of the world's population lives in affluent economies. Poor African and Asian countries perceive the poor of the United States as living in abundance and affluence. Citizens of Russia and Ukraine have seen their modest standards of living collapse to the levels of poor African and Asian economies in just one decade. How we organize and manage our economies explains why some are rich and others are poor. Countries with stable democracies, economic freedom, and low corruption tend to be affluent, whereas those with unstable governments, limited economic freedom, and high rates of corruption are poor and not improving. Economies that were once affluent, such as Argentina, have become poor. It is the strength of economic institutions that creates affluence. A society that makes the wrong choices runs the risk of losing its prosperity.

If we understand economics, we can protect ourselves against wrong choices. We must understand that affluent economies solve complex economic problems in a fluid manner that is largely unseen. We take for granted the fact that the 25 cent pencil is made from materials from Washington State, Sri Lanka, and Brazil. We do not wonder why each successive computer we buy is not only cheaper but also more powerful, that every year new jobs are created, that the products we want are in the stores when we want them. How and by whom have all these things been organized? Most economic activity, like the 25 cent pencil, the cheaper and more powerful computer, and the new job, is organized by "unseen" forces acting without any central direction or control. We shall analyze these forces throughout the chapters of this text, as we strive to bring the unseen into focus.

Economies work in complex and sometimes puzzling ways. To understand economics requires that you "think like an economist." This is an exciting and challenging task. Economics did not spring forth from a vacuum; it was developed over many years by economists in response to various events and ideas. This chapter is the first step on your journey to understanding the major ideas of economics—their evolution and their impact on the economic events of today.

[1]Alan Greenspan, chairman of the U.S. Federal Reserve System, quoted in the *Wall Street Journal,* Tuesday, September 21, 1999, A27.

LEARNING OBJECTIVES

After completing this chapter you should be able to:

1. Understand the general definition of economics.
2. Be able to describe the five Defining Moments of Economics: The Industrial Revolution, the rise and fall of socialism, the Great Depression, Globalization, and the Information Revolution.
3. Understand how economics uses the scientific method to test economic theories.
4. Distinguish between positive and normative economics.
5. Recognize the logical fallacies.

CHAPTER PUZZLE: Will the Internet have as much of an effect on the next 500 years as the fifteenth century invention of the printing press had on the past 500 years?

WHAT IS ECONOMICS?

The most fundamental fact of economics is that people must make choices. We cannot have everything we want. This simple fact applies to societies as well as to individuals. It applies to the rich and to the poor. Simply stated:

Economics is the study of how people choose to use their limited resources (land, labor, and capital) to produce, exchange, and consume goods and services. It explains how these scarce resources are allocated among competing ends by the economic system.

We shall expand on this definition in the next chapter when we discuss the meanings of resources, production, and exchange.

During the past one and a half centuries, as nations and their citizens have made economic choices, they have been influenced by one of two competing philosophies. The philosophy of *capitalism* maintains that private ownership and private decision making provide the best framework for creating growth and prosperity; that is, if people are simply left alone to pursue self-interests, good things will happen. The competing philosophy of *socialism* teaches that private ownership and self-interest lead to bad economic results—inequality, poverty, and depressions. Socialism argues that the state can better look after the interests of society at large through state ownership and central planning.

How we organize our economic affairs—the blend of capitalism and socialism that we select—depends on how we understand the events that shape our lives. Economists offer a framework for interpreting such events. Robert Heilbroner called the great economists of the past the "Worldly Philosophers" because, while they command no armies, they influence the way we run our world by determining what we believe about the economy and how it works.[2]

DEFINING MOMENTS OF ECONOMICS

Our understanding of the economic aspects of our lives is conditioned by past events and ideas. Our material circumstances were not created overnight. We didn't wake up one day to discover high-technology factories, a complex legal system, an information superhighway, a transportation network, and sophisticated financial markets. All these resources and institutions are the consequence of past events.

Change occurs sometimes gradually, sometimes rapidly. Sometimes monumental changes take place that we recognize only after the fact. There are even times when we think change has occurred when it has not—and so it is with economic change.

Over the past two centuries there have taken place a number of changes so important that they have defined the direction of economics and influenced the lives of millions of people. These "defining moments" have provided the stimulus for the great economic thinkers to provide explanations that became the great theories of economic science.

A **Defining Moment of economics** is an event or idea, or a set of related events or ideas over time, that has changed in a fundamental way the manner in which we conduct our everyday lives and the way in which we think about the economy.

[2]Robert Heilbroner, *The Worldly Philosophers,* 6th. ed. (New York: Simon and Schuster, 1986), esp. p. 13.

We focus on five Defining Moments of economics:

1. The Industrial Revolution
2. The Rise (and Fall) of Socialism
3. The Great Depression
4. Globalization
5. The Information Revolution

Each of these Defining Moments illustrates a fundamental idea of economics. The Worldly Philosophers developed powerful and influential theories to explain why each moment happened and what its consequences were. You will frequently encounter these Defining Moments throughout the text, for they define the basic themes, concepts, problems, and puzzles not only of the past but also of contemporary economic life. The issues raised by the Defining Moments—growth, affluence, poverty, cycles, trade, ownership, economic institutions—constitute the major economic issues of the past, the present, and the future.

1. The Industrial Revolution: The Benefits of Voluntary Exchange

In the early eighteenth century, enormous economic changes began to take place, first in England and then in Europe and North America. These changes are now known as the Industrial Revolution.

The **Industrial Revolution** occurred as a result of extensive mechanization of production systems that shifted manufacturing from the home to large-scale factories. This combination of scientific and technological advances and the expansion of free-market institutions created, for the first time, sustained economic growth.

In 1700, England was primarily an agricultural nation of only 10 million people. Most of its citizens were peasants tilling the soil with simple plows; a few were merchants and artisans; a very few were the ruling aristocracy living on large estates. Their lives were not much different from those of their ancestors a century or two earlier.

At first slowly and then more quickly, factories powered by water mills and later by steam engines sprang up. Employment in industry began to outpace employment in agriculture. People flocked from the countryside to the industrial centers of London, Birmingham, and Glasgow. Inventors and scientists sought and found better ways of making products that people wished to buy. With the development of mass production techniques, costs of production fell. Products that had previously been inaccessible to the average household became affordable. The Industrial Revolution created the conditions for those increased levels of living standards that we enjoy today.

Adam Smith (1723–1790), the founder of modern economics, explained simply and eloquently the Defining Moment of the Industrial Revolution. Smith's 1776 masterpiece, *An Inquiry into the Nature and Causes of the Wealth of Nations,* combined simple theory with his prodigious learning and insights. One of the most important books ever written, *The Wealth of Nations* brought Smith lasting fame and changed forever the way we view the economy.

In his work, Smith explained the ongoing Industrial Revolution with one powerful insight. He realized through careful observation that a massive increase in production and wealth could take place spontaneously without government direction and control. Smith proposed that self-interest could be relied upon to organize our economic affairs. He wrote:

> It is not from the benevolence of the butcher, the brewer, or the baker, that we expect our dinner, but from their regard to their own interest.

Adam Smith's key insight was that two parties to a voluntary exchange will both benefit. It is not necessary to direct people to engage in transactions from which they benefit. Through the pursuit of self-interest, individuals voluntarily engage in those activities in which they themselves earn the most income. Individuals contribute to the well-being of the entire society not just through charitable impulses but by self-interest. Each person, as Adam Smith said, "intends only his own gain," but is "led by an invisible hand" to promote the general interest of society through the magic of the marketplace.

Smith argued that free enterprise solves economic problems better than did the pervasive government monopolies and intrusive regulations of his day. Individuals must be allowed to make their own decisions in the pursuit of their self-interest. If they make the right decisions, the result will be profit; wrong decisions mean losses. This insight paved the way for a hands-off approach of government that allowed England, through the benefits of the Industrial Revolution, to become the world's most prosperous nation.

Much of this book describes how we compete with one another in the marketplace. One Internet service provider competes with another for customers by trying to offer better prices and better quality. Airlines fight for survival by learning how to provide safe service at a cost lower than that offered by their competitors. One architect competes with another by offering more original designs at a better price. In such a system, success is measured by profit; failure is measured by losses. It is this competition that guides the invisible hand.

> Adam Smith's lesson of history is that economic growth and progress come from spontaneous interaction of self-interested individuals.

2. The Rise (and Fall) of Socialism

Spontaneous interactions create change. The Industrial Revolution was an event of monumental change. It increased the real wages of workers and created a middle class. People began to live longer. Birth rates rose, death rates fell, and population grew. Farmers and villagers voluntarily left their homes to seek a better life in the city. The Industrial Revolution benefited many more people than just the rich. From 1760 to 1860, the poorest 65 percent of the British population increased their average real income by over 70 percent.[3]

Adam Smith taught that economic life consists of successes and failures. We must compete to prosper. We pursue our self-interest, while others pursue their self-interest. There will be winners and there will be losers.

The supporters of socialism, however, chose to focus on the misfortunes imposed by the Industrial Revolution. Whereas Smith saw economic progress, they saw struggle and failure. The Industrial Revolution centralized production by shifting workers from the farm or household shop to the factory.

Industrial workers in the coal mines of England, the steel mills of Germany and France, and the textile factories of New England began to question the fairness of a system in which they performed the work and only the owners appeared to reap the rewards. They saw themselves in a class struggle with the capitalists. They formed labor unions, struck factories, and formed political parties to represent the interests of workers. The ground was fertile for socialism, our second Defining Moment.

The foremost philosopher of socialism, Karl Marx (1818–1883), wrote about the unfairness of the capitalist system in his masterwork *Das Kapital.* He explained why class struggle would lead to the eventual overthrow of capitalism and its replacement by a superior economic system called *communism.* In 1848, 72 years after the publication of *The Wealth of Nations,* Marx issued his *Communist Manifesto,* calling for the workers of the world to revolt against their capitalist bosses. Marx promised that, under communism, class conflicts would disappear, people would work for pleasure, and distribution would reflect need.

After several failed attempts, socialism's next Defining Moment came with the formation of the world's first socialist government in Russia as a consequence of the Bolshevik Revolution in 1917. The Soviet communists under Lenin and Stalin began the twentieth century's greatest social experiment—the creation of a socialist economy based on state ownership and the use of state planning to replace the market. The state actions of Marx replaced the spontaneous interactions of Smith. Instructions came from the state and from the Communist party; personal initiative and innovation were discouraged; and people were told to think of the interests of society, not of their own interests.

The Soviet experiment at first appeared to yield successes. Russia escaped the Great Depression that overwhelmed the capitalist world in the 1930s. Communism spread to one-third of the world's population, engulfing Eastern Europe, China, Vietnam, Cuba, and North Korea. By the late 1950s, the leaders of the Soviet Union promised to "bury capitalism." The reverse has happened: capitalism buried communism, not by waging war, but by providing living standards to ordinary people far above those available under communism. The Soviet Union was disbanded in 1991, and other countries from the former socialist world soon followed suit. The former socialist countries now face the difficult task of transition from socialism to capitalism.

The failure of socialism was predicted as early as the 1920s by two powerful economic thinkers. Ludwig von Mises and Friedrich Hayek, both Austrian economists, were early skeptics concerning the ability of a socialist economy to sustain itself. Like Adam Smith, von Mises and Hayek taught that we can best

[3]See Nicholas Crafts, *British Economic Growth During the Industrial Revolution* (Oxford: Clarendon Press, 1985).

understand economic behavior by logically analyzing the actions of individuals. Capitalism works by making people pay for failure and benefit from success. Rewarding success and penalizing failure encourage people to work effectively. Under capitalism, the shoe manufacturer that produces at a high cost shoes no one wants will fail and disappear. Von Mises and Hayek predicted that socialism must fail because in that system, errors of judgment need not be corrected. If a shoe manufacturer loses money in a socialist state, the losses will be covered by the state. After all, it was the state that told the shoe manufacturer what to do in the first place. There is little or no incentive to keep costs low or to produce a product that people want. Unlike the capitalist shoe manufacturer, whose investment and property are at stake, under state ownership everyone and hence no one is the owner. And, thus, no one really cares. Indeed, we shall discuss the importance of incentives throughout this text.

> The lesson of socialism regarding economics is that if people do not have the incentives to use goods and services efficiently, then waste and inefficiency will result. Capitalism corrects mistakes by forcing those who make them to pay for them.

The Soviet Union was socialism's great experiment, but it was not socialism's only legacy. While Russia reacted to socialism's appeal with revolution in 1917, the rest of Europe reacted by introducing the welfare state.

The **welfare state** provides substantial benefits to the less fortunate—unemployment insurance, poverty assistance, old-age pensions—to protect them from further economic misfortune.

First in Germany and then in other parts of Europe, governments enacted social security legislation, government health insurance, progressive income taxes, worker safety laws, and unemployment insurance. This legislation was designed to make capitalism more humane—to reduce the risks of capitalism and to make the state responsible for those bearing the costs of capitalism.

The welfare state raises a fundamental question: To what extent are the enormous benefits of capitalism, as described by Adam Smith and Ludwig von Mises, jeopardized by a mixed economic system that makes the state rather than individuals responsible for its risks?

3. The Great Depression: The Cost of Progress

The Industrial Revolution in England, Western Europe, and North America created long-term economic growth. Prior civilizations (for example, the Greeks and Romans) had achieved growth but could not sustain it. The economic growth that followed the Industrial Revolution was not perfectly even, but occurred in cycles. Although newspaper headlines spoke of financial panics and depressions, each downswing seemed to correct itself and upward progress continued. Throughout the nineteenth century and during the early part of the twentieth century, bad times were followed by good times in a seemingly endless cycle—until the late 1920s.

The Great Depression—our third Defining Moment—took hold first in Europe, and then in the United States. Overnight, people saw their paper fortunes disappear. On Wall Street, bankrupt investors hurled themselves out of skyscrapers in despair. Banks closed. Ordinary citizens lost their homes. The stock market crash of 1929 was only a financial manifestation of a larger economic phenomenon. The Great Depression itself constituted a severe and sustained drop in output and jobs.

The **Great Depression** was a sustained period of high unemployment and falling output that occurred in Europe and North America in the 1920s and 1930s.

Those who did not live through the Great Depression cannot possibly comprehend its effects on millions of lives. Some three years after the start of the Depression, output in the United States had fallen by one-third, and one of four people who wished to work did not have a job. It was not until the late 1930s that the economy recovered to the level of output before the market crash, and it was not until 1942 and the beginning of World War II that the unemployment rate recovered to its previous low.

The main effect of the Great Depression was to cause many Americans and Europeans to question whether growth and prosperity are automatic. The Depression created a sense of concern about the future. Prosperity was no longer something to be taken for granted. The government came to be viewed as an instrument of good to protect people against further economic downturns, both large and small.

The Great Depression was an unanticipated event of such magnitude that it required a great economist to develop a new theory explaining it. That economist was John Maynard Keynes (1883–1946), an English intellectual, teacher, journalist, and statesman.

Smith and his followers had argued that the free market would promote economic progress. In his 1936 *General Theory of Employment, Interest and Money,* Keynes advanced a theory that showed why capitalist economies are subject to periodic breakdowns that can be corrected only by massive doses of government spending. While Smith emphasized the incentives to produce goods and services, Keynes emphasized the incentives of people to buy goods and services.

Keynesian economics is the source of the idea that buying a car or a house is "good for the economy." The importance of spending was hard to deny in the years following the Great Depression. Keynes argued that the Great Depression occurred because we did not spend enough. If there is not enough private spending, then government spending must make up the difference.

Keynes provided a justification for government spending to achieve macroeconomic objectives: If government spending is needed to keep the economy healthy, politicians can spend more without taxing. They can make their constituents happy without the pain of higher taxes. While households and businesses must be subject to financial discipline, the government need not be. Indeed, most of us are aware that until 1998 the federal government had been running deficits year after year for 50 years.

> The rise in government spending and the expansion of the welfare state raise the question of the extent to which we can reap the benefits of capitalism if we protect individuals from the risks and competition of capitalism.

Another great economic thinker presented a different picture of the Great Depression. The Austrian-born American economist Joseph Schumpeter (1883–1950) developed the theory that the Great Depression had roots in technological changes that were transforming the twentieth century. His main insight was that the *business cycle* is necessary for economic progress. New products always displace old products. The automobile replaced the horse-drawn carriage; the personal computer replaced the typewriter. Schumpeter considered the Great Depression to be an event in which many different forces converged. According to Schumpeter, it was no accident that the Soviet Union escaped the Great Depression, because it also escaped the opportunity for economic progress. Progress requires the freedom to develop new goods and new markets. Progress requires the competition of old and new ideas; progress requires winners and losers.

4. Globalization

Archaeologists are astonished by evidence of trade in remote times. Bronze artifacts cast in the Middle East in 3500 B.C.E. have been found thousands of miles away in ancient French villages. Through the ages, school children have been fascinated by Marco Polo's thirteenth-century accounts of traveling from his native Venice to China in search of exotic silks and spices. Human beings have always sought out for their own use new and exotic products produced by other societies. Human beings have, as Adam Smith remarked, a "propensity to truck, barter, and exchange one thing for another." He wrote:

> Nobody ever saw a dog make a fair and deliberate exchange of one bone for another with another dog. Nobody ever saw one animal by its gestures and natural cries signify to another, this is mine, that yours; I am willing to give this for that.

Although we are naturally drawn toward trading with one another, trade has grown unevenly. Trade depends on the ease of communication and the costs of transporting goods and services long distances. Marco Polo's journey to China consumed more than half his lifetime; today, the same trip can be made in one day on a commercial jet. His letters from China to Venice took years to deliver; now, such messages can be delivered in seconds by fax or e-mail.

Like the Industrial Revolution, the socialist revolution, and the Great Depression, the globalization of the world economy is a Defining Moment.

Globalization refers to the degree to which national economic markets and international businesses are integrated and interrelated into a world economy.

The participation of any economy in global markets may not take place swiftly and continuously; it may be a long-term process with stops and starts.

Globalization, like the other Defining Moments, was a response not only to inexorable events but also to a powerful economic insight—that trade benefits both parties irrespective of their strengths and weaknesses. This insight had already paved the way for the expansion of trade in Great Britain in the nineteenth century.

Adam Smith had to argue against those who claimed that trade with other nations could lead to national bankruptcy. However, the great English economist David Ricardo (1772–1823) demonstrated that both weak and powerful nations benefit from trade by doing those things they do relatively more efficiently than others. His discovery of the surprisingly simple yet subtle law of comparative advantage (explained in later chapters) is perhaps one of the greatest contributions economics has made to our understanding of the world about us. As we will show, this law demonstrates that every country can specialize in those goods in which it has a comparative advantage, regardless of how rich or poor the country might be or how high or low its wages.

It was Ricardo's law of comparative advantage that persuaded the English Parliament to adopt a free trade policy in the first half of the nineteenth century, with the passage of the Corn Laws. The remarkable success of England's experiment with free trade forced other countries to reduce barriers to trade imposed by narrow special interest groups.

The Industrial Revolution brought forth the first strong and sustained wave of globalization of the world economy. Coal-powered boats and railroads linked markets; the telegraph and later the telephone made long-distance communication possible. The Industrial Revolution was accompanied by strong and sustained growth in international trade. Two world wars and the Great Depression halted the globalization of the world economy. However, the major powers entered the postwar era determined to avoid the mistakes of the past and to promote the growth of trade and commerce.

Thus, in the past 50 years we have experienced an explosion of international commerce and trade. We can rightly say that we are a world economy, made possible by the revolutionary developments in transportation and communication and the conscious decisions of countries to lower their barriers to trade. In the 1990s agreements to create common markets in Europe and North America provided new impulses for globalization.

A world economy has benefited our lives in a variety of ways. We now have a wealth of choices among cars, foodstuffs, computers—almost every product that we consider. Companies are no longer national in nature: A Japanese company located in Germany can be headed by an American president. Stocks of U.S. companies are traded in Japan as we sleep, continue to be traded in London as we begin our day, and complete their trading in New York as we finish lunch. The car you drive might be made in Korea, your neighbor might work for British Petroleum, and your business loan could be from a Canadian bank. Despite its complexities, globalization has enriched our lives not only in terms of economic opportunities and options but also in a broader philosophical sense.

International trade brings broad benefits, but it hurts special interest groups. Markets that were secure are threatened by foreign competitors. Everyone must take part in competition to win customers with superior products, lower prices, or a combination of both. For example, domestic beef producers are threatened by lower-cost foreign producers. Automobile companies and their unions warn against the threat of foreign imports.

Although it brings broad benefits, globalization is opposed by special interest groups. Thus, the progress of globalization is not steady or guaranteed.

5. The Information Revolution

We require information to carry out economic activity. If I don't know you want to buy my product, I cannot sell it to you. The better the information businesses have on prices and competitive products, the more efficiently they can be run. Stock markets cannot function without up-to-date information on who wants to buy, who wants to sell, and at what prices. When information is costly, economic activity is limited; when the costs of information decline, prosperity should increase. Economists also have long recognized that improving knowledge is the major factor behind rising living standards. If information on newly created knowledge can be spread and used rapidly, prosperity should increase. Information is like the cost of labor and materials. Producers and consumers get the same benefits when information becomes cheaper that they get when material costs become cheaper.

The monumental increase in information technology over the past two decades is our fifth Defining Moment:

The staggering improvements in our ability to create, use, and exchange information that have accompanied the vast improvements in information technology (computerization, the Internet, wireless telephones) are termed the **Information Revolution.**

The Information Revolution is entering its third decade. Therefore, we still do not know what its long-run effects will be. It was initiated by a series of inventions—the transistor, the semiconductor, the silicon chip, fiber optics, microprocessors, cable TV—all of which brought together the computer's ability to generate and process information with telecommunications' ability to transmit it.

The Information Revolution was not caused by science alone; it would not have occurred without changes in economic policy. Key steps in creating the Information Revolution were the U.S. government's decision to deregulate telecommunications and television broadcasting—steps followed by governments in England, Europe, Japan, and Latin America. Competition in telecommunications created new broadcast frequencies, which provided entrepreneurs with new ways to transmit information by regular phone lines, wireless transmissions, and underground television cable. Improvements in our ability to transmit information would have been meaningless if there were no one to receive this information. Our ability to receive and process vast amounts of information was made possible by the spread of ever cheaper and ever more powerful personal computers.

As with the Industrial Revolution, the Information Revolution was spurred by farsighted entrepreneurs and entrepreneurial companies, such as Bill Gates (Microsoft), Gordon Moore (Intel), Steve Jobs (Apple Computer), CompuServe and AOL, the inventor of the World Wide Web, Timothy Berners-Lee, or the developer of the Web browser, Marc Andreeson, all of whom saw profit opportunities in information technology.[4] A short 15 years ago, callers could make their local or long distance calls through only one provider, and international long distance calls cost several dollars per minute—if they could be placed at all. Documents could be sent only by the U.S. Postal Service: there was no FedEx or UPS to promise overnight delivery. There were no fax transmissions. A business wishing to send papers across town had to use messenger services. Businesses used to have throngs of clerks, armed with pencils and paper, to keep track of inventories; now inventories are tracked by electronic scanners that place automatic orders for goods in short supply. Retailers previously could sell goods only by setting up expensive stores; now they can sell through the Internet. Scientists can disseminate their latest results instantaneously on the World Wide Web.

When economists are confronted with a new Defining Moment, like the Information Revolution, they must study its effects. Some economists, such as Nobel laureate George J. Stigler, anticipated the effects of an Information Revolution by pointing out the advantages of reducing the cost of information. Others, such as Paul Romer, are currently studying the effects of an Information Revolution on long-term economic growth and concluding that the future of the world economy is bright. At some point in the future, we will have a new Defining Moment economist, whose work will be forever associated with the Defining Moment of the Information Revolution.

Economic Theory and the Scientific Method

The economy is a complex mixture of many types of decision makers, each with different goals and knowledge about how things work. The U.S. economy is made up of millions of households and firms, and thousands of separate federal, state, and local governments. Each makes production and consumption decisions. Consumers want to pay low prices for the things they buy and earn high wages. Firms want to charge high prices and pay low wages. Automobile companies want low-priced steel; steel companies want high-priced steel. Gathering information about all these choices is a complex task. It is essential to abstract from the irrelevant or unimportant facts in

[4]Tim Berners-Lee, *Weaving the Web* (San Francisco: Harper, 1999).

order to gain an understanding of the way the economy works.

Economic Theories and Models

Smith, Marx, Keynes, Schumpeter, and Ricardo all explained events by formulating economic *theories* of how the world works. Theories can cover the workings of an entire economy or limit their scope to explain, for example, what happens to consumer spending when prices change. Simply defined:

A **theory** is a simplified and coherent explanation of the relationship among certain facts.

The most important economic theories explain in a logical manner the Defining Moments we have just discussed. Adam Smith explained how an industrial revolution could occur using a system of free enterprise. Karl Marx explained how people might turn to socialism. Von Mises and Hayek explained why socialism would fail. John Maynard Keynes sought to explain the Great Depression. When the industrialized countries experienced rising inflation and rising unemployment in the 1970s and 1980s, new and powerful theories were put forward to explain this unusual phenomenon.

The world is so complicated that all theories, economic or physical, must be devised by eliminating irrelevant facts and concentrating on only the most important relevant ones. For example, in explaining the demand for gasoline, the color of cars—black, white, or red—is not important and should be ignored. Other things, however, like the price of gasoline or the incomes of automobile owners, may be important and should be considered. Economic theories focus on the most important systematic factors that explain economic behavior.

For example, we might theorize that the demand for coffee depends inversely on the price of coffee and positively on the price of tea. A model illustrating this theory might show that an increase in the price of coffee by $1 would reduce worldwide sales by one million pounds. Models can be illustrated by graphs, equations, or words; they show the concrete workings of the theory.

The Scientific Method

Economic theories are not fanciful abstract exercises; they must explain the real world to be useful. If a theory is not supported by the facts, it should be discarded in favor of one that is. How do we know that a theory is correct? A theory is a simplified explanation of the relationship between two or more facts. You observe that when the price of videocassettes rises, the number that are sold falls. To explain this observation, you come up with the following theory: "People have allocated so many dollars to the purchase of videocassettes. Thus, if the price rises, people must buy fewer units in order to keep from exceeding their budget." You check the actual facts and find that as the price of videos fell, people spent more dollars on videos. This finding would refute your theory, which requires that people spend the same amount.

The **scientific method** is the process of formulating theories, collecting data, testing theories, and revising theories.

This simple example shows that the scientific method requires confronting theories with additional facts. The scientific method enables us to evaluate our beliefs in a way that can be tested by others. The Nobel physicist Richard Feynman put it this way:

> If you make a theory, . . . and advertise it, or put it out, then you must also put down all the facts that disagree with it, as well as those that agree with it. . . . You want to make sure, when explaining what it fits, that those things it fits are not just the things that gave you the idea for the theory; but that the finished theory makes something else come out right, in addition.[5]

The advantage of learning a theory is that you are freed from having to learn the facts of each situation covered by the theory. If the theory is correct, the facts of each situation will be consistent with it.

According to the scientific method, a theory that does not work in practice cannot be a good theory. Finding that a theory does not fit the facts leads to new theories that cover more experience. In science, this process represents progress. The Italian economist Vilfredo Pareto (1848–1923) once remarked,

> Give me a fruitful error anytime, full of seeds, bursting with its own corrections. You can keep your sterile truth for yourself.

[5]Richard Feynman, *"Surely You're Joking, Mr. Feynman!" Adventures of a Curious Character* (New York: Bantam Books, 1986), pp. 311–312.

Logical Fallacies

Logical fallacies plague all scientific thinking. The three most common to economics are the *ceteris paribus fallacy,* the *false-cause fallacy,* and the *fallacy of composition.*

Economic phenomena are complicated; they are generally caused by several factors. Consider a videocassette example in which you observe that the number of units that are sold increases when the price rises. Does this mean that price increases cause customers to buy more? In this case, we might suspect that the number of videocassettes sold depends on something other than the price. Income may be increasing, so the number of buyers may be increasing along with the prices of videocassette recorders. To understand the true relationship between the price of cassettes and units sold (which we presume to be negative), we must hold these other factors constant. To conclude from these facts that a higher price brings about greater sales is a *ceteris paribus* fallacy.

Ceteris paribus is a Latin term meaning "other things being equal." Any attempt to establish the relationship between two factors must hold constant the effects of other factors to avoid confusing the relationship; otherwise, the *ceteris paribus* problem will occur.

To understand how one factor affects another, we must be able to sort out the effects of all other relevant factors. An entire branch of economics, econometrics, combines economic theory and statistics to deal with the *ceteris paribus* problem.

The ***ceteris paribus*** **problem** occurs when the effect of one factor on another is masked by changes in other factors.

Consider the odd fact that in 20 of the last 23 years, the stock market rose when the National Football Conference team won the Super Bowl and fell when it lost. To conclude that the one event (the NFC team wins the Super Bowl) caused the other event (a rise in stock market prices) is a false-cause fallacy. Some people even buy or sell in the stock market on the basis of which team wins the Super Bowl!

The **false-cause fallacy** is the assumption that because two events occur together, one event has caused the other.

Economic theory tries to establish in a scientific manner whether a cause-and-effect relationship exists. Since there is no logical reason for a football game to affect the stock market, we must reject a cause-and-effect relationship. Economics, however, can offer a number of logical theories that specify cause-and-effect relationships between variables (such as the overall state of the economy, interest rates, expectations of inflation) and the stock market.

The third major fallacy involves reasoning from special cases to the general case, or the reverse. Imagine a fire in a crowded movie theater. If *one* of us runs to the exit, he or she will escape unharmed. If *all* of us run to the nearest exit, few will escape unharmed. It is a *fallacy of composition* to suppose that what is true for one is true for all.

If your employer replaces you with a robot, you would rightly complain that the robot has put you out of a job. But beware of committing a fallacy of composition. If you say, "robots are destroying American jobs," you have fallen into a logical trap. For the whole economy, robots might be increasing the number of jobs of all types. It is only correct for you to say that the robot took your particular job, and now you have to find a new one!

The **fallacy of composition** is the assumption that what is true for each part taken separately is also true for the whole or, in reverse, that what is true for the whole is true for each part considered separately.

Positive and Normative Economics

We often hear people joke about getting "six different answers from five economists." This image of disagreement is a distortion of the truth. There is, in fact, considerable agreement among economists about what *can* be done.

Economists agree that widespread freezes in citrus-growing areas raise citrus prices, that rising gas prices reduce gas consumption, and that price controls cause shortages. Disagreements about "what is" focus primarily on complex phenomena like inflation, unemployment, and business cycles. We can use the scientific method to test the theories of positive economics.

Positive economics is the study of how the economy works; it explains the economy in measurable terms.

There is, however, considerably more disagreement over what *ought to* be done. You will find economists disagreeing on whether we should have government-mandated universal health insurance; whether income taxes should be lowered for the middle class, the rich, or the poor; whether there should be job programs for the poor. These disagreements are only partly over "what is." We may agree on what will happen if program A is chosen over program B, but we may disagree sharply over the desirability of those consequences.

Normative economics is the study of what ought to be in the economy; it is value based and cannot be tested by the scientific method.

Disagreements in other sciences are less visible than in economics. Theoretical physicists still disagree about the physical nature of the universe, but this controversy is understood by only a few theoretical physicists. On the other hand, economic disputes attract immediate attention. We are concerned about whether inflation will accelerate, whether we will lose our jobs, or whether interest rates will fall. We all want to know what the future holds in store.

Should economists be able to foresee the future? If they cannot correctly predict what will happen, does this mean that economics has failed? Some events can, indeed, be predicted. If gas prices rise sharply, we shall eventually buy less gas. Other events—such as stock market fluctuations, inflation, or the business cycle—are difficult if not impossible to predict. As we shall see in later chapters, economic principles themselves imply that systematically correct predictions about complex economic phenomena are not possible.

Unanswered Questions

The five Defining Moments of economics we have discussed reveal the major issues of economics that will occupy our attention in this text—growth, business cycles, unemployment, inflation, competition, incentives, economic systems, and technology.

Economics is constantly evolving as events unfold. There will be new Defining Moments, and future economists must establish important theories to explain them. In fact, today there is much economists do not know or can explain only poorly. For example:

1. They do not understand well how to dismantle socialist economic systems to return them to capitalism. This task will probably occupy us for the next quarter century.
2. They do not fully understand the business cycle—why economies are still subject to ups and downs—despite the powerful explanations of Keynes and Schumpeter.
3. They do not understand how to measure the links between technological advances, the business cycle, and the true rate of economic growth.

If we knew the answers to these and other economic questions, economics would not be the exciting field of study it is. Because we are still searching for answers, we require building blocks of knowledge to formulate explanations.

In the next chapter let us use some of the tools of the scientific method to understand how economic choices are made in a world of scarce resources. What are the costs of making choices? What arrangements are used to resolve the problem of choice? Graphical analysis makes these questions easier to answer. As an aid to using these tools, we shall review the guidelines for working with graphs in the appendix to this chapter.

Summary

1. The Defining Moments of economics are the Industrial Revolution, the rise (and fall) of socialism, the Great Depression, the globalization of the world economy, and the Information Revolution. Each Defining Moment is associated with a great economic idea. Adam Smith explained the Industrial Revolution; Karl Marx, the appeal of socialism; John Maynard Keynes and Joseph Schumpeter, the Great Depression; David Ricardo, the benefits of globalization; and Ludwig von Mises and Friedrich von Hayek, the weaknesses of socialism. The economist identified with the Information Revolution is yet to be determined.

2. Theory allows us to make sense of the real world and to learn how the facts fit together. There is no conflict between good theory and good practice. Economic theories are based on the scientific

method of hypothesis formulation, collection of relevant data, and testing of theories.

3. The *ceteris paribus* problem occurs when it is difficult to determine relationships between two factors because other factors have not been held constant.

4. Two other logical fallacies plague economic analysis: the false-cause fallacy (assuming that event A has caused event B because A is associated with B) and the fallacy of composition (assuming that what is true for each part taken separately is true for the whole or, conversely, assuming that what is true for the whole is also true for each part).

5. Economists tend to agree on positive economic issues (what is), whereas they tend to disagree on normative issues (what ought to be). Disagreements among economists are more visible to the public eye than disagreements in other scientific professions.

KEY TERMS

economics 5
Defining Moment of economics 5
Industrial Revolution 6
welfare state 8
Great Depression 8
globalization 10
Information Revolution 11
theory 12
scientific method 12
ceteris paribus problem 13
false-cause fallacy 13
fallacy of composition 13
positive economics 13
normative economics 14

QUESTIONS AND PROBLEMS

1. In what ways has the growing globalization of the economy changed our everyday lives?
2. Explain how you would use the scientific method to determine what factors cause the grade point averages of students in your class to differ.
3. "If I stand up at the game, I will see better." Explain under what conditions this statement is true and under what conditions it is a logical fallacy. Also explain which logical fallacy is involved.
4. "The price of corn is low today because people are now watching too much TV." This statement is a potential example of which logical fallacy (or fallacies)?
5. Economists are more likely to agree on the answers to which of the following questions? Why?
   a. Should tax rates be lowered for the rich?
   b. How would lowering tax rates for the rich affect economic output?
   c. How would an increase in the price of VCRs affect purchases of VCRs?
   d. Should government defense expenditures be reduced?
   e. How would an increase in military spending affect employment?
6. "The severe heat and drought this summer substantially reduced revenue from wheat and corn crops in the Midwest. The incomes of all wheat and corn farmers therefore will fall." Which logical fallacy may be involved in this statement and why?
7. Use the data in Table A to devise some simple theories and to test them against "the facts."

TABLE A

	1990	*1997*
New passenger cars (millions sold)	9.3	8.3
New car prices (1990 = 100)	100	120
Personal income (billions of dollars)	4977	7132

Source: http://www.Economagic.com

8. Can we say that the data in Table A "prove" the theory? Is it better to say that they "support" the theory?
9. Identify which of the following statements are theories (or hypotheses).
   a. The U.S. population rose more rapidly in the 1950s than in the 1990s.
   b. People who get severely sunburned are more likely to develop skin cancer.
   c. An increase in income causes people to buy more consumer goods.
   d. The United States and Western Europe have the highest incomes among the world's nations.
   e. Cats can see better in the dark than dogs.
   f. If people believe that a product is hazardous to their health, they will consume less of it.

10. Marx, von Mises, and Hayek had quite different views of socialism. Explain their basic differences of opinion.
11. What was the Industrial Revolution? How does it differ from the Information Revolution?

INTERNET CONNECTION

12. Using the links from http://www.awl.com/ruffin_gregory, read the article "Economic Development for the 21st Century: New Measures of Well-Being" on the Federal Reserve Bank of Minneapolis Web site.
    a. According to the author, how should one measure well-being?
    b. According to the author, how has the Industrial Revolution contributed to our well-being?
    c. According to Adam Smith, what determines wealth?
13. Using the links from http://www.awl.com/ruffin_gregory, download the World Bank's data on commodity prices. Then, plot the price of cotton from 1980 to 1998.
    a. What do you observe about the trend in cotton prices if any?
    b. How do you think an economist would explain these movements?

PUZZLE ANSWERED: Most historians of science and technology credit Gutenberg's invention of the movable printing press in 1450 as the most important invention of the millennium. It changed our lives by lowering the costs of disseminating information. We do not yet know whether the Internet's invention will prove more important than the printing press. However, it is already clear that the Internet will dramatically change lives in the twenty-first century in the following ways: People will be able to work anywhere, and they may choose to leave large cities. More people will locate in the best locations, near seas or mountains and in pleasant climates. The Internet will equalize world income insofar as Indian or Chinese software developers will be valuable to companies and can ply their trade just as well in their home countries as in an affluent country. The Internet is already changing the way we buy goods and services. We can shop more efficiently by the Internet. Retail malls could easily be a thing of the past.

Appendix 1A

Understanding Graphs

Appendix Insight

Economics makes extensive use of graphs. In Chapter 1 we discussed economic theories and models. Graphs are tools we use to illustrate economic models. A graph is a visual scheme for picturing the quantitative relationship between two variables.

This appendix reviews graph construction, positive and negative relationships, and dependent and independent variables, and it details how we calculate the areas of rectangles and triangles. It explains slopes for both linear and curvilinear relationships and shows how we can use them to find maximum and minimum values. It distinguishes between time series and cross section data. Finally, it describes three common pitfalls of using graphs.

The Use of Graphs in Economics

Graphs can efficiently describe quantitative relationships. As the Chinese proverb says, "a picture is worth a thousand words." A graph is easier both to understand and to remember than the several hundred or perhaps thousands of numbers that the graph represents.

Positive and Negative Relationships

The first important characteristic of a graph is whether it shows a positive (direct) or a negative (inverse) relationship between the two variables.

A **positive (direct) relationship** exists between two variables if an increase in the value of one variable is associated with an *increase* in the value of the other variable. A **negative (inverse) relationship** exists between two variables if an increase in the value of one variable is associated with a *reduction* in the value of the other variable.

Panel (*a*) of Figure A1 depicts how an increase in horsepower will increase the maximum speed of an automobile. The *vertical axis* measures the maximum speed of the car from the 0 point (called the *origin*); the *horizontal axis* measures the horsepower of the engine. When horsepower is 0 (the engine is off), the maximum speed the car can attain is obviously 0; when horsepower is 300, the maximum speed is 100 miles per hour. Intermediate values of horsepower (between 0 and 300) are graphed. When a line is drawn through these points, the resulting curved line describes the effect of horsepower on maximum speed. Since the picture is a line that goes from low to high speeds as horsepower increases, it is an *upward-sloping curve.*

Now let's consider an example of a negative (inverse) relationship. As the horsepower of the automobile increases, the gas mileage will fall. In panel (*b*) of Figure A1, gas mileage is now measured on the vertical axis. Since the graph is a curve going from high to low values of gas mileage as horsepower increases, it is an example of a *downward-sloping curve.*

Dependent and Independent Variables

In relationships involving two variables, one variable is the dependent variable and the other is the independent variable. The dependent variable—denoted by *Y*—changes as a result of change in the value of another variable. The independent variable—denoted by *X*—causes the change in the dependent variable.

In panel (*a*) of Figure A1, an increase in engine horsepower causes an *increase* in the maximum speed of the automobile. In panel (*b*), a horsepower increase causes a *reduction* in gas mileage. In both examples, horsepower is the independent variable. The other two variables depend upon horsepower because the changes in horsepower bring about changes in speed and gas mileage.

(*a*) A Positive Relationship

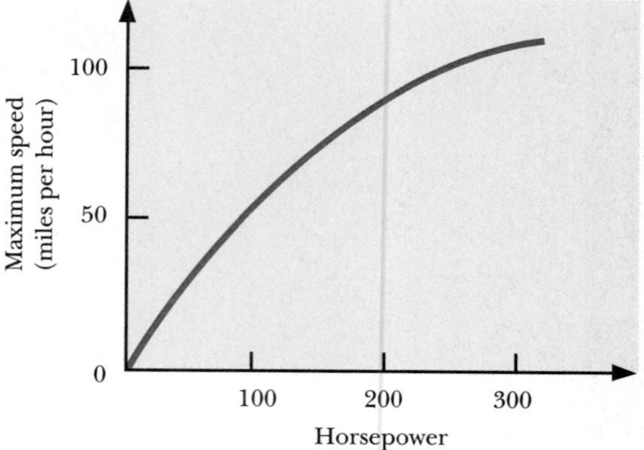

(*b*) A Negative Relationship

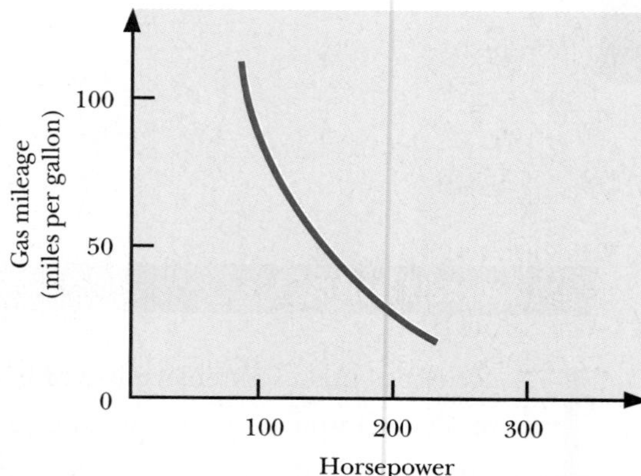

FIGURE A1 Graphing Positive and Negative Relationships

Panel (*a*) shows a positive relationship. As the horizontal variable (horsepower) increases, the value of the vertical variable (maximum speed) increases. The curve rises from left to right. Panel (*b*) shows a negative relationship. As the horizontal variable (horsepower) increases, the vertical variable (mileage) decreases. The curve falls from left to right.

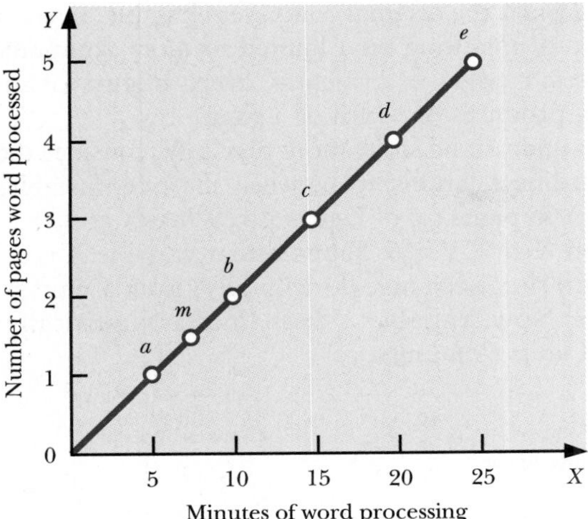

FIGURE A2 Constructing a Graph

Advantages of Graphs

We can tell from a quick glance at a graph whether a curve is positive or negative. We have to work harder to reach this conclusion if the same information is presented in a table. Table A1 details the quantitative relationship between minutes of word processing and number of pages processed. (The quantitative relationship between minutes and pages is that every 5 minutes of word processing produces 1 page of manuscript. Thus 5 minutes produce 1 page, 15 minutes produce 3 pages, and so on.) The data are graphed in Figure A2.

Points *a, b, c, d,* and *e* completely describe the data in Table A1. Indeed, a graph of the data acts as a substitute for the table. This is the first advantage of graphs over tables: Graphs provide an immediate visual understanding of the quantitative relationship between the two variables just by the plots of points. Since the points in this case move upward from left to right, there is a *positive relationship* between the variables.

TABLE A1 THE RELATIONSHIP BETWEEN MINUTES OF WORD PROCESSING AND NUMBER OF PAGES PROCESSED

	Minutes of Word Processing (X axis)	*Number of Pages Processed (Y axis)*
	0	0
a	5	1
b	10	2
c	15	3
d	20	4
e	25	5

TABLE A2 THE RELATIONSHIP BETWEEN MINUTES OF WORD PROCESSING AND NUMBER OF PAGES PROCESSED (DATA REARRANGED)

	Minutes of Word Processing (X axis)	*Number of Pages Processed (Y axis)*
b	10	2
a	5	1
	0	0
e	25	5
c	15	3
d	20	4

This advantage may not seem to be great for such a simple and obvious case. However, suppose the data had been arranged as in Table A2.

After looking at the data, we should eventually see that there is a positive relationship between X and Y; however, it is not immediately obvious. A graph makes it easier for us to see the relationship.

A large table would be required to report all intermediate values in Table A1. In a graph, however, all these intermediate values can be represented simply by connecting points *a, b, c, d,* and *e* with a line. A second advantage is that large quantities of data can be represented more efficiently in a graph than in a table.

The data in Tables A1 and A2 reveal the relationship between minutes of word processing and number of pages processed (Figure A2). The relationship can change, however, if other factors change that affect word-processing speed. Table A1 shows minutes and pages input on a computer with an old keyboard. If the word processor works with an improved keyboard, a different relationship will prevail. He or she can now process 2 pages instead of 1 page every 5 minutes. Both relationships are graphed in Figure A3. Thus, if factors that affect speed of word processing (for example, the quality of the computer) change, the relationship between minutes and pages can shift. Because economists frequently work with relationships that shift, it is important to understand shifts in graphs.

> The first advantage of graphs over tables is that it is easier to see the relationship between the variables.

> The second advantage of graphs over tables is that large quantities of data can be represented efficiently in a graph.

UNDERSTANDING SLOPE

The magnitude of the reaction of a dependent variable *(Y)* to a change in an independent variable *(X)* is represented by the *slope* of the curve depicting their relationship. Many central concepts of economics require an understanding of slope.

> The **slope of a curve** reflects the response of one variable to changes in another. The **slope of a straight line** is the ratio of the rise (or fall) in *Y* over the run in *X*.

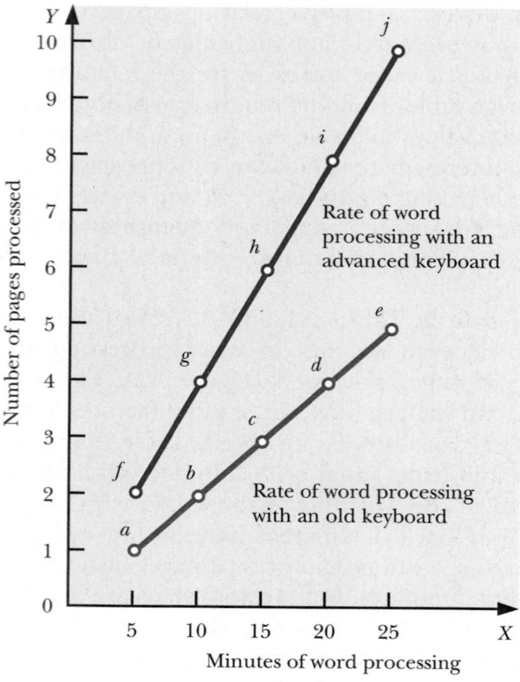

FIGURE A3 Shifts in Relationships

The curve *abcde* graphically illustrates the data in Table A1 that shows the relationship between minutes and pages with an old keyboard. The new (higher) curve *fghij* shows the relationship between minutes and pages with an advanced keyboard. As a consequence of the upgraded computer, the relationship has shifted upward. Any given X is now associated with a higher Y value.

Consider the original computer example. Every 5 minutes of inputting on a limited memory computer produces 1 page; equivalently, every minute of inputting produces one-fifth of a page.

To understand slope more precisely, consider the straight-line relationship between the two variables X and Y in panel (*a*) of Figure A4. When $X = 5$, $Y = 3$; when $X = 7$, $Y = 6$. Suppose that variable X is allowed to *run* (to change horizontally) from 5 units to 7 units. Now, variable Y rises (increases vertically) from 3 units to 6 units.

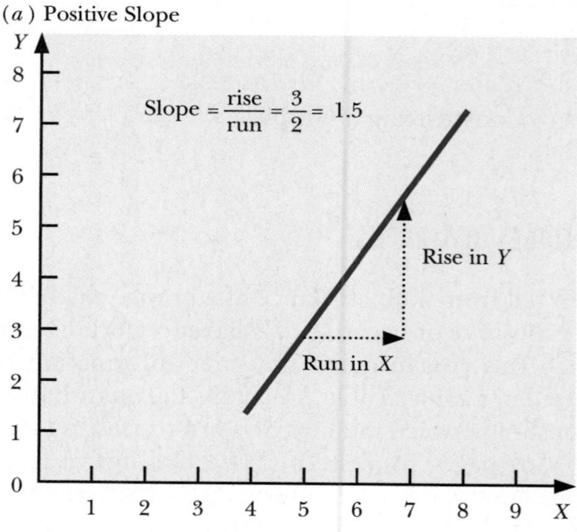

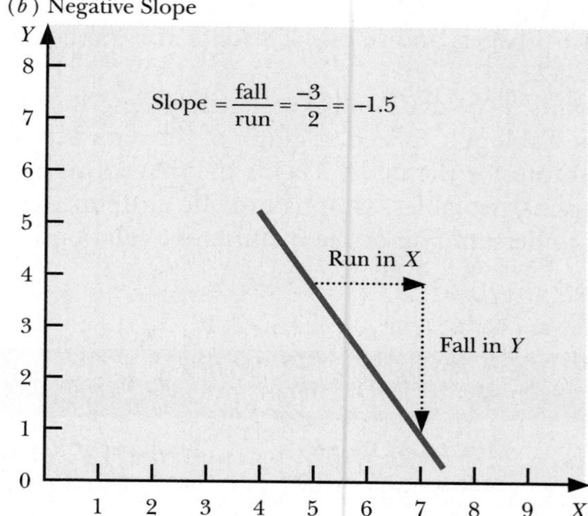

FIGURE A4 Positive and Negative Slope

The slope is measured by the ratio of the rise in Y over the run in X. In panel (*a*), Y rises by 3 and X runs by 2, and the slope is 1.5. In panel (*b*), the fall in Y is −3, the run in X is 2, and the slope is −1.5.

The slope of the line in panel (*a*) is

$$\frac{\text{Rise in } Y}{\text{Run in } X} = \frac{3}{2} = 1.5$$

A *positive value of the slope* signifies a *positive relationship* between the two variables.

This formula works for negative relationships as well. In panel (*b*) of Figure A4, when X runs from 5 to 7, Y falls from 4 units to 1 unit, or rises by −3 units. Thus, the slope is:

$$\frac{\text{Rise in } Y}{\text{Run in } X} = \frac{-3}{2} = -1.5$$

A *negative* value of the slope signifies a *negative relationship* between the two variables.

If ΔY (delta Y) stands for the change in the value of Y and ΔX (delta X) stands for the change in the values of X,

$$\text{Slope} = \frac{\Delta Y}{\Delta X}$$

This formula holds for positive or negative relationships.

Let us return to the word-processing example. What slope expresses the relationship between minutes of inputting and number of pages? When minutes increase by 5 units ($\Delta X = 5$), pages increase by 1 unit ($\Delta Y = 1$). The slope is therefore $\Delta Y/\Delta X = 1/5$. In Figures A2, A3, and A4, the points are connected by straight lines. Such relationships are called *linear relationships*.

Figure A5 shows how the slope is measured when the relationship between X and Y is curvilinear. When X runs from 2 units to 4 units ($\Delta X = 2$), Y rises by 2 units ($\Delta Y = 2$); thus the slope between *a* and *b* is 2/2 = 1. Between *a* and *c*, however, X runs from 2 to 6 ($\Delta X = 4$), Y rises by 3 units ($\Delta Y = 3$), and the slope is 3/4. In the curvilinear case, the value of the slope depends on how far X runs. The slope changes as we move along a curve. In the linear case, the value of the slope will *not* depend on how far X runs, because the slope is constant and does not change as we move from point to point.

There is no single slope of a curvilinear relationship and no single method of measuring slopes. An individual slope can be measured between two points (say, between *a* and *b* or between *b* and *c*) or at a particular point (say, at point *a*). A uniform standard must be adopted to avoid confusion. This standard requires that tangents be used to determine the slope at any single point on a curve.

A **tangent** is a straight line that touches the curve at only one point.

To calculate the slope at *a,* let the run of X be "infinitesimally small" rather than a discrete number of units such as 1/2, 2, or 4. An infinitesimally small change is difficult to conceptualize, but the graphical result of such a change can be captured simply by drawing a tangent to point *a*.

If the curve is really curved at *a,* there is only one straight line that just barely touches *a* and only *a*. Any other line cuts the curve at two points or none. The tangent to *a* is drawn as a straight line in Figure A5.

The **slope of a curvilinear relationship** at a particular point is the slope of the tangent to the curve at that point.

The slope of the tangent at *a* is measured by dividing the rise by the run. Because the tangent is a straight

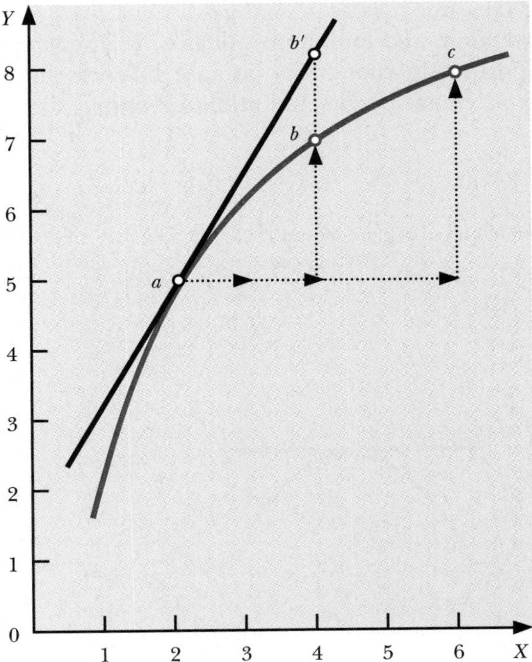

FIGURE A5 Calculating Slopes of Curvilinear Relationships

The ratio of the rise over the run yields a slope of 1 from *a* to *b* but a slope of 3/4 from *a* to *c*, and 1/2 from *b* to *c*. To compute the slope at point *a,* the slope of the tangent to *a* is calculated. The value of the slope of the tangent is 3/2, since between *a* and *b′* $\Delta Y = 3$ and $\Delta X = 2$.

line, the length of the run does not matter. For a run from 2 to 4 ($\Delta X = 2$), the rise (ΔY) equals 3 (from 5 to 8). Thus the slope of the tangent is 3/2, or 1.5.

Maximum and Minimum Values

Figure A6 shows two curvilinear relationships that have distinct high points or low points. When a curvilinear relationship has a zero slope, at the X value where slope is zero the value of Y reaches either a high point, or maximum, as in panel (*a*), or a low point, or minimum, as in panel (*b*). In panel (*a*) of Figure A6, the relationship between X and Y is positive for values of X less than 6 units and negative for values of X more than 6 units. The exact opposite holds for panel (*b*): The relationship is negative for values of X less than 6 and positive for X greater than 6. Notice that at the point where the slope changes from positive to negative (or vice versa), the slope of the curve will be exactly zero; the tangent at point $X = 6$ for both curves is a horizontal line that neither rises nor falls as X changes.

Maximum and minimum values of relationships are important in economics because business firms seek to *maximize* profits and *minimize* costs.

Scatter Diagrams

Statisticians may have more powerful tools with which to measure relationships, but the scatter diagram is a convenient analytical tool to examine whether a positive or negative relationship exists between two variables.

A **scatter diagram** consists of a number of separate points, each plotting the value of one variable against a value of another variable for a specific time interval.

In Figure A7, mortgage interest rates are measured along the horizontal axis, and new housing starts (the number of new homes on which construction has started) are measured along the vertical axis. Each of the dots on the scatter diagram shows the combination of mortgage rate and number of housing starts for a particular year. The pattern of dots provides visual information about the relationship between the two variables. If the dots show a pattern of low mortgage rates and high housing starts but high mortgage rates and low housing starts, the scatter diagram indicates a *negative relationship*, indi-

(*a*) *Y* Is Maximized When Slope Is Zero

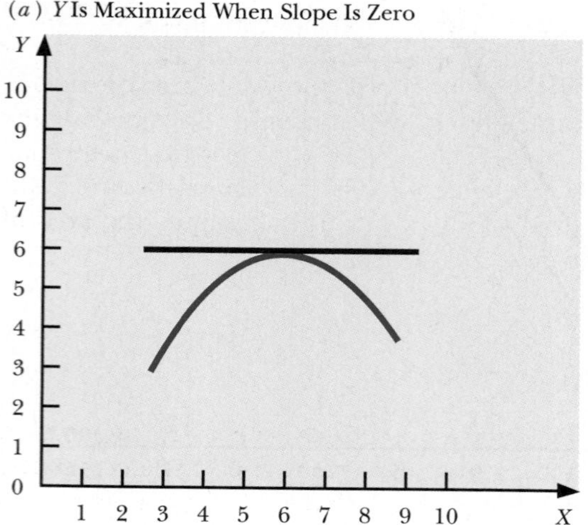

(*b*) *Y* Is Minimized When Slope Is Zero

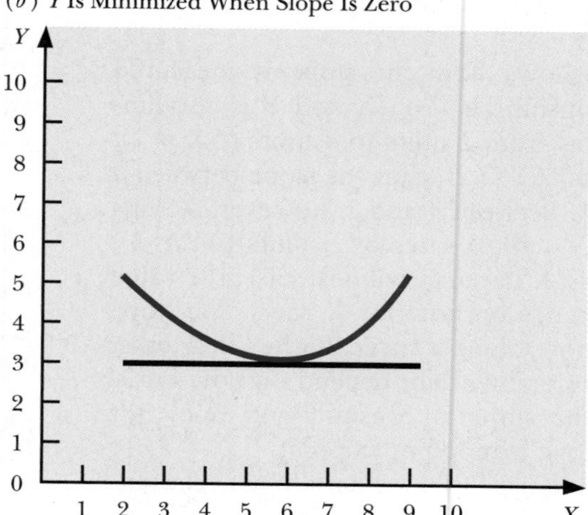

FIGURE A6 Maximum and Minimum Points

Some curvilinear relationships change directions. Notice that in panel (*a*), when the curve changes direction at $X = 6$, the corresponding value of Y is *maximized*. In panel (*b*), when $X = 6$, Y is *minimized*. In either case, the slope equals zero at the maximum or minimum value.

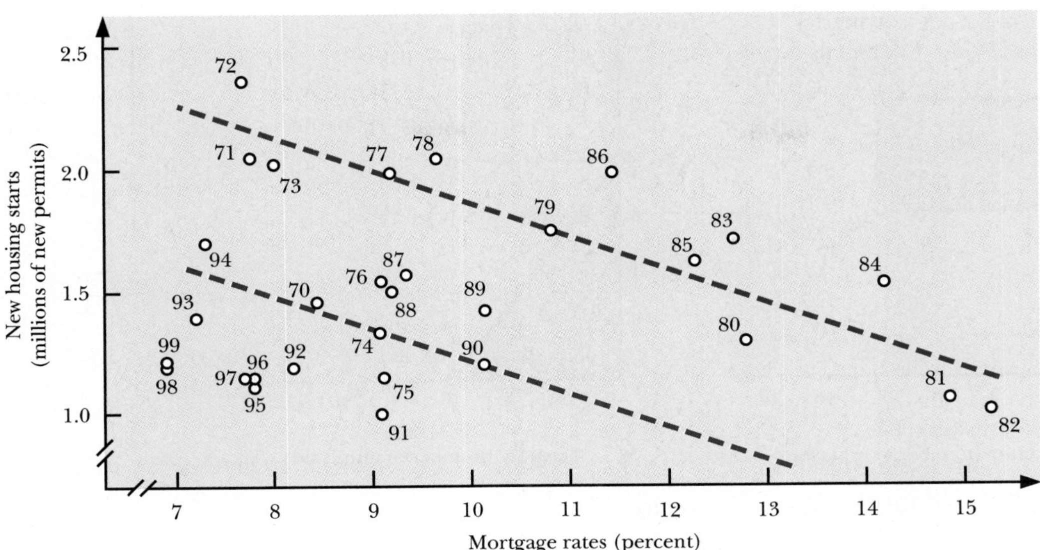

FIGURE A7 A Scatter Diagram of Mortgage Rates and Housing Starts, 1970–1999

The generally falling pattern of dots suggests that there is a negative relationship between these two variables. The fact that not all dots lie on a single line suggests that other factors besides the independent variable (mortgage rates) affect the dependent variable (housing starts). *Source:* http://www.gpo.ucop.edu/catalog/erp_appen_b.html.

cated by a generally declining pattern of dots from left to right. A generally rising pattern of dots from left to right shows a *positive relationship.* If there were no relationship, the dots would be distributed randomly.

Figure A7 shows a negative relationship between mortgage rates and housing starts. The broad, negatively sloped band traces out the general pattern of declining dots. Such a pattern makes sense: The number of houses being built should drop when the cost of borrowing to buy a home rises.

Areas of Rectangles and of Triangles

In economics, it is important to understand how to calculate areas of rectangles and of triangles. Panel (*a*) of Figure A8 shows the area of a rectangle, and panel (*b*) shows the area of a triangle. In panel (*a*), a firm sells 8 units of its product for a price of $10, and it costs $6 per unit to produce the product. How much profit is the firm earning? The firm's profit is the area of the rectangle *abcd.* To calculate the area of a rectangle, we must multiply the height of the rectangle (*ad* or *bc,* or $10 – $6 = $4 per unit) by the width of the rectangle (*ab* or *dc,* 8 units). The area of the rectangle is $4 per unit times 8 units, or $32 of total profit.

Panel (*b*) of Figure A8 shows the area of triangle *efg.* Because this triangle accounts for one-half the area of the rectangle *efgh,* we must first determine the area of the rectangle (which equals $8 \times 6 = 48$) and multiply it by $^1/_2$. In this example, the area of the triangle is $0.5 \times 48 = 24$.

The Pitfalls of Graphs

When used properly, graphs help us to understand complex data in a convenient and efficient manner. They may, however, be used to confuse or even misinform. Factions in political contests, advertisers of competing products, or rivals in lawsuits can take the same set of data, apply the standard rules of graph construction, and yet create graphs that support their own positions.

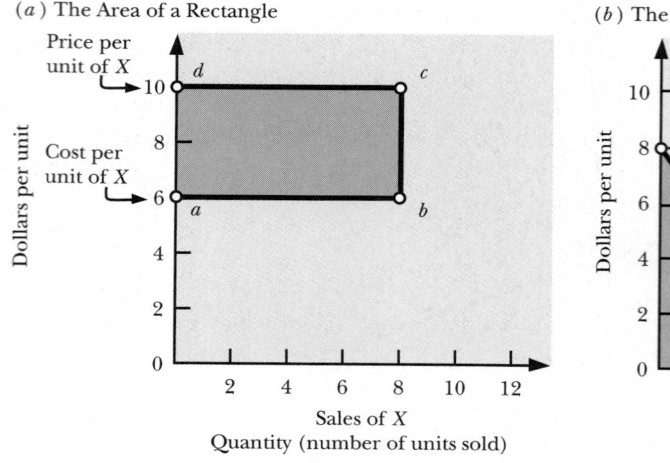

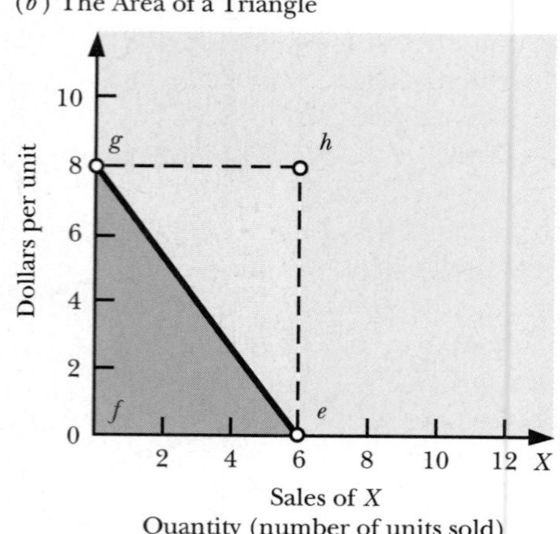

FIGURE A8 Calculating Areas of Rectangles and Triangles

The area of the rectangle *abcd* in panel (*a*) is calculated by multiplying its height (*ad*, or equivalently, *bc*) by its width (*ab*, or equivalently, *dc*). The height equals $4, and the width equals 8 units; therefore, the area of the rectangle equals $32. Thus, $32 is the amount of this firm's profits. The area of the triangle *efg* in panel (*b*) is one-half the area of the corresponding rectangle *efgh*. The area of the rectangle is 8 × 6 = 48. The area of the triangle *efg* is therefore 0.5 × 48 = 24.

This section warns us about three of the many pitfalls of using and interpreting graphs: (1) the ambiguity of slope, (2) inflation and growth distortion, and (3) unrepresentative data.

The Ambiguity of Slope

The steepness of the rise or fall of a graphed curve can be an ambiguous guide to the strength of the relationship between the two variables. The slope is affected by the scale used to mark the axes, and the slope's numerical value depends upon the unit of measure.

In Figure A9, on pages 26 and 27, panel (*a*) provides an example of the *ambiguity of slope*. If you look carefully, you will see that both the left-hand and right-hand graphs plot exactly the same numbers: the annual sales of domestically produced cars for the years 1978 to 1986. In the left-hand graph, because each unit on the vertical axis represents 1 million cars, the decline in sales appears to be small. In the right-hand graph, because each unit now measures a half-million cars, the decline appears to be steep. The impression you would get of the magnitude of the decline in auto sales is affected by the choice of units on the vertical axis even though both graphs depict identical information.

Inflation and Growth Distortion

A variable may give the appearance of measuring one thing while in reality it measures another. In economics, two common types of improper measurement are (1) inflation-distorted measures and (2) growth-distorted measures. These are encountered in *time series graphs,* in which the horizontal *X* axis measures time (in months, quarters, years, decades, and so forth) and the vertical *Y* axis measures a second variable whose behavior is plotted over time.

Panel (*b*) of Figure A9 gives an example of the importance of inflation distortion by showing graphically the per capita national debt before and after adjustment for inflation.

Inflation distortion is the measurement of the dollar value of a variable over time without adjustment for inflation over that period.

Per capita national debt (without adjustment for inflation) increased more than five times between 1950 and 1994. The red line shows the per capita national debt *adjusted for inflation*. The rather surprising result is that, after the effects of inflation are removed, the per capita national debt actually decreased over the 30-year period from 1950 to 1980. From 1980 to 1994, per capita debt rose sharply after adjustment for inflation. If we look at the entire 44-year period, per capita debt in 1994 was only moderately above that of 1950 after adjustment for inflation.

Output, employment, and the like tend to rise over time even after adjustment for inflation. They rise because population grows, the labor force expands, the number of plants increases, and the technology of production improves. To look at the growth of one thing without taking into account this overall expansion can lead to growth distortion.

Growth distortion is the measurement of changes in a variable over time that does not reflect the concurrent change in other relevant variables with which the variable should be compared, such as population size or the size of the economy.

People who want to demonstrate alarming increases in alcohol consumption or crime can point to increases in gallons of alcohol consumed or crimes reported without noting that population may be increasing at a rate that is as fast or faster. Panel (*c*) of Figure A9 shows the problem of growth distortion. The left-hand graph shows the inflation-adjusted output of the 100 largest manufacturing concerns. By looking at this graph, we might conclude that the dominance of American manufacturing by giant concerns has risen by a considerable amount. However, by looking at the output *share* of the 100 largest manufacturing companies (the right-hand chart), we find that the output of these companies has just been keeping up with the manufacturing output in general.

Unrepresentative Data

A third pitfall of graphs is the use of *unrepresentative* or *incomplete data*. A graphed relationship may depend upon a time period or a choice of regions or countries. For example, panel *(d)* of Figure A9 shows how unemployment data can be manipulated. Suppose the agenda is to demonstrate that the U.S. unemployment rate was lower than the rates of other countries. The left-hand chart, comparing U.S. unemployment with that of three other industrialized countries, suggests that U.S. unemployment is lower. However, in the right-hand chart of nine industrialized countries, the U.S. unemployment rate appears about in the middle.

We all use statistics. We see them in our newspaper; we hear them on news broadcasts. Because they can be abused, it is important that we know how to use them, and to interpret them, correctly.

SUMMARY

1. Graphs are useful for presenting positive and negative relationships between two variables. A positive relationship exists between two variables if an increase in one is associated with an *increase* in the other; a negative relationship exists between two variables if an increase in one is associated with a *decrease* in the other. In a graphical relationship, one variable may be an independent variable and the other may be a dependent variable.

2. Graphs have certain advantages over tables: The relationship between the variables is easier to see, and graphs can accommodate large amounts of data more efficiently.

3. The slope of a straight-line relationship is the ratio of the rise in Y over the run in X. The slope of a curvilinear relationship at a particular point is the slope of a tangent to the curve at that point. When a curve changes slope from positive to negative as the X values increase, the value of Y reaches a *maximum* when the slope of the curve is zero; when a curve changes slope from negative to positive as the X values increase, the value of Y reaches a *minimum* when the slope of the curve is zero. Scatter diagrams are useful tools for examining data for positive or negative relationships between two variables.

4. The area of a rectangle is calculated by multiplying its height by its width. The area of a triangle is calculated by dividing the product of height times width by 2.

5. There are three pitfalls to be aware of when using graphs: (1) the choice of *units* and *scale* affects the apparent steepness or flatness of a curve,

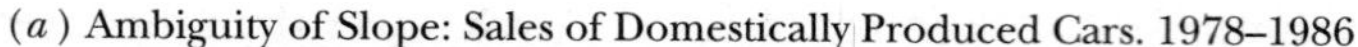
(*a*) Ambiguity of Slope: Sales of Domestically Produced Cars. 1978–1986

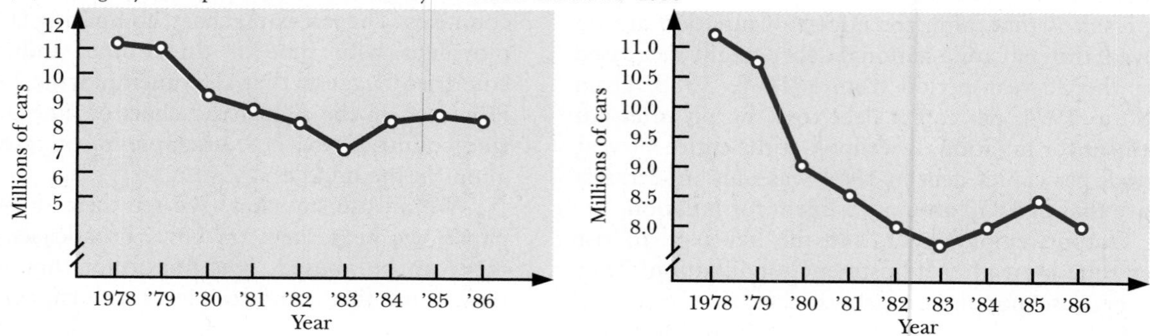

(*b*) Inflation-Distorted Measures: Per Capita Government Debt. 1950–1998

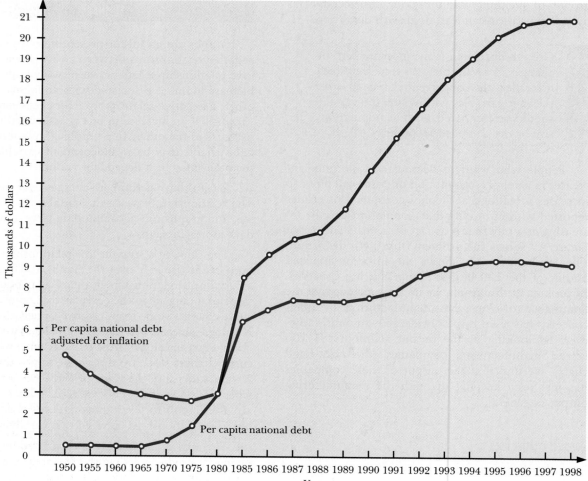

Thousands of dollars

21
20
19
18
17
16
15
14
13
12
11
10
9
8
7
6
5
4
3
2
1
0

Per capita national debt adjusted for inflation

Per capita national debt

1950 1955 1960 1965 1970 1975 1980 1985 1986 1987 1988 1989 1990 1991 1992 1993 1994 1995 1996 1997 1998

Year

(*c*) Growth-Distorted Measures:
Output of 100 Largest Manufacturing Companies

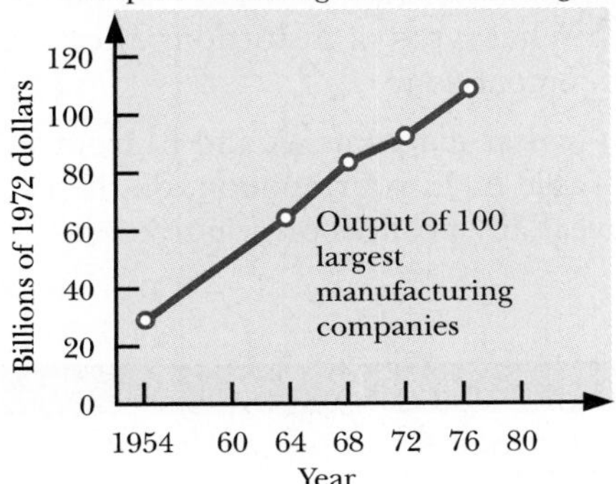

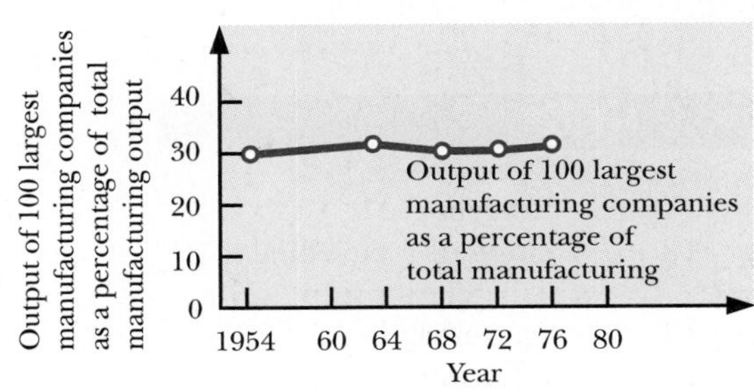

(*d*) Unrepresentative Sample:
U.S. Employment in International Perspective in 1990

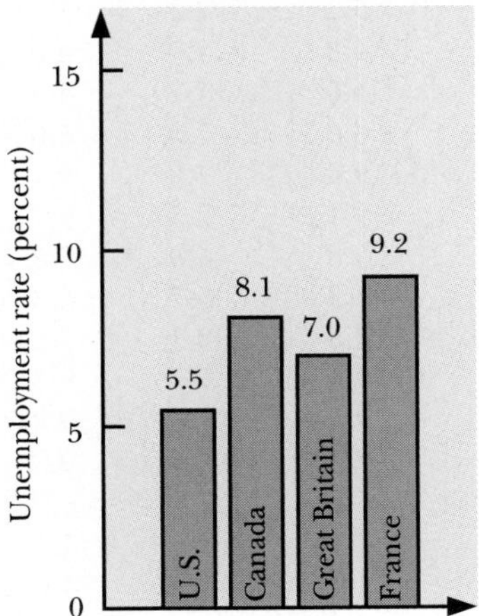

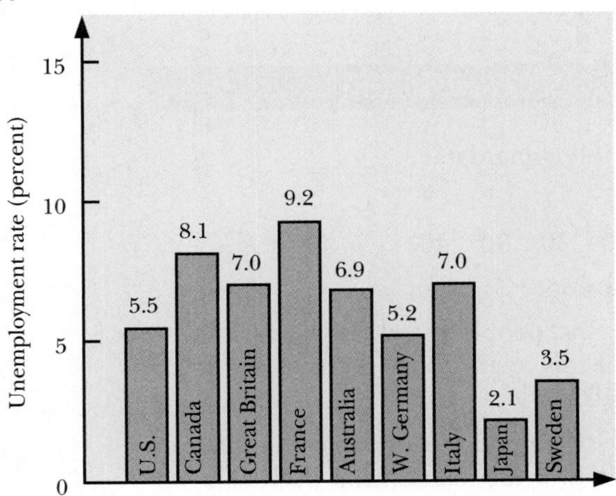

FIGURE A9 Examples of Pitfalls in the Use of Graphs

In panel (*a*), the choice of units on the vertical axis determines the steepness of slope. Although both figures plot the same data, the graph on the right appears to yield a steeper decline in domestic auto sales. In panel (*b*), the graph of per capita government debt (not adjusted for inflation) shows a steady rise in per capita debt. After the inflation distortion is removed (the red line), we find that per capita debt actually declined over the 50-year period from 1950 to 1998. From 1980 to 1998, per capita debt rose moderately over the 50-year period. In panel (*c*), the left-hand graph shows that the output of the 100 largest manufacturing firms has been increasing since 1954 by substantial amounts. This graph, however, fails to reflect the overall growth of the economy, including the growth in total manufacturing. The right-hand graph adjusts for growth distortion and shows that the share of output of the 100 largest manufacturing firms has barely changed since 1954. In panel (*d*), when the sample is limited to four high-unemployment countries (the left-hand graph), the U.S. unemployment rate does not appear to be high by international standards. When a broader and more representative sample is taken of nine countries (as shown in the right-hand graph), the U.S. unemployment rate appears to be average by international standards.
Source: http://www.stls.frb.org/fred.

(2) the variables may be inflation-distorted or growth-distorted, and (3) omitted data or incomplete data may result in an erroneous interpretation of the relationship between two variables.

KEY TERMS

positive (direct) relationship 18
negative (inverse) relationship 18
slope of a curve 20
slope of a straight line 20
tangent 21
slope of a curvilinear relationship 21
scatter diagram 22
inflation distortion 24
growth distortion 25

QUESTIONS AND PROBLEMS

1. Graph the following data:

X:	0	1	2	3
Y:	10	20	30	40

   What is the slope?
2. As income falls, people spend less on cars. Is the graph of this relationship positively or negatively sloped?
3. As the price of a good falls, people buy more of it. Is the graph of the relationship positively or negatively sloped?
4. Answer the following questions using Figure A.
   a. What is the slope?
   b. What is area *A* (shaded in green)?
   c. What is area *B* (shaded in pink)?

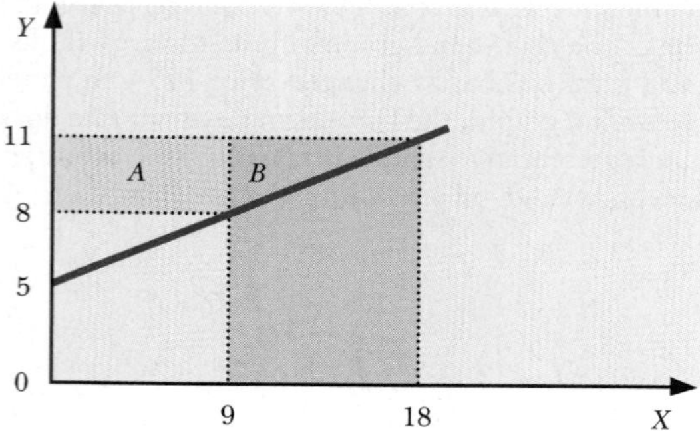

FIGURE A

5. The federal government spent $96 billion in 1970 and almost $1.5 trillion in 1999 on goods and services. What types of distortions affect this kind of comparison?
6. Prepare two scatter diagrams (A and B) from the data in Table A. In your opinion, do these diagrams reveal any positive or negative relationships?

TABLE A

	Diagram A		*Diagram B*	
	Unemployment Rate	*Inflation Rate*	*Interest Rate*	*Inflation Rate*
1970	4.8	5.2	7.3	5.2
1971	5.8	4.8	5.7	4.8
1972	5.5	4.0	5.7	4.0
1973	4.8	6.0	7.0	6.0
1974	5.5	9.4	7.8	9.4
1975	8.3	9.1	7.5	9.1
1976	7.6	5.8	6.8	5.8
1977	6.9	6.3	6.7	6.3
1978	6.0	7.8	8.3	7.8
1979	5.8	9.5	9.7	9.5
1980	7.0	9.8	11.6	9.8
1981	7.5	9.3	14.4	9.3
1982	9.5	6.2	12.9	6.2
1983	9.5	4.1	10.5	4.1
1984	7.4	4.0	11.9	4.0
1985	7.1	3.6	9.6	3.6
1986	6.9	2.7	7.1	2.7
1987	6.1	3.4	7.7	3.4
1988	5.5	3.3	8.3	3.3
1989	5.3	4.1	8.6	4.1
1990	5.5	4.2	8.3	4.2
1991	6.7	2.9	6.8	2.9
1992	7.4	3.0	5.3	3.0
1993	6.8	3.0	4.4	3.0
1994	6.1	2.6	6.3	2.6
1995	5.6	2.8	6.3	2.8
1996	5.4	3.3	6.0	3.3
1997	4.9	1.7	6.1	1.7
1998	4.4	1.6	5.1	1.6
1999	4.3	2.0	5.3	2.0

Source: http://www.stls.frb.org.

7. During the 2000 U.S. presidential debate, suppose the incumbent party faces an increase in unemployment last year of 240,000 workers, or

approximately 0.1 percent. Which figure will the incumbent party's candidate mention in his public statements? To which will his opponent refer?

8. Suppose thefts in a small town rise from a total of 1 to 2 cases in a given year. A sheriff running for reelection will refer to which change in her public speeches—the absolute change ("only" 1 additional break-in last year) or the percentage change (a 100 percent increase)?

INTERNET CONNECTION

The Economy at a Glance; Basic Statistics of U.S. Economy
http://stats.bls.gov/eag/eag.us.htm

Chapter 2

Unlimited Wants, Scarce Resources

Chapter Insight

There are 2.5 physicians in the United States for every thousand persons. In Mexico the number is 1.3, and in Brazil it is 0.3. Thus, in the United States there are 400 men, women, and children for every doctor. In Mexico there are 769 people, and in Brazil there are 3333 people for every physician. The number of physicians is a measure of one of the most important medical resources a country has. In all countries the number of physicians is limited; hence, we must make choices about how to use the scarce resource. Both rich and poor countries must decide on the best use of their scarce supply of doctors. In the United States, the problem may be less acute, but, judging from the heated political and social debates, it is a matter about which we feel strongly. Should we share our doctors equally, or should the rich have easier access? Should we pay physicians ourselves or should they be paid by the government through a form of socialized medicine? Brazil must answer the same questions. When one person or group of persons uses a scarce resource, there is less of it for others. If doctors spend all their time caring for wealthy patients, they have less time for other patients. If doctors decide to see patients based on how long they are willing to stand in line, those at the back of the line have less access than those at the front. This chapter describes the concepts of scarcity and choice.

LEARNING OBJECTIVES

After studying this chapter, you will be able to:

1. Define scarcity and why scarcity requires choices of what, how, and for whom.
2. Understand why economics is the study of allocating scarce resources among competing ends by the economic system.
3. Explain opportunity costs and their measurement.
4. Use the production possibilities frontier to illustrate efficiency, growth, and the law of increasing cost.
5. Differentiate macroeconomics from microeconomics.
6. Understand the law of diminishing returns.

CHAPTER PUZZLE: Explain why, in 2000, military recruiters were not able to recruit enough qualified young men and women to meet the manpower requirements of the U.S. volunteer army. (Hint: 1999 was a year of low unemployment and high prosperity.)

The Economic Problem

Only a few scarce goods concern the difference between life and death, but all raise the same economic problem. There is not enough Black Sea caviar to satisfy all who want it; therefore, some system must be established to determine who will get it and who will not.

How shall we use our scarce resources? Because we cannot produce enough to meet our virtually unlimited wants, we must choose among alternatives, and we must make these hard choices in an orderly fashion. We must use our limited resources to decide *what* to produce, *how* to produce, and *for whom* to produce.

What? Should we devote our limited resources to producing civilian or military goods, luxuries or necessities, goods for immediate consumption or goods that increase the wealth of society (capital goods)? Should small or large cars be produced? Should buses and subways be produced instead of cars? Should the military concentrate on strategic or conventional force?

How? What combination of the factors of production will be used to produce the goods that we want? Will coal, petroleum, or nuclear power be used to produce electricity? Will bulldozers or workers with shovels build dams? Should automobile tires be made from natural or synthetic rubber? Should Diet Coke be sweetened with saccharin or another sugar substitute? Should tried-and-true methods of production be replaced by new technology?

For Whom? Will society's output be divided equally or unequally? Will differences in wealth be allowed to pass from one generation to the next? What role will government play in determining allocation? Should government change the way the output is distributed?

The *for whom* question also addresses the future. How do we go about providing for the future—building the roads and power plants, and finding the technologies that will benefit future generations?

The imbalance between what people want and what they are able to acquire illustrates the most basic facts of economic life: the economic problems of *scarcity* and *choice*. The economy cannot fulfill everyone's wants; therefore, someone or something must decide which wants will be met. There will never be enough resources to meet everyone's wants.

The Defining Moment economists of Chapter 1 wrote about how we, as consumers, owners of businesses, or employees deal with scarcity and choice. As consumers, we are motivated to spend our money wisely, including saving some of it. As owners of businesses, we must combine resources wisely and produce products that customers will buy. We must do this to make a profit. As employees, we must find and keep jobs and put in a satisfactory performance. All these actions create the spontaneous interactions described by Adam Smith.

THE DEFINITION OF ECONOMICS

As we know from Chapter 1, economics is the study of how people allocate their scarce resources among competing ends within a specific economic system, to produce, exchange, and consume goods and services. To understand this definition, however, we must also know the exact economic meanings of *scarcity, choice, resources, allocation, competing ends,* and *economic systems.*

Scarcity

If there were no scarcity, there would be no need to study economics. Scarcity is present wherever virtually unlimited wants are greater than available resources can supply. Scarcity does not imply that most of us are poor or that our basic needs are not being met. Scarcity exists simply because it is human nature for us to want more than we can have.

Along an Idaho highway stands an amusing sign: "Tumbleweeds are free, take one." Idaho tumbleweeds are free because the number of tumbleweeds available far exceeds the number people want. In Alaska, however, tumbleweeds may be such a rarity that the number people want exceeds the number available. Exotic orchids can be freely picked in some remote Hawaiian islands, but they command high prices elsewhere.

Congested airports like New York's LaGuardia, Washington's Ronald Reagan, London's Heathrow, and Tokyo's Narita can handle only a limited number of takeoffs and landings per day. More planes wish to use these airports than can be accommodated. Committees allot takeoff and landing slots, and competing airlines intensely negotiate to obtain them. Landing slots are scarce at these major airports. At uncongested airports, on the other hand, landing slots are a free good because there are more slots than the airlines want.

An item is a **scarce good** if the amount available is less than the amount people would want if it were given away free of charge.

An item is a **free good** if the amount available is greater than the amount people want at a zero price.

These examples show that goods may be scarce even if their price is zero, and goods may be free at one time and place and scarce in another time and place. (See Example 1.)

Choice

Choice and scarcity go together. We all face *tradeoffs*. To have more of one thing, we must have less of another. An individual must choose between taking a job and pursuing a college education, between saving and consuming, between going to a movie and eating out. Businesses must decide where to purchase supplies, which products to offer on the market, how much labor to hire, and whether to build new plants. Nations must choose between spending more for

Tumbleweed/Airports

EXAMPLE 1

The Pacific Yew and Cancer: Scarcity, Allocation, and Opportunity Costs

The Pacific yew, a shrublike tree native to the Pacific West Coast, was long regarded as a weed, which loggers would burn. So uninteresting was this tree that no one kept inventories on the number in existence. It was a free good—until recently.

Studies by the National Cancer Institute revealed that taxol, a substance that comes from the Pacific yew, is effective in treating advanced cases of ovarian and lung cancer. However, it takes six 100-year-old trees to treat a single cancer patient, and most of the mature Pacific yews have been destroyed; they can be found only in one of every 20 acres of Oregon's forests.

Although scientists have discovered ways to make synthetic taxol, there is still not enough taxol to treat all patients who need it. The Pacific yew's scarcity meant that an allocation system had to be used to distribute the available taxol. The National Cancer Institute continues to determine which patients will receive the drug. However, as the production of synthetic taxol increases, its distribution will be handled by doctors' prescriptions, and payments will be made by insurance companies or by the patients themselves.

Sources: Taxol Synthesized, http://www.hort.purdue.edu/newcrop/NewCropsNews/94-4-1/ taxol.html; The Taxol Story: An Overview, http://www.pfc.cfs.nrcan.gc.ca/ecosystem/yew/taxol.html; Also see http://www.pfc.nrcan.gc.ca/ecosystem/yew/taxol.html.

defense or more for public education, they must decide whether to grant tax reductions to businesses or to individuals, and they must decide how much freedom their citizens should have to buy or sell goods in foreign countries.

Resources

Resources, also known as **factors of production**, are the inputs used to produce goods and services.

Resources are divided into four categories: land, capital, labor, and entrepreneurship. They include the natural resources, the capital equipment (plants, machinery, and inventories), the human resources (workers with different skills, qualifications, and ambitions), and the skills to organize production that are used as *inputs* to produce scarce goods and services. These resources represent the economic wealth of society because they determine how much *output* the economy can produce. The limitation of resources is the fundamental source of scarcity.

Land is a catchall term that covers all of nature's bounty—minerals, forests, land, and water resources.

Land includes all natural resources—unimproved and unaltered—that contribute to production. Desert land that has been irrigated is not "land" by this definition because labor and capital are used to alter its natural condition. Other items such as air and water are in this category, as long as they are in their natural state.

Capital includes equipment, buildings, plants, and inventories created by the factors of production; that is, capital is used to produce goods both now and in the future.

When capital is used to produce output, it is not consumed immediately; it is consumed gradually in the process of time. An assembly plant can have a life of 40 years, a lathe a life of 10 years, and a computer a life of 5 years. In 2000, the total value of all U.S. capital was slightly in excess of $490 trillion.[1]

Capital means physical capital goods— computers, trucks, buildings, plants—rather than *financial capital,* which represents ownership claims to physical capital.

AT&T shareholders own financial capital, but their shares really represent ownership of AT&T's physical capital.

Economists also make a distinction between the stock of physical capital and additions to that stock. The stock of capital consists of all the capital (plants, equipment, inventories, and buildings) that exist at a given time. This stock grows when new plants come on line, new equipment is manufactured, and additions are made to inventories. Through *investment* we add to our stock of capital.

Labor is the combination of physical and mental talents that human beings contribute to production.

Labor resources consist of the people in the work force, with their various natural abilities, skills, education, and ambitions, who contribute to production in various ways. The loading-dock worker contributes muscle power; the computer engineer contributes mental abilities; the airline pilot contributes physical coordination and mental talents. In the United States today, the labor force consists of more than 120 million individuals.

Capital investment adds to the stock of human capital just as it adds to the stock of physical capital.

Human capital is the accumulation of past investments in schooling, training, and health that raise the productive capacity of people.

Investment in training and education raises the wealth of society because, like investment in physical capital, it increases production capacity.

Entrepreneurs organize the factors of production to produce output, seek out and exploit new business opportunities, and introduce new technologies and inventions. The entrepreneur takes the risk and bears the responsibility if the venture fails.

The Defining Moment economists all understood that the entrepreneur creates economic progress. The entrepreneur is the one who sees an opportunity that

[1]OECD (Organization for Economic Cooperation and Development), Department of Economics and Statistics, *Flows and Stocks of Fixed Capital* (Paris: OECD, 1983), p. 9. Figures updated by the authors.

others do not see, is prepared to accept risk, raises the capital to take advantage of the opportunity, and then organizes production. Without the entrepreneur, there would have been no Industrial Revolution.

The entrepreneur accepts the vast responsibility of risk. The entrepreneur who makes a wrong decision loses money, assets, and reputation. If we do not allow appropriate rewards for the entrepreneur, such as profits from successful ventures, there is no reason for the entrepreneur to assume risk. The failure of the Soviet experiment to allow appropriate incentives for the entrepreneur contributed to its downfall. Von Mises and Hayek predicted that socialism would fail because of the lack of incentives for entrepreneurs.

Allocation

Allocation is the apportionment of scarce resources to specific productive uses or to particular persons or groups.

Consider what would happen without organized allocation. We would have to fight with one another for scarce resources. The timid would compete ineffectively; the elderly or weak would be left out. Such free-for-all allocation was common in ancient times, but it is rare in modern societies. It reappears when social order breaks down. Martial law must be declared and the national guards or U.N. peacekeepers must be brought in to prevent looting and violent competition for scarce goods during floods, natural disasters, and wars. Societies cannot function effectively unless the allocation problem is resolved in a satisfactory manner. (See Example 2.)

Competing Ends

Whatever allocation system is used, it must somehow allocate scarce resources among competing ends.

Competing ends are the different purposes for which resources can be used.

Individuals compete for resources: Which families will have a greater claim on scarce resources? Who will be rich? Who will be poor? The private sector (individuals and businesses) and the government compete for resources. Even current and future consumption compete for resources: When scarce resources are

EXAMPLE 2

Should We Organize the Internet by Market or by Plan?

This chapter teaches that scarce resources can be allocated by market or by plan. Market allocation means that the suppliers of Internet services can freely offer their services to users without government intervention. In the market case, suppliers of Internet services will sell their products either directly to users, as is the case of Internet service provider (ISP) monthly access fees (AOL or CompuServe), or by attracting large numbers of viewers who are exposed to paid advertising on the Web site (the various free ISPs). Allocation by plan means that the government decides who is allowed to offer Internet services by requiring licenses and dictating rules that all Internet suppliers must follow. The closest analogy to the Internet is television broadcasting, which is currently a combination of "market" and "plan." No television broadcaster is allowed to operate without a government license that allots that broadcaster a broadcast frequency. In return for the license, the broadcaster must obey government rules and regulations concerning what can and cannot be shown. Currently, virtually anyone can set up a Web site. The government has so far not been able to license Internet operators. As complaints against Internet smut and news-gossip services have increased, there has been increasing discussion of whether the government should manage and control the Internet. Opponents of government regulation argue that such interference would violate rights to free speech.

invested in physical and human capital to produce more goods and services in the future, these same resources cannot be used in the present. Society must choose between competing national goals when allocating resources. What is most important: price stability, full employment, elimination of poverty, or economic growth? The Defining Moment economists disagreed about whether this competition for resources is harmful or helpful. Adam Smith believed that each person's pursuit of self-interest was good for society. Karl Marx thought that the pursuit of self-interest would lead to collapse.

ECONOMIC SYSTEMS

Each society uses an economic system to solve allocation problems and to maintain order.

An **economic system** is the property rights, resource-allocation arrangements, and incentives that a society uses to solve the economic problem.

Economic systems are differentiated according to the specific institutions for determining property rights and incentive systems.

The two major economic systems are capitalism and socialism, philosophies introduced in Chapter 1 as we discussed the Defining Moments in economics. Capitalism is characterized by private ownership of the factors of production, market allocation of resources, and the use of economic incentives. Socialism is characterized by state ownership or control of the factors of production, the use of noneconomic as well as economic incentives, resource allocation by central state or government plan, and centralized decision making.

No actual economy fits exactly into one of these two molds. Economies combine private and public ownership, administrative and market allocation, economic and noneconomic incentives, and centralized and decentralized decision making. The economies of most nations reflect a mixed system that combines features of both capitalism and socialism. However, in most economies, the major traits of one particular economic system dominate. Experience has shown that capitalist countries have outperformed socialist countries in terms of living standards, innovation, and technological advances.

Property Rights

Property rights are the rights of an owner to buy, sell, or use and exchange property (that is, goods, services, and assets).

In our capitalist economy, most of us take property rights for granted. We are accustomed to being able to freely buy and sell, or rent property and goods. In a socialist economy, property belongs to the state and its use and disposition are handled quite differently.

Property Rights in a Capitalist System. In a capitalist society, most property is owned by private individuals. Private owners of property are motivated by self-interest to obtain the best deal possible for themselves. The legal system protects private property from theft, damage, and unauthorized use, and defines who has property rights. With property rights, property owners will reap the benefits of using their property wisely and will suffer the consequences of wrong decisions concerning the use of their property. Obviously, property owners will try to use their property for their own economic gain.

Property Rights in a Socialist System. In a socialist society, most property (except labor) is owned by the state, and the state has rights to use and exchange that property. Individual ownership of property has been limited to a few head of livestock, a private home in some circumstances, a private car, a TV, and so on. If state property is misused, the "state" suffers the consequences. In the former Soviet Union the saying was: "Everybody and thus nobody is the owner of property. Why should we care?"

Allocation Arrangements

Resources can be allocated either by market or by plan. Capitalism uses market resource allocation. Socialism allocates resources by government decree.

Market Allocation. Market allocation allows buyers and sellers to exchange goods and services through markets. Owners of private property have the right to use the property to their best advantage and to sell the property at the best price possible. The actions of the owners of private property will be guided by markets.

A **market** brings together buyers and sellers and in doing so determines prices.

The farmer looks at the prices of corn and soybeans to decide how much of each crop to plant; the owner of an oil refinery uses the prices of gasoline, fuel oils, and kerosene to determine how much of each petroleum product to refine. The private owner of labor (that is, the individual worker) looks at wage rates, job descriptions, and different occupations to determine where to work.

These decisions are made spontaneously and without government direction. They are guided by what Adam Smith described as the invisible hand. The invisible hand (described more fully in the next chapter) ensures that these individual actions will be coordinated.

Allocation by Plan. Under planned resource allocation, a central authority determines output targets and makes the basic investment decisions. Industrial ministries issue output targets to enterprises and tell them what materials to use. Although planners cannot decide exactly for whom the output is produced, they play a significant role in determining who will get the scarce automobiles, apartments, and vacations.

Incentives

Any economic system must provide incentives for people to work hard and to take economic risks.

Incentives in a Capitalist System. A capitalist system uses economic incentives to motivate employees. Higher salaries, bonuses, and stock options are rewards for tasks that are well done. Entrepreneurs are rewarded by having the value of their businesses grow. It is economic incentives—the opportunity to earn bonuses, profits, and higher salaries—that make us work hard and take business risks. Without economic incentives, there would be little reason for us to pursue our self-interest.

Incentives in a Socialist System. A socialist system relies more heavily on nonmaterial incentives, although socialist systems quickly learned that they could not rely on nonmaterial incentives alone. In socialist systems, there is greater emphasis on "working for the good of society." Medals, honorary positions, and other noneconomic incentives are used to motivate workers. However, there is in this system little to motivate the risk-takers. Under capitalism, the entrepreneur can earn substantial rewards for taking advantage of profit opportunities. Under socialism, the state must be the entrepreneur. Any rewards from successful entrepreneurship will go to the state—to everyone and hence to no one.

With the fall of socialism in the Soviet Union and Eastern Europe and the dramatic economic reforms of the Chinese economy, few countries of the world now follow the socialist ideal. The appeal of socialism, however, has been with us for almost two centuries, and even earlier. We have not seen the last of socialism. The major socialist experiment has failed. However, socialist principles still have appeal on the grounds that they can make capitalism more humane or even make capitalism work better. Whether socialism's appeal continues will depend on the solutions to the ongoing transitions of the former socialist economies.

Opportunity Costs

Whenever we make choices among competing ends, we must sacrifice valuable alternatives. The value of such a sacrifice is an opportunity cost.

The **opportunity cost** of a particular action is the loss of the next-best alternative.

If you buy a new car, its opportunity cost might be a trip, an investment in the stock market, or enrollment in a university. To find the true cost of the car you must consider the cost of losing your next-best alternative. If the government increases health spending, the opportunity cost is the next-best alternative that had to be sacrificed (such as more spending on public education or a tax reduction).

Opportunity costs provide a shortcut method of differentiating free goods from scarce goods.

The Idaho tumbleweed had no opportunity cost. If one tumbleweed is taken, nobody has to go without a tumbleweed. A 9 A.M. landing slot at Heathrow Airport has a positive opportunity cost: If American Airlines gets it, British Airways must do without it.

The opportunity cost of an action can involve the sacrifice of time as well as goods. To gather the free tumbleweed, the traveler must sacrifice time (although the time cost may be very small). Attending a football game with a free ticket is not necessarily free. The three hours you spent at the game you could have devoted to alternative activities such as studying. If a major exam were scheduled for the next day, the opportunity cost of the game could be quite high.

Economic decisions are based on opportunity costs. In committing its resources to a particular action (such as producing cars), a business must consider the opportunities it forgoes by not using these resources for another activity (such as producing trucks). Before signing a contract to work for Ford Motor Company, workers must consider the other employment opportunities that they are passing up. People with savings must weigh the various alternatives before they commit their funds to a particular investment, such as certificates of deposit, stocks, or bonds.

> Every choice involved in the allocation of scarce resources has opportunity costs. Free goods have an opportunity cost of zero. Scarce goods have a positive opportunity cost.

Production Possibilities

Economists use the concept of the production possibilities frontier (PPF) to illustrate the function of scarcity, choice, and opportunity costs. The PPF reveals the economic choices open to society. An economy can produce any combination of outputs on or inside the PPF.

> The **production possibilities frontier (PPF)** shows the combinations of goods that can be produced when the factors of production are used to their full potential.

Suppose an economy produces only two types of goods: compact discs and wheat. Figure 1 shows the amounts of wheat and compact discs that this hypothetical economy can produce with its limited supply of factors of production and technical knowledge.

The economy has resources that can be used for either wheat or compact discs. Land may be better suited for wheat; compact discs may require more capital. If the economy chooses to be at point *a* on Figure 1, it will produce no compact discs and the maximum of 18 tons of wheat from the factors of production available. At point *f*, the economy produces no wheat and the maximum of 5000 compact discs. At point *c*, 2000 compact discs are produced; the maximum number of tons of wheat that can be produced is therefore 15. Each intermediate point on the PPF between *a* and *f* represents a different combination of wheat and compact discs that are produced using the same resources and technology.

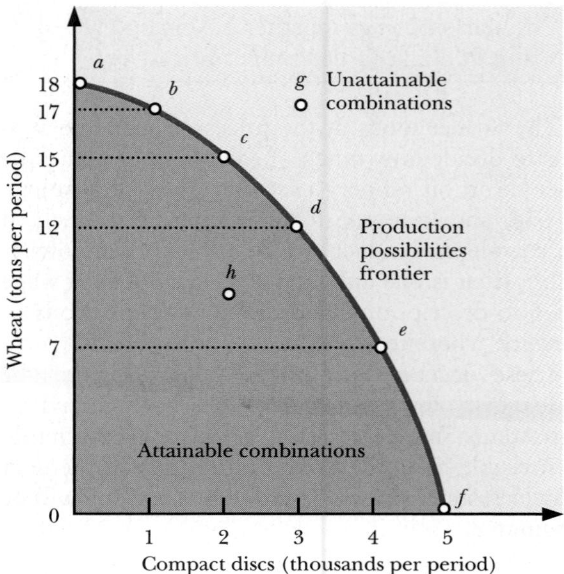

FIGURE 1 The Production Possibilities Frontier (PPF)

The PPF shows the combinations of outputs of two goods that can be produced from society's resources when these resources are used to their maximum potential. Point *a* shows that if 18 tons of wheat are produced, no compact disc production is possible. Point *f* shows that if no wheat is produced, a maximum of 5000 compact discs can be produced. Point *d* shows that if 3000 compact discs are produced, a maximum of 12 tons of wheat can be produced. Point *g* is beyond society's PPF. With its available resources, the economy cannot produce 17 tons of wheat and 3000 compact discs. Points like *h* inside the PPF represent an inefficient use of resources.

Combination	*Compact Discs (thousands)*	*Wheat (tons)*	*Opportunity Cost of Compact Discs (in tons of wheat)*
a	0	18	0
b	1	17	1
c	2	15	2
d	3	12	3
e	4	7	5
f	5	0	7

Although this hypothetical economy is capable of producing output combinations *a* through *f*, it cannot produce output combination *g* (17 tons of wheat and 3000 compact discs) because *g* uses more resources than the economy has. It can, on the other hand, produce the output combination at point *h*, which is inside the frontier, because it requires fewer resources than the economy has.

The Law of Increasing Costs

When the economy is at point *a* in Figure 1, it is producing 18 tons of wheat and no compact discs. The opportunity cost of increasing the production of compact discs from zero to 1000 is the 1 ton of wheat that must be sacrificed in the move from *a* to *b*. The opportunity cost of 1000 more compact discs (moving from *b* to *c*) is 2 tons of wheat. The opportunity cost of the move from *e* to *f* is a much higher 7 tons of wheat. In other words, the opportunity cost of compact discs rises with the production of more compact discs. This tendency for opportunity costs to rise is the law of increasing costs.

The **law of increasing costs** states that as more of a particular commodity is produced, its opportunity cost per unit increases.

The bowed-out shape of the PPF shows the law of increasing costs. Suppose the economy starts at *a*, producing only wheat and no compact discs. People now want compact discs, and the economy must suddenly increase its production of compact discs. Because the amount of resources available is not altered, the increased compact disc production must be at the expense of wheat production. The economy must move along its PPF in the direction of more compact disc production.

As compact disc production increases, the opportunity costs of a unit of compact disc production rises. At low levels of production, the opportunity cost of a unit of compact disc production is relatively low. Some factors of production are suited to producing both wheat and compact discs; they can be shifted from wheat to compact disc production without a significant increase in opportunity cost. As compact disc production increases further, resources suited to wheat production but ill-suited to compact disc production (experienced farmers make inexperienced workers in the disc industry) must be diverted into compact disc production. Ever-increasing amounts of these resources must be shifted from wheat production so that compact discs keep expanding at a constant rate. There will be a rise in the opportunity cost of a unit of compact disc production (the amount of wheat sacrificed), reflecting the law of increasing costs.

The Law of Diminishing Returns

Underlying the law of increasing costs is the law of diminishing returns. Wheat is produced by using land, labor, and tractors. Suppose a farm has a fixed amount of land (1000 acres) and a fixed amount of capital (10 tractors). Initially, 10 farmworkers are employed. Each has 100 acres to farm and 1 tractor. If the number of farmworkers increases to 20, each worker will have 50 acres to farm and 2 workers will have to share 1 tractor. If the number of farmworkers increases to 1000, each worker will farm 1 acre and 100 workers will share each tractor. Obviously, workers will be less productive if each has only an acre to farm and has to wait for 99 other workers to use the tractor. When labor is increased in equal increments, with the amount of land and tractors constant, the corresponding increases in wheat production will be smaller and smaller.

The **law of diminishing returns** states that when the amount of one input is increased in equal increments, holding all other inputs constant, the result is ever smaller increases in output.

The law of diminishing returns recognizes that output is produced by combinations of resources. Vegetables are produced by labor, farm machinery, and chemical fertilizers. Compact discs are produced by skilled labor, microelectronic equipment for stamping circuits, and managerial talent. The law of diminishing returns applies whenever one or more factors are fixed, and output must be expanded by an increase in the factors that can be varied. As more and more of the variable factors are used, there will eventually be too much of them relative to the fixed factors. Accordingly, the extra output produced by additional inputs of the variable factor will decline. (See Example 3.)

Efficiency

An economy operates on its production possibilities frontier only when it uses its resources with maximum efficiency.

EXAMPLE 3

Diminishing Returns and American Wines

The best wine-growing regions of the world are in France, Germany, Austria, and Italy. These wine-growing regions combine the right soil, temperature, and rainfall conditions to produce the grapes for vintage wines and champagne. With the exception of some parts of California, U.S. land is not as well suited to wine production as are these parts of Europe. Nevertheless, U.S. vintners produce more than 600 million gallons of wine for sale each year—some in states like Texas and Oklahoma, which are definitely not known for their wines.

The law of diminishing returns explains why not all wine is produced in Germany, France, Austria, Italy, and California. As wine production expands in established regions, new acreage must be cultivated that is less suited to wine production. As diminishing returns set in for established wine-producing areas, the marginal acre of land devoted to wine production eventually becomes inferior to new wine-growing regions such as Texas and Oklahoma. Instead of being produced in Europe or California, new wine is produced in Texas or Oklahoma.

If our taste for wine continues to grow, eventually we will be buying wine from Kansas and Nebraska—an event explained by the law of diminishing returns.

In Figure 1, if the economy produces output combinations that lie on the PPF, the economy is efficient. When an economy is operating on its PPF, it cannot increase the production of one good without reducing the production of another good. If the economy operates at points inside the PPF, such as *h,* it is *inefficient* because more of one good could be produced without cutting back on the other good.

Efficiency occurs when the economy is using its resources so well that producing more of one good results in less of other goods. No resources are being wasted.

If workers are unemployed or if machines stand idle, the economy is not operating on its PPF because available resources are not being employed. If these idle resources were used, more of one good could be produced without reducing the output of other goods. Misallocated resources are those that are not used to their best advantage. Except for the most unusual of circumstances—if a surgeon works as a ditch digger, if cotton is planted on Iowa corn land, or if supersonic jets are manufactured in Tahiti—resources are misallocated. If resource misallocations are removed, more of one good could be produced without sacrificing the production of other goods. How to best achieve economic efficiency is a core question of economics. Our resources are limited; we should make best use of them. Adam Smith argued that an economy will operate efficiently if people are allowed to pursue their self-interest. Von Mises argued that socialist economies cannot be efficient. In later chapters we shall consider the conditions required for economic efficiency.

Economic Growth

When the fabled traveler Marco Polo reached China in 1275, he was amazed at the riches he saw. Compared to his native Venice, China was a much richer and more prosperous country. Although modern China has been growing rapidly, it is today a much poorer country than Italy. A modern Marco Polo would be surprised by China's poverty, not by its wealth.

This example shows the importance of economic growth. The economic reality is that Italy grew more rapidly than China over the long run. Italy participated in the Industrial Revolution (see the Defining Moments of Chapter 1); China did not. In fact, China may even have failed to grow for centuries after its power and prosperity had peaked. Economic growth is not synonymous with rising living standards. For living standards to rise, the output of goods and services must expand more rapidly than population.

Economic growth occurs when an economy expands its outputs of goods and services.

Prosperity can be achieved only if economic growth is sustained for a long period of time. Relatively few countries of the globe have experienced such growth, and prosperity remains limited to a small percentage of the world's population. Economic growth has not been steady even in the advanced industrialized countries. England, the country in which the Industrial Revolution began, experienced rapid growth in the eighteenth and nineteenth centuries but relatively slow growth in the twentieth century. Germany and Japan grew so rapidly after World War II that they were both called "economic miracles."

Economic Growth and the PPF

Economic growth is an expansion of the PPF outward and to the right. The PPF can expand for two reasons: The capital and labor resources of the economy can expand, or the efficiency of the use of those resources can improve. The first type of growth is extensive growth; the second type is intensive growth. *Extensive economic growth* is the result of the expansion of the economy's resources. *Intensive economic growth* is the result of the more efficient use of available resources. Improvements in technology, better management techniques, and the creation of better legal and economic institutions—as first witnessed during the Industrial Revolution—are all sources of intensive economic growth.

Economic growth can be influenced by policy. Policies promote economic growth when they encourage the formation of capital, the improvement of science and technology, and the development of new business techniques. Some economic growth is not controllable. There can be periods of slow technological progress or there can be unanticipated breakthrough inventions—such as the steam engine or the computer—that change the economy forever.

Capital Accumulation. Deciding where to locate on the PPF represents a choice between capital goods and consumer goods. As you know, capital goods are the equipment, plants, and inventories added to society's stock of capital. These goods satisfy wants in the future. Consumer goods are food, clothing, medicine, and transportation that satisfy consumer wants in the present.

The choice between capital goods and consumer goods is shown in Figure 2. In this figure, the economy

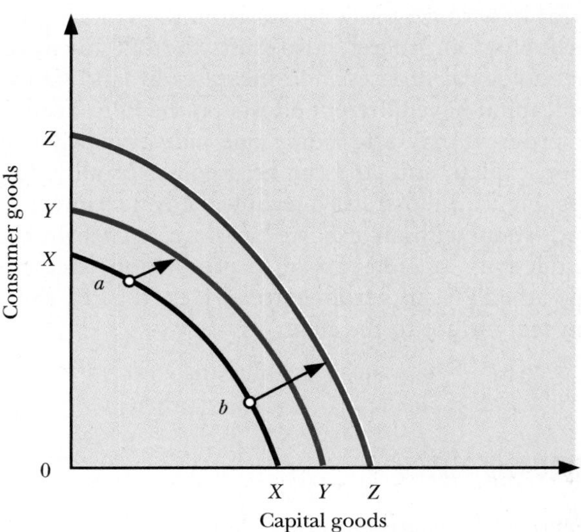

FIGURE 2 The Effect of Increasing the Stock of Capital on the PPF

The initial PPF is curve *XX*. If the economy chooses point *a*, allocating most resources to the production of consumer goods and few to the production of new capital goods, the PPF in the future will shift out to curve *YY*. But if the economy chooses point *b*, with comparatively little consumption and comparatively high production of new capital goods, the future PPF will shift out further to *ZZ*.

with the PPF labeled *XX* must choose among the combinations of consumer goods and capital goods located on *XX*. If *b* is selected over *a,* fewer wants are satisfied today, but additions to the stock of capital are greater. More capital today means more production in the future. The society that selects *b* will therefore experience a greater outward shift of the PPF and will be able to satisfy more wants in the future.

If a society chooses *a,* the PPF expands from *XX* now to *YY* in the future. If it chooses *b,* the PPF expands more: from *XX* now to *ZZ* in the future. The economy will be able to satisfy more wants at *ZZ* than at *YY*.

There are limits to the rule that less consumption today means more consumption tomorrow. If all resources were devoted to capital goods, the labor force would starve. If too large a share of resources is put into capital goods, worker incentives might be low and efficiency might be reduced.

Shifts in the PPF. Figure 2 shows extensive growth due to capital accumulation. Increases in labor or land or discoveries of natural resources also shift the PPF outward. Intensive growth occurs when society learns how to get more output from the same inputs. Technological progress also shifts the PPF outward. Technological progress and increases in land, labor, and capital have different effects on the PPF. Technical progress may affect only one industry—whereas labor, capital, and land can be used across all industries. Figure 3 illustrates a technical advance in wheat production without a corresponding change in the productivity of compact disc production. Accordingly, the PPF shifts from *af* to *bf*. Here the PPF shifts upward but not to the right.

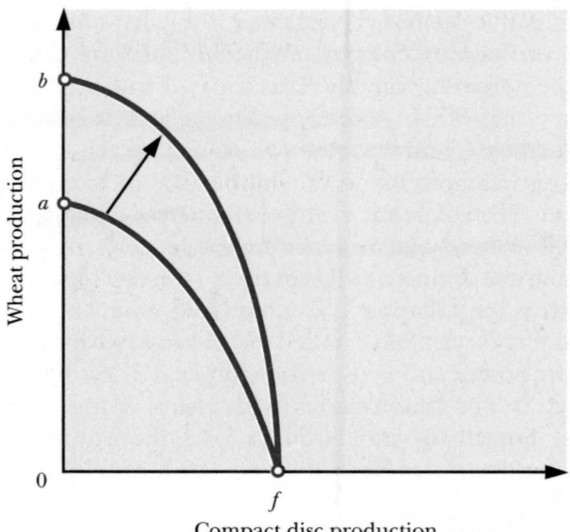

FIGURE 3 Technical Progress in Wheat Production

If a higher-yielding strain of wheat is discovered, a larger quantity can be produced with the same resources. Since this increase in wheat production will not influence compact disc production, the PPF will rotate from *af* to *bf*.

Microeconomics studies the economic decision making of firms and individuals in a market setting; it is the study of individual decision making and its impact on resource allocation.

Micro and Macro

Economics concerns scarcity, choice, allocation, economic systems, and growth. We can study these core issues from either a micro or a macro perspective.

Microeconomics

Economics is divided into two main branches called *microeconomics* and *macroeconomics*. These branches deal with economic decision making from different vantage points.

Microeconomics focuses on the individual participants in the economy: the producers, workers, employers, and consumers. In everyday economic life, things are bought and sold. People decide where and how many hours to work. Managers decide what to produce and how to organize production. These activities result in *transactions* that take place in markets where buyers and sellers come together. Individuals are motivated to do the best they can for themselves in these transactions, with the limited resources at their disposal.

Microeconomics considers how businesses operate under different competitive conditions and how the combined actions of buyers and sellers determine prices in specific markets.

Microeconomics assumes that the individual economic actors weigh the costs and benefits of their actions. Households spend their limited income to gain maximum satisfaction; they decide where to work and how much to work in the same fashion. Businesses choose the type and quantity of products and the manner of production in order to obtain maximum profits.

In effect, microeconomics studies the spontaneous interactions of Adam Smith's invisible hand—how individuals and businesses come together in markets. Because microeconomics studies the results of our weighing costs and benefits, it has expanded into areas outside the traditional realm of economics. Economists use microeconomics to deal with environmental problems, to explain how voters and public officials make their political decisions, and to analyze marriage, divorce, fertility, crime, and suicide. Even the court system uses microeconomic analysis to determine legal settlements and compensation for personal injuries.

Macroeconomics

Macroeconomics is the study of the economy as a whole, rather than individual markets, consumers, and producers. It concerns the *general* price level (rather than individual prices), the national employment rate, government spending, government deficits, trade deficits, interest rates, and the nation's money supply.

Macroeconomics uses measures called *aggregates,* which add together (or aggregate) individual microeconomic components. These aggregates include gross domestic product (GDP), the consumer price index (CPI), the unemployment rate, and the government surplus and deficit. Macroeconomics studies relationships between aggregate measures, such as the relationship between inflation and interest rates, the effects of government deficits on prices and interest rates, and the relationship between money and inflation.

The Coming Together of Micro and Macro

When modern economics was born more than 200 years ago with the publication of Adam Smith's *Wealth of Nations,* there was no distinction between micro- and macroeconomics. Early economic thinkers believed that it was necessary only to study consumers and producers in the marketplace to understand the economy as a whole. After all, the macroeconomy is nothing more than the sum total of individual decisions. These early pioneers did not realize that generalizing from the part to the whole can lead to mistakes (the fallacy of composition we discussed in Chapter 1).

Macroeconomics was not formally born until the late 1930s, with the publication of Keynes's *General Theory.* Specifically, macroeconomics was formed to explain the Great Depression. Why should an economy suddenly produce much less output and supply many fewer jobs?

Modern economics reemphasizes the importance of understanding individual behavior as a basis for understanding the behavior of the economy as a whole. Macroeconomists study how individuals behave to explain how the economy as a whole behaves.

In the next chapter, we shall consider how the price system solves the economic problem of *what, how,* and *for whom;* how it facilitates specialization and exchange; and how it provides for the future.

SUMMARY

1. Wants are unlimited; there will never be enough resources to meet unlimited wants.

2. The economic problem is what to produce, how to produce, and for whom. All economies must resolve this economic problem.

3. Economics is the study of how scarce resources are allocated among competing ends by an economic system. A good is *scarce* if the amount available is less than the amount people would want if it were given away free. A good is *free* if the amount people want is less than the amount available at zero price. The ultimate source of scarcity is the limited supply of resources. The resources that are factors of production are land, capital, labor, and entrepreneurship. Because scarcity exists, some system of allocating goods among those who want them is necessary.

4. The opportunity cost of any choice is the next-best alternative that was sacrificed to make the choice. Scarce goods have a positive opportunity cost; free goods have an opportunity cost of zero.

5. The production possibilities frontier (PPF) shows the combinations of goods that an economy is able to produce from its limited resources when

these resources are used to their maximum potential and for a given state of technical knowledge. If societies are efficient, they will operate on the production possibilities frontier. If they are inefficient, they will operate inside the PPF.

6. The law of increasing costs says that as more of one commodity is produced at the expense of others, its opportunity cost will increase. According to the law of diminishing returns, when the amount of one input is increased in equal increments, if all other inputs are constant, successive increases in output become smaller.

7. Economic growth occurs because the factors of production expand (extensive growth), or because technological progress raises productivity (intensive growth). The choice of consumer goods over capital goods is a choice between meeting wants now and meeting them in the future.

8. Economics is divided into microeconomics, the study of the behavior of markets, consumers, and producers; and macroeconomics, the study of the economy as a whole.

KEY TERMS

scarce good 33
free good 33
resource 34
factors of production 34
land 34
capital 34
labor 34
human capital 34
entrepreneur 34
allocation 35
competing ends 35
economic system 36
property rights 36
market 37
opportunity cost 37
production possibilities frontier (PPF) 38
law of increasing costs 39
law of diminishing returns 39
efficiency 40
economic growth 41
microeconomics 42
macroeconomics 43

QUESTIONS AND PROBLEMS

1. In the early nineteenth century, land in the western United States was given away free to settlers. Was this land a free good or a scarce good, according to the economic definition? Explain your answer. Explain why land in the United States is no longer given away free.

2. The town of Hatfield charges each resident $75 per year for water. The town is running out of water.
   a. What is the opportunity cost of water to the individual customer?
   b. What is the opportunity cost of water to the town?
   c. Is water scarce?
   d. How might prices be used to solve the water shortage?

3. "Desert sand will always be a free good. More is available than people could conceivably want." Evaluate this statement.

4. A local millionaire buys 1000 tickets to the Super Bowl and gives them away to 1000 Boy Scouts. Are these tickets free goods? Why or why not?

5. In the American West, irrigation has turned desert land into farmland. Does this example demonstrate that nature's free gifts are not fixed in supply?

6. Determine in which factor-of-production category—land, capital, or labor—each of the following items belongs.
   a. A new office building
   b. A deposit of coal
   c. The inventory of auto supplies in an auto supply store
   d. Land reclaimed from the sea in Holland
   e. A trained mechanic
   f. An automated computer system

7. Using Figure 1 as your model, draw two production possibilities curves for compact disc production as opposed to wheat production. In the first, show what would happen if the technology of compact disc production improved while the technology of wheat production remained the same. In the second, show what would happen if the technologies of compact disc production and wheat production improved simultaneously.

8. Consider an economy that has the choice of producing either bricks or bread. There are exactly 100 workers available. Each worker can

produce one brick or one loaf of bread. There is no law of diminishing returns. Sketch the economy's production possibilities curve?

9. By purchasing a new big-screen TV set, I pass up the opportunity to buy a personal computer, to take a vacation trip, to paint my home, or to earn interest on the money paid for the TV. What is the opportunity cost of the TV? How would I determine the opportunity cost?

10. How does the production possibilities curve illustrate the choices available to an economy?

11. If widgets were given away free, people would want to have 5 million per month. When would widgets be free goods and when would they be scarce goods? Under what conditions would the opportunity cost of widgets to society be positive?

12. Using the data in Table A, explain whether these data illustrate the law of diminishing returns. Show how much extra corn can be produced by different numbers of farmhands, each working an 8-hour day.

TABLE A

Number of Farmhands	*Output of Corn (thousands of bushels)*
1	50
2	100
3	140
4	160
5	170

13. The data in Table B describe a production possibilities frontier (PPF) for a hypothetical economy.
    a. Graph the PPF.
    b. Does the PPF have the expected shape?
    c. Calculate the opportunity cost of guns in terms of butter. Calculate the opportunity cost of butter in terms of guns. Do your results illustrate the law of increasing costs?
    d. If this economy produces 700 guns and 3 tons of butter, will it solve the *how* problem efficiently?
    e. If at some later date this economy produces 700 guns and 12 tons of butter, what do you conclude has happened?

TABLE B

Hundreds of Guns	*Tons of Butter*
8	0
7	4
5	10
3	14
1	16
0	16.25

14. Which of the following topics falls under macroeconomics? Which under microeconomics? Explain your answer in each case.
    a. The price of fish
    b. The interest rate
    c. Employment in the computer industry
    d. The general price level
    e. The national unemployment rate
    f. Unemployment in Oklahoma
    g. The number of new homes built in the United States

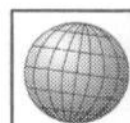

INTERNET CONNECTION

15. Using the links from http://www.awl.com ruffin_gregory, read the article "Speed Doesn't Kill" from the Milkin Institute Review, 4Q 1999. *Note:* Go to the magazine bar and the issues will drop down.
    a. Why does the author argue that the 55 mph speed limit was a failure?
    b. What is the economic cost of the 55 mph speed limit? *Hint:* What is the opportunity cost here? What benefits are there to the 55 mph limit? How would you weigh the two?

PUZZLE ANSWERED: This chapter teaches that all resources have their opportunity cost as measured by what they could earn in their next-best use. The year 2000 was one of considerable economic prosperity, low unemployment, and rising wages. Military recruiters found that young men and women, who a couple of years earlier were willing to sign up for the all-volunteer army, now had better options in the civilian economy. What had been their second-best option (civilian employment) now became their best option, and the number of volunteers dropped.

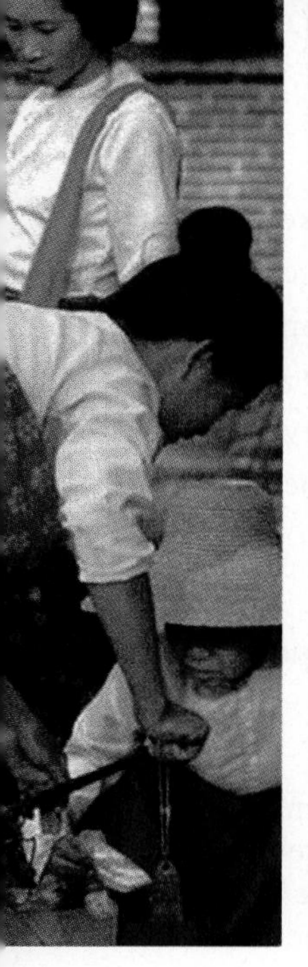

Chapter 3

THE PRICE SYSTEM AND THE ECONOMIC PROBLEM

Chapter Insight

In 1973, the Organization of Petroleum Exporting Countries (OPEC) pushed up the price of oil by restricting its supply to world markets. Panic set in as the price of oil rose from $2 per barrel in the early 1970s to $35 per barrel in 1981. The price of a gallon of gasoline rose from 36 cents in 1972 to $1.31 in 1981. Pundits warned that we might not survive this crisis. It was said that we could not do without gas to run our cars or without fuel oils to run our industry. We did indeed survive—through the workings of the price system. The dramatic rise in gas prices told us that we must economize on gas. No government pronouncement was required. In 1973, the average passenger car consumed 736 gallons per year. By 1981, this figure had dropped to 557 gallons. Despite a growing population and more cars on the road, total gas consumption by cars fell from 78 billion gallons in 1973 to 72 billion in 1981. The price system "solved" the energy crisis of the 1970s.

Nobel laureate Friedrich Hayek (one of the Defining Moment economists of Chapter 1) described this phenomenon as follows:

> The marvel is that in a case like that of a scarcity of one raw material, without an order being issued, without more than perhaps a handful of people knowing the cause, tens of thousands of people whose identity could not be ascertained by months of investigation, are made to use the material or its products more sparingly; i.e., they move in the right direction.[1]

[1]Friedrich Hayek, "The Use of Knowledge in Society," *American Economic Review* 35, 4 (September 1945): 519–530.

Does the price system protect us from future energy crises? Between early and mid-1999, oil prices doubled (from $11 per barrel to $24) as OPEC countries, especially Saudi Arabia, again cut back on production. Notably, the world press did not warn of a new energy crisis that would threaten the world economy. All realized that the price system builds in limits to price increases. If oil prices rose too high, new production from non-OPEC countries like Mexico would come on the market, and also consumers would again cut back on energy consumption. The relatively low gas prices of the mid-1990s encouraged us to buy gas-guzzling sport utility vehicles. When gas prices rise again, we'll switch back to more fuel-efficient cars.

LEARNING OBJECTIVES

After completing this chapter, you will be able to:

1. See how the economy is a circular flow of goods and money from consumers to firms and from firms to consumers.
2. Understand how solving the economic problem for any economy involves answering the three questions *what, how,* and *for whom.*
3. Know the difference between relative prices and money prices.
4. Appreciate how relative prices guide decisions through the principle of substitution.
5. Understand how the price system coordinates economic activity and solves the economic problems of what, how, and for whom.
6. Explain the determinants of specialization and the role of money.
7. Know the Law of Comparative Advantage.
8. Know the limits to the invisible hand.

CHAPTER PUZZLE: When the North American Free Trade Agreement (NAFTA) was passed by Congress, critics warned of a "huge sucking sound" of American jobs disappearing to Mexico, where labor is cheap. Now, more than five years after NAFTA's passage, the number of jobs has grown in both the United States and Mexico. How can this be, given that Mexican workers earn only a small percentage of what American workers earn?

THE PRICE SYSTEM AS A COORDINATING MECHANISM

Our economy is made up of millions of consumers, millions of resource owners, and hundreds of thousands of enterprises. Each participant makes economic decisions to promote his or her self-interest. How are the decisions of all these people and businesses coordinated? What prevents the economy from collapsing if these decisions clash? Is it necessary to have someone or something in charge? The Defining Moment economists focused on these questions.

The Invisible Hand

Let us consider in detail how Adam Smith (whom we met in Chapter 1) answered these questions. He described how market allocation solves the economic problem efficiently without conscious direction:

> Every individual endeavors to employ his capital so that its produce may be of greatest value. He generally neither intends to promote the public interest, nor knows how much he is promoting it. He intends only his own security, only his own gain. And he is led by an *invisible hand* to promote an end which was no part of his intention. **By pursuing his own interest he frequently promotes that of society more effectively than when he really intends to promote it.** [Emphasis added.][2]

Smith's "invisible hand" works through the price system.

The **price system** coordinates economic decisions by allowing resource owners to trade freely, buying and selling at whatever relative prices emerge in the marketplace.

---

[2]Adam Smith, *The Wealth of Nations,* ed., Edwin Cannan (New York: Modern Library, 1937), p. 423.

EXAMPLE 1

Where Did All the Goods Come From? Russia's Move to a Market Economy

Prior to 1992, the Russian government set the prices of goods and services and ran all retail stores. Prices were usually set very low, and people had to stand in line to buy goods and services. Often, when they reached the front of the line they found there was nothing to buy. On January 1, 1992, the Russian government decided to distribute goods and services through markets, and they decontrolled prices of most consumer goods. Prices rose sharply from the low levels that the state had set. Almost overnight, the lines disappeared, and miraculously goods appeared on shelves. Electronics stores that a few weeks earlier had stocked only electric light bulbs were now full of toasters, radios, CD players, and Korean-made television sets. Although the Russian economic transformation has been deeply flawed and corrupt, at least consumers now have a wide choice of goods they can buy (if they have the money) without standing in line.

Our experience—which includes the rise and fall of socialism, a Defining Moment in Chapter 1—shows that the invisible hand usually works better than the "visible hand" of the state. The invisible hand works through the price system, which provides necessary information for informed decision making. (See Example 1.)

Relative Prices and Money Prices

How do we know whether prices are high or low? A relative price indicates how one price stands in relation to other prices. It is quite different from a money price.

A **relative price** is a price expressed in terms of other goods.

A **money price** is a price expressed in monetary units (such as dollars, francs, etc.).

If a textbook sells for 60 dollars and a compact disc (CD) player for 120 dollars, two textbooks is the relative price of a CD player, or one-half of a CD player is the relative price of a textbook.

Figure 1 illustrates the money prices and relative prices of attending different types of higher educational institutions—community colleges, public universities, and private universities. Panel *(a)* shows that the money prices of attending colleges and universities rose between 1992 and 1999 from an average of $5300 for community colleges to an average of $9250 for public universities to an average of $19,750 for private universities. All money prices rose, but they rose fastest in private universities. Panel *(b)* shows the relative prices of community colleges and public universities as a percent of private universities (the cost of private universities equals 100). In both 1992 and 1999, community colleges (31 percent as expensive as private universities) and public universities (48 percent as expensive as private universities) were bargains compared to private universities. Over this time period, they became even more of a bargain. By 1999, their relative prices fell to 28 percent and 46 percent as expensive as private universities.

Money prices are most meaningful when they are compared to prices of *related* goods. For example, it makes sense to compare the price of electricity to that of natural gas because commercial and residential users make choices between natural gas and electricity. Should we heat and air condition our homes with electricity or natural gas? Should manufacturers use electricity or natural gas as fuel?

Example 2 on page 51 shows how the price system responds to changes in relative prices, even in "nonbusiness" activities like higher education. When relative prices change, consumers will substitute relatively less expensive products for those products whose prices have increased. The business that loses customers must therefore protect its market.

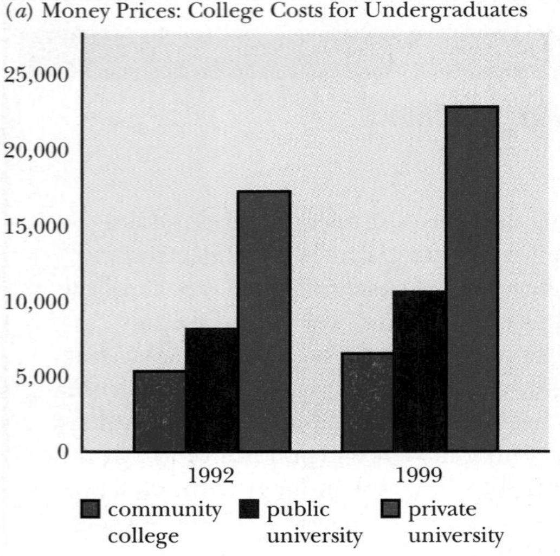

(b) Relative Prices: College Costs for Undergraduates As a Percent of Private Universities

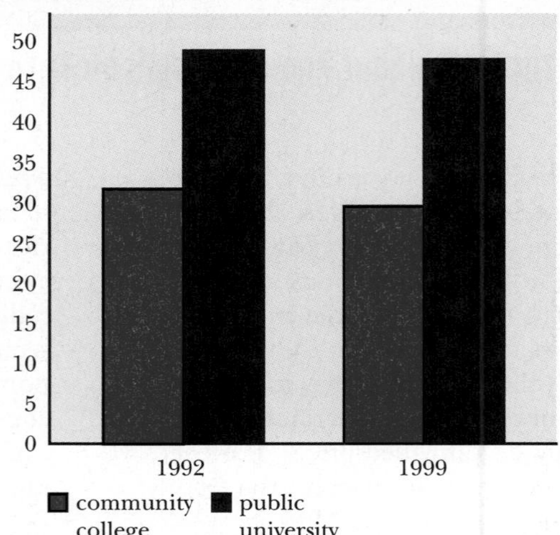

FIGURE 1 Money Prices and Relative Prices of Attending Different Types of Higher Educational Institutions
Sources: http://www.collegeboard.org; *Statistical Abstract of the United States.*

> The money price of a commodity can rise while its relative price falls. The money price can fall while its relative price rises. Money prices and relative prices need not move together.

Relative prices play a prominent role in resolving the economic problem of *what, how,* and *for whom* raised in the previous chapter. Money prices do not. Relative prices signal to buyers and sellers what goods are cheap or expensive. *Buying and selling decisions are based on relative prices.* If the relative price of one good rises, buyers substitute other goods whose relative prices are lower. For example, the lowering of the relative price of electricity will encourage consumers to use electricity rather than natural gas.

The emphasis on relative prices does not mean that money prices are unimportant. Money prices—or the price level—are important in macroeconomics. It is here that the concept of inflation plays an important role.

> **Inflation** is a general increase in money prices over time.

Elections are won or lost on the basis of inflation; the living standards of people on fixed incomes can be damaged by inflation. Inflation drives up interest rates. But even in the case of inflation, money prices are not considered in isolation. Instead, the level of money prices today is compared with the level of money prices yesterday. Ultimately, this is also a form of relative price.

> In microeconomics there is greater interest in relative prices than in money prices. In macroeconomics, there is greater interest in the level of money prices than in relative prices.

The Principle of Substitution

Virtually no good is fully protected from the competition of substitutes. Aluminum competes with steel, coal with oil, electricity with natural gas, labor with machines, movies with video rentals, one brand of toothpaste with another, and so on. The only goods for which there are no substitutes are minimal quantities of water, salt, or food and certain life-saving medications, such as insulin. Rela-

EXAMPLE 2

Even Harvard, Princeton, and Yale Must Protect Their Markets

Figure 1 showed the money prices and relative prices of college education. Premier private universities, like Harvard, Princeton, and Yale, are much more expensive than premier public universities, like Berkeley, UCLA, the University of Michigan, and the University of Texas, and they are becoming relatively more expensive over time. Students who have the academic achievements to attend either premier private or public universities can substitute public for private universities if the relative price of private universities becomes too high. If too many qualified students choose public universities, private universities will not be able to meet their enrollment objectives. Like other businesses, private universities lower their prices when confronted with the lower-priced substitutes. To quote a report of the Congressional Budget Office: "For many students, institutionally provided financial aid reduces the actual price of tuition to well below \$3000. Only 12 percent of students had tuition bills of more than \$14,000. And at those few high-priced institutions that are the focus of so much media attention, financial aid offsets the price even more: Colleges and universities that charge \$20,000 or more for tuition provide an average of \$12,000 in institutional aid to their financial aid recipients." In other words, private universities are forced to lower their prices—which they do through generous scholarships—in order to compete with public universities.

Source: http://www.tulane.edu/~aau/Iken Tuition7.24.97.html.

tive prices guide resource allocation through the principle of substitution.

The **principle of substitution** states that practically no good is irreplaceable. Users are able to substitute one product for another when relative prices change.

To say that there is a substitute for every good does not mean that there is an *equally good* substitute for every good. One mouthwash may be a close substitute for another; a television show may be a good substitute for a movie; rental apartments may be good substitutes for private homes. However, carrier pigeons are a poor substitute for telephone service; public transportation is a poor substitute for the private car in sprawling cities; steel is a poor substitute for aluminum in the production of jet aircraft.

Increases in relative prices (like the increase in gas prices discussed in the Chapter Insight) provide signals for consumers to consider possible substitutes. When the relative price of coffee increases, people consume more tea. When the relative price of beef rises, people buy more poultry and fish. There is no single recipe for producing a cake, a bushel of wheat, a car, recreation, comfort, or happiness. Increases in relative prices motivate consumers and firms to search out substitutes. Changes in relative prices signal producers to look for substitutes. When the relative price of crude oil rises, utilities switch from oil to coal. Airlines buy more fuel-efficient aircraft when the relative price of jet fuel rises.

Equilibrium

Households and business firms make buying and selling decisions on the basis of relative prices. The family decides how to spend its income; the worker decides where and how much to work; the factory manager decides what inputs to use and what outputs to produce. Insofar as these decisions are made individually, what guarantees that there will be enough steel, bananas, foreign cars, domestic help, steelworkers, copper, and lumber for homes? What ensures that there will not be too much of one good and too little of another? How will Adam Smith's invisible hand prevent shortage or surplus?

Let's consider an example: If automobile producers decide to produce more cars than buyers want to buy *at the price asked by the automobile producers,* there will be many unsold cars. Since dealers must pay their bills and earn a living, they must sell cars at lower prices. As the money price of cars falls, the relative price tends to fall, and customers begin to substitute automobiles for vacations, home computers, or remodeled kitchens. The decline in the relative price of automobiles signals automobile manufacturers to produce fewer cars. Eventually, a balance between the number of cars people are prepared to buy and the number offered for sale will be struck, and the corresponding price is called an equilibrium price.

The **equilibrium price** is that price at which the amount of the good people are prepared to buy (demand) equals the amount offered for sale (supply).

The economy itself requires enormous information about how to produce different goods, product qualities, product prices, worker efficiencies, and so forth. The price system allows us to make decisions by knowing only the relative prices that are important to us. Each participant will specialize in information that is personally relevant. We buy more of a good that has become relatively cheap; we economize on goods that have become relatively expensive. We need not know why the good has become cheap or expensive.

Just as checks and balances in an ecological system prevent one species of plant or animal from overrunning an entire area and extinguishing itself, relative prices provide the checks and balances in the economic system. If one product is in oversupply, its relative price will fall; more will be purchased and less will be offered for sale. If one product is in short supply, its relative price will rise; less will be purchased and more will be offered for sale.

The Circular Flow of Economic Activity

Let us consider all of the activity that must be coordinated with the invisible hand. Economic activity is circular. Consumers buy goods with the incomes they earn by supplying land, capital, and labor to the business firms that produce the goods they buy. The circular-flow diagram in Figure 2 shows how output and input decisions involving millions of consumers, hundreds of thousands of producers, and millions of resource owners fit together.

The **circular-flow diagram** summarizes the flow of goods and services from producers to households and the flow of the factors of production from households to business firms.

As the circular-flow diagram illustrates, the flows from households to firms and from firms to households occur in two markets: the goods market and the factors market. The *goods market* is the market in which buyers and sellers come together to buy and sell goods and services. The *factor market* is the market in which buyers and sellers come together to buy and sell land, labor, and capital.

The circular-flow diagram consists of two circles. The outer circle shows the *physical flows* of goods and services and productive factors. The inner circle shows the *flows of money* expenditures on goods and services and on productive factors. The physical flows and money flows go in opposite directions. When households buy goods and services, goods flow to the households, but the sales receipts flow to businesses. When workers supply labor to business firms, productive factors flow to businesses, but the wage income flows to households.

For every physical flow in the economy, there is a corresponding financial transaction. To obtain goods, the consumer must pay for them. When firms sell products, they receive sales revenues. When businesses hire labor or rent land, they must pay for it. When individuals supply labor, they receive wages.

Two types of goods and services are omitted from the circular flow diagram. *Intermediate goods* are goods that businesses sell to other businesses. For example, the steel industry supplies steel to the automobile industry, which produces the automobiles that enter the circular flow. The other goods and services that are not included in the circular flow diagram are those produced and used within the household, such as the cooking, cleaning, transportation, and other services provided by one family member to another.

The amount of activity in the circular flow of economic activity is staggering. There are more than 20 million business firms in the U.S. economy, inter-

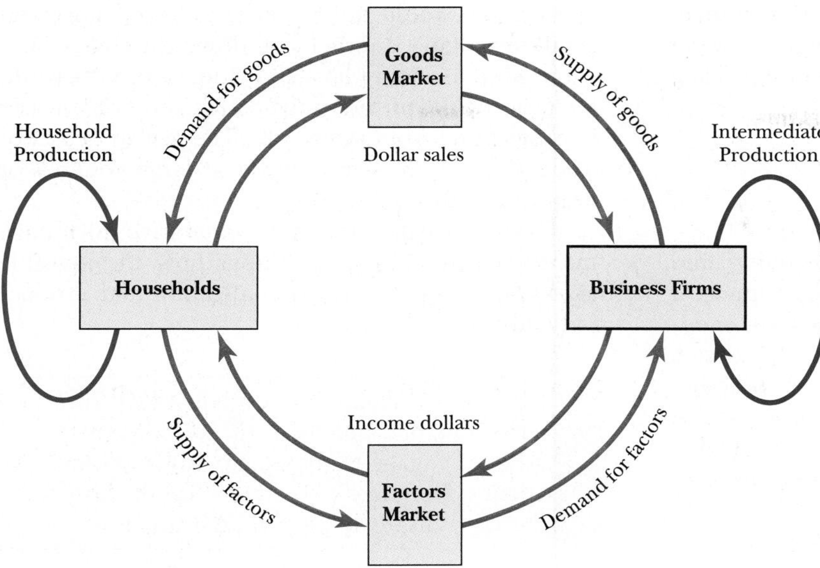

FIGURE 2 The Circular Flow of Economic Activity

Economic activity is circular. The outside circle describes the flow of physical goods and services and productive factors through the system: business furnishes goods to households, who furnish land, labor, and capital to business. The inside circle describes the flow of dollars: households provide dollar sales to business, whose costs become incomes to households. These two circles flow in opposite directions. The circular-flow diagram shows that flows of intermediate goods remain entirely within the business sector and do not enter the circular flow. It also shows that because household-production services are produced and consumed within the family, they do not enter the circular flow.

acting with 80 million households. Business firms employ 120 million persons. The value of capital resources in the circular flow is more than $40 trillion. The annual value of goods and services that flow from business firms (including government) to households is over $10 trillion. We cannot even count the millions of distinct goods and services the economy produces. The field of economics called *national income accounting* explains how economists measure the total flow of goods and services from businesses to households and the flow of factor resources from households to businesses.

Specialization, Productivity, and Exchange

Adam Smith's invisible hand does far more than simply balance supply and demand. As the economic problem suggests, the price system needs to determine *how* we produce output and *how* we provide for the future. In a market economy, the price system encourages specialization, which raises efficiency and allows economies to produce ever-larger outputs from their available inputs.

Specialization is the tendency of participants in the economy (people, businesses, and countries) to focus their activity on tasks to which they are particularly suited.

Exchange complements specialization by permitting individuals to trade the goods in which they specialize for those that others produce.

Exchange is everywhere. We exchange our specialized labor services for money; then we exchange money for a huge variety of goods. The United States exchanges its wheat for videocassettes made in Japan. Within a business, different departments exchange skills in engineering, purchasing, and marketing to produce and sell the firm's output. A travel agency exchanges its ability to market group tours for discounted airline tickets. A foreign-car manufacturer agrees to supply fuel-efficient engines to an American-auto manufacturer in return for marketing and repair outlets.

Productivity and Exchange

The best way to understand productivity and exchange is to consider a simple example. Suppose a sailor is stranded on an uninhabited island—a modern Robinson Crusoe. The sailor has to decide whether to make fish nets or fish hooks or whether to sleep or break coconuts. The sailor would not be specialized; he would be a jack-of-all-trades. Solving the *for whom* problem is easy—everything he produces is for himself—and the problems of *what* and *how* are solved without having to know relative prices, being concerned about ownership, or using markets.

In the modern economy, a jack-of-all-trades is rare; a specialist is commonplace. A typical household consumes thousands of articles, yet one member of the household may specialize in aligning suspension components on an automobile production line. Everyone in our economy (except hermits) is dependent on the efforts of others. We produce one or two things; we consume many things.

Specialization gives rise to exchange. If people consumed only those things that they produced, there would be no trade and there would be no need for money. Money, trade, and specialization are all characteristics of a modern economy.

Specialization raises productivity. Increased productivity was defined in Chapter 2 as the production of additional output from the same amount of resources. As Adam Smith noted in *The Wealth of Nations,* specialization is a basic source of productivity advances. Specialization raises productivity in two ways. First, specialization allows resources, which have different characteristics, to be allocated to their best use. Land, capital, and people come in different varieties. Some machines can move large quantities of earth; others can perform precision metal work. Some land is moist; other land is dry. Some people are agile seven-footers; others are small and slow. These differences offer opportunities for specialization.

Second, by concentrating certain resources in specific tasks, we can produce large amounts of output at a lower cost per unit of output. Even if all people in an automobile manufacturing plant had identical skills, it would still be better to have one person install the engine, another bolt down the engine, and so on in an assembly line. Individuals who focus on one task can learn their jobs better and don't waste time switching from job to job. The per unit costs of production are frequently lower at large volumes of output. (See Example 3.)

David Ricardo's law of comparative advantage (mentioned in Chapter 1) shows how the invisible hand of prices promotes specialization and productivity advances.

The **law of comparative advantage** is the principle that people, firms, or countries should engage in those activities for which their advantages over others are the largest or their disadvantages are the smallest.

Suppose Sally is twice as good at making hats as Harry, but three times better at making shoes. Sally can make $100 a day in hats and $120 a day in shoes. Harry can make $50 a day in hats and $40 a day in shoes. Sally will specialize in shoe production because this gives her more income even though she has an advantage over Harry in hat production. Harry will specialize in hats because that maximizes his income even though he is at a disadvantage in hat production compared to Sally. What matters is not whether you can make more or less than somebody else in some activity, but whether you can make more in that activity than in some other activity. Sally has a comparative advantage in shoe production because she can do better in that employment than in hats; and Harry has a comparative advantage in hats because he can make more in hats than in shoes.

Thus, a mediocre computer programmer could possibly be the best clerk in a local supermarket. The clerks in the local supermarket may not be able to stock shelves and work a cash register as well as the programmer, but they have a comparative advantage in that occupation. An attorney may be the fastest typist in town, yet the attorney is better off preparing deeds than typing them. (See Example 4 on page 56.)

The law of comparative advantage applies to countries as well as people. A country's resources are best committed to those activities for which its advantages are the largest or its disadvantages are the smallest. It does not matter that one country has low wages and another country high wages. What matters is how the resources are best used within a coun-

EXAMPLE 3

Specialization and the Pin Factory

Economic science seeks to explain the facts of economic life. Perhaps the most basic question is why some people and countries are rich while others are poor. One of Adam Smith's key insights was that people and countries that effectively specialize will be wealthy.

In his classic *Wealth of Nations,* Adam Smith used the pin factory to illustrate the benefits of specialization. In his day (the late nineteenth century), pins were manufactured through a large number of separate operations. Then (and now) pin making consisted of (1) drawing wire, (2) straightening, (3) pointing, (4) twisting, (5) cutting heads and heading the wire, (6) tinning and whitening, and (7) papering and packaging. The major advantages of specialization were achieved by separating pin production into many operations: One set of workers would do the straightening, another the pointing, another the twisting, another the cutting of heads, and so on.

According to Adam Smith's calculations, the average specialized worker could produce 5000 pins a day (the number of pins per day divided by the number of workers in the pin factory). If each person worked alone, only a few pins would be produced by each worker. The specialized worker, in this case, could produce almost 1000 times more wealth than the unspecialized worker.

Source: Clifford Pratten, "The Manufacture of Pins," *Journal of Economic Literature* 18, 1 (March 1980): 93–96.

try. We will see in the chapter on international trade that every country has goods that it can profitably export—even if the country had the highest overall wage level or the lowest overall productivity level.

Let us use a simple numerical example to illustrate the law of comparative advantage as applied to international trade and specialization. Table 1 shows the quantities of two products (commercial jets and computer motherboards) that can be produced in either the United States or Taiwan with 100,000 hours of skilled labor.

The United States has an *absolute advantage* in both jets and computer motherboards. With the same amount of labor, it can outproduce Taiwan in both products. The United States is twice as productive in jet production and 1.5 times as productive in computer motherboard production. The United States has a comparative advantage in jets as is seen in the lower opportunity costs of jets in the United States, where the production of one jet causes the loss of 3.75 units of motherboards. In Taiwan, the opportunity costs of jets is much higher: The Taiwanese economy must sacrifice 5 units of motherboards to produce one jet. The law of comparative advantage states that the United States will specialize in jets, Taiwan in computer motherboards, and that they

TABLE 1 ILLUSTRATION OF COMPARATIVE ADVANTAGE

	(1) Number of commercial jets produced with 100,000 hr of labor	*(2) Number of computer "motherboards" produced with 100,000 hr of labor*	*(3) Opportunity costs of jets (2 ÷ 1)*
United States	4	15	3.75
Taiwan	2	10	5.00

EXAMPLE 4

Comparative Advantage and Hawaiian Pineapples

The law of comparative advantage states that people and, by extension, countries specialize in those activities that they perform relatively better than others do. What matters is comparative, not absolute, advantage.

For more than 60 years, the Hawaiian island of Lanai had a comparative advantage in growing pineapples. Lanai soil, climate, and workers produced pineapples for world markets at prices that yielded large profits for the Dole Company, owner of more than 90 percent of the island.

Even though Lanai workers remain among the world's most productive pickers of pineapple, 1991 was the last year that a pineapple crop was planted on Lanai. Why? Lanai pineapple pickers earned $8.23 per hour; those in Thailand, however, earned less than $.90 per hour. Lanai workers therefore had to be almost nine times more productive than Thai workers for their pineapples to remain competitive. Even though Lanai pickers were more productive than Thai workers in absolute terms, they lacked a sufficient margin to offset lower Thai wages.

It might appear that Lanai pineapple pickers are losers from changing comparative advantage. In fact, Hawaii has a greater absolute advantage in tourism than in pineapples. Lovely beaches, friendly people, and a warm climate attract visitors from all over the world. Thus, the development of tourism, an activity in which Lanai has comparative advantage, raised wages throughout the island to such an extent that the Dole Company could no longer operate a profitable pineapple business. As Lanai's comparative advantage shifted from pineapples to tourism, pineapple pickers became bartenders, hotel maids, and concierges. It was the profitability of tourism that made growing pineapples unprofitable!

Source: "After a Long Affair, Pineapple Jilts Hawaii for Asian Suitors," *New York Times,* December 26, 1991.

will sell to each other the product they produce at the low opportunity cost.

Even though Taiwan has an absolute disadvantage in both products, its labor can compete by working for a wage between half and two-thirds that of American workers. At a wage of 60 percent of the United States, Taiwan can produce computer motherboards more cheaply than American workers, but American workers can produce jet aircraft more cheaply than Taiwanese workers. Indeed, this is the pattern of trade observed: Our computer manufacturers import computer motherboards and chips from Taiwan, and Taiwan's airlines buy commercial aircraft from the United States.

Money and Exchange

Money is essential in an economy where people are specialized because it reduces the cost of transacting with others.

Money is anything that is widely accepted in exchange for goods and services.

Money can take many forms. In simple societies, fishhooks, sharks' teeth, beads, or cows have been used as money. In modern societies, money is issued and regulated by government, and money may (gold coins) or may not (paper money) have an intrinsic value of its own.

Money enables us to trade with anyone else, unlike a barter system in which we must trade with someone who wants what we specialize in.

Barter is a system of exchange where products are traded for other products rather than for money.

In barter, for example, it would be necessary for barefoot bakers to exchange goods with hungry shoemakers. A successful barter deal requires that the two (or more) traders have matching wants. Money is essential precisely because such coincidences of wants are rare.

If one form of money were abolished by law, another form would replace it. The costs of barter are so high that societies must have something to serve as money. If we did not have something that served as money, we would have to barter for everything. Barter would be so inefficient that the economy might actually not survive under such a condition.

The Industrial Revolution (a Defining Moment of Chapter 1) was accompanied by the development of banking. Banking created new forms of money called checks, which facilitated the growth of modern industry and trade. The development of international banking prompted the rapid rise of globalization after World War II. International banking made it possible for the money of one country to be electronically converted and to be instantaneously transferred to a bank or other firm in another country thousands of miles away.

Provision for the Future

The invisible hand uses the price system to balance supply and demand and to promote specialization and exchange. But can the invisible hand provide for the future? Our high living standards today are the result of past investment in physical and human capital. What is there in the price system that encourages us to make such investments?

The stock of capital goods is one generation's legacy to the next. The interstate highway system will be enjoyed not only by the generation that built it, but also by future generations. The ultimate benefits of space exploration will accrue to generations far in the future. As future chapters will show, we must save in order to invest. We are able to invest only as much as we are able to save. We save by not spending all our income. We sacrifice consumption today to save; we would not be willing to make this sacrifice unless saving allowed us to increase our consumption in the future. The sacrifice of current consumption is the cost of saving. The benefit of saving is that interest will be earned on savings.

The **interest rate** is the price of credit that is paid to savers who supply credit.

If the interest rate is 10 percent per annum, $1000 of saving today will give us $1100 a year hence. A dollar sacrificed (saved) today yields more than a dollar tomorrow. The higher the interest rate, the greater the inducement to save.

The interest rate not only acts as an inducement to save, it also signals to businesses whether they should borrow for investment. Like any other price, the interest rate provides a *balance*—in this case, balancing the amount we are willing to save with the amount businesses want to borrow for investment. If the interest rate is low, businesses will want to invest because they find it cheap to add to their capital stock. However, at a low interest rate few are willing to save. The reverse is true at high interest rates: Few businesses will want to invest, but households will be quite willing to save.

The interest rate balances the saving offered by households with the investment businesses wish to undertake. The price system uses interest rates to solve the problem of allocating resources between present and future consumption.

Limits of the Invisible Hand

We have emphasized the virtues of resource allocation through the price system. The price system solves the problems of *what, how,* and *for whom* without centralized direction. It balances the actions of millions of consumers and thousands of producers, and it even solves the difficult problem of providing for the future. The price system has great strength, but it has weaknesses as well. These weaknesses must be examined to determine the costs and benefits of interfering with the workings of the price system and possibly creating unintended consequences.

Income Distribution

There is no guarantee that resource allocation through the price system will solve the *for whom* problem in such a way as to satisfy the ethical beliefs of members of society. Some people believe that income should be distributed fairly evenly; others believe that the gap between rich and poor should be substantial. Many believe that it is unfair for people to be rich just because they were lucky enough to inherit wealth or intelligence.

Economics can shed little light on what is a "good" or "fair" solution to the *for whom* problem because such decisions require personal value judgments. Economics is broad enough to accommodate virtually all views on the desirability of differing distributions of income; judgments about income distribution are in the realm of normative economics.

Public Goods

Another weakness of the price system is that it cannot supply certain goods—called public goods—that are necessary to society. Public goods include defense, the legal system, highways, and public education. In the case of private goods, there is an intimate link between costs and benefits: The one who buys a car enjoys the benefits of the car; the one who buys a loaf of bread eats that loaf. Public goods, on the other hand, are financed not by the dollar votes of consumers but by taxes. In most cases, the benefits each individual derives from public goods will not be known. Moreover, it is difficult to prevent nonpayers from enjoying public goods. National defense protects nontaxpayers just as well as it protects the taxpayers.

Externalities

The invisible hand also may not handle well cases where private costs and benefits differ from social costs and benefits—when there are costs and benefits that are external to the price system. If a polluting factory makes nearby residents ill or causes housing values to fall without having to consider these external costs on others, it will produce more than it should. One of the big issues of economics involves how to deal with externalities and whether government action is required.

Monopoly

The invisible hand may not function well when a single firm controls the supply of a particular commodity. What makes Adam Smith's invisible hand work so well is that individual buyers and sellers compete with one another; no single buyer or seller has control over the price. The problem with monopoly—a single seller with considerable control over the price—is that the monopolist can hold back the amount of goods, drive up the price, and enjoy large profits. While the monopolist would benefit from such actions, the buyer would not.

Macroeconomic Instability

The invisible hand may solve the economic problem of scarcity but may provide a level of overall economic activity that is unstable. It is a historical fact that capitalist economies have been subject to fluctuations in output, employment, and prices—called business cycles—and that these fluctuations have been costly to capitalist societies. A key question is: Are they the price of progress?

In later chapters, we shall discuss in detail not only the advantages of the invisible hand but also these limits.

SUMMARY

1. The "invisible hand" of Adam Smith describes how a capitalist system allows individuals to pursue their self-interest and yet provides an orderly, efficient economic system. If too much of a product is produced, its relative price will fall. If too little of a product is produced, its relative price will rise. The balance of supply and demand is called an equilibrium.

2. Relative prices guide the economic decisions of individuals and businesses. They signal to buyers and sellers what substitutions to make.

3. The principle of substitution states that users substitute one good for another in response to changes in relative prices.

4. The circular-flow diagram summarizes the flows of goods and services from producers to households and the flows of factors of production from households to producers. Transactions take place in goods markets and in factors markets.

5. Specialization increases productivity. It occurs because of the differences among people, land, and capital and because of the economies of large-scale production. The law of comparative advantage states that the factors of production will specialize in those activities where their advantages are greatest or their disadvantages are smallest. Comparative advantage applies to people and to countries.

6. The price system provides for the future by allowing people to compare costs now with benefits that will accrue in the future. The interest rate balances the amount of saving offered with the amount of investment businesses wish to undertake.

7. The invisible hand may not solve the problems of income distribution, public goods, externalities, monopoly, or macroeconomic instability.

KEY TERMS

price system 48
relative price 49
money price 49
inflation 50
principle of substitution 51
equilibrium price 52
circular-flow diagram 52
specialization 53
exchange 53
law of comparative advantage 54
money 56
barter 57
interest rate 57

QUESTIONS AND PROBLEMS

1. "The principle of substitution states that virtually all goods have substitutes, but we all know that there are no substitutes for telephone service." Comment on this statement.
2. Explain why you can usually find the items you want at a grocery store without having ordered the goods in advance.
3. In 1963 an average car cost about $2000; in 1995 an average car cost about $20,000. But on the average, what cost $100 in 1963 cost about $375 in 1995. Did the relative price of a car increase or fall compared to most goods and services?
4. Not every product has a good substitute. Which of the following are good substitutes for one another? Which are poor substitutes? Explain the general principles you used in coming up with your answers.
   a. Coffee and tea
   b. Compact Chevrolets and compact Fords
   c. Cars and city buses
   d. Electricity and natural gas
   e. Telephones and express mail
5. Computer manufacturers want to sell more personal computers than customers want to buy at the current price. What do you expect to happen to the price?
6. You own a one-carat diamond ring that you no longer like. In fact, you would like to have a new television set. How would you get the television set in a barter economy? Discuss the efficiency of exchange in a barter economy versus a monetary economy.
7. "Specialization takes place only when people are different. If all people were identical, there would be no specialization." Evaluate this statement.
8. Assume that while shopping, you see long lines of people waiting to buy bread, while fresh meat is spoiling in the butcher shops. What does this tell you about prevailing prices? What is your prediction about what will happen to the relative price of bread?
9. Bill can prepare 50 hamburgers per hour or wait on 25 tables per hour. Mike can prepare 20 hamburgers per hour or wait on 15 tables per hour. If Bill and Mike open a hamburger stand, who should be the cook? Who should be the waiter? Would Bill do both?
10. Why would private industry find it difficult to organize national defense? How would private industry charge each citizen for national defense?
11. In an hour's time, Jill can lay 100 tiles or can mortar 50 bricks. Tom can lay 10 tiles or mortar 20 bricks in an hour's time. Each tile laid or brick mortared pays $1. According to the law of comparative advantage, in which activity should each specialize? Explain why it is

that Jill should not do both activities and let Tom rest simply because Jill is better at both activities.

12. Why in the circular-flow diagram do physical quantities move in one direction and dollar quantities move in another direction?
13. Which of the following transactions would enter the circular flow and which would not?
    a. U.S. Steel sells steel to General Motors.
    b. General Motors sells a car to Jones.
    c. Jones takes a job from General Motors and receives $100 in wages.
    d. Jones has his suit cleaned at the local dry cleaner and pays $5.
    e. Jones washes his dress shirt.
14. Explain how an increase in the interest rate alters society's provision for the future.
15. What is the opportunity cost of saving? What is the benefit?
16. Explain why, when you go to a store, there is not a surplus or a shortage of 25¢ pencils.

INTERNET CONNECTION

17. Using the links from http://www.awl.com/ruffin_gregory, read the article "Health Care: Let's Face Reality" on the Brookings Institution Web site.
    a. How is health care rationed in the U.S. system? Do we use a market system? Explain your answer.
    b. If we were to use a market system, would the problem that the article describes still occur?

PUZZLE ANSWERED: As was pointed out in the discussion of comparative advantage, U.S. workers earn higher wages because they are more productive. Mexican workers, who produce less per hour of work, compete with American workers by working for less. There will be no massive sucking noise of jobs moving from the United States to Mexico because wages will adjust to allow both countries to compete according to comparative advantage.

Chapter 4

Demand and Supply

Chapter Insight

Prior to the deregulation of the airline industry in the 1980s, airlines unceremoniously bumped passengers on overbooked flights according to the order in which they arrived at the airport. This practice meant that passengers who urgently needed to be on that flight might have had to wait for the next flight, whereas passengers who cared little whether they were on that particular flight or the next remained on board the first flight. Involuntary bumping caused enormous inconvenience for bumped passengers.

Economists, using the tools of demand and supply, came up with a simple solution: Today, if a flight is overbooked, the airline offers bonuses—free tickets, cash, or some other inducement—to those who volunteer to take the next flight. First, a low bonus is offered, and, if insufficient, it is raised as the flight time approaches until the number of remaining passengers equals the number of available seats. In effect, a price is paid to reduce the number of passengers to the seating capacity of the plane. When the plane takes off, everyone usually is benefited.

Incentives offered by airlines to induce passengers to volunteer are free tickets for future flights or cash, ranging up to $400. Currently slightly over one in every 10,000 passengers is involuntarily bumped. There are 677 Internet listings advising passengers how to play the "airline bumping" game, including instructions on how to earn cash by booking flights on holidays with the hope of receiving cash or free tickets.

Sources: http://www.dot.gov; http://www.bestfares.com/travel_center/desks/public/199907/10012559L.asp.

LEARNING OBJECTIVES

After studying this chapter you will be able to:

1. Define competitive markets.
2. State the law of demand.
3. Understand the difference between changes in demand and changes in quantity demanded.
4. See why the supply curve is usually upward sloping.
5. Understand the difference between changes in supply and changes in quantity supplied.
6. Appreciate the meaning of the equilibrium price.
7. Understand the causes of shortages and surpluses.
8. Be able to apply supply and demand analysis to unconventional markets.

CHAPTER PUZZLE: Schoolteachers in Houston, Texas, are currently being offered cash bonuses for signing employment contracts. Why do these schoolteachers receive sign-on bonuses when others do not?

WHAT IS A MARKET?

To understand demand and supply, we shall focus on how a *single market* works.

A **market** is an established arrangement that brings buyers and sellers together to exchange particular goods or services.

Markets comprise demanders (or buyers) who are motivated by different factors (or goals), and suppliers (or sellers). The prices discussed in the previous chapter are determined in markets. In each market, buyers and sellers base their decisions on price.

Types of Markets

Video rental stores; gas stations; farmers' markets; real estate firms; the New York Stock Exchange (where stocks are bought and sold); auctions of works of art; gold markets in London, Frankfurt, and Zurich; labor exchanges; university placement offices; and thousands of other specialized arrangements are all markets. The New York Stock Exchange uses modern telecommunications to bring together the buyers and sellers of corporate stock. The university placement office brings together university graduates and potential employers. The video rental store brings together the buyers and sellers of videos.

Some markets are local, others are national or international. Residential real estate is usually bought and sold in local markets; houses cannot be shipped from one place to another. The growing globalization of the world economy—a Defining Moment of economics—has made more and more markets international in character. United States companies hire marketing specialists from Europe and Asia; U.S. consulting firms sell their services to companies in Latin American and Africa. The New York Stock Exchange, the various gold exchanges, and the Chicago commodity exchanges bring together buyers and sellers from around the world. (See Example 1.)

Markets and Competition

In economics, we distinguish among different types of markets according to the amount of competition. Some markets comprise numerous buyers and sellers, buying and selling products that are identical or nearly identical. An example is agricultural markets, such as the markets for wheat or corn, in which there are literally hundreds of thousands of suppliers. These markets are highly competitive. Other markets are dominated by one or several suppliers; here, buyers have fewer choices. Examples are the local natural gas or electricity company. Most markets are somewhere in between highly competitive markets and markets with little competition. There are a number of suppliers; they offer products that are differentiated from one supplier to the next.

Virtually no market is spared competition. All goods have substitutes: The question is whether the substitute is a good one or not. Natural gas substitutes for electricity, wheat for corn, and Chevrolets for Mazdas. The amount of competition determines how buyers and sellers in that market behave. Later chapters will analyze four distinct market models.

This chapter describes how buyers and sellers behave in a highly competitive market—which a later chapter will identify as a perfectly competitive market. In this market, there are a large number of buy-

EXAMPLE 1

The NASDAQ Stock Exchange

Trading on the National Association of Securities Dealers Automated Quotation System (NASDAQ) stock exchange began in 1971. The NASDAQ exchange is the world's first electronic stock market. It is the fastest stock growing exchange, often trading 1 billion shares of stock per day of the approximately 6000 companies listed on NASDAQ. In 1998, the annual dollar volume of trading equaled almost 6 trillion dollars. NASDAQ lists almost 500 non-U.S. companies, including exotic companies like Russia's Lukoil.

An electronic stock market determines stock prices that equate supply and demand. Orders to buy (bids) or to sell (offers) are entered into a single computer. NASDAQ displays "inside quotations" (the market's best bids and offer prices) on-screen for all market participants to see. On the other hand, the New York Stock Exchange, NASDAQ's major competitor, operates on the basis of auctions managed by specialists, who balance supplies and demands of the stocks in which they specialize to determine the market prices.

The NASDAQ stock exchange operates according to rules that it sets itself, such as accounting and disclosure standards, and according to the general rules of the U.S. Securities and Exchange Commission.

Source: http://www.nasdaq.com.

ers and sellers, buying and selling a homogeneous product, such as wheat, corn, gold, frozen orange juice concentrate, plywood, or pork bellies.

Demand

We know that we all want more than the economy can provide. But the goods and services that we *want*—those that we would take if they were given away free—are quite different from the goods and services we demand.

The **demand** for a good or service is the amount people ar e prepared to buy under specific circumstances such as the product's price.

What we are actually prepared to buy depends on price and various other factors we shall discuss in this chapter.

The Law of Demand

The most important factor affecting the quantity of a good or service purchased by consumers is its price. We buy more if the price falls; we buy less if the price rises, holding other factors constant (*ceteris paribus*). This is a fundamental law of economics, the law of demand.

The **law of demand** states that there is a negative (or inverse) relationship between the price of a good or service and the quantity demanded, if other factors are constant.

EXAMPLE 2

M&Ms AND THE LAW OF DEMAND

The law of demand states that the quantity demanded will increase as the price is lowered, so long as other factors that affect demand do not change. In the real world, factors that affect the demand for a particular product change frequently. Tastes change, income rises, and prices of substitutes and complements change. The makers of M&M candy conducted an experiment that illustrates the law of demand. Over a 12-month test period, the price of M&Ms was held constant in 150 selected stores, and the content weight of the candy was increased. When the price is held constant and the weight increased, the price per ounce is lowered. In the stores where the price per ounce was dropped, sales rose by 20 to 30 percent almost overnight, according to the director of sales development for M&Ms. As predicted by the law of demand, a reduction in price causes the quantity demanded to rise, *ceteris paribus.*

Source: "Why Do Hot Dogs Come in Packs of 10 and Buns in 8s and 12s?" *Wall Street Journal,* September 21, 1984.

Demand for a good or service also depends on other factors, like the prices of related goods (for example, the demand for tea depends on the price of coffee), income, and tastes. We shall consider these other factors later. For the moment, we want to concentrate on the price of the good or service itself.

The main reason that the law of demand holds true is that we tend to substitute other, cheaper goods or services as the price of any good or service goes up. If the price of airline tickets rises, we cut back on less essential flying, and we drive rather than fly. If the price of movie tickets rises, more people will rent videos or watch TV, or movie addicts will cut back on the number of visits to the movie theater. The quantity demanded is negatively related to the price of a good or service. (See Example 2.)

The **quantity demanded** is the amount of a good or service consumers are prepared to buy at a given price (during a specified time period), if other factors are held constant.

When a price rises enough, some of us may even stop buying altogether. As the price rises, the number of actual buyers may fall as some of us switch entirely to other goods.

As the price of a good goes up, we also buy less because we are poorer. If you buy a new car every year for $15,000 (after trade-in), and the price rises to $19,000, you would need an extra $4000 per year of income to maintain your old standard of living. The $4000 increase in the price of the car is like a cut in income of $4000.

The law of demand shows why the concept of *need* is not very useful in economics. A "need" implies that we cannot do without something. But when the price changes, the law of demand says that the quantity demanded will change. For example, "need" for a daily shower would likely disappear if it costs $50 to take one!

The *demand curve* or the *demand schedule* shows the negative (or inverse) relationship between quantity demanded and price. To avoid confusion, we shall refer to the *demand schedule* when the relationship is in tabular form and the *demand curve* when the relationship is in graphical form.

The Demand Curve

Figure 1 shows both a demand curve and a demand schedule for corn. Buyers in the marketplace demand 20 million bushels of corn per month at the price of $5 per bushel. At a lower price—say, $4 per bushel—the quantity demanded is higher. In this case, the

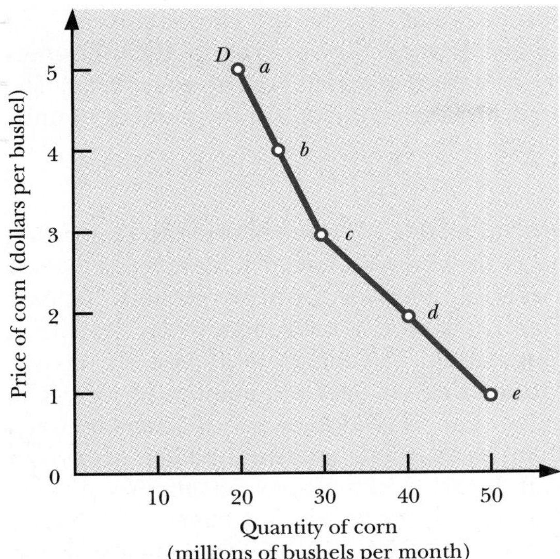

FIGURE 1 The Demand Curve for Corn

This figure shows how the quantity of corn demanded responds to the prices of corn, holding all other factors constant. At *a,* when the price of corn is $5 per bushel, the quantity demanded is 20 million bushels per month. At *e,* when the price of corn is $1, the quantity demanded is 50 million bushels. The downward-sloping demand curve (*D*) shows the amounts of corn consumers are willing to buy at different prices.

DEMAND SCHEDULE FOR CORN

	Price (dollars per bushel)	*Quantity Demanded (millions of bushels per month)*
a	5	20
b	4	25
c	3	30
d	2	40
e	1	50

quantity demanded at the lower price of $4 is 25 million bushels. By continuing to decrease the price, buyers are persuaded to purchase more and more corn. Thus, at the price of $1, quantity demanded is 50 million bushels.

Note that in graphs showing demand curves, price is placed on the vertical axis and quantity demanded on the horizontal axis. When price is $5, quantity demanded is 20 million bushels (point *a*). Point *b* corresponds to a price of $4 and a quantity of 25 million bushels. When price falls from $5 to $4, quantity demanded rises by 5 million bushels from 20 million to 25 million bushels.

The demand curve *D* drawn through points *a* through *e* shows how quantity demanded responds to changes in price. Along *D,* price and quantity are *negatively* related; that is, the curve is downward sloping.

The demand curve shows that as larger quantities of corn are put on the market, lower prices are required to clear the market (to sell that quantity). The price needed to sell 25 million bushels of corn is $4 per bushel. To sell the larger quantity of 30 million bushels, a lower price of $3 is required.

In this book we shall encounter two types of demand curves: the demand curves of individuals (households) and the market demand curve.

The **market demand curve** is the demand of all buyers in the market for a particular product.

The demand curve for corn in Figure 1 refers to all buyers in the corn market, an international market that brings together all buyers of corn both at home and abroad. The demand curve for Hawaiian real estate brings together all buyers of Hawaiian real estate; the demand curve for Microsoft's Windows 2000 software brings together all buyers from around the globe.

Shifts in the Demand Curve

The demand curve shows what would happen to the quantity demanded if *only the good's own price* were to change. The good's own price is not the only determinant of demand; other factors can play an important role. The factors that can shift the demand curve include (1) the prices of related goods, (2) consumer income, (3) consumer preferences, (4) the number of potential buyers, and (5) expectations.

The Prices of Related Goods. Goods can be related to each other as either substitutes or complements.

Two goods are **substitutes** if the demand for one rises when the price of the other rises (or if the demand for one falls when the price of the other falls).

Examples of substitutes are coffee and tea, two brands of soft drinks, stocks and bonds, Macintosh and IBM-compatible computers, pay TV and movie rentals, foreign and domestic cars, natural gas and electricity. Some goods are very close substitutes (two different brands of fluoride toothpaste), and others are very distant substitutes (cars and supersonic aircraft).

Two goods are **complements** if the demand for one falls when the price of the other increases.

Examples of complements are automobiles and gasoline, food and drink, dress shirts and neckties, airline tickets and automobile rentals. Complements tend to be used jointly (for example, automobiles plus gasoline equals transportation). An increase in the price of one of the goods effectively increases the price of the joint product of the two goods.

Income. It is easy to understand how income influences demand. As our incomes rise, we spend more on normal goods and services. But as income increases, we also spend less on inferior goods.

A **normal good** is one for which demand increases when income increases, holding all prices constant. An **inferior good** is one for which demand falls as income increases, holding all prices constant.

For most of us, lard, day-old bread, and second-hand clothing are examples of inferior goods. For some people, inferior goods might be hamburgers, margarine, bus rides, or black-and-white TV sets. But most goods—from automobiles to water—are normal goods.

Preferences. *Preferences* are what people like and dislike without regard to budgetary considerations. You may *prefer* to live in your own ten-room home but can afford only a two-bedroom apartment. You may prefer a Mercedes-Benz but can afford only a used Chevrolet. Preferences plus budgetary considerations (price and income) determine demand. As preferences change, demand changes. If we learn that oat bran muffins lower weight and cholesterol, we will increase our demand for oat bran muffins. Business firms try to influence preferences by advertising. The goal of advertising is to increase the number of units sold at each price.

The Number of Potential Buyers. If more buyers enter a market, the market demand will rise. The number of buyers in a market can increase for many reasons. Relaxed immigration laws or a baby boom may lead to a larger population. The migration of people from one region to another changes the number of buyers in each region. The relaxation of trade barriers between two countries may increase the number of foreign buyers. If Japanese restrictions on imports of U.S. rice are removed, the number of buyers of U.S. rice will increase. Lowering the legal drinking age would increase the number of buyers of beer.

Expectations. If we believe that the price of coffee will rise substantially in the future, we may decide to stock up on coffee today. During periods of rising prices, we often start buying up durable goods, such as cars and refrigerators. The mere expectation of an increase in a good's price can induce us to buy more of it. Similarly, we can postpone the purchase of things that are expected to get cheaper. During the 1990s, as personal computers became cheaper and cheaper, some buyers deliberately postponed their purchases on the expectation of even lower prices in the future.

Shifting Demand. Figure 2 shows the demand curve for dress shirts. This curve, *D*, is based on a $10 price for neckties (a complement), a $20 price for sport shirts (a substitute), a certain income, given preferences, and a fixed number of buyers.

An increase in the price of neckties (a complement for dress shirts) from $15 to $15 shifts the entire demand curve for dress shirts to the left from D to D′ in panel (*a*). Dress shirts are usually worn with neckties. If neckties increase in price, consumers buy fewer of them and substitute less-formal shirts for shirts that require neckties. As a result, the demand for dress shirts decreases, shifting left.

An increase in the price of sport shirts (a substitute for dress shirts) from $20 to $30 shifts the

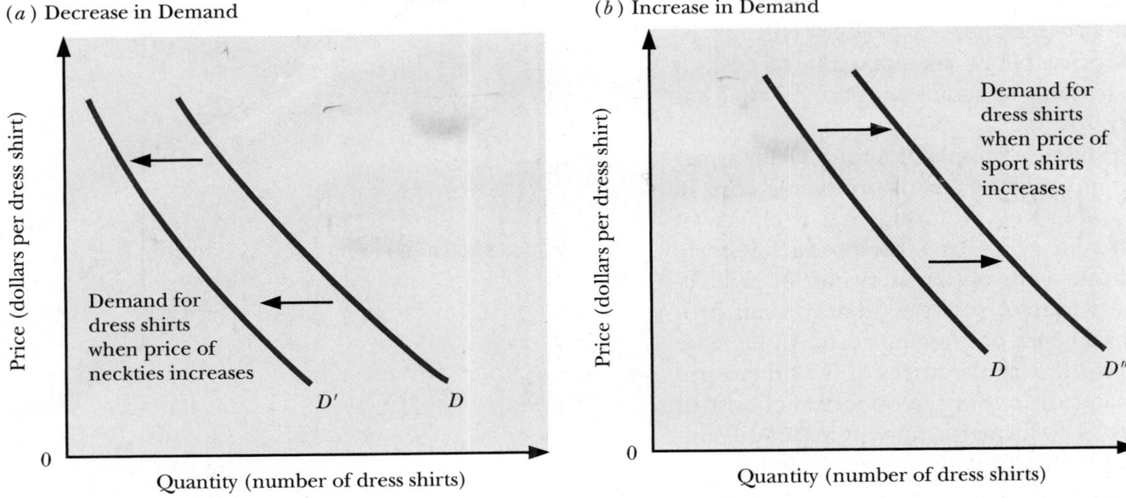

FIGURE 2 Shifts in the Demand Curve: Changes in Demand

The demand curve for dress shirts depends on the price of neckties and the price of sport shirts. When the price of neckties is $10 and the price of sport shirts is $20, the demand curve for dress shirts is *D*. In panel (*a*), if the price of neckties rises to $15, holding the price of sport shirts at $20, then at each price for dress shirts the demand falls. The demand curve shifts to the left from *D* to *D′*. In panel (*b*), keeping the price of neckties at $10 and raising the price of sport shirts to $30 will raise the demand for dress shirts. The demand curve will shift rightward to *D″*. A rightward shift depicts an increase in demand, and a leftward shift illustrates a decrease in demand.

demand curve for dress shirts to the right of *D* to *D″* in panel (*b*). When the price of sport shirts increases, consumers substitute dress shirts for sport shirts. As a result of this substitution, the demand for dress shirts increases, shifting right.

If consumer income increases and if dress shirts are a normal good, demand will increase (*D* will shift to the right). If preferences change and dress shirts fall out of fashion, demand will decrease (*D* will shift to the left). If buyers expect prices of dress shirts to rise substantially in the future, demand today will increase.

Supply

Supply depends on a variety of factors, just as demand depends on a number of factors. One of these factors is price.

The **supply** of a good or service is the amount that firms are prepared to sell under specified circumstances.

The **quantity supplied** of a good or service is the amount offered for sale at a given price, holding other factors constant.

There are a number of reasons why firms *will* offer more of the product if its price rises. Chapter 2 introduced opportunity cost and the law of diminishing returns. You will recall that opportunity costs are the value of the next-best alternative sacrificed in taking an action, and that the law of diminishing returns states that the resource cost per unit of output rises as more and more output is produced (when there are fixed factors). Both of these facts explain why, under normal circumstances, firms supply more output at a higher price.

Supply decisions are based upon a simple rule: Under normal circumstances, a product will not be supplied at a price below its opportunity cost. It doesn't make sense to sell something for $3 that has an opportunity cost of $5.

Let's use a simple example of a farm. The farmer can measure opportunity costs of producing corn in different ways. First, if the farmer has a choice of producing different types of farm products—corn, wheat, or soybeans—the opportunity cost of producing corn is the wheat or soybeans that are not produced as a consequence of growing corn. An increase in the price of corn (with the prices of the other farm products unchanged) *lowers* the opportunity cost of producing corn. The farmer is now prepared to supply more corn because of its lower opportunity cost. Second, if the farmer could produce only one product—corn—the farmer would not supply more corn unless the price of corn were to rise. The law of diminishing returns states that the cost of producing a bushel of corn rises as more corn is produced. This cost of resources used, such as tractors, fertilizers, and labor costs, is the opportunity cost of producing corn under these circumstances. Insofar as the opportunity cost of producing a bushel of corn rises as more corn is produced, the only way to get the farmer to supply more corn is to offer a higher price—to cover the farmer's higher opportunity cost of producing more corn.

> Opportunity costs and the law of diminishing returns explain why firms are prepared to supply more output at higher prices.

The Supply Curve

Figure 3 shows a supply schedule for corn. When the price of corn is $5 per bushel, farmers are prepared to supply 40 million bushels per month (point *a*). As the price falls to $4, the quantity supplied falls to 35 million bushels (point *b*). Finally, when the price is $1, farmers are prepared to sell only 10 million bushels (point *e*).

The smooth curve drawn through points *a* through *e* is the supply curve, *S*. It shows how quantity supplied responds to price, all things being equal—in other words, how much farmers are prepared to offer for sale at each price. Along the supply curve, the price and supply of corn are positively related: A higher price is needed to induce farmers to offer a larger quantity of corn on the market.

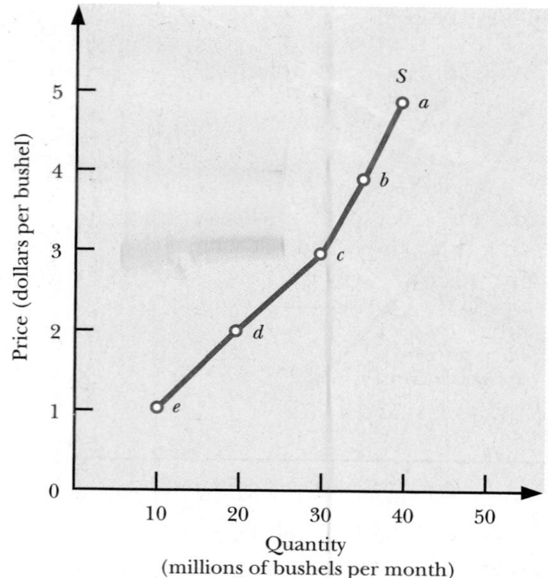

FIGURE 3 The Supply Curve for Corn

This figure depicts how the quantity of corn supplied responds to the price of corn. At *a*, when the price of corn is $5 per bushel, the quantity supplied by farmers is 40 million bushels per month. In the last situation, *e*, when the price is $1 per bushel, the quantity supplied is only 10 million bushels per month. The upward-sloping curve (*S*) drawn through these points is the supply curve of corn.

SUPPLY SCHEDULE FOR CORN

	Price (dollars per bushel)	*Quantity Supplied (millions of bushels per month)*
a	5	40
b	4	35
c	3	30
d	2	20
e	1	10

Shifts in the Supply Curve

Factors other than a good's own price can change the relationship between price and quantity supplied, causing the supply curve to shift. These other factors include (1) the prices of other goods, (2) the prices of relevant resources, (3) technology, (4) the number of sellers, and (5) expectations.

Prices of Other Goods. The resources used to produce any particular good can almost always be used elsewhere. Farmland can be used for corn or soybeans; engineers can work on cars or trucks; unskilled workers can pick strawberries or lettuce; trains can move coal or cars. As the price of a good rises, resources are naturally attracted away from other goods that use those resources. Thus, the supply of corn will fall if the price of soybeans rises; if the price of lettuce rises, the supply of strawberries may fall. If the price of trucks rises, the supply of cars may fall. If the price of fuel oil rises, less kerosene may be produced.

The Prices of Relevant Resources. As resource prices rise, firms are no longer willing to supply the same quantities of goods produced with those resources at the same price. An increase in the price of coffee beans will increase the costs of producing coffee and decrease the amount that coffee companies are prepared to sell at each price; an increase in the price of corn land, tractors, harvesters, or irrigation will reduce the supply of corn; an increase in the price of cotton will decrease the supply of cotton dresses; an increase in the price of jet fuel will decrease the supply of airline seats at each price.

Technology. *Technology* is knowledge about how different goods can be produced. If technology improves, more goods can be produced from the same resources. For example, if a new, cheaper feed allows Maine lobster farmers to lower their costs of production, the quantity of lobsters supplied at each price will increase. If an assembly line can be speeded up by rearranging the order of assembly, the supply of the good will tend to increase. Technological advances in genetic engineering can increase the supply of medicines and foods such as milk and tomatoes.

The Number of Sellers. If the number of sellers of a good increases, the supply of the good will increase. For example, the lowering of trade barriers (such as licensing requirements for foreign firms) may allow foreign sellers easier entry into the market, increasing the number of sellers.

Expectations. It takes a long time to produce many goods and services. When a farmer plants corn or wheat or soybeans, the prices that are expected to prevail at harvest time are actually more important than is the current price. A college student who reads that there are likely to be too few engineers four years from now may decide to major in engineering in expectation of a high income. When a company decides to establish a plant that takes five years to build, expectations of future business conditions are crucial to that investment decision.

Expectations can affect supply in different directions. If oil prices are expected to rise in the future, oil producers may produce less oil today to have more available for the future. In other cases, more investment will be undertaken if high prices are expected in the future. This greater investment will cause supply to increase and may result in lower prices for the company's product.

Shifting Supply. Figure 4 illustrates shifts in the supply curve for corn. The supply curve is based on a $10-per-bushel price of soybeans and a $2000 yearly rental on an acre of corn land. If the price of soybeans rises, the supply curve for corn will shift leftward in panel (*a*) because some land used for corn will be shifted to soybeans. If the rental price of an acre of corn land goes down, the supply curve will shift to the right—*S″* in panel (*b*). The reduction in the land rental price lowers the costs of producing corn and makes the corn producer willing to supply more corn at the same price as before.

> A leftward shift of the supply curve signifies that producers are prepared to sell smaller quantities of the good at each price: It indicates a *decrease in supply*. A rightward shift signifies that producers are prepared to sell larger quantities at each price: It indicates an *increase in supply*.

Table 1 summarizes the factors that cause demand and supply curves to shift.

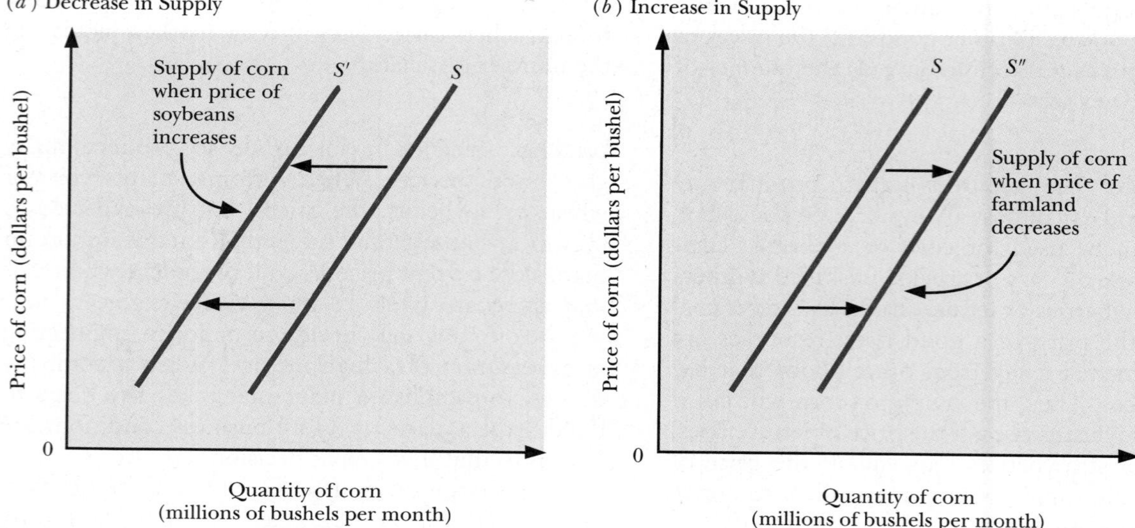

FIGURE 4 Shifts in the Supply Curve: Changes in Supply

The supply curve of corn depends on the price of soybeans and the price of farmland. When farmland is $2000 an acre per year and soybeans are $10 per bushel, *S* is the supply curve for corn. Panel (*a*) shows that if farmland stays at $2000 per acre per year but soybeans fetch $15 instead of $10, farmers will switch farmland from corn to soybeans and cause the supply curve for corn to shift to the left from *S* to *S*′ (a decrease in supply). Panel (*b*) shows that if soybeans remain at $10 per bushel and farmland falls from $2000 to $1000 per acre, the supply curve for corn will shift to the right from *S* to *S*″ (an increase in supply).

TABLE 1 FACTORS THAT CAUSE DEMAND AND SUPPLY CURVES TO SHIFT

Demand Factor	*Example*
Change in price of substitutes	Increase in price of coffee shifts demand curve for tea to right.
Change in price of complements	Increase in price of coffee shifts demand curve for sugar to left.
Change in income	Increase in income shifts demand curve for automobiles to right.
Change in preference	Judgment that cigarettes are hazardous to health shifts demand curve for cigarettes to left.
Change in number of buyers	Increase in population of City X shifts demand curve for houses in City X to right.
Change in expectations of future prices	Expectation that prices of canned goods will increase substantially over the next year shifts demand curve for canned goods to right.
Supply Factor	*Example*
Change in price of another good	Increase in price of corn shifts supply curve of wheat to left.
Change in price of resource	Decrease in wage rate of autoworkers shifts supply curve of autos to right.
Change in technology	Higher corn yields due to genetic engineering shift supply curve of corn to right.
Change in number of sellers	New sellers entering profitable field shift supply curve of product to right.
Change in expectations	Expectation of a much higher price of oil next year shifts supply curve of oil today to left; expectation of higher ball-bearing prices in the future causes more investment, shifting supply curve to right.

Equilibrium of Demand and Supply

Along a given demand curve, such as the one in Figure 1, there are many price-quantity combinations from which to choose. Along a given supply curve, there are also many different price-quantity combinations. Neither the demand curve nor the supply curve is sufficient by itself to determine the *market* price-quantity combinations.

Figure 5 puts the demand curve of Figure 1 and the supply curve of Figure 3 together on the same diagram. We should remember that the demand curve indicates what consumers are prepared to buy at different prices; the supply curve indicates what producers are prepared to sell at different prices. For the most part, these groups of economic decision makers are entirely different. How much will be produced? How much will be purchased? How are the decisions of consumers and producers coordinated?

Suppose that the price of corn is $2 per bushel. At a $2 price, consumers want to buy 40 million bushels and producers want to sell only 20 million bushels. This discrepancy indicates that at $2 there is a shortage of 20 million bushels.

A **shortage** results if at the current price the quantity demanded exceeds the quantity supplied; the price is too low to equate the quantity demanded with the quantity supplied.

At a $2 price, 20 million bushels will be traded. Consumers who wish to buy 40 million will be able to buy only the 20 million bushels corn producers are willing to sell. At a price of $2 per bushel, some people who are willing to buy corn cannot find a willing seller. The demand curve shows that a number of consumers are willing to pay more than $2 per bushel. Such buyers will try to outbid one another for the available supply. As buyers compete with one another, they will bid up the price of corn as long as there is a shortage of corn.

The increase in the price of corn in response to the shortage has two main effects. On the one hand, the higher price discourages consumption. On the other hand, the higher price encourages production. Thus the increase in the price of corn, through the actions of independent buyers and sellers, leads both buyers and sellers to make decisions that will reduce the shortage of corn.

What will happen if the price is $4 per bushel? At that price, consumers want to buy 25 million bushels and producers want to sell 35 million bushels. Thus, at $4 there is a surplus of 10 million bushels on the market.

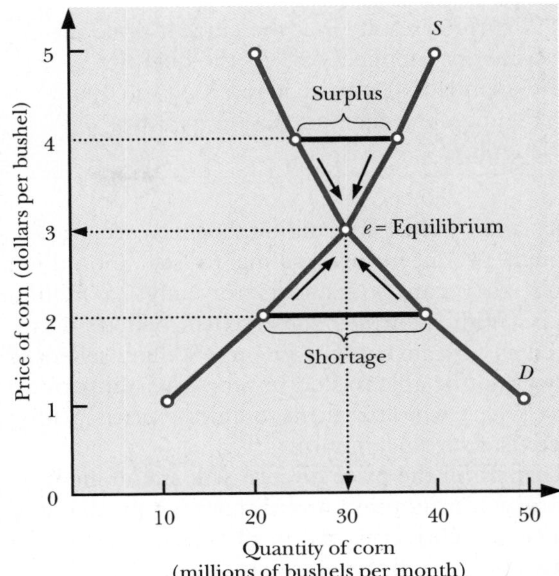

FIGURE 5 Market Equilibrium of Corn

This figure shows how market equilibrium is reached. The demand curve for corn is that from Figure 1 and the supply curve for corn is that from Figure 3. When the price of corn is $2, the quantity demanded is 40 million bushels, but the quantity supplied is only 20 million bushels. The result is a shortage of 20 million bushels of corn. Unsatisfied buyers will bid the price up. Raising the price will reduce the shortage. If the price of corn is raised to $4 per bushel, the quantity supplied is 35 million bushels. The result is a surplus of 10 million bushels of corn. This surplus will cause the price of corn to fall as unsatisfied sellers bid the price down. As the price falls, the surplus will diminish. The equilibrium price is $3 because the quantity demanded equals the quantity supplied at that price. The equilibrium quantity is 30 million bushels.

A **surplus** results if at the current price the quantity supplied exceeds the quantity demanded: The price is too high to equate the quantity demanded with quantity supplied.

At a $4 price, 25 million bushels are traded. Although producers are willing to sell 35 million bushels, they can find buyers for only 25 million bushels. With a surplus some sellers will be disappointed as corn inventories pile up. Willing sellers of corn will not be able to find buyers. The competition among sellers will lead them to cut the price as long as there is a surplus of corn.

This fall in the price of corn will simultaneously encourage consumption and discourage production. Through the corrective fall in the price of corn, the surplus of corn will therefore disappear.

According to the demand and supply curves portrayed in Figure 5, when the price of corn reaches $3 per bushel, the shortage (or surplus) of corn disappears completely. At this equilibrium (market-clearing) price, consumers want to buy 30 million bushels and producers want to sell 30 million bushels.

The **equilibrium (market-clearing) price** is the price at which the quantity demanded by consumers equals the quantity supplied by producers.

There is no other price-quantity combination at which quantity demanded equals quantity supplied—any other price brings about a shortage or a surplus of corn. The arrows in Figure 5 indicate the pressures on prices above or below $3 and show how the amount of shortage or surplus—the size of the brackets—gets smaller as the price adjusts.

The equilibrium of demand and supply is stationary in the sense that once the equilibrium price is reached, it tends to remain the same so long as neither supply nor demand shifts. Movements away from the equilibrium price will be restored by the bidding of frustrated buyers or frustrated sellers in the marketplace. The equilibrium price is like a rocking chair in the rest position; after a gentle push its original position will be restored.

What the Market Accomplishes

An equilibrium price does three things. First, it *rations* the scarce supply of the good among all the people who would like to have it if it were given away free. Some people must be left out if the good is scarce. The price determines who will be excluded by limiting consumption.

Second, the system of equilibrium prices *economizes on the information required to match demands and supplies.* Buyers do not have to know how to produce a good, and sellers do not need to know why people use the good. Buyers and sellers need only be concerned with small bits of information, such as price, or small portions of the technological methods of production. The market accomplishes its actions without any one participant's knowing all the details. In all these examples, producers make their decisions without knowing what consumers are doing and consumers make their decisions without knowing what producers are doing.

Third, the market coordinates the actions of a large number of independent buyers and sellers through equilibrium prices. In such a situation, every single buyer or seller is making the best possible decision.

Changes in the Equilibrium Price

Sometimes prices go up, and sometimes they go down. In this section we shall investigate the reasons for price changes. Thus far we have seen that the equilibrium price is determined by the intersection of the demand and supply curves. The only way for the price to change is that the demand or supply curves themselves shift, and this occurs only if one or more of the factors that affect demand and supply *besides the good's own price* change.

Change in Demand (or Supply) versus Change in Quantity Demanded (or Supplied)

We make a careful distinction between movements along a demand curve and shifts in the entire curve. A change in the good's own price—as from p_2 to p_1 in panel (*a*) of Figure 6—causes a movement along the demand curve referred to as a change in quantity demanded. When a change in a factor other than the

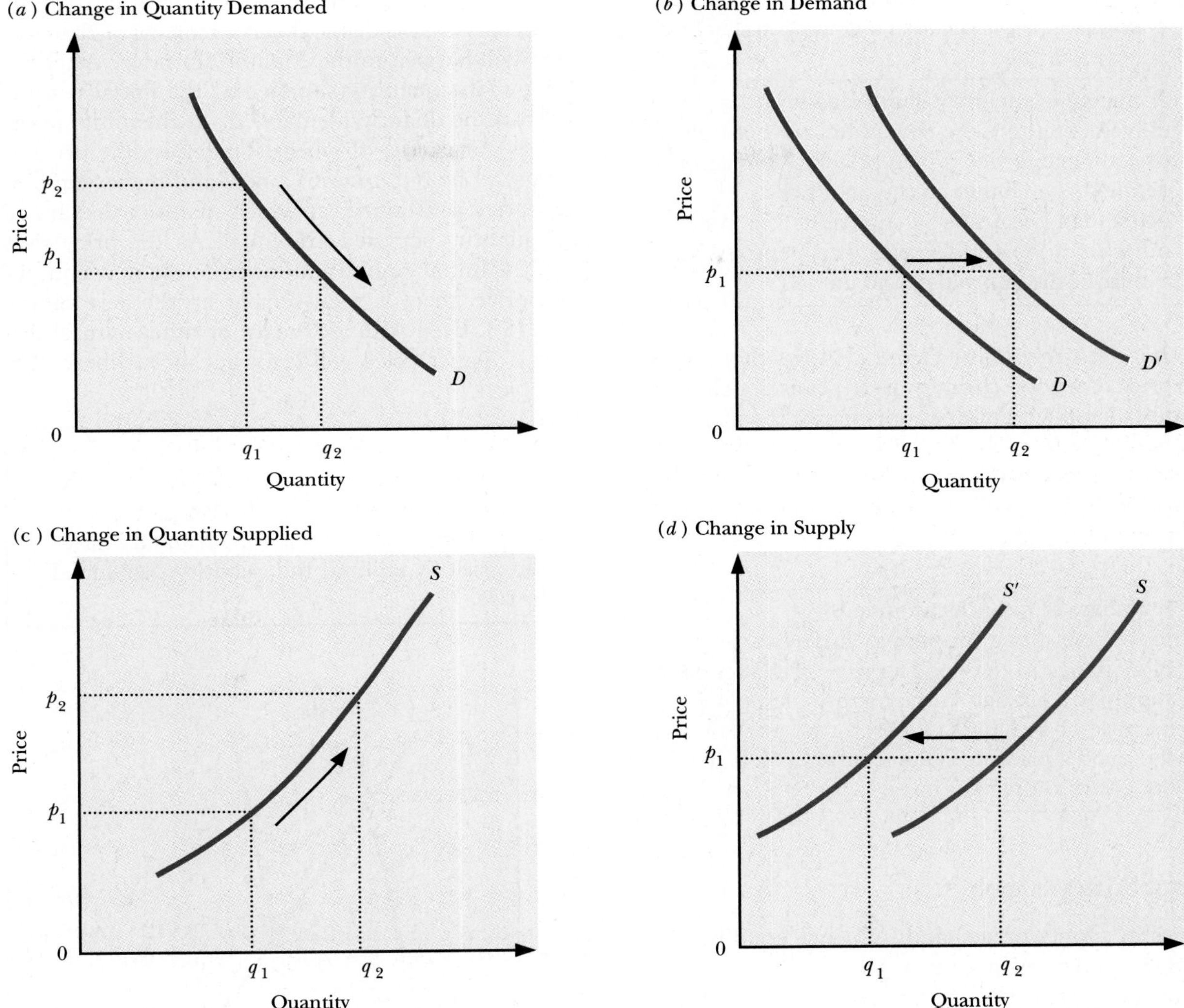

FIGURE 6 Changes in Demand/Supply Versus Changes in Quantity Demanded/Supplied

In panel (*a*), the increase in quantity demanded (from q_1 to q_2) is the result of the drop in price (from p_2 to p_1). The change in price causes the movement along the demand curve (D). In panel (*b*), the increase in quantity (from q_1 to q_2) is the result of a shift in the demand curve (an increase in demand) to D', holding price constant. When demand increases, the whole demand curve shifts as the result of some change that leads consumers to buy more of the product at each price.

In panel (*c*), the increase in quantity supplied (from q_1 to q_2) is the result of a rise in price (from p_1 to p_2). The change in price causes a movement along the supply curve (S). In panel (*d*), the decrease in supply (from q_2 to q_1) is the result of the shift in the supply curve (decrease in supply) from S to S', holding price constant. Firms wish to sell less at the same price.

good's price shifts the entire curve to the left or to the right, as in panel (*b*), it is called a change in demand.

A **change in quantity demanded** is a movement along the demand curve because of a change in the good's price. A **change in demand** is a change in the quantity demanded because of a change in a factor other than the good's price. It is depicted as a shift in the entire demand curve.

Similarly, panel (*c*) of Figure 6 shows that a rise in the price of a good (from p_1 to p_2) causes a change in quantity supplied but does not change the location of the supply curve. A change in supply, shown in panel (*d*), occurs when a factor other than the good's own price changes, shifting the entire supply curve to the left or to the right.

A **change in quantity supplied** is a movement along the supply curve because of a change in the good's price. A **change in supply** is a change in the quantity supplied because of a change in a factor other than the good's price. It is depicted as a shift in the entire supply curve.

The Effects of a Change in Supply

Changes in supply or demand influence equilibrium prices and quantities in given markets.

Consider the severe drought in the United States in the summer of 1999, a natural disaster that reduced the supply of wheat. Figure 7 shows the demand curve, *D*, and the supply curve, *S*, before the drought. After the drought destroyed part of their crops, farmers offer 25 million bushels at a \$5 price, whereas earlier they had offered 50 million bushels at that price. The supply curve for wheat has shifted to the left, to *S′*.

When the supply curve changes for a single good—like wheat—the demand curve normally does not change. The factors influencing the supply of wheat *other than its own price* have little or no influence on demand. In our example, the drought does not shift the demand curve. The demand and supply curves are independent in the analysis of a single market.

The supply curve has shifted to the left (supply has decreased); the demand curve remains unchanged. What will happen to the equilibrium price? After the drought, the quantity supplied at the initial price is less than the quantity demanded. At the initial price, there is a shortage of wheat. Therefore, the price of wheat will be bid up until a new and higher equilibrium price is attained, at which quantity demanded and quantity supplied are equal. As the price rises from the initial equilibrium price to the new equilibrium price, there is a movement up the new supply curve (*S′*). Even with a drought or other natural disaster, a higher price will coax out more wheat. (See Example 3.)

A decrease in supply without a change in demand causes the price to rise and the quantity demanded to fall. An increase in supply without a change in demand causes the price to fall and the quantity demanded to rise.

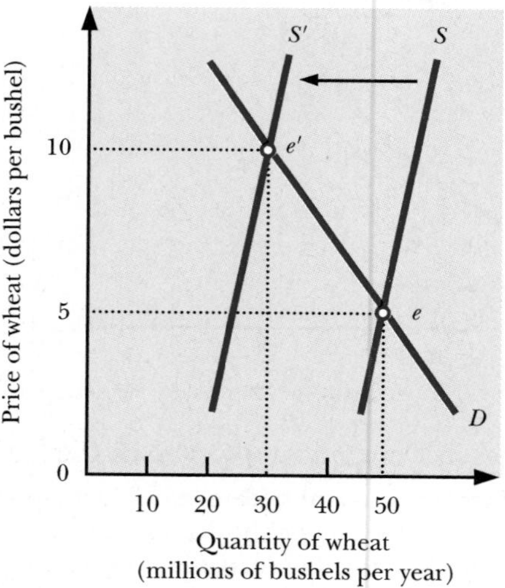

FIGURE 7 The Effects of a Drought on the Price of Wheat

In this figure, a drought shifts the supply curve of wheat from *S* to *S′*. Where a price of \$5 per bushel formerly brought forth 50 million bushels of wheat (on *S*), the same price now brings forth only 25 million bushels of wheat (on *S′*). This decrease in supply raises the equilibrium price from \$5 to \$10. The movement from *e* to *e′* is a movement along the demand curve. Although the demand curve does not change, quantity demanded decreases from 50 million to 30 million bushels as the price rises from \$5 to \$10 per bushel.

EXAMPLE 3

The Taiwan Earthquake and Computer Stocks

The 7.6 magnitude earthquake that struck Taiwan on September 21, 1999, sent shock waves through the toy and computer industries worldwide, which rely on Taiwanese semiconductors. Taiwan produces 10 percent of the world's chips and 80 percent of the motherboards used to run personal computers. Most of Taiwan's semiconductor plants were not destroyed by the quake, but a number of key precision instruments (many made of glass) were damaged. U.S. stock markets responded to the Taiwan earthquake by bidding down the share prices of U.S. computer manufacturers.

Supply and demand explain the reaction to the Taiwan earthquake. The threatened disruption of chip and motherboard supplies means that their prices should rise. Higher chip and motherboard prices will raise the cost of producing personal computers, causing their supply curves to shift to the left, driving up the prices of computers. Higher prices mean lower equilibrium quantities and a halt (or slowing) to growth of annual computer sales. Buyers of computer company stocks like to see rapid growth of sales, which, in the past, have been spurred by lower costs and lower prices. Anything that would cause costs to rise and the growth of sales to decline will drive down the stock prices of computer manufacturers.

Sources: http://www.ohio.com:80/bj/business/docs/030843.htm; http://www.bergen.com:80/biz/taiecon199909281.htm.

The Effects of a Change in Demand

A change in demand for wheat is illustrated in Figure 8. The initial equilibrium is depicted by the demand curve, *D*, and the supply curve, *S*. The equilibrium wheat price is $5, and the equilibrium quantity is 50 million bushels. *D* and *S* are the same curves as in Figure 7. Now let's imagine a change on the demand side. For example, new medical evidence shows that eating whole grain wheat will increase longevity. This news shifts the demand curve sharply to the right (from *D* to *D′*). This increase in demand for wheat would drive up the price of wheat. When the price rises, the quantity supplied rises. *There has been no increase in supply, only an increase in quantity supplied* in response to the higher price.

Notice that when the demand curve shifts as a result of a change in a demand factor other than the good's price, there need be no shift in the supply curve. As we have seen, demand and supply curves are considered independent in a single market. If a market is small enough relative to the entire economy, the link between the factors that shift demand curves (summarized in Table 1) and those that shift supply curves is weak. In our example, the change in preferences should not affect the willingness of farmers to supply wheat at different prices during any given time period.

> An increase in demand without a change in supply causes the price to rise and the quantity supplied to rise. A decrease in demand without a change in supply causes the price to fall and the quantity supplied to fall.

Simultaneous Changes in Demand and Supply

Figure 9 combines the two previous cases and illustrates what happens to price and quantity if the two events (the drought and the change in preferences) occur together. The demand curve shifts to the right from *D* to *D′* (demand increases), and the supply curve shifts to the left from *S* to *S′* (supply falls).

Prior to these changes, equilibrium price was $5, and equilibrium quantity was 50 million bushels. The shifts in demand and supply disrupt this equilibrium. Now at a price of $5, the quantity supplied equals 25 million bushels and the quantity demanded equals 90

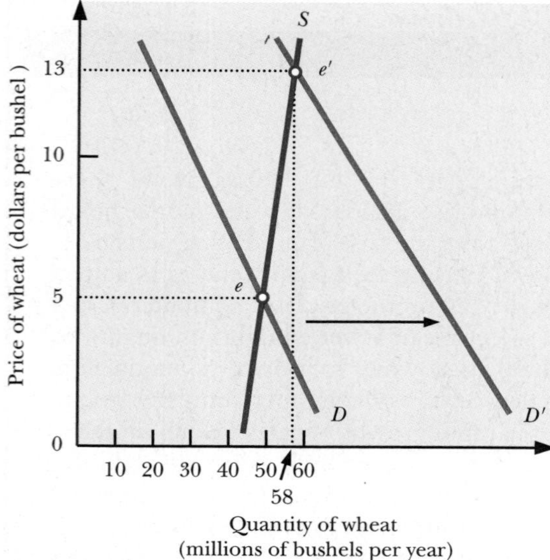

FIGURE 8 The Effects of an Increased Preference for Whole Grain Wheat on the Price of Wheat

If for some reason we want to eat more whole grain wheat as the result of a change in preferences, the demand curve for wheat will shift to the right. The shift in the demand curve from *D* to *D′* depicts an increase in demand. This increase in demand drives up the equilibrium price from $5 per bushel to $13 per bushel. As price rises from $5 to $13, quantity supplied increases from 50 million to 58 million bushels resulting in movement along the supply curve, *S*.

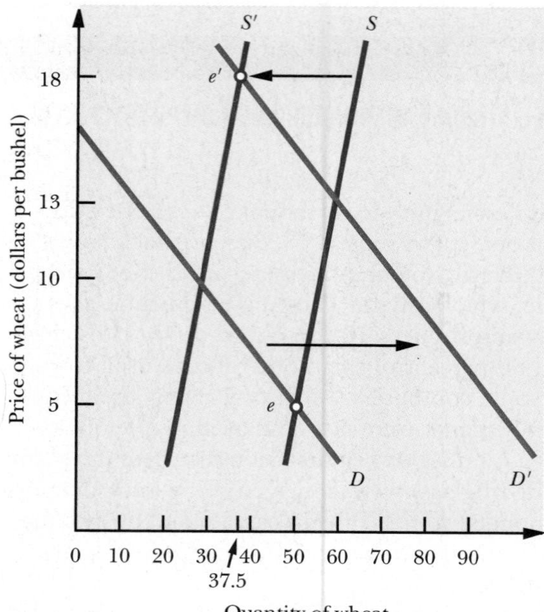

FIGURE 9 The Effects of an Increase in Demand and a Decrease in Supply on the Price of Wheat

This graph combines the supply change in Figure 7 and the demand change of Figure 8. The original equilibrium was at a price of $5 and a quantity of 50 million bushels. After the shift in supply (from *S* to *S′*) and the shift in demand (from *D* to *D′*), there is a shortage at the old price (quantity supplied equals 25 million bushels, and quantity demanded equals 90 million bushels). The equilibrium price rises to $18, and the equilibrium quantity falls to 37.5 million bushels.

million bushels—a shortage. The new equilibrium occurs at a price of $18 and a quantity of 37.5 million bushels. In this example, the two shifts magnify each other's effects. As we have shown, if there had been only the supply change, price would have risen to $9. If there had been only the demand change, price would have risen to $13. The combined effects cause the price to rise to $18. In this case, the causes of the changes in demand and supply are independent.

Figure 10 summarizes the effects of all possible combinations of shifts in demand curves and supply curves. As panels *(e)*, *(f)*, *(h)*, and *(i)* demonstrate, the effects of simultaneous changes in demand and supply are sometimes indeterminate. If supply increases (shifts right) and demand decreases (shifts left), the price will fall. If supply decreases and demand increases, the price will rise. If, however, both demand and supply curves move in the same direction (if both increase or if both decrease), the price effect depends upon which movement dominates.

Novel Applications of Demand and Supply

The concepts of demand, supply, and equilibrium price apply to a wide range of exchanges. Almost anything that admits to being priced and exchanged freely can be analyzed by the tools of this chapter.

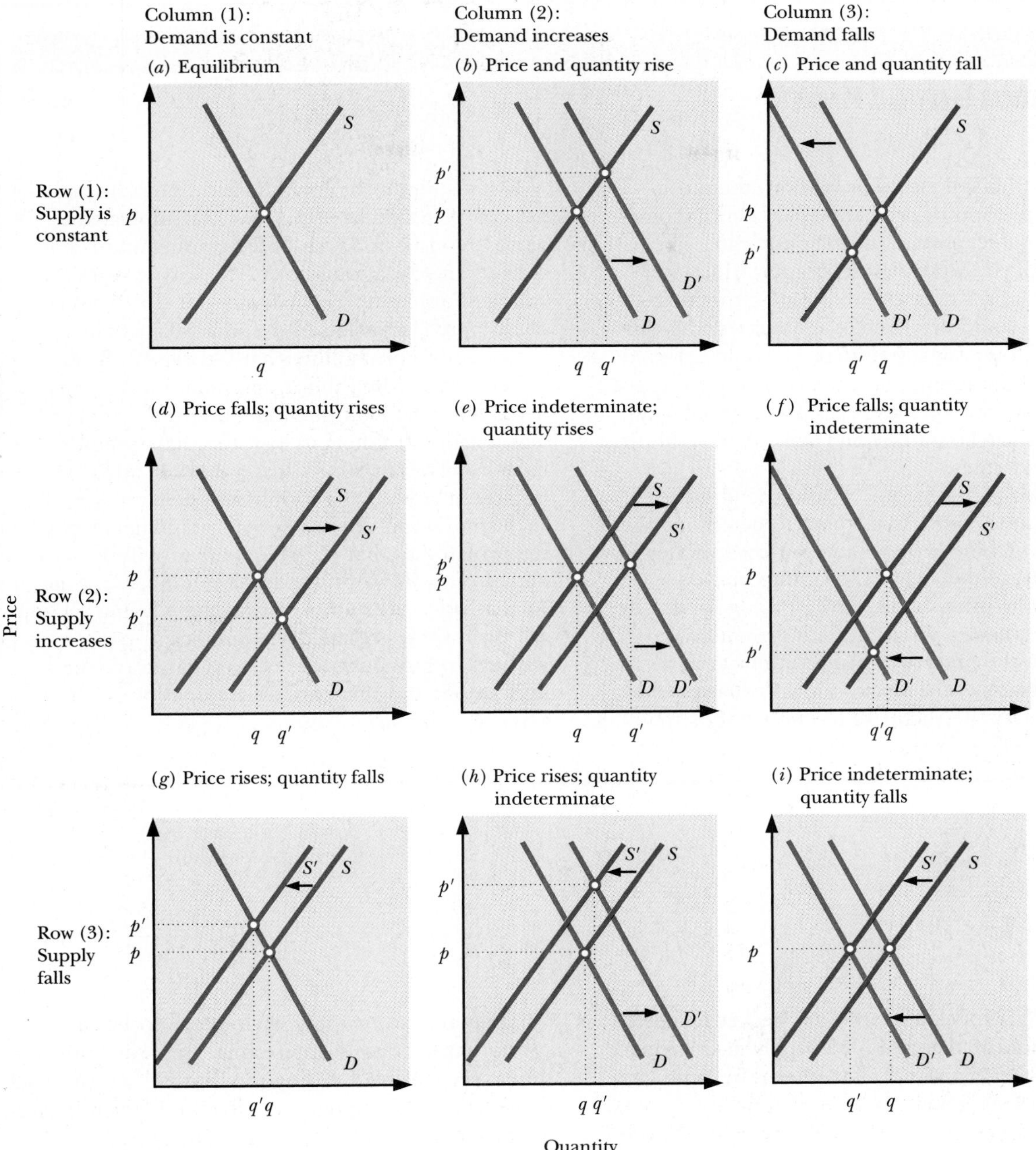

FIGURE 10 Summary of the Effects of Shifts in Supply Curves and Demand Curves

This figure gives the results of all possible combinations of shifts in supply curves and demand curves. To read it, match the rows and columns. For example, the figure in panel (*e*), at the intersection of row 2 and column 2, shows what happens when supply and demand increase simultaneously. The figure in panel (*i*), at the intersection of row 3 and column 3, shows what happens when both supply and demand fall.

EXAMPLE 4

The Political Elections Market

Until the political elections market, the most accurate method of predicting election outcomes was to conduct surveys of the electorate. The public looked to prestigious organizations such as Gallup and Roper to predict who the next president would be. Then economists at the University of Iowa suggested that we could get even more accurate predictions of election outcomes if an "election market" were set up in which buyers and sellers could buy and sell "shares" in different candidates.

The idea is that people would spend more thought, time, and effort trying to determine the election outcome if they had their own money on the line. Respondents to the Gallup or Roper polls, on the other hand, have nothing to lose by providing vague or inaccurate information.

Indeed, the predictions of economists have been borne out. The election market has been a more accurate predictor of election results than national polling organizations.

Details about the Iowa Political Elections market can be found at http://www.biz.uiowa.edu/iem/. It consists of Web-based trading and is considered an educational tool. The way it works is simple. For example, on August 10, 1999, you could purchase a share for about $0.75, which indicated the probability that George W. Bush would win the Republican nomination for president. When he won the nomination, the share was worth $1; if he had lost, the share would have been worth $0.00. It is a market price because it reflects the supply and demand for such shares and offers a summary judgment of the probability that a certain person will be nominated. The $0.75 price was an equilibrium price. At that price the number of people wishing to sell Bush shares equaled the number of people wishing to buy Bush shares. You can trade for as little as $5, and there are no transaction costs for active accounts.

Economist and Nobel laureate Gary Becker pioneered the application of demand and supply to marriage, crime, and other economic phenomena. In some societies, marriage is a market transaction—the groom may pay a bride price or the bride's family might provide a dowry. The bride price or dowry equates demand and supply. If there are too many brides, the bride price will fall. In the market for crime, the price of crime is the punishment that criminals expect to receive if they break the law; they balance this punishment against the amount they expect to earn from mugging, robbing, or burglarizing. A reduction in the price of crime increases the amount of crime.

Demand and supply even apply to betting. The sports pages contain interesting "market" information every weekend during the football season. Each game has a point spread, in which one team is given an advantage over the other. The purpose of the point spread is to provide equilibrium in the market for betting so that the number of people betting on the favored team equals the number of people betting on the underdog team. (See Example 4.)

In the next chapter, we will look at the unintended consequences of economic decisions.

SUMMARY

1. Markets differ according to the degree of competition.

2. The law of demand states that quantity demanded falls as price goes up, if other things are equal, and vice versa; the demand curve is a graphical representation of the relationship between price and quantity demanded—again, if other things are equal. The demand curve is downward sloping. The demand schedule shows the relationship between quantity demanded and price in tabular form.

3. As price goes up, quantity supplied usually rises; the supply curve is a graphical representation of the relationship between price and quantity supplied. The supply curve tends to be upward sloping because of the law of diminishing returns.

4. The equilibrium combination of price and quantity occurs where the demand curve intersects the supply curve or where quantity demanded equals quantity supplied. Competitive pricing rations goods and economizes on the information necessary to coordinate supply and demand decisions. A shortage results if the price is too low for equilibrium; a surplus results if the price is too high for equilibrium.

5. A change in quantity demanded signifies a movement along a given demand curve; a change in demand signifies a shift in the entire demand curve. A change in quantity supplied is shown by a movement along a given supply curve; a change in supply, by a shift in the entire supply curve.

6. The demand curve will shift if a change occurs in the price of a related good (substitute or complement), income levels, preferences, the number of buyers, or the expectation of future prices.

7. The supply curve will shift if a change occurs in the price of another good, the price of a resource, technology, the number of sellers, or the expectation of future prices. A change in the equilibrium price-quantity combination requires a change in one of the factors held constant along the demand or supply curves. Demand-and-supply analysis allows one to predict what will happen to prices and quantities when demand or supply schedules shift.

8. The concepts of demand, supply, and equilibrium price can be applied to a wide range of exchanges.

KEY TERMS

market 62
demand 63
law of demand 63
quantity demanded 64
market demand curve 65
substitutes 65
complements 66
normal good 66
inferior good 66
supply 67
quantity supplied 67
shortage 71
surplus 72
equilibrium (market-clearing) price 72
change in quantity demanded 74
change in demand 74
change in quantity supplied 74
change in supply 74

QUESTIONS AND PROBLEMS

1. Explain the relationship between the principle of substitution discussed in the previous chapter and the law of demand.
2. "People need medicine. If the price rises, people will not buy less medicine." Evaluate this statement in terms of the reasons demand curves are downward sloping.
3. Plot the demand and supply schedules for jeans in Table A as demand and supply curves.

TABLE A

Price (dollars)	*Quantity Demanded of Jeans (units)*	*Quantity Supplied of Jeans (units)*
10	5	25
8	10	20
6	15	15
2	20	10
0	25	5

a. What equilibrium price would this market establish?

b. If the state were to pass a law that the price of jeans could not be more than $2, how would you describe the market response?
c. If the state were to pass a law that the price of jeans could not be less than $8, how would you describe the market response?
d. If preferences changed and people wanted to buy twice as much as before at each price, what will the equilibrium price be?
e. If, in addition to the above change in preferences, there is an improvement in technology that allows firms to produce this product at lower cost than before, what will happen to the equilibrium price?

4. American baseball bats do not sell well in Japan because they do not meet the specifications of Japanese baseball officials. If the Japanese change their specifications to accommodate American-made bats, what will happen to the price of American bats?

5. "The poor are the ones who suffer from high gas and electricity bills. We should pass a law that gas and electricity rates cannot increase by more than 1 percent annually." Evaluate this statement in terms of demand-and-supply analysis, assuming that equilibrium prices rise faster than 1 percent annually.

6. Much of the automobile rental business in the United States is done at airports. How do you think a reduction in airfares would affect automobile rental rates?

7. If both the demand and the supply for coffee increase, what would happen to coffee prices? If the demand fell and the supply increased, what would happen to coffee prices?

8. "People are buying more burgers because the price has fallen." Is this an increase in demand?

9. Which of the following statements uses incorrect terminology? Explain.
   a. "The fare war among the major airlines in the summer of 1999 increased the demand for air travel."
   b. "The economic expansion of the 1990s caused the demand for air travel to rise."

10. What factors are held constant along the demand curve? Explain how each can shift the demand curve to the right. Explain how each can shift the demand curve to the left.

11. What factors are held constant along the supply curve? Explain how each factor can shift the supply curve to the right. Explain how each factor can shift the supply curve to the left.

12. Why is the demand curve downward sloping?

13. Why is the supply curve normally upward sloping? Can you think of any exceptions?

14. What is the effect of each of the following events on the equilibrium price and quantity of hamburgers?
   a. The price of steak (a substitute for hamburgers) increases.
   b. The price of french fries (a complement) increases.
   c. The population becomes older.
   d. The government requires that all the ingredients of hamburgers be absolutely fresh (that is, nothing can be frozen).
   e. Beef becomes more expensive.
   f. More firms enter the hamburger business.

15. "As a general rule, if *both* demand and supply increase or decrease, the change in price will be indeterminate." Is this statement true or false? Illustrate with a diagram.

16. "As a general rule, if demand increases and supply decreases, or vice versa, the change in quantity will be indeterminate." Is this statement true or false? Illustrate with a diagram.

17. Let us assume that the number of compact discs sold in markets has more than quadrupled over the past three years. The average price of a compact disc, however, has fallen. Use demand-and-supply analysis to explain this phenomenon.

INTERNET CONNECTION

18. Using the links from http://www.awl.com/ruffin_gregory, read "Trends in Youth Smoking" on the Cato Institute's Web site.
   a. According to the authors, what has happened to teenage smokers' demand for cigarettes over the past 20 years?

   b. In recent years, cigarette prices have increased markedly. How would this influence the teenage demand for smoking?

19. Using the links from http://www.awl.com/ruffin_gregory, read "Can U.S. Oil Production Survive the 20th Century?" on the Federal Reserve Bank of Kansas City Web site.
   a. What happened to the relationship between supply and demand during the 1990s?
   b. Has the cost of finding petroleum increased or decreased? What influence do you think this will have on long-term supply? Illustrate your answer using supply and demand curves.

PUZZLE ANSWERED: The starting pay of teachers in Houston is set by formulas approved by the school board. During periods of rapid growth in the demand for new teachers, these pay rates do not adjust quickly to equate supply and demand, creating a "shortage" of new teachers. Schools respond to this shortage by offering signing bonuses.

Chapter 5

UNINTENDED CONSEQUENCES

Chapter Insight

All policies must be considered with great care because they may cause unintended consequences. To choose the right economic policies, we must contemplate both the intended and the unintended consequences. As Friedrich A. Hayek, one of the Defining Moment economists, noted: "The pursuit of our most cherished ideals . . . [can produce] results utterly different from those we expected."[1]

Robert Malthus (1766–1835) was one of the first economists to discuss how unintended consequences could change the outcome of poorly designed policies. According to Malthus, "First appearances . . . are deceitful . . . and the partial and immediate effects [of policy] . . . are often directly opposite to the general and permanent consequences."[2] In 1800, he wrote an essay on the high price of food. Malthus, who was a minister of the Church of England, pointed out that food prices were higher in England than in Sweden because of the allowances (welfare payments) that English parishes were giving to the poor. By giving the poor these allowances, the price of food was being bid up, making it more difficult for all, including the poor, to buy food.

We don't have to go back to 1800 to find examples of unintended consequences. Our welfare system has encouraged the breakup of welfare families. Well-

[1]*The Road to Serfdom,* Chicago: University of Chicago Press, 1944, p. 11.
[2]*An Investigation of the Present High Price of Provisions,* London: L. Johnson, 1800.

intended efforts to improve access to medical care has caused its quality to deteriorate in affluent countries like England and Canada. Efforts to supply the poor with low-cost housing has reduced its availability.

LEARNING OBJECTIVES

After completing this chapter, you will be able to:

1. Relate marginal costs to marginal benefits and understand the principle of optimal choice.
2. Know the definition of game theory and understand the prisoner's dilemma.
3. Use the principle of unintended consequences to explain the failures of price controls, rent controls, and the unintended effects of government health insurance programs.

CHAPTER PUZZLE: A classmate comes to you with the following proposition: "Our teacher grades on a curve. All other 50 students agree that they will not study hard for the next test. We'll all make poor grades but no one will suffer because of the curve." How would you react? Would you react differently if there were only 4 students?

MARGINAL ANALYSIS

The economy is just people making decisions about the ordinary business of earning a living. The decisions of households, governments, and corporations are made by individuals trying to do the best they can, given the circumstances. Because individuals are the main actors of economics, the student of economics has an advantage over the struggling physics student, who cannot ask, "What would I do if I were a molecule?" The student is one of the "molecules" economists study.

Our behavior is affected by the *incentives*—the carrots and sticks—that we face in any given situation. The "carrots" are the benefits we receive from an economic activity; the "sticks" are its costs. We are guided in our economic decisions by costs and benefits.

In one of the Defining Moments of economics, as discussed in Chapter 1, Adam Smith pointed out that "it is not from the benevolence of the butcher, the brewer, or the baker that we expect our dinner, but from their regard to their own self-interest. In other words, we do things if we perceive that the benefits of what we are doing will exceed their costs.

The tool most used by economists to study economic decision making is the comparison of costs and benefits, or marginal analysis. (See Example 1.)

Marginal analysis examines the costs and benefits of making small changes from the current state of affairs.

Marginal Costs and Benefits

Let's start with a simple example: You might use marginal analysis to decide how much studying is "enough." First, you examine the benefits of a slight (marginal) increase in your present amount of studying. If you increase your study time by, say, one hour per day, you will probably earn higher grades and a better job upon graduation. Although you will not be able to measure these results exactly, you would have a general idea of the benefits of additional study. Simultaneously, you consider the costs of one more hour of studying per day. You might have to sacrifice earnings from a part-time job, or you might have to give up your gym workout, your favorite television program, or an extra hour of sleep.

Whether you are studying "enough" depends upon whether you conclude that the benefits of the extra studying outweigh the additional costs. If they do, you conclude that you are not studying enough, and you will study more. If the extra costs are greater than the extra benefits, you conclude that you should not increase your study time.

Businesses make choices in a similar fashion. Consider a local fast-food restaurant. Its owners must

EXAMPLE 1

THE RENT GRADIENT AND MARGINAL ANALYSIS

Economics teaches that people make decisions using marginal analysis, weighing costs and benefits at the margin. Consider the choices of housing locations in cities like Atlanta, Houston, or Los Angeles, where people commute to work on congested freeways. Houses and apartments located closer to the city center offer benefits in the form of shorter commuting times. Thus, the closer the location to the city center, the higher the price or the rent. In cities like Houston, for example, housing prices drop by $5000 for each additional mile from the city center.

Along with additional factors like schools and other amenities, marginal analysis says that people weigh the extra costs of more centrally located homes against the benefits of shorter commuting times. People tend to balance the marginal costs and benefits, typically choosing that location where they perceive the extra benefits of shorter commuting times to roughly equal the extra costs in the form of higher prices or rents.

decide if its current hours of operation (11 A.M. to midnight) are "enough." Before taking action, the restaurant's owners have to make a decision at the margin. They must estimate how much extra revenue will be gained by opening for breakfast. They also estimate the extra costs of opening earlier (the extra supplies, larger payroll, higher utility bills, more advertising). If the extra benefits from opening earlier (the additional revenue) exceed the extra costs, the owners will decide to open early for breakfast. If the extra benefits are less than the extra costs, the owners will not increase their hours of operation. People and businesses make all kinds of economic decisions by comparing the extra costs with the extra benefits associated with making changes in their plans.

> To make decisions, we must consider the extra (or marginal) costs and benefits of an increase or decrease in a particular activity. If the marginal benefits outweigh the marginal costs, we undertake the extra activity.

Marginal Analysis and Optimal Choice

Marginal analysis dictates that we should carry out any activity whose marginal benefit is greater than its marginal cost. We should cut back on any activity whose marginal cost exceeds its marginal benefit. If we combine these rules, we see that the *optimal level* of activity (how many hours to work, how many units of output to produce, how much time to devote to study, and so forth) occurs where marginal costs and marginal benefits are equal.

In the studying example, let's say that if we study two additional hours, the marginal benefit of each extra hour is greater than the marginal cost. We should study these extra hours. If we now consider studying a third hour, the marginal cost equals the marginal benefit; a fourth hour, however, yields marginal costs greater than marginal benefits. The conclusion: We should continue to increase our study time until the marginal costs and marginal benefits of extra study are equal. The choice of the optimal study time—in this case, three hours—is shown in Figure 1.

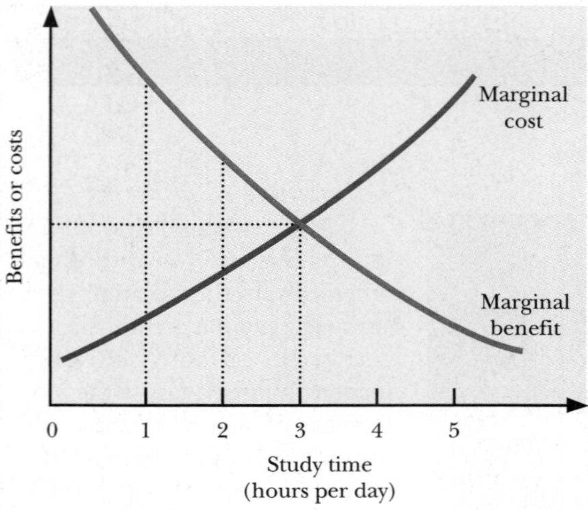

FIGURE 1

The optimal amount of studying is three hours per day. When less time is allocated, the marginal benefit exceeds the marginal cost; thus, it pays to study more.

In later chapters we shall apply this rule to many different types of economic choices—consumption, labor supply, unemployment, acquisition of information, and production. The rule is a powerful one that we can use to explain a wide variety of economic phenomena.

Marginal Analysis and Incentives

Whenever anything happens to change the marginal costs and benefits of economic actions—changes in prices, wages, incomes, regulations—we respond by changing our economic behavior. In the restaurant example, if the wages of restaurant employees rise, the marginal costs of opening early for business increase, and the restaurant is less likely to decide to open early. If the price of breakfasts rises, the marginal benefits of opening earlier are greater, and the restaurant is more likely to open early. Let's suppose the city government, wishing to encourage more restaurants to open early, lowers the local taxes of restaurants that open early. This action also gives the restaurant an extra incentive to open early. Or let's suppose that the federal government mandates an increase in the minimum wage. (The fast-food restaurant hires primarily teenagers working at the minimum wage.) This mandate raises the restaurant's marginal cost and provides an incentive to open fewer hours.

We, as consumers and employees, alter our behavior in response to changes in incentives. If the government raises income tax rates, the marginal benefits of working overtime or taking second jobs are reduced. The tax increase causes us to change our behavior; we are less likely to work overtime, and our spouse is less likely to work.

Actions that affect the marginal costs and benefits cause people and businesses to alter their behavior. Accordingly, actions that alter costs and benefits have both primary and secondary effects.

> The secondary (or indirect) effect of an action that alters marginal costs and benefits is that people and businesses alter their economic behavior.

Secondary or indirect effects are often hard to predict and difficult to measure. The direct effect of an increase in income tax rates is to raise government tax revenues. Its secondary effect is quite different. If the tax increases cause us to work less, or to reduce taxable market activities, taxable income will tend to fall. If the government increases the minimum wage, the direct effect is to raise the income of those working at the minimum wage. The secondary effect is to reduce the employment of minimum wage workers and hence to reduce their income.

Secondary effects make it difficult to predict the *net* effect of government actions, which is the sum of direct and indirect effects. The net effect of lowering income tax rates on government revenue is the negative effect of lower tax rates minus the positive secondary effect of more taxable income. The net effect of raising the minimum wage on the incomes of low-skilled workers is the positive effect of higher wages of employed workers minus the loss of income of those who become unemployed as a consequence.

Games and the Prisoner's Dilemma

When you play chess, checkers, or poker, the result depends on how well your opponent plays compared to your play. Many economic situations are similar. What we can do depends on our expectations about what others are going to do. If we expect others to cheat or harm us in some way, we will take action to minimize the cost we expect others to try to impose on us. In a word, our behavior is social: What we do depends on others.

The study of how we interact with others in our economic and social behavior is called **game theory.**

Economists use game theory to analyze situations in which economic players must use strategies against each other. Economists have used game theory for over fifty years, and John Nash's 1994 Nobel Prize honored his contributions to game theory.

A game is simply a situation in which each player (including you) can follow different strategies (what you will do in any situation) and receives a reward or penalty depending on strategies adopted by the other players. The game's outcome depends not only on you but also on others.

In many cases, we are in complete control over the outcome, independent of the actions of others. When you go to the grocery store, whether you buy that gallon of milk or not makes no real difference to anybody else—but it does to you. If you study an extra hour and get a higher grade, you benefit and no one else is affected.

In other cases, however, your actions affect others and vice versa. If there are only two persons in your class and your instructor grades on a curve, your additional studying affects the second student's grade. Your grade now depends on how much the other student studies. Any action you take must now consider how the other student will behave. If you study more and the other student does not, your grade will improve. If you study more and the other student also studies more, your grade will be unchanged. With such interdependence, calculation of marginal costs and benefits can become complex.

The prisoner's dilemma game is used to describe many types of "games" that we must play in our economic lives. It is so called because it describes a situation in which the police are questioning two suspected bank robbers. The suspects can either cooperate with each other through silence or confess to the police. In the prisoner's dilemma game, self-interest leads people to do something that is not in their collective interest. In other words, when people are involved in a prisoner's dilemma, no one has an incentive to do what is best for all concerned.

A **prisoner's dilemma** is a game in which all would gain by cooperating, but self-interest causes them not to cooperate.

Figure 2 shows the prisoner's dilemma. Jesse James and Billy the Kid are arrested on suspicion of robbing a bank. Billy's two possible strategies are shown by the rows; Jesse's by the columns. Each square cell shows the payoffs to Billy and Jesse for any particular combination of strategies. Billy's payoff is in the lower left corner of each cell; Jesse's payoff is in the upper right corner of each cell. If both confess, they each get 3 years in jail. The reward or payoff for each is therefore -3. If one confesses while the other remains silent, the one who remains silent gets 6 years while the one who confesses goes free (0 years). If both remain silent (they cooperate), they each get 1 year for carrying a concealed weapon.

What should each do? If Jesse confesses, Billy is better off confessing; otherwise, he gets 6 years. If Jesse remains silent, Billy is better off confessing because he goes free. *No matter what Jesse does, it is better for Billy to confess.* The same is true for Jesse. Thus, self-interest causes both bank robbers to confess, and they each spend 3 years in jail. They would both be better off remaining silent, but self-interest leads to an outcome that is worse for both players.

The prisoner's dilemma game applies to a broad range of economic, political, and social actions. It applies to any situation in which players are driven to strategies or actions that are inferior to cooperative solutions. The prisoner's dilemma explains, among other things, why price wars take place among sellers, why governments engage in deficit financing, and why shortages cannot be solved by voluntary cooperation.

Hence, economic decision making can be studied in two contexts. In one context, your decisions do not affect others. You can decide upon your best

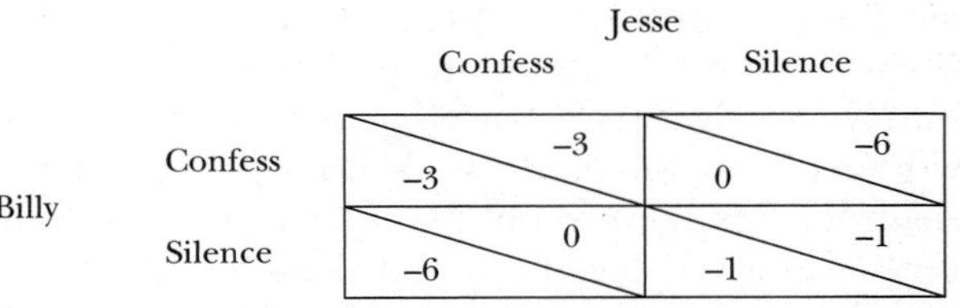

FIGURE 2 The Prisoner's Dilemma

course of action using marginal analysis without worrying how others will react. In the second context, your actions affect others and vice versa. You must consider how others will react. In effect, you are involved in a strategic game with others.

The Principle of Unintended Consequences

Economics deals with real economic problems—inflation, poverty, unemployment, or inadequate medical care. When public concern grows, pressure usually grows to pass legislation that will correct the problem, but economic problems usually are not easy to solve. The principle of unintended consequences warns that because people will always try to do the best they can given the circumstances, the ultimate effects of economic policies may be different from the intended effects. Indeed, the "cure" can sometimes be worse than the "disease."

The **principle of unintended consequences** holds that economic policies may have ultimate or actual effects that differ from the intended or apparent effects.

Consider some examples: The Aid to Families with Dependent Children Program (AFDC) provides financial assistance to families with dependent children according to demonstrated need. If welfare authorities determine that a family with young children has "enough" income, no assistance will be provided. An unintended consequence of the AFDC program has been to encourage the breakdown of the U.S. poor family. Poor households qualify for more AFDC assistance if the father is absent. Many poor families are better off if fathers desert their families to increase the amount of AFDC assistance. A program intended to stabilize the family has had the unintended consequence of breaking it apart.

The Social Security Act was intended to supplement the retirement incomes of older Americans. What has been the result? If the Social Security Act simply gave us back what we put into it during our working years, the result would not have been different from that if we simply saved for our retirement years. However, the Social Security Act did not just promise to repay us for our contributions: It promised to repay early participants more than they put in. To finance social security, future workers had to be taxed! As an unintended consequence, many Americans stopped saving. About 50 percent of all Americans save nothing toward retirement and plan to rely exclusively on social security. To finance the program, it was necessary to raise social security taxes from minuscule amounts (about 1 percent of payrolls) to the present 15 percent of payrolls. As we Americans stopped saving for our retirement, and as the U.S. population aged, the social security system is now facing a crisis: Sometime in the first half of the twenty-first century, it will be bankrupt unless we change the system.

Third-Party Payments and Copayments

In some cases, we decide that a good or service is so essential that a third party (often the government or an insurance company) should pay part of the cost for the user. Examples are goods and services such as medical care or education, where the actual consumer pays only part of the cost, the remainder being paid by another party.

Third-party payments occur when the consumer pays only part of the cost. The consumer's share is called a **copayment**. The remainder of the cost is paid by a third party, such as the government.

Figure 3 shows the effects of third-party payments and copayments on prices and equilibrium quantities. The demand curve *D* shows demand when consumers pay the full costs themselves. If consumers pay only half the costs (a 50 percent copayment), they can obtain the good at half the price as before, so the demand curve shifts left to *D′*. If the third party pays the entire cost (a zero copayment), the good is free to consumers, and consumers demand the quantities they would want at a zero price (*D″*). The supply curve has a positive (upward) slope, showing that the product is supplied by a competitive market.

The result of third-party payments is an increase in price. The smaller the consumer copayment, the greater the increase in price. The increase in equilibrium quantities depends on the slope of the supply curve. If supply is fixed (a vertical supply curve),

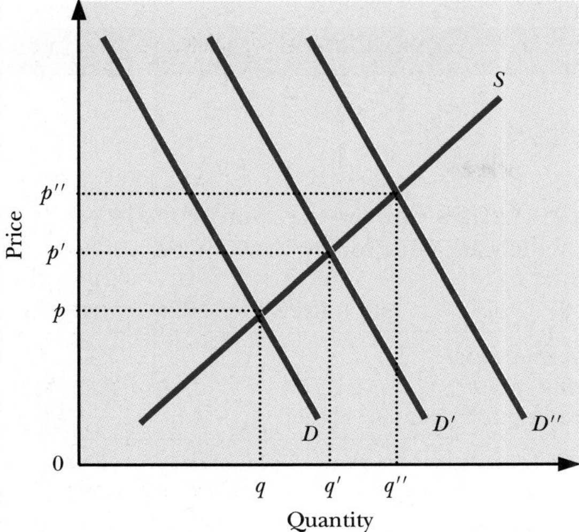

FIGURE 3 Equilibrium Prices and Quantities with Third-Party Payments

We begin with no third-party payments. The demand curve D yields a price of p and an equilibrium quantity of q. Demand curve D' shows third-party payments with a 50% copayment rate. Consumers are, in effect, getting the good for half price, so they demand more. The new price is p', and the new equilibrium quantity is q'. Demand curve D'' shows the demand curve with full third-party payments. Consumers demand what they would want if the good were given away free. The result is an even higher price (p''). Note that if the supply curve had been vertical, the increases in demand would have raised only prices, not quantities.

third-party payments cause prices to rise, without any increase in quantity. (See Example 2.)

Economists are critical of third-party payments for a simple reason: Assume that we can buy a product for $1 by paying half its price (50 cents) while someone else pays the other half. The producer of the good has had to expend $1 worth of society's resources to produce the good, but the consumer places only a 50 cent value on the good. The result: We have used up $1 worth of society's scarce resources to produce something that we value only at 50 cents.

> Third-party payments lead to the result that we use up society's scarce resources to produce goods that are valued by users at less than the cost of these resources.

PRICE CONTROLS AND UNINTENDED CONSEQUENCES

We dislike high prices when we are buyers and we love high prices when we are sellers. As a consequence, buyers bring political pressure for government control to lower prices below the prices that would prevail in a market equilibrium. The principle of unintended consequences shows that, if the government intervenes in price setting—even for a worthy cause—unintended results usually emerge, which may defeat the intent of the policy.

We studied the rationing function of prices in the last chapter. Briefly, if a good is scarce, it is necessary to find some way of allocating the scarce supply among all of the competing claimants. Fights, favoritism, first-come-first-served, or ration booklets are possible solutions. Market prices have an enormous advantage over the other allocation mechanisms: they are more efficient.

Figure 4 distinguishes between equilibrium and disequilibrium prices. The price at which the demand and supply curves intersect is the equilibrium price.

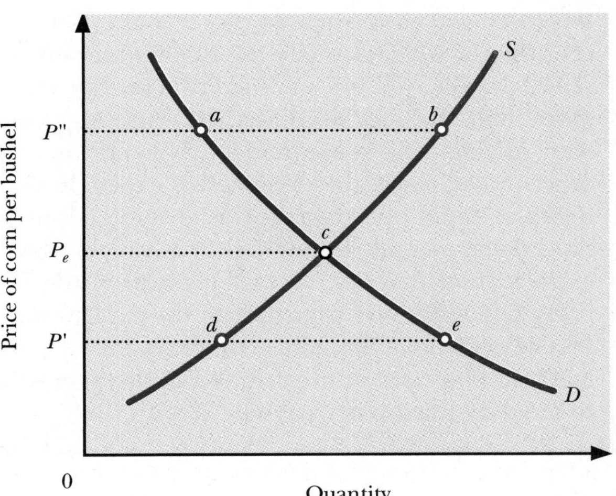

FIGURE 4 Disequilibrium Prices

The demand (D) and supply (S) curves intersect at c, which yields an equilibrium price of P_e, at which the quantity demanded equals the quantity supplied. At a higher price, say P'', there is a surplus where the quantity demanded (a) is less than the quantity supplied (b). At a lower price, say P', there is a shortage where the quantity demanded (e) exceeds the quantity supplied (d).

EXAMPLE 2

Third-Party Payments and Medical Costs

The provision of high-quality medical care to all—rich and poor alike—is a laudable social goal. Most industrialized countries, the United States included, have government programs to ensure that almost everyone has access to medical care. Since July 1966, Medicare has provided government-sponsored health insurance for people age 65 and over. The states provide Medicaid services to the poor, disabled, and families with dependent children. Currently, we spend almost $4500 on medical care for each man, woman, and child in the United States. The accompanying figure shows that only 17 cents of every health care dollar is paid by persons out of their own pockets. The vast bulk is paid by third parties: Medicare and Medicaid account for over one-third, and another one-third is paid by private health insurance.

The discussion of third-party payments suggests that we demand more of a product when third parties pay for a portion of it. We demand more medical care when we pay less than 20 percent than if we had to pay the full amount ourselves. Indeed, the price of medical care has risen more than 10 times since Medicare and Medicaid were introduced—more than twice as fast as other prices.There are a number of explanations for these rapid price increases (the aging population, rising income, technological advances), but experts agree that the increasing use of third-party payments is a large part of the explanation.

The accompanying table compares the increases in prices of prescription drugs, typically covered by third-party payments, with the increase in prices of over-the-counter medications, which are paid for by consumers.

	1990	*1996*	*1998*
Prescription drugs (1982–84 = 100)	182	243	259
Nonprescription drugs	121	143	148

This table suggests that the price of medical care would rise much less rapidly if we had to pay for medical care ourselves.

Sources: Joseph Newhouse, "Medical Care Costs: How Much Welfare Loss?" *Journal of Economic Perspectives,* Vol. 6, No. 3 (summer 1992). For information from the U.S. Health Care Financing Administration, see http://www.hcfa.gov.

The Nation's Health Dollar
Where It Came From

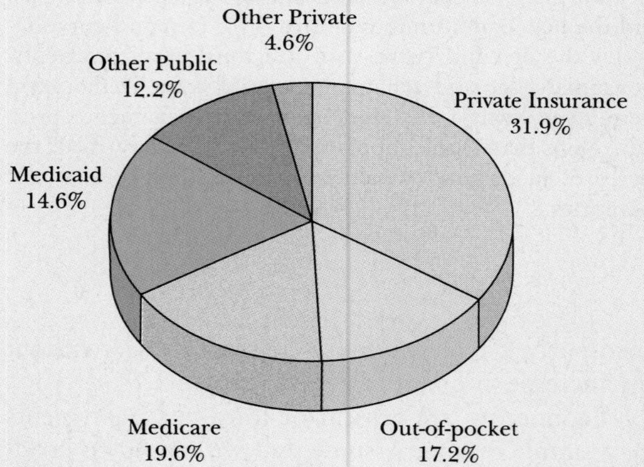

Source: http://www.hcfa.gov/stats/nhe-oact/tables/chart.htm.

An **equilibrium price** is that price at which the quantity demanded of the product equals the quantity supplied.

A **disequilibrium price** is one at which the quantity demanded does not equal the quantity supplied.

Any price other than the one at which the demand and supply curves intersect is a disequilibrium price.

As Figure 4 shows, if the price is above the equilibrium price, a surplus will result. If the price is not allowed to fall, sellers will not be able to make decisions that reflect the actual demand for the good. They will want to produce more than buyers want to buy. They are experiencing the prisoner's dilemma because each seller has an incentive to sell more but cannot because the price is too high. If the price is allowed to fall, this incentive will lower the price further until the incentive vanishes.

At any price below the equilibrium price, a shortage will result. If there is a shortage, buyers want to purchase more of the good or service than is available. If the price is not allowed to rise, each buyer faces a prisoner's dilemma. They want to buy more but cannot. Thus, each buyer acts against the collective interests of all buyers.

Adam Smith's invisible hand is based on the principle that we should allow prices to find their equilibrium levels without interference. Equilibrium prices coordinate the actions of buyers and sellers even though each is following self-interest.

Price Controls: The Gas Panic of 1973

In October 1973, the Organization of Petroleum Exporting Countries (OPEC) placed a total ban on oil exports to the United States after the outbreak of an Arab-Israeli conflict. The United States, heavily dependent upon imported oil, faced the prospect of running short of oil.

President Nixon responded by introducing a complicated system of government allocation that set the price of gasoline far below the equilibrium price. Gasoline stations were allowed to raise their prices only to price ceilings set by the government. Violators were punished by fines and imprisonment.

The intended consequence of the gas price controls was to prevent undue hardship, especially on the poor, by limiting increases in the price of gasoline at the pump. The unintended consequence was that people had to stand in line at gas stations, often starting at 4 A.M. Arguments broke out at gas stations over who was in line first, a number of people were killed in these confrontations, and many gas station attendants carried firearms. Importantly, car owners protected themselves against the shortage of gasoline by trying to keep their gas tanks as full as possible all of the time. The limited supply of gasoline was being driven around in the form of full gasoline tanks.

The prisoner's dilemma in this case is clear-cut. If the available supply (at the controlled price) equalled, say, 60 percent of desired usage, we would not have to wait in lines for gasoline if everybody voluntarily cut their usage to 60 percent. But each person has an incentive, at the controlled price, to use more than 60 percent. Thus, long lines developed, and enormous resources were wasted just trying to find gas.

The reaction of the nations of Western Europe was different. They simply allowed gasoline prices to rise to their new equilibrium level. European car owners reluctantly paid the higher prices, and the unintended consequences that took place in the United States were avoided.

Rent Controls

Rent controls also reveal the unintended effects of disequilibrium pricing. (See Example 3.) Municipal governments under pressure from renter groups can freeze rents (that is, prevent rents from rising). Many cities have rent control ordinances. Figure 5 shows the market for rental housing in New York City. As

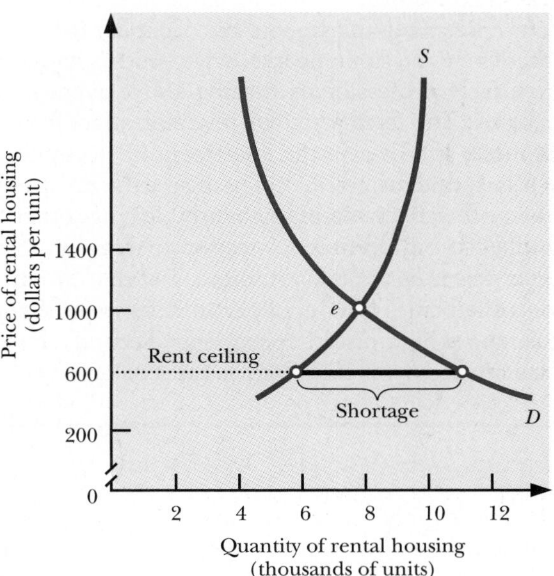

FIGURE 5 The Effect of Rent Ceilings on the Market for Rental Housing

If the equilibrium price-quantity combination for the rental market is \$1000 per unit and 8000 units (point *e*), a rent ceiling of \$600 per month on a standard housing unit would lower the quantity supplied to 6000 units and raise the quantity demanded to 11,000 units, creating a shortage of 5000 units of rental housing.

EXAMPLE 3

The Unintended Consequences of Rent Controls: Apartmentless in Santa Monica

Rent controls were introduced as temporary wartime price controls during World War II. They remain a force in many U.S. cities, ranging from New York City and Washington, D.C., to San Francisco and Santa Monica. Cities with rent controls account for about 20 percent of the U.S. population. It is rare for rent controls to be abolished. In January 1997 Cambridge and Brookline, Massachusetts, became the first major U.S. cities to abandon rent controls. In New York City, 1.1 million of the city's 1.6 million apartments are rent controlled, creating a huge constituency of families that favor rent control's continuation.

Rent controls were ostensibly introduced to make cheap housing available to poor families. The result has been the opposite: First, rent controls create shortages of affordable housing. Rent-controlled apartments are occupied for decades by the same people, who, studies show, are largely professionals earning above-average incomes. The former mayor of Cambridge, for example, still lives in the apartment he occupied as a law student in 1973. These apartments are taken off the market permanently, leaving other families to bid up rental rates for apartments that are not rent controlled. Studies show that in rent-controlled cities the only apartments available for leasing are high-priced apartments. Second, cities with rent controls have higher rates of homeless people. Third, the stock of housing in rent-controlled cities tends to shrink because owners cannot afford the upkeep on rent-controlled properties, and there is little new construction because of the fear of extending rent controls throughout the housing market. Fourth, occupants of rent-controlled apartments hoard the available supply, meaning that vacancy rates are much lower in rent-controlled cities. New York has not had a vacancy rate in excess of 5 percent since World War II. San Francisco has a vacancy rate of only 2 percent. Other cities have vacancy rates between 10 and 15 percent. Low-priced housing units simply are not available in cities with rent controls. Families in cities without rent control have an easier time finding moderately priced rental units. Fifth, rent controls have been used in some cities, such as Santa Monica, to exclude outsiders. Once rent controls were applied in Santa Monica, construction stopped, and it became impossible for newcomers to find an apartment there. One professional woman looked for an apartment for a year and solved her problem by marrying someone who already had an apartment.

Source: William Tucker, "How Rent Controls Drive Out Affordable Housing," *Cato Policy Analysis,* No. 274, May 21, 1997. http://www.cato.org/pubs/pas/pa-274.html.

usual, the supply curve is upward sloping; the demand curve is downward sloping. In a free (unregulated) market, the rent would settle at $1000 per month for a standard rental unit. But suppose a price ceiling of $600 is established by the city council. As long as landlords are free to supply the number of apartments they wish, a lower price will mean a correspondingly smaller number of units offered for rent. Figure 5 shows that 6000 units are supplied at a price of $600 and 8000 units at a price of $1000. The quantity demanded rises to 11,000 units as the price falls from $1000 to $600. Accordingly, the price ceiling results in a shortage of 5000 units. If the price could rise from $600 to $1000, there would be no shortage. This is the equilibrium price.

Each of the 11,000 New York City residents who wants an apartment has an incentive to be one of the lucky 6000 residents who gets one of the rent-controlled apartments. The socially responsible act would be for the 11,000 to agree to give the 6000 available apartments to those who place the highest value on them. But the prisoner's dilemma prevents this from happening. The lucky 6000 who actually get rent-controlled apartments will not willingly give up their apartments to those who value the apartments more. Indeed, it is usually the case that the rent control ordinances prevent people from legally subletting their apartments at a higher price.

Consider the unintended consequence of rent controls. The intent is to ensure an adequate supply of affordable housing. The result is that, although a few people get cheap housing, fewer cheap housing units are available overall. Many people have to do without; others must pay more by renting high-priced non-rent-controlled apartments. The quality of the housing stock drops because developers have no interest in improving apartments with fixed rents that cannot be increased; although it may be in the social interest to improve the housing stock, with rent controls it is not in the private interest of the landlords.

Marginal Analysis and Unintended Consequences

As discussed earlier in this chapter, we make decisions by weighing the marginal costs and marginal benefits of our actions. If a government policy changes marginal costs and benefits, we will respond, often in ways that defeat the original intent of the policy.

Consider the government policy of insuring bank deposits. The intent is to prevent depositors from losing their hard-earned money and to create a "sound" banking system. Government deposit insurance, however, changes marginal costs and benefits and has unintended consequences: If we know that we cannot lose our bank deposits no matter what happens, the marginal benefit of spending the time to determine whether our bank is solvent or not disappears. We no longer gain advantage from keeping our funds out of poorly run banks, and deposits flow into banks that are risky and poorly managed. As these banks fail, confidence in the banking system is reduced and the policy intended to create confidence in the banking system actually serves to reduce confidence.

If people lose their jobs, through no fault of their own, it would seem unfair for them to be without income. It is for this reason that most governments have unemployment insurance. Unemployment compensation changes the marginal costs and benefits of being unemployed. If you live in a country that pays 75 percent of lost income, the marginal cost of remaining unemployed is low and you will not search as hard to find a new job. Accordingly, unemployment compensation—a program designed to make unemployment less onerous—can have the unintended consequence of worsening the unemployment problem.

Economic Policy and Unintended Consequences

The existence of unintended consequences is not a counsel for despair. Rather, unintended consequences tell us that the challenge is to develop good economic policies, not to pose superficial solutions to difficult problems. In economics, as in medicine, recognizing a problem does not mean knowing its solution. At one time, doctors made their patients worse off by bleeding them; they recognized the illness but did not know the cure. Economic policy makers may commit the same error.

Economists can make important contributions to sound economic and business policies. It was economists who suggested that we deal with pollution by setting up a market for pollution rights. This market has reduced the costs of pollution control. Economists have pointed out that solutions to such problems as poverty and the lack of adequate medical care require an economic approach that emphasizes the incentives created by the policies designed to correct these problems. Beginning with Adam Smith, economists have warned against interfering with the invisible hand of markets without a very careful consideration of the possible unintended consequences.

Above all, economists teach that "there is no such thing as a free lunch." The law of scarcity simply cannot be repealed. Anyone, therefore, who promises to solve the problems of poverty, unemployment, health, or safety by simply passing a law that is the result of complicated political pressures is either stupid or not telling the truth. The sober message is this: All actions have costs and benefits. To make the right decision, we must know all of the costs and benefits—even if they come through indirect effects. The bias of economists is to select policies in which the marginal benefits exceed the costs, without regard for or influence from narrow interest groups. We devote a later chapter to consider why this choice is difficult.

SUMMARY

1. The principle of unintended consequences states that well-intended economic policies may have unintended consequences. Their ultimate effects may differ from their intended effects.

2. Marginal analysis states that people make economic decisions by weighing the consequences of making changes from the current state. People have an incentive to undertake actions as long as the marginal benefits of those actions exceed the marginal costs.

3. Game theory concerns social or economic interactions in which individuals must take into account the behavior of others before they can determine their costs or benefits. The most important game is called the prisoner's dilemma, in which everybody would gain from cooperation but nobody has an individual incentive to do so.

4. Failure to understand the incentives people have in any situation can lead to unintended consequences, such as in the cases of federal bank deposit insurance, unemployment insurance, social security, and free medical care.

5. If the price is above the equilibrium price, a surplus will exist in which the quantity supplied exceeds the quantity demanded. If the price is below the equilibrium price, the quantity demanded exceeds the quantity supplied and a shortage will prevail. Policies that cause the price to deviate from the equilibrium price have unintended consequences because society now faces a prisoner's dilemma.

6. According to the principle of unintended consequences, policy makers must be careful in their policy decisions and take into consideration both the intended and unintended effects of their policies.

KEY TERMS

QUESTIONS AND PROBLEMS

1. The current welfare system has the unintended consequence of breaking up poor families. Explain why this is so and try to devise a system that avoids this unintended consequence.
2. Consider the study example of marginal analysis. Apply it to another type of activity and use it to explain the optimal level of that activity.
3. What do you think would happen to the rate of unemployment if unemployment benefits were lowered and people could qualify for such benefits for only two weeks instead of six months? Use marginal analysis to explain your answer.
4. If a wealthy benefactor declared that he would pay for everyone's medication, what effect would this have on the prices of medication? Explain your answer.
5. Bread is currently selling for \$1.50 per loaf. The government now declares that all stores must sell it for \$0.50 per loaf to everyone to help the poor. Consider the effects of this action and its possible unintended consequences.
6. Explain why minimum wages could hurt teenage workers. Would the amount of hurt depend upon where the minimum wage was set?
7. If you were a loan shark would you favor or oppose usury laws (legal interest rate ceilings)?
8. The equilibrium price of gas rises to \$2 from \$1 a gallon. A price ceiling of \$1 is imposed. If each person drives less, the benefits are \$100 a year. If one person drives more, while the rest of society drives less, that person benefits by \$200 a year. If all try to drive more, the benefits to each are only \$50 a year because of the time wasted looking for gas. What will happen?
9. Use supply and demand diagrams to show the effects on prices and quantities of a government program that copays 10 percent of rents for low-income families versus a program that pays 90 percent.
10. Consider the prisoner's dilemma game described in this chapter. Explain what might be the result if the players played the game a large number of times.

INTERNET CONNECTION

11. Many cities, such as San Francisco, have adopted "living wage" ordinances, which mandate that certain employers must pay their employees a minimum living wage. Using the links from http://www.awl.com/ruffin_gregory, read the article on living wages on the Federal Reserve Bank of San Francisco Web site.
    a. Using supply and demand diagrams, show the effect of a living wage ordinance on San Francisco. Assume that the living wage is above the market-clearing wage.
    b. Using supply and demand diagrams, show the effect on the labor market in adjacent areas. What should happen to wages in neighboring towns?
    c. Do you think the author is in favor of a living wage?

PUZZLE ANSWERED: The students in the class are caught in a prisoner's dilemma. If they study less and the other students "cheat" by studying more, their grades will suffer. If there are a large number of students who do not know each other well, it will be hard to arrange an effective agreement that all will obey. If the number of students is small and all know each other well, it will be easier to reach an agreement to "cooperate."

Part II

Product Markets

Chapter 6

Elasticity of Demand and Supply

Chapter Insight

The state of Texas once attempted to raise revenues with a 20 percent increase in tuition and fees at state universities and a 25 percent increase in the charge for vanity license plates. One year later, the state treasurer reported that revenues from tuition and fees from state universities were up 15 percent, while revenues from vanity license plates were down 10 percent.

This chapter uses the concept of price elasticity, which shows that the sensitivity of buyers to price increases varies from product to product, to explain why raising prices increased revenues from tuition and fees but decreased revenues from vanity license plates. The tuition raise at state universities caused only a few students (at least in the short run) to go out of state or switch to private universities, so revenues increased. However, when the price of vanity license plates was raised, many people switched to regular license plates (a perfectly good substitute), so revenues fell.

The elasticity concept applies not only to the responsiveness of quantity sold to changes in the good's own price but also to the responsiveness of demand to changes in income and in the prices of other goods. In addition, there are elasticity measures of the responsiveness of quantity supplied to changes in price.

LEARNING OBJECTIVES

After completing this chapter you will be able to

1. Measure the price elasticity of demand.
2. Understand the relationship among price elasticity, price, and total revenue or expenditure.
3. Understand how the income elasticity of demand is used to determine the dividing line between necessities and luxuries.
4. Predict how the price elasticity of supply will differ in the immediate run, the short run, and the long run.
5. Discuss the effects of an excise tax.

CHAPTER PUZZLE: Each state imposes cigarette taxes, ranging from less than \$2 a carton in Alabama to \$10 a carton in Hawaii. There is also a federal excise tax of \$2.40 a carton. Would cigarette smokers in a particular state be hurt more by an additional \$1 state tax or an additional \$1 federal tax (which all states must pay)?

THE PRICE ELASTICITY OF DEMAND

Remember that the demand curve shows how quantity demanded responds to different prices, if all other things are equal, and the supply curve shows how quantity supplied responds to different prices, if all other things are equal. In panels (*a*) and (*b*) of Figure 1, the equilibrium intersection of the supply curve (*S*) and the demand curve (whether *D* or *D*′) is at point *e*, where price is \$10 and quantity is 100 units. The only difference between the two diagrams is in the demand curve. *D* in panel (*a*) is much flatter than *D*′ in panel (*b*). The supply curves (*S*) are identical.

Suppose that there is a reduction in supply. The leftward shifts of the supply curve from *S* to *S*′ are the same in panels (*a*) and (*b*). When supply decreases, equilibrium price rises and equilibrium quantity falls. The equilibrium point *e* moves in panel (*a*) to *e*′ and in panel (*b*) to *e*″. In panel (*a*), the price increase (from \$10 to \$14) is relatively small compared to the substantial reduction in quantity demanded (from 100 units to only 20 units). In panel (*b*), on the other hand, the price increase (from \$10

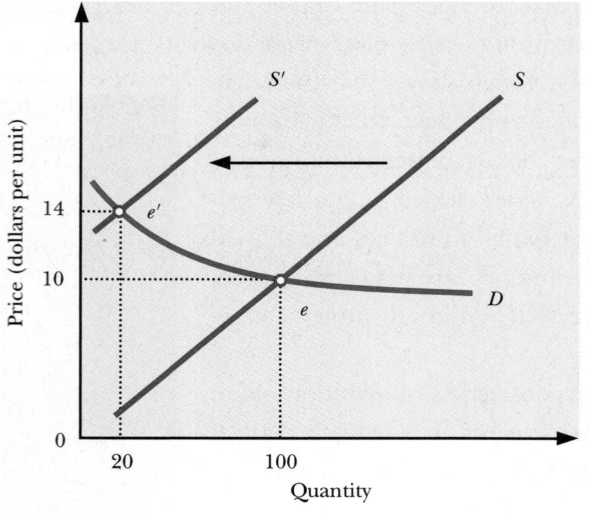

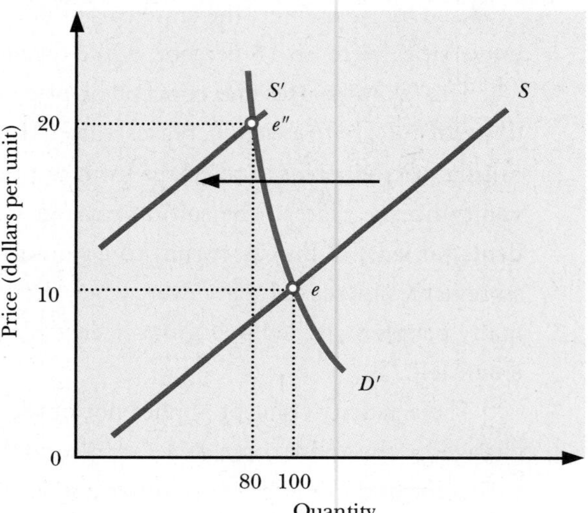

FIGURE 1 Response to a Reduction in Supply

In both panels (*a*) and (*b*), *S* intersects the demand curve at the equilibrium price–quantity combination of \$10–100 units. The supply conditions are exactly the same in each diagram, but the quantity demanded is less responsive to price changes in panel (*b*) than in panel (*a*). A decrease in supply from *S* to *S*′ causes a sharper increase in the equilibrium price when quantity demanded is less responsive to price. Although the price increase in (*b*) from \$10 to \$20 is greater than the price increase in (*a*) from \$10 to \$14, quantity demanded falls more in (*a*) than it does in (*b*).

to $20) is relatively large compared to the small reduction in quantity demanded from 100 to 80 units. The difference between the two demand curves in panels (*a*) and (*b*) is in the *responsiveness of quantity demanded to a price increase*. In panel (*a*), quantity demanded is quite responsive to the price change; in panel (*b*), it is less responsive. The price elasticity of demand (E_d) is a measure of this responsiveness.

The **price elasticity of demand** (E_d) is the percentage change in the quantity demanded divided by the percentage change in price.

Absolute changes in price or quantity demanded are poor measures of responsiveness. If a $1 increase in the price of coal lowers quantity demanded by 1 ton, we cannot determine whether these changes are large or small unless we know the initial price and quantity. If the initial price is $2 per ton, a $1 change in price represents a 50 percent increase in price. If the initial price is $1000, a $1 change in price is minuscule. The same principle applies to quantity changes. The measure of the response of quantity demanded to change in price must therefore be the relative (or percentage) change in price or quantity demanded.

The Coefficient of the Price Elasticity of Demand

Because of the law of demand, the quantity demanded rises when the price falls, and the quantity demanded falls when the price rises. Thus the sign of the price elasticity of demand will be negative. It is a convention in economics that, when calculating the *coefficient* of the price elasticity of demand, you drop the negative sign and use the *absolute value* of the elasticity.

The coefficient of the price elasticity of demand (E_d) is the absolute value of the percentage change in quantity demanded (%ΔQ) divided by the percentage change in price (%ΔP):

$$E_d = \frac{\%\Delta Q}{\%\Delta P}$$

where %Δ stands for percentage change.

For example, if P rises by 10 percent and Q falls by 20 percent, E_d equals 20 percent divided by 10 percent, or 2. An elasticity coefficient of 2 means that if prices were raised from the prevailing level, the percentage change in quantity demanded would be 2 times the percentage change in price. The elasticity coefficient measures the percentage change in quantity demanded for each 1 percent change in price. With an elasticity coefficient of 2, a 5 percent increase in price means a 10 percent reduction in quantity demanded.

Calculating the Price Elasticity of Demand

Table 1 shows how to calculate the price elasticity of demand. The price of wheat per bushel changes from $4.50 to $5.50, and the quantity demanded responds by falling from 105 to 95 bushels. We determine the price elasticity of demand by calculating the percentage changes in quantity demanded and price. This

TABLE 1 HOW TO CALCULATE THE PRICE ELASTICITY OF DEMAND

	Prices (dollars per bushel)	*Symbols*
Initial price	$4.50	P_0
Change in price	1.00	ΔP
New price	5.50	$P_1 = P_0 + \Delta P$
Average price	5.00	$P = (P_0 + P_1)/2$
Percentage change in price	20%	$(\Delta P/P) \times 100$
	Quantities (bushels of wheat)	
Initial quantity demanded	105	Q_0
Change in quantity demanded	−10	[illegible]
New quantity demanded	95	[illegible]
Average quantity demanded	100	[illegible]
Percentage change in Q	10%	[illegible]
Price elasticity of demand	10%/20% = 0.5	[illegible]

may seem simple, but there is a trick: We must calculate the percentage change on the basis of *average* quantity and *average* price. Why? The price elasticity should be the same whether the price rises or falls. If we use the initial price or quantity, this would not be the case. When the price rises from \$4.50 to \$5.50, the percentage increase is (\$1/\$4.50) × 100 = 22 percent. When the price falls from \$5.50 to \$4.50, the percentage decrease is (\$1/\$5.50) × 100 = 18 percent. To avoid one price elasticity for rising prices and another for falling prices, we calculate the percentage change on the basis of the average price, \$5 = (\$4.50 + \$5.50)/2. Thus, the percentage change in the price is (\$1/\$5) × 100 = 20 percent for both price increases and price reductions. The change in quantity demanded is 10 bushels; the average quantity demanded is 100 = (95 + 105)/2. The percentage change in quantity demanded is (10/100) × 100 = 10 percent for both quantity increases and quantity decreases. Accordingly, the price elasticity is E_d = 10 percent/20 percent = 0.5.

The use of the average price and average quantity to calculate the price elasticity of demand is the midpoint elasticity formula. This formula yields the same elasticity coefficient for an increase from a lower price to a higher price as for the decrease from the higher price to the lower price.[1]

The **midpoint elasticity formula** for determining the elasticity of demand (E_d) for a given segment of the demand curve is

E_d = Percent change in quantity demanded / ...cent change in price

...ntity demanded

... quantities

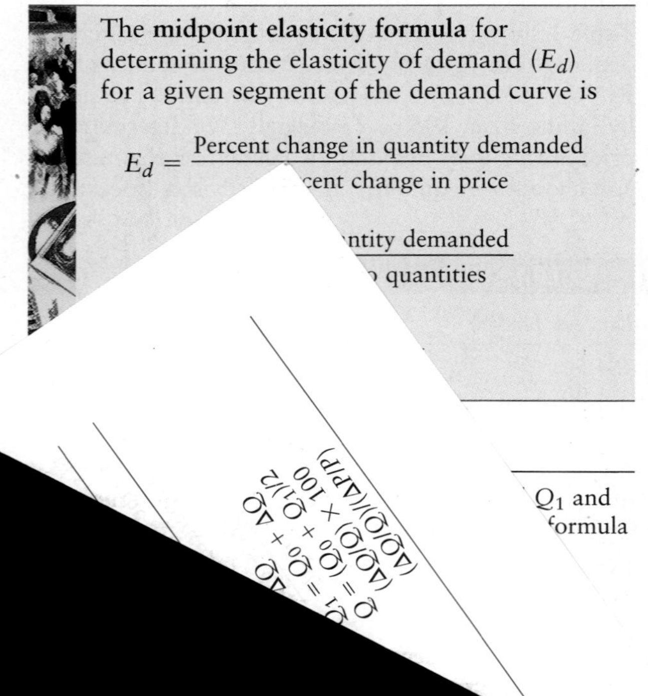

... Q_1 and ...formula

Elasticity and Total Revenue

Economists divide elasticity coefficients into three broad categories:

1. When $E_d > 1$, demand is *elastic* (Q is strongly responsive to changes in P).
2. When $E_d < 1$, demand is *inelastic* (Q responds weakly to changes in P).
3. When $E_d = 1$, demand is *unitary elastic* (a borderline case).

The above distinctions are made because the coefficient of the elasticity of demand shows what will happen to the total revenue (TR) of sellers when price changes along a given demand curve.

The **total revenue (TR)** of sellers in a market is the price of the commodity times the quantity sold:

$$TR = P \times Q$$

Along a demand curve, price and quantity demanded move in opposite directions. While a fall in price lowers total revenue, the resulting rise in quantity demanded raises total revenue. The direction of total revenue is determined by a tug-of-war between these conflicting forces. The outcome depends on the extent to which quantity demanded responds to changes in price. For example, a relatively small rise in quantity demanded will not offset the decline in revenue caused by a fall in price, but a substantial rise in quantity demanded could offset the revenue loss caused by a lower price. Thus, the response of total revenue to price changes depends on the price elasticity of demand.

Elastic Demand. If $E_d > 1$, the percentage rise in quantity demanded is greater than the percentage fall in price. Revenue *increases* because the increase in quantity demanded more than offsets the *decrease* in price. Price and revenue move in opposite directions.

When $E_d > 1$, $|\%\Delta Q| > |\%\Delta P|$; thus TR will move in the opposite direction of price.

Inelastic Demand. If $E_d < 1$, the percentage rise in quantity demanded is less than the percentage fall in price. Revenue *falls* because the *decline* in price is not offset by the relatively small rise in quantity. Price and revenue move in the same direction.

> When $E_d < 1$, $|\%\Delta Q| < |\%\Delta P|$; thus TR will move in the same direction as price.

Unitary Elastic Demand. If $E_d = 1$, the percentage rise in quantity demanded equals the percentage fall in price. Revenue is unchanged because the decline in price is just offset by the rise in quantity.

> When $E_d = 1$, $|\%\Delta Q| = |\%\Delta P|$; thus TR will not change.

We can always determine whether demand is elastic, inelastic, or unitary elastic by the total revenue test, which simply checks what happens to total revenue when the price changes. Just to know that demand is inelastic or elastic is very important to the business firm.

The **total revenue test** uses the following criteria to determine elasticity:

1. If price and total revenue move in different directions, $E_d > 1$ (demand is elastic).
2. If price and total revenue move in the same direction, $E_d < 1$ (demand is inelastic).
3. If total revenue does not change when price changes, $E_d = 1$ (demand is unitary elastic).

Elasticity Along a Demand Curve

Figure 2 applies these tests for determining elasticity to the case of a linear demand schedule in which a given change in price always causes the same change in quantity demanded. In the accompanying table, column 3 shows total revenue (price times quantity) at different prices. In panel (*a*), the price is reduced from \$9 to \$7; 15 units were sold at \$9, and now 25 units are sold at \$7. The green area indicates the loss in revenue that occurred because the first 15 units had to be sold at the lower price of \$7. But more units are sold at \$7 than at \$9. The red area indicates the revenue gained from the sale of more units. Total revenue rises because the red area is larger than the green area when demand is *elastic*. The revenue lost through the lower price is more than offset by the revenue gained by the sale of substantially more units.

The midpoint formula also confirms that demand is elastic when price falls from \$9 to \$7. The percent change in quantity demanded (50 percent) divided by the percent change in price (25 percent) equals 2.

If price now falls from \$7 to \$5, as in panel (*b*), demand is unitary elastic; in this case, revenue remains constant because the revenue lost (the green area) equals the revenue gained (the red area). As price falls further from \$5 to \$3, demand is inelastic. In panel (*c*), the revenue lost (the green area) exceeds the revenue gained (the red area) from selling a few more units, so total revenue falls. The midpoint formula confirms that the coefficient of price elasticity is inelastic (0.5).

Perfectly Elastic or Perfectly Inelastic Demand Curves

The highest degree of elasticity possible—the greatest responsiveness of quantity demanded to price—is a perfectly horizontal demand curve. In Figure 3 on page 99, any amount on demand curve *D* can be sold at the indicated price (\$5). Such a horizontal demand curve describes perfectly elastic demand.

A horizontal demand curve illustrates **perfectly elastic demand** ($E_d = \infty$), a condition in which quantity demanded is most responsive to price.

The elasticity formula shows that E_d is infinitely large ($E_d = \infty$) when the demand curve is horizontal: The quantity demanded can be increased indefinitely without a decrease in price. As a result, the elasticity formula yields an infinitely large coefficient of price elasticity of demand.

Perfectly elastic demand curves are actually common in the real world. In competitive markets in which no single producer is large enough to influence the market price, each seller can sell all he or she wants to sell at the market price. American wheat farmers can sell all they want at the prevailing market price and can't sell anything at a higher price. Thus each seller faces a horizontal demand curve even though the market demand curve is downward sloping.

The lowest degree of inelasticity possible—the least sensitivity of quantity demanded to price—occurs when the demand curve is perfectly vertical.

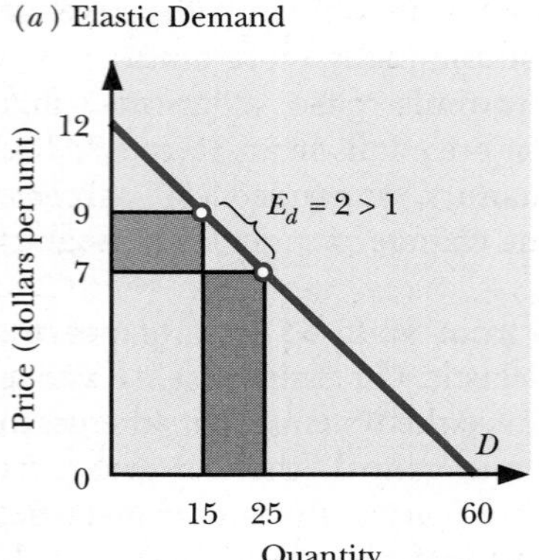

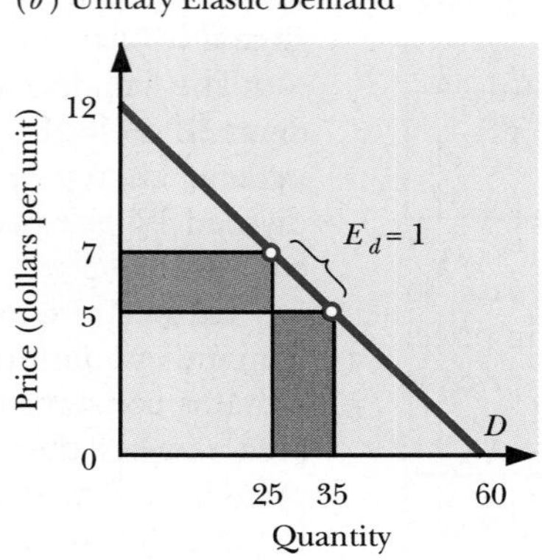

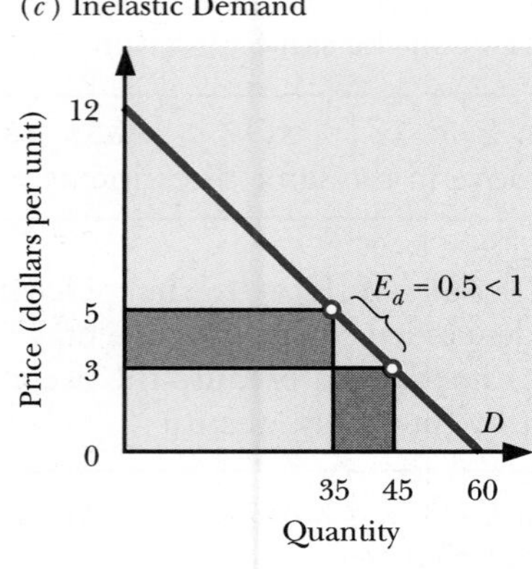

FIGURE 2 Total Revenue and Elasticity

The linear demand curve, *D*, is the same in panels (*a*), (*b*), and (*c*). Between the prices of $9 and $7, the elasticity of demand (E_d) is 2; demand is elastic. Panel (*a*) shows that a reduction in price raises revenue. The green rectangle shows the revenue lost due to the lower price, and the red rectangle shows the revenue gained due to the greater number of units sold. Because the red rectangle has a greater area than the green rectangle, more revenue is gained than lost. Between prices of $7 and $5, E_d equals 1; panel (*b*) shows that the reduction in price has no impact on revenue. Finally, between the prices of $5 and $3, E_d is 1/2; demand is inelastic. Panel (*c*) shows that the reduction in price lowers revenue because more revenue is lost (green area) than gained (red area). Thus, the elasticity of demand varies along a linear demand curve with constant slope. *Elasticity and slope are different.*

	Price (dollars per unit) P *(1)*	*Quantity (units)* Q *(2)*	*Total Revenue* TR = $P \times Q$ *(3) = (1) × (2)*	*Percentage Change in Quantity Demanded* $\frac{\Delta Q}{(Q_1 + Q_2)/2}$ *(4)*	*Percentage Change in Price* $\frac{\Delta P}{(P_1 + P_2)/2}$ *(5)*	*Coefficient of Price Elasticity,* E_d *(6) = (4) ÷ (5)*
(*a*)	9	15	135			
	7	25	175	$\frac{10}{20} = 50\%$	$\frac{2}{8} = 25\%$	$\frac{50}{25} = 2$
(*b*)	5	35	175	$\frac{10}{30} = 33.3\%$	$\frac{2}{6} = 33.3\%$	$\frac{33.3}{33.3} = 1$
(*c*)	3	45	135	$\frac{10}{40} = 25\%$	$\frac{2}{4} = 50\%$	$\frac{25}{50} = 0.5$

Columns 1 and 2 show the demand schedule graphed above. Column 3 is the total revenue of sellers. Column 4 shows the percentage change in quantity using the midpoint formula. Column 5 shows the percentage change in price using the midpoint formula. Finally, column 6 shows the elasticity of demand, E_d.

A vertical demand curve illustrates **perfectly inelastic demand** ($E_d = 0$), a condition in which quantity demanded is least responsive to price.

In Figure 3, with the vertical demand curve *D′*, 75 units of the good will be sold regardless of the price. The coefficient of the elasticity of demand is zero because if the price were to rise above $5, the percentage change in the quantity demanded would be zero. When zero is divided by the percentage change in price, E_d is zero.

With a perfectly inelastic demand curve, no matter how high the price rises, consumers will not cut back on the quantity demanded. The demand

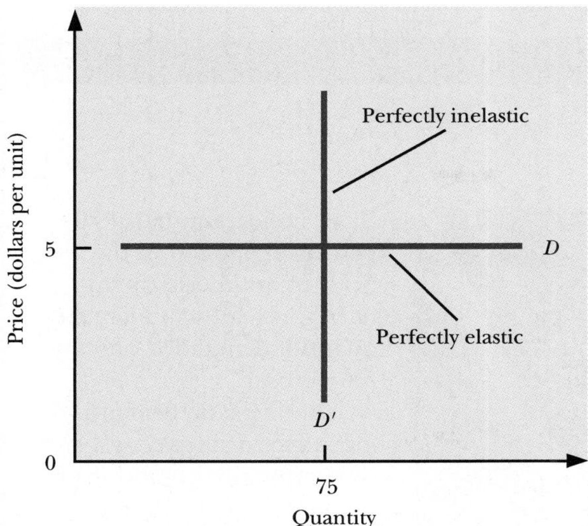

FIGURE 3 Perfectly Elastic and Perfectly Inelastic Demand Curves

The demand curve D is perfectly elastic; it is perfectly horizontal, or parallel to the quantity axis. The demand curve D' is perfectly inelastic; it is perfectly vertical, or parallel to the price axis. The elasticity-of-demand coefficient of D is infinitely large along the entire demand schedule. The elasticity-of-demand coefficient of D' is zero along the entire demand curve.

curve of insulin for the diabetic is probably as close to perfectly inelastic as possible, but even in this case if the price rose higher and higher, diabetics would have to reduce their dosages and accept some health loss or change their behavior by eating less or exercising more.

Elasticity Versus Slope Along a Demand Curve

Perfectly elastic and inelastic demand curves describe very special circumstances: the extremes of infinite response and no response. A vertical demand curve shows perfect inelasticity; a horizontal demand curve shows perfect elasticity. It might be tempting to conclude, by analogy, that demand is more elastic when the demand curve is "flat" than when the demand curve is "steep." This conclusion would be wrong.

The price elasticity of demand is different from the slope of the demand curve. Although both elasticity and slope measure the response of quantity demanded to change in price, the slope of the demand curve does not indicate the size of the response. In Figure 2, each time the price falls by $2, quantity demanded rises by 10 units. The slope of the demand curve is constant because the curve is a straight line. We showed earlier that as the price falls from $9 to $7, from $7 to $5, and from $5 to $3, the price elasticity of demand falls. Why? For each successive $2 price reduction, the percentage change in price rises since P is falling; and for the same increases in quantity demanded, the percentage change in quantity demanded falls since Q is rising.

Typically, price elasticity of demand falls as prices fall: Consumers are more responsive to price changes at high prices than at low prices. When hand calculators were introduced in the 1970s, they sold for about $200. The demand for them was very price elastic: When their price started to fall, consumers eagerly increased the quantity demanded as they substituted hand calculators for slide rules. Today, the price of hand calculators is very low ($10 or less). A reduction in price would bring about a comparatively small increase in quantity demanded. (See Example 1.)

Determinants of Price Elasticity of Demand

What determines the sensitivity of consumers to price? The three important determinants of the price elasticity of demand for a good are (1) the availability of substitutes, (2) the relative importance of the good in the budget, and (3) the amount of time available to adjust to the price change.

The Availability of Substitutes. Every good has substitutes, but some goods have excellent substitutes and others have very poor ones. The price elasticity of demand depends upon how easily people can turn to substitutes.

Consider the price elasticity of demand for postal service. The elasticity of demand has increased substantially with the introduction of new substitutes—fax machines and electronic mail. Sending an E-mail is cheaper and faster than sending a letter.

The availability of substitutes depends upon how broadly a good is defined. The elasticity of demand for automobiles is lower than that for Chevrolets. The demand for energy is less elastic than the demand for natural gas. The demand for entertainment will be less elastic than the demand for movie tickets. The more narrowly defined the product (Chevrolets versus automobiles, natural gas versus energy, movie tickets versus entertainment), the greater the number of close substitutes (Plymouths

EXAMPLE 1

The Demand for International Telephone Calls

One of the fundamental features of demand is that as prices drop there is a tendency for demand to become less elastic. This happens because as price falls, there are fewer good substitutes. A good example is the tremendous reduction in the price of international phone calls. In 1979, a one-minute telephone call to Europe cost about $4; but in 2000 it was possible to pay as low as $0.11 for a one-minute call to Europe. Such a telephone call would have cost almost $100 in 1929 (all prices in 2000 dollars). We would expect that in modern times the demand for international telephone calls would be quite inelastic, and this is the case. A recent study estimated that the price elasticity of demand is only 0.36, indicating that a 10 percent reduction in the price of an international telephone call will increase quantity demanded only by 3.6 percent.

An inelastic demand for a product or service is a sign of competitive conditions in the marketplace. When demand is inelastic, a single seller of a good or service will raise the price because revenue will increase, holding other factors constant. We know this to be the case because there are many providers of international phone calls.

Source: Jan Acton and Ingo Vogelsang, "Telephone Demand over the Atlantic: Evidence from Country-Pair Data," *Journal of Industrial Economics* 40 (September 1992): 305–323.

for Chevrolets, natural gas for electricity, cable TV for movies) and the higher the elasticity of demand. (See Example 2.)

> The greater the number of close substitutes for a good, the *more elastic* its demand. The smaller the number of close substitutes for a good, the *more inelastic* its demand.

The Relative Importance of the Good in a Consumer's Budget. Both gasoline and salt have few close substitutes. Which one should be more elastic?

An increase in the price of salt from $0.40 to $0.50 a package (a 22 percent increase by the midpoint method) would not have a substantial percentage effect on purchases of salt. The average household buys two boxes of salt per year, so a 22 percent price increase would raise the family's cost of living by only $0.20 per year. A 22 percent increase in the price of gasoline, however, translates into a price increase from $1.20 per gallon to $1.50 per gallon. The average family consumes about 1000 gallons of gas per year, so its cost of living would be increased by $300 per year. Consumers would scarcely notice the salt price increase, so their purchases would hardly be affected, but the gasoline price increase would hit their pocketbooks hard and would therefore depress gasoline purchases.

As this comparison shows, the price elasticity of demand depends upon the relative importance of the good in the consumer's budget.

> Goods that represent a small fraction of the consumer's budget (salt, pepper, drinking water, matches) are more inelastic in demand than products that constitute a large fraction of the consumer's budget (automobiles, fuel oil, mortgage payments, personal computers), other things being equal.

EXAMPLE 2

The Importance of Substitutes: Call Forwarding

Many people with telephones have call waiting and call forwarding features. Call waiting notifies you of incoming calls while you are on the telephone; call forwarding forwards your calls to another telephone if you are not at home. The existence of voice mail and answering machines means that call forwarding has more substitutes than call waiting. Many voice mail systems allow a caller to leave a message even if you are on the phone. Although an answering machine is of no use when you are on the phone, if you are gone, it is a good substitute for call forwarding. Economic theory predicts that, since the two features cost about the same, the demand for call forwarding (the feature with more substitutes) should be more elastic than the demand for call waiting.

Fortunately, call waiting has an elasticity of demand of 1.5; and call forwarding has an elasticity of demand of 2.5. Economic theory is vindicated in this case!

Source: Donald J. Kridel and Lester D. Taylor, "The Demand for Commodity Packages: The Case of Telephone Custom Calling Features," *The Review of Economics and Statistics* 75 (May 1993): 362–368.

Time to Adjust to Price Changes. Demand becomes more elastic as consumers have more time to adjust to price changes. This pattern is explained by a number of factors. Consider the response of consumers to higher electricity prices. Immediately after electric utility rates are increased, we can do little more than lower our heating thermostats in the winter and raise our air-conditioning thermostats in the summer. As time passes, additional substitutes for electricity become available. Extra insulation and more energy-efficient heating and air-conditioning equipment can be installed. If natural-gas prices have not risen as much, we can convert to natural-gas appliances when our old system needs to be replaced.

Many expenditures are determined by habits, which are often hard to break. A family may be used to setting the thermostat at 72 degrees in the winter: They may need time to adjust to cooler temperatures when energy prices rise.

> Generally speaking, demand becomes more elastic as consumers have more time to adjust to changes in prices.

The principles discussed in this section are illustrated by actual price elasticities, such as those described in Table 2. Two variants are presented: the *short-run* E_d (where the consumer has not had more

TABLE 2 SHORT-RUN AND LONG-RUN PRICE ELASTICITIES

	E_d *in Short Run*	E_d *in Long Run*
Cigarettes	0.44	0.78
Jewelry	0.41	0.67
Toilet articles	0.20	3.04
Owner-occupied housing	0.04	1.22
China and glassware	1.55	2.55
Electricity	0.13	1.89
Water	0.20	0.14
Medical care and hospitalization	0.31	0.92
Tires	0.86	1.19
Auto repairs	0.40	0.38
Durable recreation equipment	0.88	2.39
Motion pictures	0.88	3.69
Foreign travel	0.14	1.77
Gasoline	0.15	0.78

Sources: Hendrick S. Houthakker and Lester D. Taylor, *Consumer Demand in the United States: Analyses and Projections* (Cambridge, MA: Harvard University Press, 1970), 166–167; James L. Sweeney, "The Demand for Gasoline: A Vintage Capital Model," Working Paper, Department of Engineering Economics, Stanford University; Gary S. Becker, Michael Grossman, and Kevin M. Murphy, "An Empirical Analysis of Cigarette Addiction," *American Economic Review* 84 (June 1994): 396–418.

time to adjust to price changes) and the *long-run* E_d (where the consumer has had more time to adjust to price changes).

The elasticities show that long-run elasticities are larger than short-run elasticities. The elasticities in the table also illustrate the important role of substitutes. Medical care has fewer substitutes than most of the other products, and it has lower short-run and long-run elasticities than products such as motion pictures, recreation equipment, and china. Electricity has no good short-run substitutes, and short-run electricity E_d is low.

Other Elasticities of Demand

We know from Chapter 4 that consumer demand depends not only on the product's own price, but also on consumer preferences, the prices of substitutes and complements, and consumer income. Although economists devote most of their attention to price elasticity of demand, the elasticity concept is also applied to the other factors affecting demand. Economists measure the responsiveness of demand to the prices of related goods (cross-price elasticity) and the responsiveness of demand to consumer income (income elasticity). The concepts of cross-price elasticity and income elasticity provide insights into the interrelationships of prices and the effects of income changes on consumer demands.

Cross-Price Elasticity

A change in the price of one product affects the demand schedules of related products. This responsiveness of demand to other prices is measured by the cross-price elasticity of demand (E_{xy}).

The **cross-price elasticity of demand (E_{xy})** is the percentage change in demand of the first product (x) divided by the percentage change in the price of the related product (y).[2]

Unlike the price elasticity of demand, which is negative, the cross-price elasticity can be either positive or negative.

A positive cross-price elasticity of demand means that an increase in the price of one product will cause an increase in the demand for *substitutes*. As the price of beef rises, the quantity of beef demanded falls, in part because substitutes have been purchased in place of beef. For example, an increase in the price of beef causes an increase in the demand for chicken. Generally speaking, the *closer* the substitutes, the *higher* the cross-price elasticity.

A negative cross-price elasticity means that an increase in the price of one product will cause a decrease in the demand for the other product. Airline travel and auto rentals are *complements* because many auto rentals are made by airline travelers. If the price of airline tickets falls, auto rental companies can expect an increase in rentals from the larger number of travelers. Table 3 contains a few estimates of some actual cross-price elasticities.

> If the cross-price elasticity of demand is positive, the two products are *substitutes*. If the cross-price elasticity is negative, the two products are *complements*. If the cross-price elasticity is zero, the products are unrelated.

Income Elasticity

A rise or fall in consumer income will affect the demands for different products. As consumer income rises, the demand for most products increases. The responsiveness of demand to consumer income is measured by the income elasticity of demand (E_i).

The **income elasticity of demand (E_i)** is the percentage change in the demand for a product divided by the percentage change in income, holding all prices fixed.[3]

The income elasticity of demand is usually positive for most goods because higher consumer income

---

[2]The cross-price elasticity of demand is calculated by the same midpoint elasticity formula as the elasticity of demand. The only difference is that instead of the "own price" (P_x), the price of the related product (P_y) is in the denominator.

$$E_{xy} = \frac{Q_{x2} - Q_{x1}}{Q_{x1} + Q_{x2}} \div \frac{P_{y2} - P_{y1}}{P_{y1} + P_{y2}}$$

[3]The midpoint elasticity formula for the income elasticity of demand is

$$E_i = \frac{Q_2 - Q_1}{Q_1 + Q_2} \div \frac{I_2 - I_1}{I_1 + I_2}$$

where I denotes consumer income.

TABLE 3 SELECTED CROSS-PRICE ELASTICITIES

Good No. 1	*Good No. 2*	*Elasticity Coefficient*
Butter[a]	Margarine	0.67
Natural gas[b]	Fuel oil	0.44
Beef[a]	Pork	0.28
Cigarettes[c]	Liquor	0.10
Cheese[d]	Butter	−0.61

Sources: [a]H. Wold and L. Jureen, *Demand Analysis* (New York: Wiley, 1953); [b]L. Taylor and R. Halvorsen, "Energy Substitution in U.S. Manufacturing," *The Review of Economics and Statistics* (November 1977);[c]R.K. Goel and M.J. Morey, "The Interdependence of Cigarette and Liquor Demand," *Southern Economic Journal* (October 1995); [d]L. Philips, *Applied Consumption Analysis* (Amsterdam: North-Holland, 1974).

TABLE 4 SELECTED INCOME ELASTICITIES

Good	*Elasticity Coefficient*
Motion-picture tickets[a]	3.4
Foreign travel[a]	3.1
Toys[a]	2.0
Automobiles and parts[b]	1.7
Wine[c]	1.6
Clothing and shoes[b]	1.1
Furniture[b]	0.9
Beef[d]	0.5
Beer[a]	0.4
Pork[d]	0.3
Lard[d]	−0.1

Sources: [a]H.S. Houthakker and L.D. Taylor, *Consumer Demand in the United States* (Cambridge, MA: Harvard University Press, 1970); [b]L. Philips, *Applied Consumption Analysis* (Amsterdam: North-Holland, 1974); [c]J. Johnson, E. Oksanen, M. Veall, and D. Fretz, "Short-Run and Long-Run Elasticities for Canadian Consumption of Alcoholic Beverages," *The Review of Economics and Statistics* (February 1992); [d]G.E. Brandow, "Interrelations among Demands for Farm Products and Implications for Control of Market Supply," Pennsylvania State University Agricultural Experiment Station Bulletin 680, 1961.

usually means increased spending. If the income elasticity equals unity, each 1 percent increase in income will lead to a 1 percent increase in the demand for the good. Hence consumers would continue to spend the same fraction of their income on the good as before their income increased. For example, a consumer spends \$10 on soft drinks out of \$100 weekly income. If the income elasticity is 1, an increase in income to \$110 will increase spending on soft drinks to \$11; therefore, the fraction spent is still 10 percent. If the income elasticity exceeds 1, people will spend a larger fraction of their income on the good as income rises. If the income elasticity is less than 1, people will spend a smaller fraction of their income on that good as income rises. We can define the terms *necessities* and *luxuries* using the income elasticity of demand concept.

Necessities are those products that have an income elasticity of demand less than 1.

Luxuries are those products that have an income elasticity of demand greater than 1.

Based on these criteria, goods such as food items are necessities, and recreational vehicles are luxury items. Notice, though, that the economist allows the terms *luxury* and *necessity* to be defined by the market choices people make rather than by individual perceptions about what is more "necessary" than something else. See Table 4 for some selected income elasticities ranging from movies (3.4) to lard (−0.1). (See also Example 3.)

THE PRICE ELASTICITY OF SUPPLY

The price elasticity of demand measures the responsiveness of *consumers* to price change. The price elasticity of supply (E_s) measures the responsiveness of *producers* to price changes.

The **price elasticity of supply (E_s)** is the percentage change in the quantity supplied divided by the percentage change in price.

We calculate the elasticity of supply in the same way as the elasticity of demand; however, now Q refers to quantities *supplied*, not quantities demanded.

According to the midpoint formula, E_s is calculated as

$$E_s = \frac{Q_2 - Q_1}{(Q_1 + Q_2)/2} \div \frac{P_2 - P_1}{(P_1 + P_2)/2}$$

Like the elasticity of demand, the E_s coefficients are divided into three categories: elastic ($E_s > 1$), unitary elastic ($E_s = 1$), and inelastic ($E_s < 1$). The direction of movement of total revenue along a supply curve, however, will not depend upon the value of E_s. The E_s coefficient is positive except in rare

EXAMPLE 3

ENGEL'S LAW AND INCOME ELASTICITIES: WHERE HAVE ALL THE FARMERS GONE?

The income elasticity of demand is the percentage change in demand divided by the percentage change in income. If a product's income elasticity of demand is less than 1, its purchases tend to rise more slowly than income, and its share of total consumer spending falls.

The nineteenth-century German statistician Ernst Engel noted a statistical regularity in his studies of family budgets in different countries. Engel found that as a family's income increases, the percentage of the budget spent on food declines. Subsequent statistical studies have confirmed this finding. This statistical regularity has come to be called *Engel's law*. In terms of income elasticity, Engel's law simply means that the income elasticity of demand for food is less than 1.

The inelastic income elasticity of demand explains a trend that characterizes virtually all economies. As income grows, the share of income devoted to purchases of agricultural goods falls. A smaller share of income is spent on goods produced by agriculture, and larger shares are spent on manufacturing and services. The factors of production therefore shift in relative terms from agriculture to manufacturing and services in response to the relative change in consumer demand.

Engel's law explains (at least partially) the declining shares of the farm population in industrialized societies. At the turn of the century, U.S. families spent $0.30 of every dollar on food. In 1929, they spent $0.25 of every dollar on food; and in 1999, they spent about $0.15 of every dollar on food. At the beginning of the twentieth century, one in three workers was employed in agriculture. On the eve of World War II, only one in ten workers was employed in agriculture. By 1999, only two in every hundred workers were employed in agriculture.

Source: Historical Statistics of the United States.

cases because firms usually respond to a higher price by producing more.

Perfectly Elastic and Perfectly Inelastic Supply Curves

The highest degree of elasticity possible for a supply curve is a perfectly horizontal supply curve.

A horizontal supply curve illustrates **perfectly elastic supply** ($E_s = \infty$); quantity supplied is most responsive to price.

In Figure 4, supply curve *S* illustrates a case in which, at the price of $10, producers of the good are willing to supply any amount of the good to the market at that price.

Most of the supply curves that the average consumer encounters are perfectly elastic. The grocery store is willing to sell any person all the bread, canned goods, and dairy products that person wants to buy at the set prices. Under normal circumstances, however, all buyers together (the market) must offer

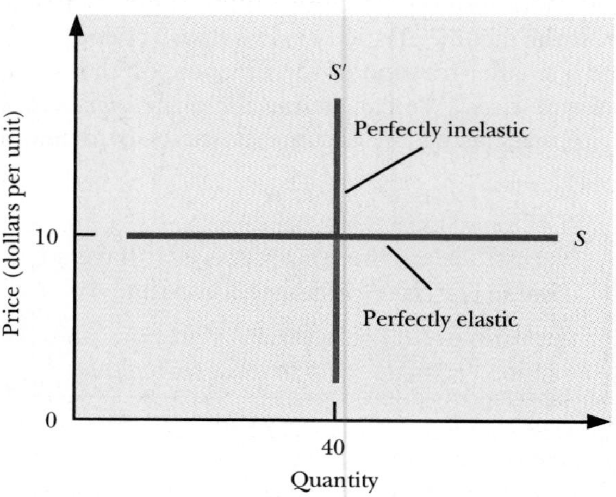

FIGURE 4 Perfectly Elastic and Perfectly Inelastic Supply Curves

The supply curve *S* is perfectly elastic because at a price of $10 any quantity of output can be offered on the market by sellers. The supply curve *S′* is perfectly inelastic because no matter how much the price rises, the quantity supplied remains the same.

higher prices to induce producers to increase the quantity supplied.

The lowest degree of elasticity occurs when the supply curve is perfectly vertical, as shown in Figure 4 by supply curve S'.

A vertical supply curve illustrates **perfectly inelastic supply** ($E_s = 0$); quantity supplied is least responsive to price.

The coefficient of E_s in this case is zero. An increase in price has no effect on quantity supplied; therefore, the percentage change in quantity supplied is zero. A good example would be the fisher's catch of fresh fish at the end of the day. Here the supplier cannot go back out on the boat to increase that day's supply of fresh fish if the price rises.

Most market supply curves fall between the two extremes of perfect elasticity ($E_s = \infty$) and perfect inelasticity ($E_s = 0$).

Elasticity of Supply in Three Time Periods

Like elasticity of demand, elasticity of supply depends upon, among other things, the amount of time the producer has to respond to price changes.

In general, the elasticity of supply increases as the producer has more time to adjust to changes in prices.

When prices change, economists distinguish between three time periods during which producers adjust their supply to the new prices: the immediate run, the short run, and the long run.

The **immediate run** is a period of time so short that the quantity supplied cannot be changed at all. In the immediate run—sometimes called the *momentary period* or *market period*—supply curves are perfectly inelastic.

The **short run** is a period of time long enough for existing firms to produce more goods but not long enough for existing firms to expand their capacity or for new firms to enter the market. Thus output can be varied, but only within the limits of existing plant capacity.

The **long run** is a period of time long enough for new firms to enter the market, for old firms to disappear, and for existing plants to be expanded. In the long run, firms have more flexibility in adjusting to price changes.

The amount of calendar time required to move from the short run to the long run varies with the type of industry. The electric power industry may require a decade to expand existing power-generating facilities and bring new plants on line. On the other hand, the fast-food industry can construct and open a new outlet in a few months.

The long-run elasticity of supply is determined primarily by the specificity of the factors used in the production of the good or service in question. Products that use factors of production similar to those in use throughout the economy will have high elasticities of supply. In this case, it is easy to expand production of the particular product because additional supplies of the required inputs are readily available. But products that use highly specialized resources will tend to have lower elasticities of supply because additional production puts upward pressure on the prices of the required inputs. For example, Table 5 shows some estimated long-run elasticities of supply in the U.S. economy. Products like oil and natural gas have relatively low supply elasticities compared to urban housing.

TABLE 5 SELECTED ESTIMATES OF LONG-RUN SUPPLY ELASTICITIES

Good	*Elasticity Coefficient*
Wheat[a]	0.93
Lumber[b]	0.90
Corn[a]	0.18
U.S. oil[c]	0.76
Drugs[b]	0.33
Natural gas[d]	0.20
Urban housing[e]	5.30

Sources: [a]M. Nerlove, "Estimates of the Elasticities of Supply of Selected Agricultural Commodities," *Journal of Farm Economics* (May 1956); [b]John Shea, "Do Supply Curves Slope Up?" *Quarterly Journal of Economics* (February 1993); [c]E.W. Ericson, S.W. Millsaps, and R.M. Spann, "Oil Supply and Tax Incentives," *Brookings Papers on Economic Activity* (1974); [d]J.D. Khazzoom, "The FPC Staff's Econometric Model of Natural Gas Supply in the United States," *The Bell Journal of Economics* (Spring 1971); [e]B.A. Smith, "The Supply of Urban Housing," *Journal of Political Economy* (1976).

ELASTICITY AND THE TAX BURDEN

Local, state, and federal governments tax a variety of goods and services, including tobacco, alcohol, gasoline, and various foreign imports. Elasticity of demand and supply explains how the burden of such taxes falls on consumers or producers. The group with the lowest sensitivity to price pays the largest share of the tax.

How the Tax Burden Is Shared

We shall consider a tax imposed only on producers because we will discover that a tax on consumers has exactly the same effects. A tax on all producers of a product will simply shift up their supply curve by the amount of the tax, because every point on the supply curve shows the lowest net price the producers are willing to accept for the corresponding quantity.

Suppose that a tax is imposed on a luxury good like perfume. Figure 5, panel (*a*), shows the supply curve and the demand curve for perfume before the tax is imposed. The equilibrium price is $2 per gram, and the equilibrium quantity is 5 million grams per month at point *e* before the tax is imposed.

For a tax of $1 per gram, sellers must now charge $3 to earn $2; they must charge $2.15 to earn $1.15. The tax will shift the supply curve *up* by exactly $1—the amount of the tax. Before the tax, suppliers were prepared to supply 5 million grams per month at a price of $2 per gram, but after the tax, suppliers will be prepared to supply the same 5 million grams per month only if the price is $3. The tax does not change the demand curve. At each price (where the price now includes the $1 tax), consumers will continue to demand the same quantities. Therefore, the new price will be higher than the original $2 price.

The new equilibrium point is *e'* at a price of $2.15 and a quantity of 4 million grams. Buyers pay $2.15 for perfume, and sellers receive $1.15 after paying the $1.00 tax to the government. The government gets $4 million ($1.00 × 4 million grams) in taxes. The equilibrium price *paid* by consumers goes up $0.15 (from $2.00 to $2.15), but the net price (price minus tax) received by producers goes down by $0.85 (from $2.00 to $1.15). In this particular

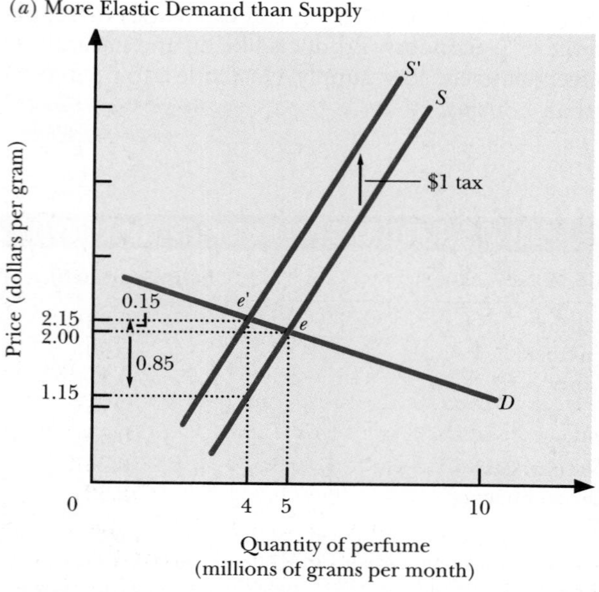

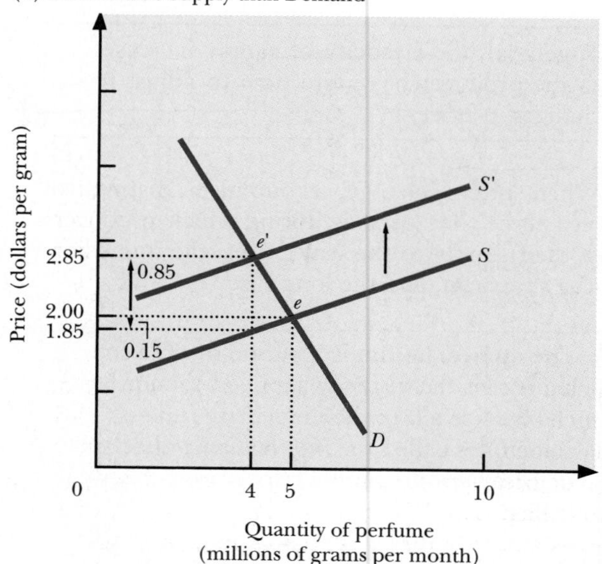

FIGURE 5 The Burden of a Tax

Panel (*a*) shows a more elastic demand than supply. A $1 tax shifts the supply curve up vertically by the amount of the tax. The price rises from $2 to $2.15. Consumers pay $0.15 of the $1 tax because of the higher price. Producers pay $0.85 because their price (after tax) falls to $1.15. Panel (*b*) shows a more elastic supply than demand. The $1 tax still shifts up the supply curve by the amount of the tax, but now the price rises by $0.85. Hence consumers pay $0.85 of the tax and producers $0.15.

case, the greater burden of the tax is on the sellers, who pay three-quarters of the tax. Buyers pay only one-quarter of the tax.

Elasticities Determine Who Bears the Burden

Why does the producer bear a greater part of the burden than the consumer in our perfume example? The answer is found in the elasticities of demand and supply.

The demand curve in Figure 5, panel (*a*), is more elastic than the supply curve in the vicinity of the equilibrium point *e*, as evidenced by the fact that curve *S* is steeper than curve *D*. Consumers therefore respond more to the price than do producers. Hence, consumers have a greater opportunity to avoid the tax.

Had the supply curve been more elastic than the demand curve, the consumer would have borne a greater burden of the tax. If consumers have an inelastic demand, it is easier to shift the tax forward to them and harder to reduce the price paid to producers. (See Example 4.)

Panel *(b)* shows the case of a supply that is more elastic than demand. In this case, the consumer pays more of the tax ($0.85) than does the producer ($0.15).

Figure 6 illustrates the case of a perfectly elastic supply curve. In fact, in the long run, there are many industries with perfectly elastic supply curves. In this case, the entire burden of the tax is on the buyer or consumer. The reason is simple: If supply is perfectly elastic at a particular price, producers will not provide the good at any lower price. A tax cannot lower the net price received by producers and the entire tax must be paid by the consumer. Thus, we can see that it makes no difference whether the tax is imposed on the producer or on the consumer; the final burden simply depends on the relative size of the elasticities of demand and supply.

The main reason why taxing authorities prefer to tax goods with relatively low elasticities is that they are interested in the total tax revenue. When a tax is imposed, the revenue equals the tax multiplied by the number of units sold. Every tax reduces the number of units sold. Therefore, by imposing taxes on goods with relatively low elasticities, the authorities can collect more tax revenue.

The concept of elasticity allows us to understand the extent to which changing prices and income affect demand and supply. In the next chapter we will look behind the demand curve to understand the law of demand and consumer surplus.

EXAMPLE 4

Cigarettes and Marijuana: Complements or Substitutes?

Elasticities tell us what happens to the use of substitutes and complements when prices increase. Take the case of the effects of increased cigarette prices: Studies of annual surveys conducted by the Institute for Social Research at the University of Michigan find that cigarettes and marijuana are complements. When a price rises, the demand for complements falls. The study concluded that a 10 percent increase in cigarette prices cuts marijuana use among young people by an average of about 6 percent. Thus the cross-price-elasticity is about −0.6. Similar findings have been published by the Centers for Disease Control and Prevention.

What are the policy implications? Since the demand for cigarettes is inelastic (about 0.4) and the supply elasticity is much higher, an increase in cigarette taxes will raise the price to consumers by a substantial amount. An unanticipated result is that higher cigarette taxes will also control substance abuse by young people. Many have argued that significant increases in the price of cigarettes may cause youths to substitute marijuana for cigarettes, but this evidence suggests that cigarette smoking is a prelude to marijuana use, just as drinking coffee may stimulate the demand for doughnuts!

Source: F. Chaloupka, R. Pacula, M. Farrelly, L. Johnston, P. O'Malley, and J. Bray, "Do Higher Cigarette Prices Encourage Youth to Use Marijuana?" *NBER Working Paper No. 6939* (February 1999).

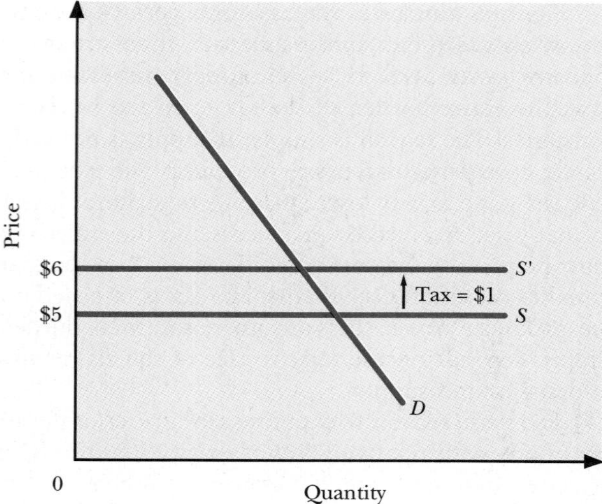

FIGURE 6 The Effect of a Tax with Perfectly Elastic Supply

A tax of $1 on suppliers shifts the supply curve up by $1 in order to recoup the required supply price. Market price will rise from $5 to $6 when supply is perfectly elastic. The tax on producers is shifted entirely to buyers.

SUMMARY

1. The price elasticity of demand (E_d) is a measure of the responsiveness of consumers to changes in price. It is the absolute value of the percentage change in quantity demanded divided by the percentage change in price. The price elasticity of demand can be either elastic ($E_d > 1$), unitary elastic ($E_d = 1$), or inelastic ($E_d < 1$). If demand is elastic, price and total revenue move in opposite directions. If demand is inelastic, price and total revenue move in the same direction. If demand is unitary elastic, total revenue is not affected by price changes. E_d can be calculated by the midpoint elasticity formula; the change in quantity is divided by the average quantity, and the change in price is divided by the average price. The price elasticity of demand is determined by the availability of substitutes (more substitutes mean higher elasticity), the amount of adjustment time (more time means higher elasticity), the importance in the consumer's budget (the more important the good, the higher the elasticity), and the status of the good as a necessity or a luxury (necessities tend to have lower elasticities).

2. Elasticities can also be used to measure the responsiveness of consumer demand to changes in income and the prices of other goods. Cross-price elasticity is the percentage change in the demand of one good divided by the percentage change in the price of the other good. If this number is positive, the two goods are substitutes; if it is negative, the two goods are complements. Income elasticity of demand is the percentage change in the demand divided by the percentage change in income. If this number is greater than 1, the good is a luxury; if it is less than 1, the good is a necessity.

3. The price elasticity of supply is the percentage change in quantity supplied divided by the percentage change in price. Supply is perfectly elastic when the supply curve is horizontal; supply is perfectly inelastic when the supply curve is vertical. The price elasticity of supply depends upon the time period of adjustment. In the immediate run, supply is fixed and the supply schedule is perfectly inelastic. In the short run, firms can produce more or fewer goods, but they do not have sufficient time to alter their capital stock or enter or leave the industry. In the long run, supply can be altered through changes in capital stock and through the entry and exit of firms. Elasticity of supply is greater in the long run than in the short run.

4. Elasticity analysis explains whether producers or consumers will bear the greater burden of a tax on a particular good. The group with the smallest price elasticity pays the largest share of the tax.

KEY TERMS

price elasticity of demand (E_d) 101
midpoint elasticity formula 102
total revenue (TR) 102
total revenue test 103
perfectly elastic demand 103
perfectly inelastic demand 104
cross-price elasticity of demand (E_{xy}) 108
income elasticity of demand (E_i) 108
necessities 109
luxuries 109
price elasticity of supply (E_s) 109
perfectly elastic supply 110
perfectly inelastic supply 111
immediate run 111
short run 111
long run 111

QUESTIONS AND PROBLEMS

1. Using the demand schedule in Table A, calculate the price elasticities of demand for each successive pair of rows.

TABLE A

Price (dollars)	*Quantity (units)*
5	1
4	2
3	3
2	4
1	5

2. Suppose the price elasticity of demand for rental housing is 0.6 and the average rent increases from $500 per month to $700 per month. At $500 per month, 100,000 rental units are rented. What percentage decrease in quantity demanded would you predict from this information? Approximately how many units would be rented at $700 per month?
3. Suppose the price of gasoline falls from $1.20 per gallon to $0.60 per gallon. Why would a consumer's short-run adjustment to this price change be different from the long-run adjustment?
4. Assume that the basic monthly charge for a private telephone is $10.50 per month. If the rate were to rise to $11.00, would you expect a substantial reduction in the quantity demanded? Explain your answer. If, on the other hand, the basic monthly charge were $250 per month and the rate were to rise by the same percentage as the lower rate, what is your prediction for the change in quantity demanded?
5. The Chapter Insight related that after the state of Texas raised the price of personalized license plates, the state's revenue from personalized license plates fell. From this information, what can you say about the price elasticity of demand for personalized plates?
6. If the price of tennis balls goes up, what impact will this price increase have on the quantity demanded of tennis rackets? What sign (+ or −) will the cross-price elasticity have? What sign will the cross-price elasticity of tennis balls and golf balls have?
7. The income elasticity of demand for all services taken together is greater than 1. As the economy grows, what would you expect to happen to the share of service industries in total output?
8. During economic recessions, used car sales typically rise and new car sales decline. Explain why.
9. Assume that oranges have the following characteristics. The elasticity of demand is 0.2, and the elasticity of supply is 2. If government imposes a tax of $1 per crate of oranges, who will end up paying more of the tax (bearing the larger burden of the tax): the consumer or the producer? Why? Draw a diagram illustrating your argument.
10. Evaluate the validity of the following statement: "The elasticity of demand for oranges is 0.2; therefore, California orange growers could raise their income by restricting their output."
11. Suppose the supply curve for product *X* shifts to the right (supply increases). What happens to the total expenditure of consumers under each of the following conditions?
    a. The demand for *X* is price elastic.
    b. The demand for *X* is price inelastic.
    c. The demand for *X* is perfectly elastic.
    d. The demand for *X* is perfectly inelastic.
12. Suppose the supply curve for product *X* shifts to the left (supply decreases). What happens to the total expenditure of consumers under each of the following conditions?
    a. The demand for *X* is price elastic.
    b. The demand for *X* is price inelastic.
    c. The demand for *X* is perfectly elastic.
    d. The demand for *X* is perfectly inelastic.
13. Suppose the demand for product *X* increases. What happens to the total revenue of sellers under each of the following conditions?
    a. The supply of *X* is elastic.
    b. The supply is *X* is inelastic.
14. Using the determinants of the price elasticity of demand, indicate which item in each of the following pairs of goods has the higher elasticity.
    a. Wheat or grains
    b. Soft drinks or beverages
    c. Cars or clothing
    d. Toothpicks or beef

15. Double the quantities demanded at each price in Table A (for example, when the price is $5, assume 2 units are demanded; when the price is $4, assume 4 units are demanded; and so on). What happens to the slope of the demand curve? What happens to the elasticity of demand between each successive pair of prices?
16. Who bears the burden of a tax on a good in each of the following circumstances?
    a. The supply curve is upward sloping; demand is perfectly inelastic.
    b. The supply curve is upward sloping; demand is perfectly elastic.
    c. The demand curve is downward sloping; supply is perfectly inelastic.
    d. The demand curve is downward sloping; supply is perfectly elastic.
17. Calculate the price elasticity of demand for the market demand curve $Q = 100 - 2P$ when the price changes from $P = \$42$ to $P = \$38$.
18. After studying Table 4, would you agree with the statement "Beer is a necessity; wine is a luxury"?

INTERNET CONNECTION

19. Using the links from http://www.awl.com/ruffin_gregory, read the abstract on cigarettes and alcohol on the National Bureau of Economic Research Web site. (Do not download the article.)
    a. From reading the abstract, what do you think will happen to the quantity demanded for alcohol if the price of cigarettes increases? Is the cross-price elasticity positive or negative?
    b. From reading the abstract, what do you think will happen to the quantity demanded for cigarettes if the price of alcohol increases? Is the cross-price elasticity of demand positive or negative?
    c. Do you have an explanation for this result?

PUZZLE ANSWERED: The cigarette smokers in a state would be hurt more by a $1 state tax than by a $1 federal tax because the supply of cigarettes to a state is more elastic than the supply of cigarettes to the country. Accordingly, a $1 state tax should raise the price of cigarettes in the state by approximately $1, whereas a federal tax would raise the price by less than $1. This ignores the possibility of border residents buying the cigarettes in an adjacent state.

Demand and Utility

Chapter Insight

To the economist, a rational person is one who carefully weighs the costs and benefits of different actions. The theory of consumer behavior is the classic description of a rational person.

This theory would not be useful if it did not explain the facts of everyday experience. Adam Smith once observed that "nothing is more useful than water; but it will purchase scarce anything; scarce anything can be had in exchange for it. A diamond, on the contrary, has scarce any value in use; but a very great quantity of other goods may frequently be had in exchange for it."

In this chapter we shall consider a theory of consumer behavior that will not only explain Adam Smith's diamond/water paradox, but will also explain the law of demand. Motivating the theory is the idea that we try to do the best we can with what we've got. The explanation of the law of demand also directly provides a method for measuring consumer gains and losses that result from lower or higher prices.

LEARNING OBJECTIVES

After completing this chapter, you will be able to:

1. Understand how consumer preferences differ from demand.
2. Know the law of diminishing marginal utility.
3. Explain the principles under which the consumer's choices are in equilibrium.
4. See how the law of demand is related to the law of diminishing marginal utility.
5. Define the difference between income and substitution effects.
6. Understand how to go from individual demand to market demand.
7. Calculate the consumer surplus gain or cost from price changes.

CHAPTER PUZZLE: Kathy buys 50 pizzas a year at $10 each. The price rises to $11, and her purchases drop to 45 pizzas a year. Her total expenditures drop from $500 to $495 a year. What happens to her consumer surplus?

The Concept of Utility

Economists like to make a distinction between *preferences* and *demand*. A consumer's preferences are what he or she likes; a consumer's demands are what he or she buys. You might prefer a Porsche to a Chevrolet, but you buy the cheaper car because that is what your budget will allow. You buy the Chevrolet from the list of cars you can afford. Preferences and demand are different, yet what we demand depends on our preferences. The amount of goods and services that households purchase depends not only on prices and income, but also on preferences and tastes.

A simple way of representing preferences is to follow the late-nineteenth-century writers on economics. The treated *utility* as a property of some good or service that tended to give pleasure or happiness to the consumer. Indeed, every producer or seller of a good or service tries to anticipate the wants or preferences of customers. If a product gives little utility to anyone, the seller will fall on hard times. Similarly, economics must have a theory of consumer behavior that fits a broad range of human experience.

Utility is that property of a good or service that gives satisfaction or happiness to the consumer.

One of the key features of consumption is that some wants are more important than others. For example, hunger and thirst must be satisfied first; next, there must be shelter from the weather. In advanced societies, preferences extend to creature comforts, faster modes of transportation, exotic foods, efficient means of communication, and even consumption for purposes of ostentation and display. The love of variety is one of many enduring characteristics of human beings. Moreover, people have different tastes. (See Example 1.)

These facts can be summarized by a very simple idea: Each person enjoys utility from the goods and services he or she consumes; the more of any good or service a person consumes, the less useful an additional unit becomes. The appendix to this chapter shows that it is not necessary to actually measure the utility people get from consumption. However, it is useful to quantify preferences in order to measure differences in the utility of goods. For example, if we say that your utility of consuming 10 sodas per week is 400 and your utility from consuming 11 sodas per week is 420, then we can quantify the marginal utility of increasing soda consumption by 1 bottle per week as 20 "utils."

The **marginal utility** (MU) of any good or service is the increase in utility that a consumer experiences when consumption of that good or service (and that good or service alone) is increased by 1 unit. In general,

$$MU = \frac{\Delta TU}{\Delta Q}$$

where TU is total utility and Q is the quantity of the good.

As we shall see, however, this absolute measure of marginal utility is only a tool for comparing the relative marginal utilities for two or more goods.

The Law of Diminishing Marginal Utility

The more of something a person consumes, the less valuable it becomes at the margin.

EXAMPLE 1

De Gustibus Est Disputandum

Economists like to say that "there is no disputing of tastes," or in Latin, *de gustibus est disputandum.* One person may like a toothpaste that tastes terrible to another person, so different brands are used to satisfy both. Differences between people hold for just about anything. We might think that this tremendous diversity of preferences would defeat the scientific analysis of consumer tastes. But it turns out that subgroups of the human population seem quite consistent in their differences. In September 1999 a poll of men, women, Democrats, Republicans, and Independents showed that although individuals have different tastes, it makes little difference which *group* is studied. In other words, there is very little between-group variation. If the results of any study of the population dramatically changed from one population group to another, the study of human behavior would be more difficult. Here are the results for the survey question, *What is your favorite sport?*

	Men	*Women*	*Democrats*	*Republicans*	*Independents*
Baseball	23%	24%	22%	24%	21%
Basketball	12	21	19	14	16
Football	52	38	44	48	46
Not sure	13	17	15	14	17

Although there was a slight difference between men and women over basketball and football, there were no significant differences among the subgroups.

The similarities in preference were even more striking for the question, *If you could choose, would you rather have:*

	Men	*Women*	*Democrats*	*Republicans*	*Independents*
An extra day of pay	12%	11%	13%	10%	11%
An extra day with family	67	63	61	66	66
An extra day of rest	18	23	23	20	19
Not sure	3	3	3	4	4

There may be no accounting for tastes, but small subgroups can be studied for the characteristics of the entire population. The scientific study of consumer demand is possible.

The **law of diminishing marginal utility** states that as more of a good or service is consumed during any given time period, its marginal utility eventually declines, if the consumption of everything else is held constant.

Thus, the first gallon of water we consume in a given week, for example, has an enormous marginal utility. If we have no water, we will consider 1 gallon to be very valuable. The twentieth gallon of water has a relatively small marginal utility for a person who already has 19 gallons. The *total utility* from all 20 gallons of water is the sum of the marginal utilities of

EXAMPLE 2

Marginal Utility, "All You Can Eat for $10," and the Daily Newspaper

Many restaurants offer buffets where customers can eat all they want for a specified price. Such offers are possible because the marginal utility of food diminishes rapidly. Depending upon the individual's appetite, extra helpings yield smaller and smaller marginal utilities. In fact, they rather quickly yield negative marginal utility, in which the consumer's utility decreases with an extra helping. Although more food costs the consumer nothing, people will limit the amount of food they consume.

Rapidly diminishing marginal utility explains why the daily newspaper is dispensed from coin-operated boxes that permit people to take as many copies as they want. Newspaper companies know that the marginal utility of a second newspaper is zero for most people, so they don't worry about people taking more than one. Owners of coin-operated dispensers of other products (soft drinks, candies, etc.) know that they cannot give the consumer the opportunity to take more than one.

all units. Why does the marginal utility of water decline so rapidly as more water is consumed? The first gallon of water is essential to sustaining life; its marginal utility is therefore astronomical. As more water becomes available, water can be applied to less urgent uses: bathing, washing clothes, feeding pets, and eventually even to watering the lawn. By the time sufficient water is available for watering the lawn, the marginal utility of the last gallon is much smaller than the marginal utility of the first gallon.

The rate at which marginal utility declines varies. For food products, for example, marginal utility declines rapidly. The marginal utility of the second hamburger is much less than that of the first. The marginal utility of the third hamburger is very small or even negative. For other goods, such as collectors' items, marginal utility may decline slowly as consumption increases. (See Example 2.)

The Diamond/Water Paradox

In the quotation at the start of this chapter, Adam Smith poses the famous *diamond/water paradox.* The paradox questions why prices often fail to reflect the usefulness of goods. Water and salt, without which we would perish, have low relative prices, whereas goods that have little practical value, such as diamonds, gold, and high fashion, have high relative prices.

Why is it that diamonds, whose total utility is much less than that of water, have a higher relative price than water? The law of diminishing marginal utility provides the answer to this paradox. On the one hand, the consumption of water usually takes place at a low marginal utility because the supply of water is large; on the other hand, the supply of diamonds is usually so limited that consumption takes place at a relatively high marginal utility. Although water's total utility is high, its marginal utility is low. Therefore, no one will sacrifice very much for an additional gallon.

The terms of the diamond/water paradox hold under normal supply conditions, but what happens when these conditions are disrupted? At the end of World War II, people in parts of Europe gladly exchanged diamonds and precious metals for bread and potatoes. The availability of food products was so limited that food products yielded a higher marginal utility (by preventing malnutrition) than did diamonds and precious metals. Similarly, when the American West was being settled in the nineteenth century, range wars were fought (and people were killed) over the control of water holes, and in arid parts of the world, such as Somalia and Rwanda, armed conflicts still break out over water.

Marginal Utility and the Law of Demand

The law of diminishing marginal utility explains the diamond/water paradox; relative prices reflect marginal utility rather than total utility. In this section we shall examine the exact relationship between the law of diminishing utility and the law of demand.

The theory of consumer demand is simply that we, as consumers, try to arrange our pattern of spending so that we are getting the most out of our limited budgets. To achieve maximum utility, we allocate our budgets on goods in such a way that it is impossible to obtain more utility by spending a bit more on one good and a bit less on another.

The central concept of the best allocation of the consumer's limited resources is the "bang per buck." Suppose the marginal utility of another pizza is 50 utils. If the price of a pizza is $5, then another dollar spent on pizza yields 10 (= 50/5) utils.

The **marginal utility per dollar** for any good or service is the ratio of its marginal utility to its price (MU/P).

Note that the concept of marginal utility per dollar is a rate measure similar to miles per hour. Just as you can drive 50 miles per hour without driving a full hour, marginal utility per dollar need not involve the expenditure of exactly $1, as in the pizza example, where an extra pizza costs $5.

The best allocation of a consumer's limited budget is achieved when the last dollar spent on each good has the same marginal utility.

A **consumer equilibrium or optimum** requires that (1) all income be spent and (2) the marginal utilities per dollar for each good purchased are equal. Thus, if goods A, B, C, . . . and so forth, are being purchased, it must be that

$$MU_A/P_A = MU_B/P_B = MU_C/P_C = \dots \text{ for all goods.}$$

At this point, the consumer is not inclined to change purchases unless some other factor (such as prices, income, or preferences) changes.

Why must the MU/*P*s be equal? The MU/*P* ratio can be thought of as either the utility gained when another dollar is spent on the good, or the utility lost when spending on the good is cut by a dollar. For example, suppose one more dollar spent on pizza raises utility by 10 utils but spending one less dollar on hamburgers lowers utility by only 4 utils. Switching a dollar from hamburgers to pizza will bring about a net increase of 6 utils—the 10 util gain from more pizza and the 4 util lost from fewer hamburgers. Why? The MU/*P*s of each good must be the same; if not, utility can be increased with the same total expenditure. On the other hand, when all the MU/*P*s are the same, any reallocation of spending will make the consumer worse off. The reason is the law of diminishing marginal utility: More spent on a good lowers its MU/*P;* less spent on a good raises its MU/*P*. Starting from a situation of equality of all MU/*P*s, spending more on pizza and less on hamburgers causes MU_{pizza} to fall and $MU_{hamburger}$ to rise. Because $MU_{pizza}/P_{pizza} < MU_{hamburger}/P_{hamburger}$, the consumer has an incentive to substitute hamburgers for pizzas until equality is restored.

The equal MU-per-dollar rule explains the water/diamond paradox. When you note that the MU/*P*s of water and diamonds are the same to the average consumer, you find an explanation for the water/diamond paradox. The marginal utility of a diamond is in the same proportion to its price as the marginal utility of water is to its price, but the total utility from water far exceeds the total utility from diamonds. Remember that total utility is the sum of the marginal utilities. The total utility of water will be enormous because of the high marginal utility of the first and second units of water.

The equal MU-per-dollar rule explains why demand curves are downward sloping. Let's say you are buying ale and bread. In equilibrium, $MU_A/P_A = MU_B/P_B$. If the price of ale falls, at that moment the ratio MU_A/P_A must rise above MU_B/P_B. You have an incentive to buy more ale. According to the law of diminishing marginal utility, MU_A must fall. In this way the equality between the MU/*P*s is established once again, with a larger amount of ale purchased at the lower price. The law of demand is therefore a consequence of the law of diminishing marginal utility.

Another consequence of the equal marginal utilities rule and the law of diminishing marginal utility is that we do not spend all our money on one good or service. If we tried to spend all our money on one or two goods, we would drive down their marginal utilities. We choose instead a variety of goods and services. We sometimes eat chicken, sometimes beef, and sometimes fish. Few of us like to wear the same clothes day after day. Almost all of us spend some money on shelter, clothing, and food.

A Numerical Example

A numerical example will reinforce how the equal MU-per-dollar rule leads to the law of demand.

Consider an individual consumer, Mr. Ruffgreg, who purchases only two goods, ale and bread. Ruffgreg's preferences for both goods are summarized in Table 1. Columns 2 and 6 show the total utility of ale (TU_A) and bread (TU_B), respectively; columns 3 and 7 show the marginal utility of ale (MU_A) and bread (MU_B), respectively. These utility schedules apply to Ruffgreg's consumption over a particular time period—say, a week. The utility of ale does not depend on the consumption of bread, or vice versa. Both ale and bread obey the law of diminishing marginal utility.

Ruffgreg's marginal utility schedule for ale, depicted in Figure 1, is based on the data in column 3 of Table 1. The first pint of ale (per week) yields Ruffgreg a marginal utility of 40 utils; the second, 30 utils; the third, 20 utils; and the fourth, 10 utils. The total utility from consuming different quantities of ale is the sum of the marginal utilities up to the quantity of ale consumed. The total utility from consuming 3 pints of ale during a week, for example, is 90 (= 40 + 30 + 20).

We cannot determine Ruffgreg's demands for ale and bread from his preferences alone. As we know from Chapter 4, demand depends not only on consumer preferences but also on consumer income and prices. Let's keep our example simple: Ruffgreg has $8 to spend on ale and bread per week. The price of ale (P_A) is $2 per pint, and the price of bread (P_B) is

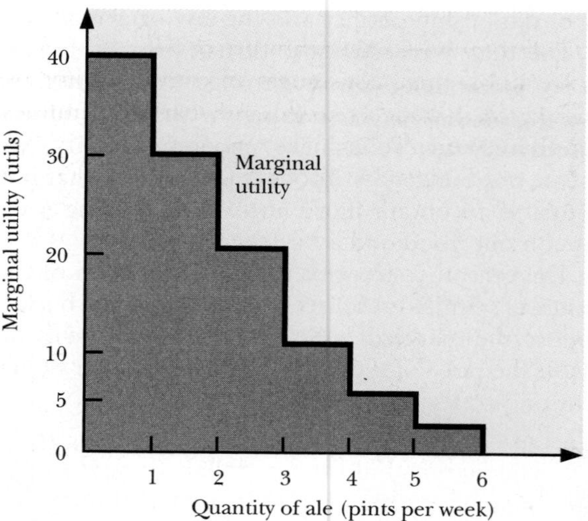

FIGURE 1 Marginal Utility Schedule

This figure graphs the data in columns 1 and 3 of Table 1. The width of each bar represents 1 pint of ale. The vertical height or area of each bar represents marginal utility for that extra unit of ale. Total utility up to some quantity of ale is the sum of the areas of the bars to the left of that quantity of ale. For example, the total utility of 2 pints equals 70 (= 40 + 30); the total utility of 5 pints equals 105 (= 40 + 30 + 20 + 10 + 5).

TABLE 1 THE UTILITY OF ALE AND BREAD

Quantity of Ale (pints), Q_A *(1)*	*Total Utility of Ale (utils),* TU_A *(2)*	*Marginal Utility of Ale (utils),* MU_A *(3)*	*Marginal Utility of Ale per Dollar (utils),* MU_A/P_A *(4)*	*Quantity of Bread (loaves),* Q_B *(5)*	*Total Utility of Bread (utils),* TU_B *(6)*	*Marginal Utility of Bread (utils),* MU_B *(7)*	*Marginal Utility of Bread per Dollar (utils),* MU_B/P_B *(8)*
1	40	40	20	1	15	15	30
2	70	30	15	2	23	8	16
3	90	20	10	3	30	7	14
4	100	10	5	4	35	5	10
5	105	5	2.5	5	38	3	6
6	107	2	1	6	40.5	2.5	5

This table lists the quantities of ale and bread consumed per week by Ruffgreg, along with the utility Ruffgreg attaches to each quantity. The price of ale equals $2 per pint and the price of bread equals $0.50 per loaf. The marginal utility columns illustrate the *law of diminishing marginal utility:* the marginal utility of each product falls as the amount consumed increases.

$0.50 per loaf. Ruffgreg can spend the entire $8 allowance on ale, buying 4 pints of ale, or he can spend all $8 on bread, obtaining 16 loaves of bread. The most likely case, however, is that Ruffgreg will spend part of the money on ale and part on bread. For instance, he can purchase 3 pints of ale per week, costing $6, and 4 loaves of bread per week, costing $2, for a total weekly expenditure of $8.

We know that consumers maximize utility by spending their budgets to equate marginal utilities per dollar. We calculate marginal utility per dollar by dividing marginal utility by the price. For each quantity of ale, priced at $2 per pint, the marginal utility per dollar in column 4 of Table 1 is half the marginal utility in column 3. For each quantity of bread, priced at $0.50 per loaf, the marginal utility per dollar in column 8 is twice the marginal utility in column 7.

Table 2 illustrates a step-by-step process through which Ruffgreg maximizes utility by making incremental expenditures for bread and ale until all of his income is allocated. At the point of the initial purchase, a loaf of bread, which costs $0.50, yields a marginal utility of 15 and a marginal utility *per dollar* of 30 (= 15/$0.50), and a pint of ale, which costs $2, yields a marginal utility of 40 but a marginal utility *per dollar* of only 20 (= 40/$2). Because bread has a higher marginal utility per dollar, Ruffgreg's first purchase is one loaf at a cost of $0.50, leaving $7.50 to spend. Ruffgreg now finds that the marginal utility per dollar is higher for a pint of ale (20) than for a second loaf of bread (16), so he purchases one pint for $2, leaving $5.50 to spend. Marginal utility per dollar is higher for a second loaf of bread (16) than for a second pint of ale (15), so Ruffgreg's third purchase is a second loaf of bread. Ruffgreg continues to

TABLE 2 THE STEPS TO CONSUMER EQUILIBRIUM

	Available Choices	*Decision*	*Income Remaining*	
1st Purchase	1st pint of ale: $MU_A/P_A = 20$ 1st loaf of bread: $MU_B/P_B = 30$	Buy 1st loaf of bread for $0.50	$8.00 – $0.50 = $7.50	
2nd Purchase	1st pint of ale: $MU_A/P_A = 20$ 2nd loaf of bread: $MU_B/P_B = 16$	Buy 1st pint of ale for $2.00	$7.50 – $2.00 = $5.50	
3rd Purchase	2nd pint of ale: $MU_A/P_A = 15$ 2nd loaf of bread: $MU_B/P_B = 16$	Buy 2nd loaf of bread for $0.50	$5.50 – $0.50 = $5.00	
4th Purchase	2nd pint of ale: $MU_A/P_A = 15$ 3rd loaf of bread: $MU_B/P_B = 14$	Buy 2nd pint of ale for $2.00	$5.00 – $2.00 = $3.00	
5th Purchase	3rd pint of ale: $MU_A/P_A = 10$ 3rd loaf of bread: $MU_B/P_B = 14$	Buy 3rd loaf of bread for $0.50	$3.00 – $0.50 = $2.50	
6th Purchase and 7th Purchase	3rd pint of ale: $MU_A/P_A = 10$ 4th loaf of bread: $MU_B/P_B = 10$	Buy 3rd pint of ale for $2.00 and 4th loaf of bread for $0.50	$2.50 – $2.00 = $0.50 $0.50 – $0.50 = $0	Equilibrium

This table shows the step-by-step process by which a consumer makes purchasing decisions to maximize satisfaction. In this example, with data taken from Table 1, the consumer has $8 to spend. At each step, the consumer chooses the commodity that has the higher marginal utility per dollar. The consumer ends up buying 3 pints of ale and 4 loaves of bread, which is the equilibrium combination because marginal utility per dollar is equal for the two goods at the last purchase, and all income is spent.

select the product with the higher marginal utility per dollar until his budget is exhausted.

Ruffgreg achieves consumer equilibrium when he buys 3 pints of ale and 4 loaves of bread; he has spent his entire income of $8 (3 pints at $2 each and 4 loaves at $0.50 each), and the marginal utility per dollar is 10 utils for both ale and bread. Total utility is 135 utils (90 for ale and 35 for bread). If Ruffgreg spent his $8 differently, his total utility would drop. For example, if he bought 2 more units of bread at a cost of $1 and paid for them by buying only 0.5 unit less of ale, his total utility would drop to 120.5 utils—40.5 for 6 units of bread and 80 for 2.5 units of ale.

The law of demand can be derived from this example. When the price of ale is $2, Ruffgreg purchases (demands) 3 pints of ale, given that his income is $8 and the price of bread is $0.50. The price/quantity combination of $2 and 3 pints of ale is point *r* on Ruffgreg's demand curve (Figure 2).

We can calculate other points on the demand curve by repeating the whole process at different prices of ale, keeping income at $8 per week and the bread price at $0.50 per loaf.

If the price of ale falls from $2 to $1 per pint, the marginal utility per dollar for ale becomes greater than the marginal utility per dollar for bread at the old equilibrium of 3 pints of ale and 4 loaves of bread. Expenditures will consequently be reallocated between the two goods until the $8 is spent and marginal utilities per dollar are again equal—this time at 5 pints of ale and 6 loaves of bread. Thus, when the price of ale is $1, the quantity demanded is 5 pints. This price/quantity combination of $1 and 5 pints is point *t* on the demand curve. As the law of demand asserts, holding all other factors constant, a decrease in the price causes an increase in the quantity demanded.

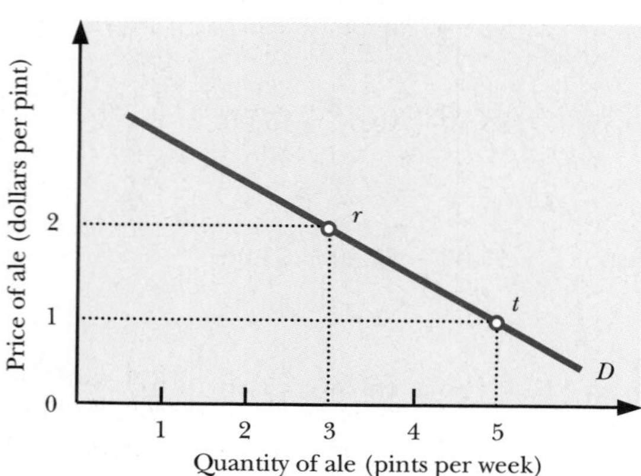

FIGURE 2 The Individual Demand Curve Derived from Ruffgreg's Marginal Utility Schedule

This curve shows Ruffgreg's demand curve for ale calculated from Table 1. Say the price of bread is $0.50 per loaf and weekly income is $8. The quantity required for consumer equilibrium when the price of ale equals $2 per pint is 3 pints (point *r*). The equilibrium quantity when the price of ale equals $1 per pint is 5 pints (point *t*).

> Every point on a consumer's demand curve satisfies the conditions that MU/*P* be the same for all goods purchased and that all income be spent. In other words, the consumer is maximizing utility at each price/quantity combination on the curve.

Income and Substitution Effects

A reduction in the price of a good has two effects. First, the savings that we gain can be used as income to purchase more goods. The part of the total increase in the quantity demanded of the reduced-price good that can be attributed to this extra income is called the **income effect**. Second, the cheaper good yields a higher marginal utility per dollar, so consumers bent on maximizing satisfaction will substitute this now-cheaper good for other products. This part of the increase in the quantity demanded of the cheaper good is called the **substitution effect**.

> When the price of a good falls, we buy more of it because (1) the price reduction is like an increase in income that in itself normally results in larger demands for all goods and services (the **income effect**); and (2) we tend to substitute that good for other, relatively more expensive goods (the **substitution effect**).

If we refer again to Table 2, we can see that, before the price of ale dropped from $2 to $1, Ruffgreg purchased 3 pints of ale and 4 loaves of bread for a total of $8 worth of ale and bread. At the lower price of ale, Ruffgreg can purchase the same 3 pints of ale and 4 loaves of bread for $5, leaving $3 extra. This $3 represents an increase in real income that can be spent on either ale or bread. The effect of this increase on purchases of ale constitutes the income effect.

EXAMPLE 3

Are Consumer Tastes Stable?

If consumer tastes were unstable, the theory of demand would be of little use. What the theory says is that the amount of a good sold changes only if certain underlying factors change, such as the price of the good, the prices of other goods, income, or the population. But what if tastes change? It is difficult to measure tastes; for practical purposes tastes are an invisible determinant of demand. Thus, if tastes were highly erratic, we would observe changes in the demand for a good or service that are unrelated to changes in the things we can observe, such as the price of the good or other goods.

The theory of income and substitution effects actually tells us that tastes are stable. How? If tastes were unstable, we would find in our studies of demand that the measured substitution effect would be contrary to economic theory. We can easily account for the income effect of a price change by multiplying the price change by the importance of the good in the economy or population being studied; thus, the income effect of price changes can be used to adjust the data. If the adjusted data show that an increase in the price of a good raises the demand for the good (controlling for all other factors), we would conclude that the theory of consumer demand is wrong. But in study after study this does not appear to happen. People don't change their tastes that often for (non-fad) goods. For example, a study of individual households in the United Kingdom shows that an increase in the price of food, alcohol, fuel, clothing, transport, and services lowers the quantity demanded of each of these categories when all other factors are held constant. Another finding is that when all income and all prices are doubled, so that the consumer is in the same real position, consumer demand does not change, just as predicted by economic theory. Therefore, we conclude that tastes must be relatively stable, or at least not so unstable as to contradict economic theory. Finally, the same study concluded that demand is price inelastic for all the above broad categories except for alcohol.

Source: R. Blundell, P. Pashardes, and G. Weber, "What Do We Learn about Consumer Demand Patterns from Micro Data?" *American Economic Review* (1993).

The price reduction is also accompanied by a drop in the relative price of ale (the ratio of ale price to bread price falls from 4 to 2). As a result, Ruffgreg receives more marginal utility per dollar from ale than from bread and, therefore, switches to buying more ale. This switch from bread to ale constitutes the substitution effect. (See Example 3.)

The size of the income effect from a price change depends on the amount of the good being consumed. A change in the price of a Rolls-Royce has no income effect for the vast majority of people because that ultra-luxury car lies far outside the limits of their budgets. However, a rise in the price of gasoline affects all drivers according to the amount they use. Thus, the income effects of price changes for food, clothing, and housing can be substantial. The income effects of price changes for goods that are relatively unimportant in the consumer's budget are small or trivial.

The size of the substitution effect also depends on the ease with which other goods can be substituted for a good. A Ford has more substitutes than a Rolls-Royce, so the substitution effect of a price change for Fords is correspondingly larger.

Is the Theory Realistic?

Do we really behave in the mechanical fashion depicted by the theory of consumer behavior? We do not carry marginal utility schedules in our heads or calculate the marginal utility per dollar on each and every good. But we most certainly think in terms of "best buys." Advertisers often stress the fact that their product gives the consumer "more for the dollar" than the competitive products. We shop at different stores before we buy a product; and we buy magazines such as *Consumers' Report* that compare different products and even recommend "best buys."

Thus, it is not surprising that on average we behave as predicted by the theory. We have downward-sloping demand curves. As price falls we find less valuable uses for the good. If we buy a variety of goods instead of just one or two, we must spread our spending among lots of goods in order to avoid the diminishing marginal utility or satisfaction we receive from consuming more of one particular good.

MARKET DEMAND

The law of diminishing marginal utility implies that rational consumers will purchase less of a product, all other things being equal, if its price rises. According to the law of demand, the demand schedules of individual consumers will have negative slopes.

The individual consumer, however, is usually only a small part of the total market in which prices are established. Individual demand curves must be combined to determine the market demand curve for a particular good.

The **market demand curve** shows the total quantities demanded by all consumers in the market at each price. It is the horizontal summation of all individual demand curves in that market.

Figure 3 shows the demand curves for ale for two consumers, Smith and White, who, for simplicity, constitute all the buyers in the market for ale. At a price of $3 per pint, Smith demands 0 pints and White demands 1 pint. We obtain the total market demand at the $3 price by adding the two individual demands (0 + 1 = 1 pint). At a price of $2 per pint, Smith demands 2 pints and White demands 3 pints. The total market demand at the $2 price is 2 + 3 = 5 pints.

The market demand curve in Figure 3 is downward sloping for the same reasons that the individual

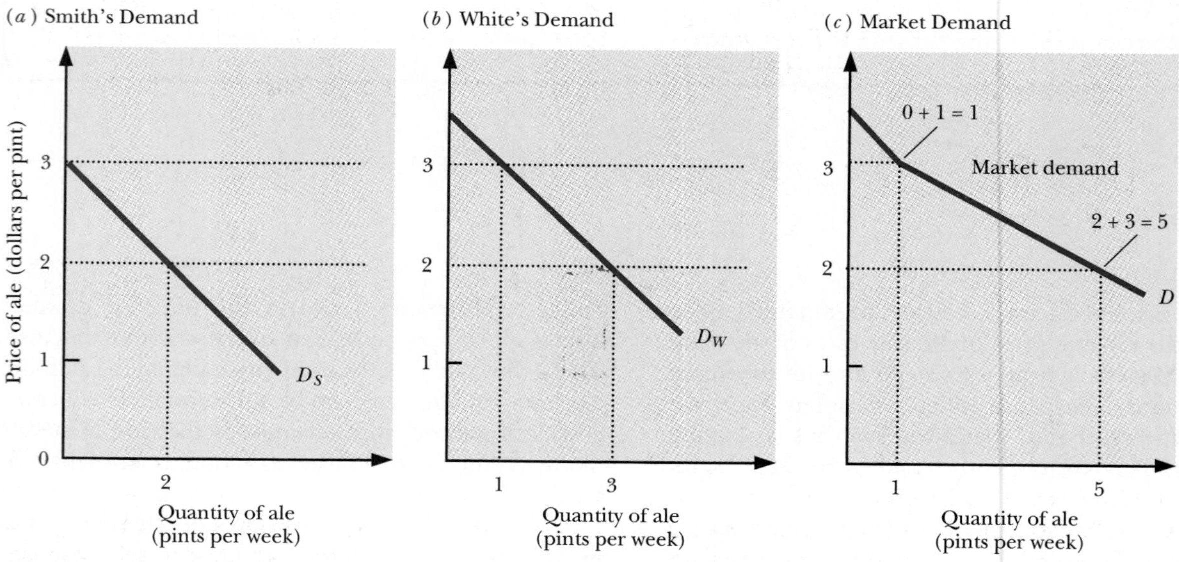

FIGURE 3 From Individual to Market Demand

The market demand curve is the *horizontal* summation of all individual demand curves; it is calculated by summing the individual quantities demanded by all individuals at each price. Here, the market has only two consumers, but the principle applies to markets with any number of consumers.

demand curves are downward sloping. Likewise, at each point along the market demand curve, just as along an individual demand curve, consumers are maximizing their satisfaction. Also, as price decreases, more consumers might be enticed to buy a product. In Figure 3, for example, when the price of ale is above $3, Smith is not in the market; at a price of $0.50, even more buyers may enter.

Consumer Surplus

We know that a high-priced good (diamonds) has a proportionately higher marginal utility than a low-priced good (water). When we, as consumers, maximize our satisfaction, we push the consumption of each good to the point where the marginal utility per dollar (MU/*P*) is the same for all the goods consumers are buying. *The theory of consumer demand shows that price reflects marginal utility.*

When consumers are in equilibrium, the price of a good is a *dollar measure* of the value of the *last unit* of the good (its marginal benefit).

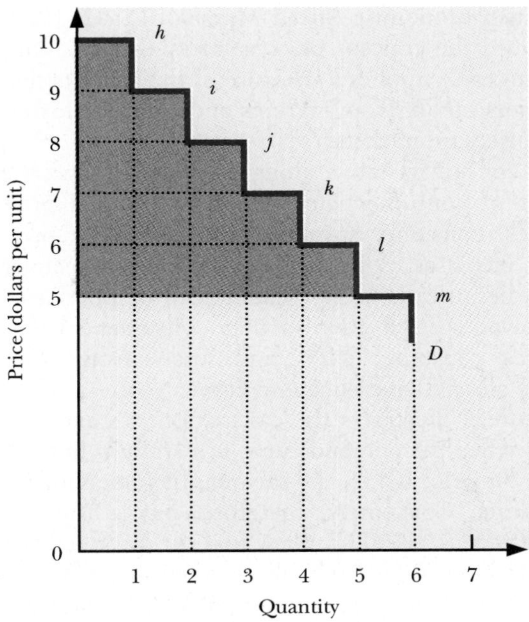

FIGURE 4 Consumers' Surplus

Say that the current market price is $5 and the quantity demanded is 6 units. According to the demand curve, consumers were prepared to spend $10 for the first unit, $9 for the second unit, $8 for the third unit, $7 for the fourth unit, and $6 for the fifth unit. When a total of 6 units are bought, however, consumers need pay only $5 each for all 6 units. Thus, they pay for each of the 6 units only what the sixth unit is worth to them. The difference between what each unit is worth to consumers and what the consumers actually pay is shown by the height of the green area for each unit. Adding these surpluses for all units yields a total consumers' surplus of $5 + $4 + $3 + $2 + $1 = $15.

Figure 4 pictures a market demand curve that describes a series of steps because the product is available only in whole units (such as a radio or a piano). According to the demand curve, if only 1 unit of the product is available, some consumer is willing to pay $10 for it (point *h*). If only 2 units of the product are available, someone is willing to pay $9 for the second unit (point *i*). If 6 units are available, someone is willing to pay a price of $5 for the sixth unit. The current market price therefore reveals what consumers are willing to pay for the *last unit* of the product sold.

When the market price is $5 and the quantity demanded is 6 units (point *m*), the price paid by each consumer reflects the value of the sixth unit to the last purchaser, even though the first of those 6 units is still worth $10 to someone, the second is still worth $9 to someone else, and so on. The total value of the 6 units to consumers ($10 + $9 + $8 + $7 + $6 + $5 = $45) is greater than the total amount that consumers pay for them (6 × $5 = $30). Consumers enjoy a surplus on all the earlier units because they have a higher marginal value than later units. The surplus on each unit is the difference between the consumer's maximum willingness to pay and what the consumer must actually pay.

Consumer surplus is the excess of the total consumer benefit that a good provides beyond consumer cost.

For example, at a price of $5 the first unit is worth $10 to someone but costs $5, so that person enjoys a surplus of $5 on the first unit. Someone enjoys a surplus of $4 on the second unit because the second unit is worth $9 to that person but costs $5. Only the last unit sold (the sixth) will yield no surplus, for its price will reflect exactly what that unit is worth to the consumer. Adding these surpluses together, one obtains a total consumer surplus of $15.

British economist Alfred Marshall (1842–1924) introduced the concept of consumers' surplus. This powerful tool supplies a measure of the benefits that consumers obtain from markets and from the lowering of prices in markets.

As consumers move along a demand curve, the amount of consumer surplus changes: If the price increases, consumer surplus decreases; if the price falls, it increases. A lower price increases consumer surplus because the same benefits can be purchased at a lower cost. It follows that consumer surplus measures consumer gains and losses from price changes along a given demand curve.

Figure 5 illustrates the calculation of consumer surplus when the demand curve is a straight line. At point *f*, the price is $15 and the quantity demanded is 1000 units. Consumers, therefore, pay a total of $15,000 ($15 × 1000 units) for the product. At quantities less than 1000 units, consumers would have been willing to pay more than $15. This difference, measured by the vertical distance between the demand curve and the horizontal line at $15, constitutes the surplus for each unit. For instance, the purchaser of the 500th unit would have been willing to pay $20 instead of the $15 actually paid (point *e*). Adding all the surpluses together for quantities less than 1000 yields the consumer surplus, or the area of the red triangle labeled *A*.[1]

What will happen to consumer surplus if the market price drops to $10? It will increase because a surplus will exist at all quantities less than 1500, whereas the surplus previously stopped at a quantity of 1000. Consumer surplus at point *g*, where price is $10, is the area of the triangle formed by the demand curve and the horizontal line at $10, or the sum of the three areas *A* + *B* + *C*. Consumer surplus at a price of $15 was area *A;* therefore, the *increase* in consumer surplus as a consequence of the drop in price is *B* + *C* = $5000 (area of *B*) + $1250 (area of *C*) = $6250.[2] (See Example 4.)

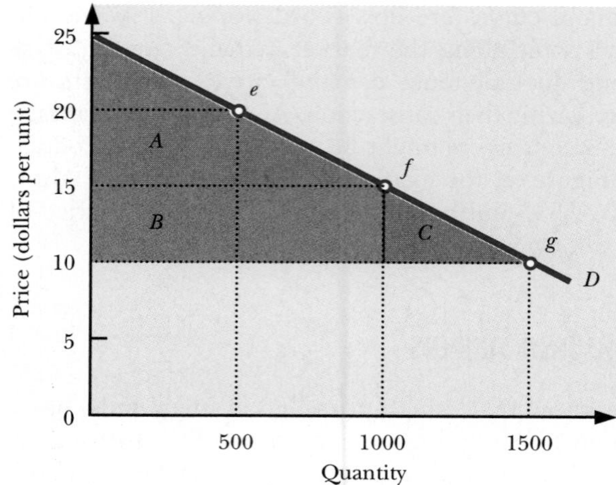

FIGURE 5 The Gain in Consumer Surplus Resulting from a Reduction in Price

When price is $15 and quantity demanded is 1000 units, the consumer surplus is the red triangle *A*, the excess of what people would be willing to pay beyond the actual cost. If the price falls to $10, quantity demanded increases to 1500 units and consumer surplus is the area *A* + *B* + *C*. Consumer surplus, therefore, increases by *B* + *C*, or by $6250.

The Role of Consumer Surplus

We can think of consumer surplus as the incentive for each person to engage in voluntary exchange. People buy many things, and each purchase yields a surplus over and above what it costs. Without this incentive people would not be eager to participate in the market.

[1]By changing quantity demanded in very small increments, the demand schedule approximates a smooth line. Thus, consumer surplus is measured by the smooth area of triangle *A*, instead of by adding a series of rectangles together as in Figure 4.

As explained in Appendix 1A, areas of *rectangles* are computed by multiplying the horizontal width of the rectangle times the vertical height of the rectangle. The width of rectangle *B* is 1000; the height is $5. Areas of triangles are calculated by multiplying the width of the triangle by its height and dividing by 2 (or multiplying by 1/2). The area of the the triangle will be 1/2 that of the rectangle formed by the height and width of the triangle.

[2]The segment of the demand curve between *f* and *g* in this example was deliberately constructed to have an elasticity of demand of unity, so that the amounts of consumer spending at both points are equal. At both prices, consumers spend $15,000, but consumer surplus is $6250 greater at the lower price than at the higher price.

EXAMPLE 4

Consumer Surplus and Your Television

Consumers enjoy consumer surplus when they can buy something for less than they would have been willing to pay. We pay $20 per month for local telephone service; many of us would be willing to pay much more if we had to. We pay $75 per month for our electricity; if we had to, we would be willing to pay more.

A survey conducted by *TV Guide* asked people how much they would be willing to pay to keep their television sets. Television, after all, is the major source of entertainment for most of us, giving instant access to news, situation comedies, and cable programming. Although respondents answered differently, some people would have been willing to pay over $100,000 to avoid being deprived of television. For the person willing to pay $100,000 for television, the $350 price of a color television set provides a consumer surplus of $99,650!

In order to have a market—sellers of the goods people want—it is equally necessary to offer sellers an income that more than compensates them for the toil and trouble of providing those goods. People make an income in a capitalist society by providing what others want and are willing to pay for. Both sides of the market are engaged in voluntary exchange. Nobody forces you to work as a lawyer, teacher, or mechanic. Nobody forces you to buy bread, milk, or personal computers. Having the means to purchase what you want in a capitalist society acts as a certificate to show that you have provided services to others.

Consumer surplus enhances our understanding of two Defining Moments in economics. The Industrial Revolution created immense consumer surpluses. The new technologies of mass production lowered costs of production and made goods that had been unheard-of luxuries accessible to the masses. Factories could now produce textiles at a fraction of the cost of homespun garments. Textile prices dropped and consumer surplus grew. As the Industrial Revolution proceeded, science and technology created new products—electric lights, phonographs, telegraph services. Earlier consumers would have gladly purchased these products; prior to scientific advances, however, such products either could not be produced at all or entailed too high a price for consumers. New products at affordable prices, therefore, created vast sums of consumer surpluses.

Globalization, another Defining Moment, is motivated by producers in one country being able to offer goods at higher quality and lower prices to consumers in another country. Trading goods and services according to comparative advantage creates substantial consumer surpluses and provides the gains that encourage the growth of international trade.

The consumer surpluses provided by the Industrial Revolution and by globalization constitute the vast rises in living standards that consumers have experienced over the past two centuries.

To earn an income in a capitalist society people must overcome an obstacle: costs. Goods and services are seldom free. Somebody—firms—must produce them by having the incentive—profits—to gather the required resources. It is to this story that we will turn in the next chapter.

SUMMARY

1. *Utility* is a numerical measure of a consumer's satisfaction from different commodity bundles. *Marginal utility* is the increase in total utility obtained when consumption of a good is increased by 1 unit. The *law of diminishing marginal utility* states that the marginal utility eventually declines as more of a good or service is consumed, holding the consumption of other goods constant. The fact that market prices reflect marginal utility rather than total utility explains the diamond/water paradox.

2. The law of diminishing marginal utility is consistent with the law of demand. When the rational consumer equates marginal utility per dollar on the last purchases of each commodity, the consumer is in equilibrium. If the price of one good falls, its marginal utility per dollar initially rises, and more of the commodity will be consumed. Rational consumers spend their money in a way that maximizes their satisfaction (utility). A drop in the price of a good has two effects: First, the use of the resulting increase in real income to purchase more of the good constitutes the *income effect*. Second, the increase in the amount of the good purchased that is due to the decrease in its relative price constitutes the *substitution effect*.

3. The *market demand schedule* is the horizontal summation of the demand schedules of all individuals participating in the market. The market demand schedule will have a negative slope because its individual components have negative slopes.

4. *Consumer surplus* measures the extent to which consumer benefits exceed consumer costs for a particular product. Consumer surplus follows from the law of diminishing marginal utility. Consumers pay the same market price for each unit they buy, but the market price reflects only the value of the last unit sold. The marginal benefit of earlier units, therefore, exceeds the market price. Adding these surpluses together yields total consumer surplus. The concept of consumer surplus permits the measurement of consumer losses and gains from price changes.

KEY TERMS

utility 118
marginal utility (MU) 118
law of diminishing marginal utility 119
marginal utility per dollar 121
consumer equilibrium or optimum 121
income effect 124
substitution effect 124
market demand curve 126
consumer surplus 127

QUESTIONS AND PROBLEMS

1. In some parts of the world, sick people seek the help of witch doctors. In the United States, most people seek medical doctors when they are ill; a few seek out faith healers. Does this variation mean that consumer preferences for medical care are basically unstable?
2. In the late 1970s and early 1980s, Americans began to buy smaller, fuel-efficient vehicles instead of large "gas guzzlers." In the 1990s, they switched back to buying larger vehicles; even Japan started exporting larger vehicles to the United States. Do these changes indicate that consumer preferences are unstable?
3. If the marginal utility of a good *A* were to increase as consumption of the good increased (in opposition to the law of diminishing marginal utility), would $MU_A/P_A = MU_B/P_B$ still be the equilibrium condition?
4. Use the marginal utility information in Table 1 to calculate the demand for ale at the price of $4 per pint. What do you do when marginal utility per dollar cannot be exactly equated for two goods on the last unit sold?
5. Again using Table 1, calculate the demand for ale at the price of $2 but at a weekly income of $11. Compare this result with the answer at $8. Which is larger? Why?

6. Assume that there are 1000 identical consumers in the market, each with the same income and the same preferences. When the price of *X* is $50 per unit, the typical consumer is prepared to purchase 20 units. When the price is $40 per unit, the typical consumer is prepared to purchase 25 units. Construct from this information the market demand curve for *X* (assume the demand curve is a straight line). Then calculate the loss of consumer surplus when the price rises from $40 to $50 per unit.

7. A consumer is spending an entire weekly income on goods *A* and *B*. The last penny spent on *A* yields a marginal utility of 10; the last penny spent on *B* yields a marginal utility of 20. Is it possible for the consumer to be in equilibrium? If so, what are the exact conditions?

8. Lisa White consumes only goods *X* and *Y*. Column 1 of Table A shows the marginal utility she derives from various units of *X;* column 2 shows the marginal utility she derives from various units of *Y*. Her income is $20, the price of *X* is $2 per unit, and the price of *Y* is $4 per unit. Use Table A to answer the following questions:
   a. How much of *X* and *Y* will Lisa White demand?
   b. Check your answer by using the consumer equilibrium conditions. (Is all income spent? Does $MU_X/P_X = MU_Y/P_Y$?)

TABLE A

(1)		(2)	
Units of X	MU_X	*Units of Y*	MU_Y
1	20	1	2000
2	16	2	200
3	12	3	20
4	10	4	10
5	6	5	4

9. Can the equilibrium conditions be applied to more than two goods? How?

10. The price of ale is $10, the price of bread is $5, and the marginal utility of bread is 50 utils when the consumer is in equilibrium. Can you determine how much is spent on ale? Can you determine the marginal utility of ale?

11. The price of oranges is $0.25 each, and the price of grapefruit is $0.50 each. Assuming that all income is spent in each case, determine whether or not the consumer is in equilibrium in each of the following circumstances. If consumer equilibrium does not occur, determine which good the consumer will purchase in greater quantity and explain why.
    a. The marginal utility of oranges, MU_O, equals 10, and the marginal utility of grapefruit, MU_G, equals 15.
    b. $MU_O = 50$ and $MU_G = 100$.
    c. MU_O is twice that of MU_G.
    d. MU_G is twice that of MU_O.

12. *Optional Question.* Income and substitution effects can be measured. Suppose that the income elasticity of demand for housing is 1 and that the price elasticity of demand is 0.3 (these numbers are close to actual estimates). Furthermore, suppose that housing accounts for 20 percent of the average household's budget. A decrease in income of 2 percent would decrease the demand for housing by 2 percent because the income elasticity is 1. Now suppose that income is held constant and that the price of housing rises by 10 percent. Since the price elasticity is 0.3, a 10 percent increase in price will lower quantity demanded by 3 percent. What portion of this 3 percent decrease in quantity demanded is due to the income effect? What portion is due to the substitution effect? (*Hint:* A 10 percent increase in the price of housing raises the cost of living by 2 percent since there is a 10 percent increase in 20 percent of the budget. Observe also that a 2 percent increase in the cost of living has the same effect as a 2 percent reduction in income. Therefore, a 10 percent increase in the price of housing, holding income and other prices constant, is like a 2 percent reduction in real income.)

INTERNET CONNECTION

13. Using the links from http://www.awl.com/ruffin_gregory, read the article on utilitarianism.
    a. Why have economists today rejected utilitarianism?
    b. Does the author suggest any practical alternatives?

PUZZLE ANSWERED: Kathy buys 50 pizzas each year at \$10 each, spending \$500; when the price rises to \$11 she buys 45 pizzas, spending \$495. How much is she affected? She is buying 5 fewer pizzas. The first she gives up is worth \$10, the last \$11. The 5 pizzas have an average value of \$10.50. While she spends \$5 less per year, the cost to her is \$2.50 in lost consumer surplus. She was spending \$10 each on the 5 sacrificed pizzas, with each worth \$10.50 on the average. Thus, she lost \$2.50 (=\$.50 × 10) in consumer surplus on the 5 she gives up. But she pays \$1 more for each of the 45 pizzas she still consumes. Total loss in consumer surplus = \$47.50. See Figure A.

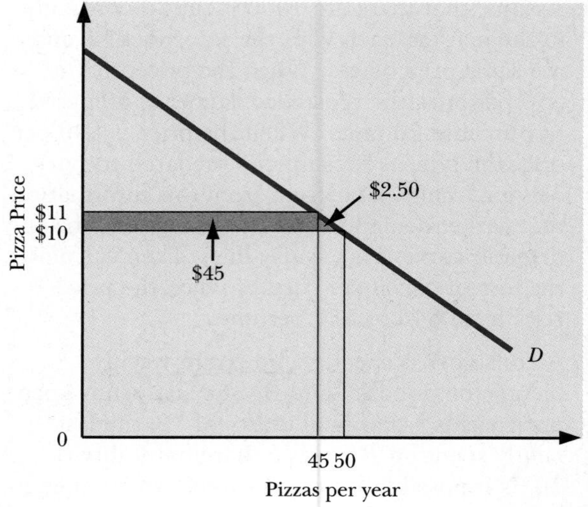

FIGURE A

Appendix 7A

Indifference Curves

Appendix Insight

The preceding chapter based the law of demand on the nineteenth-century conception of utility—a measure that reflects the magnitude as well as the rank of a consumer's satisfaction from different commodity bundles. Skepticism about the quantification of utility prompted economists to seek an alternative approach to understanding consumer behavior. The culmination of this search is the *indifference curve theory.* This theory assumes that consumers are able to *rank* their preferences for combinations of goods, but it does not require that utility be measured in absolute terms. A consumer who does not prefer one combination to another is said to be *indifferent.* Indifference curve theory provides a convenient graphical approach for illustrating consumer response to income and price changes, and for analyzing the breakdown of consumer behavior into substitution and income effects.

Consumer Preferences

The indifference curve approach is based on an analysis of the amount of one good a consumer is willing to give up in exchange for 1 unit of another good without experiencing a loss in total satisfaction. When one combination of goods yields the same satisfaction as another, the consumer is indifferent between the two combinations.

Figure A1 diagrams the preferences of a particular consumer. The horizontal axis measures the quantity of ale consumed by the individual per week. The vertical axis measures the quantity of bread consumed by the individual per week. At point *a,* 6 loaves of bread and 1 pint of ale are consumed. At point *a,* the consumer is willing to give up 3 loaves of bread for 1 more pint of ale. Making this trade would move the consumer to point *b,* where 3 loaves of bread and 2 pints of ale are consumed. At point *b,* the consumer is willing to give up only 1 loaf of bread to acquire 1 more pint of ale. Making this trade would move the consumer to point *c,* where 2 loaves of bread and 3 pints of ale are consumed per week. Finally, to acquire 1 more pint of ale, the consumer at point *c* is willing to give up only half of a loaf of bread, which would result in the combination at point *d.* Among points *a, b, c,* and *d,* the consumer is indifferent.

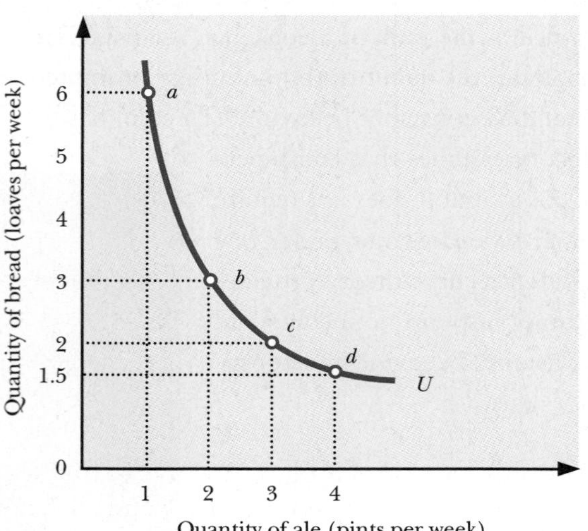

FIGURE A1 An Indifference Curve

When given the choice among the commodity bundles along an indifference curve, the consumer is indifferent. Consumption pattern *a* yields the same satisfaction to the consumer as *b, c,* or *d.* The absolute value of the slope of an indifference curve is the marginal rate of substitution and shows—in this case—how much bread the consumer is just willing to sacrifice for one more pint of ale.

A curve (*U*) can be drawn through points *a, b, c,* and *d* to represent all possible consumption patterns that keep the consumer at the same level of satisfaction. The consumer is indifferent among these patterns.

An **indifference curve** shows all the alternative combinations of two goods that yield the same total satisfaction to a particular consumer and among which the consumer is indifferent.

An indifference curve is downward sloping because both goods yield satisfaction. The consumer's satisfaction will remain constant when the consumption of one good increases only if consumption of the other good decreases.

The Law of Diminishing Marginal Rate of Substitution

When indifference curves are used to analyze consumer preferences, the concept of marginal utility is no longer required.

The **marginal rate of substitution (MRS)** is how much of one good a person is willing to give up to acquire one unit of another good.

Thus, the marginal rate of substitution is simply a fancy name for an acceptable trade-off between two goods, for a person's *valuation* of an additional unit of one good in terms of another. For example, the amount of pizza a person would be willing to sacrifice for an additional hot dog indicates that person's valuation of hot dogs in terms of pizza.

An indifference curve is always convex when viewed from below (that is, the curve bulges toward the origin). This convex curvature follows from the law of diminishing marginal rate of substitution.

The **law of diminishing marginal rate of substitution** states that as more of one good (*A*) is consumed, the amount of another good (*B*) that the consumer is willing to sacrifice for one more unit of good *A* declines.

As more ale is consumed relative to bread, the consumer is willing to give up less and less bread to acquire additional units of ale because bread is getting more valuable and ale is getting less valuable. In Figure A1, from point *a* down to point *d* and beyond, the indifference curve gets flatter and flatter because the relative valuation placed on ale is decreasing compared to that of bread.

The flatter the slope of the indifference curve, the lower the relative valuation the consumer places on *A* (compared to *B*) when *A* is on the horizontal axis. The slope of the tangent at any point on the indifference curve measures the marginal rate of substitution of good *B* for good *A*.

Indifference curves can be drawn to represent any level of satisfaction. Each consumer has an entire map of indifference curves, one for every level. Figure A2 shows three indifference curves for the same consumer. Higher indifference curves for any one consumer represent higher levels of satisfaction because more is usually better.

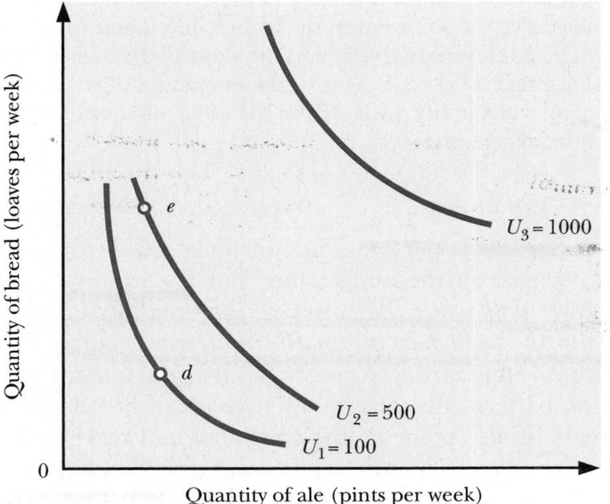

FIGURE A2 Map of Indifference Curves

Each consumer has an infinite number of indifference curves. Three indifference curves for a particular consumer are shown here. The higher the indifference curve is, the greater is the well-being of the consumer. The indifference map shows that commodity bundle *e* is preferred to bundle *d* because the former is on a higher indifference curve. Indifference curve U_3 represents a higher level of satisfaction than U_2, and U_2 represents a higher level than U_1. The level of satisfaction along each indifference curve is constant.

Indifference curves are subjective and unique to each person. Nevertheless, all indifference curves have the following five properties in common:

1. Indifference curves between two goods for which consumers derive positive benefits are downward sloping.
2. Indifference curves are bowed toward the *origin* (the point where the axes meet), reflecting the law of diminishing marginal rate of substitution.
3. The consumer is better off when he or she moves to a higher indifference curve.
4. Indifference curves cannot intersect each other because an intersection would indicate that the consumer is simultaneously worse off and better off. (Even though indifference curves cannot intersect, they need not be parallel.)
5. The entire pattern of indifference curves is independent of changes in market circumstances (income or prices), just as a map is fixed regardless of your location.

The Budget Line

What a consumer can afford is determined by the consumer's budget. Suppose the price of ale is \$2 per pint and the price of bread is \$0.50 per loaf, as in the preceding chapter. Assume the consumer has \$8 to spend per week on ale and bread. If the entire \$8 is spent on ale, the consumer can buy 4 pints of ale (point *m* in Figure A3). If the entire \$8 is spent on bread, 16 loaves can be purchased (point *n*).

The **budget line** represents all the combinations of goods the consumer is able to buy, given a certain income and set prices. The budget line shows the consumption possibilities available to the consumer.

The budget line connecting points *m* and *n* indicates all possible combinations of ale and bread that the consumer is able to purchase by allocating the entire \$8 income between the two goods.

The budget line in Figure A3 has a slope with an absolute value of 16/4 = 4. This slope is the price of ale (the good on the horizontal axis) in terms of bread (the good on the vertical axis): P_A/P_B = \$2/\$0.50 = 4; it indicates that a consumer who wants to buy 1 more pint of ale must give up 4 loaves of bread.

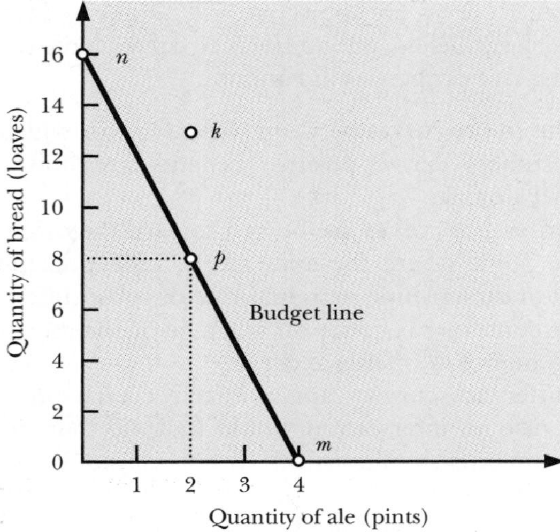

FIGURE A3 The Budget Line

With a budget of \$8, the consumer can buy 16 loaves of bread at a price of \$0.50 per loaf or 4 pints of ale at a price of \$2 per pint. Spending \$4 on each good would buy 8 loaves of bread and 2 pints of ale (point *p*). The budget line shows the choices open to the consumer. The consumer can afford to buy any combination of goods on the budget line. Points above the budget line, such as *k*, cannot be purchased with the consumer's income. The slope of the budget line is the ratio of the price of ale to the price of bread—here, 4.

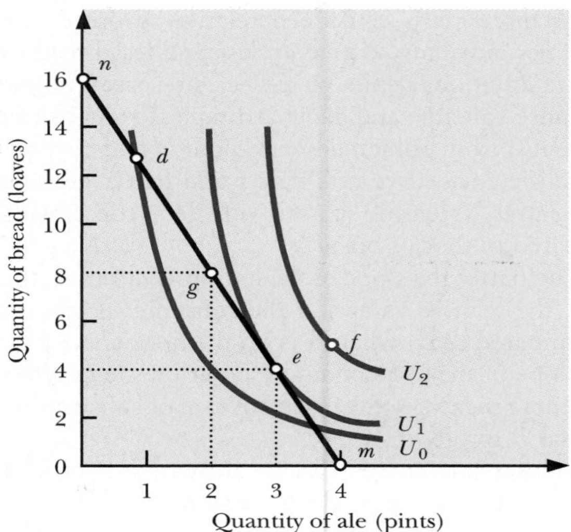

FIGURE A4 Consumer Equilibrium

The consumer's optimal consumption pattern is at point *e*. A point like *d* is attainable (on the budget line) but is inferior to *e* because it places the consumer on a lower indifference curve (U_0). Point *f* is preferable to *e* (the consumer is on a higher indifference curve, U_2) but is not attainable with the given set of income and prices. At *e*, the indifference curve U_1 is tangent to the budget line. Thus, the slope of the indifference curve equals the slope of the budget line. This tangency is equivalent to the marginal utility rule for maximizing utility ($MU_A/P_A = MU_B/P_B$) discussed in the preceding chapter.

Algebraically, point *m* in Figure A3 is income divided by the price of ale (Income/P_A) because it represents the maximum possible consumption of ale. Point *n* is income divided by the price of bread (Income/P_B). Then, the absolute value of the slope of the line *nm* is as follows:

$$\text{Slope} = \frac{\text{Income}}{P_B} \div \frac{\text{Income}}{P_A} = \frac{P_A}{P_B}$$

An indifference curve shows how the consumer ranks various commodity bundles; the budget line shows which bundles the consumer *is able to buy*. Combining the information represented by an indifference curve and the budget line reveals which combination the consumer *will buy*.

CONSUMER EQUILIBRIUM

The consumer achieves equilibrium by choosing a consumption pattern that maximizes satisfaction and lies on the budget line. The consumer is *able* to locate anywhere on the budget line, but *the rational consumer will select the consumption combination that falls on the highest attainable indifference curve*. Figure A4 illustrates the choice of an optimal consumption pattern. By consuming 4 loaves of bread and 3 pints of ale (point *e*), the consumer can reach indifference curve U_1. Any other point on the budget line will fall on a *lower* indifference curve. At this optimal consumption point, the budget line is tangent to (touches the curve only at one point and has the same slope as) the indifference curve.

In equivalent terms, consumer equilibrium occurs at that point on the highest attainable indifference curve where the marginal rate of substitution equals the price ratio. At point *e*, the consumer's marginal rate of substitution is 4 because the consumer is willing to trade off 4 units of bread for 1 unit of ale. The price ratio, as we have shown, is also 4.

The consumer is in equilibrium when the budget line is tangent to the highest attainable indifference curve. Two conditions are then satisfied: (1) The consumer is on the budget line. (2) The consumer's marginal rate of substitution of bread for ale equals the price ratio of ale to bread (P_A/P_B).

The marginal rate of substitution of bread for ale ($MRS_{B/A}$) equals the ratio of the ale's marginal utility (MU_A) to the bread's marginal utility (MU_B):

$$MRS_{B/A} = \frac{MU_A}{MU_B}$$

Indifference Curves and Utility

Utility is a numerical measure of consumer satisfaction. By assigning numerical levels of utility to indifference curves, we can relate the two concepts. (We must not, however, confuse the convenient language of utility theory with the assumption that utility is measurable.) Any numbers can be assigned as long as they are increasing for higher indifference curves. Thus, in Figure A2, we assign a higher number (1000) to indifference curve U_3 than to U_2 (500) or to U_1 (100).

Also in the preceding chapter, the quantification of utility allowed us to define the marginal utility (MU) of a good as the increase in utility per unit change in the consumption of the good, holding the consumption of other goods constant. Marginal utility theory and indifference curve analysis are linked by the ability to use the marginal utilities of two goods to calculate the marginal rate of substitution. For example, if the marginal utility of ale (MU_A) is 20 and the marginal utility of bread (MU_B) is 5, it takes 4 extra loaves of bread to compensate the consumer for the loss of only 1 pint of ale. But if $MU_A = 10$ and $MU_B = 5$, the marginal rate of substitution of bread for ale is only 2.

We can translate the conditions for equilibrium outlined in the preceding section into the equal marginal utility-per-dollar rule for consumer equilibrium described in the preceding chapter. At point e in Figure A4, the slope of the indifference curve is MU_A/MU_B, and the slope of the budget line is P_A/P_B. The indifference curve equilibrium rule is equivalent to

$$MU_A/MU_B = P_A/P_B$$

Some algebraic manipulation shows that this equation is equivalent to the marginal utility per dollar rule for equilibrium:

$$MU_A/P_A = MU_B/P_B$$

The Effect of an Income Change

The consumer's equilibrium position is affected by changes in income, the price of ale, and the price of bread. Figure A5 shows that a reduction in the consumer's income from \$8 to \$4 leads to a reduction in the demand for both ale and bread. We assume the price of ale stays at \$2 per pint and the price of bread remains at \$0.50 per loaf. The budget line shifts downward from *nm* to *hj* because the consumer can purchase a maximum of only 2 pints of ale or 8 loaves of bread with an income of \$4. Consumption decreases from 4 loaves of bread and 3 pints of ale to only 2 loaves of bread and 1.5 pints of ale at the new equilibrium (point e_0).

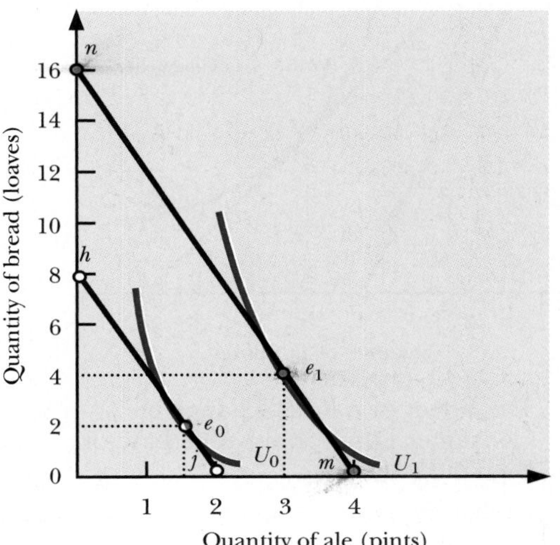

FIGURE A5 The Effect of an Income Change

When the price of ale is \$2 per pint and the price of bread is \$0.50 per loaf, a fall in income from \$8 to \$4 causes a parallel shift in the budget line from *nm* to *hj*. The equilibrium point moves from e_1 to e_0, which is on a lower indifference curve (U_0).

Notice that because prices are held constant, the slope of the budget line, P_A/P_B, remains the same. Thus, all budget lines for a given set of prices are parallel, shifting downward when income falls and upward when income rises. Clearly, utility also rises and falls in concert with income.

THE EFFECT OF A PRICE CHANGE

Now consider the effects of a change in the price of one of two goods, holding income and the other price constant. Figure A6 shows that a fall in the price of ale from \$2 to \$1 per pint leads to an increase in the quantity of ale demanded. The initial equilibrium situation is represented by point e_1, where the price of ale is \$2 and the price of bread is \$0.50. Reducing the price of ale to \$1 allows the consumer to purchase as many as 8 pints of ale with the same income of \$8. The budget line swings outward from *nm* to *nr*.

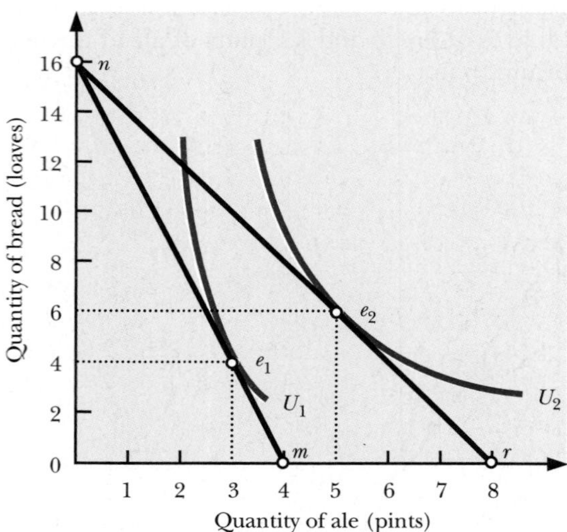

FIGURE A6 The Effect of a Price Change on Consumer Equilibrium: The Law of Demand

If we assume that income is \$8 and the price of bread is \$0.50, when the price of ale falls from \$2 to \$1 per pint, the budget line swings outward from *nm* to *nr* because the consumer is able to buy as many as 8 pints of ale. The consumer finds a new equilibrium combination, e_2, where indifference curve U_2 is tangent to the new budget line *nr*. A fall in the price of ale from \$2 to \$1, thus, increases the quantity of ale demanded from 3 pints at point e_1 to 5 pints at point e_2.

At the new equilibrium position, point e_2, the consumer buys 5 pints of ale and 6 loaves of bread. Before the price change, the consumer bought 3 pints of ale and 4 loaves of bread. The law of demand is reconfirmed: lowering the price of ale increases the quantity of ale demanded.

Moreover, the consumer is made better off (moves to a higher indifference curve) by the fall in the price of ale. The lower the price of a good bought by a consumer, holding income and other prices constant, the greater the consumer's welfare.

> When the price of one good falls, an increase in real income occurs, represented by an outward swing of the budget line.

An analysis of the effect of a price change illustrates why demand curves are downward sloping. A downward slope on a demand curve implies that as the price of a good falls, the quantity demanded rises. The preceding chapter outlined two reasons for the law of demand: the substitution effect and the income effect. When the price of a good falls, people tend to substitute that good for other goods because its relative price decreases. Thus, the substitution effect tends to increase the quantity of a good demanded when its price falls. In addition, when the price of a good falls, people have more money to spend on all goods. For a person who is accustomed to buying one \$20,000 car per year, a reduction in price to \$18,000 is like a \$2000 increase in income. If a good is normal, increases in income raise the demand for it. Thus, the income effect of a decrease in the price of a good further increases the quantity demanded.

Figure A7 shows a consumer with an initial budget line *vw* and an initial equilibrium at point *e*, where the consumer is purchasing *q* units of ale. When the price of ale falls, the budget line shifts to *vz*. The quantity of ale demanded is now q'' at the new equilibrium point, e''. The consumer is better off after the drop in the ale price because curve U'' is higher than curve *U*. Indifference curve analysis can be used to isolate the roles of the substitution effect and the income effect on the change in the equilibrium position.

When the price of ale falls, the ratio of the price of ale to the price of bread changes. This new ratio is reflected by the budget lines *vz* and *st*. A consumer interested only in maintaining the same level of utility achieved on curve *U* would increase the quantity of ale demanded until he or she reached point e',

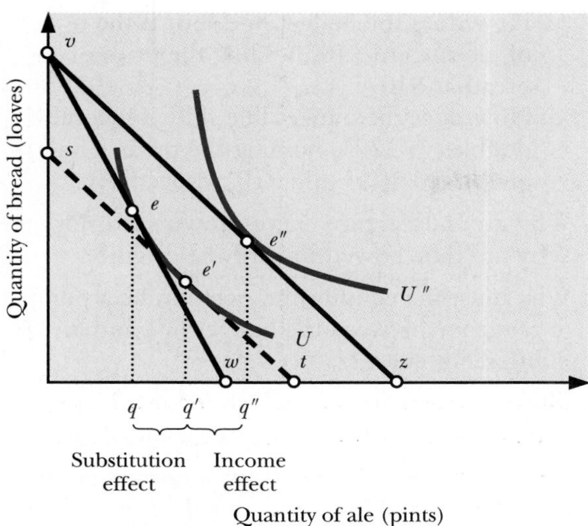

FIGURE A7 Substitution and Income Effects

When income is \$8 per week, bread costs \$0.50 per loaf, and ale costs \$2 per pint, the initial equilibrium is point e. When the price of ale falls from \$2 to \$1 per pint, the budget line swings outward from vw to vz. The new equilibrium is point e''. The substitution effect is obtained by drawing the budget line st parallel to vz but tangent to the original indifference curve, U. Thus, the substitution effect is the distance qq' and the income effect is the distance $q'q''$. In the case of a normal good, the income effect augments the substitution effect.

where line st is tangent to U. At e', the consumer buys more ale and less bread without changing the level of satisfaction. This change in the quantity of ale demanded, from q to q', constitutes the substitution effect of the change in the price of ale.

At point e', however, the consumer is not spending all available income. The drop in the price of ale shifts the budget line outward to vz, which has the same ale price/bread price ratio as st but enables the consumer to choose a position on a higher indifference curve. Instead of remaining at e', a consumer who wishes to maximize satisfaction will choose e'', a point on the highest indifference curve attainable given budget line vz. A consumer making this choice will further increase the quantity demanded of ale from q' at e' to q'' at e''. This new equilibrium, unlike e', does satisfy all the conditions of consumer equilibrium. The increase in quantity demanded from q' to q'' constitutes the income effect of the change in the ale price.

The importance of the distinction between the substitution and income effects is that if a good is normal, the income effect reinforces the substitution effect. In Figure A7, the price of ale falls and the substitution effect increases quantity demanded from q to q' along the convex indifference curve U. The move from e' to e'' is like any income increase. If ale is a normal good, more ale will be consumed. In effect, a reduced price of ale gives the consumer more income to spend on both ale and bread. It follows from the above analysis that if a good is normal, the demand curve for the good must be downward sloping.

SUMMARY

1. Indifference curve analysis requires only that consumers be able to state whether they prefer one combination of goods to another or whether they are indifferent. An indifference curve plots those combinations of goods that yield the same level of satisfaction to the consumer. In indifference curve analysis, the law of diminishing marginal rate of substitution replaces the law of diminishing marginal utility. It states that the greater the quantity of good X that the individual consumes relative to good Y, the smaller will be the quantity of good Y that the consumer is willing to sacrifice to obtain 1 more unit of good X. The budget line shows the choices of goods open to the consumer.

2. Maximizing satisfaction requires that the consumer seek out the highest indifference curve that can be attained while remaining on the budget line. This point occurs at the tangency of the indifference curve and the budget line.

3. Indifference curves can be related to marginal utilities. The marginal rate of substitution of bread for ale is the marginal utility of ale divided by the marginal utility of bread.

4. A change in income causes a parallel shift in the budget line. The budget line shifts downward if income decreases and upward if income increases. The new equilibrium is simply the point of tangency between the new budget line and an indifference curve.

5. A reduction in the price of one commodity swings the budget line outward. The new equilibrium occurs at the point of tangency between a higher indifference curve and the new budget line.

The consumer is made better off by the price reduction because the consumer is able to locate on a higher indifference curve. The effects of a price change on quantity demanded can be broken down into a substitution effect, which maintains the existing utility level, and an income effect, which results from the change in the consumer's level of utility.

KEY TERMS

indifference curve 134
marginal rate of substitution (MRS) 134
law of diminishing marginal rate of substitution 134
budget line 135

QUESTIONS AND PROBLEMS

1. Assume that a consumer's income is $100, the price of ale is $5 per pint, and the price of bread is $4 per loaf.
   a. Draw the consumer's budget line.
   b. How does the budget line shift if the price of bread rises to $10, holding the price of ale at $5?
   c. How does the budget line shift if the price of ale rises to $10, holding the price of bread at $10?
   d. How does the budget line shift if income doubles to $200, holding the prices of ale and bread at $5 and $10, respectively?
2. Why are indifference curves downward sloping? Why are they bowed toward the origin?
3. Why must the equilibrium position be a point of tangency between the budget line and an indifference curve?
4. Illustrate a situation in which income increases and the demand for one of two goods falls.
5. Derive the law of demand for a normal good using the distinction between substitution and income effects when the price of the good rises.
6. Assume that the marginal rate of substitution of good *X* for good *Y* is $MRS_{X/Y} = 6$, that the price of good *X* is $1 per unit, and that the price of good *Y* is $3 per unit.
   a. Illustrate the consumer's current position on the budget line relative to an indifference curve.
   b. Explain why the consumer would buy more of good *Y*.

Chapter 8

Economic Organization: Property Rights and the Firm

Chapter Insight

Scarcity means that there must be competition for resources. To avoid physical conflicts over the use of scarce resources, societies establish property rights that are policed and enforced by the state or by strong customs. How resource conflicts are resolved is crucial to the success or failure of an economic organization. In an advanced capitalist society, the conflicts are resolved peaceably through widely accepted laws, customs, and institutions. It is in this framework that the price system coordinates supply and demand. We buy or sell, borrow or lend, enter contracts, and start businesses with the expectation that we can enjoy certain future benefits. When you purchase a shirt or dress, you expect future benefits peculiar to yourself. If someone stole your shirt or dress, you would be robbed of all your future benefits. When economists assume that people maximize utility, it is understood they do not maximize their utility through theft of someone else's goods. Clearly, there must be rules of the game or property rights that specify what people can and cannot do. You can buy bricks to build a fireplace, but you cannot throw a brick through your neighbor's window. Without rules of the game, society would break down.

In most advanced societies, economic activity takes place in markets, where things are bought and sold, or borrowed and lent. Business firms operate organized markets. This is obvious when you go to stores to buy things. Business firms come in all shapes and sizes. The vast majority are operated for profit. Some, like the New York Stock Exchange, have historically been nonprofit firms, but have recently become for-profit.

It is impossible to have an efficient economy without business firms. It is, therefore, necessary for us to study the basic nature of the business firm.

Nobel Prize–winning economist Ronald Coase asked the question, Why do business firms exist? This penetrating question has turned out to be one of the basic questions as to how we organize an economy. Once you understand why a business firm exists, you can turn your attention to all kinds of firms. There are big and small corporations, partnerships, and sole proprietorships. But most economic activity takes place within or between corporations or between individuals and corporations. Why?

A corporation is jointly owned. It is developed without government direction but under a set of rules on the shared use of private property. By the time of the Industrial Revolution, corporations had reached a level of maturity. It was corporations that raised the capital and provided the business management that made the Industrial Revolution possible.

LEARNING OBJECTIVES

After completing this chapter, you will be able to:

1. Define property rights.
2. Unravel the role of the entrepreneur in the economy.
3. Explain the basic reasons business firms exist.
4. Understand the advantages and disadvantages of corporations, partnerships, and sole proprietorships.
5. Explain the difference between stocks and bonds.
6. Understand how stocks are valued on the stock market.
7. Explain how the stock market promotes profit maximization.

CHAPTER PUZZLE: If interest rates rise, the value of corporations on the stock markets falls. Why?

Property Rights

Property is anything that has an exchange value, that is, a price for the marketplace for goods, services, and ideas. Every society through its laws, customs, and social conventions specifies the rules of the game. These rules are the property rights that people have over the use of all goods and services. The right to use a piece of land to grow wheat, the right to use a particular frequency to broadcast a radio program, and the right to create an Internet site are valuable resources that can be exchanged.

Property rights specify how resources can be used, who can use them, and how they can be transferred to other people.

Private property prevails in resources if the owner or owners have the exclusive right to use the resources and sell or transfer those rights to other people. Property is anything that has value to another person, and property rights include the power to use the property according to the will of the owners. It is property rights that give value to all the future uses to which goods or services can be put. How property rights have developed is a long and complicated story.[1] According to the Fourteenth Amendment to the U.S. Constitution, "No State . . . can deprive any person of life, liberty, or property, without due process of law." The word *liberty* means that the citizen is free to enjoy his or her faculties in all lawful ways, choosing where to live and how to earn his or her livelihood, and to enter contracts that achieve these objectives. Generally speaking, an economic activity is lawful so long as it does not interfere with someone else's right to use their property. For example, it is illegal for you to set up an Internet site that sends a computer virus to someone using your site. If you set up a business firm that is so noisy that another business firm cannot operate, you have infringed on the other firm's physical right to use its property.

The right to use your property as you see fit *does* allow you to reduce the exchange value of someone

[1]See John R. Commons, *The Legal Foundations of Capitalism* (New York: The Macmillan Co., 1924), ch. 2.

else's property through your own access to markets. For example, if you invent a new operating system (such as Linux) that competes with Microsoft's Windows operating system, and thereby lower the profits of Microsoft and the wealth of Bill Gates, you have not infringed on Bill Gates's property rights. Private property rights are merely a promise to have access to markets. You can open a restaurant next door to an established restaurant, driving it bankrupt by offering better food or service at a reasonable price, but you cannot drive a truck through its kitchen.

Entrepreneurs

In a private enterprise economy, entrepreneurs are the driving force of the economic system. The entrepreneur is the one who tries to peer into the future, gather the financing to attract the resources necessary for the project, and then direct those resources to produce the corresponding goods and services. To accomplish the goals of the entrepreneur, a business firm is created or a new product or service is made available through an established business firm. The entrepreneur cannot be sure that there is a profit in this endeavor. It is not possible to know in advance whether the venture will be profitable. The farmer must buy the seed and rent the land before selling the wheat; the software company must pay someone to develop the new word processing program before selling it. Many people will try, and only a few will succeed.

The **entrepreneur** sets up a business firm or creates a new product or service for the purpose of making a future profit.

Famous entrepreneurs of the late twentieth century include Steve Jobs (Apple Computer), Bill Gates (Microsoft), ad Sam Walton (Wal-Mart). In earlier days it was Andrew Carnegie (steel) and Henry Ford (cars). We hear about the handful of successes but not about the many failures. The Forbes 400, a listing of the 400 richest Americans, has shown an average annual turnover rate (new members) of about 10 percent.[2] In 1985, the traditional industries of manufacturing, oil, and real estate made up 60 percent of the Forbes 400. The recent explosion in high-tech and the Internet has shaken things up considerably. In 1999, traditional industries such as steel or cars comprised only 16 percent of the Forbes 400, with technology, finance, and media/entertainment dominating the list. The turnover rate on the Forbes 400 rose from 10 percent to 20 percent. Most people on the list are self-made. We live in a dynamic society totally unlike the feudalism of the Middle Ages in which people simply did what their parents did and lived within a twenty-mile radius for their entire lives.

Economist Joseph Schumpeter (1883–1950) stressed the role of the entrepreneur in both the creative and destructive forces in the economy: "The fundamental impulse that keeps the capitalist engine in motion comes from new consumers' goods, new methods of production or transportation, the new markets, the new forms of industrial organization that capitalist enterprise creates." To Schumpeter the essential fact about capitalism is the process of "creative destruction" that takes place when new goods and processes replace old goods and processes.

Why Business Firms Exist

The business firm is the organizational device by which entrepreneurs carry out their manifold activities. Although it is possible for entrepreneurs to work entirely through markets without organizing business firms, such instances are rare. An entrepreneur could build a home by contracting through markets with carpenters, plumbers, electricians, and lumber and glass suppliers. Most homes are not built this way. They are built by construction firms, whose owners or managers direct employees—carpenters, electricians, and unskilled laborers—to perform particular tasks.

Almost all output is produced by business firms. Business firms have common features irrespective of their specific form of organization. They have an owner or owners. They have a manager, who may or may not be the same as the owner. Most have employees, and they have resources that can be directed by the firm's managers.

Resources are allocated within the firm by managerial coordination.

Managerial coordination is the disposition of the firm's resources according to the directives of the firm's manager(s).

[2]"America's 400 Richest People," *Forbes* (October 11, 1999), p. 49.

All business firms need a person or persons to make managerial decisions. The firm's managers allocate the capital and land owned or leased by the firm and issue directives to employees who work according to written or unwritten contracts.

A **principal** has controlling authority and engages an agent to act subject to the principal's control and instruction.

An **agent** acts for, on behalf of, or as a representative of a principal.

If IBM signs a contract with American Airlines to upgrade its computer reservations, American Airlines is the principal and IBM the agent. If Jim, the owner of Jim's Motorcycle Repair, hires Bob to work as a repairman and sales clerk, Jim is the principal and Bob is the agent.

Once the principal and agent agree on terms, the principal must ensure that the agent fulfills the terms of the agreement. If the principal and agent have different goals, conflicts between the principal and agent are possible. Business firms must find effective ways of monitoring and controlling their agents.

There are four main reasons for having business firms: They can limit the costs of market transactions, take advantage of economies of scale, bear risk individuals are unwilling to bear, and provide monitoring of team production.

Limiting the Costs of Using Markets

Nobel laureate Ronald Coase[3] argued that as long as the cost of organizing an activity inside the firm is below the cost of organizing that activity using markets, the task will be carried out within the firm. Market coordination has its costs. Market-coordinated activities require contracts, paperwork, searching for the best prices, and paying legal expenses if contracts are not fulfilled. Imagine, for example, the enormous transactions costs of using market coordination to produce a modern commercial jet aircraft. Thousands of subcontracts would have to be negotiated to produce the instruments, the hydraulic control systems, the airframe, and the interior furnishings. Managerial coordination can reduce these transactions costs. Instead of negotiating thousands of market contracts, the manager simply directs employees to perform designated tasks, allocates the plant and equipment of the business enterprise, and works with fewer subcontractors. It is easier for Jim to hire Bob as a repairman/sales clerk on a year's contract than to go out and hire someone on a daily basis in the labor market.

A major cost reduction from using an identifiable business firm is the cost of acquiring information about new products, processes, and workers. Workers and ideas are attracted to business firms. Few people would take a good idea to someone outside of a firm—both large and small. Moreover, a firm is a specialized institution for collecting information that is relevant to the particular goods or services being provided. IBM is famous for the motto "Think," which it posts at various points in the workplace. The people working for IBM are thinking about a narrow range of issues and accumulating information specific to the firm's products. There are also benefits from working close to people in the same field. In universities, for example, it is better to have everyone in an economics or mathematics department in close proximity than to have department members spread all over the campus. In a firm, the manager may have a comparative advantage or experience in finding information. When the manager shares her sources with employees, they can contribute more to the discovery of relevant information about markets or products. Having people work in the same place or under a central management is a cheaper way to collect in formation than going to outside markets to discover information on a piece-by-piece basis.

Taking Advantage of Economies of Scale

As Adam Smith pointed out more than 200 years ago, business firms can take advantage of *economies of scale.*

Economies of scale are present when large output volumes can be produced at a lower cost per unit than small output volumes.

Economies of scale are present in many production processes (you are already acquainted with Smith's example of a pin factory). The business firm brings together workers, land, and capital: The manager directs workers to specialize in different tasks;

[3]Ronald H. Coase, "The Nature of the Firm," *Economica* 4 (1937): 386–405. Reprinted in George Stigler and Kenneth Boulding, eds., *Readings in Price Theory* (Homewood, IL: Richard D. Irwin, 1952).

output is produced in larger production runs and at a lower cost per unit. In order for Jim to repair motorcycles at a reasonable cost, he may need a number of employees in addition to Bob to perform specialized repair tasks and handle a larger volume of business.

Bearing the Risk

In his classic study, Frank Knight emphasized that some individuals are more willing to bear risk than others.[4] Business ventures typically involve risk (demand can change, prices can fluctuate, and so on). The owner of the enterprise (the principal) is willing to bear the risk. The employees (the agents) are not. The employer hires workers and rents land and equipment at negotiated prices. In return for this security, employees agree to follow the owner's business directives. If the business is successful, the owner will reap the rewards; if it fails, the owner will suffer the consequences. The business firm exists because it provides a convenient way for those who are willing to bear risk—the entrepreneurs—to do so.

Monitoring Team Production

In another classic study of business organization, Armen Alchian and Harold Demsetz noted that business enterprises are formed when there are gains from team production.[5] In many cases, employees working as a team can produce more output than can employees working alone.

If team production is used, the performance of individual employees must be monitored by the owner/manager to ensure that no employees are shirking their responsibility. Because the owner of a firm is paid out of the gains of team production, the owner will be motivated to do a good job of monitoring. If Bob and Julie work together as a team to repair motorcycles, Jim, the owner, may have to monitor their work to make sure that both members of the team are working effectively.

Team monitoring is essential when agents and principals have different goals. The principal wants to earn a maximum profit. Employees may want a lighter work load. Hired managers may value job security more than profits.

Profit Maximization

Capitalism and socialism provide different visions of the way economies should work. In Adam Smith's view of capitalism, it is healthy for business firms to pursue their self-interest in the form of profits. The profit motive causes them to pursue society's interests while pursuing their own narrow goals. In Karl Marx's view of capitalism, the selfish pursuit of profits will lead to exploitation, misery, and socialist revolution.

What is the goal of a business firm? The objective of business firms is profit maximization.

Profit maximization is the search by firms for the product quality, output, and price that give the firm the highest possible profits.

Some economists have questioned whether firms do indeed maximize profits. Perhaps firms are interested in other things, like maximizing sales or growth of employment.

Natural selection theory argues that profit maximization must be the overriding objective of business firms. (See Example 1.)

According to the **natural selection theory**, if business firms do not maximize profits, they will be unable to compete with other firms and will be driven out of the market or taken over by outsiders.

Any firm that does not seek to maximize profits may be forced to close its doors when competitors offer higher-quality products at lower cost. The natural selection argument is compelling in the case of firms that face competition. It is less compelling for businesses that are insulated from competition. Business firms that do not earn maximum profits run another risk: They can be taken over by outsiders who can earn higher profits.

Our experience of the last century is that the profit motive is indeed the prime motivator for business. The industrial pioneers who initiated the Industrial Revolution were motivated by profits. The founders of the great businesses over the past century have been motivated by profits. Experience

---

[4] Frank H. Knight, *Risk, Uncertainty, and Profit* (New York: Harper Torchbooks, 1957).

[5] Armen Alchian and Harold Demsetz, "Production, Information Costs, and Economic Organization," *American Economic Review* 57, no. 5 (December 1972): 777–795.

EXAMPLE 1

The Profit Motive Spurs Flexibility

The two largest stock markets in the United States, the New York Stock Exchange and the Nasdaq market, switched from being nonprofit to for-profit corporations in 1999. Why, after more than a century of being organized as a country club, would the New York Stock Exchange want to become a for-profit, publicly traded company? The basic reason is technological change: The rise of electronic trading on the Internet and the growing popularity of dividend reinvestment plans, in which the public can buy stock directly from companies, made it necessary for the stock exchanges to reorganize themselves along for-profit lines.

In a country club atmosphere, decision making becomes bogged down in committees, and without the pressure to maximize profits that comes from being a publicly traded company, adaptation to change takes place at a snail's pace. Country clubs cover expenses by charging fees to members, and to provide more tennis courts or better greens on the golf course, a large board must make a decision without the force of profit pushing them in the right direction. The decision may be made on the basis of who has the loudest voice.

When a company is for-profit and the company can be purchased on the open market (the definition of a publicly traded company), the company management must try to maximize profit in order to keep the stockholders happy. This goal makes for quicker and better decision making because those in control have a clearer objective than that of making a few club members happy. For example, if a nonprofit corporation wants to expand, it must raise its member fees. But a for-profit corporation can sell stock in the company. Profit is a clear objective; if a company is for-profit and it does not maximize profit, the board of directors may find itself on the outside looking in.

Source: "Two Top Markets Ready to Become Public Companies," *New York Times* (July 24, 1999).

also confirms Joseph Schumpeter's insight about creative destruction, discussed earlier in this chapter. No firm's profits are secure forever. All businesses must eventually face the "creative destruction" of competition.

Forms of Business Organization

Business enterprises are classified into three categories: sole proprietorships, partnerships, and corporations. The form a business enterprise takes determines who makes business decisions, how capital is raised, who bears the risk of business failures, and how principal/agent problems are resolved.

Sole Proprietorships

The sole proprietorship is the least complex form of business enterprise.

The **sole proprietorship** is owned by one individual.

Advantages. The first advantage of the sole proprietorship is that decision-making authority is clear-cut: It resides with the owner. In making business decisions, the owner need not consult anyone.

The second advantage of the sole proprietorship is that it is easy to establish—there are no agreements with other owners.

The third advantage is that the profits of the company accrue to the owner; unlike the profits of a corporation, the earnings of a sole proprietorship are taxed only once as personal income.

Disadvantages. The main disadvantage of the sole proprietorship is that the owner must assume unlimited liability (responsibility) for the debts of the company.

The owner enjoys the profit of the business if it is successful; the owner is personally liable if the business suffers a loss. Unlimited liability explains why most proprietorships are small. Their owners raise capital by reinvesting profits; by dipping into personal wealth to invest in the company; or by borrowing from relatives, friends, and lending institutions. The firm's borrowing power is limited by the owner's earning capacity and personal wealth. Lending to an individual proprietorship can be risky. If the proprietor dies, becomes incapacitated, or declares bankruptcy, the lender must stand in line with other creditors.

Partnerships

A partnership is much like an individual proprietorship, but it has more than one owner.

A **partnership** is owned by two or more people called partners, who make all the business decisions, share the profits, and bear the financial responsibility for any losses.

Advantages. The advantages of partnerships are much like those of the sole proprietorship. Partnerships are usually easy to set up. The profits of the company accrue to the partners and are taxed only once as part of their personal income.

Partnerships, however, provide greater opportunity to specialize and divide managerial responsibility. The partner who is the better salesperson will be in charge of sales. The partner who is a talented mechanical engineer will be in charge of production. Each partner offers different talents. A partnership also can raise more financial capital because the wealth and borrowing power of more than one person can be mobilized. If a large number of wealthy partners can be assembled, large sums of capital can be raised.

Disadvantages. First, the partners have unlimited liability for the debts of the partnership. A business debt incurred by any of the partners is the responsibility of the partnership. Each partner stands to lose personal wealth if the company is a failure. A conflict in goals can arise when one partner is more risk-averse (or lazier) than another. For this reason, partnerships are often made up of family members, relatives, and close personal friends.

Second, decision making can become complicated if partners disagree. Partnerships can be immobilized when partners disagree on fundamental policy. Decision making becomes more complicated as the number of partners grows.

Third, partnerships can be unstable. If disagreements over policy cause one partner to withdraw, the partnership may have to be reorganized. When one partner dies, the partnership agreement may have to be renegotiated.

Corporations

The *corporation* came into existence to overcome the disadvantages of the sole proprietorship and the partnership.

A **corporation** is a business enterprise that has the status of a legal person and is authorized by federal and state law to act as a single person.

The corporation is owned by stockholders who possess shares of stock in the corporation. The stockholders elect a board of directors that appoints the management of the corporation. A stockholder's share of ownership of the corporation equals the number of shares owned by that individual divided by the total number of shares outstanding (owned by stockholders). If you own 100,000 shares of AT&T stock and there are 630 million AT&T shares outstanding, then you own 0.016 percent of AT&T. The corporate management determines whether to reinvest profits or disburse them as dividends. The stockholder who owns 1 percent of the stock of AT&T will receive 1 percent of the dividends paid to shareholders.

Common stock, preferred stock, and convertible stock are three types of corporate stock.

Common stock confers voting privileges and the right to receive dividends only if they are declared by the board of directors.

Preferred stock does not give voting privileges, but corporations must pay dividends on preferred stock before paying those on common stock.

Convertible stock pays the owner fixed interest payments and gives the privilege of converting the convertible stock into common stock at a fixed rate of exchange.

Corporations can have thousands or millions of shares outstanding, owned by a large number of stockholders. Billionaire H. Ross Perot's 11 million shares of General Motors stock made him GM's largest shareholder (with 2 percent of GM stock) before he sold his shares. In closely held corporations, the number of stockholders is limited, and each stockholder owns a substantial share of the corporation's stock.

Stockholders typically do not participate directly in the running of most corporations. There are too many shareholders, and they are too involved in their own business affairs. For these reasons, there is usually a separation of ownership and management. The board of directors appoints a management team that makes decisions for the corporation. If the corporation is unsuccessful, the stockholders may vote out the current board of directors, or the board of directors itself may decide to bring in a new management team.

Stockholders, however, can exercise substantial indirect control over management by simply selling their stock. The sale of stock by enough dissatisfied stockholders will depress the share price.

Advantages. The first advantage of the corporation is that its stockholders are not personally liable for its debts. If a corporation cannot meet its debts, its creditors can lay claim to its assets (bank accounts, equipment, supplies, buildings, and real estate holdings), but they cannot file claims against the stockholders. The worst case for stockholders is that their stock becomes worthless. (See Example 2.)

Limited liability contributes to a second advantage: Corporations can raise large sums of financial capital by selling corporate bonds, issuing stock, and borrowing from lending institutions. (We shall discuss the details of how corporations raise capital later in the chapter.)

The third advantage of the corporation is its status as a legal person distinct from the officers of the corporation. A change in the board of directors, the resignation of the current president, or a transfer of ownership can destroy a partnership or sole proprietorship, but these events do not alter the legal status of the corporation. Continuity is also an advantage in raising financial capital. Lending institutions are willing to make long-term loans to a corporation because they expect the corporation to outlive its current owners and officers. Continuity also makes it easier for the corporation to hire a career-minded labor force.

The fourth advantage of the corporation is that owners (individuals with money to invest) do not always make the best managers. Talented officers who own little company stock can be brought into the corporation as managers.

Disadvantages. A first disadvantage of the corporation is its complexity. A modern corporation can have thousands or even millions of stockholders. Ownership can be so dispersed that it is difficult to mobilize the owners or get them to resolve important issues. Power struggles among shareholder factions can paralyze decision making. The costs of gathering information about the complex dealings of the corporation are high to individual shareholders, who are often poorly informed about the corporation.

A second disadvantage of the corporation is the possibility of conflicting objectives between the principals (the shareholders) and the agents (the management team). Shareholders are interested in maximizing the long-run profits of the corporation (thereby getting the best return from their shares of stock). The management team may be more interested in preserving their jobs or in maximizing their personal income or fringe benefits than in profit maximization.

A third disadvantage of the corporate form in the United States is the double taxation of corporate profits. The profits of the corporation can either be distributed to shareholders as dividends or be kept as retained earnings to be reinvested. The corporation must pay corporate income taxes on its profits. If the corporation chooses to reinvest all profits, corporate profits will be taxed only once, but if it distributes some of its profits to shareholders as dividends, shareholders must pay personal income tax on these dividends. Therefore, a portion of corporate profits can be taxed twice—first by the corporate income tax and second by the personal income tax.

The advantages and disadvantages of each business form are summarized in Table 1.

However, the disadvantages of the corporation are insignificant compared to its ability to grow far beyond what is practical with proprietorships or partnerships. A corporation is fundamentally a way to share property rights among many people without being overwhelmed by the principal/agent problem. Separating ownership from control saves on the cost of coordinating the decisions of millions of stockholders; and putting the stock of the company for

EXAMPLE 2

How Unlimited Liability Almost Ruined Lloyd's of London

Lloyd's of London was founded in the late seventeenth century by a group of merchants, ship-owners, and insurance brokers who met regularly at the coffee house of Edward Lloyd. It grew to become the largest international provider of marine insurance and other types of risk insurance, such as airline insurance.

Lloyd's of London made its reputation on its willingness to insure virtually anything. Lloyd's insured an actress's legs, renowned jewels, and hazardous shipments. Lloyd's was one of the last great businesses that operated on the basis of unlimited liability. Various insurance packages were underwritten by "Names"—individual investors who had to make good on claims, even if they had to use all their personal assets to do so.

The Names were organized into some 300 syndicates or partnerships that would insure various activities.

The years 1991 and 1992 were disastrous for the insurance industry. The Gulf War, numerous natural disasters and airline crashes, and product liability claims caused billions of dollars of losses for Lloyd's of London insurance syndicates. Lloyd's of London Names had to sell virtually all their personal assets to cover these losses. One Name—a former heavyweight boxing champion—had to sell his championship belts. Other Names had to sell their noble titles and their estates.

As a consequence of these losses, Lloyd's of London is no longer willing to insure many high-risk activities. Policies that were previously sold by Lloyd's of London are no longer available. Lloyd's of London is now considering restructuring the company because of the feature of unlimited liability. In the future, the venerable company could well be a corporation with its stock listed on major stock exchanges.

Source: "Clubhouse for Sale," *The Economist* (August 14, 1999)

sale in a free and open market causes the management to have the same goal as the stockholder.

The Stock Market and the Goals of the Corporation

The major principal/agent problem faced by the corporation is that the management and stockholders may have different goals. The management is the agent of the stockholders. The management wants to maximize its income; the stockholders want to maximize the value of the stock. Suppose, to take the extreme case, that management owns only a few percent of the outstanding stock and that the rest of the stock is held by millions of investors. How can the millions control the few? What is to prevent the managers from paying themselves exorbitant salaries, milking the corporation of its assets, and retiring to beach homes in Hawaii?

This problem of the separation of ownership (stockholders) from control (management) is neatly solved by the stock market and the institutional practices of corporations. Here's how it works: The management knows that a corporate raider can buy enough shares to oust them. Managers can lose their jobs very quickly, as the president of Compaq Computer Corporation learned in 1999, even though

TABLE 1 TYPES OF BUSINESS ORGANIZATION

Type of Firm	*Advantages*	*Disadvantages*
Sole Proprietorship	1. The business is simple to set up. 2. Decision making is clear-cut; the owner makes the decisions. 3. Earnings are taxed only once, as personal income.	1. The owner has unlimited liability; the owner's personal wealth is at risk. 2. The company has a limited ability to raise financial capital.
Partnership	1. The business is relatively easy to set up. 2. More management skills are available; two heads are better than one. 3. Earnings are taxed only once, as the personal income of the partners.	1. There is unlimited liability for the partners. 2. Decision making can be complicated. 3. Partnerships can be unstable.
Corporation	1. There is limited liability for owners. 2. The company is able to raise large sums of capital through issuing bonds and stock. 3. The company has an eternal life. 4. The company is able to recruit professional management and to change bad management.	1. There are greater possibilities for management disagreements. 2. There is the possibility of conflicting goals between the owners of the corporation (the *principals*) and management (the *agents*). 3. Corporate income is taxed twice: first as corporate profits and second as personal income (dividends).

there is no takeover attempt. The mechanism is the stock price. First, the board of directors decides to give the management team stock options that enable the top executives to buy the stock for a set price at a specified future date. If the company is highly profitable, the stock price will rise, giving a bonus to the holders of stock options. This may sound like opportunism, but it is a device that forces the top executives to have the same objectives as the stockholders. Second, if the stock price falls too low, a group can buy the stock and install a new board of directors and management team. When the stock price falls due to poor performance, the board of directors will try to replace the management team before they themselves are replaced. Thus, stock options give the management team the incentive to be as productive as possible in order to prevent a corporate takeover and to increase the value of their stock options.

Business Enterprises in the U.S. Economy

In the United States, there are about 20 million business enterprises. The overwhelming majority of these are proprietorships (70 percent); the rest are corporations (20 percent) and partnerships (10 percent). Although proprietorships dominate in number, their share of total business revenues is relatively small, accounting for only 6 percent. Corporations, on the other hand, account for 90 percent of business revenues.

Proprietorships are concentrated in the trade and services industries, where small family businesses are common. Corporations are prevalent in manufacturing and trade. Partnerships are active in trade, finance, and services industries.

The large corporation accounts for the most business sales and profits. The absolute size of giant U.S. corporations is awesome. The annual sales of large U.S. industrial corporations—such as General Motors, IBM, and ExxonMobil—exceed the annual output of many industrial economies. The annual sales of General Motors, for example, equal the annual production of Belgium. The combined annual sales of the six largest U.S. industrial corporations exceed the annual production of the United Kingdom. The sales rankings of giant U.S. corporations change with the fortunes of the company and the industry.

The Multinational Corporation

As early as the late 1800s, many large U.S. companies operated internationally. Singer licensed a French company to manufacture its sewing machines, Westinghouse started a shop in Paris, Western Electric set up an affiliate in Belgium, and Eastman incorporated a company in London to manufacture film. These international ventures were early examples of multinational corporations.

A **multinational corporation** engages in foreign markets through its own affiliates located abroad, and it pursues business strategies that transcend national boundaries.

As we discussed in Chapter 1, globalization of the world economy is a Defining Moment of economics. The first multinational corporations were formed during the Industrial Revolution. Since World War II, the barriers to international trade and capital movements have been reduced. International markets for goods, services, and capital are replacing national markets. Business enterprises that previously had to compete only with other domestic companies now must compete with companies from Japan, Germany, Taiwan, or Mexico. (See Table 2.)

The multinational corporation moves capital, technology, and entrepreneurial skills from areas where they are abundant to areas where they are scarce; it spreads throughout the world new ideas, new products, and new ways of organizing production. German and Swiss chemical companies introduce their products, ideas, and management skills to their affiliates in Taiwan and Brazil. Japanese automobile manufacturers introduce their manufacturing and quality control techniques to their U.S. affiliates.

Large corporations are no longer confined to the borders of their home country. They have foreign affiliates and foreign employees, and nationals from other countries are on their boards of directors. The multinational corporation has become an important instrument of change in the world economy.

Raising Capital for the Corporation

Corporations have an advantage in raising financial capital. Like proprietorships and partnerships, corporations can borrow and they can reinvest profits. In addition, corporations can raise capital by selling bonds or additional shares of stock.

Corporate **bonds** are obligations to repay the principal at maturity and to make annual interest payments until the maturity date.

Selling Bonds

By selling bonds, corporations acquire funds to finance business expansions. Once a bond is sold, the buyer can resell it, but such sales in the bond market do not add to the corporation's financial capital.

The interest or principal payments on corporate bonds represent a legal obligation for the corporation, just as with any other debt. The purchaser of the bond has loaned the corporation money, and the corporation has promised to pay specified interest payments until maturity. Interest payments on corporate bonds have a claim on company earnings prior to dividends.

Issuing Stock

A second means of raising financial capital is for the corporation to sell additional shares of stock. Suppose XYZ Corporation has 100,000 shares of stock that are already owned by stockholders. Each share of stock currently sells for $10 on the secondary market

TABLE 2 THE LARGEST 25 GLOBAL COMPANIES, 1999

Rank	*Global Company*	*Revenues, $ Millions*
1	General Motors	161,315.0
2	DaimlerChrysler	154,615.0
3	Ford Motor	144,416.0
4	Wal-Mart Stores	139,208.0
5	Mitsui	109,372.9
6	Itochu	108,749.1
7	Mitsubishi	107,184.4
8	Exxon	100,697.0
9	General Electric	100,469.0
10	Toyota Motor	99,740.1
11	Royal Dutch/Shell Group	93,692.0
12	Marubeni	93,568.6
13	Sumitomo	89,020.7
14	Intl. Business Machines	81,667.0
15	AXA	78,729.3
16	Citigroup	76,431.0
17	Volkswagen	76,306.6
18	Nippon Telegraph and Telephone	76,118.7
19	BP Amoco	68,304.0
20	Nissho Iwai	67,741.7
21	Nippon Life Insurance	66,299.6
22	Siemens	66,037.8
23	Allianz	64,874.7
24	Hitachi	62,409.9
25	U.S. Postal Service	60,072.0

Source: Fortune, April 1999.

for stock. (We shall discuss financial markets in the next section of the chapter.)

The corporation decides that it needs to raise $500,000 to build a new plant and arranges with an investment bank or an underwriter to sell 50,000 new shares of stock to investors. The company prepares a prospectus to describe to potential buyers the financial condition of the company and the proposed uses for the funds.

The amount of money investors will be willing to pay for the 50,000 new shares reflects their assessment of how the proposed investment will affect the earnings of XYZ Corporation. If investors expect the new plant to raise company earnings substantially, they will offer a higher price than if they expect the investment to have a small effect.

Suppose that XYZ Corporation can sell the 50,000 new shares at the $10-per-share price. XYZ Corporation raises $500,000 through the stock issue. By contrast with corporate bonds, which legally obligate the corporation to pay fixed interest payments, stocks convey no obligation to pay dividends.

Stocks or Bonds?

The main advantage of issuing new stock is that it does not obligate the corporation to make interest payments. If the corporation is doing well, it can declare a dividend for its shareholders; if it is doing poorly, shareholders must do without a dividend.

Such is not the case with bonds. Bonds obligate the corporation to make interest payments no matter what. During bad times, the corporation may not be able to afford these interest payments. The selling of bonds is thus risky for corporations. If they have large amounts of interest payments to make each year, they become very susceptible to the ups and downs of business. (See Example 3.)

EXAMPLE 3

The Market for High-Yield Bonds

High-yield or "junk" bonds have a higher risk of default than bonds of the highest quality. Credit rating agencies consider the financial strength of a company. The highest quality bonds are rated AAA. The credit scale descends to C and, finally, to the D or default category.

Before the 1980s, junk bonds were considered "fallen angels" that resulted from a decline in the credit quality of former higher quality bonds. But then modern economics showed that bonds of lower quality can actually reduce the overall risk of a portfolio that contains a variety of assets. If an asset pays a risky return that is not correlated with the returns of other less risky assets, combining the assets in a portfolio can actually lower overall risk and raise returns.

In light of this new theory, financiers or underwriters began to be more creative, leading to the issuance of junk bonds to finance all sorts of businesses. For example, Ted Turner's cable television networks were started by the creative efforts of Michael Milken, who led a revolution in the junk financing business. Although this ended in scandal, the variety and number of high-yield bonds are currently a valuable part of the U.S. capital market. Today, investors are advised to keep a small portion of their portfolio in higher-risk bonds. Some consider Milken a predator; others consider him a benefactor of humanity because he financed many new businesses that have contributed to the great efficiency of the U.S. economy.

The big question that any economy must answer is, What will be produced? This is determined by profit-seeking capitalists investing in different enterprises and businesses. Because of the risk characteristics of different businesses, a wide variety of financial instruments are necessary. Junk bonds are one way to finance profitable businesses that have a chance of going bankrupt or making large profits.

Source: Daniel Fischel, *Payback: The Conspiracy to Destroy Michael Milken and His Financial Revolution* (New York: HarperCollins, 1995).

FINANCIAL MARKETS

Corporate stocks and bonds are traded in financial markets, often called capital markets. It is capital markets that provide the funds required for industrial expansion and growth. Corporate stocks are traded in stock markets, or stock exchanges; corporate bonds are traded in bond markets. The prices of stocks and bonds are determined in these markets.

A **bond market** is a market in which bonds of different types are traded. Bond markets buy and sell corporate bonds and bonds of governmental organizations.

A **stock exchange** is a market in which shares of stock of corporations are bought and sold and in which the prices of shares of stock are determined.

Although there are many organized financial markets around the world, the most important stock and bond exchanges are located in New York City, London, Denver, Frankfurt, Tokyo, Zurich, and Paris. The world's largest stock exchange is located on New York City's Wall Street: the New York Stock Exchange (NYSE). The NYSE lists about 50 billion shares of stock, and most days millions of shares worth billions of dollars change hands. The shares of the largest American and multinational corporations are traded on the NYSE.

Present Value

Because bonds make specified payments over a specified period of time, there must be a common denominator. A \$100 interest payment made today has a different value from one made 10 years from now. We cannot understand bond pricing without first understanding the present value of money.

For the sake of simplicity, assume that the annual interest rate is 10 percent. If you deposit \$100 in a savings account, it will earn \$10 interest at the end of 1 year. At 10 percent interest, \$100 today will be equal to \$110 a year from now. If the interest rate is 5 percent, \$100 today will be equal to \$105 a year from now.

What should you be willing to pay today in order to receive \$110 in 1 year? At 10 percent interest, the most you should be willing to pay is \$100. Why? Investing more than \$100 at 10 percent interest yields more than \$110 at the end of 1 year. Thus, the present value (PV) of \$110 in one year's time is \$100 at 10 percent interest.

The **present value (PV)** is the most anyone would pay today to receive the money in the future.

The price of a bond that promises to make specified payment at specified future dates will be the present value of those payments. The present value (PV) of each dollar to be paid in 1 year at the interest rate i (i stands for the rate of interest in decimals) is

$$PV = \frac{\$1}{1 + i}$$

If the interest rate is 10 percent, then $i = 0.10$ and $1 + i = 1.10$. The PV of each dollar equals \$0.9091. If \$10,000 is to be paid in 1 year, its PV today equals \$9,091 (\$10,000 times 0.9091).

The present-value formula becomes more complicated when the repayment period is greater than 1 year.[6] We can generalize to show that the present value of a sum to be received in 3 years is that sum divided by $(1 + i)^3$; the present value of a dollar to be received in n years is

$$PV = \frac{\$1}{(1 + i)^n}$$

At a 10 percent interest rate, \$100 received 1 year from now has a present value of \$90.91; \$100 to be received 5 years from now has a present value of only \$62.27. The longer the repayment period, the lower the present value.

The farther in the future the money is to be paid, the lower is its present value.

---

[6]To understand this general formula, consider the following: At an interest rate of 10 percent, how much money do you have to deposit today to have \$121 at the end of 2 years? If the sum PV is deposited at interest rate i, it will be worth $PV \times (1 + i)$ 1 year from now. At the end of the second year, it will be worth $PV \times (1 + i) \times (1 + i)$, or $PV(1 + i)^2$. Setting the sum $PV(1 + i)^2$ equal to \$121 and dividing by $(1 + i)^2$ yields

$$PV = \frac{\$121}{(1 + i)^2}$$

At 10 percent interest, the present value of \$121 to be received 2 years from now is \$100 (= \$121/1.1[2]).

Bond Prices

Present value falls as the interest rate rises. In the preceding example, the present value of \$121 to be received in 2 years is \$100 at an interest rate of 10 percent—that is, $\$121 \div 1.1^2 = \$100$. At an interest rate of 20 percent, the PV of \$121 to be received 2 years from now falls to \$84; that is, $\$121 \div 1.2^2 = \$84$.

> The present value of a dollar to be received in the future falls as the interest rate rises, and rises as the interest rate falls.

Bond prices fall when interest rates rise; they rise when interest rates fall. Buyers and sellers in bond markets therefore try to anticipate whether interest rates will rise or fall in the future. If bond dealers suspect that interest rates are going to rise, they sell their bond holdings and bond prices drop. It is for this reason that bond dealers and speculators expend so much effort trying to anticipate what will happen to interest rates.

Because corporate bondholders have prior claim on company earnings, bonds offer a relatively secure return. Bondholders will receive their interest and principal payments so long as the corporation does not become bankrupt.

Corporate bonds are not riskless because bond prices fluctuate in the bond market. If the bond owner sells the bond before the date of maturity, the price received for the bond may well be less than the price paid for the bond. Bond prices are the present value (PV) of interest and principal payments. However, there is an inverse relationship between interest rates and present values. As interest rates rise, investors will pay less for the stream of interest payments offered by a bond. As interest rates fall, investors will pay more for the stream of interest payments offered by the bond.

Stock Prices

Stock exchanges bring together buyers and sellers of a particular stock—for example, shares of IBM. The number of shares of IBM stock outstanding is fixed (unless IBM decides to issue new shares of stock), and the current owners of these shares will be prepared to sell their shares at different prices. The supply curve of IBM shares is shown as curve *S* in Figure 1. The higher the price, the greater the number of IBM shares current owners will be prepared to sell; thus, the supply curve is positively sloped. The demand curve for IBM shares, curve *D*, is negatively sloped. The lower the share price, the greater the number of IBM shares people will be prepared to buy. The equilibrium price of IBM shares is that price at which the number of shares demanded equals the number of shares supplied. The equilibrium number of shares traded is referred to as the volume of IBM transactions.

The different assessments of the future profits of the corporation determine the supply and demand curves of Figure 1. The share owner receives dividends that the corporation pays out of profits (if any) and benefits from reinvested profits, which may increase future profits. Share prices, therefore, depend upon the present and future earnings of the corporation. Present earnings are known, but future earnings are uncertain. People have different views of the future of a particular corporation. Some see a

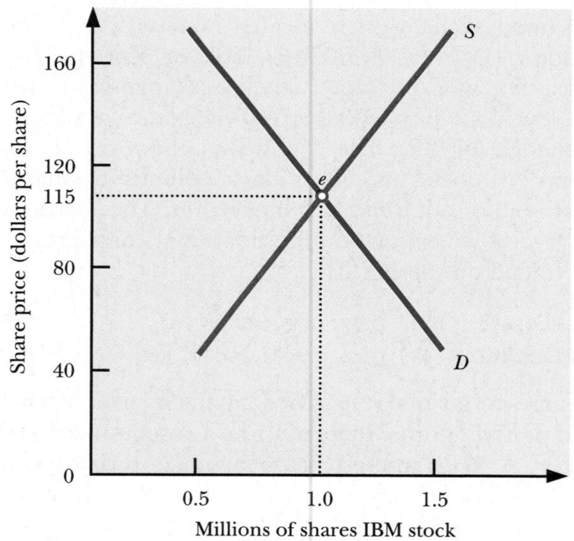

FIGURE 1 Determination of IBM Stock Prices

This figure diagrams the supply (*S*) and demand (*D*) curves for shares of IBM stock on February 11, 2000. The supply curve is positively sloped because owners of IBM stock offer more shares for sale at high prices than at low prices. The demand curve is negatively sloped because buyers of IBM shares are prepared to buy more at low prices than at high prices. The equilibrium price is that price at which the quantity demanded equals the quantity supplied. Share prices fluctuate daily because of shifts in demand and supply. The equilibrium price reflects the consensus present value of the future earnings per share of IBM.

bright future of rising profits and dividends; others, a bleak future of declining economic fortunes.

The price of a share of stock depends upon the anticipated future profits per share of outstanding stock, called earnings per share. *Earnings per share (EPS)* is the annual profit of the corporation divided by the number of shares outstanding. Suppose Jones, an optimist, expects earnings per share of XYZ Corporation to be \$10 from now until eternity. Smith, a pessimist, expects earnings per share of XYZ Corporation to be \$5 from now until eternity. The anticipated future profits of XYZ Corporation need to be converted by both Jones and Smith into a present value.

Take Jones's assumption that one share of XYZ Corporation will earn \$10 per year forever—that is, it will provide a *perpetual stream* of income. How much is that \$10 per year worth in present value? If the interest rate is 10 percent, \$100 will earn \$10 per year. This \$100 is the *present value* of the \$10 perpetual stream. If the interest rate fell to 5 percent, \$200 will earn \$10 a year in perpetuity. Hence \$200 is the present value at 5 percent interest.

The general formula for calculating the present value (PV) of a perpetual stream of corporate earnings per share is:

$$PV = \frac{R}{i}$$

where R = the annual earnings per share. At an interest rate of 10 percent, the present value of \$10 a year in perpetuity is \$10 ÷ 0.10, or \$100.

Applying the perpetuity formula (at a 10 percent interest rate), the present value of the anticipated earning's stream of one share of stock is \$100 (\$10/0.10) for Jones and \$50 (\$5/0.10) for Smith. Jones would be a willing seller of XYZ stock at a price greater than \$100 and a willing buyer at a price less than \$100. Smith would be a willing seller at a price above \$50 and a willing buyer at a price below \$50. At a \$75 price, Smith would sell and Jones would buy.

The share price settles at that price at which the quantity of shares demanded equals the quantity supplied. This equilibrium price is the consensus of participants in the market concerning the present value of the future earnings of the corporation.

> The price of a share of stock is the anticipated present value of the future earnings per share of the stock.

The price/earnings (P/E) ratio signals whether investors believe the profits of the company, or earnings per share, will rise or fall from current profit levels.

> The **price/earnings (P/E) ratio** is the price of a share of stock divided by the earnings per share.

If the average company has a P/E ratio of 6, companies with a P/E ratio greater than 6 are expected to have profits rising at above-average rates. Companies with a P/E ratio less than 6 are expected to have profits rising at below-average rates.

> A high P/E ratio indicates that investors believe that current profits understate the future profits of the corporation. A low P/E ratio indicates that investors believe that current profits overstate the future profits of the corporation.

Stock Prices and Resource Allocation

The buying and selling of stock does not have a direct effect on the corporation's financial capital. However, the price of stocks does affect the allocation of capital resources. (See Example 4.) For example, if XYZ Corporation develops a promising anticancer drug and obtains Food and Drug Administration approval to market it, investors assume that XYZ Corporation earnings will rise substantially; therefore, the price of XYZ stock will rise rapidly. Assume that prior to the development of this new drug the price of XYZ stock was \$10. The company can raise \$500,000 by selling 50,000 new shares of stock. However, if the prospect of the new drug raises the stock price to \$50 the issue of 50,000 new shares will raise \$2.5 million instead of \$500,000.

As stock prices rise, corporations find it less expensive to raise financial capital. Likewise, corporations with falling stock prices find it more expensive to raise money for expansion. In this sense, the secondary markets for corporate stocks serve as barometers that signal the direction of the allocation of financial capital. Stockholders can express their dissatisfaction by selling their shares, which drives down the price of the stock. If dissatisfaction is widespread, the falling stock price prevents the firm from raising capital by selling new shares.

This chapter considered business organization as a first step in the study of the supply of goods and services. The next chapter will examine the role of production costs.

SUMMARY

1. Property rights specify how resources can be used, who can use them, and how they can be transferred to other people. Private property rights give an individual the exclusive right to use the good in any way he or she sees fit and to sell those rights to anyone.

2. Entrepreneurs are central to the economic process by setting up new business firms, producing new goods and services, and directing the resources to new and expanded uses.

3. Firms exist to take advantage of economies of scale, to bear risk, to limit transaction costs, and to provide for team production.

4. Business firms allocate their land, labor, and capital resources through managerial coordination. Business firms work both through market allocation in their dealings with other firms and consumers and through managerial allocation.

5. An agency relationship exists when one party—the agent—acts on behalf of another party—the principal. Principal/agent relationships are useful in describing the behavior of business firms.

EXAMPLE 4

TULIP MANIA

In late 1999 there was much talk of a stock market "bubble" among economists as well as stock market gurus. The Dow Jones average had risen from about 3000 in 1991 to 11,000 in mid-1999—an increase of 366 percent in the face of corporate profits rising 225 percent, from $400 billion in 1991 to about $900 billion. A bubble occurs when the price of something sold on market goes beyond its fundamental value. For a stock, this would mean that the price of the stock exceeded the present value of the risk-adjusted future earnings. It is not always easy to spot a bubble—until it bursts. Examples of bubbles that burst are the stock market crashes of 1929 and 1987 for the United States, the Japanese stock market crash in the 1990s, and the tulip mania of 1637.

The tulip mania is the classic market bubble. Tulips became popular in the 1500s, and there was a demand for different varieties. The supply of some rare varieties could not keep up with the demand, and the prices shot up. The rise in prices convinced ordinary citizens that this was a way to get rich. In Holland, the center of the tulip market (as it is today), people went so far as to mortgage their homes and businesses to invest in tulips. One bulb sold for as much as $20,000. When the prices reached outlandish levels in 1637, people began to take profits, that is, to sell. The smart money people got out first. Prices collapsed. Families lost their businesses and even their homes.

Thus, when economists speak of market bubbles they often refer to the tulip mania of 1637 as an example of speculation gone wild. Economist Edward Yardini pointed to magazine articles in 1999 about "Dow 36,000" and "Get Rich on Mutual Funds" as examples of the grandiosity and magical thinking that characterize bubbles. The problem with a stock market bubble is that it redirects resources from areas of high productivity to areas of low productivity, reducing economic efficiency. In the late 1990s, capital moved from old-line companies with solid profits to Internet companies with negative profits and, perhaps, no hope of positive profits. Whether the stock market boom of the 1990s can be considered a "bubble economy" will be known with hindsight.

Sources: http://www.Economagic.com; Charles Kindelberger, *Manias, Panics, and Crashes: A History of Financial Crises* (Wiley Investment Classics Series), 3d ed., (New York: Wiley, 1996); Jonathan Laing, "Half-Full, Half-Empty," *Barron's* (October 4, 1999).

6. Most economists assume that the goal of business firms is the maximization of profits. Natural selection theory says that firms that do not maximize profits cannot survive.

7. The three forms of business organization are the sole proprietorship (a business owned by one individual), the partnership (a business owned by two or more partners who share in making business decisions), and the corporation (a business enterprise owned by stockholders). Although there are more sole proprietorships in the United States than there are partnerships or corporations, corporations (due to their larger average size) account for the bulk of business sales and profits.

8. A multinational corporation uses foreign affiliates to engage in foreign economic activities. It exercises direct control over these foreign affiliates to pursue business strategies for the world market.

9. Corporations can raise capital by selling bonds or issuing more stock. Corporate bonds are IOUs that obligate the corporation to make fixed interest payments and to repay the principal at the date of maturity. The amount of money a corporation can raise will depend upon its stock market price.

10. Prices of stocks and bonds are determined in stock exchanges and in bond markets. The price of the stock will reflect the present value of its earnings per share. Bond prices are inversely related to interest rates.

11. Stock prices affect the cost of raising capital to the corporation. Rising stock prices cause capital to be allocated in favor of the corporation with rising share prices.

KEY TERMS

property rights 142
entrepreneur 143
managerial coordination 143
principal 144
agent 144
economies of scale 144
profit maximization 145
natural selection theory 145
sole proprietorship 146
partnership 147
corporation 147
common stock 147
preferred stock 147
convertible stock 147
multinational corporation 151
bond 151
bond market 153
stock exchange 153
present value (PV) 153
price/earnings (P/E) ratio 155

QUESTIONS AND PROBLEMS

1. You are deciding whether to build a home yourself or hire an established building firm. What are the transaction costs of arranging to have the home built without the use of the building company? Under what circumstances would these costs be low enough for you to decide to build the home yourself?
2. Risk bearing is one function served by business firms. What risk does the owner of a new restaurant bear?
3. Generally, sole proprietorships are smaller than partnerships and partnerships are smaller than corporations. From what you know about the legal features of business organizations, explain why.
4. In limited partnerships, the liability of each partner for the debts of the company is limited. Explain why such partnerships may be more attractive than the traditional form of partnership.
5. Explain why corporations can issue bonds that mature in decades while partnerships and proprietorships can borrow for only short periods of time.
6. Explain why a corporation would be reluctant to issue new shares of stock to raise capital when the price of the stock is at an all-time low.
7. One stock has a price/earnings ratio of 2; a second stock has a price/earnings ratio of 20. The average P/E ratio is 6. What would be the investment community's best guess as to the course of future profits for each company?
8. ZYX Corporation offers to sell bonds maturing in 20 years at an interest rate of 7 percent. If you buy a $10,000 bond from ZYX, what will be the annual interest payment? Are you more likely to buy the bond if you expect the interest rate to fall?
9. For the following transactions, explain which party is the principal and which is the agent, and why.
   a. Smith hires a remodeling company to add a room to her house.
   b. A university buys a computer from IBM.
   c. An engineer signs a contract with Aramco to work for a year in Saudi Arabia.

10. The price of one share of an airline stock is $4. The airline has not made a profit for 4 years. If share prices reflect corporate profitability, why is the price not $0?
11. Professional football teams take detailed films of each football game so that they can observe the performance of each player on each play. Using the Alchian/Demsetz theory, explain why they are monitoring player performance.
12. Assume an aerospace corporation does not manufacture its own jet engines. Instead, it buys them on subcontracts from other manufacturers. Using Coase's arguments about why firms exist, explain why the aerospace corporation would make this decision.
13. There are two plots of land. They are identical in all respects but one. Plot A can be used for anything; plot B cannot be used for a shopping center or for growing wheat. Which plot will have the highest value in the marketplace?
14. How does the stock market discipline the behavior of corporate management?

INTERNET CONNECTION

15. Using the links from http://www.awl.com/ruffin_gregory, look at the Fortune 500 list.
    a. What are the top 10 Fortune 500 companies? What is the total revenue of these companies? Assuming that the gross national product (GNP) of the United States is $8 trillion, what percentage of this $8 trillion do the top 10 firms represent?
    b. Where does Microsoft rank in this list? Why isn't it in the top 10 even though its market value (the value of its stock) is higher than any of the companies in the top 10 list? *Hint:* How does the Fortune 500 rank companies?
16. Using the links from http://www.awl.com/ruffin_gregory, look at the Census Bureau's County Business Patterns Web page.

    Select your state and county. Create a table using the data from the Establishments by Employment-Size Class columns. Calculate the percentage of firms in each employment category. What size firm has the largest share? (For most counties the smallest firms, with 1–4 employees, will have the largest share.)
17. Using http://www.awl.com/ruffin_gregory, read "Who Should Be in Charge?" on the Federal Reserve Bank of Boston Web site.
    a. According to the author, do shareholders always control the companies they own? Why or why not?
    b. What suggestions does the author give to address the issue of corporate governance?

PUZZLE ANSWERED: Stock prices fall because the value of a corporation depends on the future profits of the company; and higher interest rates today mean that those future profits have a smaller present value. With higher interest rates a smaller amount of money (present value) needs to be invested to earn the same income.

Chapter 9

PRODUCTIVITY AND COSTS

Chapter Insight

There is no free lunch. The law of scarcity implies that it costs us something to produce the things we want. But the costs of basic products like television sets, wheat, cars, and personal computers are constantly changing. Ultimately, the prices we pay reflect these costs. As prices fall or rise, we buy more or less of the product.

Why do costs change? In this chapter we shall study the role of the law of diminishing returns, the scarcity of the resources used in production processes, and the impact of technological progress itself over long periods of time, such as several decades. Technological progress is the major determinant of costs. For example, in the 1930s a tire cost about $13 (in today's prices) and today a tire costs about $70. However, because modern radial tires last more than 10 times longer than the old two-ply tires of the past, the actual cost of a tire per 1000 miles driven has fallen to about half of what a tire cost in the 1930s. This calculation does not even take into consideration the opportunity cost of frequently changing tires: Flat tires were commonplace in the 1930s and are rare today.

In this chapter we also explore the costs that firms bear in producing the goods we want. But what are costs? How are they measured? How are they related to production? The costs that we study in this chapter will become in future chapters the basis for supply and how markets work.

LEARNING OBJECTIVES

After completing this chapter, you will be able to:

1. See why opportunity costs include explicit and implicit costs.
2. Explain the difference between economic profits and accounting profits.
3. Understand the average/marginal rule.
4. Define marginal physical product and use it to explain the law of diminishing returns.
5. Distinguish between fixed and variable costs.
6. Discuss average variable, average total, and marginal costs.
7. Explain the difference between the short-run and the long-run cost curves (and the shape of the long-run curve).

CHAPTER PUZZLE: You own a clothing store and instruct your salesclerk to raise the price of a certain line of women's clothing because you were just told that the next time you order that line the cost to the store will increase. Your salesclerk objects that the stock in house still costs the same, and it would be cheating the customers to raise the price on old stock. "Wait for the new goods to come in," he claims. Is your salesclerk's argument valid?

PRODUCTIVITY

Once a business firm has chosen its basic organizational form (sole proprietorship, partnership, or corporation) it must get down to the main task—making a profit. Business activities can be complicated (for example, a corporation producing a commercial jet airliner) or simple (a teenager mowing lawns for summer earnings). To make a *profit* the business firm must earn revenues in excess of costs. The firm must understand revenues and costs to make sound business decisions.

Production costs depend upon input prices and productivity. Production costs rise as input prices rise, and they fall as productivity improves. Let us look at what happens to the costs of production as firms expand the level of output.

The Short Run Versus the Long Run

A business firm expands the volume of its output by using additional resources. Every good or service is produced by a combination of resources (land, labor, capital, raw materials, entrepreneurial or managerial talent). The combination of resources used depends upon three factors: (1) the productivity of the resources, (2) the prices of the resources, and (3) the time available to the firm for altering output. The first two are important because the business firm will try to keep costs as low as possible. The last is important because time is required to change the level of resource use. Some resources can be adjusted immediately. Other resources require considerable time to change.

A firm can obtain more labor resources quickly by asking each employee to work overtime. The firm might also be able to acquire additional raw materials immediately.

The **short run** is a period of time so short that the existing plant and equipment cannot be varied; such inputs require planning, building, and installation.

Additional output can be produced if the variable inputs of labor and raw materials are expanded. But the installation of a new piece of capital equipment or the construction of a new plant can require a significant amount of time.

The **long run** is a period of time long enough to vary all inputs.

The long run is not a specified amount of calendar time; it can be as short as a few months for a fast-food restaurant, a couple of years for a new automobile plant, or a decade or more for an electrical power plant. In the case of manufactured goods, engineering complexity determines whether the long run is a matter of weeks or years in actual calendar time.

The Law of Diminishing Returns

To understand the meaning of productivity, we must understand the concept of a production function.

A **production function** summarizes the relationship between labor, capital, and land inputs and the maximum output these inputs can produce for a given state of knowledge.

A production function is a technological recipe. A simple analogy is a cake recipe. It tells how much output can be produced from a given combination of inputs and tells by how much output will increase if one (or all) input(s) increase(s). For example, doubling the ingredients in a cake recipe will produce two cakes.

The production function for cars, computers, or wheat is more complicated than a cake recipe. The firm's production function is determined by the engineering and technical knowledge relevant to the firm's business. The firm's production function dictates the relationship between increases in inputs and increases in outputs in the short run—a relationship that follows a distinctive pattern, called the *law of diminishing returns*. As you know from Chapter 2, the law of diminishing returns states that as ever-larger amounts of a variable input are combined with fixed inputs, the extra product attributable to each additional amount of the variable input must eventually decline.

The extra product that is attributed to an additional unit of an input, if other inputs are fixed, is the most basic concept of productivity.

The **marginal physical product (MPP)** of a factor of production is the change in output divided by the change in the quantity of the input, if all other inputs are constant.

The law of diminishing returns asserts that as more of a variable input is used in the short run, diminishing MPP must eventually be encountered by any firm. Alternatively, the law states that additional units of output require more resources when the point of diminishing returns is reached.

A shrimp boat along the Texas Gulf Coast illustrates the law of diminishing returns. The fixed inputs are the boat, nets and other fishing equipment, and the ocean. The variable inputs are the number of workers (shrimpers) employed. Table 1 shows the daily output (in bushels) as a function of the number of shrimpers. Figure 1, panel *(a)*, shows the total output curve; Figure 1, panel *(b)*, shows the marginal product curve.

If the boat is operated by only one shrimper, his or her time must be divided among piloting the boat, setting the nets, pulling in the nets, and unloading the nets. A lone shrimper catches 2 bushels per day. A second shrimper brings the total output to 12 bushels per day. The additional shrimper allows each person

TABLE 1 THE LAW OF DIMINISHING RETURNS, SHRIMP FISHING

Number of Shrimpers	*Daily Output (in bushels)*	*Marginal Physical Product*
0	0	
		2
1	2	
		10
2	12	
		20
3	32	
		30
4	62	
		20
5	82	
		10
6	92	
		5
7	97	
		3
8	100	
		2
9	102	
		1
10	103	

to specialize and save time switching from job to job. A third shrimper proves even more valuable, raising daily output to 32 bushels. The fourth shrimper raises output to 62 bushels, the fifth to 82, the sixth to 92, and so on.

The MPP is the change in output per unit change in the input. Raising the input of shrimpers from 0 to 1 raises output by 2 bushels. Adding the sixth shrimper raises output from 82 to 92 bushels for an MPP of 10 bushels. Adding the tenth shrimper raises output from 102 to 103 bushels for an MPP of 1 bushel.

As Figure 1, panel *(b)*, shows, diminishing returns set in after the fourth shrimper. Up to the fourth shrimper, each additional shrimper has a higher MPP. Starting with the fifth shrimper, each additional shrimper has a lower MPP than the previous one. As more shrimpers are added to the fixed inputs of a boat and fishing equipment, the benefits from specialization by each shrimper are exhausted. With the addition of the fifth shrimper, the variable inputs start to get in each other's way.

The law of diminishing returns applies to the production of any good or service. When some

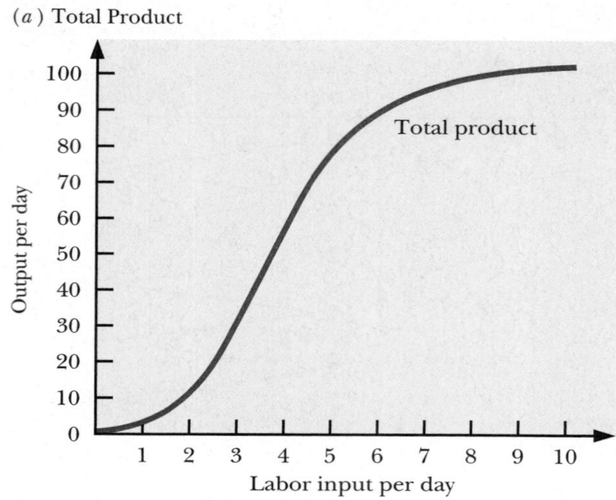

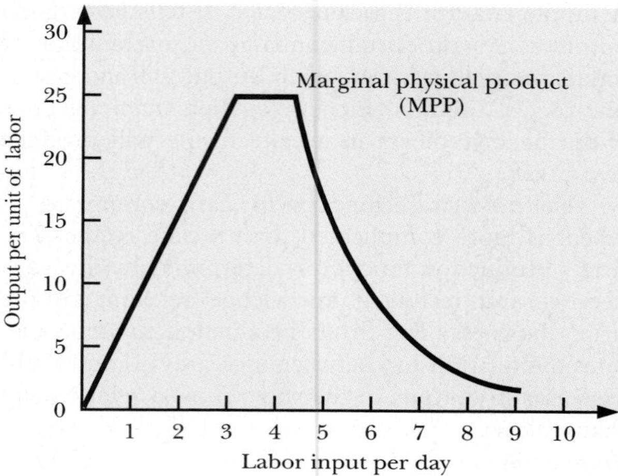

FIGURE 1 The Law of Diminishing Returns

Panel *(a)* shows the total daily output; panel *(b)* shows the marginal physical product. Both graphs are based on the data in Table 1. When the total daily output is increasing rapidly, the marginal physical product curve (MPP) is increasing. When the total daily output is increasing, but at a slower and slower rate, the MPP curve is declining.

inputs are fixed, adding variable inputs causes each variable input to have less of the fixed input with which to work. When the fixed input becomes "crowded" with variable inputs, the law of diminishing returns sets in.

Opportunity Costs

The land, labor, and capital used by the firm are costly. But what are these costs? Costs are not always what they seem. Indeed, we shall see that it is not always what the firm paid for its inputs that counts as much as what the firm must give up in the future. In economics and commerce, as the economist William Stanley Jevons (1835–1882) put it, "bygones are forever bygones; and we are always starting clear at each moment, judging the values of things with a view of future utility."

Suppose your rich aunt gives you a brand-new Miata sports car, which has a market value of $20,000. She tells you, "This car is yours. You may keep it or sell it. If you sell it, the $20,000 is yours. As long as you keep it, I'll pay for all gas, oil, maintenance, repairs, and your insurance. The car is yours—free in every way." This car is a generous gift. But the car is not free. There is a cost to *using* the car, a cost that may actually be higher than the annual cost of a small car that you would have to buy yourself.

Suppose that you could put into a savings account the $20,000 that the "free" sports car is worth. If the account earns 6 percent interest per year, $20,000 would bring you $1200 per year in interest income. Suppose that your using the car for 1 year will reduce its resale value from $20,000 to $16,000—a cost to you of $4000. The total yearly *cost* of using the car is therefore $5200.

The lesson is that *costs are not necessarily what has been paid but what must be given up by taking one action rather than another.* Opportunity cost is the measure of what has been given up.

The **opportunity cost** of an action is the value of the next-best forgone alternative.

The concept of opportunity costs was embodied in the production possibilities frontier we discussed in Chapter 2. When more of one good (such as cars) is produced, a certain amount of some other good (such as wheat) must be given up.

Consider a business firm that makes personal computers. To produce the personal computers requires resources. To acquire these resources, the firm must pay the owners of the resources because the resources have alternative uses. The minimum payments that are necessary to attract resources into personal computer production are the opportunity costs of production. Some of these payments are *explicit* (as money changes hands) and some may be *implicit*. The manager of the firm must also consider the implicit costs (the value of those resources if used elsewhere) of the resources owned by the firm. In the Miata example, the entire $5200 yearly cost is implicit.

Short-Run Costs

Fixed and Variable Costs

In the short run, some factors (such as plant and equipment) are fixed in supply to the firm; even if the firm wanted to increase or reduce them, this is not possible in the short run. The firm pays these *fixed costs (FC)* even if it produces no output. In the short run, it produces greater output by using more of its *variable inputs* such as labor and raw materials. The costs of these variable factors are *variable costs (VC)*. The sum of variable and fixed costs is *total costs (TC)*.

Fixed costs (FC) are those costs that do not vary with output.

Variable costs (VC) are those costs that do vary with output.

Total costs (TC) are variable costs plus fixed costs:

$$TC = VC + FC$$

The short run is defined as a period of time so short that some costs must be fixed. As the time horizon expands, more and more inputs can be varied. Thus, in the long run, all costs are variable—that is, fixed costs are zero.

Fixed costs and variable costs play different short-run roles in the behavior of the firm, as you will see in the next chapter. (See Example 1.)

Marginal and Average Costs

The behavior of costs in the short run depends on the law of diminishing returns. Indeed, productivity and costs are inversely related. The higher the productivity, the lower costs are; the lower the productivity, the higher costs are.

Marginal Costs. As output increases, both total cost and variable cost increase by the same amount. Suppose, for example, that when the output of shrimp increases by 2 bushels, total (and variable) costs rise by $10. The change in costs divided by the change in output is called the marginal cost (MC) of production.

Marginal cost (MC) is the change in total cost (or equivalently in variable cost) divided by the increase in output or, alternatively, the increase in costs per unit of increase in output.

$$MC = \frac{\Delta TC}{\Delta Q} = \frac{\Delta VC}{\Delta Q}$$

In this example, MC is $5 ($10 ÷ 2). In other words, MC is the increase in cost per unit of increase in output. If the increase in output is only one unit, the MC is simply the increase in costs associated with increasing output by one unit. You can determine MC for any increase in output.

Average Costs. While marginal costs reflect the change in costs per unit of change in output, average costs spread total, variable, or fixed costs over the entire quantity of output.

In the short run the most important average cost is the firm's average variable cost (AVC). To obtain AVC, divide variable costs by output. Fixed cost per unit produced is called average fixed cost (AFC) and is calculated by dividing fixed costs by output. Average total cost (ATC) is total cost divided by output. Alternatively, ATC is the sum of AFC and AVC.

Average variable cost (AVC) is variable cost divided by output:

$$AVC = VC \div Q$$

Average fixed cost (AFC) is fixed cost divided by output:

$$AFC = FC \div Q$$

Average total cost (ATC) is total cost divided by output, or the sum of average variable cost and average fixed cost:

$$ATC = TC \div Q = AVC + AFC$$

EXAMPLE 1

What Are Marginal Costs in the New Economy?

The law of diminishing returns maintains that when one holds fixed inputs constant, and when technological knowledge itself is also held constant, adding more of a variable input eventually becomes less effective at the margin. In fiber optics, technological advances are pushing the point of diminishing returns further into the future.

Telecommunications, high-speed data communications, and high-definition television require enormous transmission capacity. The first fiber-optic cables simply sent a single laser down a glass fiber tube. But light comes in different colors. Now many different-colored lasers travel down a fiber-optic cable, tremendously increasing the amount of information a fiber-optic cable can carry. Using 160 different colors, it is possible to send 1.6 trillion bits of data per second down a single fiber-optic cable. The problem is no longer speed but controlling the colors so they don't get mixed up. After the fixed cost of installing controllers, called routers, the capacity of a fiber-optic system is extraordinary.

What are marginal costs in an enhanced fiber-optic system? It costs an Internet company about $10 a month to link a customer to the World Wide Web. But the additional cost to the company of a customer using the service 100 hours a month versus 20 hours a month may be trivial or even zero. There may be a possibility of congestion—slow access at peak periods—but on average it may make little difference to the company how many hours are used. Thus, the appropriate marginal costs are how much it costs a company to link a customer to the Internet. The same is true for local telephone calls and, perhaps soon, for long distance calls. It is marginal cost per customer-month that matters to the company, rather than marginal cost per hour of customer usage. Greater capacity of the fiber-optic cable may reduce this marginal cost. But in each case the question is, for a given technology, do marginal costs rise as more and more customers are signed up? The law of diminishing returns says that eventually those marginal costs will rise for a given telecommunications technology.

Source: "New Rules for the New Economy," *Wired* (September 7, 1997); "In Wired World, Much Is Free at the Click of a Mouse," *New York Times* (October 14, 1999).

The Average/Marginal Relationship

The relationship between *average* values and *marginal* values is an important one. In this chapter we examine the relationship between average costs and marginal costs; in later chapters we shall discuss the relationship between average revenues and marginal revenues. There is a common arithmetical background to all average/marginal relationships. It will be useful to examine this arithmetical relationship before discussing costs.

We all know what an average is: It is the total amount of something divided by the number of instances. The margin is simply the increase in the total as the number of instances increases. Suppose you are budgeting your meals for five days. You have a food budget of $50. You can spend no more than $10 a day. If in the first 2 days you have spent $20, your daily average is $10. The third day you see a luscious dessert and spend $13 (the margin). Now you have spent $33 for an average of $11. You know at this point that the fourth and fifth days will require cutting back. On the fourth day, you spend exactly $11; your average is now $11 because your total spending is $44. You don't need a course in economics to tell you that your fifth day will be tough—you will have to give up one of your favorite drinks or snacks. Clearly, the last day you must spend much less than $11—that is, $6—to reach your goal. To raise the average, you spend more than the preceding average; to lower the average, you spend less. This rule applies to all average/marginal relationships.

> The average/marginal rule states that whenever the marginal value exceeds, equals, or falls short of the preceding average value, the new average value rises, remains the same, or falls, respectively.

Another example: Suppose the average height of the students in your classroom is 5′8″. If a new student arrives, what happens to the average? If the new (marginal) student has a height that exceeds 5′8″, the average height of the class will increase; if the student has a height that is less than 5′8″, the average will fall; and if the student is exactly 5′8″, the average will remain the same.

The Cost Curves

The average/marginal relationship can help us to understand costs. Table 2 and Figure 2 show cost and output information for the Texas Hat Company, which produces only hats. The costs shown include all opportunity costs (explicit and implicit). The firm has fixed costs of $48 per day. The fixed costs consist primarily of the interest on the Texas Hat Company's capital, lease payments, and depreciation. As more hats are produced, variable costs must rise because more inputs, such as labor and raw materials, are needed. Figure 2, panel (*a*), graphs total costs, variable costs, and fixed costs; Figure 2, panel (*b*), graphs average variable costs, average total costs, and marginal costs.

In Table 2, variable and total costs are shown in columns 2 and 4. The marginal cost figures in column 5 are shown *in between* the various output levels, because they are in this case the extra cost of going from one output level to another.

In the Texas Hat Company example, MC at first falls and then rises. When MPP is rising, each

TABLE 2 THE SHORT-RUN COSTS OF THE TEXAS HAT COMPANY

Quantity of Output (units), Q (1)	*Variable Cost (dollars), VC (2)*	*Fixed Cost (dollars), FC (3)*	*Total Cost (dollars), TC (4) = (2) + (3)*	*Marginal Cost (dollars), MC (5)*	*Average Variable Cost (dollars), AVC (6) = (2) ÷ (1)*	*Average Fixed Cost (dollars), AFC (7) = (3) ÷ (1)*	*Average Total Cost (dollars), ATC (8) = (4) ÷ (1) = (6) + (7)*
0	0	48	48			∞	∞
				20			
1	20	48	68		20	48	68
				10			
2	30	48	78		15	24	39
				6			
3	36	48	84		12	16	28
				4			
4	40	48	88		10	12	22
				8			
5	48	48	96		9.6	9.6	19.2
				12			
6	60	48	108		10	8	18
				20			
7	80	48	128		11.4	6.9	18.3
				32			
8	112	48	160		14	6	20
				44			
9	156	48	204				

This table shows the family of cost schedules for the Texas Hat Company operating in the short run with total fixed cost of $48. The table shows the basic data. *Variable cost* (column 2) rises with the level of output. *Total cost* (column 4) is the sum of total fixed cost and total variable cost. *Marginal cost* is shown in column 5, and *average variable, average fixed,* and *average total cost* are shown in the remaining columns.

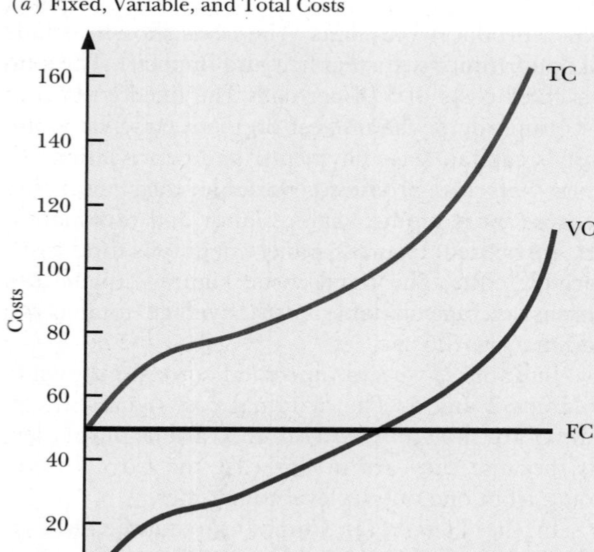

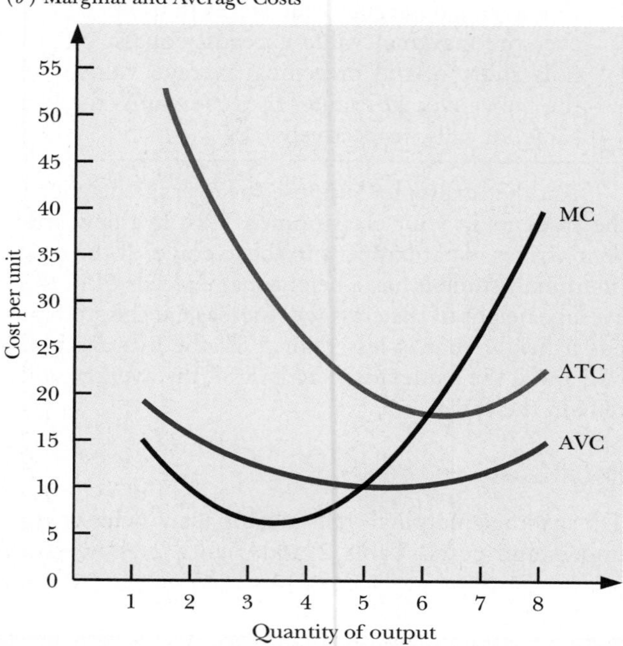

FIGURE 2 The Short-Run Costs of the Texas Hat Company

In panel (*a*), total and variable costs are graphed from data in Table 2. In panel (*b*), the marginal and average figures (except for average fixed cost) are graphed from the data. Average total cost is the sum of average variable cost and average fixed cost. Note that ATC approaches AVC as output grows and that MC intersects both curves at their minimum points.

additional worker produces a larger addition to output than the previous worker. If the firm pays each worker the same wage, the addition to cost (MC) will then decline. When MPP is falling, each additional worker produces a smaller addition to output; therefore, the addition to cost (MC) will rise. Thus, according to the law of diminishing returns, MC will eventually rise in the short run as output is expanded.[1]

> According to the law of diminishing returns, marginal physical product will fall as output expands in the short run. But marginal cost rises when marginal physical product falls. Therefore, marginal cost will rise as output expands in the short run.

In column 6 of Table 2, variable costs are divided by output to arrive at AVC. In column 7, fixed costs are divided by output to arrive at AFC. Notice that AFC declines throughout because the same fixed cost is being spread out over more units of output. In column 8, total cost—column 4—is divided by output to obtain ATC.

Figure 2, panel (*b*), shows the graphical relationship between MC and AVC and between MC and ATC. Recall that when MC is below AVC (or ATC), the margin is pulling down the average. Thus, when output increases from 3 units to 4 units, AVC falls from $12 to $10, and ATC falls from $28 to $22. The MC of $4 is below AVC and ATC and pulls them both down. When output is 5 units, MC is slightly above AVC, and so just begins to pull AVC upward. When output is larger than 5 units, MC exceeds AVC and is pulling AVC up. When output is smaller than 5 units, MC falls short of AVC and is pushing AVC down.

Cost curves show what happens to costs of production as the level of output changes. Figure 2, panel (*b*), illustrates an important principle: the MC curve intersects the AVC and ATC curves at their minimum points because of the average/marginal rule. At the minimum point, the average value is nei-

[1]The formula for calculating marginal cost from MPP is MC = *W*/MPP, where *W* denotes the wage rate.

ther rising nor falling; therefore, the marginal and average values must be equal.

Minimum ATC occurs after the minimum AVC because when AVC reaches its minimum point, MC is equal to AVC and is still below ATC. Thus, when AVC is minimized, the ATC curve must still be falling by the average/marginal rule. When the ATC curve reaches its minimum point, the plant is being operated at its most efficient level.

Because ATC = AVC + AFC, the distance between the AVC and ATC curves represents AFC. As a given fixed cost is spread over a larger output, AFC gets smaller. Thus, the AVC and ATC curves get closer together as output rises.

> The MC curve intersects the AVC curve and the ATC curve at their respective minimum values. AVC is at its lowest value when marginal cost equals average variable cost. ATC is at its lowest value when marginal cost equals average total cost.

Long-Run Costs

Firms have no fixed factors of production in the long run; therefore, they do not have any fixed costs. In the long run, the business enterprise is free to choose any combination of inputs to produce output. All costs are variable. However, once a business makes its long-run decisions (the company completes a new plant, the commercial-farming enterprise signs a 10-year lease for additional acreage), it again has fixed factors of production and fixed costs. Long-run cost-minimizing decisions are based on the prices the firm must pay for land, labor, and capital. (See Example 2.)

Shifts in Cost Curves

The Texas Hat Company can determine the ATC curves it would face with different size plants. With a small plant and highly unspecialized machinery, Texas Hat would face the cost curve ATC_1 (see

EXAMPLE 2

Flight Management Systems and Cost Minimization

Businesses combine resources to minimize the cost of providing a particular good or service. Finding minimum-cost combinations is one of management's most important functions.

Advanced commercial aircraft produced by Boeing and Airbus, the two major producers, have on-board computers that help airlines minimize their operating costs. The flight management system (FMS) contains several dozen microprocessors that analyze the entire flight plan.

First, the pilot types in the route, wind information, altitude, and the plane's weight. The FMS regulates the speed to achieve the most efficient fuel budget. There is even a cost index that balances the cost of paying a flight crew against the cost of fuel. When fuel is relatively cheap, the computer increases the airspeed to reduce pilot and crew hours; when fuel is relatively expensive, the computer lowers airspeed. The FMS finds the optimal speed that minimizes the total cost of fuel and flight crew hours.

In other businesses, management uses similar procedures to minimize operating expenses. Pipeline and electrical power plants have automated systems that minimize costs.

Source: Scientific American (July 1991), p. 99.

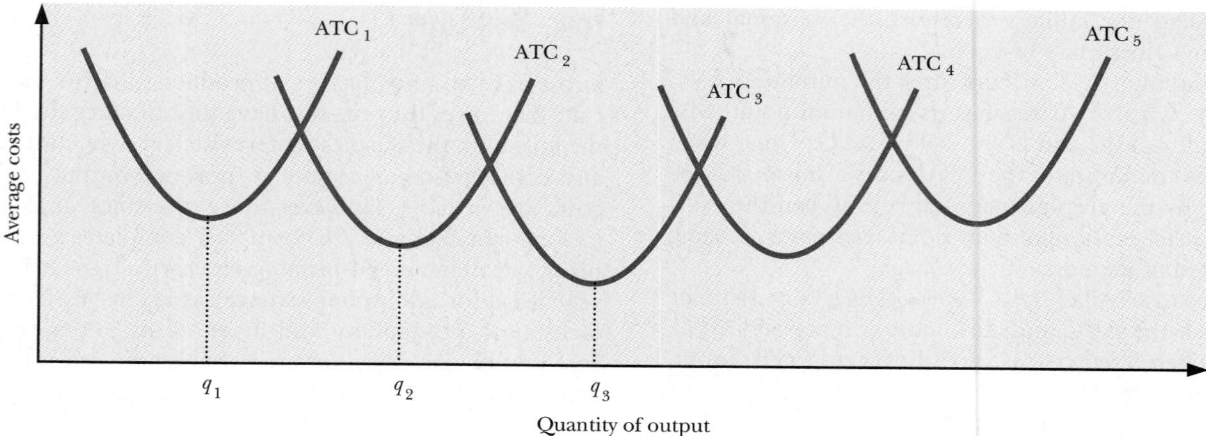

FIGURE 3 Shifts in Cost Curves with Changing Plant Size

Economies of scale are achieved with larger plant sizes up to the plant size ATC_3. When diseconomies of scale are encountered, larger plant sizes entail larger unit costs, as with ATC_4 and ATC_5.

Figure 3), whose lowest point is at output level q_1. With a slightly larger plant and more specialized equipment, Texas Hat's cost curve, ATC, would be lower for sufficiently larger levels of output, such as at q_2. The remaining ATC curves show the average costs for even larger plants. The curve ATC_3 yields the most efficient plant size, because at output level q_3, ATC is at its lowest point. (See Example 3 on page 170.)

The Long-Run Cost Curve

For each level of fixed input such as plant size, there is a different ATC curve. If there are an infinite number of fixed input levels from which to choose, there are an infinite number of associated ATC curves. Because all costs are variable in the long run, there is no distinction between long-run variable costs and long-run total costs.

Long-run average cost (LRAC) consists of the minimum average cost for each level of output when all factor inputs are variable (and when factor prices and the state of technology are fixed).

In the long run, the enterprise is free to select the most effective combination of factor inputs because none of the inputs is fixed. The LRAC curve "envelopes" the short-run average total cost (ATC) curves, forming an LRAC curve that touches each ATC curve only at one point, as shown in Figure 4. In the short run, the fact that some factors of production are fixed causes the ATC curve to be U-shaped. The law of diminishing returns does not apply in the long run because all inputs are variable.

Economies and Diseconomies of Scale

The LRAC curve will also be U-shaped, as shown in Figure 4. Long-run average costs first decline as output expands and then increase as output expands even further. Firms experience first economies of scale, then constant returns to scale, and finally diseconomies of scale as output expands.

Economies of Scale. The declining portion of the LRAC curve is due to economies of scale that arise out of the indivisibility of the inputs of labor and physical capital goods or equipment.

Economies of scale are present when an increase in output causes long-run average costs to fall.

The division of labor is much more specialized in a large firm than in a small firm. People are indivisible; it is difficult for an employee of a small firm to be one part mechanic, two parts supervisor, and three parts electrician and still remain as efficient as an employee who specializes in just one task. In a large firm, workers increase their productivity or dexterity through experience and save time because they do not move from one task to another.

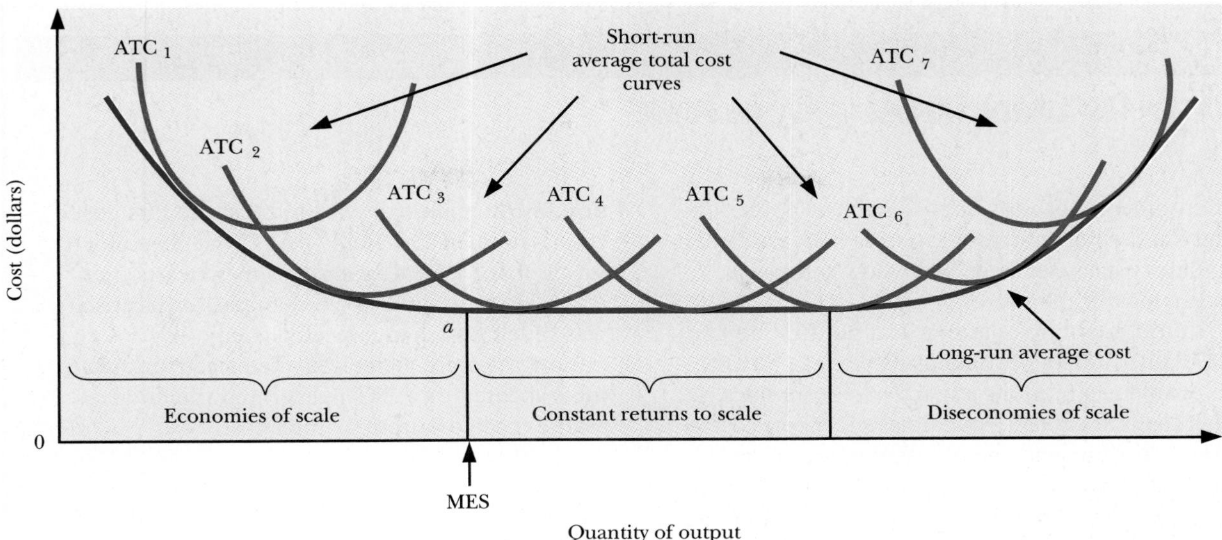

FIGURE 4 The Long-Run Average Cost Curve as the Envelope of the Short-Run Average Total Cost Curves

For each level of fixed input, there is a corresponding short-run average total cost curve. The long-run average cost curve is the envelope of the short-run average total cost curves. The long-run average cost curve is U-shaped. The declining portion shows economies of scale. The rising portion shows diseconomies of scale. The horizontal portion shows constant returns to scale.

The principles of specialization also apply to machines. A small firm might have to use general-purpose machine tools whereas a large firm might be able to build special equipment or machines that will substantially lower costs when large quantities are produced. Small-scale versions of certain specialized machines simply cannot be made available.

Economies of scale can occur because specialization allows for greater productivity in any of a variety of areas, including technological equipment, marketing, research and development, and management. The optimal rate of utilization for some types of machinery may occur at high rates of output. Some workers may not be able to perfect specialized skills until a high rate of output allows them to concentrate on specific tasks. As the output of an enterprise increases with all inputs variable, average costs will decline because of the economies of scale associated with increased specialization of labor, management, plant, and equipment.

Constant Returns to Scale. Economies of scale will become exhausted at some point when expanding output can no longer take advantage of specialization. At this point constant returns to scale set in.

Constant returns to scale are present when an increase in output does not change long-run average costs of production.

Diseconomies of Scale. As output continues to expand after experiencing constant returns, the size of the firm becomes a problem, and long-run average costs will begin to rise. At this point diseconomies of scale set in.

Diseconomies of scale are present when an increase in output causes long-run average costs to increase.

Diseconomies of scale can be caused by a series of factors. As the firm continues to expand, management skills must be spread over a larger and larger firm. Managers must assume additional responsibility, and managerial talents may eventually be spread so thin that the efficiency of management declines. The problem of maintaining communications within a large firm grows, and red tape and cumbersome bureaucracy become commonplace. Large firms may find it difficult to correct their mistakes. Employees of large firms may lose their identity and feel that

EXAMPLE 3

Shifts in Cost Curves: The Case of Nuclear Power

Environmental groups oppose nuclear power on safety and environmental grounds. Government regulatory agencies have been slow to license nuclear power plants.

Although public relations and politics are usually blamed for the problems of nuclear power, the problems are more a matter of economics. When capital capacity expands, short-run cost curves shift out and the industry operates on a new cost curve suited to greater demand. In the case of electrical power, there is a substantial lag between the decision to build generating plants and their completion. Most nuclear power plants were planned during the late 1960s and early 1970s when the long-run demand for electricity was expected to expand rapidly. New plants would meet the increased demand at lower average costs. In fact, the first nuclear power plants that became operational during a period of expanding demand proved quite profitable.

The energy crisis of the mid- and late 1970s had a profound impact on electricity demand in the 1980s and 1990s. With rising energy prices, consumers cut back and the new power plants could not be operated efficiently at the lower-than-anticipated demand levels.

Figure A shows an electrical utility that expected to be generating 600 megawatts of electricity in 1996. Therefore, it built a nuclear power plant to expand its capacity. The completion of the nuclear power plant shifted its cost curve from ATC to ATC′. ATC′ yields a much lower cost for generating 600 megawatts than ATC. However, the 1996 demand for electricity was much less than expected. Only 400 megawatts were generated. The electrical utility (now located on ATC′) generated this lower-than-expected output at high cost.

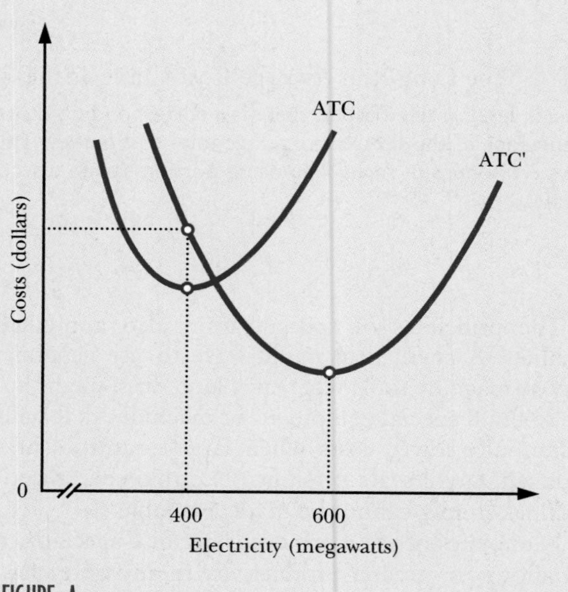

FIGURE A

their contributions to the firm are not recognized. As the output of an enterprise continues to increase, average cost will eventually rise because of the diseconomies of scale associated with the growing problems of managerial coordination.

Minimum Efficient Scale

Why are some companies more profitable than others? Why are some industries more concentrated than others? Why is a particular company doing well or poorly? Economies of scale can help provide answers for these questions.

The LRAC curve in Figure 4 is flat over a large range. Empirical studies for a number of industries suggest that such constant returns to scale occur over a significant range of output. The output level at which average costs are minimized (at point *a*) is called the minimum efficient scale (MES) of the firm.

The **minimum efficient scale (MES)** is the lowest level of output at which average costs are minimized.

TABLE 3 ESTIMATES OF THE MINIMUM EFFICIENT SCALE (MES) IN SELECTED U.S. INDUSTRIES

Industry	*MES as a Percentage of U.S. Demand*
Diesel engines	21–30
Computers	15.0
Refrigerators	14.1
Cigarettes	6.6
Beer brewing	3.4
Bicycles	2.1
Petroleum refining	1.9
Paints	1.4
Flour mills	0.7
Bread baking	0.3
Shoes (nonrubber)	0.2

Sources: F.M. Schere, Alan Beckenstein, Erich Kaufer, and R.D. Murphy, *The Economics of Multiplant Operation* (Cambridge, MA: Harvard University Press, 1975), 80–94. Leonard W. Weiss, "Optimal Plant Size and the Extent of Suboptimal Capacity," in Robert T. Masson and P.D. Qualls, eds., *Essays on Industrial Organization in Honor of Joe S. Bain* (Cambridge, MA: Ballinger, 1975), 128–131; adapted in part from C.F. Pratten, *Economies of Scale in Manufacturing Industry* (Cambridge, U.K.: Cambridge University Press, 1971).

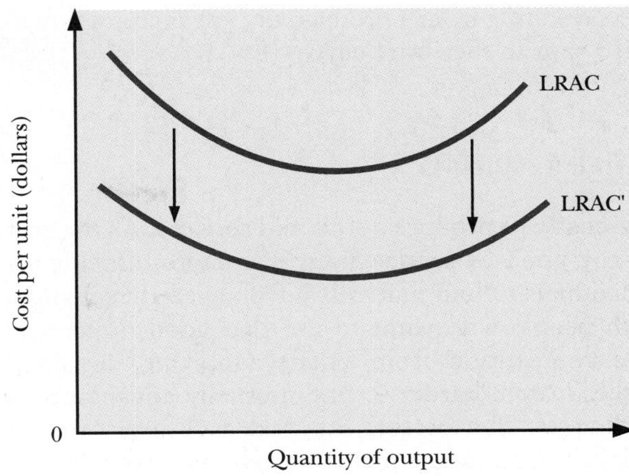

FIGURE 5 The Effect of a Productivity Advance on the Long-Run Average Cost Curve

An improvement in technological knowledge can cause an advance in productivity, where more output can be produced with the same inputs or where the same output can be produced with fewer inputs. The basic consequence is that the long-run average cost (LRAC) curve shifts down. Thus, productivity advances imply that unit production costs fall for each level of output, given the assumption that factor prices are constant.

Economies of scale differ substantially among industries. Some industries experience economies of scale up to output levels that are a high proportion of total industry sales. These industries tend to have a small number of firms because larger firms can drive smaller firms out of business. Studies show, for example, that the electricity and automotive industries have significant economies of scale, while others, such as garments and concrete, do not. Table 3 reports the results of studies of selected industries showing that the minimum efficient firm size is as high as a 21 to 30 percent market share in the case of diesel engines and as low as a market share of only 0.2 percent in the case of shoes.

Productivity Advances and the Cost Curves

The cost curves reflect the productivity and prices of the factors of production. A factor's *productivity* is the amount of output that can be obtained from a given level of its input. The production function shows how much output can be produced from any given set of inputs. A *productivity advance* results when *more* output can be produced with the *same* inputs. For example, when American farm productivity increased by over 50 percent from the 1960s to the 1990s, the production functions for grains, dairy products, poultry and eggs, and meat animals changed in such a way that fewer inputs were needed to obtain the same output. As a consequence, for any level of output and for given prices of the inputs, productivity advances will result in lower unit costs of production.

Figure 5 shows what happens to the LRAC curve as productivity improves, if input prices are constant. For each level of output, unit production costs fall. Thus, the entire LRAC curve shifts downward. The minimum efficient scale of the firm can rise or fall, depending on the type of technological breakthrough that has taken place. To illustrate, Henry Ford's assembly-line production of the famous Model T required a larger scale of plant, but a move away from assembly-line production with the use of modern industrial robots can involve a smaller minimum efficient scale.

Because unit production costs fall for each level of output, productivity advances are different from cost reductions arising from economies of scale. The fall in costs arising from economies of scale is a movement along a given LRAC curve, while a fall in costs resulting from a productivity advance is a downward shift in the entire curve.

Defining Moments

It is costly to produce goods and services. As the cost of any good or service rises, it is more difficult for individuals to find mutually advantageous exchanges with people who want to use that good or service. The competition from others supplying the good makes it even harder to find mutually advantageous exchanges. If a person can find a cheaper way of doing something, either through an invention or through better use of a particular plant or economies of scale, then surviving the challenges of competition becomes easier.

We discussed in the first chapter that the Industrial Revolution switched production from the household to the factory. This change caused production costs to drop enormously. Adam Smith's pin factory is the classic example of how, through economies of scale and the division of labor, production costs can be brought down to extremely low levels. Pin making then and now required a large number of separate operations in which each worker specialized. According to Smith's calculations, the average worker in an eighteenth-century factory could produce almost 5000 pins a day, but alone could produce only a few pins per day. Today, the average worker in a modern pin factory produces around 80,000 pins a day!

Competition keeps firms alert. Henry Ford was considered the genius of his age. He produced the famous Model T Ford in 1912 in only one color—black. He beat out his competitors by developing mass production methods that kept the price of a Model T within reach of the average person—about $10,000 in current dollars. In the mid-1920s General Motors offered a Chevrolet that was faster, easier to drive, and obtainable in a variety of colors. To compete, Henry Ford offered the Model A in 1927. The process has continued up to the present. An entry-level 2000 Ford Escort can still be purchased for about $11,000, which is about 10 percent more expensive than a new Model T in 1912. The current Ford is much better than a Model T Ford in terms of its durability, safety, comfort, and speed.

In the next few chapters we shall see how costs are harnessed by the market.

SUMMARY

1. In the short run, plant and equipment cannot be varied; in the long run, all inputs are variable.

2. The marginal physical product is the increase in output divided by the change in the quantity of an input, if all other inputs are constant. The law of diminishing returns states that as one input is increased (if other inputs are constant), the marginal physical product of the variable input will eventually decline.

3. The opportunity cost of an action is the value of the next best forgone alternative. The average of a series of values falls when the marginal value is below the previous average value; the average stays constant when the marginal value equals the previous average; the average rises when the marginal value exceeds the previous average.

4. Variable costs are those costs that vary with output; fixed costs do not vary with output. In the long run, all costs are variable. Marginal cost (MC) is the increase in cost divided by the increase in output. Average variable cost (AVC) is variable cost divided by output; average total cost (ATC) is total (fixed plus variable) cost divided by output. The AVC and ATC curves tend to be U-shaped with the MC curve intersecting the AVC and ATC curves at their minimum values.

5. In the long run, a firm can alter the size of its plant. For each plant size, there is a particular average total cost (ATC) curve. The envelope of all such ATC curves is the long-run average cost (LRAC) curve, which gives the minimum unit cost of producing any given volume of output. Along the LRAC curve, the firm is choosing the least-cost combination of inputs.

6. Economies of scale prevail when increasing output lowers average costs of production. Constant returns to scale prevail when increasing output does not change average costs of production—in which case, the LRAC curve is horizontal. Diseconomies of scale prevail when increasing output lowers the average unit costs of production. A firm's minimum efficient scale is the lowest level of output at which average costs are minimized.

7. Advances in productivity shift the LRAC curve down (assuming input prices are constant).

KEY TERMS

short run 160
long run 160
production function 160
marginal physical product (MPP) 161
opportunity cost 162
fixed costs (FC) 163
variable costs (VC) 163
total costs (TC) 163
marginal cost (MC) 163
average variable cost (AVC) 163
average fixed cost (AFC) 163
average total cost (ATC) 163
long-run average cost (LRAC) 168
economies of scale 168
constant returns to scale 169
diseconomies of scale 169
minimum efficient scale (MES) 170

QUESTIONS AND PROBLEMS

1. Your uncle gives you a "free" car and pays for the insurance, gas, oil, and repairs. You are told you may sell the car at any time. Assume the car is now worth $20,000 and will have an estimated value of $12,000 after 1 year. If the interest rate is 10 percent, how much does it cost you to use the car for 1 year?
2. Explain the distinction between explicit costs and opportunity costs. Why are opportunity costs a better guide to resource-allocation decisions?
3. A firm's out-of-pocket costs are $15,000 per month. In addition, the firm's implicit opportunity costs are $5000. What are the firm's total opportunity costs? How much revenue must the firm generate in sales in order to stay in business over the long run?
4. If a baseball player enters a game with a batting average of 0.250 (25 hits per 100 times at bat) and gets 2 hits out of 4 tries on that day, what happens to his batting average? Why?
5. Contrast the average total cost (ATC) curve of a firm that has very large fixed costs relative to variable costs with the ATC curve of a firm that has very small fixed costs relative to variable costs.
6. For a given production plan, a firm's fixed costs are zero and its variable costs are $1 million. Is the plan short-run or long-run? Explain.
7. Answer the following questions using the production-function information in Table A. Assume that 1 unit of labor costs $5 and 1 unit of capital costs $10.
   a. Derive the marginal physical product (MPP) schedule. Does it obey the law of diminishing returns?
   b. Derive the short-run cost schedules.
   c. Derive the MPP and short-run cost schedules if labor productivity doubles (with 1 labor unit, for example, being used to produce an output of 10 units instead of 5 units).
   d. Explain why the short-run cost curves shift if the amount of capital input changes.

TABLE A

Labor (units)	*Capital (units)*	*Output (units)*
0	2	0
1	2	5
2	2	15
3	2	20
4	2	23
5	2	24

8. At the current output level, ATC is $25, AVC is $10, and marginal cost (MC) is $15. If output increases by 1 unit, what happens to the new ATC? To the new average variable cost (AVC)? If ATC stays at $25 and MC increases to $25, what happens to the next ATC?
9. Suppose FC = $25, VC = Q^2, and MC = $2Q$. Draw the AFC, AVC, MC, and ATC curves. At what output level does the minimum ATC occur?
10. What is the role of the law of diminishing returns in explaining the shape of the cost curves? Construct a numerical example.
11. If MC rises, what conclusion can you draw about whether ATC or AVC is rising or falling?
12. What is the opportunity cost of a worker to a firm that mistakenly pays the worker $40 an hour instead of the worker's wage of $25 an hour?

13. Industry A, with $10 million in sales, comprises three equal-sized large firms. Industry B, also having $10 million in sales, is made up of 50 equal-sized firms. From this information, make rough sketches of the long-run average-cost curve of a typical firm in each industry. Also make predictions about the minimum efficient scale as a given percentage of industry output in both cases.

14. Suppose that the MPP of the third worker is 100 units of output per week and that the MPP of the fifth worker is 50 units of output per week. If each worker is paid $25 per week and labor is the only variable input, what is the MC associated with the output of the third worker? Of the fifth worker?

15. Using Table B, plot all the short-run total-cost and average-cost curves discussed in this chapter. Do the cost curves have the expected shapes? Explain your answer.

TABLE B

Output (units)	*Fixed Costs (dollars)*	*Variable Costs (dollars)*
1	10	5
2	10	8
3	10	12
4	10	20
5	10	40

16. With a *cable* modem, a computer is always attached to the Internet. What is the appropriate unit for marginal cost?

INTERNET CONNECTION

17. Using the links from http://www.awl.com/ruffin_gregory, read the article on the Red Herring magazine Web page.
    a. What does the author think are the reasons why productivity has increased?
    b. In terms of the cost curves that you have studied, how would an increase in productivity affect total cost? Average total cost? Please show this using a diagram.

PUZZLE ANSWERED: According to the principle of opportunity cost, the cost of the line of clothing has increased. Why? It is not the explicit cost or the historical cost that matters, but what it costs the firm to sell the good; to replace the item the firm must buy the good from the manufacturer at the new, higher price. Opportunity cost to a retailer is replacement cost.

Appendix 9A

Production Isoquants

Appendix Insight

To choose the right combination of resources, a firm should use the *least-cost method* of production. In this appendix we shall discuss how firms determine the level of output that uses the least costly combination of resources.

The Production Function

A production function shows the maximum output that can be achieved by a given combination of inputs. Figure A1 shows a hypothetical firm that employs only two factors—capital and labor—to produce its output. The horizontal edge measures the labor input from 1 to 8 workers; the vertical edge measures the capital input from 1 to 8 machines. The amount of output that can be produced from any combination of labor and capital is shown in the cells corresponding to the intersection of a row of capital input and a column of labor input. For example, 8 machines and 1 worker produce 50 units of output; 8 machines and 2 workers produce 71 units of output. Thus, the production function shown in Figure A1 gives the possible methods of producing the outputs shown at each intersection.

Marginal Physical Product

The marginal physical product (MPP) of a factor is the extra output associated with increasing the input of the factor by 1 unit, if all other factors are constant. Suppose that the amount of capital is held constant at 4 machines. With 1 worker, output is 35 units; with 2 workers, output is 50 units; and so on. Clearly the marginal product of labor is 35 for the first worker and 15 for the second worker (because output rises from 35 to 50 units). We can read the MPP of labor in the figure simply by noting the difference between consecutive outputs along a given

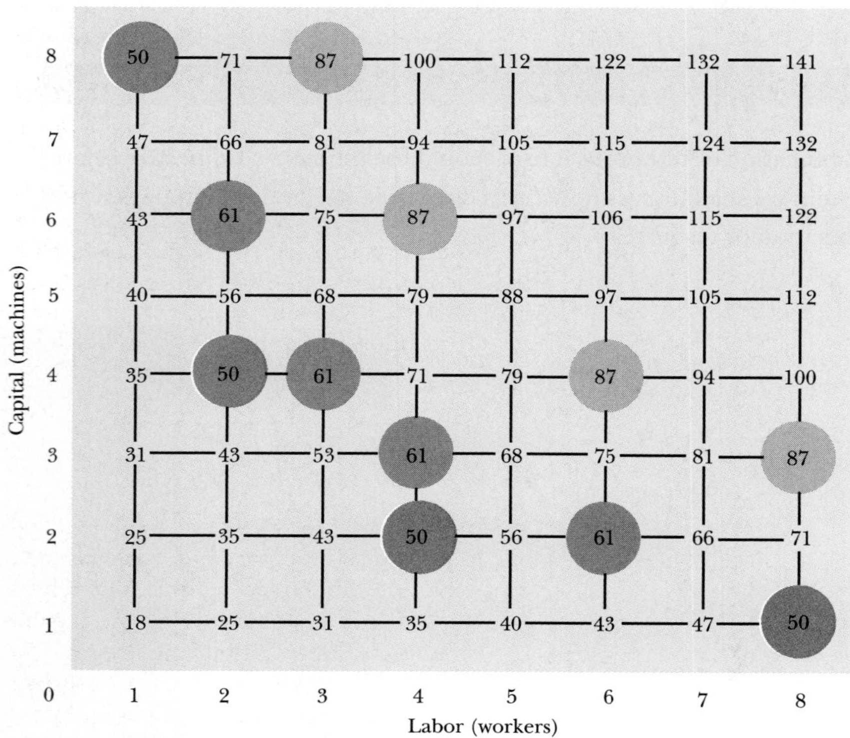

FIGURE A1 The Production Function

Capital inputs are measured vertically; labor inputs are measured horizontally. The number at the intersection of a row and column shows the output for that level of capital and labor input. For example, 4 machines and 2 workers produce 50 units of output. The law of diminishing returns can also be seen because, when the input of machines is held constant at 4 units, additional units of labor bring about smaller additions to output; thus, along a given row, output *increases* but at a *decreasing* rate.

row. Using similar reasoning, we can determine the marginal product of capital by varying the machine input, if labor is constant.

The Law of Diminishing Returns

According to the law of diminishing returns, the MPP of a factor eventually declines as more of the factor is used, if all other productive inputs are constant. In Figure A1, when capital equals 4 machines, the MPP of the second worker is 15 and the MPP for the third worker is only 11.

The production function summarized in Figure A1 assumes constant returns to scale. When there are 3 units of capital and 3 units of labor, output is 53 units; when inputs double to 6 units of capital and 6 units of labor, output doubles to 106 units. When there are 3 units of capital and 3 units of labor, the fourth unit of labor has an MPP of 8 units, as output rises from 53 to 61. When there are 4 units of capital and 4 units of labor, the fifth unit of labor also has an MPP of 8 units, as output rises from 71 to 79. Thus, *the MPP of labor remains the same as long as the ratio of capital to labor remains the same.* The source of the law of diminishing returns is the increasing ratio of workers to machines.

The Principle of Substitution

We know from Chapter 3 that there are substitutes for nearly everything. This principle of substitution is also illustrated in Figure A1, which shows that 50 units of output can be produced by four different combinations of capital and labor. These combinations are listed in columns 2 and 3 of Table A1.

From the information provided so far, there is no reason to choose the combination of 8 units of capital/1 unit of labor over the combination of 1 unit of capital/8 units of labor to produce 50 units of output. *The production function alone cannot tell us how to produce the 50 units of output.* We must also consider cost information.

TABLE A1 FACTOR COMBINATIONS FOR PRODUCING 50 UNITS OF OUTPUT

	Output (units), Q *(1)*	*Capital (machines),* C *(2)*	*Labor (workers),* L *(3)*	*Total Cost (dollars),* TC *(4)*
a	50	8	1	250
b	50	4	2	200
c	50	2	4	250
d	50	1	8	425

Note: The price of capital is $25 per machine; the price of labor is $50 per worker.

Least-Cost Production

The price of labor (P_L) and the price of capital (P_C) help us determine what combination of capital and labor the firm will use. (Think of the price of capital as the implicit or explicit rental on a machine, truck, or building.) Suppose P_L = $50 per worker and P_C = $25 per machine. Column 4 of Table A1 shows the costs of each combination of labor and capital that yields 50 units of output. For example, combination *a* costs $250 because 8 machines cost $200 (8 × $25) and 1 worker costs $50. From Table A1 we can determine that the minimum-cost combination is *b*. This combination calls for 4 units of capital and 2 units of labor, the total cost (TC) of which is $200. The average total cost of production is ATC = TC/Q = $200/50 = $4 per unit, which is the lowest possible cost per unit when total output is 50 units.

In moving from combination *a* to combination *b*, the firm can substitute an extra unit of labor for 4 machines without a loss of output. Labor costs $50, but 4 machines cost $100. Thus, the firm saves $100 in machine costs by substituting 1 worker for 4 machines and spends $50 on the added worker for a net gain of $50 (without a loss in output). Clearly, it pays the firm to select *b* over *a*.

The Isoquant

These principles of least-cost production can be illustrated by graphs. Figure A2 plots combinations *a,b,c,* and *d* from Table A1 and connects these points by a smooth curve. The curve *abcd* shows all the combinations of capital and labor input that produce 50 units of output; hence, it can be called the isoquant for 50 units of output. (*Iso* means same; *isoquant* means same quantity.)

An **isoquant** shows the various combinations of two inputs (such as labor and capital) that produce the same quantity of output.

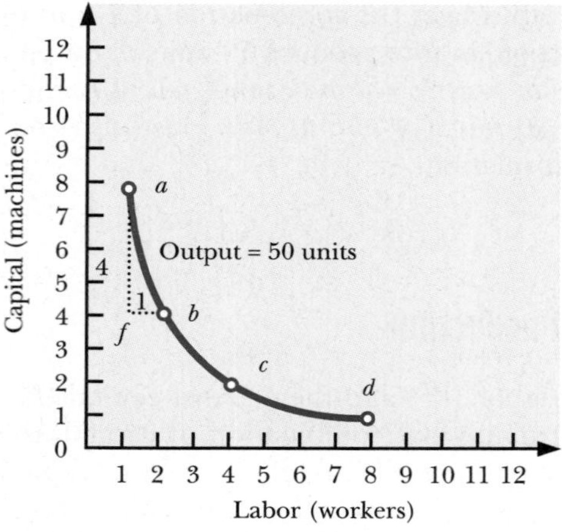

FIGURE A2 The Isoquant

The isoquant shows all the combinations of labor (number of workers) and capital (number of machines) that produce the same amount of output. It is bowed toward the origin because the law of diminishing returns dictates that substituting capital for labor becomes easier as the ratio of workers to machines increases.

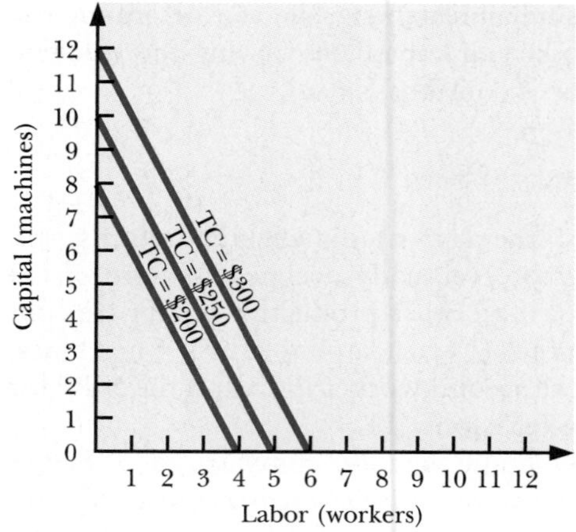

FIGURE A3 Isocost Lines

Isocost lines show all the combinations of labor and capital that cost the same amount. The line for TC = \$300 shows all the combinations costing \$300. The slope of each equal-cost line is measured by the ratio of the price of labor to the price of capital; in this case, labor is \$50 per worker and capital is \$25 per machine; thus, each equal-cost line has an absolute slope of 2.

Isoquant curves are similar to the indifference curves studied in the appendix to the chapter on demand and utility. Just as the indifference curves were convex to the origin, so isoquants are convex to the origin. The ratio of the line segment *af* to *fb* is the amount of capital that can be substituted for the extra unit of labor. The slope of the curve between *a* and *b* reflects the fact that the MPP of labor is four times the MPP of capital. The vertical distance *af* is four times the horizontal distance *fb,* which reflects the rate at which capital must be substituted for labor to keep output constant. The ratio of the marginal physical products measures the marginal rate of substitution (or the rate at which capital can be substituted for labor). This ratio equals the slope (in absolute value) of an isoquant between two points or the absolute slope of the tangent to any point of the equal-output curve.

> The marginal rate of substitution of capital for labor
>
> $$= \frac{\text{MPP of labor}}{\text{MPP of capital}}$$
>
> = The (absolute) slope of the isoquant

The isoquant is bowed toward the origin because when workers are substituted for machines, the MPP of labor falls relative to the MPP of capital; to keep output constant as labor is substituted for machines, fewer and fewer machines can be given up for each worker acquired.

Isocost Lines

If we assume that the price of labor (P_L) is \$50 per worker and the price of capital (P_C) is \$25 per machine, the total cost (TC) of production is

$$TC = (P_L \times L) + (P_C \times C) = \$50L + \$25C$$

where L = the number of workers and C = the number of machines. In Figure A3, the line TC = \$300 consists of all the combinations of labor and capital that cost \$300. For example, if $C = 12$ and $L = 0$, TC = \$300; if $C = 0$ and $L = 6$, TC = \$300; the combination of 6 machines and 3 workers also costs \$300. Thus, line TC is the isocost line for costs of \$300.

> The **isocost line** shows all the combinations of labor and capital that have the same total costs.

Figure A3 gives three illustrative isocost lines, but there is one for every level of total costs. These isocost lines are parallel because each has the same slope. The absolute slope of any isocost line is simply P_L/P_C. In this example, the (absolute) slope is 2 since the price of 1 unit of labor is twice that of 1 unit of capital; therefore, 2 units of capital can be substituted for 1 unit of labor without increasing or decreasing total costs.

> The (absolute) slope of the isocost line is the price of labor divided by the price of capital, which represents the rate at which firms can substitute labor for capital without affecting total costs.

The Least-Cost Rule

Figure A4 shows how the firm minimizes the cost of producing a given volume of output (in this case, output is 50 units). When the isoquant for 50 units of output and the isocost lines for three representative cost levels appear on the same graph, we can determine the least-cost combination by observing where the isoquant *abcd* just touches the *lowest* isocost line (at point *b*). The lowest isocost line that curve *abcd* can reach is TC = \$200. All other combinations of labor and capital on *abcd* cost more than \$200. Thus, point *b* is the least-cost production point; it is the best combination of labor and capital (4 machines and 2 workers) for producing 50 units of output.

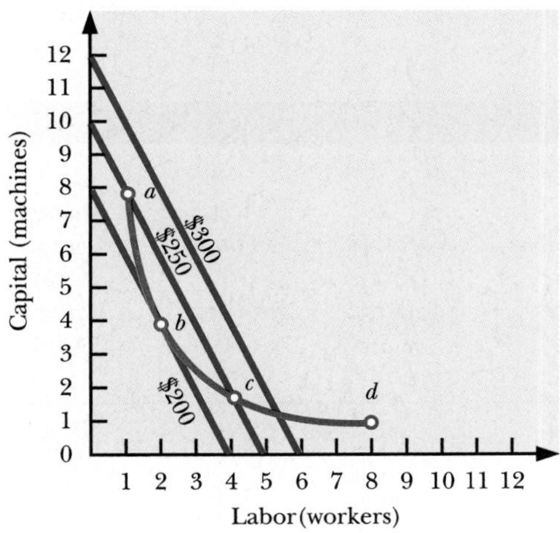

FIGURE A4 The Least-Cost Rule

The least-cost method of producing 50 units of output can be found at the point where the isoquant, *abcd*, touches the lowest equal-cost line, TC = \$200. At point *b*, the slope of the isoquant equals the slope of the isocost line because the two curves are tangent; here the ratio of the marginal physical product of labor to that of capital equals the ratio of the price of labor to the price of capital.

In Figure A4, the slope of the isoquant is the same as the slope of the isocost line because both are tangent (they touch without crossing) at that point. Thus

$$\frac{MPP_L}{MPP_C} = \frac{P_L}{P_C} \tag{1}$$

We can write the least-cost rule in a second way:

$$\frac{MPP_L}{P_L} = \frac{MPP_C}{P_C} \tag{2}$$

In other words, the least-cost rule requires that the extra output from the last dollar spent on labor must equal the extra output from the last dollar spent on capital. A third way of writing the least-cost rule, by taking the reciprocals of equation (2), is

$$\frac{P_L}{MPP_L} = \frac{P_C}{MPP_C} \tag{3}$$

> The **least-cost rule** is that the least-cost combination of two factors can be found at the point where a given isoquant is tangent to the lowest isocost line. In other words, the least-cost combination of two factors can be found where
>
> $$\frac{P_L}{MPP_L} = \frac{P_C}{MPP_C}$$

The price of labor divided by the MPP of labor is labor cost per additional unit of output, which is simply the marginal cost of output using labor. (Recall that marginal cost is the extra cost of producing 1 more unit of output.) Similarly, the price of capital divided by the MPP of capital is the marginal cost of production using capital. According to equation (3), least-cost production (in the long run) requires using capital and labor in such a way that the marginal cost of production is the same whether output is increased using capital or using labor. If these two were not equal, one would be substituted for the other.

When $P_L/\text{MPP}_L = P_C/\text{MPP}_C$, since all cost-lowering substitution possibilities are exhausted, the long-run marginal cost of production is equal to the common value of the two ratios.

The Link Between the Short Run and the Long Run

The least-cost rule gives us the link between the short run and the long run. The long run is a period of time so long that both workers and machines can be varied. In the short run, the number of machines is fixed. It takes time to find the right machine, install it, and train workers to use it properly. Thus, fixed costs are the machine costs, and variable costs are the labor costs. In the short run, marginal cost is the ratio P_L/MPP_L.

As shown in Table A2, the number of machines is fixed at 4 in the short run, and the number of workers can be varied from 0 to 5. The first four columns of Table A2 are derived from Figure A1. Column 5 of Table A2 is the short-run marginal cost. Columns 6 through 9 show the short-run costs of production. Column 9 illustrates the average total cost (ATC) of production. Note that ATC hits its minimum at an output of 50 units where ATC = $4.00.

Applying the Least-Cost Rule

What would the firm do if the price of capital rises from $25 per machine to $100 per machine, while the price of labor remains at $50 per worker? If the firm continues to use 4 machines and 2 workers to produce 50 units of output, the new factor prices cause total costs to be ($100 × 4) + ($50 × 2) = $500; average costs rise from $4 to $10 ($500/50). The firm, of course, would begin to substitute the now cheaper labor for the now more expensive machinery. The price of capital is now twice as great as the price of labor, so the slope of the new isocost lines is 1/2 instead of 2. Figure A5 shows what happens. The old TC line was *mn*—with the minimum-cost point *b*. The new minimum TC line is *m'n'*, which is tangent to point *c* on the isoquant. The least total cost of production is now $400 (4 units of capital now costs $400 and 8 units of labor costs $400). Because 50 units are still produced, the average cost of production is now $8 ($400/50). The firm saves $2 per unit of output by substituting labor for capital. Quadrupling the price of capital causes the average cost of production to double (from $4 to $8). The optimal ratio of machines to workers is now 2 machines per 4 workers, or 1/2 machine per worker. The production process has become less capital intensive and more labor intensive.

TABLE A2 PRODUCTIVITY AND COSTS

Capital (machines), C (1)	*Labor (workers),* L (2)	*Output (units),* Q (3)	*Marginal Physical Product of Labor (units),* MPP_L (4)	*Marginal Cost (dollars),* MC (5)	*Fixed Cost (dollars),* FC (6)	*Variable Cost (dollars),* VC (7)	*Total Cost (dollars),* TC (8)	*Average Total Cost (dollars),* ATC (9)
4	0	0			0	0	0	0
			35	1.43				
4	1	35			100	50	150	4.29
			15	3.33				
4	2	50			100	100	200	4.00
			11	4.54				
4	3	61			100	150	250	4.10
			10	5.00				
4	4	71			100	200	300	4.23
			8	6.25				
4	5	79			100	250	350	4.43

Note: The price of labor is $50 per worker; the price of capital is $25 per machine.

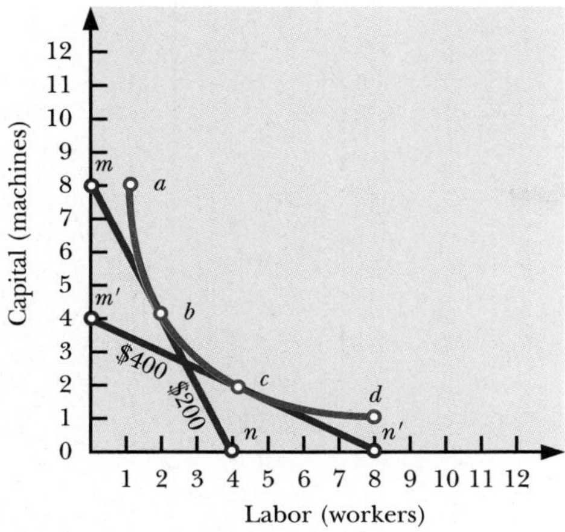

FIGURE A5 A Change in Factor Price

The isocost line *mn* shows the minimum cost of producing 50 units of output when capital is $25 per machine and labor is $50 per worker. (Line *mn* is the same as TC = $200.) If the price of capital rises to $100 per machine, the equal-cost line *m′n′* shows that the lowest cost of producing 50 units of output rises to $400 and the least-cost combination of capital and labor shifts from point *b* to point *c* as cheaper labor is substituted for machines.

SUMMARY

1. An isoquant shows all the combinations of two factors that will produce a given level of output. The production function can be described by the isoquant map. Its slope is the marginal rate of substitution.

2. An isocost line shows all the combinations of two factors that have the same total costs. Its slope is the relative factor cost, wage/rent.

3. The least-cost combination of two factors can be found at the point where an isoquant is tangent to the lowest isocost line.

KEY TERMS

isoquant 177
isocost line 178
least-cost rule 179

QUESTIONS AND PROBLEMS

1. Why is an isoquant convex to the origin? Why is it downward sloping?
2. What should be the cost objective of the firm?
3. Show that raising the price of capital relative to labor will lead a firm to choose more labor-intensive techniques of production.
4. Assume a firm is hiring labor and capital until $MPP_L = 3$ and $MPP_C = 15$ units. Suppose $P_C = \$4$ per unit and $P_L = \$10$ per unit.
   a. Is the firm minimizing costs?
   b. Should the firm hire more capital and less labor or more labor and less capital? Explain your reasoning.

Chapter 10

Perfect Competition

Chapter Insight

The law of scarcity invites us to try to produce what we want at the lowest possible cost. If not, we are wasting resources that might be used to feed, clothe, and shelter our population, especially the poor. It is a worthy objective. But scarcity requires competition.

Competition is often misunderstood. Social critics frequently lament the fact that our society is "competitive" rather than "cooperative." Competition, however, is unavoidable: In a world of scarcity, few of us will freely give up our claims to a share of the wealth.

The theory of perfect competition tells us how the goods that people want are produced at the lowest cost to society. Competition, thus, lightens the burden of scarcity. If a business firm does not sell at the lowest cost, it goes out of business. If firms in an industry are making positive economic profits, new firms enter the market and drive the price down to the lowest cost possible. Firms come and go in the race for the consumer dollar. In this chapter, we shall encounter the fascinating tale of how firms and consumers are forced to cooperate by following the trail of price.

LEARNING OBJECTIVES

After completing this chapter, you will be able to:

1. See why perfectly competitive firms are price takers and why price equals marginal revenue.
2. Understand the profit maximization conditions for the firm under perfect competition.
3. Discuss how the supply curve of the market is related to the marginal cost curves of each firm.
4. Determine the shape of the long-run supply curve for both constant-cost and increasing-cost industries.
5. Apply the theory of perfect competition to services with low marginal costs.
6. Explain why perfect competition is efficient.

CHAPTER PUZZLE: Is it better for the economy that new firms are created or that old firms are going out of business?

SCARCITY AND COMPETITION

Competition can take a variety of forms. A free-for-all system of catch-as-catch-can or steal-as-much-as-one-can constitutes one possible scheme. In such a system, property rights do not exist; each person takes whatever he or she can find. It is easy to see that such a system will not work well. If property rights are not protected by law, people will have little incentive to buy or produce property. Likewise, such conditions will create a demand for security guards or mafia-style protection against the bullies and thugs who might prevail. Such conditions actually exist today in Russia.

A system that allows people to buy and sell property rights *freely,* with those rights protected by the state, will be more orderly. Firms will find it profitable to enter into market transactions with buyers, and all participants will attempt to strike the best deal for themselves. Such a system can exist under varying degrees of competition. In this chapter we shall study firms operating in the most competitive markets possible.

COMPETITION AS A MARKET MODEL

An *industry* is a collection of firms producing a similar product or service (such as steel, aluminum, milk, wheat, haircut, or tax preparation). A crucial characteristic of each industry is the extent to which competition is present. Economists recognize four basic market models, from the most to the least competitive: *perfect competition, monopolistic competition, oligopoly,* and *monopoly.* (See Table 1.) Perfect competition is the subject of this chapter. The other three market models will be discussed in detail in the following chapters.

As a brief preview of these models, perfect competition exists when individual firms in an industry have no control over the market price and new firms are free to enter the industry. Perfect competition is most likely found in an industry where there are many small producers of a homogeneous product. Farming and low-priced clothing are classic examples of perfect competition. Monopolistic competition prevails when there are many small producers of a differentiated product and new firms can enter freely. Local supermarkets and service stations are good examples of monopolistic competitors. When firms are large relative to the market and some impediments to the entry of new firms exist, the industry is oligopolistic. For example, there are only a handful of large automobile companies, steel companies, soap manufacturers, and cereal producers in the United States. Finally, a monopoly exists when an industry's product is supplied by only one firm. Some examples of monopolies may include local telephone service or the local newspaper; frequently, only one company in each industry is able to serve a community.

Firms in an industry may be price takers or price makers.

TABLE 1 MARKET MODELS

Type	*Number of Firms*	*Product*	*Entry*
Perfect competition	Many	Homogeneous	Easy
Monopolistic competition	Many	Heterogeneous	Easy
Oligopoly	Few	Not specified	Not easy
Monopoly	One	Irrelevant	Difficult

A firm that is a **price taker** considers the market price as something over which it has no control.

In the real world, almost every seller exercises some influence over price; but the more competition the seller faces, the less control each individual seller can exercise over the prices charged. In the extreme case, the seller has absolutely no control over price.

Perfect competition prevails in an industry when each individual seller faces so much competition from other sellers that the market price is taken as given.

This type of behavior tends to prevail when there are many firms selling a homogeneous product to an informed public, and new firms are free to enter or old ones to leave the industry. The conditions for perfect competition are four:

1. The industry contains so many buyers and sellers that no single one can influence the price of the product.
2. Each buyer or seller is perfectly informed about prices and the quality of the product.
3. The product is homogeneous; that is, it is not possible or even worthwhile to distinguish the product of one firm from that of another in the industry.
4. No barriers obstruct entry into or exit from the market; that is, there is complete freedom of entry and exit.

As a consequence of these conditions, no firm in the industry can sell the product at a price higher than that of another firm—people will always try to buy from the firm with the lowest price. This competition will cause every firm to sell at the same price.

The difference between the perfectly competitive firm and the industry as a whole is illustrated in Figure 1. Panel (*b*) shows the industry demand curve, *D*, for the product. When the market price is \$7, the quantity demanded in the industry is 10,000 units. The individual firm, shown in panel (*a*), can sell all it wants (from a practical standpoint) at the going industry price of \$7. Whether the firm sells 3 units or 10 units, the price is still the \$7 market price. (See Example 1.)

The demand curve facing the perfectly competitive firm is *horizontal* or *perfectly elastic* at the going market price.

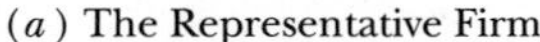

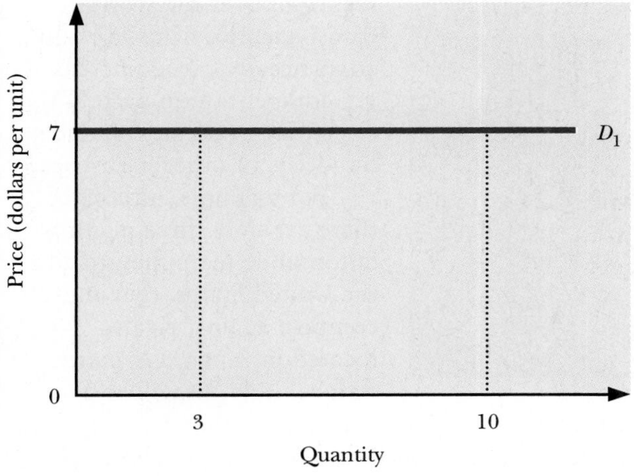

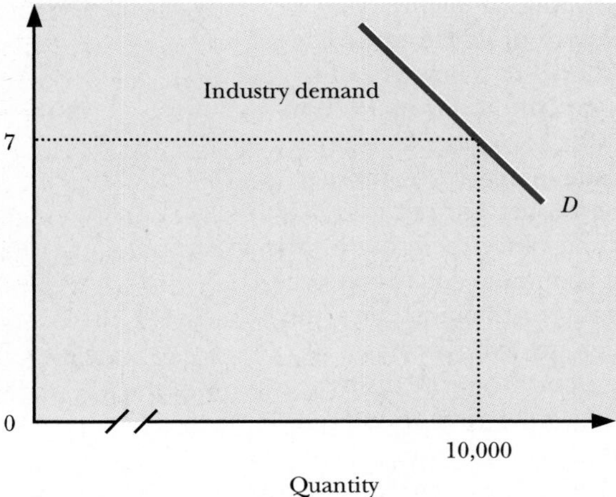

FIGURE 1 Firm Demand Versus Market Demand

The industry demand curve *D* in panel (*b*) shows the total industry demand for a homogeneous product being produced by many relatively small firms. The demand curve D_1 in panel (*a*) shows how this demand is perceived by the individual firm. Because the individual firm is so small relative to the market, it cannot significantly influence the market price. The firm is thus a price taker and can sell all it wants at the going price.

The individual firm in a perfectly competitive industry produces very small amounts relative to the industry as a whole. Thus, an individual firm cannot change the industry price by altering the quantity of the good it offers in the marketplace. Because the individual firm faces a perfectly elastic demand schedule, the firm is a price taker. If the firm tries to sell at a price higher than the market price, it will sell nothing.

Economic Profits

The theory of perfect competition, as well as other market models, rests on the assumption that firms seek to maximize profits. Therefore, in order to analyze how markets operate, we must first understand the concept of profits.

Economists do not use the general term *profits* in the way most people do, nor do they always measure profits in the same manner as accountants. Economic profits indicate whether or not resources are being directed to their best use.

Economic profits represent the amount by which revenues exceed total opportunity costs.

For example, pharmacist Smith is the owner and operator of Smith's Drugstore. Smith has put $120,000 of her own money into the business. She could, however, earn $4000 per month working as a pharmacist in a chain drugstore. Moreover, Smith's capital investment in her own drugstore might earn $1000 per month if invested elsewhere. This sum of $5000 (= $4000 + $1000) is an *implicit* cost of doing business. (Although this $5000 is a true opportunity cost, no money changes hands.) The *explicit* (accounting) costs involved are Smith's rent pay-

EXAMPLE 1

Growth of World Trade and Competition

The opening up of domestic markets to international competition is always a Defining Moment. The growth of world trade has ushered in a new era of competition. From 1970 to 2000, for example, world trade increased by more than 6 percent per year, about twice the growth rate of economic activity in general. For the most part, the high growth rate has resulted from the dismantling of barriers to international competition. Three important forces have been at work. First, explicit trade barriers such as tariffs and quotas have been relaxed by many countries. Second, international communications are now much cheaper because of the development of satellite technology, which allows telephone, television, and radio transmissions to be beamed almost anywhere in the world. Third,

computer technology now makes it possible for companies to monitor developments all over the world. Consequently, firms in many countries are facing increasing competition in auto, TV, electronics, computers, and hundreds of other industries.

For example, although there are only three major automobile manufacturers in the United States, they must compete against rivals located in Japan, Germany, France, Italy, Brazil, and Korea for customers throughout the world. Likewise, restaurants in Paris and Tokyo must compete for customers with McDonald's and Burger King. Increasing international competition in the last several decades has expanded the number of industries to which the perfectly competitive model is applicable.

ments on the building, inventory costs, business taxes, and wage payments to clerks and other pharmacists. These add up to $74,000 per month. Smith's total monthly opportunity cost for operating her own drugstore is the sum of explicit costs ($74,000) and implicit costs ($5000), or $79,000.

Now suppose Smith's Drugstore has monthly sales of $80,000. Smith's accounting profits are $6000 per month (that is, sales = $80,000; accounting costs = $74,000). Smith's economic profit, however, is only $1000 because total opportunity costs are $79,000. Accounting costs ignore the implicit costs that must be assigned to the use of Smith's entrepreneurial talents and funds. These implicit costs must be paid for the entrepreneur/owner to commit entrepreneurial resources and financial capital to the business. In this case, if accounting profits had been below $5000, Smith would not have entered the business because she would not earn a normal profit, which equals the cost of doing business.

A **normal profit** is the return that the time and capital of an entrepreneur would earn in the best alternative employment. It also is the return that is earned when total revenues equal total opportunity costs.

Perfect Competition in the Short Run

Perfectly competitive firms have no control over price; they are price takers. Therefore, the major decision they face is how much output to produce. In the short run, a perfectly competitive firm makes its output decisions by varying the quantities of variable inputs (such as labor, raw material, energy) that are combined with its fixed plant and equipment. The fixed level of plant and equipment is both a burden and a blessing. It is a blessing to established firms because in the short run fixed costs prevent new firms from entering the industry. Time is needed to build more plants or install more equipment. Yet, the fixed level of plant and equipment is also a burden. In the short run, the firm is obliged—even if it shuts down temporarily—to make certain contractual payments (taxes, rent payments, contractual obligations to some employees) and to forgo interest receipts that it could earn if it could sell the plant and equipment.

In the short run, the firm must make two decisions: first, whether to temporarily shut down, and second, how much to produce if it decides not to shut down. In the long run, the firm has the additional options of building more plants and acquiring more equipment or leaving the business permanently. We shall consider the long run in a later section.

The Two Rules of Profit Maximization

When calculating the appropriate level of output, firms are guided by the goal of profit maximization (or loss minimization). To maximize profit, firms must follow some simple rules.

The Shutdown Rule. The first decision faced by the perfectly competitive firm is whether to shut down temporarily or produce some output. Surprisingly, it is not important whether the revenues that the firm earns cover fixed costs. In the short run, firms must live with fixed costs. Thus, fixed costs should not affect decision making in the short run because they must be paid even if the firm shuts down. Only in the long run can fixed costs be avoided. Instead, according to the shutdown rule, the decision to shut down for the short run depends on the relationship between revenues and variable costs.

The **shutdown rule** states that if a firm's revenues at all output levels are less than variable costs, it can minimize its losses by shutting down. If there is at least one output level at which revenues exceed variable costs, the firm should not shut down.

For example, brick manufacturer Smith has fixed costs of $1000 per week. She can sell $3000 worth of bricks per week while incurring a variable cost (VC) of $2900. Should the bricks be produced or should the plant be shut down? If no bricks are produced (the shutdown case), the fixed costs of $1000 must be paid anyway, so the manufacturer will incur a loss of $1000. By producing $3000 worth of bricks, the manufacturer can *reduce* her losses to $900 because producing bricks results in an excess of $100 of revenues ($3000) over variable costs ($2900). The reasoning behind the shutdown rule is that any excess of revenues over variable costs can be applied to cover a portion of fixed costs.

The Profit-Maximization Rule. Once the firm has decided not to shut down, what rule should it follow to maximize profits or minimize losses? The decision about *how* *much* to produce is guided by marginal analysis, as we discussed in Chapter 5. If at any point producing another unit of output *raises the profit of the firm (or reduces its losses)*, more output should be produced. Marginal adjustments in the level of output will be made as long as each change increases profit or reduces losses.

What is the best output? As we learned in the preceding chapter, marginal cost (MC) is the increase in costs that results from increasing output by 1 unit. The marginal benefit of producing 1 more unit of output is the revenue it generates.

Marginal revenue (MR) is the increase in total revenue (TR) that results from each 1-unit increase in the amount of output:

$$MR = \frac{\Delta TR}{\Delta Q}$$

As long as an extra unit of output adds more to revenue than to costs, the profits of the firm increase (or its losses diminish) with greater production. If the marginal cost of an additional unit of output exceeds its marginal revenue, the firm's profits will be reduced (or its losses increased) by producing that extra unit. It follows that the profit-maximization rule holds that marginal revenue should equal marginal cost. This rule applies to all firms, be they perfectly competitive or monopolistic.

The **profit-maximization rule** states that a firm will maximize profits by producing that level of output at which marginal revenue (MR) equals marginal cost (MC).

What is MR for a competitive firm? Because the competitive firm can sell all it wants without depressing the going market price, that price (*P*) is equivalent to the marginal revenue. Thus, for a competitive firm, the rule is to produce where *P* = MC.

The Cost Curves Again. Consider the Texas Hat Company, described in Table 2, the same firm that you met in Table 2 of the previous chapter. The firm's average variable costs (AVC) for different levels of output are listed in column 2; average total costs (ATC) in column 3; total costs (TC) in column 4; and marginal costs (MC) in column 5. Figure 2 presents the same information in graphical form. Remember that the difference between the ATC and AVC curves measures average fixed cost (AFC) and the MC curve

TABLE 2 THE PROFIT-MAXIMIZING FIRM: THE TEXAS HAT COMPANY

Output (1)	*Average Variable Cost* (2)	*Average Total Cost* (3)	*Total Cost* (4)	*Marginal Cost* (5)	*P = Marginal Revenue* (6)	*Revenue* (7)	*Profit* (8)
0	—	∞	$48		$26	$0	−$48
				$20			
1	$20	$68	68		26	26	−42
				10			
2	15	39	78		26	52	−26
				6			
3	12	28	84		26	78	−6
				4			
4	10	22	88		26	104	16
				8			
5	9.6	19.2	96		26	130	34
				12			
6	10	18	108		26	156	48
				20			
7	**11.4**	**18.3**	**128**		**26**	**182**	**54**
				32			
8	14	20	160		26	208	48
				44			
9	17.3	22.7	204				

When MR = MC, profit is maximized. If *P* = MR = $26, the firm should produce 7 units.

intersects both the AVC and ATC curves at their minimum points.

The minimum points on the AVC and ATC curves are important to keep in mind. In Table 2, the minimum average variable cost listed in column 2 is $9.60—which occurs when the output equals five units. The minimum average total cost listed in column 3 is $18—which occurs when the output equals six units.

Whether or not the firm can make a profit depends upon the price. The competitive firm can sell all it wants at the going price. When the price exceeds the minimum ATC of $18, the firm can make a profit by producing six units of the good.

The Firm's Short-Run Supply Curve

In the short run, the competitive firm's objective is either to maximize profits or, if necessary, to minimize losses. The firm's supply curve indicates how much it is prepared to sell at each price. Once the market price is set, the firm will find itself in one of three positions:

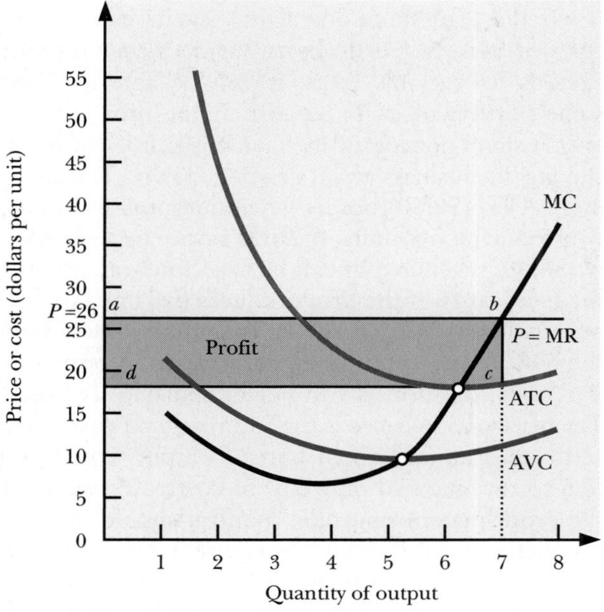

FIGURE 2 The Profit-Maximizing Firm

The market price is $26. The firm maximizes profit at an output level of seven units (where *P* = MC). At *P* = $26, price exceeds ATC by the distance *bc*. Total profit is the rectangle *abcd*.

1. The price is high enough that the firm can make economic profits.
2. The price is low enough that the firm stays in business but produces at a loss.
3. The price is so low that the firm's best option is to temporarily shut down and hope for the price to rise.

The Profitable Firm. Let us start with a price of $26. Because the firm is perfectly competitive, *P* = MR = $26. Columns 4, 7, and 8 in Table 2 show the total cost, total revenue, and profit (positive or negative) of the firm. If the firm produces six units, minimizing average total costs at $18, it can make a profit of $48. However, at this output, the MC of the seventh unit equals $20. Since MR = $26, the firm can increase its profit by producing more units; the increase in revenue will exceed the increase in costs. If output is raised to seven units, profit increases to $54. This $6 increase represents the difference between the increase in revenue ($26) and the increase in costs ($20). Profit is maximized at $54 because the MC of the eighth unit is $32, which exceeds MR = $26.

The graph in Figure 2 shows us the same results. At any point along the line *P* = MR, the firm's total revenue equals the price times the quantity produced. Profit is maximized where the *P* = MR line intersects the MC curve; when *P* = $26, this occurs at an output level of seven units. On the graph, the MC curve is filled in for all levels of output. The vertical difference between the *P* = MR line and the ATC curve at that point—the distance *bc*—indicates profit per unit of output. Total profit is determined by multiplying this difference by the output of seven units and is measured by the rectangle *abcd*. Profit will not be maximized at any output other than seven units because MC will not equal *P* or MR.

The Loss-Minimizing Firm. Let us turn to the second case, in which the market price is not high enough for the firm to make a profit. A market price lower than the minimum ATC of $18 will result in losses. Consider a price of $16. Table 3 and Figure 3 use the same cost figures as the previous example, but columns 6, 7, and 8 of the table now reflect the lower price. The firm cannot make a profit; instead, it must worry about minimizing its losses. If the firm produces an output of zero, column 4 shows that total costs will still be $48—the firm's fixed costs do not disappear if it shuts down. The firm's revenue will be zero, as

TABLE 3 THE LOSS-MINIMIZING FIRM: THE TEXAS HAT COMPANY

Output (1)	Average Variable Cost (2)	Average Total Cost (3)	Total Cost (4)	Marginal Cost (5)	P = Marginal Revenue (6)	Revenue (7)	Profit (8)
0	—	∞	$48		$16	$0	−$48
				$20			
1	$20	$68	68		16	16	−52
				10			
2	15	39	78		16	32	−46
				6			
3	12	28	84		16	48	−36
				4			
4	10	22	88		16	64	−24
				8			
5	9.6	19.2	96		16	80	−16
				12			
6	**10**	**18**	**108**		**16**	**96**	**−12**
				20			
7	11.4	18.3	128		16	112	−16
				32			
8	14	20	160		16	128	−32
				44			
9	17.3	22.7	204				

When P = $16, losses are minimized when output is 6 units.

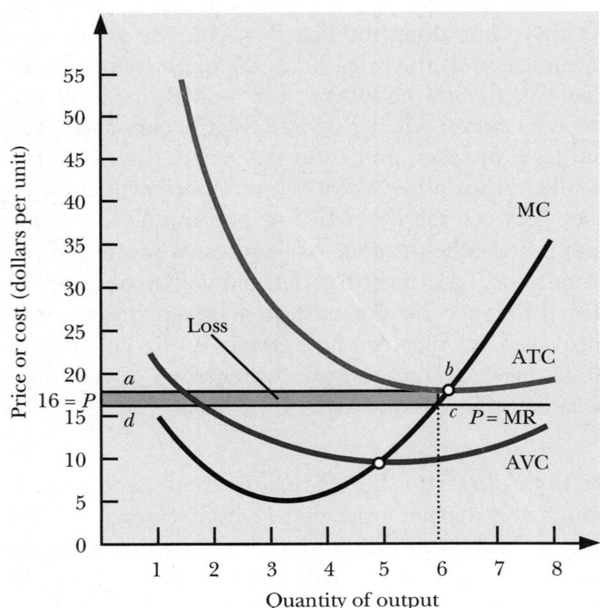

FIGURE 3 The Loss-Minimizing Firm

In this case, minimum ATC is $18 and P = $16, so the firm loses money. But the firm minimizes its losses by adjusting output to 6 units, where P = MC. At this level, it is able to cover not only its variable costs but also some portion of fixed costs. By shutting down, the firm would lose its fixed costs of $48.

shown in column 7, and its loss (its negative profit) will be $48.

If the firm shuts down, it loses its entire fixed costs of $48. Can it do better? If the firm's revenue exceeds its variable costs, it will be able to cover some portion of its fixed cost. If the firm can pay even a small portion of its fixed costs, it is better off staying in business than shutting down. The minimum AVC ($9.60) occurs when output is five units. By producing five units, the firm's price exceeds AVC by $6.40, revenue that can be used to cover some of the fixed costs. If the firm produces five units of output, its loss is $16, as shown in column 8, less than the $48 loss of shutting down. Yet, at an output of five units, the firm is still not minimizing its losses. The price of $16 exceeds the $12 marginal cost of the sixth unit; an additional unit of output would add $16 to revenue and only $10 to costs. According to the profit-maximizing rule, the firm should increase production until P = MC. In Figure 3, when the MC curve is filled in or smoothed, this occurs at point *c*, where the P = MR line intersects the MC curve yielding an output of six units. At this point, the firm's losses per unit of output are measured by the distance *bc*, or P − ATC = $16 − $18 = − $2. The firm's total losses of $12 (the six units times the $2 loss per unit) are shown by the red rectangle.

> Perfectly competitive firms choose that level of output where P = MC—or, in graphical terms, where the P(= MR) line intersects the MC curve—provided price is greater than the minimum level of AVC. This rule holds whether the firm is maximizing its profit or minimizing its losses.

The Shutdown Case. In the previous two cases, the price of the product exceeded the minimum AVC of $9.60. If, however, the price falls short of the minimum AVC, what should the firm do? A price below the average variable cost causes the firm's revenues to fall short of variable costs, so the firm should temporarily shut down. If the firm does not shut down, it loses not only its fixed cost, but also the portion of its variable cost that is not covered by dollar sales.

Table 4 and Figure 4 illustrate the situation of the competitive firm when the price is only $8. Column 8 in Table 4 shows that its losses are minimized when output is zero. When the firm produces nothing, its losses are limited to its fixed cost of $48. Any additional output, since the price does not cover AVC, will increase the firm's losses. By producing the first unit, for example, the firm's AVC is $20. Since

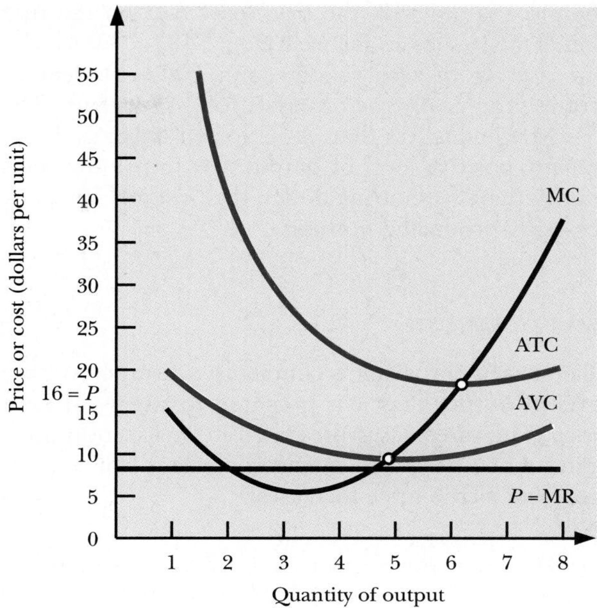

FIGURE 4 The Shutdown Case

In this case, P = $8 and the minimum AVC is $9.60. The firm minimizes its losses by shutting down because the price is less than AVC.

TABLE 4 THE SHUTDOWN CASE: THE TEXAS HAT COMPANY

Output (1)	*Average Variable Cost (2)*	*Average Total Cost (3)*	*Total Cost (4)*	*Marginal Cost (5)*	*P = Marginal Revenue (6)*	*Revenue (7)*	*Profit (8)*
0	—	∞	$48		$8	$0	−$48
				$20			
1	$20	$68	68		8	8	−60
				10			
2	15	39	78		8	16	−62
				6			
3	12	28	84		8	24	−60
				4			
4	10	22	88		8	32	−56
				8			
5	9.6	19.2	96		8	40	−56
				12			
6	10	18	108		8	48	−60
				20			
7	11.4	18.3	128		8	56	−72
				32			
8	14	20	160		8	64	−96
				44			
9	17.3	22.7	204				

When P = $8 (< AVC), losses are minimized by shutting down.

the price is only \$8, the firm loses \$12 on the first unit. Thus, its losses increase from \$48 to \$60 as output rises from zero to one unit. Figure 4 demonstrates graphically the rationale for a shutdown. The P = MR line is less than AVC for all outputs. Thus, for any positive level of output, the firm loses more money than by shutting down; the firm minimizes its losses by producing nothing.

The Firm's Supply Curve

The supply curve for a competitive firm shows the level of output that it is prepared to supply at each price. The three cases presented in this section illustrate that the profit-maximizing level of output increases as the price increases.

> The competitive firm's supply curve is that portion of the firm's MC curve that lies above the AVC curve. It indicates the profit-maximizing level of output for the firm at different price levels. Because the marginal cost curve is positively sloped, the competitive firm's supply curve is also positively sloped.

A graphical summary of the competitive firm's supply curve is shown in Figure 5. The P = MR line intersects the MC curve above the minimum point on the AVC curve. If output is short of the intersection (point e), the firm can make the additional profit shown by the green area, which represents MR in excess of MC. If the firm pushes output above point e, it loses the amount shown by the red area, which represents MC in excess of MR. We know the firm is better off producing at point e than shutting down because P exceeds AVC. Since the firm is more than covering its variable costs, it is paying off at least some of its fixed costs.

The Industry's Short-Run Supply Curve

The behavior of the profit-maximizing firm explains the short-run behavior of the perfectly competitive industry of which it is a part. Recall that the short run is a period so short that old firms cannot build new plants and equipment; new firms cannot enter; old firms cannot leave. Thus, there are a fixed number of competitive firms of given sizes. Each individual firm's supply curve is its MC curve above its AVC curve. The industry supply curve is just the horizontal sum of the supply curves of all the firms in the industry.

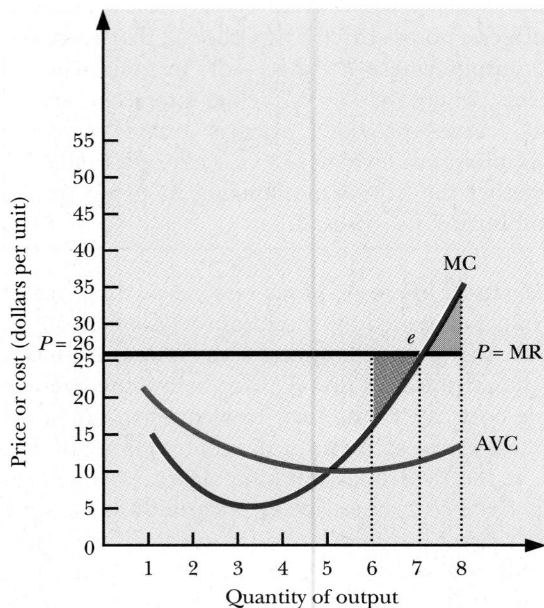

FIGURE 5 Profit Maximization
Profit is maximized where MR = MC. The green area is lost if output is too low, and the red area is lost if output is too high.

> In the short run, the **industry** or **market supply curve** is the horizontal summation of the supply curves of all firms in the industry, which in turn are those portions of the firms' MC curves located above minimum AVC.

Figure 6 illustrates how the industry supply curve is derived in the case of four identical firms, but the principles are the same for any number of firms. We have considered an even simpler marginal cost curve than in the previous example. The marginal cost curve (above AVC) for a single firm is shown as S_1 = MC. The firm wishes to sell zero units at a price of \$15, two units at a price of \$20, three units at a price of \$25, four units at \$35, and five units at \$50. The curve S_4 is the market supply curve for all four firms.

Graphically, the industry supply curve is the *horizontal* summation of the supply curves of all firms.

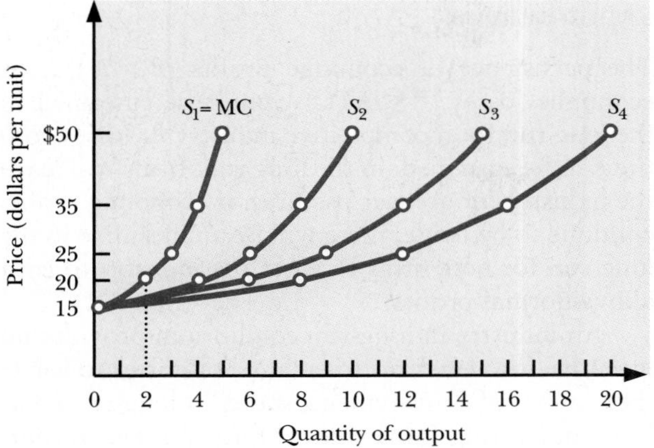

FIGURE 6 The Industry Supply Curve

The industry supply curve is the horizontal summation of all individual firms' supply curves. In the present case, there are four identical firms. Each firm has the MC curve S_1. As additional firms are added, the supply curve shifts rightward to S_2 (for two firms), S_3 (for three firms), and finally to the market supply curve S_4 for all four firms.

With four identical firms, no industry output is supplied at a price of $15. At a price of $20, eight units are supplied (the four firms at two units each). At a price of $50, the industry is prepared to supply 20 units (four firms at five units each). The supply curves S_2 and S_3 show what the industry supply curves would be with only two and three firms in the industry. The addition of firms simply shifts the market supply curve to the right.

Short-Run Equilibrium

The market or industry equilibrium occurs at the market price that balances the market supply with the market demand for the good. Figure 7 demonstrates how the short-run equilibrium price is determined, for the firm of Figures 2 through 4. Panel (*a*) of Figure 7 shows the individual firm, and panel (*b*) an industry consisting of 1000 such firms. The supply curve *S* in panel (*b*) is the horizontal summation

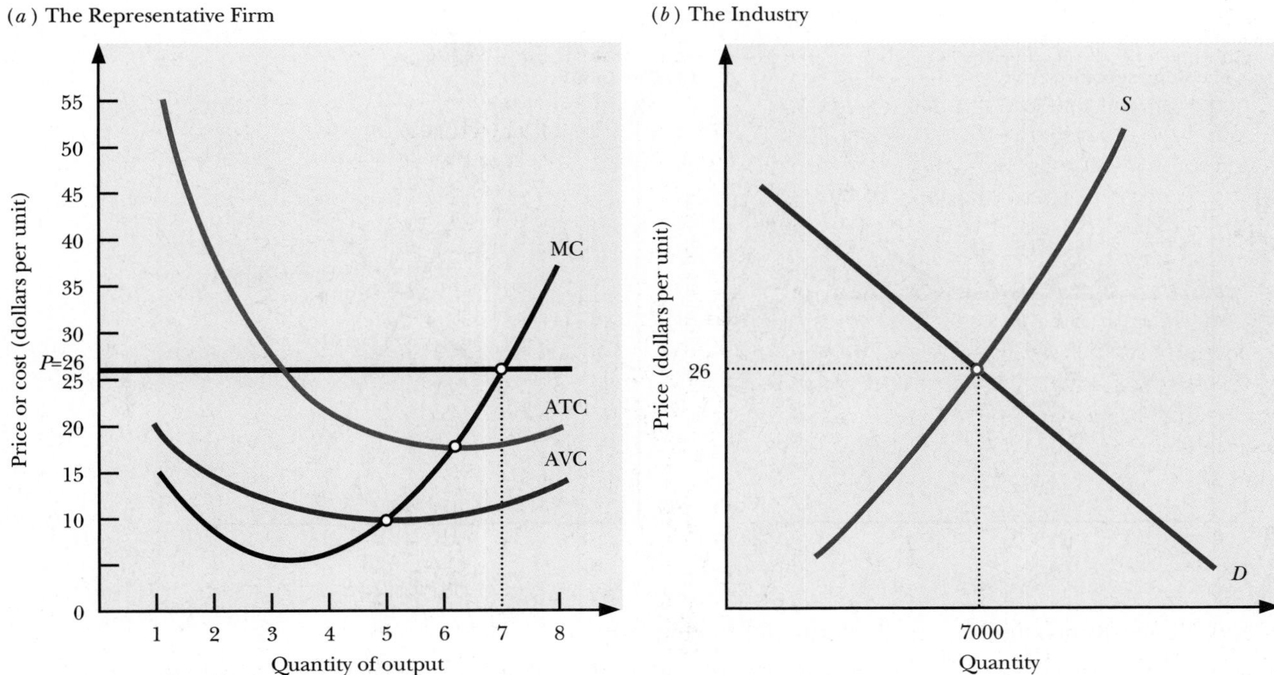

FIGURE 7 Short-Run Equilibrium: The Firm and the Industry

Panel (*a*) shows the representative firm; panel (*b*) shows the industry, in which there are 1000 firms. Firm demand occurs at the point where industry demand and supply are in equilibrium, in this case at a price of $26 and an output of 7000 units. The individual firm in panel (*a*) is making a short-run profit.

of all firms' MC curves above AVC. For example, at a price of $26 each firm sells seven units and the industry sells 7000 units. If the market demand curve D intersects the market supply curve at the price of $26, then the quantity demanded also equals the quantity supplied (7000), and the $26 price becomes the individual firm's horizontal demand curve. In response to this price, the firm produces seven units, at the point where the MC curve intersects its demand curve. The profit-maximizing behavior of the individual firm is consistent with the profit-maximizing behavior of all the firms in the market.

Perfect Competition in the Long Run

The effect of economic profits on perfectly competitive industries occurs primarily in the long run, when new firms can enter the industry and established firms can exit. As competitive firms respond to economic profits or losses, the industry short-run supply schedule shifts, and prices change.

Long-Run Equilibrium

The persistence of economic profits ($P > \text{ATC}$) or economic losses ($P < \text{ATC}$) cannot be sustained in the long run for a competitive industry. If losses continue to be sustained, in the long run, firms will leave the industry for greener pastures. If economic profits continue to be made, there will be an incentive in the long run for new firms to enter the industry to earn above-normal profits.

An industry in long-run equilibrium provides no incentive for new firms to enter or old firms to leave; the number of firms remains static. In long-run equilibrium, existing firms will operate at a level of output at which average total cost equals the price.

Figure 8 diagrams a perfectly competitive industry in long-run equilibrium. In the long run, the firm operates at an efficient scale of operation. Thus, the ATC curve for the optimal plant will have a minimum average cost equal to the minimum average cost on the long-run average cost curve (LRAC). The long-run equilibrium for the representative firm occurs at q_0, where $P = \text{ATC} = \text{LRAC}$.

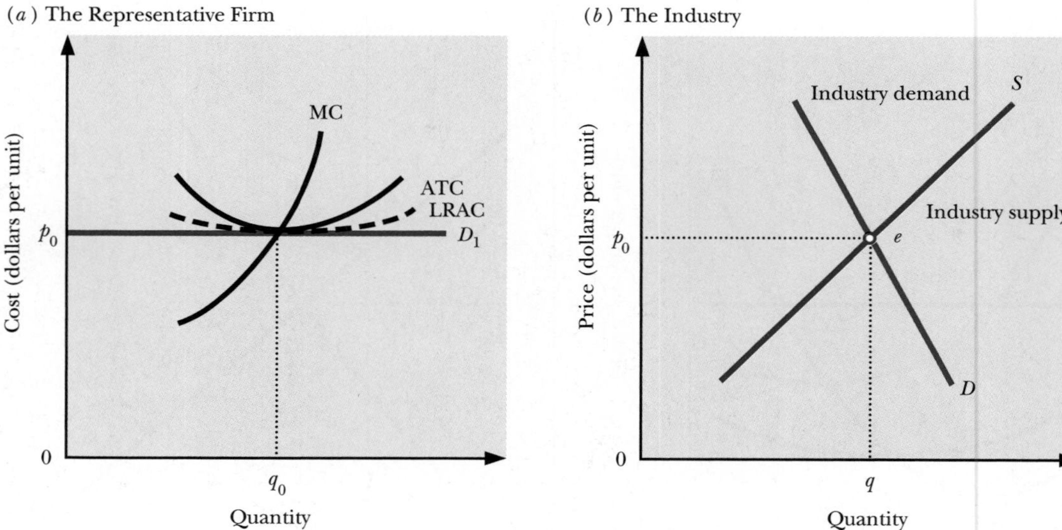

FIGURE 8 Long-Run Equilibrium: The Firm and the Industry

These graphs illustrate the relationship between the firm and the industry in long-run equilibrium. Notice that three conditions are satisfied: (1) quantity supplied equals quantity demanded; (2) price equals marginal cost; and (3) price equals average total cost, which equals long-run average cost. (The representative firm makes zero economic profit.) The representative firm in panel (*a*) produces at the point where the D_1 curve intersects the MC curve ($P = \text{MC}$). Its profits are zero because price just covers the minimum average total cost of production. The industry supply curve in panel (*b*) is based on the number of firms in existence in long-run equilibrium.

When $P = \text{MC}$ and $P = \text{ATC} = \text{LRAC}$ at the long-run equilibrium output, and when MC intersects ATC at its *minimum point,* the perfectly competitive firm is producing at the lowest average cost in the long run.

> Long-run equilibrium occurs for the competitive industry when economic profits are zero and long-run average costs are minimized.

This finding suggests that perfectly competitive firms will operate at maximum efficiency (produce at minimum LRAC) in the long run.

The Mechanism of Entry and Exit

A perfectly competitive industry adjusts toward a long-run equilibrium of zero economic profits through entry and exit. For the economy as a whole, entry and exit are opposite sides of the same coin. If it is profitable to enter one industry, resources must be exiting another industry. In other words, if revenue exceeds opportunity costs in some industries, it falls short of opportunity costs in others.

This mechanism is difficult to see in a large economy, such as that of the entire United States. But in a small economy it would be obvious. For example, in the state of Hawaii the success of the tourist industry crippled the pineapple industry through the effect of higher wages in the former.

Entry. In the long run, the mechanism of free entry eliminates economic profits and ensures that goods are produced at minimum average cost with an efficient plant size.

Consider the perfectly competitive industry in Figure 9. Panel (*a*) graphs the ATC and MC curves of a typical firm in this industry; we assume ATC is the short-run average total cost curve for an efficient scale of plant. Panel (*b*) graphs the market supply curve derived by summing the supply curves of the 100 firms in the industry. When the market demand curve is *D*, the equilibrium price is $10. At this price, the representative firm makes zero profits (a normal return). The demand curve facing the representative

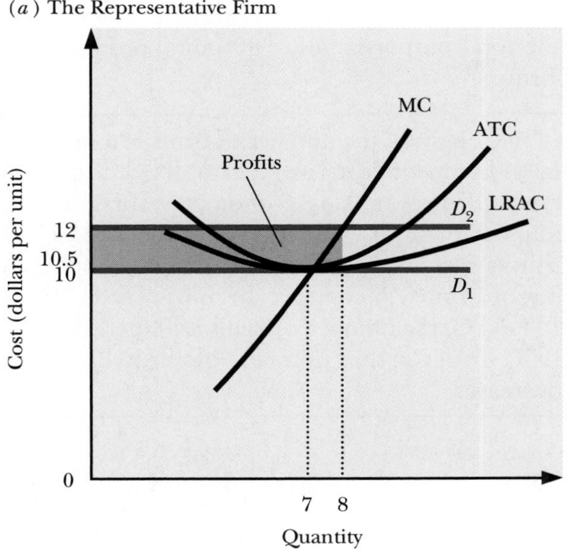

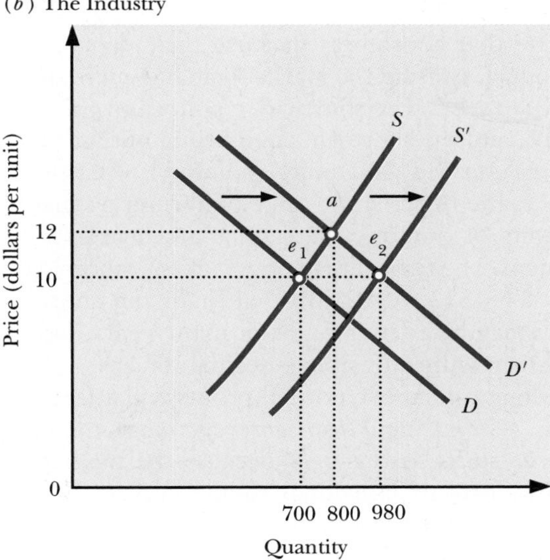

FIGURE 9 Free Entry of Firms Drives Economic Profits to Zero and Unit Costs to a Minimum

The initial long-run equilibrium is e_1, at the intersection of *D* and *S* in panel (*b*). When demand shifts to *D′*, the short-run equilibrium price rises to $12 (point *a*), creating economic profits for the individual firm facing the new demand curve D_2 in panel (*a*). In the long run, new firms enter the market until the supply curve shifts to *S′*. The long-run equilibrium is established at point e_2, where price again equals $10. Each firm returns to producing seven units of output, but the number of firms rises from 100 (700 ÷ 7) to 140 (980 ÷ 7).

EXAMPLE 2

Entry Is Easy on the Internet

The Internet has changed the conditions of entry in retailing. It is now possible to start a business within hours. A 16-year-old recently started an Internet site dealing with the selling of sports products in just two hours: he constructed a marketplace with brand-name products, prompt shipping, and even secured credit-card transactions. It is not even necessary to build a warehouse for the goods; for that can be outsourced to other suppliers or wholesalers. The World Wide Web is used by eBay as an auction site; and it has quickly become a mall for retailing. The biggest Internet retail industry is probably that for books, represented by amazon.com and bn.com. But ingenious entrepreneurs will figure out how to sell just about everything online, saving customers a great deal of fuel and shoe leather.

This example shows how technological change can shorten the long run. The shortened calendar time involved in the long run means that the economy will work more efficiently. When the long run takes less time, the shift of resources from relatively unproductive areas to relatively productive areas also will be quicker. Greater efficiency means higher incomes for the average person.

Source: "Now You Can Open Up Shop from the Comforts of Home," *Wall Street Journal* (October 4, 1999).

firm is D_1; each of the 100 firms produces seven units of the product, yielding a market output of 700 units. Point e_1 represents both a short-run and a long-run equilibrium.

Suppose that consumers increase their demand for the product, causing the market demand curve to shift from D to D'. The short-run equilibrium price rises to \$12, and the short-run equilibrium output of the industry rises to 800 units (point a).[1] At this higher price, the firm's short-run equilibrium occurs at eight units of output, where price and marginal cost are equal. The typical firm now makes economic profits [$= 8 \times (\$12 - \$10.50) = \$12$]. In the short run, which may be a few months or many years, the individual firm will enjoy above-normal returns.

In the long run, above-normal profits will attract more firms. *As these new firms enter the market, the supply curve shifts to the right* because the market supply is the sum of individual supply curves. The entry of new firms will continue as long as economic profits remain positive. (See Example 2.) But as the supply curve shifts to the right (to S'), the market price falls, shrinking profits. Eventually, economic profits disappear. The new long-run (and short-run) equilibrium is point e_2, at the old equilibrium price of \$10. The individual firm again produces seven units; but the total output is now 980 units, produced by 140 firms.

> In the long run, the number of firms in a perfectly competitive industry is not fixed. If the typical firm is making economic profits, the number of firms will expand. If the typical firm is sustaining economic losses, the number of firms will contract. In other words, if $P >$ ATC, the number of firms will increase. If $P <$ ATC, the number of firms will decrease.

Exit. The entry of some firms into profitable industries implies a simultaneous exit of other firms from unprofitable industries. As with entry, the mechanism of exit leads to a long-run equilibrium, with the average firm producing at the minimum average cost and with price equal to marginal cost. Just as entry into profitable industries is healthy for an economy, so is exit from unprofitable ones. Indeed, to say that economic profit attracts new entrants implies that those entrants were making economic losses else-

[1]Remember that in the short run, the number of firms is fixed. As market demand increases, movement occurs along the short-run supply schedule S. In the long run, new firms can enter; the result is a rightward shift of the supply curve to S'.

where. Greater profits in one industry become the opportunity costs of other industries.

> One of the most important lessons in all of economics is that entry and exit are different sides of the same economic mechanism.

In Figure 10, the initial demand and supply curves are D and S in panel (b). Point e_1 is both a short-run and a long-run equilibrium for an industry with 100 firms. Point e_1 is a short-run equilibrium because, in panel (b), the market quantity supplied equals the market quantity demanded and because, in panel (a), P = MC for the representative firm. The market is in long-run equilibrium because when price is $10 (the firm demand curve is D_1), the representative firm makes zero profits.

Suppose now that consumers reduce their demand for the product, causing the market demand curve to shift from D to D' in panel (b). As a result, the short-run equilibrium shifts from point e_1 to point *a*, where the price is $7 and the quantity is 500 units. The representative firm produces five units. Because $7 is less than ATC, the representative firm has economic losses. In the long run, firms will begin to exit, shifting the industry supply curve to the left until economic losses are eliminated (at S') and price is driven back up to the original $10. The new equilibrium is at point e_2, where total output is 336 units, and there are now only 48 firms who again produce an average of seven units each.

Capitalism the Creator

In Chapter 1 we discussed the Industrial Revolution as one of the Defining Moments of economics. But there are mini-industrial revolutions going on all of the time. When people demand the new products that new technologies create, their demand for old products must fall. The old industries must shrink or disappear. If resources are allocated politically rather than economically, vested interests will seek to preserve the old. But an unintended consequence of preserving old industries is the slowing down of the development of new industries. Capitalism is creative. It is an economic system that allows changes to take place in the most efficient way possible. The entry of new firms and the exit of old firms is the mechanism that keeps the economy up to date with the latest technologies, fashions, and fads. (See

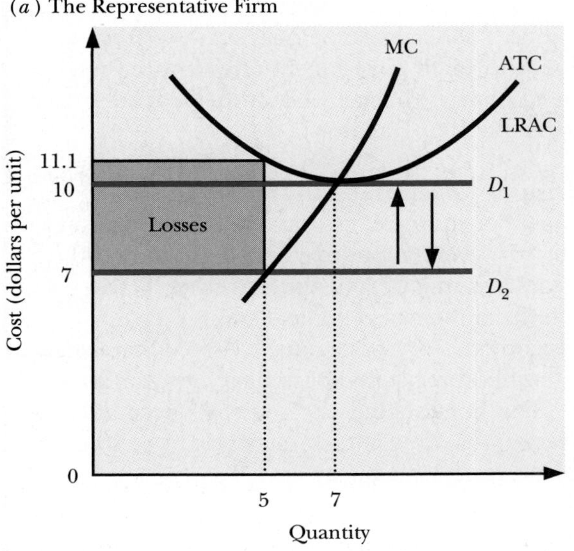

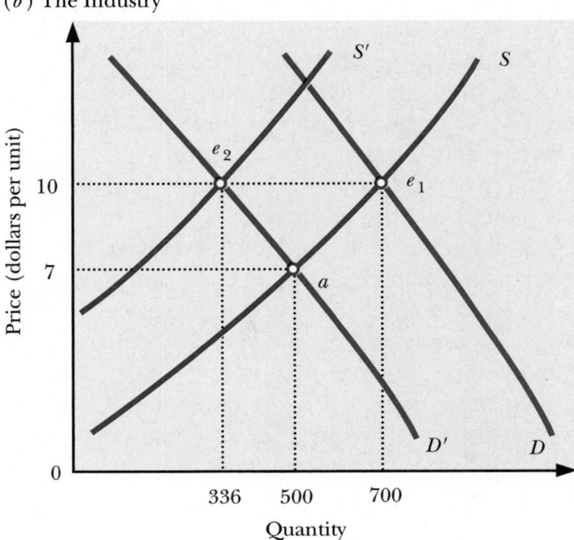

FIGURE 10 Exit of Firms Eliminates Losses and Drives Unit Costs to a Minimum

The initial long-run equilibrium is e_1, the intersection of D and S in panel (b). Demand drops to D', causing the short-run equilibrium price to fall to $7 (point a). The representative firm incurs losses as D_1 shifts downward to D_2. The exit of firms in the long run shifts the supply curve to S', which lifts the price back to $10 and eliminates losses. Each firm returns to producing seven units of output, but the number of firms falls from 100 (700 ÷ 7) to 48 (336 ÷ 7).

Example 3.) Socialism, as an economic system, broke down in part because it could not adapt to the incessant change that goes on in the world.

The Gains from Voluntary Exchange or Trade

The theory of perfect competition demonstrates that both producers and consumers can gain from voluntary exchange between many independent buyers and sellers.

Figure 11 shows an industry that is in equilibrium when price is $9 and output is 400 units. Because the industry supply curve begins at $5, the first unit can be coaxed out of some supplier by paying just $5; any price less than $5 would result in a zero output. To coax the hundredth unit out of another supplier, a price of $6 must be paid; to elicit the four hundredth unit requires a price of $9. Although the market price is $9, some production of this good would have occurred even at a price less than $9. Those firms that would have been willing to supply the good at lower prices obtain a surplus

EXAMPLE 3

The Invisible Hand: The Paradox of Progress

As the U.S. economy entered the 1990s, Adam Smith's invisible hand brought about stunning downsizing in America's best-known companies. General Motors cut its labor force by 74,000, Sears by 83,000, IBM by 25,000, and Boeing by 27,000. Such layoffs are big news and frightening to all of us.

But the invisible hand creates as well as destroys. While Sears downsized, Wal-Mart added 260,000 jobs; while IBM cut back, Microsoft, Intel, and Dell Computer expanded. General Motors downsized, but some 29,000 Americans were employed at new jobs with Honda, Toyota, Nissan, and other new Japanese plants built in the United States.

Every day jobs are created and destroyed. In the short run, the process seems cruel. But in the long run, it is integral to economic progress. In 1900, for example, 40 out of every 100 Americans worked on farms. Today, only 3 out of 100 need be farmworkers, while the remaining 97 out of 100 workers are involved in providing new homes, computers, pharmaceuticals, appliances, movies, video games, and many other goods and services.

Joseph Schumpeter called this process "creative destruction." In 1920, there were over 2 million railroad employees; now there are but 230,000. In 1900 only 51,000 workers repaired electronic equipment; today, 711,000 people do such work on much more advanced equipment. There are hardly any blacksmiths, boilermakers, or milliners today, but there are plenty of engineers, computer programmers, and truck, bus, and taxi drivers.

The entire process is led by the invisible hand. Most people fear the process because it leads to lost jobs. Politicians sometimes want to freeze old jobs through government intervention. As pointed out by Michael Cox of the Federal Reserve Bank of Dallas:

> History demonstrates the futility of saving jobs. For instance, it's hard to miss the absurdity of a well-intentioned program that 100 years ago might have aimed to keep blacksmiths and harness makers employed. As recently as 70 years ago, the United States had 10 million registered passenger cars but 20.5 million horses. Had our ancestors been able to freeze jobs, the United States would be stuck in the horse-and-buggy era.

Source: Adapted from "The Churn: The Paradox of Progress," Federal Reserve Bank of Dallas, 1992 Annual Report, and Joseph Schumpeter, *Capitalism, Socialism and Democracy*, 3d ed. New York: Harper and Brothers, 1950.

return when the market price is \$9. The supplier of the first unit receives a surplus of \$4 (= \$9 − \$5); the supplier of the 100th unit, a surplus of \$3 (= \$9 − \$6). The total surplus obtained by the suppliers of this good equals the area of the triangle *ceb*. Alfred Marshall, the great nineteenth-century British economist, called this area above the supply curve and below the price the producers' surplus.

Producers' surplus represents the amount that producers receive in excess of the minimum value the producers would have been willing to accept.

In Figure 11, when the market price is \$9, producers' surplus is the area *ceb,* which equals \$800.

The concept of producers' surplus is similar to the concept of consumers' surplus discussed in an earlier chapter.

Consumers' surplus represents the consumer benefits (the dollar value of total utility) from consuming a good in excess of the dollar expenditure on the good.

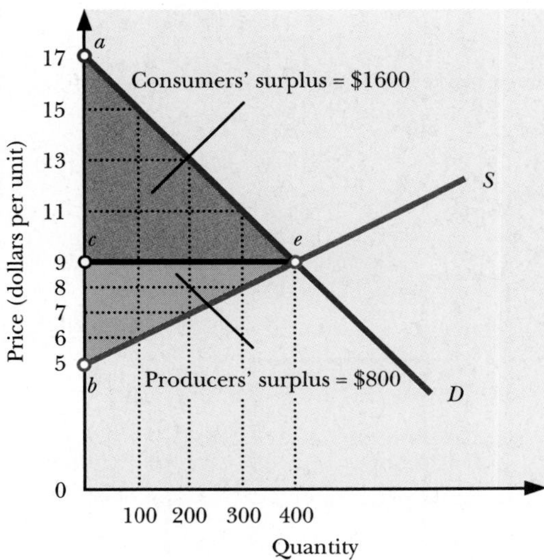

FIGURE 11 The Gains from Trade

When the price is \$9, producers' surplus is the area *ceb,* and consumers' surplus is the area *cea*. The first unit is worth \$17 to buyers and costs \$5; it yields a gain of \$12 to society from trade. All 400 units of output at the \$9 price are worth the sum of the consumers' surplus and the producers' surplus, or area *aeb*. The total of consumers' and producers' surplus is \$2400 (area of triangle *aeb* = 1/2 × base × height = 1/2 × \$12 × 400 = \$2400).

In Figure 11, when the market price is \$9, the consumer surplus is the area *aec,* which equals \$1600.

What is the value of an industry? In Figure 11, the first unit is worth \$17 to some consumer because the demand curve intersects the vertical axis at \$17. The first unit can be coaxed out of some producer for \$5. Thus, the first unit is worth approximately \$12 to society [(\$17 − \$9) + (\$9 − \$5)]. This \$12 that is gained from trade is shared by the supplier who values the first unit at only \$5 and the buyer who values the first unit at \$17. Similarly, the hundredth unit is worth \$15 to some buyer and \$6 to some supplier, yielding a net gain of \$9 [(\$15 − \$9) + (\$9 − \$6)] at a market price of \$9. The four hundredth unit squeezes out all the gains from trade.

The value of a free market, or the benefit of trade or voluntary exchange, to the economy is measured by the sum of producers' and consumers' surplus. It is important to realize that the sum of the two surpluses is the value to society of the product net of the costs of production. Because the consumers' surplus *aec* = \$1600 and the producers' surplus *ceb* = \$800, society's net gain in the market illustrated in Figure 11 is \$2400. The triangle area *aeb* can be interpreted as the potential loss to society if this market industry were eliminated.

In the real world, the gains from trade are enormous. Think of the cost to society of prohibiting the purchase and sale of a simple product like tomatoes, forcing about two-thirds of the population that does not now engage in gardening to grow their own tomatoes. The opportunity cost of forcing a multitude of busy electricians, lawyers, and doctors to weed, seed, and tend tomatoes, and the lost profits of those farmers with a comparative advantage in tomatoes, would amount to many billions of dollars.

Buffet Pricing: Application to the Internet Market

When a firm sells many items—as on a lunch buffet—or many pieces of a single item—as with Internet and telephone services—it may be optimal for the firm to charge a fixed price for unlimited usage or access. Such "buffet" pricing occurs when the marginal cost of an additional unit is small relative to the cost of monitoring how much is being used. The marginal cost of a diner in a buffet restaurant taking an extra helping is less than the cost of hiring extra waiters to serve each new item. In the case of a lunch buffet, the cost saved is the cost of employing additional service personnel. In the case of Internet usage, the marginal cost of another minute online is so low that the Internet service provider simply charges a monthly fee for unlimited usage. Cell phones are now priced this way as well, as are the subway systems in New York—riders can pay a monthly fee for unlimited usage. These examples have one thing in common: Once the consumer is admitted, the marginal cost of extra usage is very low compared to the cost of itemized pricing.

How does buffet pricing affect the theory of competitive pricing? In buffet pricing, the good being sold is unlimited access. Consider an Internet service provider (ISP). Let's assume in this case that providing Internet services is perfectly competitive. (In reality America Online is the dominant player. In the chapter on oligopoly, we shall examine a market with a dominant firm.)

ISPs have fixed setup costs. For example, they usually pay about $10 a month to the telecommunications company for each customer. Variable costs may be associated with maintaining the account as well. Because more customers mean slower access, most ISPs use a monitoring technology to automatically disconnect customers who leave the computer idle. Providers also must provide for more capacity. Thus, we should expect marginal costs to rise as the number of customers increases.

The demand side works much as for other competitive firms, but the interpretation is different. Panel (*a*) of Figure 12 shows a particular consumer's demand curve for Internet time. She is willing to pay $2 for the first hour and $0 for the fiftieth hour each month. Her demand curve (*dd'*) is linear. If the consumer has unlimited usage, her consumer surplus (not counting the monthly access fee) is $50 a month—the area of the triangle underneath the demand curve and above a $0 price. Presumably, $50 is the maximum amount she would be willing to pay for unlimited monthly usage.

Panel (*b*) shows the market demand curve for unlimited access by five consumers. The vertical axis shows the price of unlimited access; the horizontal axis shows the number of customers demanding such access. The first consumer—shown in panel (*a*)—is willing to pay $50 a month for Internet service. The second consumer will pay $40, the third and fourth $30, and the fifth $20. The height of each vertical section shows each consumer's total benefits from unlimited access.

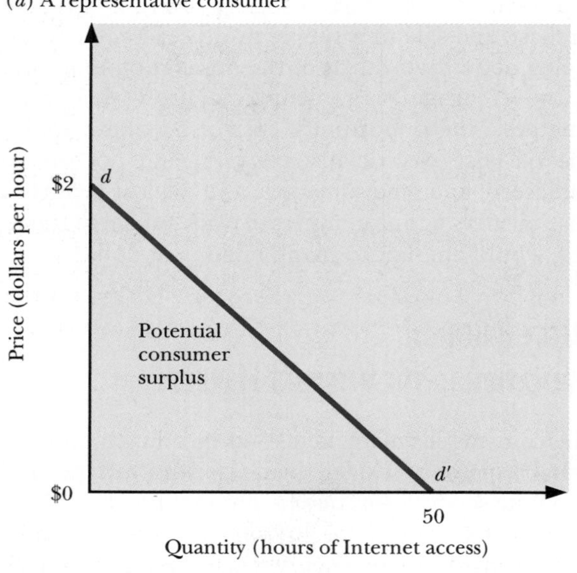

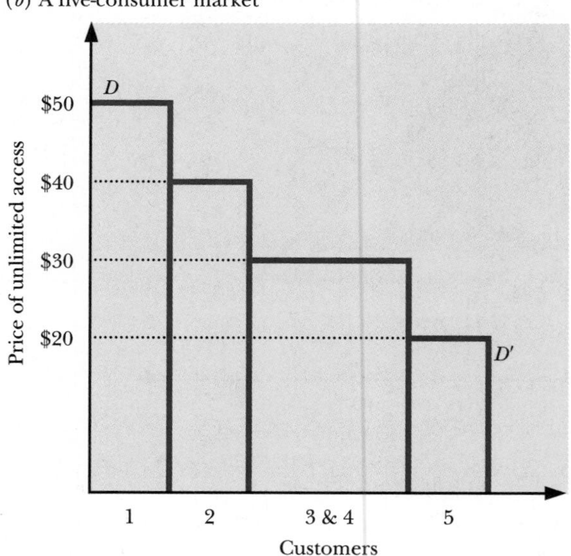

FIGURE 12 Consumer Demand for Internet Access Hours

Panel (*a*) shows a consumer's demand curve *dd'*, with potential consumer surplus of $50 (area under demand curve and above a $0 price per hour of Internet use). Panel (*b*) shows the market demand curve, the stair-step demand curve *DD'*, for five distinct consumers with potential consumer surpluses of $50, $40, $30 (two), and $20. These surpluses represent the maximum price any consumer is willing to pay for unlimited access.

Figure 13 shows that in a large market with many consumers there would be a smooth, generally downward-sloping demand curve. As the price falls, more and more customers are brought into the market. People who receive fewer benefits are now willing to pay for unlimited access. The short-run market supply curve is, as before, the horizontal sum of all marginal cost curves above average variable costs. Thus, in Figure 13 the short-run equilibrium price is $20.

The long-run analysis would be substantially the same as shown for the other industries, but in the ISP industry entry may be much quicker than for a complicated manufacturing firm. However, entry is not instantaneous, as it might be with online retailers, for providing Internet connections requires technology other than just setting up a Web page. The key question is whether providing Internet connections is subject to rising or falling marginal costs as new technologies become available. Can competition be relied on as a resource allocation mechanism? Technologies are changing so fast that we can expect the costs of linking people to the Internet to fall over time. We can expect prices to fall. Indeed, we have assumed in the above analysis that an ISP receives no other source of income, but we know that some providers also sell advertising space. This operation tends to shift the supply curve to the right, because including advertising revenues with a given monthly service fee increases the amount of service the ISP is willing to sell. Indeed, it is conceivable that the price of limited Internet connections might fall to zero. For example, in August 1999, Microsoft offered free Internet connections in Europe.

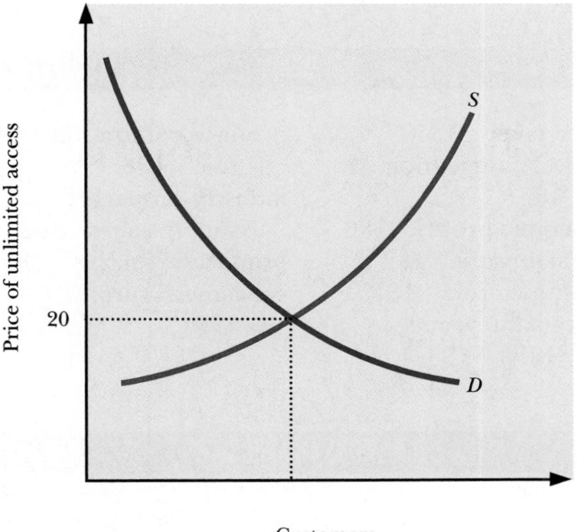

FIGURE 13 The Market for Internet Service Providers

This figure shows the market demand for Internet service providers in a competitive market. The appropriate price is the price of unlimited access. The demand curve is downward-sloping because with many consumers there will be hierarchy in which consumers can be ranked by how much they are willing to pay for unlimited access. The competitive equilibrium price of $20 separates those willing to pay at least $20 from those unwilling to pay $20. Anything that shifts the supply curve to the right will lower the price and bring in more users.

Perfect Competition in the Real World

Most industries are not perfectly competitive, but the conditions of perfect competition are met in a number of markets. Most agricultural markets—fibers, grains, livestock, vegetables, fruits—are perfectly competitive. Stock markets and commodity markets are also perfectly competitive. More important than these purely competitive markets are industries that closely *approximate* the conditions of perfect competition. In such industries, the number of producers may not be large enough to make each firm a perfect price taker, but the degree of control over price may be negligible. Information on prices and product quality may not be perfect, but consumers may have a significant amount of that information at their disposal. The product may not be perfectly homogeneous, but the distinctions between products may be inconsequential. The number of firms in the industry may not be exceptionally large, but many firms may be waiting in the wings to enter on short notice if economic profits are earned. An industry need not meet all the conditions of perfect competition for the theory of perfect competition to apply to its business behavior.

An Overview of Perfect Competition

The theory of perfect competition tells us that economic profits will be eliminated in the long run by the entry of new firms and that when the markets are in equilibrium, price and marginal cost will be equal. It also states that short-run behavior will differ from long-run behavior. In the short run, firms will stay in business as long as the price covers average variable cost; in the long run, if the price fails to cover average costs (remember that in the long run there are no fixed costs), firms will leave the industry. In the short run, demand increases will lead to price increases; in the long run, the price will ultimately depend upon the costs of the representative firm. Finally, the theory tells us that competition will result in rising and declining industries and that these changes are the source of progress in an economy.

Two of the most important characteristics of perfectly competitive industries are (1) that perfectly competitive firms will operate at minimum average cost in the long run; and (2) that perfectly competitive firms will produce that quantity of output at which price equals marginal cost in both the short run and the long run. These characteristics are important for us to remember when we evaluate the other types of markets—monopoly, oligopoly, and monopolistic competition—that we shall consider in subsequent chapters. In the next chapter we shall examine the behavior of firms that are able to exercise some control over price. Monopolists exercise considerable control over their prices; monopolistically competitive firms have only limited control over their prices.

SUMMARY

1. A market is perfectly competitive when it contains a large number of sellers and buyers, when buyers and sellers have perfect information, when the product is homogeneous, and when there is freedom of entry and exit. These conditions ensure that each seller will be a price taker. The price will be dictated to sellers by the market.

2. In the short run, the number of firms in an industry is constant, and the firm has fixed costs. In the long run, the number of firms can change through entry and exit, and fixed costs become variable costs. Profit-maximizing competitive enterprises face two decisions in the short run: first, whether or not to shut down: second, how much to produce, provided the enterprise does not shut down. If the market price covers average variable cost, the competitive firm will produce a positive level of output, the quantity at which price and marginal cost are equal. The firm's supply curve is its marginal cost curve above average variable cost. The industry supply schedule is the horizontal summation of all the supply schedules of individual firms in the industry. The price at which the quantity supplied equals the quantity demanded is the market price. Each firm takes this market price as given.

3. In the long run, firms enter competitive industries where economic profits are being made and exit from industries where a below-normal profit is being earned. Economic profits must be zero for the competitive industry to be in equilibrium. In the long run, goods are produced at minimum average cost, with price equal to marginal cost for the average competitive firm.

4. Capitalism is a creative process, allowing economic systems to respond to change. The response of firms to profits and losses is what creates change and progress.

5. The sum of consumers' surplus and producers' surplus represents the gain from voluntary exchange or trade.

6. The theory of perfect competition can explain the behavior of firms in an industry even when that industry does not meet all the conditions of perfect competition.

KEY WORDS

price taker 185
perfect competition 185
economic profits 186
normal profit 187
shutdown rule 187
marginal revenue (MR) 188
profit-maximization rule 188
industry or market supply curve 192
producers' surplus 199
consumers' surplus 199

QUESTIONS AND PROBLEMS

1. Explain why each firm may not be a price taker in an industry in which there is product differentiation among firms.
2. A firm that is contemplating whether to produce its tenth unit of output finds its marginal costs for the tenth unit are $50 and its marginal revenue for the tenth unit equals $30. What advice would you give this firm?
3. A firm has fixed costs of $100,000. It receives a price of $25 for each unit of output. Average variable costs are lowest (equal to $20) at 1000

units of output. What advice would you give this firm in the short run? In the long run?

4. Explain the relationships between accounting profits, normal profits, and economic profits. Will they always be different amounts?

5. The representative firm in the widget industry, which is perfectly competitive, is making a large economic profit. What predictions can you make about what will happen in this industry in the long run?

6. Evaluate the following statement: "The theory of perfect competition claims that economic profits will disappear in the long run. This assumption is incorrect because I know a family that has a farm that earns more than $1 million per year."

7. When will the long-run price be less than the current price?

8. Jones is a genius at farming, knowing exactly what to plant and when. As a result, Jones's farm consistently earns higher profits than do other farms. From the economist's perspective, do these represent higher profits or something else?

9. In Table 2, fixed costs are $48. If fixed costs were raised to $100, how would the supply schedule be affected in the short run?

10. Imagine that a firm faces the cost schedule given in Table A.

TABLE A

Quantity, Q	*Variable Cost, VC*	*Fixed Cost, FC*	*Total Cost, TC*
0	$0	$5	$5
1	6	5	11
2	14	5	19
3	24	5	29
4	36	5	41

a. Calculate the firm's profit or loss for each level of output when the price is $5.99, when the price is $6.01, and when the price is $10.01.
b. Calculate how many units of output the profit-maximizing or loss-minimizing firm will produce at each of those three prices.
c. Graph the firm's supply schedule.

11. You observe that the (competitive) airline industry is incurring economic losses. What do you expect to happen to ticket prices, to the quantity of airline passengers, and to the number of airline companies as time passes?

12. You observe that a highly profitable new industry is manufacturing a product of advanced technology (such as computers). What do you expect to happen to the price of the product, to profits, to the industry's output, and to the number of firms as time passes?

13. The demand and supply curves for a product are $Q = 10 - P$ for the former and $Q = P$ for the latter. What are the equilibrium values of P, Q, and the total of consumer and producer surpluses?

14. In Figure A, if the competitive price is $15, what are the firm's profit, total revenue, total costs, fixed costs, and variable costs?

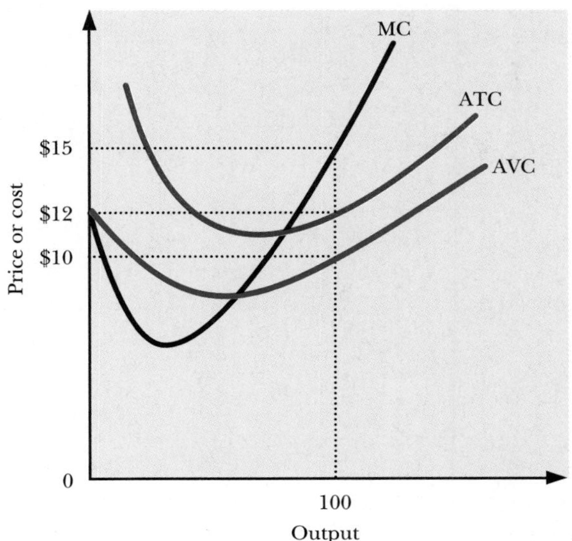

FIGURE A

15. Analyze the effects of the following on the price of unlimited Internet access:
a. Increased advertising revenues to Internet service providers
b. A law prohibiting Internet service providers from selling advertising
c. A discovery that would make online shopping easier

INTERNET CONNECTION

16. Using the links from http://www.awl.com/ruffin_gregory, read the article about the average age of farmers on the United States Department of Agriculture Web page.
    a. According to the article, what is the average age of farmers today? What reasons does the article suggest for this age?
    b. The article also suggests that there has been insufficient entry into the farm sector and that more farmers under 35 years of age need to be attracted to farming. Applying what you have learned in this chapter, suppose that agriculture is competitive; thus, you can use the model of perfect competition. Further suppose that farm prices have been declining. Using the model of perfect competition, show what will happen to the number of farms in the United States.
    c. Do you agree with the article's premise that more entry in the market is necessary?

PUZZLE ANSWERED: A key lesson of economics is that bankruptcy and the creation of new firms are often opposite sides of the same coin. When demand shifts from one industry to the next, it is necessary to shift resources to the growing industry. Both profits *and* losses are key to an efficient economy.

Chapter 11

Monopoly and Monopolistic Competition

Chapter Insight

Competition is considered good because it drives prices down to the level of minimum unit cost; thus, consumers are able to buy the good or service as cheaply as possible. The chief bane of capitalism is monopoly. When Netscape wanted the federal government to control its competitor, Microsoft, the company called its rival a monopoly. When consumers complain of cable television rates, they assert that there is a monopoly. When a pharmaceutical company has drugs that are coming off patent, Wall Street worries that its stock price may fall; or when a pharmaceutical company receives a patent on a blockbuster drug, like Pfizer with Viagra, the stock price increases. In waging famous antitrust cases against such industry giants as IBM and Microsoft, the Justice Department maintained that those firms had too much monopoly power.

In this chapter we shall examine monopoly and monopolistic competition. Monopoly exists when a firm faces no competition and can charge any price it wants. How does a firm achieve a monopoly? How does it decide on the price? Monopolistic competition exists when a firm faces competition but has some control over price. How does such a market compare to perfect competition?

LEARNING OBJECTIVES

After completing this chapter, you will be able to:

1. Discuss the conditions giving rise to monopoly.
2. Calculate marginal revenue for a monopolist.
3. See how the monopolist maximizes profit.
4. Understand that a profit-maximizing monopoly cannot be efficient from a social standpoint.
5. Apply monopoly theory to monopolistic competition.

CHAPTER PUZZLE: You own a company that sells electrical generators. Your market research informs you that a 1 percent increase in price would lower quantity demanded by exactly 1 percent. What would you do?

Conditions for Monopoly

Monopoly literally means "single seller." A pure monopoly has the following characteristics.

A **pure monopoly** exists when

1. There is one seller in the market for some good or service that has no close substitutes.
2. Barriers to entry protect the seller from competition.

As with perfect competition, examples of pure monopoly are rare, but the theory of pure monopoly does shed light on the behavior of firms that approximate the conditions of pure monopoly. Monopoly power allows the seller to have some control over the price of the product; this power is possessed to some degree by many firms. For example, a certain corner at a busy intersection may be the best spot in a town for a service station, giving one firm a locational monopoly at that spot. Such a service station could charge a higher price than its competitors.

The Sources of Monopoly

There are three basic theories about how monopolies can come about. Monopolies can arise because (1) one large firm may have lower costs than many smaller firms, (2) the government grants a monopoly to a single individual or corporation, or (3) a single firm controls a critical raw material.

The Natural Monopoly

A firm has a natural monopoly if its costs of production are less than the total costs of production of two or more separate firms producing the same total output. Large-scale production may be cheaper because of *economies of scale* or *economies of scope.*

A **natural monopoly** prevails when industry output is cheaper to produce with one firm than with two or more firms.

In the case of economies of scale, as the firm produces more its average costs fall. Economies of scale usually result from the use of costly specialized equipment. Economies of scope are similar, but they include the production of many similar products. For example, because automobiles and trucks are produced by the same types of equipment, a firm that produces a large number of trucks will have a lower cost of producing automobiles.

Throughout all levels of output, the natural monopoly's long-run average cost curve is declining. Clearly, in this case, there is room for only one firm because it will have the lowest costs.

Public utilities, such as local telephone service, electric utilities, and natural gas utilities, offer the most ready examples of possible natural monopolies. In a later chapter, we shall study the regulation of natural monopolies by the state.

Government Protection

Most examples of monopoly that come to mind are situations in which the government has granted a monopoly, through patents, public franchises (such as the public utilities mentioned above), and licensing. Indeed, in most cases, monopolies exist because of government involvement in one way or another.

Patents. American *patent* laws allow an inventor the exclusive right to use the invention for a period of 20 years. The patent holder is thereby protected from competition during that period. The IBM Corporation's patents on tabulating equipment, Microsoft's patents on its software, and SmithKline Beecham's patent on the drug Tagamet are examples of this type of entry barrier. The Bell System achieved a monopoly in the nineteenth century when Alexander Graham Bell obtained a patent for the telephone just hours before a rival inventor. (See Example 1.)

Public Franchises. State, local, and federal governments grant to individuals or organizations exclusive *franchises* to be the sole operator in a particular business. Competitors are legally prohibited from entering the market. The U.S. Postal Service's delivery of mail is a classic example of a public franchise. Only the post office can use your mailbox! States grant exclusive franchises to operate restaurants and service stations along tollways. Duty-free shops in airports and at international borders are also franchise operations. Many public utilities operate under state or local franchises.

Licensing. Entry into an industry or profession may be regulated by government agencies and autonomous professional organizations. The American Medical Association licenses medical schools and allocates hospital/staff privileges to physicians. The Federal Communications Commission licenses radio and television stations and controls entry into the lucrative broadcasting industry. Most countries license airlines and thus limit entry into the industry. In the United States, nuclear power plants must be licensed by the federal government.

Exclusive Ownership of Raw Materials

Established companies can be protected from the entry of new firms by their control of raw materials. The International Nickel Company of Canada once owned almost all of the world's nickel reserves. Virtually all of the world's diamond sales are under the control of the DeBeers Company of South Africa. American Metal Climax Corporation controls most of the world's supply of molybdenum (a metallic element used in strengthening and hardening steel).

Price-Making Behavior

The most fundamental difference between monopoly and perfect competition lies in the determination of price. The perfectly competitive firm is a *price taker;* it must accept whatever price the market dictates. The monopolist, however, is a *price maker;* it has its own market demand curve along which it seeks the profit-maximizing price. An alternative term for price-making behavior is *price searcher*. Price-making behavior is not restricted to pure monopolies. Even

EXAMPLE 1

The Original Bell Telephone Monopoly

The key characteristic of a monopoly is its ability to charge a price much higher than its average costs. The original Bell patents on the telephone provided the American Telephone and Telegraph Company (AT&T) with a monopoly from 1877 to 1894. Consequently, telephone service was extremely expensive. The cost of basic telephone service for a residential customer was about 5 percent of a typical worker's wage. Today, basic local service costs less than 1 percent of a typical worker's wage.

The effect of competition on prices is illustrated by the events that occurred when the Bell patents expired in 1894. From 1894 to 1900, almost 2000 new non-Bell telephone systems sprang up around the country. The number of telephones in the United States skyrocketed, from 240,000 in 1894 to over 6 million in 1907. In those areas where a Bell company competed with a non-Bell company, the price of basic telephone service dropped by about one-half. Bell's profits on stockholder equity plunged from around 46 percent to about 8 percent.

Source: Gerald Brock, *The Telecommunications Industry* (Cambridge: Harvard University Press, 1981).

the local grocery store has some ability to set a price that maximizes profit.

A **price maker** is a firm with some degree of control over the price of the good or service it sells.

Figure 1 illustrates the difference between price takers and price makers. The price taker's demand curve is perfectly elastic because the price is dictated by the market and more units can be sold without lowering the price. In contrast, the price-making firm must lower its price on all units sold in order to sell more. In other words, the demand curve facing a price maker is downward sloping.

Like price takers, price makers want to maximize profits by producing that level of output at which marginal revenue (MR) and marginal cost (MC) are equal. For the price taker, price equals marginal revenue; for the price maker, however, price does not.

Marginal revenue (MR) is the additional revenue raised per unit increase in quantity sold; that is, MR = ΔTR/ΔDQ, where TR is total revenue.

Price in Relation to Marginal Revenue

The perfect competitor can always sell additional output at the going market price.

For the price maker, price exceeds marginal revenue. In order to sell an additional unit of output per sales period, the price maker must lower the price on the units previously sold at a higher price. Thus, the extra revenue generated per period equals the (new) price of the extra unit sold minus the revenue lost due to the lower price for the previous units of output sold. In effect, selling one more unit "spoils the market" for the earlier units.

For a price maker, because the price for all units must decrease to sell one more unit, price is greater than marginal revenue:

$$P > \text{MR}$$

There is another way to explain why price exceeds marginal revenue for the monopolist price maker. In the chapter on productivity and costs we considered the relationship between average and marginal values. Recall that an average value falls if the marginal value is smaller than the previous aver-

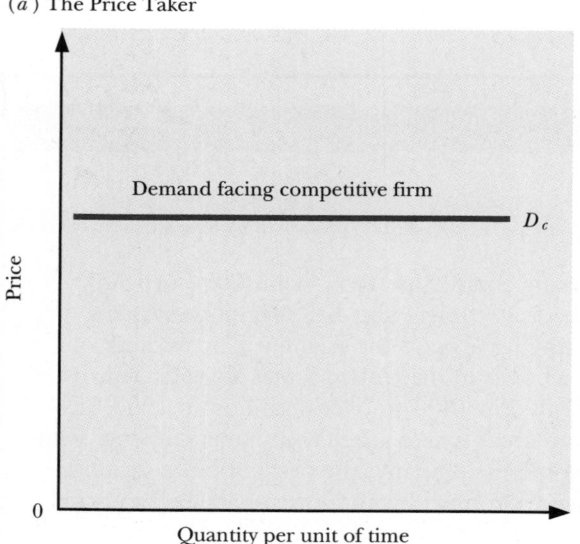

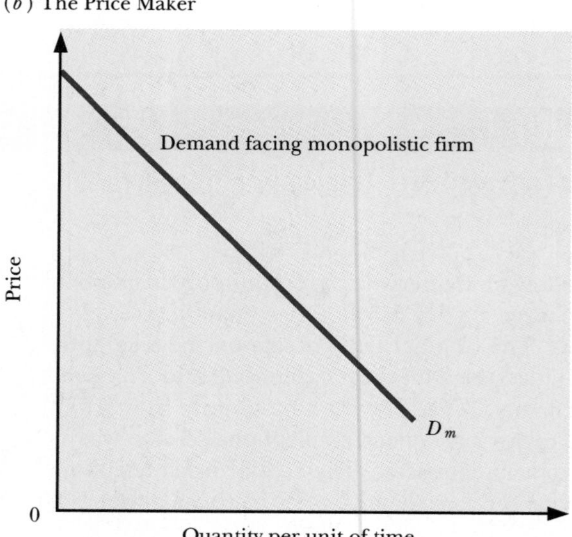

FIGURE 1 A Price Maker Versus a Price Taker

In panel (*a*), the demand curve D_c facing the competitive firm is perfectly horizontal; thus, the firm can sell as many additional units as it wants without lowering its price. In panel (*b*), the demand curve D_m facing the monopolistic firm is downward sloping; thus, the firm must lower its price in order to sell additional units.

age. Thus, if average revenue is falling, marginal revenue (MR) must be below it.

Average revenue (AR) equals total revenue (TR) divided by output.

Average revenue and price are the same when all units are sold at the same price. In general, TR = *P* × *Q*, and TR = AR × *Q*. To say that the price maker faces a downward-sloping demand schedule is to say that AR, or *P*, falls as output increases. In this case, marginal revenue must be below the previous average revenue, pulling it down. Thus, if AR is declining, MR must be less than AR. Since AR = *P*, *P* must be greater than MR.

We can measure marginal revenue per additional unit sold by taking the ratio of the change in revenue to the change in total units sold brought about by the change in price: that is, MR = ΔTR/Δ*Q*. It is not necessary to change the number of units by increments of only one unit, as in the foregoing examples. To illustrate, imagine that a producer of chocolates increases revenue by $400 when it sells another 100 boxes of chocolates. The change in revenue is $400, and the change in quantity sold is 100. Thus, the marginal revenue is MR = $400 ÷ 100 = $4.

A monopolist faces the demand schedule shown in columns 1 and 2 of Table 1. Column 3 lists the total revenue produced at each level of output (*P* × *Q*), and column 4 gives the marginal revenue schedule.

The values in column 4 that are positioned vertically between the rows correspond to the marginal revenue for each change in output level in Table 1. Since the first unit can be sold at a price of $19, the marginal revenue of that unit is also $19. To sell two units the monopolist must lower the price to $17. Total revenue is now $34; thus, MR = $34 − $19 = $15. Again, we see that MR is less than *P* for all units but the first. To sell three units requires a price of $15; total revenue rises by the MR of $11 to $45. As long as selling another unit lowers the price by $2, marginal revenue falls by $4 (twice as much).

The demand and marginal revenue schedules for the firm in Table 1 appear as demand and marginal revenue curves in Figure 2. The advantage of using

TABLE 1 MONOPOLY EQUILIBRIUM

Output (units), Q (1)	*Price or Average Revenue, P = AR (2)*	*Total Revenue, TR = Q × P (3) = (1) × (2)*	*Marginal Revenue, MR (4)*	*Total Cost, TC (5)*	*Marginal Cost, MC (6)*	*Average Cost, ATC (7)*	*Profit = TR − TC (8) = (3) − (5)*
0	$21	$0		$12			−$12
			$19		$10		
1	19	19		22		22	−3
			15		6		
2	17	34		28		14	6
			11		8		
3	15	45		36		13	9
			7		10		
4	13	52		46		11.5	6
			3		13		
5	11	55		58		11.6	−3
			−1		15		
6	9	54		72		12	−15

This table shows the demand and marginal revenue schedules of a monopolist. The demand schedule is given in the first two columns. Because all customers are charged the same price, price and average revenue are the same. Total revenue, in column 3, equals *Q* × *P*. Marginal revenue is the increase in total revenue brought about by increasing output by 1 unit. The monopolist's profit is maximized by producing 3 units of output, where profit equals $9. If the monopolist had attempted to produce 1 more unit of output, total revenue would have increased by $7 and costs would have increased by $10, so profit would have fallen by $3. If the monopolist had produced 1 less unit, total revenue would have fallen by $11 and costs would have fallen by $8, reducing profit by $3. The firm expands outputs so long as MC does not exceed MR.

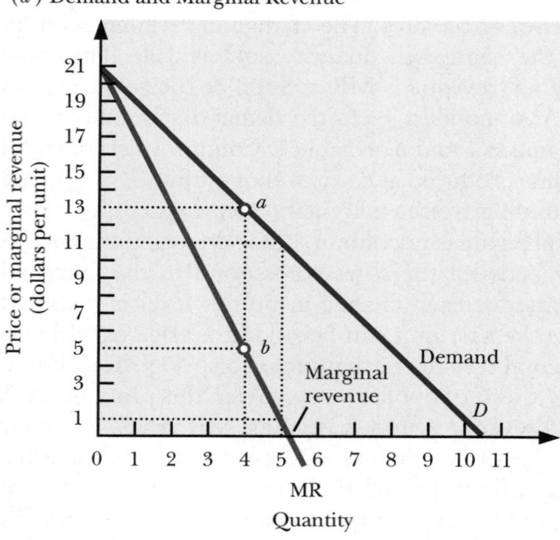

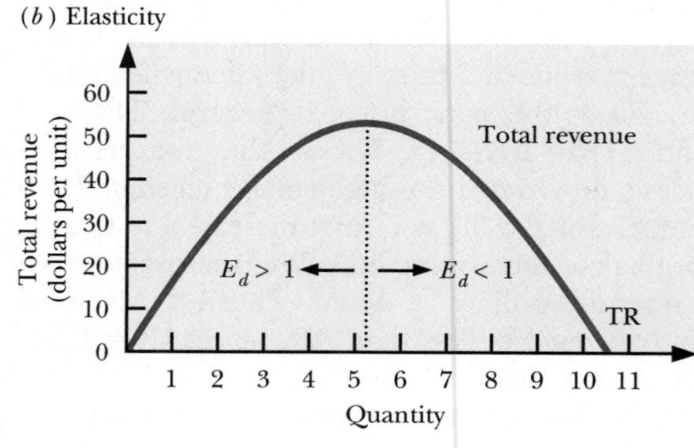

FIGURE 2 Demand, Marginal Revenue, and Elasticity

In panel (*a*), the demand and marginal revenue schedules of Table 1 are plotted as *D* and MR. At an output level of 4 units, the price is $13 and the marginal revenue is $5. In other words, the value of MR for any given price is at that point on the MR curve directly below the point on the demand curve corresponding to that price. If the demand curve is a straight line, the marginal revenue curve will be located horizontally halfway between the demand curve and the vertical axis.

In panel (*b*), the total revenue schedule of Table 1 is plotted, showing the relationship between MR and total revenue. When MR is positive, total revenue is rising; when MR is negative, total revenue is falling; when MR is zero, total revenue reaches its highest value. When the price elasticity of demand (E_d) is greater than 1, total revenue is rising; when it is less than 1, total revenue is falling. Thus, when demand is elastic, reductions in price raise total revenue; when demand is inelastic, reductions in price lower total revenue.

an MR curve rather than a numerical schedule is that on a graph we can read MR at or between different levels of output. The negative slope of the firm's demand curve, labeled *D,* shows that the firm is a price maker (it must lower price to sell a greater quantity).

The location of the MR curve below the demand curve shows graphically that price is greater than marginal revenue for any quantity of output (except for the first unit sold). Whenever the demand curve is a straight line, the MR curve will be horizontally halfway between the demand curve and the vertical axis because the slope of the MR curve is twice as steep as the slope of the demand curve. In Table 1, as we noted above, when price falls by $2, marginal revenue falls by $4. Accordingly, the marginal revenue curve intersects the horizontal axis halfway between the origin and the intersection of the straight-line demand curve with the horizontal axis, as shown in panel (*a*) of Figure 2. This relationship between the demand and marginal revenue curves is sometimes called the halfway rule.

The **halfway rule** states that when the demand curve can be represented by a straight line, the marginal revenue curve bisects the horizontal distance between the demand curve and the vertical axis.

The Theory of Monopoly

How Monopolies Determine Output

The monopolist differs from other types of price makers in two ways. As we discussed earlier, first, the monopolist is the sole producer of a product for which there are no close substitutes. Second, the monopolist is protected by barriers to entry.

The monopolist has a profit incentive to lower price and expand output when marginal revenue exceeds marginal cost. For example, if the marginal revenue of an additional unit of output is \$19 and the marginal cost of the additional unit is only \$10, the firm can add \$9 to profit by producing the additional unit. Thus, the monopolist will cut prices when marginal revenue exceeds marginal costs.

If the monopolist finds that marginal revenue is less than marginal cost, it pays to lower output and raise price. If MC = \$10 and MR = \$7, a cut in output by 1 full unit would lower costs by \$10 and revenue by only \$7, so profits would rise by \$3 (or losses would fall by \$3). Thus, the monopolist maximizes profit by choosing an output level where marginal cost (MC) equals marginal revenue (MR).

> The monopolistic firm can raise profit by expanding output (by lowering price) when MR > MC. The firm can raise profit by cutting output (by raising price) when MR < MC. The monopolist—or the price maker in general—maximizes profit by producing that quantity for which MR = MC.

Table 1 gives cost schedules for the monopolistic firm that faced the demand and revenue schedules discussed in the previous section. Like the marginal revenue values in column 4, the values in column 6 that are positioned vertically *between* the rows correspond to the marginal cost for each change in output level. What level of output will the monopolist choose to produce? Remember that the monopolist will expand output as long as marginal revenue exceeds marginal cost. The first unit of output raises total revenue by \$19 (MR = \$19) and raises costs by only \$10 (MC = \$10), thus contributing \$9 toward paying the monopolist's \$12 fixed cost and reducing a \$12 loss at zero output to a \$3 loss at 1 unit of output. The second unit of output raises revenue by \$15 and adds \$6 to costs. The second unit, therefore, turns a \$3 loss into a \$6 profit. The third unit adds \$11 to revenue and \$8 to cost, adding \$3 to profit (now \$9). If the fourth unit were produced, only \$7 would be added to revenue but \$10 would be added to cost, decreasing profit by \$3. The monopolist should therefore produce 3 units of output. Profit is maximized at $P = 15$, where profit is \$9.

Once the monopolist selects an output level of 3 units, it will charge the price of \$15 dictated by the demand schedule. The monopolist can set either price or quantity. Once one is chosen, the other will be determined by the market demand schedule. Monopolists maximize profits *either* by selecting the profit-maximizing output level and letting the market set its price *or* by selecting the profit-maximizing price and letting the demand curve determine the quantity of output.

Figure 3 shows a graph of the same monopoly profit maximization. The demand schedule is graphed as the demand curve *D;* the marginal revenue schedule is graphed as curve MR. When output is two units, marginal revenue exceeds marginal cost (point *m* is higher than point *n*), so profits rise if more than two units are produced. When output is four units, marginal revenue is less than marginal cost (point *r* is lower than point *q*), so profits rise if fewer than four units are produced.

Once again, to maximize profit the monopolist selects that output at which marginal revenue and marginal cost are equal. The MR and MC curves intersect at point *a*. We can determine the output level, price, and profit per unit of output by drawing a vertical line through *a*. The point at which the vertical line crosses the horizontal axis (point *g*) is the monopolist's output level (three units). The price corresponding to the point where the vertical line intersects the demand curve (at point *c*) is the monopolist's price (\$15). The point at which the vertical line intersects the ATC curve (at point *b*) is the average total cost of producing three units (\$12). The distance between *c* and *b* (\$15 − \$12) represents the economic profit per unit of output (\$3). Total economic profit is, therefore, profit per unit times the number of units, or the shaded area of the rectangle *cbed*. Algebraically, total economic profit = $(P - \text{ATC}) \times Q = 3 \times 3 = 9$.

Monopoly Profits in the Long Run

When there is competition in an industry, the distinction between the short run and the long run is critical. In the short run, the number of firms in the industry is fixed; in the long run, new firms can enter or old firms can exit in response to economic profits or losses. This long-run entry and exit of firms ensures that economic profits will be squeezed out of perfectly competitive industries. In the case of the monopolist, the distinction between the short run and the long run is not as important because barriers prevent new firms from entering the industry and systematically eliminating monopoly profits.

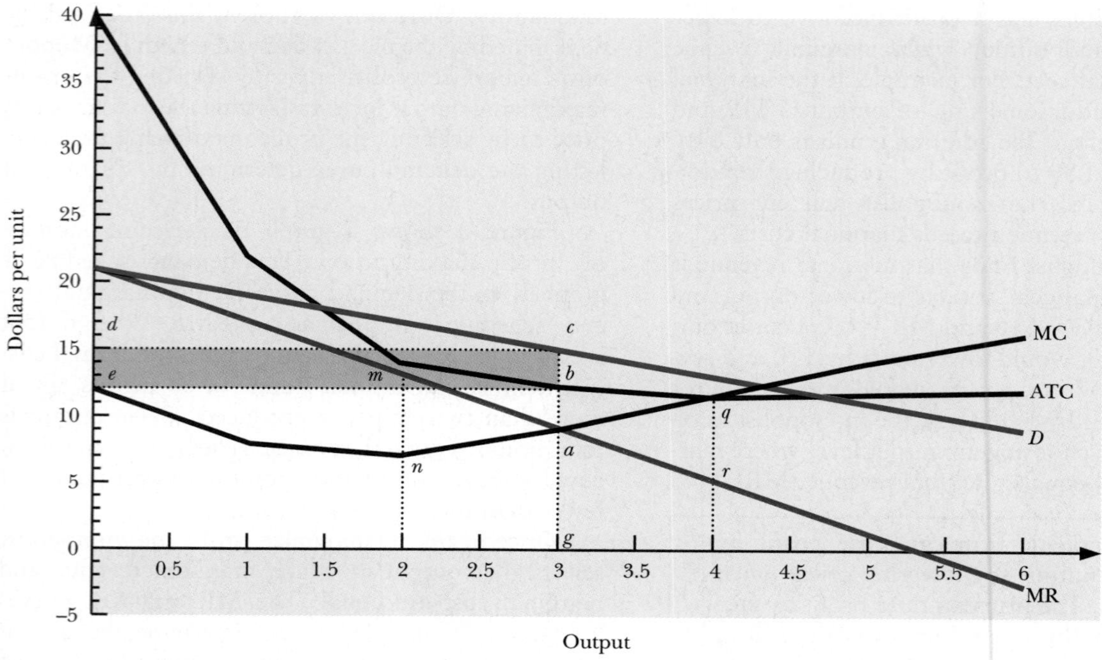

FIGURE 3 Equilibrium of a Monopoly

This monopolist has cost curves ATC and MC and faces demand curve *D*. However, the maximum profit occurs where MR = MC. The equilibrium price/quantity combination is found by drawing a vertical line from the demand curve through point *a,* where MR = MC, down to the horizontal axis. The output level represented by point *g,* where the vertical line hits the horizontal axis, gives the optimal output level (three units). The price corresponding to point *c,* where the vertical line hits the demand curve, is the optimal price ($15). Profits are represented by the rectangle *cbed.*

> Unlike competitive profits, because of barriers to entry monopoly profits can persist for long periods of time.

In the real world, it is difficult to find pure monopolies because actual or potential substitutes abound and because absolute barriers to entry are rarely present. Rather, most real-world monopolies are *near monopolies,* subject to the profit squeeze in the very long run, particularly if monopoly profits are exceptionally high.

Exceptional monopoly profits have historically inspired the development of closer substitutes for the monopolist's product. The railroads' monopoly over freight transportation was eventually broken by the emergence of trucking and air freight capabilities; the Bell System's monopoly over long-distance telephone service was broken by the advent of microwave transmission.

Although monopoly profits are not systematically driven down to the normal return, there is a tendency for high monopoly profits to inspire the development of substitutes in the very long run. (See Example 2.)

An Overview of Monopoly

Our analysis sheds light on some basic facts concerning monopoly.

1. *Monopoly profits are persistent.* Barriers to entry protect monopoly profits, although in the very long run substitutes may be developed.
2. *Monopolists need not produce where average costs are minimized.* In the long run, perfectly competitive firms will be forced to produce that quantity of output at which average costs are minimized. Monopolists, however, both in the long run and in the short run, may produce a level of output that is smaller than or larger than the level necessary to minimize average costs. In Figure 3, average total cost is

EXAMPLE 2

INTEL'S MONOPOLY

Few companies have dominated their industry as has Intel, which invented the microprocessor in the early 1970s. In 1999 Intel's microprocessors—the chips of silicon brain of every personal computer (PC)—operated over 75 percent of the several hundred million PCs operating that year. Five years earlier, Intel chips were in 90 percent of PCs. Intel achieved this dominance by learning how to manufacture better and smarter microprocessors at lower and lower prices. Intel's chips went into every IBM-compatible PC, and they became the industry standard. Now other companies, such as Advanced Micro Devices (AMD), share the market with Intel. Nevertheless, Intel still exhibits pricing power. In 1999 Intel's profit margin was close to 60 percent; thus, for every \$100 of price Intel's costs are only about \$40. This is monopoly power, but it is clearly dwindling.

Intel's greatest monopoly power is in business PCs and the high-end PCs known as servers. Other companies are chipping away at Intel's monopoly in the growing market for cheap and even free PCs. But AMD will soon be competing in the high end as well. Nobel Prize–winning economist John R. Hicks once said that the "best of all monopoly profits is the quiet life." Unfortunately, near monopolies in the technology business do not have a quiet life. Satchel Paige, one of the greatest baseball pitchers of all time as well as one of America's greatest philosophers, said, "Never look back, somebody might be gaining on you." Intel does not even have that luxury, for it faces competition on all sides.

Source: "Intel Profit for 3rd Quarter Misses Analysts' Estimates," *Wall Street Journal* (October 13, 1999).

minimized at an output of four units, but the monopolist produces only three units. In this sense, monopolists are less efficient than perfectly competitive firms.

3. *Monopolists charge a price higher than marginal cost.* The monopolist equates marginal revenue and marginal cost, and price is greater than marginal revenue. Thus, in the case of monopoly, $P > MC$.

4. *Monopolists produce where demand is elastic.* The profit-maximizing monopolist produces that quantity of output at which MR = MC. We have demonstrated that marginal revenue is positive only when demand is elastic. If the monopolist were to expand into the inelastic portion of the demand schedule, total revenue would decline and the firm's profits would fall. We can use this characteristic of monopoly pricing as a partial test for the existence of monopoly behavior. If the demand for a product is inelastic at the current price, the seller is not behaving like a profit-maximizing monopoly.

5. *There is no supply curve for monopolists.* The monopolist does not have a supply curve showing how much output will be supplied at different prices because the monopolist chooses the price. The same marginal revenue can be compatible with quite different prices, depending on the elasticity of demand.

MEASURING MONOPOLY POWER

No firm really has complete monopoly power because there are substitutes for everything. Thus, even a single newspaper in a city must compete with the Internet, *USA Today,* radio, and television. The only car company in the world would have to compete with the horse and buggy or the bicycle; at a high enough price people will switch to one of the imperfect substitutes. Given this, how do we measure the amount of monopoly power a firm faces? In the soft drink business Coke may have 50 percent of the business; in another, say, Philip Morris has 30 percent of the cigarette business. Which firm has the most monopoly power?

Economist Abba Lerner analyzed this question many years ago and concluded that the answer is very simple: The monopolist's power resides in its power to raise the price above MC. In perfect competition, the firm has absolutely no monopoly power because it must charge a price equal to marginal costs. From this reasoning, Lerner suggested that we measure the degree of monopoly power by using L (for Lerner) = $(P - \text{MC})/P$. Thus, if the price of the product is \$100 and MC = \$50, the amount of monopoly power would be 0.50. If the firm's monopoly power increased so that P = \$150, the amount of monopoly power would be (\$150 − \$50)/150 = 0.67. (See Example 3.)

> The degree of monopoly power that a firm has is measured by $L = (P - \text{MC})/P$.

Lerner's measure of monopoly power is also equal to the inverse of the elasticity of demand facing the firm. When the monopolist decides it wants to sell more of a product, it must lower the price on all units sold. Accordingly, P − MC in the above formula reflects how much the firm spoils its market by selling one more unit.[1] When divided by P, the formula just becomes $1/E$, where E is the price elasticity of demand facing the firm.

The Theory of Monopolistic Competition

In reality, few price makers are monopolies. Price makers can be anything from pure monopolies to firms that bear a close resemblance to perfect competitors. Their common characteristic is that they face a downward-sloping demand schedule for their product. In order to sell more, they must lower their price.

In the real world, there is usually some basis for distinguishing between the goods and services produced by different sellers. These distinctions may be based on the physical attributes of the product (hamburgers vary from restaurant to restaurant), on location (one gas station is more conveniently located than another), on the type of service offered (one dry cleaner offers 2-hour service; another offers 1-day service), and even on imagined differences (one type of aspirin is "better" than another). The point is that there are differences among products. Sellers of each product have some monopoly power over the customers who have a preference for their product. The extent of their monopoly power depends upon the strength of this preference.

The theory of monopolistic competition was developed by American economist Edward Chamberlin and English economist Joan Robinson in order to describe markets that produce heterogeneous products. A monopolistically competitive industry is one that blends features of monopoly and competition.

In an industry characterized by **monopolistic competition,**

1. The number of sellers is large enough to enable each seller to act independently of the others.
2. The product is differentiated from seller to seller.
3. There is free entry into and exit from the industry.
4. Sellers are price makers.

When sellers act independently, each presumes that its output or price decisions have no discernible effect on the rest of the market. Therefore, the monopolistic competitor need not worry about the reactions of rivals.

The price-making ability follows from product differentiation; because products differ, the seller has some control over price. The degree of control may be quite limited, but it exists. The seller who raises the price will not lose all customers (as would the perfect competitor) because some will have such a strong preference that they will accept the higher price.

Profit Maximization by the Monopolistically Competitive Firm

To maximize profits, firms produce that quantity of output at which marginal revenue equals marginal cost. The monopolistic competitor is no exception to this rule; that is, MR = MC. Like the monopolist, the monopolistic competitor faces a downward-sloping demand curve; marginal revenue is less than average revenue (price). It therefore selects the *quantity* at which marginal revenue equals marginal cost and charges the *price* that clears the market for its good. Analytically, in the short run the theory of

---

[1]Algebra: $\text{MR} = P + (\Delta P/\Delta Q)Q$. But MR = MC, so that $P - \text{MC} = (\Delta P/\Delta Q)Q$. Dividing by P yields $(P - \text{MC})/P = (\Delta P/\Delta Q)(Q/P) = 1/E$.

EXAMPLE 3

America Online: A Dominant Firm

The text analysis applies to the case in which one firm dominates a market so much that it determines the price at which other firms can sell their product. This might be the case, for example, with America Online, which has a large marketing advantage over its competitors. America Online had about 20 million subscribers in late 1999, before its deal to merge with the largest cable company, Time Warner. Here, the dominant monopolist knows the market demand curve and knows that it faces a competitive fringe. If it can estimate the supply curve of the competitive firm, the dominant firm's demand curve is just the market demand curve minus the supply curve of the competitive fringe. By equating the marginal revenue curve of the residual demand curve it faces to its marginal cost, the dominant firm finds its appropriate price and quantity. Thus, even though a firm may not have a strict monopoly, it can behave like a monopoly to the degree that it can price substantially above its marginal cost. America Online has a return on equity of around 40 percent, whereas its competitors, such as EarthLink and MindSpring, have negative returns on equity. Also, America Online's market value is about 70 times larger than its nearest competitor.

Source: http://biz.yahoo.com/research/indgrp/internet_servcs.html.

monopolistic competition is the same as the theory of the monopoly. The analyses of Table 1 and Figure 3 apply equally to monopolistic competition and monopoly in the short run.

Indeed, in the short run, the main difference between monopolistic competition and monopoly is the price elasticity facing the firm. Because a monopolistic competitor faces more competition from the substitute products of other firms in the industry, its price elasticity of demand will greatly exceed that of a typical monopolist.

In the long run, however, the two types of market organization are strikingly different. *Barriers to entry* protect the monopolist from competitors. The entry of new firms will not systematically squeeze out monopoly profits. Monopolistic competition, however, shares with perfect competition the characteristic of *freedom of entry*. Thus, if a monopolistic competitor earns economic profits in the short run, new firms can (and will) enter the market, gain access to those profits, and eventually drive them down to zero. Long-run equilibrium requires that price be equal to average costs.

One example of a monopolistic competitor is a service station located on a busy intersection. It may earn substantial economic profits in the short run. Like a profitable monopolist, its price is greater than average total cost after equating marginal revenue and marginal cost. If the station were a monopolist (say, a gas station with an exclusive franchise along a tollroad), new firms could not gain access to these profits, and the monopoly could continue to earn them for a long period of time. This is not the case with the monopolistic competitor.

In the long run, new firms can enter the monopolistically competitive market. Attracted by high profits, a competitor can build another service station on the opposite corner of the intersection—a close but not perfect substitute. The two stations can differ in terms of access, number of gas pumps, friendliness of service, and operating hours. The entry of the second firm will have two effects on the demand schedule of the first: (1) When customers are attracted away from the first station, the demand schedule for its product will shift to the left. (2) Because buyers now have more substitutes for the product of the first station, its demand schedule will become more elastic. If both stations continue to make economic profits, even more gas stations will be built—perhaps one or two more at the same intersection. Each new entrant will reduce the demand facing other stations and increase its price elasticity. As in the case of perfect competition, this adjustment process ends when economic profits have been eliminated.

The long-run equilibrium of a typical monopolistically competitive firm is shown in Figure 4. In the long run, new firms will enter until economic profits are driven down to zero. The relevant cost curve is the long-run average cost (LRAC) curve because revenue must cover costs in the long run. Graphically, profits equal zero at a point to the left of the lowest point on the LRAC curve, where the downward-sloping demand curve is tangent to the LRAC curve. In Figure 4, point *b*—at which output is 600 units and price is $10—is the point of zero profits and, therefore, the point of long-run equilibrium. In Figure 4, 600 units is the quantity that equates marginal cost and marginal revenue, and $10 is the price that corresponds to 600 units on the demand curve. Therefore, point *b* is the point of maximum profit. To see this differently, you might notice that because the demand curve is tangent to the LRAC curve at point *b,* price is less than long-run average cost to the left or to the right of point *b*. Thus, although profit is zero at point *b,* it is negative elsewhere. For example, at an output of 300 units, price is $13 and long-run average cost is $14; the result is a loss of $1 per unit. We know that profits are always maximized where marginal cost equals marginal revenue. Accordingly, the MC and MR curves must intersect directly below the tangency of the demand curve and LRAC curve at point *b,* as Figure 4 illustrates.

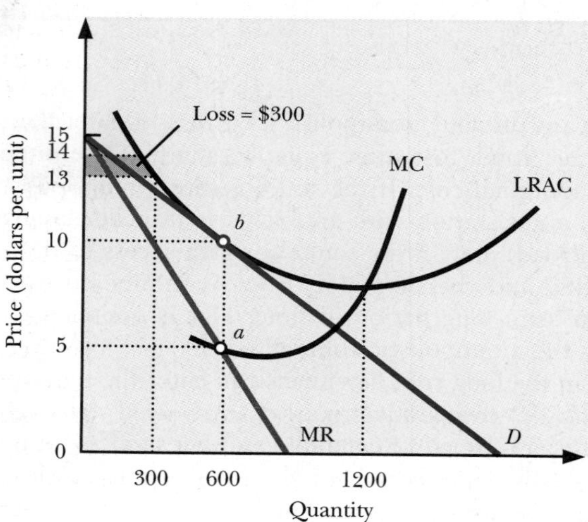

FIGURE 4 The Long-Run Equilibrium of a Monopolistically Competitive Firm

A firm engaged in monopolistic competition faces a downward-sloping demand curve such as *D*. In the long run, because of free entry, economic profits will be driven down to zero. Thus, the long-run equilibrium must be a point such as *b,* where *D* is just tangent to the LRAC curve. For any price other than $10, profits are negative. Profits, though equal to zero, are at a maximum when price is $10 and output is 600 units, indicating that marginal revenue must equal marginal cost at 600 units. Thus, the MC and MR curves must intersect directly below point *b*.

The minimum unit cost output, or optimum capacity, is clearly 1200 units in Figure 4 because at that output level, MC = LRAC. In long-run equilibrium, each firm in a monopolistically competitive industry will produce an output that is smaller than the optimal capacity. This smaller-than-optimal output results because the demand curve is downward sloping and tangent to the long-run average cost curve. Thus, there is *excess capacity,* making monopolistic competition less efficient than perfect competition. This need not mean that monopolistic competition is less socially desirable than perfect competition, since we can regard such excess capacity as the price society must pay for variety.

Product Differentiation and Advertising

The threat of the entry of new firms and the loss of economic profits are facts of life for monopolistic competitors. If they can erect artificial barriers to entry (by exclusive government franchises, licensing, or zoning ordinances), they can delay the day when their economic profits are driven down to zero. Another tactic for protecting economic profits is to engage in nonprice competition. Since monopolistic competitors, by definition, produce goods and services that are somewhat different, if they can succeed in further differentiating their products from those of their competitors, they can gain loyalty. The stronger this customer loyalty, the smaller will be the loss of customers as new firms enter and the less elastic will be the demand for a product.

Nonprice competition is the attempt to attract customers through real or imagined improvements in product quality or service, thereby shifting the firm's demand curve to the right.

Advertising is frequently used to differentiate products in monopolistically competitive markets. In fact, nonprice competition can yield considerable short-run profits for a firm and offer potential long-run profits if new entrants cannot copy the nonprice attribute. Profits on some brand-name products, such as Bayer aspirin or Borden's condensed milk, have persisted for very long periods of time. In other cases, profits are transitory. If the gas station owner differentiates the product by staying open all night or by offering a free car wash with fill-ups, then competitors can do the same.

APPLICATIONS

The theories of monopoly and monopolistic competition explain a variety of behavior patterns exhibited by price-making firms, including price discrimination and improvements in product durability. These two examples, in particular, are accounted for by the theory of price making, which holds that both monopolists and monopolistic competitors produce that quantity of output at which marginal revenue equals marginal cost.

Price Discrimination

Thus far, this chapter has assumed that the price maker charges a single price to all buyers, but this is not always the case. Customers often pay different prices for the same product. Senior citizens typically pay less for movie tickets, airline fares, and sporting events; doctors and lawyers often charge wealthy clients more than poor clients. All of these situations are examples of price discrimination.

Price discrimination exists when the same product or service is sold at different prices to different buyers.

In order for firms to price discriminate,

1. The seller must exercise some control over the price (price discrimination is possible only for price makers).
2. The seller must be able to distinguish easily among different types of customers.
3. It must be difficult for one buyer to resell the product to other buyers.

If the firm is not a price maker, it cannot control its price. The seller that cannot distinguish between customers will not know to which buyers it should charge the lower price. The electric company can readily distinguish residential from industrial users; doctors and lawyers can often identify wealthy clients on the basis of appearance, home address, and stated profession. If one buyer can sell to another, then low-price buyers can sell to high-price buyers and no one will be willing to pay the high price. Thus, poor clients cannot resell legal and medical services to the wealthy, and industrial users of electricity cannot sell their electricity to households.

If the foregoing conditions are met, the seller can divide the market into various noncompeting groups. A profit-maximizing seller will then charge prices according to the price elasticity of demand of each group. The higher the price elasticity of demand, the lower will be the price charged. For example, if working adults have a less elastic demand for newspapers than do retired adults, it pays the newspaper to charge a higher price to working adults.

Price makers see that they can achieve a substantial increase in sales by *lowering* prices in price-sensitive markets. They also see that they don't lose many sales by *raising* prices in price-insensitive markets. Hence, they will end up charging different prices in each market.

Figure 5 graphs a specific case of price discrimination. Panel (*a*) shows the demand curve of retired readers, D_R; panel (*b*) shows the demand curve of working readers, D_W. The marginal revenue curve in panel (*a*) is M_R and in panel (*b*) is MR_W. The marginal cost (MC) of weekly newspaper service is assumed to be $1.

The newspaper equates marginal revenue and marginal cost in each market by charging $3 to working readers (whose price elasticity is 1.5) and by charging $2 to retired readers (whose price elasticity is 2). The $3 workers' price corresponds to the output quantity that equates marginal cost and workers' marginal revenue; the $2 retirees' price corresponds to the output quantity that equates marginal cost and retired marginal revenue. Thus, the monopolist exploits the differences in demand elasticities by charging different prices in order to earn more profit. (See Example 4 on page 220.)

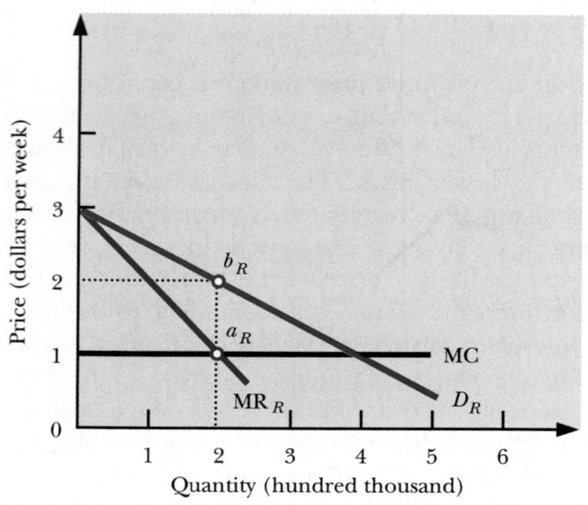

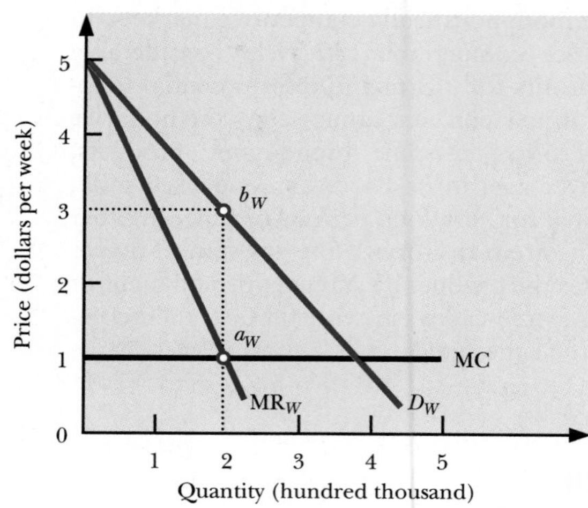

FIGURE 5 Price Discrimination: Newspapers

The demand and marginal revenue curves of retired customers are drawn as D_R and MR_R in panel (*a*). They are more elastic than the demand and marginal revenue curves (D_W and MR_W) of working customers in panel (*b*). The marginal cost of providing newspapers is the same for both customers and is constant at $1 per week. The newspaper will maximize profits in each market by equating marginal revenue and marginal cost in each market. In the workers' segment, MR = MC at a price of $3; in the retired segment, MR = MC at a price of $2.

Product Durability

Tires, cars, lightbulbs, television sets, and no-run pantyhose are just a few of the products whose durability—the amount of time they last—has been remarkably increased over the years. These improvements in durability are a prediction of economic theory. If there is competition, it is clear that firms will want to extend the life of their products in order to avoid losing business. What about monopoly? Many of us might assume that a monopoly would want to suppress durability because it would hurt future sales. But we know from the text that even monopolies will want to extend their product durability as far as costs permit.

As a simple example, let's consider a monopolist that discovers a costless method of doubling the life of a lightbulb; that is, the monopoly learns that it can continue to produce a lightbulb for the same marginal cost, but the bulb will now last twice as many hours. Will the monopolist introduce the new lightbulbs? Clearly, this discovery would cut the cost of producing a *lightbulb hour* in half. This monopolist could increase its profits just by doubling the price of the (improved) product and cutting the output in half because the price of a lightbulb hour would remain the same. To keep the example simple, if the price of a two-hour bulb were twice the price of a one-hour bulb, people could satisfy their demand by buying half as many lightbulbs each period as before. If the firm maintained the price of a lightbulb hour (by doubling the price of a lightbulb), the firm's profits would rise because revenue would stay the same while costs fell. As Figure 6 shows, however, the firm could do even better. Note that in Figure 6 everything is measured in terms of *lightbulb hours* rather than in terms of *lightbulbs.* Because the firm's marginal cost of producing lightbulb hours has fallen, it would pay the firm to reduce the price per lightbulb hour in order to equate marginal revenue and marginal cost. In Figure 6, the firm increases its profits by charging $5 per lightbulb hour ($10 per bulb) for its improved bulb.

Business firms do not extend the durability of all goods because of the cost involved. To produce a space vehicle with virtually no chance of breaking down costs millions of dollars; the cost could be reduced dramatically if all the backup systems and safety checks were eliminated. Similarly, to produce more durable cars requires certain trade-offs: either

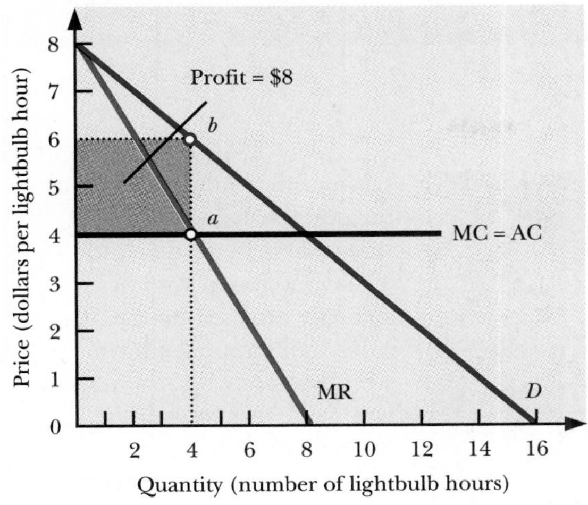

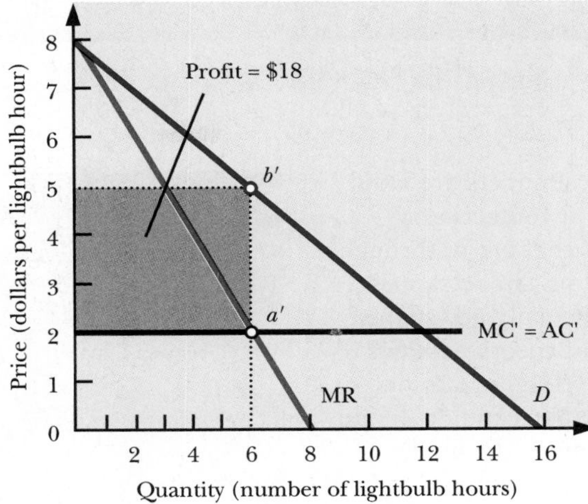

FIGURE 6 Lightbulb Durability and Monopoly Profits

The demand curve *D* shows the demand for lightbulb hours (not lightbulbs). Panel (*a*) shows a situation where 1 lightbulb equals 1 lightbulb hour (each lightbulb burns only 1 hour). If the marginal cost of a lightbulb is $4, monopoly profits are maximized where output is 4 bulbs, where marginal revenue equals $4, and where price equals $6. Monopoly profits are $8. A costless doubling of lightbulb durability (to make 1 lightbulb burn 2 lightbulb hours) is shown in panel (*b*). Marginal cost per lightbulb hour is now reduced to $2, but demand remains the same. The monopolist now maximizes profit at an output level of 6 lightbulb hours (= 3 bulbs). The monopoly price is now $5 per lightbulb hour, and monopoly profit equals $18.

the car must have a higher price (like the Mercedes-Benz or Rolls-Royce), or other characteristics—such as style and handling performance—must be sacrificed (as in the Chevrolet).

In this chapter we have examined the price-making behavior of monopolists and monopolistic competitors. In the chapter that follows we shall evaluate monopoly and monopolistic competition in relation to perfect competition. Characteristics that will be important in such a comparison include (1) the fact that monopolists are not pressured to produce at minimum average cost in the long run and (2) the fact that price makers do not equate marginal cost and price.

SUMMARY

1. A pure monopoly exists when a market contains only one seller producing a product that has no close substitutes. Barriers to entry keep out competitors. The monopolist is a price maker with considerable control over price. Pure monopoly is rare in the real world because of the existence of substitutes and the absence of absolute barriers to entry, especially in the long run. Sources of monopoly include economies of scale, economies of scope, patents, ownership of critical raw materials, public franchises, and licensing.

2. Price makers face downward-sloping demand curves; they must lower their price in order to sell more. For price makers, price exceeds marginal revenue. Marginal revenue is positive when demand is elastic; marginal revenue is negative when demand is inelastic.

3. Monopolists maximize profits by producing that output quantity at which marginal revenue and marginal cost are equal or by changing that price at which MR = MC.

4. Monopolists do not produce where price equals marginal cost. Monopolists need not produce in the long run where average costs are minimized. Monopolists produce where demand is elastic.

5. Monopoly power is measured by the excess of price over marginal cost divided by price $[(P - MC)/P]$.

EXAMPLE 4

Price Discrimination: Manufacturers' Coupons

Grocery shoppers are familiar with manufacturers' coupons that arrive through the mail or can be clipped out of the daily newspaper. Economic theory explains why some manufacturers offer coupons and others do not. In effect, the holder of the coupon is entitled to buy the product at a lower price than others. If Nabisco places a coupon offering a 50¢ discount on one of its cereals in the daily newspaper, a customer can buy the cereal at a lower price than other shoppers. Manufacturers' coupons are a form of price discrimination. The coupon issuer reasons as follows: Anyone taking the trouble to cut out the coupon has a higher elasticity of demand than other shoppers. Without the 50¢ off, many shoppers would not buy the cereal. The 50¢ reduction therefore brings about a substantial increase in quantity purchased from careful shoppers. Shoppers not taking the trouble to clip out the coupon have a lower price elasticity of demand. Their purchases are not strongly affected by the 50¢ price reduction. We have seen that price discrimination is possible only when the manufacturer has price-making power, when high-price elasticity customers can be identified, and when low-price buyers cannot resell the product. Manufacturers' coupons follow this pattern. Typically, manufacturers in highly concentrated markets (with only a few sellers), such as cereal or soap manufacturers, offer coupons. Such manufacturers exercise significant market power. Requiring coupons to obtain the lower price allows manufacturers to differentiate high-elasticity from low-elasticity customers. Although low-price buyers could theoretically sell to high-price buyers, the price difference usually is not great enough to yield this result.

6. A monopolistically competitive industry has a large number of individual firms that are price makers selling differentiated products, with freedom of entry and exit. Monopolistic competitors, like monopolists, produce where marginal revenue equals marginal cost. In the long run, the entry of new firms will drive profits down to zero. When profits are zero and MR = MC, the firm's output will be less than the minimum efficient scale; that is, unit costs are not minimized as in perfect competition. By engaging in nonprice competition—through product differentiation and advertising—monopolistically competitive firms can delay the disappearance of economic profits.

7. Price makers can raise their profits through price discrimination. Buyers with inelastic demand will pay higher prices than those with elastic demand. Product durability will depend upon the cost of supplying durability.

KEY TERMS

pure monopoly 206
natural monopoly 206
price maker 208
marginal revenue (MR) 208
average revenue (AR) 209
halfway rule 210
monopolistic competition 214
nonprice competition 216
price discrimination 217

QUESTIONS AND PROBLEMS

1. Firm A can sell all it wants at a price of $5. Firm B must lower its price from $6 to $5 to sell more output. Explain why the marginal revenue of Firm A is not the same as the marginal revenue of Firm B even though they are both charging a $5 price.
2. Evaluate the validity of the following statement: "The shutdown rule applies only to firms operating in competitive markets and does not concern monopolies."
3. Explain why a price maker can choose either its profit-maximizing output level or its profit-maximizing price. Why can it choose only one, not both?
4. A monopolist produces 100 units of output, and the price elasticity of demand at this point on the demand curve is 0.5. What advice would you give the monopolist? From this information, what can you say about marginal revenue?
5. A price maker produces output at a constant marginal cost of $5 and has no fixed costs. The demand schedule facing the price maker is indicated in Table A.
   a. Determine the price maker's profit-maximizing output, price, and profit.
   b. What will happen to profit if the firm produces more output? Less output? Why?
   c. Explain what happens to marginal revenue when output is raised from 15 to 20 units.

TABLE A

Price (dollars)	*Quantity Demanded (units)*
12	0
10	5
8	10
6	15
4	20

6. A food concession in a sports stadium makes an economic profit of $100,000 in the first year of operation. Explain what will happen to profits in subsequent years under the following conditions.
   a. The concessionaire is granted an exclusive franchise to stadium concessions.
   b. Potential competitors have the freedom to set up concession stands in the stadium.

   In the latter case, can the concessionaire do anything to protect long-run profits?
7. Prices of tickets to movies, sports events, and concerts are typically lower for children and the elderly than for working-age adults. Explain why, using the theory of price discrimination.
8. Explain why the entry of new firms into a monopolistically competitive market makes the demand curves of established firms more elastic.
9. Assume a monopoly is making an economic profit. The monopoly is sold to the highest bidder. Will the new owner make an economic profit? Why or why not?
10. Suppose the price at which a monopolist can sell its product is $P = 10 - Q$, where Q is the number of units sold per period. The monopolist's MC = ATC = $4.
    a. Graph the demand curve.
    b. Graph total revenue for output levels from 0 units to 10 units.
    c. Graph the marginal revenue at each output level.
    d. Which output level maximizes profit?
    e. How much is maximum profit?
11. A monopolist is making an economic profit of $100,000 per year. Explain what will happen to the monopolist's price and output if:
    a. The government imposes a fixed tax of $90,000 per year on the monopolist.
    b. The government imposes a fixed tax of $110,000 per year on the monopolist.
12. What advice would you give to a monopolist that is setting output to maximize revenue?
13. Evaluate the validity of the following statement: "The medical care industry is not a monopoly because the price elasticity of demand for medical care is less than unity. Monopolists would charge prices higher than current ones."
14. Explain why marginal revenue is less than price for a price maker.
15. How does monopolistic competition differ from monopoly?
16. A natural water fountain is discovered in the middle of a city. The demand schedule for the

drinking water is shown in Table B. There is no cost of production.

a. Draw the demand curve.
b. Use the halfway rule to derive the marginal revenue curve.
c. How would the city maximize its revenues from the water fountain?

TABLE B

Price (cents per drink)	*Quantity Demanded (drinks per day)*
6	0
5	10
4	20
3	30
2	40
1	50
0	60

17. Which of the following are examples of price discrimination?
    a. Discount coupons
    b. First-class airline tickets
    c. Stand-by tickets
    d. More expensive seaside rooms in a hotel

18. A monopolist has a marginal cost of $1 for each unit produced. The following table shows the demand curve. Fill in the total revenue and marginal revenue columns and calculate the firm's best price and maximum profit.

P	*Q*	TR	MR	MC
$10	1			$1
9	2			1
8	3			1
7	4			1
6	5			1
5	6			1
4	7			1

INTERNET CONNECTION

19. Using the links from http://www.awl.com/ruffin_gregory, read the article about the proposed merger between Staples and OfficeMax.
    a. If Staples and OfficeMax were to merge and create monopoly power, what would an economist predict their behavior would be?
    b. What does the article predict will happen? Specifically, where and by how much will prices rise?

PUZZLE ANSWERED: You should raise the price of generators, because by selling fewer units your cost would fall. But if you sell 1 percent fewer generators at a 1 percent higher price, total dollar sales will stay the same. Thus, with the same revenue and lower cost, profits would rise.

Chapter 12

COMPETITION, EFFICIENCY, AND INNOVATION

Chapter Insight

"Greed is good," said the fictional financier Gordon Gecko in the 1987 movie *Wall Street.* Greed drives competition, monopoly, new products, and new ways of doing things. Is greed good?

Historians write about the late nineteenth century as the period of the Robber Barons, when people such as John D. Rockefeller and J. Pierpont Morgan amassed unbelievable wealth. During the late 1870s and 1880s, workers complained of low wages, and farmers of low prices and high railroad tariffs. We might think that greed was causing the economy to collapse. Yet the United States came out of this period the greatest economic power the world has ever known.

Some analysts credit the economic growth and stock market boom of recent years to the "greed" of the Robber Barons of the 1980s, the junk bond dealers, the corporate takeover specialists, who raised capital and provided new management for the restructuring of U.S. industry.

In this chapter we explore the static and dynamic implications of profit maximization (greed?) in a world of competition and monopoly. We compare the efficiency of competition with that of monopoly, and we examine the logic of patents, the consequences of externalities, and, finally, the link between new products and the desire for profits.

LEARNING OBJECTIVES

After completing this chapter, you will be able to:

1. State why competition leads to economic efficiency.
2. Measure the amount of inefficiency caused by monopoly.
3. Understand monopoly rent-seeking behavior.
4. Discuss the difference between private and social costs.
5. Understand the role of patents.
6. Discuss the theory of dynamic competition.

CHAPTER PUZZLE: If the marginal cost to Microsoft of producing another copy of its Windows operating system is close to zero, why not allow everyone to have a copy for a price close to zero?

THE EFFICIENCY OF COMPETITION

Ever since Adam Smith argued that the invisible hand of competition would guide profit-maximizing producers and utility-maximizing consumers to an efficient allocation of society's resources, economists have been captivated by its appeal. The antitrust laws of the United States, for example, have attempted to make a competitive order the law of the land.

We know from the chapter on perfect competition that competition forces an industry to produce where the price of the product just equals the lowest unit production cost. If the price were any higher than the minimum unit cost, someone could make a profit from producing the good at that cost. Competition is efficient because it utilizes *given* resources and *given* technology in such a way that the cost of producing the desired output of the society is as low as possible. In short, all resources and all technical know-how are being used in the best possible way. Nothing is being wasted. Since the economy consists of many industries, efficiency in each industry indicates that the economy is producing the largest possible output with its given resources and technology.

Economic efficiency means that the economy is producing the maximum output of useful things with its given resources and technology.

Prices and Economic Efficiency

Prices Matter. In perfectly competitive markets, economic efficiency also results from the right balance between consumer utility and costs of production. The competitive price will reflect this balance.

Consumers buy an enormous variety of goods—milk, shirts, cars, housing, bread, and so on. As discussed in the chapter on demand and utility, well-informed, rational consumers carry out their purchases of any particular good until the ratio of its marginal utility (MU) to price is the same as that for all other goods. Individual consumers follow consumption patterns in which the prices of the goods they buy reflect the marginal utilities of those goods: low-priced goods have low MUs, and high-priced goods have high MUs. Thus, the price of a good is a dollar measure of the good's marginal utility to the individual; indeed, we can say that the marginal benefit of the good to the consumer equals its price. Because in a perfectly competitive market the price is the same for all buyers and sellers, each consumer has the same marginal benefits.

The price of a good measures its marginal benefit to society because each utility-maximizing consumer equates the good's MU/*P* ratio to that of all other goods.

Now let's consider the other side of the market, the competitive firms that produce the various goods. Each producer will expand production until price and marginal cost are equal. As long as price exceeds marginal cost, the competitive producer finds profit opportunities. These are exhausted when diminishing returns drive marginal cost up to the level of price.

In a perfectly competitive industry, every producer faces the same price and expands production to the point where marginal cost equals price. Therefore, each producer has the same marginal cost of production. The marginal cost of bread for one producer, which equals the marginal cost for other producers, is the same as the marginal cost of bread to society.

Society's cost of producing a good is minimized when each producer has the same marginal cost. If a good is produced by firms at different marginal costs, the same quantity of the total cost to society can be lowered if production is shifted from high-marginal-cost producers to low-marginal-cost producers. Market equilibrium is the state in which a good is produced at minimum cost in a quantity that yields a marginal benefit (price) equal to marginal cost. An economy at market equilibrium is efficient; $P = \text{MC}$, markets have cleared, and opportunities to increase profits have been exhausted.

The principle that $P = \text{MC}$ is the point of efficient production for any one good also means that an economy achieves an efficient allocation of resources if all goods are freely bought by consumers at prices equal to marginal costs. Consumers maximize their satisfaction or utility by arranging their consumption to equalize the satisfaction they get from a marginal dollar's worth of *every* good or service. The marginal or last dollar spent on, say, apples, is worth precisely one dollar; otherwise, the dollar would not have been spent. If prices are the same as marginal costs, these equally satisfying marginal dollars spent in all directions have exactly the same costs. But, if prices were not equal to marginal costs for every good, then goods that yield the same marginal dollar's worth of satisfaction can have widely differing costs. For example, if a dollar's worth of apples costs $0.50 and a dollar's worth of bananas costs $1.50, society would gain by shifting resources from bananas to apples. This argument assumes that marginal costs to firms reflect their marginal costs to society; it is the basis of Adam Smith's invisible hand.

> If all goods and services are produced in competitive markets with prices equal to marginal costs, the allocation of resources among all the different uses will be efficient (provided marginal costs to firms reflect their marginal cost to society).

Measuring Economic Inefficiency

It is possible to measure economic inefficiency. Let's imagine that for some reason a good is being produced at a level where $P > \text{MC}$. The difference between price and marginal cost not only represents a profit opportunity for individual producers but also signals a social opportunity. If $P > \text{MC}$, society will benefit from producing more of the good. Remember that marginal cost is the opportunity cost at the margin—the value of what is being given up elsewhere. To say that price exceeds marginal cost is to say that the resources used in the production of this particular good have a higher marginal benefit to society in this use than in any other.

In Figure 1, the equilibrium quantity is 8000 units of output. Suppose for some reason that output is only 5000 units. The marginal cost to society is $70 (at point *a*), and the marginal benefit to society is $120 (at point *b*). Moving from an output of 5000 units to an output of 8000 units benefits society by the green area *abc*. Point *c* is an efficient output level. Economic efficiency is achieved when resources are allocated such that no one can be made better off by reallocating resources without making someone else worse off.

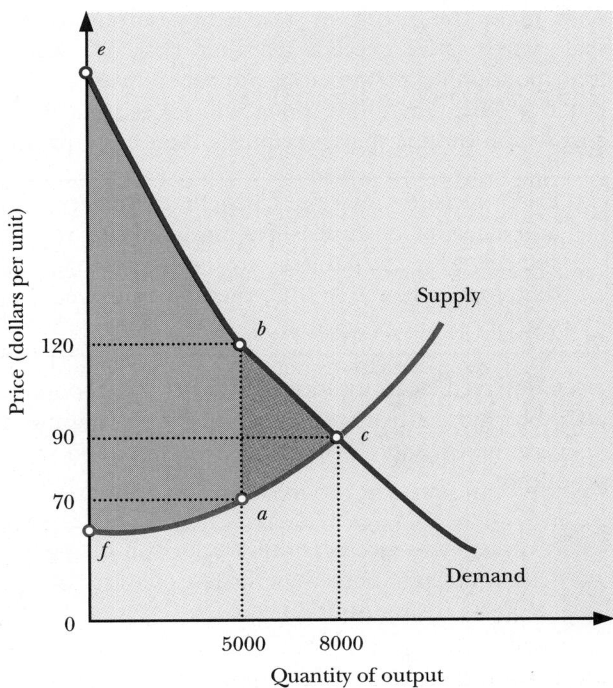

FIGURE 1 Perfect Competition and Social Efficiency

When output is restricted to 5000 units, the marginal cost of the 5001st unit of output is the price at point *a*, or $70; the marginal benefit is the price at point *b*, or $120. Moving to the equilibrium quantity of 8000 units results in a net gain to society of area *abc* because marginal benefits exceed marginal costs on the intervening 3000 units. Social efficiency is achieved when the price is $90 and the total of consumer and producer surplus equals area *ecf*.

> If price does not equal marginal cost for all goods, there is inefficiency in the system. Resources are allocated efficiently when price equals marginal cost.

Sources of Economic Inefficiency

Sources of Inefficiency in Monopoly

Monopoly has two sources of inefficiency. First, monopoly leads to contrived scarcities. Second, the resources used to acquire monopoly power can be better employed elsewhere in the economy.

Contrived Scarcity

The main argument against monopoly is that monopolies maximize profit by restricting output to the scale where price exceeds marginal cost. We know that monopolies maximize profit where MR = MC, but $P >$ MR. Therefore, price will exceed marginal cost at the output that maximizes monopoly profit.

> Price measures marginal benefit to society, and marginal cost measures marginal cost to society (if externalities are not present); therefore, when $P >$ MC, there is contrived scarcity in the economy.

Contrived scarcity occurs when the economy would be more efficient—in the sense of giving more to everyone—if more of the monopolized good were produced.

Contrived scarcity is the production of less than the economically efficient quantity of a good by a monopoly.

When $P >$ MC, 1 more unit of output adds more to social benefits than to social costs; thus, it is possible to rearrange the allocation of resources (to produce more of the monopolized good and less of other goods) to make everyone better off.

To compare monopoly with perfect competition, consider an industry in which both are possible. Figure 2 depicts an industry in which there are no economies of scale; to simplify the comparison, average costs are the same for each level of output. Therefore, average cost and marginal cost are the same: AC = MC. Either one large firm (a monopoly) or a large number of small firms (a perfectly competitive market) can satisfy consumer demand at the same average cost. Marginal cost (= AC) is a constant $4 per unit. The monopoly output (300 units) is at the level where MR is also $4 (point *a*); the monopoly price is $7. Monopoly profits are represented by the green-shaded area, which equals $900. Under conditions of perfect competition, meanwhile, free entry would squeeze out economic profits. The long-run competitive price would, therefore, be $4, and the competitive output would be 600 units (point *c*).

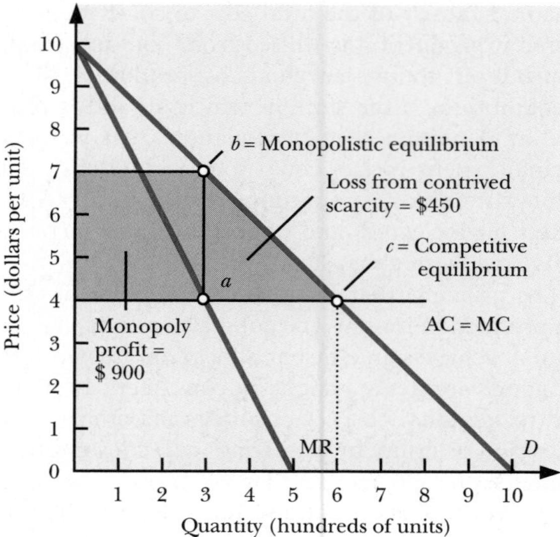

FIGURE 2 Monopoly and Competition Compared

This industry has constant returns to scale where AC = MC = $4 for all levels of output. If the industry were perfectly competitive, price would be $4 and output would be 600 units. If this industry were a single-firm monopoly, price would be $7 and output would be 300 units, with a monopoly profit of $900 (= $3 × 300). Monopoly profit is the green-shaded area. The monopolist creates profits through the contrived scarcity of 300 units (the monopolist produces 300 units less than the competitive industry). The loss from contrived scarcity is the red area, which equals $450, or the deadweight loss to society. Moving from monopoly to competition creates consumer surplus of $1350 (which is the sum of $900 + $450) while destroying only $900 worth of profits for the monopolist. More is gained by all parties taken together than is lost.

We can calculate the cost of monopoly in this case from Figure 2. If this industry is transformed from a monopoly to perfect competition, the equilibrium price/quantity combination would shift from point *b* to point *c*, and the price would fall from $7

EXAMPLE 1

Mexican Television Ad Rates

Grupo Televisa SA (TV) is Mexico's dominant media company. It had a decades-long monopoly until a smaller media company, TV Azteca SA (TZA), surfaced. But Televisa's market share rebounded to 78 percent in late 1999 as the ratings of its smaller competitor dropped. The result was that Televisa told advertisers that they were raising average rates about 40 percent in the year 2000, far outpacing the government's 10 percent inflation target. In the previous year, ad rates were increased 28 percent in the face of 13 percent inflation. Thus, it appears that costs are not the main explanation for the increase in prices.

The key to economic inefficiency is that firms with monopoly power can raise the price above marginal costs. According to the theory of monopoly, this inefficiency will grow when demand becomes less elastic because prices will be hiked to maintain equality between marginal revenue and marginal costs. This was undoubtedly the case in Mexico. Televisa not only faces less competition from its rival, but the year 2000 has witnessed a campaign spending blitz ahead of political elections, and Olympic Games, boosting the advertising market by an estimated 16.8 percent. Raising the price of advertising by 40 percent, causing ad agencies to complain, clearly reduces the quantity of ads demanded. But monopolies maximize profits by restricting supply.

Source: "Mexico's Televisa Raises Ad Rates; Agencies Balk," Dow-Jones News Wire, October 18, 1999.

to \$4. The increase in consumer surplus, defined in an earlier chapter, resulting from the shift is the sum of the green-shaded area (the monopolist's profit of \$900) and red-shaded area (\$450), equaling \$1350. But the monopolist, who is also a member of society, loses monopoly profits of \$900 in the process. Therefore, the net gain to society (the consumers' gain minus the monopolist's loss) is simply the red-shaded triangle, which equals \$450.[1] Notice that everyone involved is better off under the move to perfect competition. Because consumers gain \$1350 in consumer surplus, they can buy off the monopolist with a payment, say \$901, greater than the original monopoly profit—which would make the monopolist better off by \$1 and the consumers better off by \$449. The \$450 loss from monopoly is a deadweight loss because nothing is received in exchange for the loss. The deadweight loss of monopoly is equivalent to throwing away valuable scarce resources. (See Example 1.)

A **deadweight loss** is a loss to society of consumer or producer surplus that is not offset by anyone else's gain.

How large are losses from contrived scarcities in the American economy? Economist Arnold Harberger has estimated the deadweight loss from all monopolies to be a very small fraction of total U.S. output. A number of other researchers roughly estimate these losses at about 1 percent of GDP.[2]

---

[1]We can calculate the deadweight loss in another way. When $Q = 300$ and $P = \$7$, the difference between marginal social benefits and marginal social costs is \$3 (\$7 − \$4). Hence, it pays society to expand output beyond the 300th unit. In effect, the 301st unit adds \$3 to social welfare. The 601st unit adds nothing to social welfare because from $Q = 300$ to $Q = 600$, the extra benefit per unit declines from \$3 to \$0. Thus, on the average, the 300 additional units between 300 (the monopolist's output) to 600 (the output under perfect competition) add \$1.50 each (the average of \$3 and \$0), or \$450.

[2]Arnold Harberger, "Monopoly and Resource Allocation," *American Economic Review* 44 (May 1954): 77–87. We can mention only a few of the economists who have contributed to this estimate: David Schwartzman; Dean Worcester, Jr.; David Kamerschen; and Michael Klass.

Monopoly Rent-Seeking Behavior

The previously cited estimates of the deadweight losses from monopoly represent lower bounds to the true loss to society from monopoly.[3] In terms of Figure 2, if the industry were perfectly competitive, the price/quantity combination would be \$4/600 units, or point *c*, and there would be no deadweight loss. If someone could turn this industry into a monopoly through political activities, that person could gain the potential monopoly profit of \$900 (green-shaded area). People would be willing to spend real resources—or engage in what we will call rent-seeking behavior—to turn the industry into a monopoly and acquire the monopoly profit. We should think of the monopoly profit as the rent received in return for expending the resources needed to turn a competitive industry into a monopoly or to maintain an existing monopoly.

Monopoly rent-seeking behavior is the use of scarce resources on lobbying and influence buying to acquire monopoly rights from government.

In the extreme case, *all* monopoly profits are spent by the persons engaging in monopoly rent-seeking behavior, thereby multiplying the deadweight loss of monopoly. Not only does society lose the red-shaded area in Figure 2 (the deadweight loss) but the monopolist does *not* gain the green-shaded area (monopoly profit).

Rent-seeking behavior does not simply apply to achieving a single-firm monopoly. Any industry in which free entry is prevented by government restrictions can achieve profits that exceed competitive levels. For example, steel companies and textile unions have lobbied Congress for protection from foreign imports. Netscape lobbied government officials to protect it from Microsoft. It has been estimated that there are about 100,000 lobbyists in Washington, D.C. The offices they occupy, the secretarial services they employ, their advertising budgets, and their own labor could be used elsewhere in our world of economic scarcity. Instead, lobbyists use their resources to restrict competition through government charters, franchises, regulations, and either taxes on rival competitors or subsidies for themselves.

Rent-seeking behavior can lead to substantial social losses. To limit rent-seeking behavior, the government must act to substantially lessen the possibility of "buying" monopoly power. This, however, is not an easy task. (See Example 2 on page 228.)

[3]Anne Krueger, "The Political Economy of the Rent-Seeking Society," *American Economic Review* 64 (June 1974): 291–303; Gordon Tullock, "The Welfare Cost of Tariffs, Monopolies, and Theft," *Western Economic Journal* 5 (June 1967): 224–232.

Externalities

A perfectly competitive allocation of resources will be economically inefficient if externalities are present.

Externalities exist when an economic activity of one party results in direct economic costs or benefits for someone else who does not control that economic activity.

Externalities arise when a factory belches black smoke that raises the cost of laundry or medical care for those people living in the vicinity, when a chemical plant dumps wastes that affect fishing and agricultural production, when a pulp mill pollutes the air others must breathe, or when an airport pollutes an area with deafening noise.

When externalities are present, the total cost to society of producing a good equals the sum of its private and external costs; the total benefit to society is the sum of its private and external benefits. The total costs or benefits to society of producing a good are the social costs or social benefits.

Social costs are private costs plus external costs.

Social benefits are private benefits plus external benefits.

The main effect of an externality is that the *marginal private cost* (MPC) of production does not necessarily reflect the *marginal social cost* (MSC). The marginal social cost of producing steel includes not only the marginal private costs of the steel mill but also the marginal external costs imposed on others (the extra laundry costs, medical care costs, and so on). A steel mill might not take these external costs into account when making its economic decisions.

Figure 3 shows the effects of externalities in steel production. The MSC curve measures marginal social costs, and the supply curve measures only mar-

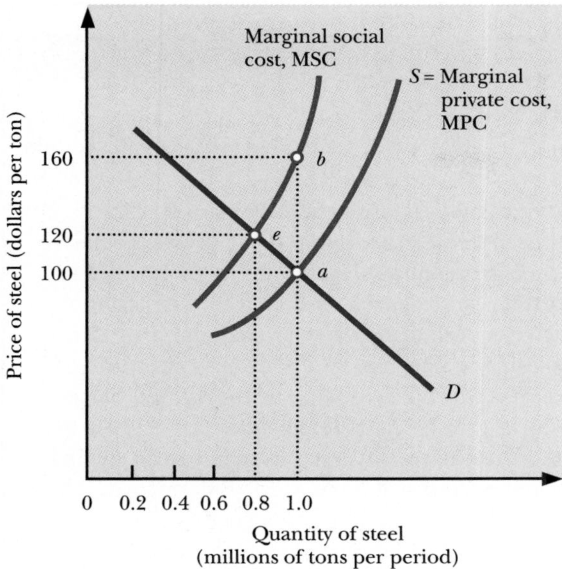

FIGURE 3 Externalities and Competition

The supply and demand curves of this hypothetical steel industry intersect at the price/quantity combination of $100 per ton and 1 million tons of steel (point *a*). The supply curve, *S*, reflects only marginal *private* costs. The MSC curve shows marginal *social* costs. At the equilibrium point *a*, the marginal social cost of an extra ton of steel is $160, but the marginal social benefit is only $100, as measured by the height of the demand curve. Too much steel is produced from the society's point of view.

ginal private costs (MPC). At competitive equilibrium, 1 million tons are produced at a price of $100 per ton (point *a*). With a marginal social cost of $160 per ton, the equilibrium output level constitutes too much steel production from the standpoint of society. Marginal social costs ($160) do not equal marginal social benefits ($100) because externalities are present. Efficiency requires that 0.8 million tons of steel be produced (point *e*), yielding both a marginal social cost and a price of $120.

Economic activities can have external benefits as well as external costs. When one neighbor plants flowers, surrounding neighbors also benefit. The person who considers personal pleasure to be the sole benefit from growing flowers will plant flowers only to the point where marginal costs and marginal benefits are equal. The marginal cost to the person growing the flowers does not equal the marginal benefits enjoyed by society (the neighborhood) because other neighbors gain some marginal benefits as well. The situation results in economic inefficiency because too few flowers get planted.

The problems created by externalities are not limited to conditions of perfect competition. All systems of resource allocation—from monopoly to planned socialism—are plagued by externalities. Pollution is more troublesome in socialist countries than it is in capitalist ones. The presence of externalities is a problem that the invisible hand of perfect competition does not automatically solve and that different economic systems may treat with varying degrees of success. We shall examine externalities in detail in a later chapter.

Technological Progress, Patents, and Competition

It is possible that competition will not be efficient in a *dynamic* (changing) situation. Perfect competition has been shown to be most efficient when resources and technology are *static* (unchanging). Some economists have argued that competition does not encourage the creation and promotion of technological change.

Patents

The major rationale for *patents*—which, in the United States, give the holder a legal monopoly on a product for 20 years—is that they are necessary to spur innovation. Why should a company or individual expend time and money on an invention that can be copied by a rival firm? Thus, patents are deemed to be a price society must pay for innovation. Basically, they protect the inventors by hindering the legal development of products related to ones that have been patented. For example, consider an electronics firm that has patented a production technology that gives it a cost advantage. Its rivals will find it difficult to develop a substitute technology that does the same thing but is different enough to avoid infringement on the patent.

A **patent** is an exclusive right granted to an inventor to make, use, or sell an invention for a term of 20 years in the United States.

Economists Edwin Mansfield, Mark Schwartz, and Samuel Wagner studied the protection a patent

EXAMPLE 2

Monopoly Rent-Seeking Behavior: Lobbying and Lawyers

The impact of monopoly rent-seeking behavior on the economy is difficult to evaluate because of the complexity of calculating the value of the resources exhausted by lobbyists attempting to create monopolies. For example, in 1991 Texas began licensing "interior designers" but not "interior decorators." This distinction in the law resulted from a seven-year effort by lobbyists aiming to protect those who meet certain requirements. This story has been repeated many times in the realm of government regulations. The efforts of a vast number of researchers would be required to evaluate this wealth of information.

Stephen Magee, William Brock, and Leslie Young have attempted to estimate the effects indirectly. They argue that lawyers are the main resource employed by monopoly rent seekers. Although lawyers are generally useful, rent-seeking increases the demand for lawyers relative to other professions. Examining a group of 34 countries, the researchers discovered a strong negative correlation between national growth rates and the national ratios of lawyers to physicians. For example, income in the United States grew at a rate of 2.3 percent between 1960 and 1980, whereas the lawyer/physician ratio during the same period was over 1.25. By contrast, Japan and Hong Kong grew at nearly 7 percent per year and had lawyer/physician ratios of only about 0.1 and 0.3, respectively.

Source: S. Magee, W. Brock, and L. Young, *Black Hole Tariffs and Endogenous Political Economy in General Equilibrium* (Cambridge: Cambridge University Press, 1989), chap. 8.

actually provides from competition in the real world. They concluded that patents provide surprisingly little protection from competition. In a survey of 48 product innovations, 31 of them patented, Mansfield and his associates found that patents increased the cost of legally imitating the original invention by only 11 percent. They also found that 60 percent of the patented inventions were successfully imitated within 4 years—far less than the 20-year life of the patent. They further discovered that patent protection was not essential for the development and introduction of at least 75 percent of the inventions they studied. In fact, patents have played a relatively small role in the most innovative fields of the past 25 years, electronics and bioengineering. Companies in these two fields have relied more on secrecy than on patents to protect their inventions. The major exception to this trend is the prescription-drug industry, in which patents have effectively protected inventions for long periods of time.

The research of Mansfield and his associates raises an important question: If patents do not effectively discourage imitation, are they really necessary to encourage innovation? Secrecy may be more effective. For example, companies like Coca-Cola and McDonald's have made large profits for years by keeping their recipes secret.

New Products and Monopolistic Competition

Perfect competition cannot really explain the introduction of new products because, by assumption, all firms produce the same product. Except for governmental research, such as that undertaken by the U.S. Department of Agriculture, new products are introduced by individual firms. One of the virtues of both monopoly and monopolistic competition is that firms have an incentive to introduce new products. Monopolies will capture a monopoly return; monopolistic competitors will capture a return on their investment in developing new products.

Enormous variety exists in the real world. Each monopolistic competitor finds it profitable to differentiate its product from rival or competitive products. When entering a supermarket or department store we are confronted with thousands of choices. There are so many types of soft drinks, breads, shirts, suits, dresses, television sets, and so forth, that few of us have tried more than a small sample of available products. There are 11,000 varieties of Seiko brand watches alone. This mind-numbing array of choices is the result of monopolistic competition.

To understand how monopolistic competition explains the introduction of new products, let's consider a case from the watch industry. A company decides that by putting a picture of George Foreman, the former heavyweight boxing champion, on a watch face its sales will soar from middle-aged male buyers who want a role model. George Foreman—for a price—gives the company the exclusive right to use his picture. This creates a short-term monopoly profit for the firm, as shown in Figure 4, panel (*a*). The profit is the area *abcd*. Other watch firms will see their sales dwindle to a precious few. They may then try to imitate the "Foreman watch" with the "Madonna watch." Some of the customers who would have bought a Foreman watch now decide to buy a Madonna watch. This shifts the demand curve for Foreman watches to the right, causing the firm to earn a normal return on its investment in Foreman watches. As a sufficient number of rivals enter the market, the long-run monopolistically competitive equilibrium is reached where the economic profits of the original innovator are reduced to zero (that is, a competitive return), as shown in Figure 4, panel (*b*).

This hypothetical story applies in reality to the thousands of new products that come out each year. Firms introduce new or better products in order to make a profit, and the free entry from rival firms keeps profits at a competitive level.

Monopolistic competition is, of course, not efficient in the sense that price equals marginal cost. It is inefficient in the static sense that the given resources could be allocated more efficiently by an all-knowing and all-powerful dictator, but in the real world it is impossible to interfere with the pricing mechanism without also destroying the ability of monopolistic competition to yield a stream of new products at ever-lower costs. Thus, the static inefficiency of monopolistic competition is the price we pay for having a workable method for generating progress.

Dynamic Competition

The theory of monopolistic competition is suggestive of a far more dynamic type of competition. The proliferation of new products is actually self-reinforcing.

(*a*) New Foreman Watch

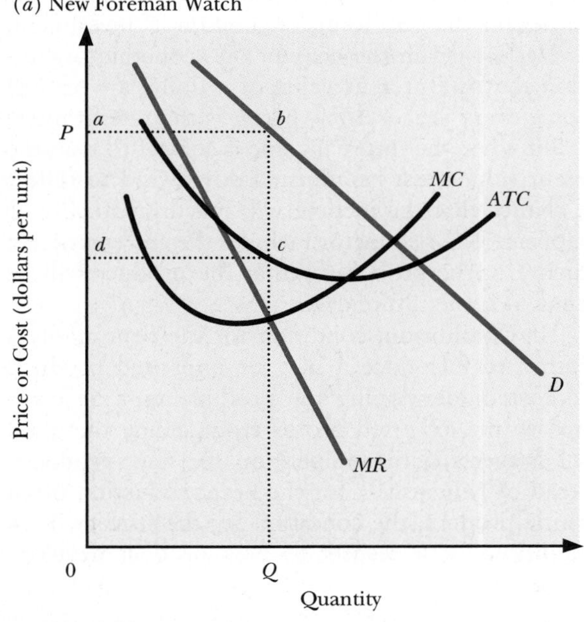

(*b*) After Entry of Competitors

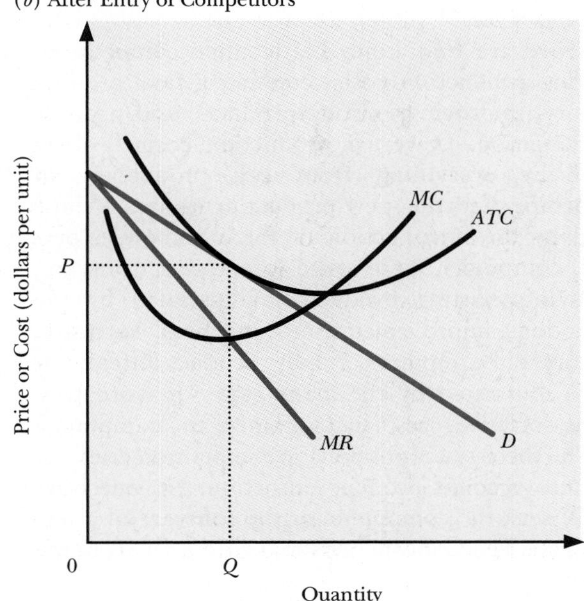

FIGURE 4 Introduction of New Products

Panel (*a*) shows a watch company that makes profits of *abcd* after introducing a new "Foreman watch." Panel (*b*) shows the long-run equilibrium after competitors drive the profits from the Foreman watch to zero.

Each new idea or invention suggests other new products that might be introduced. Sony was the first to introduce the videocassette recorder (VCR); soon, other companies introduced superior VCRs using a different format. In the 1950s, television sets had poor resolution and were bulky and expensive. In the 1980s, the application of advanced electronics led to better and cheaper television sets. Communication has evolved from the telegraph and the early primitive telephones to to today's touch-tone direct dialing to any country, satellite transmission, answering machines, call waiting, cordless phones, cellular phones, fax machines, E-mail, fax/ modems on computers, and so on, as each idea builds on the preceding one. Thus, each new product or innovation has lowered the cost of future new products or innovations. As costs fall, profit opportunities are created for ever newer products, and new products can proliferate at a faster pace.

This type of competition was best described by economist Joseph Schumpeter. He asserted that the "competition which counts [is] from the new commodity, the new technology, the new source of supply, the new type of organization (the largest-scale unit of control for instance)—competition which commands a decisive cost or quality advantage and which strikes not at the margins of profits and the outputs of existing firms but at their foundations and their very lives."[4]

There are four kinds of dynamic competition: lowering production costs, creating a new product category, improving existing products, and product differentiation. Lowering production costs is illustrated by everything from egg production to microchips. Creating new product categories is illustrated by the introduction of the automobile, personal computers, and word processing software. Improving existing products is illustrated by the tremendous improvements in cars, tires, software, and personal computers. Finally, product differentiation is illustrated by the many types of word processing software, cars, trucks, planes, and computers.

The theory of monopolistic competition does not take into account product extinction. No one buys the TV sets, the computers, or the software of a few years ago. The Osborne personal computer from the early 1980s is gone; the Model T Ford and horse and buggy are most likely found in a museum; and phonograph records are practically extinct as they have been replaced by compact discs. The theory of dynamic competition deals with the real possibility that a product will not last forever. New products leapfrog over old products. (See Example 3.) Microsoft and Intel know that they must continually innovate or other firms will drive them out of business with even better products. The guiding principle is whether to create the new product that will soon be extinct. Marginal revenue and marginal cost of production fade into the background. The key question is whether the cost of developing the product—marketing, designing, and testing—is less than the expected gains over the life of the new product.

In these circumstances marginal revenue becomes somewhat problematic. The price of the product or service must be high enough to earn a profit but low enough to keep old or new rivals out of the market. It may cost a billion dollars to develop a new kind of razor blade, as it did for Gillette to produce and market its Mach3 razor. Microsoft and Intel invest billions in research and development, yet marginal costs of production may be very small. Indeed, the marginal cost to Microsoft of producing another copy of its Windows software is close to zero. Clearly, the marginal cost of production must fall far short of the price in order for the firm to make good on its investment.

We learned in the chapter on economic organization that the present value of a dollar's worth of income every year is $1/r$, where r is the rate of interest. But when the future income is subject to risk, the present value must be adjusted downward to reflect the chance that the income will fall dramatically or disappear. The risk factor includes the entrepreneur's estimate of the probability that the product will be extinct at some future date.

The equilibrium condition for the firm involves whether to introduce a new or improved product. The cost of developing the product must be compared to the expected profits from selling the good until it meets with competition for new products. Instead of MR = MC for the best production of an existing product, the condition for the firm to be in equilibrium with respect to new product development is:

Cost of development = the risk-adjusted present value of profits

[4]Joseph Schumpeter, *Capitalism, Socialism, and Democracy,* 3d ed (New York: Harper & Brothers, 1950), p. 84.

EXAMPLE 3

Leapfrog Competition: WordPerfect Versus Microsoft Word

The theory of dynamic competition is well illustrated by the market for word processors. In 1986, WordStar shared the market with WordPerfect, with Microsoft Word a distant third. Word's share leapfrogged over WordStar by 1991 with a 28 percent market share, while WordPerfect accelerated to 48 percent of the market. An observer in 1991 may have argued that WordPerfect was the dominant player for the future. However, by 1997, Microsoft Word had 70 percent of the market, compared with only 6 percent for WordPerfect. This is an old story. After Henry Ford introduced the famous Model T, Ford had the lion's share of the automobile market. Later, General Motors took the lead, as GM produced cars that were more tailored to the individual tastes of consumers. Ford now appears to be overtaking GM once again. Would you predict that Word will be the number one word processor by 2003?

MARKET SHARE OF COMPETITIVE PC WORD PROCESSING PACKAGES, 1986–1997

Year	*WordPerfect*	*Word*	*AmiPro*	*DisplayWriter*	*MultiMate*	*WordStar*
1986	14	6		5	9	13
1987	25	6		13	11	21
1988	37	8		9	7	13
1989	41	15		9	5	11
1990	40	21	1	6	3	16
1991	48	28	6	2	1	8
1992	43	38	8			3
1993	40	46	11			1
1994	26	61	11			
1995	17	68	9			
1996	7	62	29			
1997	6	70	22			

Source: Richard Schmalensee, Microsoft Testimony, 1999.

This equilibrium condition tells us that companies will develop new products as long as their development costs equal or fall short of their benefits (risk-adjusted present value of profits). If four products have benefits in excess of or equal to development costs, but a fifth has benefits less than such costs, four new products will be introduced. Such a model explains why it is that companies such as Intel and Microsoft can grow their profits at double-digit rates and yet find that their stock prices are not infinite. For example, if a company's profit grows at 10 percent a year without risk, and interest rates are 10 percent, the stock price should theoretically be infinite. But when one adjusts for the possibility that the company's current products may disappear in a few years, it is necessary to place a finite value on the stock.

In this chapter we have examined the efficiency of competition—both perfect and monopolistic—and monopoly under the assumption that both are feasible. We have looked at the role of patents and monopolistic competition or monopoly in promoting technological progress and the introduction of new products. In the next chapter we shall examine the more complicated problems created by oligopolies.

SUMMARY

1. Perfect competition can lead to economic efficiency. Goods are produced at lowest cost and in the right amounts. The most efficient allocation of resources occurs when P = MC reflects marginal benefits and marginal costs to society at large. Interference with the P = MC condition results in economic inefficiency.

2. Monopoly is inefficient because of contrived scarcity and rent-seeking behavior. Monopolists make a profit by reducing output to the point where P exceeds MC. Rent-seeking behavior can prevent competition and can add to the social costs of monopoly power by absorbing resources in the associated lobbying.

3. Externalities exist when the decisions of one consumer or producer incidentally benefit or harm someone who does not control the decision. In this case, perfect competition does not result in economic efficiency because P and MC simply reflect private benefits and costs instead of social benefits and costs. Social efficiency requires that marginal social costs equal marginal social benefits. All market types and economic systems, however, have difficulty dealing with externalities.

4. Monopoly and monopolistic competition are more conducive to technological progress. In some cases, patents may give some firms the incentive to develop new products.

5. Dynamic competition is the competition from reducing production costs, creating new product categories, improving existing products, and product differentiation. The firm is in equilibrium with respect to new product introduction if the cost of development equals the risk-adjusted present value of the profits it generates.

KEY TERMS

economic efficiency 224
contrived scarcity 226
deadweight loss 227
monopoly rent-seeking behavior 228
externalities 228
social costs 228
social benefits 228
patent 229

QUESTIONS AND PROBLEMS

1. Restate why P = MC is the condition for economic efficiency.
2. Give examples of positive external benefits and negative external costs.
3. Why do economists claim that monopolists contrive scarcity?
4. The marginal cost of production in industry A is \$8 and is equal to the average cost. The demand schedule is linear and is given in Table A. What is the deadweight loss of monopoly that results from contrived scarcity in this case? What is the maximum monopoly rent-seeking loss?

TABLE A

Price (dollars per unit)	*Quantity (units)*
20	0
15	500
10	1000
5	1500
0	2000

5. Explain why monopolists produce too little output from the standpoint of economic efficiency.
6. Explain the resource allocation problem that would exist in a competitive market economy if the following undertakings have externalities: (a) the production of electricity by burning coal and (b) the immunization of children against

communicable diseases. Draw a supply-and-demand diagram for each undertaking, indicating both the market allocation and the correct resource allocation result.

7. What does the historical evidence indicate about the relationship between the size of business firms and technological progress? Do large business enterprises hold a "monopoly" on technological innovation?
8. What is the difference between rent-seeking losses and losses that result when the monopolist produces where marginal revenue equals marginal cost?
9. Why is production at an output level where marginal cost equals marginal revenue socially inefficient for monopolies but socially efficient under perfect competition?
10. The marginal cost of production for a new drug is $2 per dozen. The demand schedule for the drug is shown in Table B.
    a. What is the monopoly price for the drug?
    b. Compare the gains that consumers would receive to the losses that the monopolist would incur if the drug were sold competitively.

TABLE B

Price (dollars per dozen)	*Quantity (dozens)*
10	0
9	1
8	2
7	3
6	4
5	5
4	6
3	7

11. The Mafia obtains protection "rents" through the threat of violence, exacting payments in return for securing the physical or economic safety of one person against potential criminals or predators. Is this a form of economic rent seeking?
12. If competition is dynamic, can a firm's monopoly power be measured by its market share?
13. What is the difference between dynamic competition and competition in the market for wheat?

INTERNET CONNECTION

14. Using the links from http://www.awl.com/ruffin_gregory, read "Summary of Written Testimony of Microsoft Witness Professor Richard L. Schmalensee" and "Direct Testimony of Frederick R. Warren-Boulton" in the case *United States of America vs. Microsoft Corporation.*
    a. Your text argues that some markets may be dynamically competitive, even though they appear monopolistic. Briefly summarize why Schmalensee argues that Microsoft is in a dynamically competitive industry.
    b. How does Warren-Boulton respond to Schmalensee?
    c. Which side do you agree with? (There is not necessarily a correct answer here.)

PUZZLE ANSWERED: If the price were close to zero, Microsoft would not have had any incentive to invent the operating system. In dynamic competition, the firm must make profits to recover the development and marketing costs of goods that have very small marginal production costs.

Chapter 13

The Game of Oligopoly

Chapter Insight

The competition that firms face has a dramatic effect on their future prospects. In May 2000, Microsoft had a market capitalization of $320 billion (what investors think the company is worth, based on the stock price and the number of shares) on sales of $20 billion and profits of about $8 billion. Ford had a market capitalization of about $61 billion on sales of about $156 billion and profits of about $6.5 billion. The difference between these two companies reflects the perceived difference in their future profits. Ford must compete with General Motors, which is about the same size, as well as with companies all over the world. Even though Microsoft's profits are only 20 percent less than Ford's, investors value Microsoft as worth eight times more than Ford because they believe that Microsoft faces less competition. Investors expect that not only will Microsoft's profits persist into the future, but that they will grow. Microsoft's biggest competitor is Oracle, with a market capitalization of $180 billion on sales of $9 billion. Should we expect any difference in the behavior of Ford and Microsoft toward their customers and their competitors?

The theory of oligopoly is an attempt to gain insight into situations such as those in which Microsoft and Ford find themselves. *Oligopoly* is an umbrella term that describes market structures that fall between monopoly and monopolistic competition. The complex and varied behavior of oligopolies arises from the different strategic situations in which the firms may find themselves. In this chapter we will consider the forces that lead oligopolies to behave more competitively or more monopolistically. Finally, we shall discuss how game theory—the study of strategic rivalry—is used in the analysis of oligopoly.

LEARNING OBJECTIVES

After completing this chapter, you will be able to:

1. Understand the central elements of an oligopoly.
2. Explain how cartels work or don't work.
3. Apply game theory to oligopoly behavior.
4. Specify the economic obstacles to collusion.
5. Provide a possible defense of oligopoly.

CHAPTER PUZZLE: A government study finds that the computer industry is becoming more dominated by the larger firms. Is it justifiable to conclude that the economy is worse off?

OLIGOPOLY

An oligopoly is an industry in which there are so few firms that the firms are large enough to have a significant impact on the price of the product. For example, the automobile industry in the United States is certainly an oligopoly because companies like Ford, DaimlerChrysler, and General Motors can all affect the prices of cars and trucks.

An **oligopoly** is an industry (1) that is dominated by a few firms, (2) whose individual firms must consider the policies of their rivals in making their decisions, and (3) whose firms are price makers.

In contrast to perfect or monopolistic competition, individual oligopolists are deeply concerned with the policies of their rivals. Ford certainly not only must worry about its own pricing and product line, it also must formulate some plans about what prices and products will be offered by Toyota, Honda, DaimlerChrysler, and General Motors. The same is true for each of the others. Oligopolists think of themselves as engaging in a market game in which their profits depend on the behavior of rivals. They advertise, introduce new products, or change prices in their bid to entice customers away from their rivals.

Firms like IBM, Intel, General Electric, and Ford are involved in oligopolistic industries. When we speak of "big business," it is frequently an oligopoly we have in mind. Oligopolies, however, are all around us. If a city has several newspapers, each newspaper will be principally concerned with the editorial, advertising, and pricing policies of the others in the same city. Therefore, the theory of oligopoly applies to a great many business situations involving both large and small businesses.

Mutual interdependence is the key to oligopoly behavior. In making decisions on prices, quantities, and qualities of its product, an oligopolist must consider the possible reactions of rival firms. In some cases, the pattern of reaction may be easy to anticipate for all participants. In other cases, participants must engage in strategic behavior to outguess and outmaneuver their rivals.

Mutual interdependence exists when a firm recognizes that its decisions are likely to invite reactions by rivals.

Oligopolies are a diverse lot. One oligopoly will behave like a monopoly; some are far closer to perfect or monopolistic competition. Thus, there are several different ways for us to approach the study of oligopoly.

MEASUREMENT

To call an industry an oligopoly does not condemn it. But how do we identify one? Some economists believe that oligopoly is the predominant form of industrial organization because it is characterized by (1) relatively few firms and (2) limited or difficult entry. Indeed, just like monopoly, an oligopolistic industry, in order to exert some monopoly power (charging a price substantially greater than marginal cost), must be protected by some *barriers to entry*. If there are no entry barriers, any economic profits will be competed away by rival firms.

A **barrier to entry** is a legal or natural impediment that gives an advantage to existing firms over firms that might enter into the industry.

In the chapter on monopoly and monopolistic competition we encountered numerous barriers to entry, such as economies of scale, patents, public franchises, licensing, and exclusive ownership of raw materials. In oligopoly, there also are (1) financing advantages of incumbents, (2) brand loyalty caused by product differentiation, (3) access to distribution channels, and (4) a learning curve that requires product experience before costs can be competitive with established rivals. (See Example 1.)

Barriers to entry will presumably result in a number of large firms dominating an industry. If an industry can be defined in terms of its total domestic market (e.g., the pizza or software market), a convenient measure is the share of the market held by the largest firms. For example, the four-firm concentration ratio is the market share of the largest four firms (see Table 1).

A four-firm **concentration ratio** is the percentage of industry sales accounted for by the four largest firms.

Table 1 shows the latest available statistics for some selected industries. These concentration ratios are an imperfect guide to the extent of oligopoly for three reasons. First, concentration ratios do not reflect competition from foreign producers or from substitute products at home. The four-firm concentration ratio of the U.S. automobile industry is 84 percent—a figure that fails to measure the competition of foreign imports.

Second, many markets, such as newspapers, cement, and real estate, are local or regional. Concentration ratios for percentages of national sales are

EXAMPLE 1

The Learning Curve

Most economic activity takes place in offices, shops, and factories. One of the most commonly observed facts is that as the organization gains experience in producing goods and services, such as motorcycles, software, microprocessors, telephone calls, electricity, and even financial services, the cost of production falls over time. Put simply, people learn how to do things better. This precept was first systematically observed about 80 years ago by aircraft engineer Theodore White, who was responsible for cost estimates for Curtiss Aeroplane. He discovered that the cost of assembly line labor declines 20 percent for each doubling of production experience. Thus, the 100th airplane required only 80 percent of the labor cost of the 50th airplane. This became known as the "80 percent curve." In 1966 a Boston consulting group found that the unit costs of integrated circuits dropped 25 percent for each doubling of experience. The Boston group called this the "experience curve." Since then, learning curves have been published for everything from bottle caps to soft contact lenses; they show that costs tend to fall from 10 percent to 30 percent whenever production experience doubles.

Whatever it is called, the learning/experience curve provides a barrier to entry for new firms: New firms must incur higher costs than established firms; thus they are at a competitive disadvantage in the market place. Some studies have shown that experience in one firm may have spillover effects to another firm in the industry, because experienced people can move or can simply talk to individuals in other firms. Nevertheless, learning curve effects means that entry cannot be perfectly free as assumed in the theory of perfect or monopolistic competition.

Source: Michael Rothschild, *Bionomics: The Inevitability of Capitalism,* New York: Henry Holt and Company, 1990, Chap. 17.

TABLE 1 SELECTED CONCENTRATION RATIOS IN MANUFACTURING, 1992

Industry	*Four-Firm Concentration Ratio*	*Number of Firms*
Cigarettes	93	8
Malt beverages	90	160
Motor vehicles and car bodies	84	398
Aircraft	79	151
Cigars	74	25
Guided missles and space vehicles	71	24
Potato chips and similar snacks	70	333
Tires and inner tubes	70	104
Internal combustion engines	56	250
Meat packing	50	1,296
Electronic computers	45	803
Semiconductors and related devices	41	823
Blast furnaces and steel mills	37	135
Bread, cake, and related products	34	374
Petroleum refining	30	131
Industrial and organic chemicals	29	489
Men's and boys' shirts	28	527
Pharmaceutical preparations	26	583
Fluid milk	22	525
Periodicals	20	4,390
Women's and misses' dresses	11	3,943
Plastics	5	7,605
Commercial printing	7	28,485
Industrial machinery	1	22,596

Source: U.S. Census of Manufacturers, MC92-S-2, http://www.census.gov.

misleading in such markets. A local or regional firm may dominate its relevant market, and this dominance would not necessarily be reflected by the national concentration ratio.

Third, concentration ratios do not measure *potential* competition. They do not indicate in which industries new firms can find ways and means to overcome existing barriers to entry if existing firms earn extraordinary profits. One airline may account for 90 percent of the flights between two cities, but the number of potential entrants into this market may be large.

Even though the concentration ratio can be misleading, as Table 1 indicates it is certainly the case that the cigarette industry, with a four-firm concentration ratio of 93, is less competitive and has more market power than a firm in the plastics, commercial printing, or industrial machinery industry. The concentration ratio should only be used as a rough guide to the structure of industry, given the above reservations. It is even possible that a high concentration ratio is simply reflective of greater economic efficiencies on the part of the larger firms. In other words, concentration ratios or market shares should always be used with caution.

The Dominant-Firm Oligopoly

Occasionally one firm dominates an industry so much that the firm can set a price much like a monopoly after it takes into account some fringe of much smaller competitors. For example, America Online is without question the largest Internet service provider, with a market capitalization of over $140 billion (in April 2000) compared with a market capitalization of about $2 billion for its rival, DoubleClick/EarthLink. If there is a fringe of competitive firms with higher unit costs, the dominant firm can simply estimate aggregate supply of those firms, deduct it from market demand, and choose the profit-maximizing price and quantity from the remaining demand facing the dominant firm. For example, Figure 1 illustrates a dominant firm that faces demand curve DD'' and a competitive fringe with the supply curve S. The dominant firm has marginal costs MC and allows the competitive fringe full

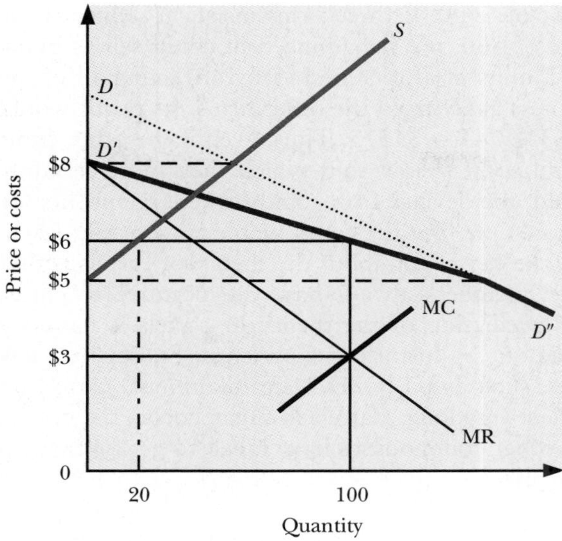

FIGURE 1 The Dominant Firm

Above the entry price of $5, the dominant firm's demand curve is flatter, or more elastic, than the market demand curve, *DD″*. The MR curve is marginal to *D′D″* rather than to *DD″*. Thus, the dominant firm charges a lower price.

freedom. At the price $8 the competitive fringe supplies the entire market, but at the price $5 the dominant firm supplies the entire market. When the supply curve *S* is deducted from the demand curve *DD″*, the remaining demand facing the dominant firm is *D′D″*. The dominant firm's demand curve has a marginal revenue curve MR; thus, at the price $6 the dominant firm maximizes its profit by setting its MR = MC, as always.

Notice three things about the dominant firm. First, because a dominant firm loses business to rivals from a higher price, its demand curve is more elastic than the market demand curve *DD″*. Thus, the price is lower than in a monopoly. Second, the dominant firm must have some sort of advantage over the competitive fringe; in the case of Figure 1 the advantage is in a much lower cost of production. At the equilibrium position, the MC of the dominant firm is $3 and that for the competitive fringe is $6 (equal to the dominant firm's price). Third, a larger number of competitors will make the dominant firm's demand curve more elastic and lower the price of the product. This third point is illustrated by the generic manufacturers of a brand-name drug that loses its patent protection; over time, more generic manufacturers enter and the price falls.[1]

Cartels

A popular approach to oligopoly is the one suggested by Adam Smith: "People of the same trade seldom meet together, even for merriment or diversion but the conversation ends in a conspiracy against the public, or in some contrivance to raise prices." Doesn't it make sense that, say, a handful of firms that completely dominate an industry simply get together and do what's best for them?

There are several ways to conspire together on pricing and output decisions. Firms can form a cartel that assigns to each member how much output to produce or what price to charge. Alternatively, firms can sell their product at the price determined by the industry price leader.

A **cartel** is an organization of producers whose goal is to operate the industry as a monopoly.

The most notable example of a cartel in the past 50 years is the Organization of Petroleum Exporting Countries (OPEC). OPEC had operated for many years as a loosely formed organization, but as the members noticed that their share of world output had grown to overwhelming proportions they began to act in unison. In 1973–1974, the OPEC countries quadrupled the price of oil. As this dramatic "oil shock" sent tremors through the industrial world, the profits rolled into the OPEC countries. OPEC again dramatically increased oil prices in 1979–1980. In the mid-1980s, however, turmoil in the Middle East and a falling share of world output controlled by OPEC led to a weakening of the cartel.

How does a cartel work? Each member must act on behalf of the group by restricting its output below what it would do if acting alone. When each firm restricts output, the cartel can maintain a price that is far above the marginal cost of production for each firm. Acting as perfect competitors, each firm would produce where P = MC. Acting as a cartel, each firm can make greater profits by producing at that level where the cartel's marginal revenue equals marginal cost.

[1]See Richard Caves, Michael Winston, and Mark Horwitz, "Patent Expiration, Entry, and Competition in the U.S. Pharmaceutical Industry," *Brookings Papers on Economic Activity: Microeconomics 1991,* pp. 1–48.

To understand cartels we must make a sharp distinction between the cartel's MR and the firm's MR. The cartel's MR is the industry MR curve that is derived from the industry's demand curve. The firm's MR depends on the firm's demand curve. By cutting the price to one slightly below the cartel price, the firm can sell much more than if the cartel reduced the price slightly, because it would take business away from those firms adhering to the cartel price. Thus, the firm's MR may be only slightly less than the market price established by the cartel. If all firms but one are charging the cartel price, the cheating or deviant firm can then sell its entire output at a price slightly below the cartel price.

Figure 2 gives a simple example of a cartel: Four firms have access to a particular mineral spring. It costs \$20 to produce and distribute each bottle of water. Thus, AC = MC = \$20. The industry demand curve is $P = 100 - Q$. The industry's MR curve is $MR = 100 - 2Q$, since for a linear demand curve it is twice as steep. Figure 2 shows that when MR = MC = \$20, the cartel produces $Q = 40$ at a price of $P = \$60$. Each firm sells exactly 10 bottles. The profit per bottle is \$40; thus, each firm makes a profit of \$400. If three firms insist on selling at the price of \$60, the remaining firm could sell as many as 45 units at a price of \$55 by attracting all of the business away from the other firms. Its profit would be $\$35 \times 45 = \$1575$. Thus, even if the other firms would soon follow suit, which they most certainly would, the deviant firm could make large profits for a short time. But the cartel would now break down.

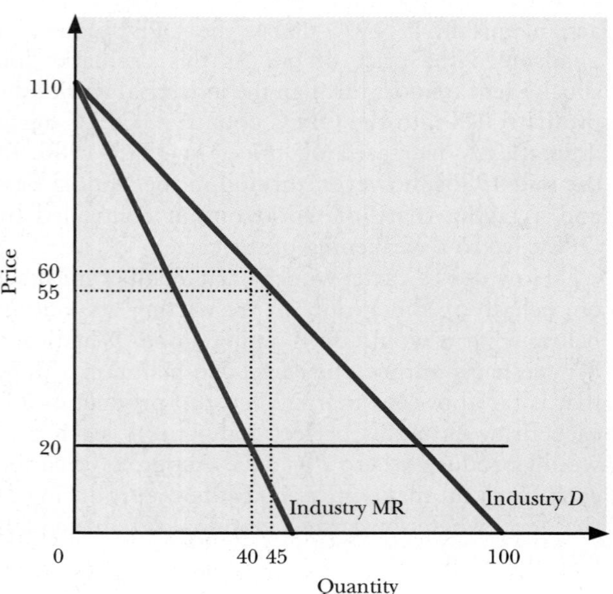

FIGURE 2 Theory of Cartels

Four identical firms with MC = \$20 could form a cartel with common $P = \$60$, with each making \$400 of a \$1600 industry profit on sales of 10 units. A cheating firm could shade price to \$55, sell at most 45 units on its own, and make at most \$1575.

The key point about the theory of cartels is that cartel members always have an incentive to cheat. This prediction of the theory of cartels is basically borne out by historical experience: Except in a few cases, such as oil (OPEC) and diamonds, cartels do not last very long. Cartels in sugar, cocoa, tin, coffee, and other commodities have failed to get a firm grip over prices.

THINKING STRATEGICALLY: GAME THEORY

Game theory was introduced in Chapter 5. Game theory provides a way of thinking about strategic situations that managers, economists, generals, and politicians find useful in making decisions against an intelligent foe.

In competitive business situations, the players are not interdependent. One firm's actions do not affect another firm in the industry. In this case, equilibrium is established at the intersection of the industry supply and demand curves. At this equilibrium, firms are selling what they want to sell and buyers are buying what they want to buy. When firms are interdependent, we must use a different concept of equilibrium, the Nash equilibrium, named for its discoverer, John Nash, a 1994 Nobel laureate in economics.

Recall from Chapter 5 that a game is really just a situation in which several players follow different possible strategies with various outcomes or payoffs.

The **Nash equilibrium** of a game is the point at which each player is doing the best he or she can given what the other players are doing.

In other words, a Nash equilibrium is achieved when the chosen game plan or strategy of each player is his or her best response to the strategies of others. Thus, in a Nash equilibrium, each person correctly anticipates what the others will do for the simple reason that there is no incentive for anyone to change from that position.

For example, in the 2000 elections, politicians were told by their advisors that negative campaigning worked. As a consequence, most politicians engaged in negative ads about their adversary (for example, "My opponent is a liar"). But why take the low road? If all politicians were to engage in positive campaigning (such as "I promise a free lunch"), no one's reputation would be smeared. It would seem just as easy for two politicians to agree to be civilized.

The reason that many of the politicians did not take the high road is the belief that negative campaigning works. Suppose two politicians think they have an equal chance of winning an election if both campaign negatively or both campaign positively. If one campaigns negatively while the other does so positively, both believe that the negative campaigner will win. Thus, there is nothing to gain from a positive campaign by one of them because it increases the perceived chances of losing the election.

In the same way, whether oligopolists collude in a cartel or act independently, they must act strategically within their understanding of the competitive situation in which they find themselves. Many examples of oligopolistic behavior can be explained as a Nash equilibrium. Let us now consider the Cournot oligopoly game, the prisoner's dilemma game, the advertising game, and the credible threat.

The Cournot Oligopoly Game

One of the most important models of oligopoly was developed by French economist Augustin A. Cournot (1801–1877) in 1838. A Cournot oligopoly occurs when each firm in a group producing a homogeneous product acts as though all other firms will continue to produce their current outputs. Thus a Cournot oligopolist supposes that if it increases its own output, the price of the product must fall by just enough to sell its planned increase in output since all rivals are expected to maintain their production levels. Similarly, if the firm cuts output, the price will rise by just enough to reduce market demand by the firm's planned reduction in output.

In a **Cournot oligopoly**, (1) the product is homogeneous, (2) each firm supposes that its rivals will continue to produce their current outputs independently of that firm's choice of outputs, and (3) there is a fixed number of firms.

Consider again the example of mineral springs supplied by an underground lake. The mineral water is accessible through two springs owned by Bob and Ted. Customers are indifferent about whether they buy mineral water from Bob or Ted, so Bob and Ted must sell at the same price. Figure 3, panel (*a*), shows Ted's output on the vertical axis and Bob's on the horizontal axis. The line *TM* describes Bob's profit-maximizing response to Ted's output, and the line *T′M′* describes Ted's profit-maximizing response to Bob's output. These *reaction curves* show the best response (or profit-maximizing response) of one firm to the other firm's output. In other words, they show the output level each firm would pick if it knew what the rival firm's output would be.

The reaction curves are easy to understand. First, they are both downward-sloping because the more Ted produces, the less of the market remains for Bob (and vice versa). Second, when the output of one is zero, the other assumes he has a monopoly and produces accordingly. In panel (*a*), the monopoly output is 3 units. Third, if one firm fully saturates the market, the other will produce nothing. This is called the *predatory output* because it drives the other firm out of business. In panel (*a*), the predatory output of each firm is 6 units. This exceeds monopoly output because in monopoly the price exceeds marginal cost, leaving room for the other firm to make some sales. Therefore, the reaction curves must appear as in panel (*a*). The two reaction curves intersect at the point where each firm's expectations about the other firm are fulfilled; it is a Nash equilibrium because each firm is doing the best it can given the other firm's choice of output. In panel (*a*), the Cournot equilibrium occurs where each firm produces 2 units; the market therefore consists of 4 units.

The world of Cournot is more competitive than monopoly but is not as efficient as perfect competition. However, as the number of firms increases, the Cournot model predicts that prices will fall and output rise, just as in the competitive model.

The Cournot game has been criticized for its assumption that firms suppose their rivals are passive, but experimental studies support this model. In a classic study, 16 pairs of undergraduates were given a Cournot game that would have resulted in a Cournot output of 40 (per subject). Surprisingly, the average output of each student firm, following their own rules, was approximately 40![2]

[2]Lawrence Fouraker and Signey Siegal, *Bargaining Behavior* (New York: McGraw-Hill, 1963).

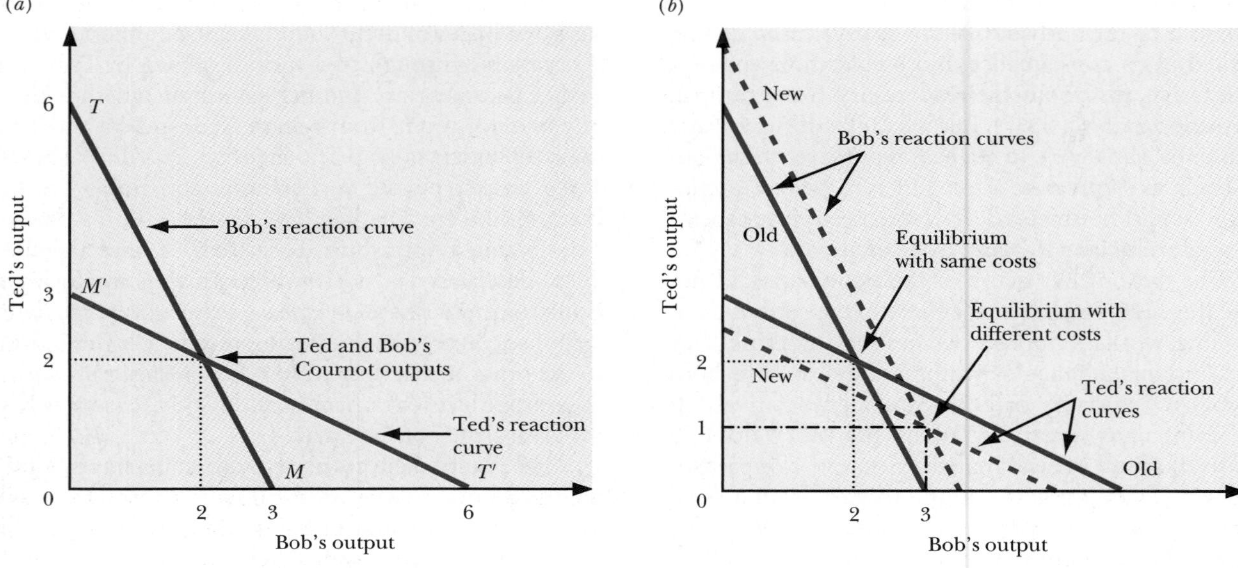

FIGURE 3 Cournot Strategies

In panel (*a*), *T′M′* is Ted's reaction curve; *TM* is Bob's reaction curve. Each person's monopoly output is 3 and each person's predatory output is 6. The Cournot solution is 2 each. Panel (*b*) illustrates the effects of different costs.

The Cournot oligopoly model has many useful features. It allows us to visualize what happens when firms have different costs. Suppose, for example, that Bob's cost of production falls while Ted's increases by the same amount. Figure 3, panel (*b*), shows that Bob's reaction curve will shift up while Ted's will shift down. Why? With lower costs than in Figure 3, panel (*a*), Bob wants to produce more for any given output for Ted; and with higher costs than in panel (*a*), Ted will want to produce less for any given output for Bob. This will result in an equilibrium in which Ted produces 1 unit while Bob produces 3 units. The market total is the same (4 units), but Bob has 75 percent of the market instead of 50 percent. This change in costs that favors one firm raises the concentration ratio but does not in any way make society worse off. Indeed, it can be argued that society is better off because the 4 units are being produced at a lower total cost to society. Thus, there are more resources to produce other good things.

Another useful feature is that in the Cournot equilibrium both firms are absolutely correct in their conjecture that the other firm will continue to produce the same amount. Indeed, market shares tend to be relatively stable. For example, the shares of General Motors and Ford in the U.S. automobile market have remained roughly the same over very long periods, with GM maintaining slightly more than one-fourth of the market and Ford slightly less than one-fourth of the market.

Another example shows that a Cournot (Nash) equilibrium is also a self-enforcing agreement. Suppose the demand curve is $P = 10 - Q$, so that every increase of 1 unit in market output lowers price by \$1. If Bob and Ted face an average and marginal cost of \$1, each would produce 3 units in the Cournot equilibrium. Why? With the given demand curve and each producing 3 units, the price of the product would be \$4 (= 10 − 6); both Bob and Ted would each earn \$9 because profits per unit are \$3 at a price of \$4. Now consider Bob's incentive to raise or lower output by 1 unit. If Bob increases output to 4 units, he expects total output to be 7 units (remember, he assumes Ted will keep output constant at 3). Thus, he anticipates that such a decision would lower the price to \$3 (= 10 − 7) and his profits would fall to \$8 (= 4 × \$2). If Bob lowers output to 2 units, he expects total output to be 5 units and price to rise to \$5. But a profit margin of \$4 and 2 units produced would yield a profit of only \$8. Thus, Bob (or Ted) would consider the profit of \$9 to be the best that can be achieved. The Cournot equilibrium is always one in which any deviation for any competing firm lowers profit. If the two firms agree to cut output to

2 units each, raising price to $6, they could each enjoy a $10 profit; but such an agreement is not self-enforceable because each would have an incentive to raise output. One firm might assume that increasing output from 2 to 3 units would raise total output to 5 units and drive the price down to $5, leaving it with an expected profit of $12. Thus, each would have an incentive to break the agreement and produce at the Cournot point.[3]

The Prisoner's Dilemma Game

The famous prisoner's dilemma game introduced in Chapter 5 was developed by game theorists as a way to analyze a situation much like that often faced by oligopolistic producers. The game assumes that two bank robbers have been apprehended by the police; they are being interrogated in separate rooms. If both talk, both go to jail but with 3-year sentences. If one talks and the other remains quiet, the one who talks gets off with a 1-year sentence and the silent bank robber gets a 6-year jail sentence. If neither talks, both get 1 year for carrying a deadly weapon. Each prisoner has a dilemma. Each knows that if he or she keeps quiet, both can get a light sentence, provided the other remains quiet; but keeping quiet is risky, because the other prisoner might talk. Moreover, if the other prisoner remains quiet, confessing lowers the sentence from 1 year to 0 years. If the other prisoner confesses, the first must confess to avoid a 6-year sentence. A Nash equilibrium occurs if both bank robbers confess. If one believes the other will confess, his or her best strategy is also to confess. If both actually confess, each has guessed correctly about the other's behavior and is able to employ the best strategy for the situation in which the other confesses. If the prisoners could communicate and make a binding agreement, they would both be better off remaining quiet.

A **prisoner's dilemma game** is a game with two players in which both players benefit from cooperating, but in which each player has an incentive to cheat on the agreement.

The prisoner's dilemma is much like an oligopolist's dilemma of deciding whether to collude or to act independently. In both cases, the consequences of one player's decision depend upon the decision of another player. Suppose Firm A and Firm B each sell a differentiated product. Suppose also that when the two products have equal prices, both firms enjoy exactly the same profit. If one charges a slightly lower price than the other, however, that firm will make large profits while the high-priced firm will make only a small profit.

Figure 4 illustrates a simple example of the oligopolist's dilemma. Each firm can choose a price of either $20 or $19. The prices Firm A might charge are shown down the left side of the figure; the prices Firm B might charge are shown along the top. The *profits* earned by each firm are the payoffs from any set of prices the *two firms together* might charge. Firm A's profit payoffs are shown in the lower left-hand corner

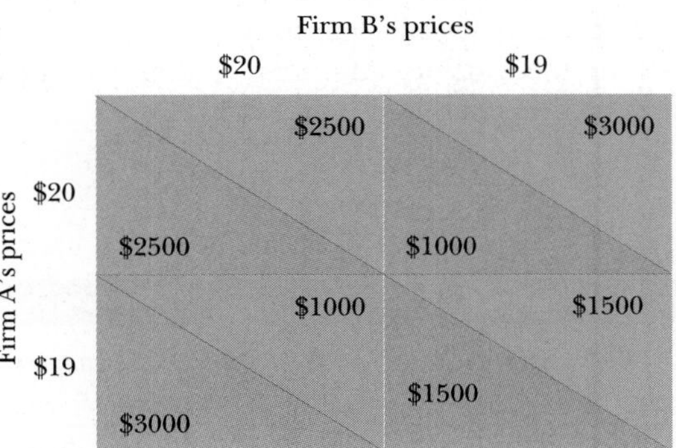

FIGURE 4 Profit Payoffs to a Two-Firm Oligopoly

Each square (cell) shows the profits that each firm would earn when various combinations of prices are charged by the two firms. Firm A's profits are shown in green in the lower left-hand corner of each cell, and Firm B's profits are shown in red in the upper right-hand corner of each cell. For example, if A charges $19 and B charges $20, A would earn a profit of $3000 and B would earn $1000. The Nash equilibrium solution is for both firms to choose a price of $19.

[3]The Cournot oligopoly solution can always be calculated as follows. If industry demand curve is $P = a - bQ$ and each of N firms has a constant marginal cost of $\$c$, then the equilibrium industry output is always $Q = N(a - c)/b(N + 1)$. Each firm thus produces $q = (a - c)/b(N + 1)$. The justification for this is easy. The firm's $MR = P - bq$ because marginal revenue is the price of the next unit sold minus the market spoiled on the previous q units due to lowering the price by $\$b$. But $P = a - bQ$, so $MR = a - bQ - bq = c$ when marginal revenue equals marginal cost. Thus, by simple algebra, $Q + q = (a - c)/b$. Substituting $Q = Nq$, we easily get $q = (a - c)/b(N + 1)$. In the example, $a = 10$, $b = 1$, and $c = 1$. Thus, $q = 3$ and $Q = 6$!

of each box (in green). Firm B's profit payoffs are shown in the upper right-hand corner of each box (in red). When both charge $20, both earn $2500; when both charge $19, both earn $1500. When one charges $20 and the other charges $19, the low-priced firm earns $3000, and the high-priced firm earns only $1000.

The two firms reach a Nash equilibrium when both firms charge $19. If each believes the other is charging $19, the best strategy for each is to charge $19. When both actually charge $19, each has guessed correctly, and each is able to employ the best strategy for the situation in which the other charges $19.

If A and B play this game repeatedly over a fairly long period of time, it is likely that A and B will eventually learn that they are both better off charging higher prices. They might learn to cooperate and choose the strategy that maximizes joint profits. In this case, both would charge $20 and earn profits of $2500 each.

The Advertising Game

If a firm's rival advertises that "my product is better than all others," it is difficult for the firm to fail to respond with its own advertising message. Let's consider a rivalry between two hypothetical hamburger giants: Big Burger and Best Burger. Table 2 shows what the strategy of each hamburger company is in response to the various amounts of daily national television commercials run by its rival.

TABLE 2 ADVERTISING STRATEGIES

Big Burger's Strategies (ads per day)		*Best Burger's Strategies (ads per day)*	
Big Burger Optimum	*Best Burger Number*	*Big Burger Number*	*Best Burger Optimum*
3	0	0	4
6	8	6	8
9	16	12	12

This table shows the profit-maximizing number of TV advertisements for each hamburger chain in response to its rival. The Nash equilibrium is reached when Best Burger runs 8 ads per day and Big Burger runs 6 ads per day because at this point each firm's profit-maximizing behavior is based on a correct guess about the other firm's behavior.

Big Burger strategists calculate that the company can maximize its profits by running 3 ads per day if Best Burger places no ads per day, by running 6 ads if Best Burger places 8 ads, and by running 9 ads if Best Burger places 16 ads. The green curve in Figure 5 graphs Big Burger's optimal strategies. On the other hand, Best Burger strategists calculate that the company can maximize its profits by running 4 ads per day if Big Burger places no ads per day, by running 8 ads if Big Burger places 6 ads, and by running 12 ads if Big Burger places 12 ads per day. The red curve graphs Best Burger's optimal strategies. The Nash equilibrium occurs where Best Burger's strategy curve intersects Big Burger's strategy curve. When Big Burger is running 6 ads per day and Best Burger is running 8 ads per day, there is a Nash equilibrium. Big Burger maximizes its profit with 6 ads when Best Burger places 8 ads; Best Burger maximizes its profit with 8 ads when Big Burger places 6 ads. At this point, each company is employing its best strategy for dealing with a correct assessment of how many ads the other company will place.

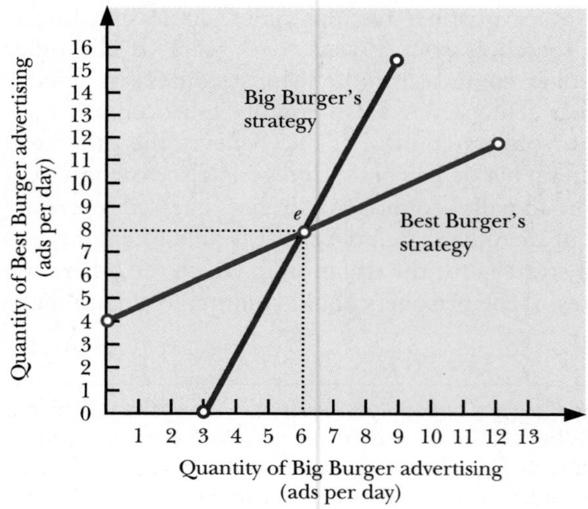

FIGURE 5 Nash Equilibrium: Advertising

The green line shows Big Burger's best response to Best Burger's ads. The red line shows Best Burger's best response to Big Burger's ads. Where the two curves intersect is a Nash equilibrium, where each firm's guess about the other firm's strategy is confirmed. In other words, Big Burger wants 6 ads when Best Burger places 8 ads, and Best Burger wants 8 ads when Big Burger places 6 ads.

EXAMPLE 2

Real-World Burger Wars

The fictional advertising game between Big Burger and Best Burger is reflected in the battle between real-world giants Burger King and McDonald's. The model predicts that when one increases advertising, the other will also. Indeed, the model works too well! In 1999, the two got in a battle over the use of the phrase "Big Kids Meal." In July 1999, Burger King introduced the Big Kids Meal designed for kids 7–12 years old. Immediately, McDonald's responded with a lawsuit claiming that they designed a Big Kids Meal in 1998 for the young-at-heart, ages 18–34.

A judge finally decided that the term was generic, and that since Burger King had spent more in advertising than McDonald's, the greater harm would be inflicted on Burger King. Thus, the judge dismissed the McDonald's case, letting the two fight it out outside the courts. The judge concluded: "It is difficult to imagine that any consumer visiting a restaurant of either party would believe that he or she is at the other party's restaurant."

Source: "McDonald's, Rival Burger King Get into Tussle over the 'Big Kids' Label," *Wall Street Journal,* July 9,1999; "Judge Rules in Burger King's Favor over Use of 'Big Kids Meals' Name," *Wall Street Journal,* October 22, 1999.

The advertising example is interesting because the firms advertise much more at the Nash equilibrium than they would if they reached an informal agreement to deliberately keep their advertising expenditures to a minimum. (See Example 2.)

The Credible Threat

Suppose an industry contains one actual monopolist and one *potential* entrant. To discourage entry, the monopolist might let the potential rival know that there would be a costly price war (prices would be set below costs) if the potential rival were to enter the industry. The rival may not believe the monopolist's threat, however, unless the monopolist makes some commitment to make this threat credible. If the potential entrant calculates that the monopolist would also lose from the price war and would eventually have to share the market, the monopolist's threat will be ignored. But the monopolist can make an irreversible commitment. For example, the monopolist might spend $10 million to secure the services of the best advertising agency before the potential rival enters the business. Or the monopolist might accumulate large cash resources to convince the potential rival of its willingness to engage in a price war. A credible threat makes it easier for the potential entrant to make a correct assumption about the monopolist's behavior.

A **credible threat** is the commitment of significant resources by existing firms to convince potential entrants to the industry that entry would result in severe losses for the entrant.

A Nash equilibrium results when the monopolist maximizes profits by making a credible threat that succeeds in keeping out the potential entrant (on the correct assumption that the potential rival would

EXAMPLE 3

Predatory Pricing and the Credible Threat

The theory of predatory pricing is quite simple. An oligopolistic firm drives out all its competitors by setting price below cost. The most famous case is the creation of the Standard Oil Company. In the nineteenth century, John D. Rockefeller supposedly lowered the price of oil, drove the small oil refineries to the brink of bankruptcy, and then bought them out at a bargain price.

The only trouble with the theory of predatory pricing is that in most cases the scenario works out differently. John McGee studied the historical record and found that Rockefeller's rivals were bought out on very favorable terms. Roland Koller examined 26 cases of alleged predatory pricing dating from 1890. Koller found only seven cases in which there was pricing below cost. Of these seven cases, only one resulted in the rival's disappearing without a trace.

Price predation is not likely to be a profitable strategy, because it does not represent a credible threat. If two oligopolistic firms have identical costs, how could one drive the other out by lowering price? Both firms can play the same game. Suppose firm A tells firm B, "I am going to lower the price until you go out of business." There is no reason why firm B could not do the same thing to firm A. Any damage firm A inflicts on firm B it also inflicts on itself. Unless B thinks that A might have lower costs, predation is not likely to work.

The Supreme Court has decided, in a key case, that

> the success of such schemes is inherently uncertain: the short-run loss is definite, but the long-run gain depends on successfully neutralizing the competition. Moreover, it is not enough simply to achieve monopoly power, as monopoly pricing may breed quick entry by new competitors eager to share in the excess profits. The success of any predatory scheme depends on maintaining monopoly power for long enough both to recoup the predator's losses and to harvest some additional gain. [Thus] predatory pricing schemes are rarely tried, and even more rarely successful.

A recent study by Lott and Opler found that for predation to be credible, managers who suffer short-term losses should be given contracts that give them long-term tenure and, hence, they should suffer less managerial turnover. But they found that managers of the 28 firms accused of predation in the 1963–1982 period experienced the same turnover rates as managers of other firms.

Sources: Matsushita Elec. Industrial Co. v. Zenith Radio, 475 U.S. 574 (1986); John McGee, "Predatory Price Cutting," *Journal of Law and Economics* (1958): 137–169; Roland Koller, "The Myth of Predatory Pricing," *Antitrust Law and Economics Review* (1971): 105–193; and John Lott and Tim Opler, "Testing Whether Predator Commitments are Credible," *Journal of Business* (1996): 339–380.

actually enter the market in the absence of the credible threat) and when the potential entrant minimizes losses by not entering the market, on the correct assumption that the monopolist would indeed start a price war. (See Example 3.)

The behavior of a wide variety of noncooperative oligopolies can be explained using the concept of a Nash equilibrium. Indeed, the Nash equilibrium concept can even be applied to many social behaviors. Game theorists are hard at work on new concepts of equilibrium that can explain even more complicated oligopolistic strategies—such as setting low prices today and high prices tomorrow.

Oligopoly: The Industrial Organization Approach

A cartel will fail if each member believes that cheating on the agreement is profitable. In the Cournot game, each oligopolist thinks that its rivals will maintain their existing outputs; in the prisoner's dilemma, each prisoner thinks the other might confess; in the advertising game, each firm thinks the other firm will maintain its current advertising budget.

Thus, the various solutions to the oligopoly problem depend on the beliefs each oligopolist has about its rivals. In these examples, collusion is not a Nash equilibrium; therefore, the oligopolists will tend to act independently.

Obstacles to Collusion

Industrial organization is the study of how industries actually behave in the real world. The industrial organization approach to understanding whether oligopolies are likely to collude is to examine the actual circumstances in which they find themselves. The chances for effective and lasting collusion decrease when there are (1) many sellers, (2) low entry barriers, (3) product heterogeneity, (4) high rates of innovation, (5) high fixed costs, (6) many opportunities for cheating, and (7) legal restrictions.

Many Sellers. The more sellers there are in the industry, the more difficult it is for the sellers to join a conspiracy to raise prices. The communication network becomes much more complicated as the number of conspirators grows. When there are two sellers, there is only one communication link. When there are three sellers, there are three different information links: A must agree with B; B must agree with C; C and A must agree. When there are 10 sellers, information must flow in 45 ways! The number of information channels increases at a far greater rate than the rate at which the number of sellers increases. It becomes far more difficult to coordinate collusive actions as the number of colluders grows. [The formula for the number of information flows is $n(n - 1)/2$, where n is the number of sellers.]

Low Entry Barriers. If it is easy for new firms to enter an industry, existing firms may not find it worthwhile to work out agreements to raise prices. Effective collusion would cause new firms to enter the industry.

High prices create profitable opportunities for new firms. For example, if an industry has constant returns to scale (no economies or diseconomies of scale), the average cost of production is the same whether there is one firm or many firms. Suppose that such an industry currently has two firms and the average cost of production—including a normal return—is $10. With complete free entry, the existing firms cannot charge more than $10 in the long run. Any price above $10 will bring in new firms to capture above-normal returns. The entry of firms will eventually drive the price down to $10, where only a normal return is earned. The two existing firms will gain no lasting benefit by conspiring to raise the price above $10.

Product Heterogeneity. The more heterogeneous (differentiated) the product is from firm to firm, the more difficult it is for the industry to achieve coordination or collusion. Reaching an agreement creates both costs and benefits. It is costlier to reach an agreement if the product is not homogeneous. Because steel is homogeneous, an agreement on prices and market shares between two major steel producers may be fairly easy to conclude. But an agreement between Airbus and Boeing over the relative prices of the *MD-11* and the Boeing 767 might be difficult because of the differences between the two planes. An agreement between the producers of high-quality goods and low-quality goods might break down because of differences of opinion over one good's quality relative to the other good's quality. It would be difficult for a fast-food chain like McDonald's to enter into a pricing agreement with a full-service restaurant chain like Red Lobster because of the difficulty of agreeing on the proper relative price.

High Rates of Innovation. If an industry has a high rate of innovation, collusive agreements are more difficult to reach. In unstable, quickly changing markets, oligopolies have more difficulty finding the joint profit-maximizing solution. The costs of reaching an agreement are higher in relation to benefits when the industry is constantly turning out new products and developing new techniques. For example, it would be difficult for Compaq and IBM to reach an agreement because of the fast pace of technological change in the personal computer market.

High Fixed Costs. As fixed costs become higher relative to total costs, collusive agreements become more likely to break down. Firms ask themselves what they can gain by cheating on the pricing agreement. If fixed costs are high, variable costs are a low percentage of total costs. As long as the price covers average variable costs, something is left over with which to pay fixed costs. By granting secret price concessions, firms may gain much in the short run if marginal costs are very low.

Many Opportunities for Cheating. If it is easy to cheat without being detected, firms will tend to break a collusive agreement. It is easier to cheat on price agreements when actual prices charged by one party cannot be known with certainty by the other parties to the agreement. For example, when the terms of price negotiations are not revealed (as in the cases of long-term oil delivery contracts or purchases of commercial aircraft by the airlines), it is easier to cheat on pricing agreements.

Legal Restrictions. In the United States, the Sherman Antitrust Act (1890) holds that combinations in restraint of trade are illegal. The Sherman Act and additional acts designed to prohibit and punish collusive behavior make up the antitrust laws of the United States (which we shall discuss in the next chapter). Antitrust laws reduce collusion by increasing the costs of forming agreements.

Unintended Consequences of Government Regulation

Government regulation of business often results in the unintended consequence of more collusive behavior on the part of oligopolists. Prohibiting cigarette advertising solved a prisoner's dilemma facing cigarette firms. Requiring all automobile firms to provide seat belts, airbags, and side-impact bags—while possibly good ideas from a social standpoint—reduces the different strategies firms might follow and therefore can lead to more collusive behavior. For example, if all firms must install passenger side airbags by a certain date, all automobile manufacturers might simply raise their prices by the cost of such airbags plus the same margin of profit. Without government guidance, firms introducing safety features on their own might be uncertain about the price they can charge. This uncertainty results in more competition. Government absolute prohibition of smoking in domestic airlines removed an opportunity for airlines to compete among themselves by offering some smoke-free flights.

In all of the above cases, government regulations created a result that would have required collusion or cooperation to achieve.

A Defense of Oligopoly

Industrial organization economists tell us that profit rates in many oligopolies dominated by large firms tend to persist over time. This fact has prompted many economists to be critical of oligopoly. Some economists, however, defend oligopoly as an efficient form of market. Harold Demsetz, for example, cited the positive relationship between profit rates and oligopoly as an indicator of the greater efficiency of large firms.[4]

Demsetz maintained that higher profits are the result of the superior cost performance of larger firms in the industry. Even if prices are set competitively so that each firm acts more or less like a price taker (exerting no monopoly power over prices), economic profits will accrue only to those firms that have lower costs, not to all firms in the industry. There is evidence that oligopoly profits are earned only by the largest firms in oligopolistic industries, not by all firms. Demsetz therefore concluded that oligopoly profits are the result not of excessive market power but of the superior efficiency of large oligopolistic firms.

Figure 6 illustrates the Demsetz argument. It takes the case of a homogeneous product that is being produced by a large low-cost producer and by small high-cost producers. Perfect competition prevails, and each firm equates marginal costs to the price. When these conditions prevail, economic profits are earned only by the large low-cost producer. The small high-cost firms earn only a normal return. Higher profits are associated with large firms because they can produce at lower costs due to significant economies of scale.

One of Chapter 1's Defining Moment economists, Joseph Schumpeter, argued that large enterprises generate more technological progress, the moving force behind economic progress that temporarily establishes some firms as dominant in their industry. Through the process of "creative destruction," Schumpeter believed that new ideas and new technologies replace the old and that the monopoly power created by technological innovation will prove to be transitory.

---

[4]Harold Demsetz, "Industry Structure, Market Rivalry, and Public Policy," *Journal of Law and Economics* 16 (April 1973): 1–10.

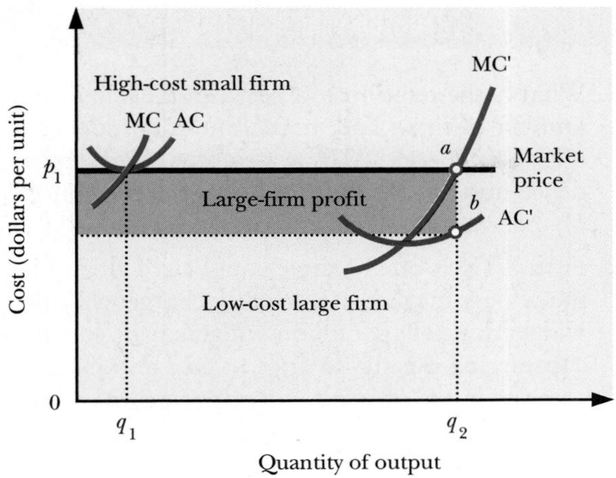

FIGURE 6 The Demsetz Thesis

The large, efficient firm produces an output of q_2 units with a per-unit profit of *ab*. The small, inefficient firm produces an output of q_1 units with a zero economic profit. According to Demsetz, perfect competition can be consistent with the positive association between concentration rates and economic profits.

It is clear that large enterprises can be the natural outcome of the competitive process. One firm may come to dominate an industry because it is more innovative, its management is more efficient, and it has taken more risks. If one or two firms tower over an industry because they have played the game better than others (Schumpeter's "creative destruction"), are not high profits their just reward? We cannot hope to answer the question, "Are concentrated oligopolies necessarily bad?" We shall consider this important policy issue in the chapter on antitrust policy.

A Comparison of the Four Market Forms

We are now finished with our study of the four market forms: perfect competition, monopoly, monopolistic competition, and oligopoly. Table 3 summarizes the key features of each.

Only perfect competition is efficient in the strict, static sense of allocating given resources with known technology. The key to efficiency is the relationship between price and marginal cost. Efficiency is achieved when price equals marginal cost. In perfect competition, $P = \text{MC}$. Monopolistic competition is mildly inefficient because $P > \text{MC}$, but nothing can or should be done about it. Oligopoly can range from a solution close to perfect competition to one close to monopoly; thus, no general conclusion is possible on static efficiency. But it is likely that $P > \text{MC}$. Monopoly is clearly inefficient because $P > \text{MC}$.

All market forms can be conducive to technological progress. We know that monopoly, monopolistic competition, and oligopoly often result in new products. But even firms engaged in perfect competition will have an incentive to discover new ways of producing their product in order to have lower operating costs than their competitors. They also have an incentive to develop new products that can be differentiated from their competitors; perfect competitors may strive to become monopolistic competitors or oligopolists.

We shall see in the next chapter, however, that the portion of the U.S. economy that is for all practical purposes "competitive" has been growing. Competition is far from dead, as some economists have claimed. The existence of different market forms also raises policy issues. We shall examine in the next chapter the use of government action in the forms of regulation and antitrust legislation to deal with monopoly power.

TABLE 3 CHARACTERISTICS OF FOUR MARKET FORMS

Market	*Static Efficiency*	*Long-Run Profit*	*Equilibrium Conditions*	*Technological Progress*
Perfect competition	efficient	zero	$P = \text{MC}$ $P = \text{AC}$	yes
Monopoly	inefficient	positive	$P > \text{MR} = \text{MC}$	yes
Monopolistic competition	mildly inefficient	zero	$P > \text{MR} = \text{MC}$ $P = \text{AC}$	yes
Oligopoly	varies	varies	varies	yes

SUMMARY

1. An oligopoly is characterized by a small number of firms, barriers to entry, mutual interdependence, and price making. The number of firms is so small that the actions of one firm have a significant effect on other firms in the industry.

2. A dominant-firm oligopoly is one that permits competitors to sell as much as they like, but because of lower costs can supply the remainder of the market at a price that equates marginal costs to the marginal revenue of the remaining demand curve.

3. Collusive agreements, if successful, allow the participating firms to earn monopoly profits. Because there are incentives to cheat on the cartel agreement, however, collusive agreements tend to be unstable.

4. Game theory analyzes the strategies that should be followed by intelligent rivals. A *Nash equilibrium* prevails in an oligopolistic market if each firm's profit-maximizing behavior is based on a correct guess about the behavior of rivals. Four examples of business games that have a Nash equilibrium are playing the Cournot oligopoly game, playing the prisoner's dilemma game, advertising, and making a credible threat.

5. Many factors can make collusion more difficult: (1) many sellers, (2) low entry barriers, (3) product heterogeneity, (4) high rates of innovation, (5) high fixed costs, (6) many opportunities for cheating, and (7) legal restrictions. However, government prohibitions or laws can sometimes promote collusion as an unintended consequence.

6. Some industrial organization economists argue that an oligopoly is an efficient form of market structure, despite its higher profits, because of economies of scale and technological innovation.

KEY TERMS

oligopoly 238
mutual interdependence 238
barrier to entry 239
concentration ratio 239
cartel 241
Nash equilibrium 242
Cournot oligopoly 243
prisoner's dilemma game 245
credible threat 247

QUESTIONS AND PROBLEMS

1. What is the relationship between the small number of firms and mutual interdependence in oligopoly theory? Why was mutual interdependence not considered in the chapter on monopoly and monopolistic competition?
2. Firm ZYX is one of three equal-sized firms in the widget market. It currently charges $20 per widget and sells 1 million widgets per year. It is considering raising its price to $22 and needs some estimate of what will happen to its widget sales. Why would it be difficult to make such an estimate?
3. Firm ZYX and the two other widget manufacturers meet in secret and agree to charge a uniform price of $50 and share the market equally (each gets one-third of sales). At the price of $50, each firm's marginal cost is $10. What are the rewards for cheating on the agreement if ZYX does not get caught? What is likely to happen if all three try to cheat?
4. The prisoner's dilemma game is also used to explain how oligopolists devise advertising strategy. Try to apply the prisoner's dilemma game to advertising.
5. In an oligopolistic industry composed of three large firms and ten small firms, the large firms earn an economic profit while the small firms earn normal profits. What do you know about the sources of economic profit in this industry?
6. How would you evaluate the following statement: "The automobile industry must be broken up because it is an oligopoly"?
7. What is a *Nash equilibrium?*
8. Which of the following are examples of a Nash equilibrium?
   a. The prisoner's dilemma game
   b. Cartel pricing
   c. The credible threat
9. Consider an industry that consists of two equal-sized firms. Their marginal cost of production is $2 at each level of output. The industry demand schedule is given in Table A. Assume that the two firms divide the market equally.
   a. What will be the cartel price and quantity?
   b. What is the incentive for each firm to cheat on the agreement?

TABLE A

Price (dollars per unit)	*Quantity Demanded (units)*
18	0
15	3
12	6
9	9
6	12
3	15
0	18

10. Which industry is more likely to collude? One with
    a. low fixed costs or high fixed costs?
    b. heterogenous product or homogeneous product?
    c. large government sales or no government sales?

    Why?
11. The market for Internet service providers is given by the demand curve $Q = 100 - P$. A competitive fringe has the supply curve $Q_c = -30 + P$. The residual demand curve facing a dominant firm is $Q_d = 130 - 2P$. If $P = 65$, for example, the competitive fringe supplies 35 units, and the dominant firm sells 0 units. The price facing the dominant firm is $P_d = 65 - 0.5Q_d$. Thus, its MR curve is $65 - Q_d$. If the dominant firm has the marginal cost of $25, how many units would it sell? At what price?

INTERNET CONNECTION

12. Using the links from http://www.awl.com/ruffin_gregory, read the Department of Justice's complaint against American Airlines.
    a. According to the government, how did American Airlines try to monopolize the market for airline services in Dallas?
    b. Do you think American Airlines has a monopoly at its Dallas hub?

PUZZLE ANSWERED: It is not justifiable to conclude that the economy is worse off because it is possible that large firms achieve their size through greater economic efficiency. Suppose one firm's costs rise by $1 per unit and another firm's fall by $1 per unit. Shifting output from one firm to the next will raise concentration ratios if the firm with falling costs is larger but the economy is producing the good more efficiently. Moreover, concentration ratios reflect only what is happening in the domestic industry; it is possible for the concentration ratio in the domestic industry to rise because of greater competition from foreign firms.

Chapter 14

Regulation and Antitrust

Chapter Insight

The institutional framework of capitalism requires that business firms follow certain rules of the game. These rules can run the gamut from minimal rules dealing with property rights to highly complex rules regarding the contracts that can be made between firms. According to one group of economists the basic rule governing contracts should simply be that any contract between agents should be legal, provided it does not interfere with someone else's liberty. If this were the case, then any set of firms could set up a cartel agreement providing for legal remedies for any member of the cartel that deviated from the agreement. Another group of economists calls for laws that declare certain business acts illegal, such as a cartel or other practices that give rise to monopoly. Under this broad category we find regulated monopolies that must charge prices or produce quantities consistent with public policy. The question underlying these views is, what should be done about monopoly? What if a monopoly exists because economies of scale make it impossible for more than one profitable firm in the market? Should such a monopoly be controlled?

In late 1999 the issue of Microsoft's domination of the software industry came under antitrust scrutiny. Economists and legal experts were in wide disagreement over whether Microsoft could legally make all the decisions that it made in bundling its Internet browser, Internet Explorer, with its Windows operating system. In 1911 the Supreme Court held that Standard Oil had a monopoly and ruled that the company should be broken up; in 1920 the Supreme Court ruled that U.S. Steel was a benevolent monopoly and should not be broken up. This chapter is concerned with the appropriate economic analysis for dealing with issues of market regulation.

LEARNING OBJECTIVES

After completing this chapter, you will be able to:

1. Describe the pricing formula of regulators and its problems.
2. Discuss why the deregulation of industries has occurred.
3. List the legislation that makes up U.S. antitrust laws.
4. Discuss the rule of reason as applied to antitrust.
5. Explain why superior innovation creates problems in interpreting the Sherman Antitrust Act.
6. Apply the antitrust laws to famous antitrust cases.

CHAPTER PUZZLE: If a firm achieves a monopoly not because it can produce the good at a lower cost but because buyers find it useful to buy the product that dominates the market, does such a monopoly run afoul of the antitrust laws?

ECONOMICS OF REGULATION

Firms may be owned by the government, be subject to price or product regulation, or be under the surveillance of antitrust laws that prohibit certain actions. The economics of regulation or government ownership differs from antitrust because the involved firm cannot follow the usual rule for profit maximization.

The Natural Monopoly

The classic justification for economic regulation or government ownership is that the industry is a natural monopoly because the firm's output can be produced at ever decreasing average costs or economies of scale even up to the size of the entire market. In the standard theory of competitive pricing, economies of scale fall substantially short of the size of the market; thus, many competing firms can be accommodated.

In an industry that is a natural monopoly, output will be produced at a lower long-run average cost by one firm than it would if the industry were made up of more than one producer. Let's consider, for example, three electric utilities that operate in the same market with three systems of power lines and underground cables. For natural monopolies, economies of large-scale production are so dominant that there is little choice but to operate as a single-firm industry. Some examples of natural monopolies are electric utilities, natural gas utilities, and local telephone service (see Figure 1).

Like other monopolies, even natural monopolies do not last forever, but can be changed by technological progress and innovation. In the case of natural monopoly, government must decide whether and how to control monopoly power. If a government chooses to control the monopoly, it has three

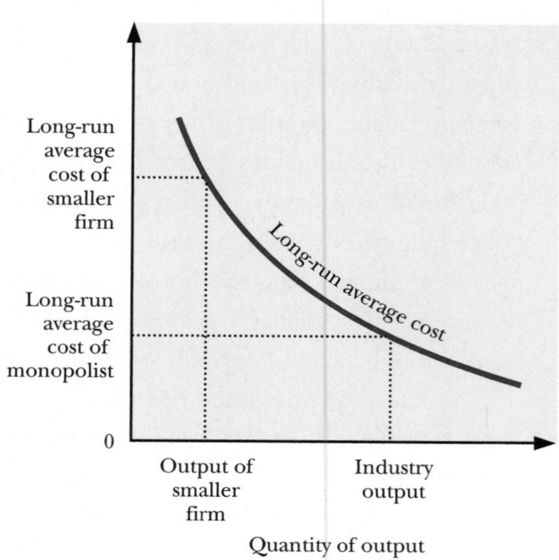

FIGURE 1 The Natural Monopoly

options: government ownership, regulation, or antitrust legislation.

Government Ownership

The government can own and operate a monopoly "in the public interest." Public ownership of business in the United States is more common at the municipal and state levels than at the federal level and is utilized for such services as local transportation, water, sanitation, gas, and electricity. During the 1990s, about one-quarter of all electricity was generated by government-owned enterprises.

At the federal level, government enterprises are fewer in number. They include, among others, the Tennessee Valley Authority (a giant, government-owned electrical utility), the U.S. Postal Service, government home mortgage programs (the Veterans Administration and Federal Housing Authority), various weapons arsenals, and the Government Printing Office. These activities account for about 2 percent of the output of the U.S. economy.

How should the government operate a public enterprise in the public interest? What instructions, for example, should be given to the public enterprise in Figure 2? One option is to produce that quantity of output at which price and marginal cost are equal (point *c*). Point *c* is *efficient* because the marginal cost (of society's resources) is equated with the marginal benefit as reflected in the price. However, the $P = MC$ rule requires that the enterprise be run at a loss to be paid by taxpayers.

Alternatively, the public enterprise can be instructed by the government to break even—to produce where price equals average total cost (at point *b*). At point *b*, price is greater than marginal cost, and the efficiency rule $P = MC$ is broken. But the customer is offered a larger quantity of output (q_b) at a lower price (p_b) than if the firm were an unregulated monopoly.

The public enterprise can also be told to operate like a private, unregulated monopoly. The enterprise then chooses the quantity, *m*, that equates marginal revenue and marginal cost. Again, the basic efficiency rule is broken: Price is more than marginal cost. The public is offered a relatively small quantity of output (q_m) for which it must pay a monopoly price (p_m). (See Example 1.)

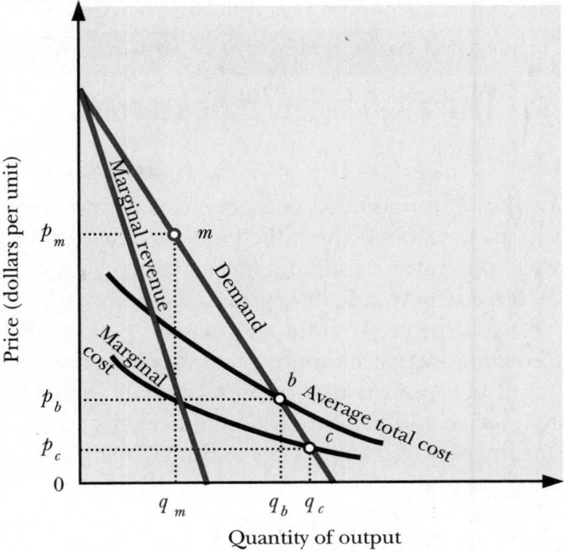

FIGURE 2 The Dilemma of a Public Enterprise

This figure depicts a monopoly that is owned by the public. It is not clear which rules the manager should follow to operate this enterprise "in the public interest." The manager could equate marginal cost and price (point *c*), but the enterprise would be operating at a loss. The manager could attempt to break even (point *b*) by operating where price and average total cost are equal, but the manager would have little incentive to economize on costs because higher costs would translate into higher prices and higher revenues. Finally, the manager could try to maximize profits (point *m*), but consumers would receive a relatively small quantity of output and pay relatively high prices while monopoly profits accrued to the state.

Just how much government (public) ownership there should be is a matter of public choice. We devote an entire later chapter to this issue.

Regulation

Regulation of prices and services is a second means of controlling monopoly.

Regulation is government control of firms, exercised by regulatory agencies through rules and regulations concerning prices and service.

EXAMPLE 1

Cable Television: Should It Be Regulated?

The law of unintended consequences is that policies can go awry if the policy maker fails to take into account the economic incentives created when some new rule or regulation is imposed. Cable television provides an interesting example. According to the theory of regulation, customers benefit because the natural monopoly is forced to lower price and increase the quantity sold to the consumer—lowering profits and increasing consumer surplus.

Studies of the impact of regulation and deregulation on the cable television industry have argued that the expectations created by a simple theory of regulation are not borne out by the evidence. Cable rates were deregulated by the Cable Communications Policy Act of 1984, which allowed cable companies the freedom to set their own prices during the 1987–1992 period. During this period, prices increased and the rate of growth of output increased as well. But the quality of service increased more than price: more channels, quicker service on the telephone, and so forth. In the next period, 1993–1994, cable rates were subject to regulation again, but the reduction in the prices of basic service was accompanied by slowing consumer growth and deteriorating quality. The authors of one study concluded that it appears that consumers may well have been better off during the period of unregulated pricing because of the cable operators' control of the quality of service. In other words, an unregulated monopoly facing no competition from entrants (arising from a government franchise) may deliver more benefits to the consumer than a regulated monopoly! Although the government can control price, it cannot control quality. When a maximum price is imposed on the provider of any service, a profit-maximizing business firm will respond by lowering quality remove the maximum price, and quality will increase to the profit-maximizing level.

Source: Thomas Hazlett and Matthew L. Spitzer, *Public Policy Toward Cable Television: The Economics of Rate Control* (Cambridge: MIT Press, 1997). See also Robert Crandall and Harold Furchtgott-Roth, *Cable TV: Regulation or Competition* (The Brookings Institution, 1996).

With regulation, the enterprise remains in private hands, but its activities are regulated by government agencies. The goals of regulation are to ensure the availability of service, establish standards for the quality of service, and guarantee that the public will be charged "reasonable" prices.

Regulation at the state and local level is largely directed at monopolies—the electric, gas, water, and telephone companies. Localities have commissions or city councils to set water and sewer rates and local telephone and cable TV rates. Most states have public utility commissions to set long distance telephone rates within the state. At the national level, federal regulatory commissions regulate a number of industries, some of which are potentially competitive. Table 1 lists the four major federal regulatory commissions.

A number of federal regulatory agencies stop short of setting prices and rates. The Food and Drug Administration is responsible for the safety of our food supplies and the safety of drugs. The National Transportation Safety Board monitors the safety of air travel. The Federal Trade Commission is charged with preventing unfair and deceptive trade practices. The Environmental Protection Agency regulates industrial pollution emissions.

Who Is Regulated?

Gas and electric companies and local telephone service are not the only industries regulated at the state and local level. Much state and local regulation is directed at competitive industries (taxicab licensing, concession franchises in sports stadiums, licensing of

TABLE 1 FEDERAL REGULATORY COMMISSIONS

1. The Interstate Commerce Commission (established in 1887) regulates railroads, interstate oil pipelines, and interstate motor and water carriers.
2. The Federal Power Commission (established in 1920) has jurisdiction over power projects and the interstate transmission of electricity and natural gas.
3. The Federal Communications Commission (established in 1934) regulates interstate telephone and telegraph service and broadcasting.
4. The Securities and Exchange Commission (established in 1934) regulates securities markets.

barbers and beauticians) and creates more rather than less monopoly power. Likewise, federal commissions regulate potentially competitive industries such as transportation and broadcasting, often limiting competition.

> Government regulation is not consistent; some is designed to combat monopoly power, but some actually discourages competition.

The amount of supervision also varies. For example, the Food and Drug Administration is stricter in its supervision of the prescription drug industry than the Environmental Protection Agency is in its regulation of the automobile industry.

Most businesses are regulated in one way or another by licenses, safety and health regulations, or occupational safety requirements. If we use this standard, then all U.S. businesses are regulated and the amount of regulation is growing daily. All businesses must comply with hiring laws, workplace regulations, and reporting laws. On the other hand, if regulated industries include only those industries in which prices are controlled by government agencies (transportation, communications, utilities, and insurance), less than 10 percent of output is produced by regulated firms.[1]

The deregulation that began in the late 1970s markedly reduced government regulation of prices and rates. We shall discuss deregulation—in particular, that in the airline industry—later in the chapter.

Principles of Rate Regulation

Regulatory commissions are required to set "reasonable" prices, establish standards for minimum quality of service, and guarantee customers access to the service without discrimination. Regulatory commissions are bound by the private property safeguards of the U.S. Constitution to protect the property rights of the owners of the regulated business. Rates must cover operating costs plus a "fair" rate of return on invested capital. If regulators do not allow regulated monopolies a fair rate of return, the monopoly can appeal to the courts for higher prices.

The Pricing Formula. The usual formula for pricing is relatively simple.

> Price of service = average operating cost + fair rate of return on invested capital.

However, the formula raises a number of questions, such as how to measure operating costs and "fair" rate of return. The formula rules out marginal-cost pricing (point *c* in Figure 2), which typically yields a loss because of declining average costs. The pricing formula, however, can encourage inefficient operating costs. The formula passes on cost increases to the consumer in the form of higher prices. Regulated firms may therefore not be motivated to minimize costs. Regulators typically do not have enough information to determine whether reported costs are legitimate, and they are reluctant to substitute their judgment for that of management.

The Rate Base. The provision of a fair rate of return on invested capital may encourage the excessive use of capital. Let's suppose that regulators have determined

[1]These figures have been updated by the authors based on earlier classic studies. Figures for 1939 and 1958 for the "government supervised" sector were from the studies of G. Warren Nutter, *The Extent of Enterprise Monopoly in the United States, 1899–1939* (Chicago: University of Chicago Press, 1951); G. Warren Nutter and Henry A. Einhorn, *Enterprise Monopoly in the United States, 1899–1958* (New York: Columbia University Press, 1969); and George Stigler, *Five Lectures on Economic Problems* (London: Longmans, Green and Company, 1949).

12 percent as a fair rate of return. The regulated firm will be allowed to earn annual profits equal to 12 percent of invested capital or the firm's rate base.

> The value of invested capital is the regulated firm's rate base.

For example, if a company has a rate base (invested capital) of $10 million and the profit rate ceiling is 12 percent, it will be allowed to earn a maximum profit of $1.2 million per year.

An unregulated company adds to its invested capital only if the present value of the resulting profits exceeds the cost of acquiring the capital. The regulated company, however, can increase its profits automatically by investing an additional $5 million, thereby expanding the rate base by $5 million, and earning a $1.8 million profit. Regulated firms have a greater incentive to acquire more capital than do unregulated firms. Because regulated firms invest at the margin in projects with rates of return lower than those realized by unregulated firms, they use capital less efficiently.[2]

The Effectiveness of Regulation

Regulation is carried out by officials, either elected or appointed, who make decisions on the basis of imperfect information.

Some experts believe that regulation cannot work because "regulation is acquired by the industry and is designed and operated primarily for its benefit."[3] Although regulators are charged with protecting the public interest, each of the consumers they protect may benefit a little by effective regulation. The regulated companies, on the other hand, stand to gain or lose a great deal at the hands of regulators. Regulated firms are big winners if they can use regulators to restrict entry into the business by licenses and other means: "Every industry that has enough political power . . . will seek to control entry."[4]

This view of regulation suggests that regulators will be proindustry, will favor the interests of the industry over those of the consuming public, and will be willing to use their power to restrict competition in that industry.

Other experts think that regulators, especially elected officials, will be more concerned about their ability to gather votes for the next election than about protecting the regulated industry. Regulators will therefore have to balance the interests of consumers and producers. How they act will depend upon politics, but a strong stand against the regulated industry may be a powerful vote-getter.[5]

These two views of regulation reflect the real world. We can find many cases in which regulators take the side of regulated industries, such as the practice of protecting established companies (such as taxi companies, dry cleaners, masseurs, etc.) from competition by restrictive licensing. (See Example 2.) We can find many cases where regulators take strong but politically popular anti-industry stances by opposing rate increases for telephone companies and electrical utilities.

Regulation provides ample examples of the law of unexpected consequences. The Food and Drug Administration's job is to protect the public from unsafe pharmaceutical drugs. If the FDA approves a drug that later proves to be harmful, heads will roll. The safe approach for FDA officials is to require years of testing and to delay certification of a new drug, sometimes until persons who could have benefited from its use have died in the meantime. The Occupational Safety and Health Administration (OSHA) is charged with promoting health and safety at the workplace, namely, to help the working man or woman. By raising the costs of paperwork and imposing new kinds of administrative burdens on companies, OSHA causes employers to cut back on the number of employees and to switch to part-time or contract workers—again an unexpected consequence of well-intentioned legislation.

Privatization

Government ownership can be reversed by privatization.

---

[2]The tendency of regulated monopolies to use too much capital was first analyzed by H. Averch and L.L. Johnson, "Behavior of the Firm Under Regulatory Constraint," *American Economic Review* 52 (December 1962).

[3]George Stigler, "The Theory of Economic Regulation," *Bell Journal of Economics and Management Science*, no. 2 (Spring 1971), p. 3.

[4]Ibid., p. 5.

[5]Sam Peltzman, "Towards a More General Theory of Regulation," *Journal of Law and Economics*, vol. 19 (August 1976), pp. 211–240.

EXAMPLE 2

Licensing Taxicabs: Who Is Protecting Whom?

City councils often restrict entry into the taxicab business, either by limiting the number of cab licenses (called medallions) or by passing ordinances identifying which cab companies are entitled to pick up passengers at municipal airports or bus terminals. Such licensing and ordinances are justified on the grounds that they ensure safety and quality.

Restrictions on entry raise the price of taxicab services to consumers. By limiting business to a small number of licensed companies, city councils create a monopoly that permits taxicabs to charge prices above the competitive price. The number of licenses or taxi medallions in New York City has remained constant at 12,189 since 1937. Medallions cost more than $120,000 in 1999. Medallion restrictions limit entry into the business, but they also create incentives for new forms of competition. "Gypsy cabs" operate without a license and offer transportation at a cheaper price. Livery services offer sleek limousines for less than the price of a licensed cab, but limousines are not allowed to roam the streets for customers.

Privatization refers to the sale of government-owned enterprises to private buyers to convert them from public to private ownership.

The public chooses privatization when it concludes that government ownership creates an inferior result to private ownership. Economic conditions such as increasing competition may change to favor private ownership. The public may become alarmed by bureaucratic inefficiency. State-owned enterprises may lack a profit motive. Bureaucratic managers often lack the incentive to combine resources efficiently; thus, public enterprises may operate at higher costs than private enterprises. The government-owned monopoly may make chronic losses that must be paid for by taxpayers. Privatization offers the chance to operate on commercial principles and to restore the company to profitability.

The failure of the socialist experiment, a Defining Moment of economics, is attributed to government ownership. If property is owned by everyone, it is, in reality, owned by no one. The Industrial Revolution, another Defining Moment, was based on private ownership. The Industrial Revolution would not have occurred without private ownership.

Deregulation

Economists favor deregulation of industries that are potentially competitive. Deregulation allows customers a broader choice of quality and price and eliminates stifling bureaucratic rules. Where the potential for competition exists, it is better for professional managers, not government bureaucrats, to make decisions about prices and services. The public will receive better service at lower cost. As a former chairman of a federal regulatory agency put it, "I have more faith in greed than in regulation."

Prior to deregulation, the Interstate Commerce Commission (ICC) forced truckers to travel roundabout routes and to return with empty trucks from long hauls. The ICC also required that prices charged by motor carriers and railroads be the same despite substantial cost differences. The Civil Aeronautics Board (CAB) required airlines to charge the same fare per passenger mile even if the plane were habitually full on one route and habitually empty on another. Consumers paid for these inefficiencies with higher prices.

Deregulation Legislation

In October 1978, President Jimmy Carter signed the Airline Deregulation Act, the first of several major deregulation acts. The Airline Deregulation Act allowed the airlines, rather than the Civil Aeronautics Board, to set their own fares and select their own routes. Service to smaller communities, financed by government subsidy when necessary, was continued until 1988. The act phased out the CAB at the end of 1984.

Three major federal deregulation acts followed in 1980. The Motor Carrier Act curbed the ICC's control over interstate trucking, allowing truckers greater autonomy in setting rates and changing routes. The Staggers Rail Act gave the railroads more flexibility in setting rates and allowed railroads to drop unprofitable routes. The Depository Institutions Deregulation and Monetary Control Act eliminated interest-rate ceilings on bank savings deposits and allowed savings and loan associates to offer checking accounts, car loans, and credit cards. The 1982 Thrift Institutions Restructuring Act enabled savings and loan institutions to operate on a more equal footing with commercial banks. The Bus Deregulatory Reform Act of 1982 allowed intercity bus lines to operate in many circumstances without applying for federal licenses.

Other deregulation was introduced by the regulatory commissions themselves. The Federal Communications Commission has allowed more channels to be available to television broadcasters. The Securities and Exchange Commission made the brokerage fees charged by stockbrokers on the New York Stock Exchange freely negotiable. The Federal Communications Commission deregulated long distance telephone service in an agreement reached with AT&T in 1982. Since then, there has been a dramatic rise in competition among rival phone companies, which is now being extended to local telephone service.

A 1992 change in federal law required electric utilities to open their transmission lines to carry a competitor's electricity. This created a vast wholesale market in electricity. From 1996 to 1998 the volume of wholesale electricity increased tenfold. In the long run, increases in such trade are estimated to reduce the average electricity bill for a family of four by about $230 a year. Since 1993, costs have fallen by 8 percent, according to the U.S. Department of Energy.

The Effects of Deregulation

The early years of deregulation were not tranquil. Airline deregulation was carried out amid two costly recessions and escalating fuel bills. Many airlines went out of business. The deregulation of trucking was fought by unions and by major trucking firms. Banking deregulation was undertaken during a period of high interest rates, numerous bank failures, and an international debt crisis. Rival long distance telephone companies did not gain equal access to local telephone exchanges until the mid-1980s.

Critics of deregulation warned that without regulation, consumers would be denied an essential service. Regulation requires access to all customers, but deregulated firms serve only profitable markets. Small communities might therefore find themselves without rail or air service. Critics also warned that competition would be eliminated by the emergence of a dominant producer, which would act as a monopolist. Critics further cautioned that deregulation would cause a loss of public control of the quality of service. Public interest programming would disappear if access to the airwaves were not regulated.

Deregulation should be judged in terms of prices, costs, and quality of service. Airlines fares fell by about 30 percent below what they would have been if regulation had continued.[6] Commissions on stock transactions dropped considerably except for small transactions. An order for 100 shares cost 20 percent less but an order for 50 shares cost 12 percent more after deregulation. Deregulation gave us a choice between discount brokers and full service brokers who offer more services at higher prices. Deregulation encouraged new firms to enter into trucking, causing rates to decrease. Rates for truckload shipments fell by 25 percent (after adjustment for inflation), and rates for less-than-truckload shipments fell by 16 percent. Airline costs fell after deregulation despite rising fuel prices. Labor productivity rose by

[6]William G. Shepherd and James W. Brock, "Airlines," in Walter Adams and James Brock, eds., *The Structure of American Industry* (Englewood Cliffs, NJ: Prentice-Hall, 1995), pp. 242, 272; Elizabeth E. Bailey, "Price and Productivity Change Following Deregulation: The U.S. Experience," *The Economic Journal* 96 (March 1986): 1–17.

20 percent during the first five years of deregulation. As competition among long distance services increased, long distance rates fell.

Deregulation imposed costs as well as benefits, however. Many airlines were unable to survive competitive pressures and went bankrupt. The earnings of airline and trucking employees fell as companies cut costs. Mergers were negotiated as healthy airlines acquired financially troubled ones. By the early 1990s, mergers and bankruptcies created a domestic airline industry consisting of three large carriers (United, American, and Delta) and one rapidly growing carrier (Southwest). Commercial banks and savings and loan institutions found themselves in a new highly competitive environment. Many of them failed, although it is difficult to blame deregulation itself. The three major television networks faced increased competition from Fox and other broadcasters. Stockbrokers from major brokerage firms had to face competition from Internet brokers.

Deregulation has done exactly what economists said it would. It reintroduced competition and the positive and negative sides of competition. Firms can no longer relax knowing that no matter what their costs or service they will make a profit. The reintroduction of competition has transformed complacent industries into dynamic instruments of change. In aviation, new low-cost airlines (such as Southwest and Reno Air) entered the market and outcompeted industry giants. The deregulation of telecommunications encouraged breathtaking advances in communications, data, and fax transmissions. The U.S. deregulation experience provides a powerful example for the rest of the world, prompting a movement toward deregulation in Europe and Japan.

ANTITRUST LAW

The major alternative to direct regulation of monopolies is legislation to control market structure and market conduct. Rather than telling monopolies what prices and services they must offer, the government sets the legal rules of the economic game.

> Antitrust law is legislation designed to control market structure and conduct.

The cornerstone of federal antitrust legislation is the Sherman Antitrust Act of 1890. The Sherman Act was passed in reaction to the public outrage against the trust movement in the railroad, steel, tobacco, and oil industries of the late nineteenth century. It was this act under which Standard Oil was broken up, as described in the Chapter Insight.

> A **trust** is a combination of firms that sets common prices, agrees to restrict output, and punishes member firms who fail to live up to the agreement.

The Sherman Act of 1890

The Sherman Act contains two sections. Section 1 provides that "every contract, combination in the form of a trust or otherwise, or conspiracy, in restraint of trade or commerce among the several states, or with foreign nations, is hereby declared to be illegal." Section 2 provides that "every person who shall monopolize, or attempt to monopolize, or combine or conspire with any other person or persons to monopolize any part of the trade or commerce among the several states, or with foreign nations, shall be guilty of a misdemeanor."

Section 1 prohibits a particular type of market conduct (conspiring to restrain trade), whereas Section 2 outlaws a particular market structure (monopoly). The vague language of Section 2 prohibits monopolization, not monopolies; although the act of creating a monopoly is clearly prohibited, the legality of existing monopolies is not resolved.

The Clayton Act and the Federal Trade Commission Act of 1914

The Sherman Act did not identify specific monopolistic practices that were in violation of the law, nor did it establish any agency (other than the existing Department of Justice) to enforce its provisions.

The Clayton Act of 1914 declared specific monopolistic practices to be illegal if their "effect was to substantially lessen competition or to create a monopoly."[7] The act gave private parties the right to

---

[7]The illegal acts are

1. Price discrimination (charging different prices to different customers for the same product),
2. Exclusive dealing and tying contracts (requiring a buyer to agree not to purchase goods from competitors),
3. Acquisition of competing companies, and
4. Interlocking directorates, in which the directors of one company sit on the board of directors of another company in the same industry.

sue—along with other penalties—for damages from injury to business or property resulting from violations of the antitrust laws.

The Federal Trade Commission Act established the Federal Trade Commission (FTC) to secure compliance with the ban on "unfair methods of competition." It was granted the authority to prosecute unfair competition and to issue cease and desist orders to violators.

The Clayton Act was revised and amended by subsequent acts. The Robinson-Patman Act—which was passed during the Great Depression in 1936, when the rate of failure for small businesses was high—protected small businesses from the competition of the growing chain stores that were receiving discounts for large purchases. The primary purpose of the Robinson-Patman Act seemed to be protection of competitors—small companies—rather than protection of competition. The Wheeler-Lea Act of 1938 extended the general ban on "unfair methods of competition" to include "unfair or deceptive" acts or practices. Under this amendment the FTC was empowered to deal with false and deceptive advertising and the sale of harmful products.

The Celler-Kefauver Act of 1950 broadened the Clayton Act's ban on corporate mergers by limiting the acquisition of one company's assets by another company, if the acquisition served to substantially lessen competition or to create a monopoly.

In 1976 Congress passed the Hart-Scott-Rodino Antitrust Improvements Act. This broadened the jurisdiction of the Sherman Act by allowing state attorneys general to sue firms for antitrust violations on behalf of their residents and, in principle, to collect treble damages (three times the estimated damage) for the state. For example, in the case against Microsoft, the federal government was joined by about 20 state attorneys general seeking treble damages. The Hart-Scott-Rodino Act also requires firms to give advance notice to the federal government of their merger plans. Thus, the Justice Department and the Federal Trade Commission can disapprove of a merger before it takes place or put restrictions on the merger, such as requiring firms to dispose of some assets before the merger.

Interpretation of the Sherman Act

American antitrust policy is determined in the courts as well as in Congress. The Sherman Antitrust Act, the mainstay of antitrust legislation, left a basic issue unresolved: Do antitrust laws prohibit only market conduct that leads to monopoly, or does monopoly by the mere fact of its existence constitute a violation?

The Rule of Reason, 1911–1945

In early rulings, the courts interpreted the Sherman Act as outlawing specific market practices that restrained trade (mergers, price fixing, price slashing to drive out competition), not the existence of monopoly in and of itself. This interpretation became known as the rule of reason.[8]

The **rule of reason** stated that monopolies were in violation of the Sherman Act if they used unfair or illegal business practices. Being a monopoly in and of itself was not a violation of the Sherman Act.

The early landmark tests of the Sherman Act were the Standard Oil and American Tobacco Company cases, both tried in 1911. In both cases, the Supreme Court ruled that these companies should be broken up into smaller companies. Both companies accounted for more than 90 percent of industry output, but they were ruled in violation of the Sherman Act for engaging in unreasonable restraint of trade, not for being monopolies. (See Example 3.)

The rule of reason was upheld in a number of cases, such as the U.S. Steel case of 1920. U.S. Steel was, in effect, ruled to be a "benevolent" monopolist. In this case, the court stated that the law did not consider mere size or the existence of "unexerted power" to be an offense.

Questioning the Rule of Reason

The rule of reason prevailed until the Aluminum Company of America (Alcoa) case of 1945, when the courts ruled that Alcoa violated the Sherman Act because it controlled more than 90 percent of the alu-

[8]This discussion of court rulings is based on Frederic Sherer, *Industrial Structure and Economic Performance,* 3d ed. (Boston: Houghton Mifflin, 1990); Oliver Williamson, *Markets and Hierarchies: Analysis and Antitrust Implications* (New York: The Free Press, 1975); and William Shepherd, *The Economics of Industrial Organization,* 3d ed. (Englewood Cliffs, NJ: Prentice-Hall, 1990).

EXAMPLE 3

Standard Oil 1911 vs. Microsoft 1999

The merger of Exxon and Mobil partially reverses the breakup of the Standard Oil Company in 1911. It is interesting to speculate whether there are parallels with the government's antitrust action against Microsoft in 1999.

Let us briefly review the facts of the original case against John D. Rockefeller's Standard Oil Trust. Rockefeller is the quintessential robber baron of the history textbooks, yet the history textbooks do not quite tell the whole story. At the beginning of the twentieth century, the major product sold by the Standard Oil Trust was kerosene, used in lamps that illuminated streets, homes, and factories. The trust consisted of so many companies that the consumer had to buy kerosene from Standard Oil, but there were few complaints because quality rose while the price fell. Competitors did complain because the low price kept their profits low. The Ohio Supreme Court broke part of the trust in 1892.

As a result of competition from the rest of the world, foreign oil companies reduced America's share of world oil production to 53 percent. Moreover, oil discoveries in Texas by rivals further eroded Standard Oil's dominance. This rival, now known as Texaco, was backed by Pittsburgh's Mellon interests, who were even richer than the Rockefellers.

But the trustbusters, aided by President Teddy Roosevelt, continued their crusade against Standard Oil, even though it was apparent that its monopoly position had been seriously eroded by competition. In 1911, the Supreme Court ordered that the trust be broken up into 33 major companies. Two of these companies later combined into what eventually was called Mobil.

Does this case have any lessons for today's action against Microsoft? Gasoline soon replaced kerosene, and here the old Standard Oil would face major competition from all sides. Microsoft faces competition from Oracle, Netscape, and Linux and is spending much of its capital entering all sorts of new businesses. The big problem with antitrust is that is often concerned with the past when what is relevant is the future—and no monopoly lasts forever.

Source: Gabriel Kolko, *The Triumph of Conservatism.* Chicago: Quadrangle Books, 1963.

minum ingot market. In a famous decision written by Judge Learned Hand, the courts ruled that size alone was a violation of the Sherman Act, thereby appearing to overturn the rule of reason.

The Alcoa case, though it may have been a correct decision, is not based on efficiency considerations. It simply stated that monopoly is illegal per se (that is, illegal on its face). In a series of decisions extending to the mid-1970s, the Supreme Court used such per se rules to evaluate antitrust violations. Antitrust decisions cannot be understood in a vacuum. These cases came after the Great Depression when many economists had developed hostility toward large-scale business firms and regarded the rule of reason with a suspicion reserved for giving hardened criminals early release from prison.

The most important case illustrating the Court's antagonism toward efficiency was the 1962 Brown Shoe case (*Brown Shoe Co. v. United States*). The Court supported the Justice Department's claim that Brown Shoe's acquisition of a local chain violated the Clayton Act. Judge Robert Bork, perhaps the most influential legal expert on antitrust in recent years, criticized the case because, although it said that mergers are not illegal simply because small stores are hurt, mergers are illegal if small stores are hurt. If this statement sounds contradictory, it is. Economist Oliver Williamson characterized the case as claiming that efficiency grounds were unimportant because smaller firms are disadvantaged. Again, in *Utah Pie Co. v. Continental Baking Co.* (1967), the Court condemned Continental's use of local price cutting to take market share away from Utah Pie, a local baker. Thus, even though it may have been economically efficient to lower prices, the Court routinely held during the post-Alcoa years that dominance of a market did not reflect superior performance.

Ironically, in *Brown Shoe* the Court also said that antitrust laws were passed "for the protection of competition, not competitors," even though that was exactly what the court was doing. Soon, the shoe would be on the other foot.

Rule of Reason Returns

Despite the Alcoa, Brown Shoe, and Utah Pie decisions, from the 1970s to the present it appears that the Court is paying attention to economic arguments in favor of efficiency. The rule of reason returned in *Continental T.V., Inc. v. GTE Sylvania Inc.* (1977). The Court held that Sylvania's restrictions on the location decisions of its dealers did not violate Section 1 of the Sherman Act. In particular, the Court cited economic efficiency as one of the reasons a manufacturer of a product facing interbrand competition (e.g., television sets produced by different manufacturers) might find it advantageous to place some restrictions on its retailers. The Court argued:

> For example, new manufacturers and manufacturers entering new markets can use the restrictions in order to induce competent and aggressive retailers to make the kind of investment of capital and labor that is often required in the distribution of products unknown to the consumer. Established manufacturers can use them to induce retailers to engage in promotional activities or to provide service and repair facilities necessary to the efficient marketing of their products, such as automobiles and major household appliances. The availability and quality of such services affect a manufacturer's goodwill and the competitiveness of his product.

The tradition of applying basic economic efficiency arguments has continued. In one of the most interesting antitrust cases, *Brooke Group Ltd. v. Brown & Williamson Tobacco Corp.* (1993) the issue focused on alleged predatory pricing of generic cigarettes by Brown & Williamson. Predatory pricing, the Court held, requires not only that prices be set below cost, but also that the firm engaging in such pricing must be able to later charge higher prices in order to compensate it for the losses sustained during the predatory pricing period. Section 2 of the Sherman Act condemns predatory pricing when it poses "a dangerous probability of actual monopolization." This case is important because (1) it affirmed an earlier decision (*Matsushita Elec. Industrial Co. v. Zenith Radio,* 1986) that predatory pricing rarely makes any sense, and (2) it did not seem to build on its 1992 decision in *Eastman Kodak Co. v. Image Tech. Svcs.* that there is per se illegality in a firm trying to take advantage of its monopoly in parts for its photocopiers even though the market in photocopiers is competitive. The Court noted in Brooke Group that monopoly power requires raising price and restricting output; but in that case, in the four years following Brown & Williamson's alleged predatory pricing, the output of generic cigarettes increased relative to the cigarette market as a whole. Thus, it was difficult to establish "a dangerous probability of actual monopolization."

In a powerful dissent in the Kodak case, Justice Antonin Scalia said: "Per se rules of antitrust illegality are reserved for those situations where logic and experience show that the risk of injury to competition from the defendant's behavior is so pronounced that it is needless and wasteful to conduct the usual judicial inquiry into the balance between the behavior's procompetitive benefits and its anticompetitive costs." He then argued that whatever Kodak might do in the market for parts to service their copy machines, they faced competition for copiers and, therefore, could not reasonably be expected to exercise prolonged monopoly power. Raising the price of its parts, or imposing restraints on the use of its parts by competitive service providers, is checked by the interbrand competition with the makers of other copy machines. "In the absence of interbrand power, . . . a rational consumer considering the purchase of Kodak equipment will inevitably factor into his purchasing decision the expected cost of aftermarket support." In other words, Scalia drew upon elementary economic theory: Rational consumers compare prices and choose the product that maximizes their utility. A firm cannot long exploit buyers of durable equipment in the market for aftermarket servicing if it faces considerable competition from other brands of the same equipment.

In 1999 the Justice Department filed a case alleging that American Airlines was dominating the Dallas/Fort Worth airlines market by charging monopoly prices. According to the Justice Department, "when small airlines try to compete against American on these routes, American typically responds by increasing its capacity and reducing its fares well beyond what makes business sense, except as a means of driving the new entrant out of the market. Once the new entrant is forced out, American promptly raises its fares and usually reduces its service. Through its predatory and monopolistic conduct, American deprives customers of the benefits of competition in violation of the antitrust laws." The language of this charge is significant; for it shows that the Justice Department is sticking to a rule of reason prosecution. Thus, the case, however decided, does not appear to change current trends in antitrust.

Definition of Market

The Alcoa decision raised a fundamental issue: If the existence of monopoly is itself a violation of the Sherman Act, how is the market to be defined?

In the Alcoa case, Alcoa controlled 90 percent of the aluminum ingot market, but it had to compete in the scrap ingot market and faced competition from stainless steel, lead, nickel, tin, zinc, copper, and imported aluminum. The court ruled that substitutes for aluminum should not be included in Alcoa's market; thus, Alcoa was characterized as a monopoly.

DuPont produced almost 75 percent of the cellophane sold in the United States but accounted for less than 20 percent of the sales of flexible wrapping materials. DuPont was accused in 1956 of monopolizing the cellophane market. The Supreme Court ruled that the flexible wrapping materials market should be defined to include "reasonably interchangeable" products such as aluminum foil or waxed paper, and that DuPont's 20 percent share of this larger market was insufficient for a monopoly.

In 1982, after more than a decade of litigation involving 66 million pages of documents, the Justice Department dropped its suit against IBM for monopolizing the "general-purpose computer and peripheral-equipment industry." By the time of the 1982 decision, IBM dominated only the mainframe computer industry (with 70 percent of the U.S. market). In its other lines of business, IBM's shares were relatively small: 20 percent of the minicomputer market, 18 percent of the word-processor market, and less than 5 percent of the telecommunications and computer services market. Based on these developments, the Justice Department decided that IBM did not monopolize the computer industry as broadly defined. In fact, in the early 1990s, IBM's share of the computer market continued to slip as it failed to keep up with its more aggressive competitors.

Also in 1982, American Telephone and Telegraph agreed to give up its regional Bell affiliates, the "Baby Bells," in return for permission to enter unregulated telecommunications and computer markets. This decision opened up the telecommunications market to the intense competition—from AT&T, Sprint, cellular telephones—that we take for granted today.

Network Effects

Many products have the feature that the more users of the product, the more useful the product is to the individual buyer. This is true for telephones, fax machines, videocassette recorders, compact discs, and many kinds of software.

There is a **network effect** when more buyers increase the marginal value of the good to any user.

One of the biggest questions in current antitrust law is whether network effects that lead to monopoly are a reason for antitrust action.

The basic reason network effects might lead to monopoly is that they raise the barriers to entry because buyers face switching costs to go from one product to the next. The classic example involves the standard typewriter keyboard, called QWERTY. It has been alleged by the creator of an alternative keyboard, DVORAK (named after its discoverer), that his keyboard is faster than the standard version. Subsequent research has failed to confirm this claim; in any case, all programmable keyboards can easily be converted to DVORAK. The switching cost would be the lost productivity while learning DVORAK. Despite the claims of superiority, people have steadfastly stuck to the QWERTY keyboard.

This example nicely illustrates the dominant position of Microsoft in the market for software. Most computers use Microsoft's operating system, Windows, which is just a software program that organizes the information on your computer and allows you to integrate many different programs in one system by merely clicking on different icons.

Competitors to Microsoft have alleged that, because of the dominance of Windows, it is difficult for other firms to get a foothold in the market for operating systems, such as the competition with Apple's Macintosh. Because of network effects, each individual has an incentive to stick with Microsoft's operating system simply because almost everyone else is using it. However, it has been argued that Window's dominance has been due primarily to the greater flexibility of Microsoft and the greater ease of upgrading to new products.[9]

Those who argue that Microsoft should be subject to the antitrust laws base their argument not so much on its dominance of the market but on the claim that Microsoft took deliberate steps to stifle competition. For example, Netscape argued that when Microsoft incorporated its Web browser, Internet Explorer, into its Windows operating system, it gave Microsoft an advantage over Netscape and, presumably, the advertising revenues that Web browsers generate. Moreover, the fact that aggressive competition leads to network effects locks existing customers into the customer base of Microsoft over its competitors. The network effects themselves may not have led to the monopoly position, but rather to Microsoft's bad behavior.[10] (See Example 4.)

Superior Innovation

Many companies gain monopoly positions not through unfair business practices but with superior innovation. Is a company that attains a dominant position through superior foresight, good planning, proper risk taking, and aggressive technological innovation violating the Sherman Act?

In decisions beginning in the 1970s involving industrial powerhouses like Eastman Kodak and DuPont, antitrust charges were dismissed on the grounds that the company had earned certain advantages by "reaping the competitive rewards attributable to efficient size,"[11] and that

> the essence of the competitive process is to induce firms to become more efficient and to pass the benefits of the efficiency along to consumers. That process would be ill served by using antitrust to block hard, aggressive competition, even if monopoly is an inevitable result.[12]

Example 4 discusses whether this view should apply to Microsoft.

Mergers

The Clayton Act of 1914 and the Celler-Kefauver Act of 1950 prohibit the acquisition of one company by another if such action reduces competition. Mergers, in which two firms combine to form one, can be of three general types: horizontal mergers, vertical mergers, and conglomerate mergers.

A **horizontal merger** is a merger of two firms in the same line of business (such as two insurance companies or two shoe manufacturers). A **vertical merger** is a merger of two firms that are part of the same materials, production, or distribution network (such as a personal computer manufacturer and a retail computer distributor). A **conglomerate merger** is a merger of companies in different lines of business.

The courts (especially since 1950) have adopted a virtual prohibition of horizontal mergers if both firms have substantial market shares. The Federal Trade Commission blocked Coca-Cola's acquisition of Dr. Pepper and Pepsico's acquisition of Seven-Up in 1986. If the mergers had been allowed, the combined market share of Coca-Cola and Pepsico would have been 80 percent. Exceptions are allowed when one firm takes over another firm that is on the verge of bankruptcy. The many airline mergers of the 1980s were motivated by the desire to keep in the airline business the assets of failing companies. The State of New York allowed the merger of Macy's and Federated Department Stores in 1994 to bring Macy's out of bankruptcy. Growing competition from European

---

[9]See Stan J. Liebowitz and Stephen E. Margolis, *Winners, Losers & Microsoft* (Washington, D.C.: The Independent Institute, 1999), pp. 127–128.

[10]See "Antitrust on Trial," *The Economist,* November 13, 1999, p. 84.

[11]This case is summarized in "FTC Dismisses Charges against DuPont in Major Statement of Its Antitrust Policy," *Wall Street Journal,* November 10, 1980.

[12]*Wall Street Journal,* November 10, 1980.

EXAMPLE 4

THE MICROSOFT CASE

In the largest antitrust suit of the 1990s, the U.S. Department of Justice (DOJ) and 19 states claimed that Microsoft monopolized the market for PC operating systems and used its monopoly power to dominate the market for Web browsers and related goods. In a preliminary finding of fact in November 1999, Judge Thomas Penfield Jackson ruled that Microsoft indeed had a monopoly in Intel-based operating systems.

How do you demonstrate monopoly power? You show that a firm has the power to raise price above a competitive level and keep it there for a sustained period of time. The DOJ must demonstrate not only that Microsoft dominated the market for operating systems, but also that it actually used its monopoly power to raise prices. It is not known, but it has been conjectured by many experts, that Microsoft sells its Windows operating system to computer manufacturers at only about $30–40. The "monopoly price" might be much higher. It may be difficult to prove monopolization in this sense. Actually, the prices of the products sold by Microsoft fell substantially. From 1985 to 1995, in 5 categories of software applications where Microsoft does not compete, prices fell by 15 percent. In the same period, in 10 categories of applications where Microsoft does compete, prices fell by 65 percent. Thus, on price alone, it is difficult to claim that Microsoft has raised prices and damaged consumers.

A key part of the DOJ's case is that Microsoft's bundling of Internet Explorer with Windows harms consumers. How to prove this is puzzling, since the browser is given away for free. Also, did Microsoft increase the price of its operating system at the time it included the browser in its operating system? This would seem to be the key question.

Perhaps the most important aspect of the case is that Microsoft engaged in anticompetitive or exclusionary contracts that prevented competitors from entering the market. Without knowledge of these contracts, it is difficult to evaluate this. Requiring computer makers to include the browser in the operating system may have led to this effect, but it must be remembered that anyone can get the Netscape browser for free just be downloading it on the Internet.

According to Nicholas Economides, an expert on network economics and antitrust, the most likely outcome of the trial is that the government will impose restrictions on the conduct of Microsoft. These will have the smallest impact on the computer industry and future innovation. The most drastic remedies would be to break up Microsoft in some way, which Economides puts at a 10 percent probability, or to force Microsoft to give away or license the code for its operating system. Either of these is unlikely because it might have a severe impact on the incentive of firms to engage in innovation in the future.

Compared to the IBM trial of the 1970s, in which IBM lost its monopoly before the trial ended and the case was dismissed, the Microsoft trial is proceeding quickly. Speed is important because Microsoft's operating system does face competition from the Linux operating system, which can be obtained free from the Internet or purchased from a distributor (Red Hat, Inc.), along with service and support. Linux is making fast inroads into the corporate market and with computer enthusiasts, as reflected in the more than doubling of Red Hat's stock price in 1999. It is possible that in a few years the market will take care of Microsoft's "monopoly."

Source: Stephen Margolis, *USA Today*, November 8, 1999; Nicholas Economides, http://raven.stern.nyu.edu/networks/ms/top.html.

EXAMPLE 5

When Is a Merger Too Big?

In 1999 the Federal Trade Commission (FTC) approved a proposed merger between Exxon and Mobil, two of the world's largest oil companies, provided that each dispose of some retail gasoline stations that competed with each other before merging. In the largest and most hotly contested merger case of the 1990s, the FTC successfully challenged the merger of Staples and Office Depot (two retailers) on the grounds they could have exerted monopoly power in specific retail markets. This may seem strange because ExxonMobil will be a $250 billion company, while Staples and Office Depot would have been a puny $15 billion company. It is therefore quite apparent that the FTC is thinking about competition not at the national level, but at the local level. According to the FTC, evidence from the companies' pricing data showed that Staples would have been able to keep prices up to 13 percent higher after the merger than without the merger. The FTC blocked the merger on the claim that it would save consumers an estimated $1.1 billion over five years. Another merger blocked by the FTC involved the proposed merger of a natural gas pipeline (Questar Corp.) company with a potential (that is, a firm planning to provide service) entrant into Salt Lake City! Clearly, the FTC is thinking small.

Source: http://www.ftc.gov/bc/compguide/mergers.htm.

aircraft manufacturers caused merger talks to begin between Boeing and McDonnell Douglas in late 1995. (See Example 5.)

Vertical mergers are in violation of the Clayton Act if merging with a supplier enables the buyer to cut out competitors, or if the vertical merger results in a transfer of significant market power. In 1957 DuPont (a major supplier of automotive fabrics and finishes) was required to sell its 23 percent ownership of General Motors stock, which gave it a competitive advantage over other automotive suppliers. Brown Shoe Company was not allowed in 1962 to acquire Kinney (a large retail shoe chain). However, in 1986, the ban on vertical mergers between moviemakers and movie theaters was eased because of increased competition from network TV, cable TV, and pay-per-view television.

Repealing Antitrust Laws

Some economists argue that the costs of applying antitrust laws outweigh the benefits to consumers. Antitrust battles force corporations to spend billions of dollars on legal expenses, and litigation can last decades. For example, before its dismissal, the IBM case lasted 13 years, costing the government more than $12 million and IBM even more. Microsoft's ongoing battles with the Justice Department in the 1990s have cost both sides millions of dollars.

The growth in international trade has largely outmoded antitrust laws, which were passed in the early part of this century. Major U.S. corporations that account for substantial shares of U.S. production must now compete with foreign companies. Moreover, modern technology facilitates the development of substitutes that pose a competitive threat to all monopolies that earn monopoly profits. Finally, monopolies may indeed be the result of superior innovation and better management. The breakup of efficient companies may actually reduce efficiency by punishing aggressive innovation.

Evolving Views of Antitrust

Why has antitrust policy changed over the years? In 1945, at the time of the Alcoa decision, economists wanted to hold the world to strict standards of perfect competition. Today, we have come to understand that it is not so much the world that is imperfect but the theory of perfect competition. The presence of information and transaction costs precludes the existence of perfect competition in its pure form. Thus, the resulting divergence of real-world industries from perfect competition does not necessarily represent a case for antitrust action. Economists realize that the world is complex, and efficient arrangements may take many forms.

We are coming to appreciate the fact that diversity may be a good thing. We may need Microsofts, Intels, and AT&Ts for certain industries and a large number of highly competitive firms for other industries. We also know that monopoly power tends to be transitory and that the threat of competition is ever-present, if not today then tomorrow.

In this chapter we have reviewed antitrust law and regulation. In the next chapter we shall consider the role of information in the economy.

SUMMARY

1. In a natural monopoly, industry output is produced by a single producer because of economies of scale over the entire range of the industry's output.

2. It is not clear how to operate government monopolies "in the public interest." Marginal-cost pricing normally leads to losses. A break-even strategy provides little incentive to reduce costs or innovate. If the government monopoly tries to maximize profits, the consumer receives no benefit.

3. Regulation of natural monopolies is aimed at limiting monopoly profits while allowing the monopoly to operate profitably, encouraging efficient operation, and preventing predatory competition. Regulated monopolies are normally allowed to charge a price that covers operating costs plus a "fair" rate of return on invested capital. This pricing formula fosters inefficiency because higher costs can be passed on to the consumer and higher investment automatically yields higher profits.

4. Regulation of potentially competitive industries creates inefficiencies and poor service. A significant deregulation movement to free competitive industries in the United States from government supervision began in the late 1970s.

5. The goal of antitrust legislation is to control market structure and market conduct by setting legal rules for businesses to follow. The Sherman Act outlaws the restraint of trade and the act of monopolization. The Clayton Act specifies which business practices illegally restrain trade. The Federal Trade Commission Act established the Federal Trade Commission and banned unfair methods of competition. The Celler-Kefauver Act toughened the antimerger provisions of the Clayton Act.

6. The "rule of reason," which held that only unreasonable restraint of trade violated the Sherman Act, was applied by the courts in antitrust cases until 1945. The rule of reason appeared to be overturned in 1945 with the Alcoa decision, when the courts judged size alone to be a violation of the Sherman Act. In subsequent cases, however, the courts have ruled that monopolies created by superior technological achievement do not violate the Sherman Act.

7. There is a network effect when more buyers increase the marginal value of the good to any user.

8. Mergers between firms in the same industry are prohibited if both have substantial market shares. Exceptions are allowed when one firm takes over another that is on the verge of bankruptcy. Conglomerate mergers are not opposed because they do not involve competing companies.

KEY TERMS

regulation 257
privatization 261
trust 263
rule of reason 264
network effect 267
horizontal merger 268
vertical merger 268
conglomerate merger 268

QUESTIONS AND PROBLEMS

1. Explain why, in the case of a natural monopoly, the industry functions most efficiently with only one producer.
2. Devise a set of rules that would, in your opinion, allow a government-owned natural monopoly to operate "in the public interest." How

would these rules be different if the firm were not a natural monopoly?

3. You are the president of a regulated monopoly. You know that the regulators will allow you to set prices to cover operating costs plus a "fair" rate of return on invested capital. How would you behave? Would you behave differently if you were not regulated?

4. One explanation offered for why regulation of electric utilities has not made much difference in utility rates is that electric utilities face competition. What kind of competition can a monopoly like an electric power utility face?

5. You operate a regulated monopoly that sells in both a competitive and a monopolistic market. How would your company's price and output decisions differ in the two markets? What steps would you take to improve your position in the competitive market?

6. Deregulation of the television broadcasting industry has been opposed by the three major networks. They wanted to keep the number of channels limited to four. How would deregulation affect their profits?

7. Should the Supreme Court follow a "per se" rule that a monopoly is illegal as long as it is established as fact or a "rule of reason" that the monopoly actually hurts consumer welfare in some way?

8. Why would innovative and risk-taking firms such as Boeing and Eastman Kodak fear the Alcoa decision?

9. Evaluate the proposal to auction off monopoly franchises to the highest bidder. Why would this return most of the monopoly profits to the government?

10. Evaluate the validity of the following statement: "Several ill-informed people have suggested doing away with our antitrust laws. To do so would return us to the days of the nineteenth-century robber barons."

11. Which of the following pairs of companies would antitrust authorities be more likely to allow to merge? Why?
    a. General Motors and Ford
    b. Prudential Insurance and McDonald's
    c. Hyatt Hotels and American Airlines
    d. U.S. Foods and Kroger Stores
    e. U.S. Steel and Ford
    f. B.F. Goodrich and General Motors

12. Economists who have studied the regulation of electric utilities have found that regulation has had little effect on prices. How do you explain the absence of a change in prices despite the ability of regulators to set prices?

13. Explain why the definition of the market has become a critical issue in antitrust law.

14. In 1992, the Supreme Court considered a case (*Eastman Kodak Co. v. Image Tech. Svcs.*, 504 U.S. 451) involving the issue of whether a company (Kodak) facing competition in the market for its durable product (in this case, photocopiers) could monopolize the market for parts and service. The majority on the Court decided that it was possible because buyers may lack adequate information and face switching costs once the durable product is purchased. The minority on the Court held that competition in the market for photocopiers makes the raw exercise of monopoly power in the parts-and-service market unlikely because when the purchase is made, buyers must take into account prospective servicing costs; and a firm that provided poor or expensive servicing would lose market position over time to competitors who would provide better or cheaper servicing. The justices introduced the concept of the "life-cycle price" of a durable good, which involves the initial cost plus the cost of future parts and services. How would you use this concept to decide the case? The case can be read at http://lawinfo.com/supremesearch.html.

15. Indicate in the following cases whether (1) the Sherman Act, (2) the Clayton Act, or (3) the Robinson-Patman Act will most likely be involved:
    a. General Motors wants to merge with Ford.
    b. Intel drives Advanced Micro Devices out of business.
    c. Microsoft sets different prices for Windows 2000 to different users, causing difficulties for other companies.

INTERNET CONNECTION

16. Using the links from http://www.awl.com/ruffin_gregory, read "Airline Deregulation" on the Cato Institute's Web page.
    a. What is the first wave of airline deregulation, and why was it important? What does the theory of perfect competition say about the effect of airline deregulation?
    b. What are the main impediments to competition in the airline industry today?

PUZZLE ANSWERED: The Sherman Antitrust Act does not declare monopolies illegal, only the act of monopolization or conduct that leads to monopoly. If a product achieves a monopoly simply because the consumers want that product over others, such a firm does not violate the law.

Chapter 15

The Economics of Information

Chapter Insight

"Speculators," "intermediaries," and others in the "information business" are often unpopular people. Farmers complain about the speculators who buy from them when the price is low and resell later at a higher price. Consumers complain about rising grocery prices, which they attribute to greedy grocers. The family that sells its home for $100,000 complains about the $6,000 fee collected by their realtor. In the former Soviet Union buying low and selling high was considered a crime.

In this chapter we shall examine the role of information in an economy. The information provided by those in the "information business"—speculators, realtors, agents, intermediaries, stockbrokers, and others—is a valuable commodity. People and businesses voluntarily pay billions of dollars to acquire information on prices, location, and quality.

The explosive growth of the Internet results in a dramatic and revolutionary reduction in information costs. We study its implications. We shall also focus on why information is a valuable commodity; the role of intermediaries, speculators, and hedgers; the costs of gathering information about markets and products; and the problems of moral hazard and adverse selection.

LEARNING OBJECTIVES

After completing this chapter, you will be able to:

1. Describe how information costs affect the contracts between parties to a business contract.
2. Understand how opportunistic behavior affects business contracts.
3. Understand the role of intermediaries as information specialists.
4. Explain how the Internet affects shopping and pricing power.
5. Discuss the function of speculation and futures markets.

CHAPTER PUZZLE: Why should the Internet cause lower markups on the goods sold by retail establishments?

Transaction Costs and Information Costs

It is costly to bring buyers and sellers together. The costs associated with making exchange possible are transaction costs. Some examples are the cost of travel, the cost of negotiation, the cost of property-rights enforcement, and the cost of acquiring information.

Transaction costs are the costs associated with bringing buyers and sellers together.

In real-world markets—even those that are highly competitive—there is considerable uncertainty about current or future prices and even about product qualities. If such information were available instantaneously at no cost of time or money, such uncertainty would evaporate. But acquiring information typically does have its costs, and information costs have a substantial effect on real-world markets.

Information costs are the costs of acquiring information on prices, product qualities, and product performance.

Information costs include the costs of telephoning, shopping, checking credentials, inspecting goods, monitoring the honesty of workers or customers, placing ads, and reading ads and consumer reports in order to acquire more economic information.

Information is costly because we have a limited capacity to acquire, process, store, and retrieve facts and figures about prices, qualities, and location of products. Information is distributed over the population in bits and pieces. The Internet has, of course, reduced information costs.

Transaction costs are affected by information costs. The buyer and seller must first find each other and then agree on the price and other terms of the contract. Knowledge of the existence and location of a willing buyer is valuable information to the seller, just as knowledge of a willing seller is valuable information to the buyer. Without this information, economic transactions cannot take place.

The microprocessor—the miniature brain behind modern computers and the so-called information superhighway—has substantially brought down the cost of communicating and processing information. Despite enormous progress, though, the computer cannot read minds, predict the future, or start a fad. For example, computer software is an enormous market, but it takes a human being to write the software and make a prediction about what people will want to buy. Bill Gates became a multibillionaire with his Microsoft Corporation. This required unique human imagination. It is information costs that makes multibillionaires possible. If information costs were zero, the billions made by Bill Gates would have been spread over millions of people.

Because information is costly, each individual accumulates information that is specific to that person's particular circumstances. For example, a farmer has detailed knowledge about local growing conditions, and consumers know a great deal about local food prices. This special information can be valuable. To quote the Nobel laureate F. A. Hayek:

> a little reflection will show that there is beyond question a body of very important but unorganized knowledge which cannot possibly be called scientific in the sense of knowledge of general rules: the knowledge of particular circumstances of time and place. It is with respect to this that every individual has some advantage over all others in that he possesses unique information of which beneficial use might be made.[1]

[1]F. A. Hayek, "The Use of Knowledge in Society," *American Economic Review* 35 (1945): 510–530.

EXAMPLE 1

SHOULD REFINERS OWN GASOLINE RETAILERS?

Six states—Hawaii, Connecticut, Delaware, Maryland, Nevada, and Virginia—have "divorcement" statutes that prohibit the vertical integration of oil refiners with gasoline retailers. These statutes provide a nice example of how economics can be used to evaluate proposed statutes. In this case, it is possible to compare prices in those six states with gasoline prices in the states that do not have such laws.

Vertical integration occurs in order to eliminate the inefficiencies that arise from the additional information costs and transaction costs of separate ownership. Vertical integration also prevents the franchised retailer from engaging in opportunistic pricing; that is, charging too high a price when the refiner is trying to increase market share. By examining the average monthly retail price net of taxes for regular unleaded gasoline and controlling for numerous differences among states, a recent study disclosed that divorcement states raised the price of gasoline by 2.7 cents a gallon. This may not seem like much, but the market for retail gasoline in the United States is about $150 billion per year. If every state imposed such laws, the cost to consumers would amount to about $2.5 billion per year in sacrificed consumer surplus (using an estimated elasticity of demand of 0.43 so that a 1 percent increase in the price lowers quantity demanded by 0.43 percent).

There are many differences among the states. For example, California has more stringent regulations on refineries; the study found that this factor was *less* important than the impact of a divorcement statute. Seemingly trivial laws can have major impacts.

Adam Smith was amused by the fact that in the eighteenth century farmers were often required to sell directly to the consumer (no middleperson), while the manufacturers were forbidden to do so and had to sell to shopkeepers who in turn sold to the consumer. Let Smith speak: "It is in the interest of every society that things of this kind should never either be forced or obstructed. The man who employs either his labour or his stock in a greater variety of ways than his situation renders necessary can never hurt his neighbor by underselling him. He may hurt himself, and he generally does so. Jack of all trades will never be rich, says the proverb. But the law ought always to trust people with the care of their own interest, as in their local situations they must generally be able to judge better of it than the legislator can do."

Source: Michael G. Vita, "Regulatory Restrictions on Vertical Integration and Control: the Competitive Impact of Gasoline Divorcement Policies," *Federal Trade Commission,* No. 227, August 1999.

By allowing people to be paid for their scarce information, the price system economizes on information costs. The auto mechanic does not have to learn nuclear physics, and the physicist does not have to know how to repair a car. (See Example 1.)

> Information is typically a scarce and valuable commodity.

THE ECONOMICS OF SEARCH

We know that a *perfectly competitive market* is one in which all buyers pay the same price for the same product. In many real-world markets, however, the prices of even homogeneous goods (milk, bread, gasoline, etc.) differ from store to store. In these real-world markets, it is more difficult for consumers to know the prices charged for the same items in different stores—even if consumers are aware of price differences, the transaction costs of always going to the cheapest store may outweigh the advantages of the lower price. As a consequence, the price for the same good differs from location to location. Such markets are usually imperfect because different buyers appear to pay different prices for the same product. From an economic viewpoint, however, the same good in a different location is considered a different product.

Information Gathering and Price Dispersion

A consumer incurs search costs while shopping, reading, or consulting experts in order to acquire pricing or quality information. Search costs explain why homogeneous products sell for different prices in different locations. A 32-inch Sony TV set may sell for different prices in stores one block apart, the same brand of milk may sell for different prices in adjacent grocery stores, and the same brand of automobile may sell at different prices in two dealerships located in the same part of town.

If information about the prices charged by different retail outlets were free (assuming that no location is more convenient than another), the same commodity would sell for the same price, as predicted by the theory of perfect competition. But information is not free; real resources must be devoted to gathering information. Therefore, in the real world, the prices of homogeneous products sold in different locations will be dispersed.

In gathering costly information, people follow the optimal-search rule.

The **optimal-search rule** states that people will continue to acquire economic information as long as the marginal benefits of gathering information exceed the marginal costs.

When a person decides to buy a new car, the more information that person has on the prices and on technical qualities of various automobiles, the better the eventual choice is likely to be. But it is costly to gather such information. It is costly to drive all over town to the various dealers; it is costly to take time off from work or from leisure activities to compare prices; it may be expensive in terms of time and money to acquire and master technical information contained in the various consumer-guide reports on new automobiles. To gather all the available information about new cars would take an inordinate amount of time and money; therefore, the prospective buyer must draw the line at the point where the marginal benefit from acquiring more information is equal to the marginal cost of acquiring more information.

Figure 1 illustrates the optimal-search rule. Suppose a consumer has just moved to a new town and is looking for the best place to buy a particular product. The consumer might visit several stores to collect valid price information. Thus, after some comparison shopping, the consumer will have a sample of the various prices charged. The vertical axis measures the benefits and costs of search per visit. The horizontal axis measures the lowest known price (S) that the consumer has collected through search. If the lowest known price is very small, the marginal benefit of search for that consumer will be low; if the lowest known price is very high, the marginal benefit of

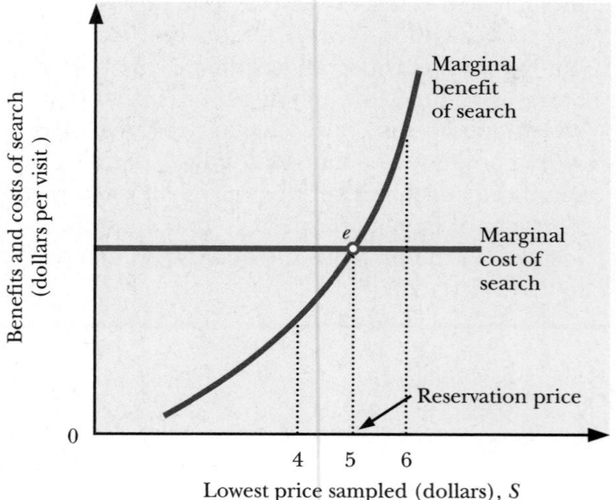

FIGURE 1 Optimal-Search Rule

The higher the lowest price sampled, the higher the marginal benefit of search. (The lowest price sampled is the best price quoted to the consumer.) The reservation price is the best price when the marginal benefit of search equals the marginal cost of search, or \$5 in the case illustrated. If the lowest price sampled is \$6, further search is required.

search will also be high. The upward-sloping curve in Figure 1 shows the marginal benefit of search for different values of the lowest sampled price. Since the marginal cost of search is assumed to be independent of the lowest price sampled, it will remain unchanged over the range of S values. The price at which the marginal cost of search equals the marginal benefit of search (at point e) is the consumer's reservation price.

The **reservation price** is the highest price at which the consumer will buy a good. Although the consumer will buy any good with a price lower than the reservation price, he or she will continue to search for a lower price only if the lowest price found exceeds the reservation price.

The reservation price in Figure 1 is \$5. If the lowest price sampled is \$6, the consumer should still search because the marginal benefit of search exceeds the marginal cost of search. If the lowest price is below \$5—say, \$4—the consumer will purchase the good because the marginal cost of search exceeds the marginal benefit of search. If the lowest price sampled is \$5, the consumer is indifferent regarding continued search, because \$5 is the highest price the consumer will pay for the product.

The reservation price occurs at a sampled price at which the marginal benefit of search equals the marginal cost of search.

We can apply the theory that consumers use a search rule where marginal benefits equal marginal costs to predict the extent of price dispersion on different products. Clearly, anything that raises the marginal benefits of search relative to the marginal costs of search will increase the amount of searching. The more resources devoted to searching, the closer will be the prices of homogeneous products sold at different stores (high-priced stores will lose business to low-priced stores). The marginal benefits of search should be greater for more expensive items; therefore, the theory of search suggests that prices of more expensive items will be less widely dispersed than those of less expensive items.

There is considerable evidence to support this proposition. In a classic study, prices were found to be less widely dispersed for identical makes of automobiles than for identical brands of washing machines.[2]

An interesting paradox is that the greater the number of people who search, the less the individual needs to search. If everyone devoted considerable resources to information searching, price dispersion—and the gains to further search—would be reduced because the sellers would be aware of the search behavior. (See Example 2.)

Information costs can be minimized for consumers by organizations such as the Consumers Union, which tests products and sells the results in a monthly magazine. Government can also reduce information costs by establishing minimum standards and carrying out inspections to ensure that these standards are being observed. Municipal governments usually have health inspectors to inspect public dining places and public swimming pools. There are universal standards of weights and measures, and inspections to ensure that the butcher's scale is accurate. Without these governmental regulations and inspections, the costs of personal inspection and information gathering would be excessive.

Information Problems

Economic dealings between individuals are governed by contracts. When a good is purchased, the seller explicitly or implicitly guarantees that the good will work according to an expected performance standard. An insurance contract stipulates that for a certain premium, the insurance company will pay out a certain amount of insurance if one or more specified events (a fire, a theft, or an automobile accident) occur. When information is costly, however, it can become difficult for one party in a contract to monitor the other party's performance, and it can be difficult to check the claims made by economic agents trying to secure favorable contracts.

The Moral-Hazard Problem

It is not possible to buy insurance against poverty. No insurance company will sell you a policy that will

[2]George Stigler, *The Theory of Price,* 4th ed. (New York: Macmillan, 1986), 4.

EXAMPLE 2

Shopping in the Twenty-First Century

In the year 2005 shopping costs could be a fraction of what they were in 1995. Just click the remote control and a couple of buttons and the TV set lights up with a menu of shopping possibilities. Click on "Grocery Stores" and then on "Price Comparison." The computer can tell you the best prices of the products you buy and can even figure out the store where it is cheapest for you to shop.

As the printing press lowered the costs of printing by 99 percent, computerized shopping will lower the costs of shopping by 99 percent. The consequence will be that no store will be able to sell an item for a price much higher than that of its competitors. Shoppers, armed with all the prices, will buy at the store with the lowest price—especially for big-ticket items. Programs might even compare the travel costs of shopping at several stores with the savings from buying at the lowest price.

This system may not work with certain products, such as fresh fish and vegetables, where shoppers might like to pick for themselves. But for the vast majority of products, the computer is revolutionizing shopping as it has revolutionized data processing and electronics.

Examples abound in which Internet commerce takes place. Amazon.com, the most famous online shopping site, allows one to buy any number of products. But markets themselves are fundamentally changed. Travel plans can be made on priceline.com. Chemconnect.com matches buyers and sellers of many chemical products used in plastics and other industries. One can now find the best deal on such rare products as ferro silicon or trichloroethylene sold anywhere in the world.

One fundamental impact is that sellers who were once protected by locational or geographic advantages must now face the competition from all sellers. This new competition will result in lower markups, as the theory of monopolistic competition shows.

Source: "Power of Internet Can Supply and Demand Forever," Dow Jones Newswires, October 18, 1999.

pay you in the event of bankruptcy or unemployment. Such insurance does not exist because it could provide an incentive for a person to quit working or seek bankruptcy.

A **moral-hazard problem** exists when one of the parties to a contract has an incentive to alter his or her behavior after the contract is made at the expense of the second party. It arises because it is too costly for the second party to obtain information about the first party's postcontractual behavior.

Moral hazard is the reason why every fire insurance policy contains a provision that fires deliberately set by a policy owner (or agent of the owner) are not covered. Indeed, insurance companies spend millions to investigate fires to determine if there was any foul play.

The basic consequence of the moral-hazard problem is that firms can offer only those contracts that will not be flagrantly abused by their customers. The kinds of contracts offered must be limited to those that will minimize the moral-hazard problem.

As an illustration of the moral-hazard problem, consider the guarantees that are offered on products. When a car is purchased, the manufacturer often gives a warranty on a car such as "the first four years or 50,000 miles, whichever comes first." The reason it does not offer a simple four-year warranty is moral hazard: there is little cost imposed on the person driving the car 200,000 miles the first year. Taxi drivers, for example, could easily take advantage of a simple four-year warranty: they would not have to worry about the car breaking down after 50,000 miles. Thus, in order for taxi drivers and the like to pay the cost of extraordinary usage, the limit of 50,000 miles is added to the basic warranty.

A second example is provided by smoking. We have known for decades that smoking cigarettes is harmful to the smoker. Some people want to make cigarette manufacturers liable for the health damage caused by smoking. However, if manufacturers are made liable for the health risks of smoking, the unintended consequence would be that the incentive to smoke would be much greater. The higher health costs would be passed from the individual to the company. This is a highly inefficient method of social engineering. If the cigarette companies had to pay some of the health costs of their customers, they would have to charge a higher price for cigarettes, whether or not they smoked one cigarette a day (presumably fairly safe) or 100 (presumably fairly unsafe). When it is known that smoking exposes the person to an additional health risk, it makes sense for society to place the cost on the individual doing the smoking.

A third example of moral hazard would be an automobile insurance policy that pays all damages if the policyholder is involved in a collision. Although it is unlikely that insured drivers would deliberately have collisions, such an insurance policy might give the driver an incentive to alter driving behavior. The driver might be less cautious in parking lots where most fender-bender accidents occur and might generally drive less defensively than normal. The insurance company cannot write into the contract that the driver must drive defensively because it is not possible to monitor the behavior of individual drivers.

The contracting parties who stand to suffer will adopt measures to minimize or prevent postcontractual opportunistic behavior. Most life insurance policies contain a clause that nullifies the contract in the case of suicide. The automobile insurer will require that drivers who have had accidents share the costs of losses by paying the first $250 or $500 to repair the damage, or by paying higher premiums in the future. If the claim is extremely large, the insurance company may even expend resources to investigate whether careless driving was involved.

In some instances, the moral-hazard problem is so severe that certain contracts cannot be written at all, at least not by private profit-maximizing companies. The poverty insurance mentioned earlier is such an example. In other cases, the moral-hazard problem is threatening enough that contracts must be limited. For example, private insurance companies find it difficult to issue general disability insurance because of opportunistic behavior. Although it is easy to establish disability in the case of lost arms or legs, it is difficult in the case of general back problems or emotional disturbances. Insurance companies expend enormous sums on information costs (maintaining a staff of physicians and investigators) to detect the opportunistic behavior that threatens their profitability.

When private markets cannot provide goods and services because of moral-hazard problems, these goods and services are sometimes provided by the state.

The Adverse-Selection Problem

The moral-hazard problem occurs when one party to a contract engages in opportunistic behavior after the contract is made. The adverse-selection problem arises prior to the making of the contract.

The **adverse-selection problem** occurs when a buyer or seller enters a disadvantageous contract on the basis of incomplete or inaccurate information because the cost of obtaining the relevant information makes it difficult to determine whether the deal is a good one or a bad one.

When a contracting party does not know the real intentions of the other party, the party with the superior information may be able to lure the other party into accepting an unfavorable contract. A contract is unfavorable if one of the contracting parties would not have entered into it if he or she had the same information as the other party.

The adverse-selection problem is encountered by those who set automobile insurance rates. Good drivers are less likely than bad drivers to have accidents that lead to costly claims against the insurance company. With full information, good drivers would not have to subsidize bad drivers, because insurance companies would be able to differentiate between good drivers and bad drivers.

Insurance companies face a different world: Smith and Jones are exactly alike except that Smith is a good driver who has never had an accident and Jones is a terrible driver who has been lucky never to have had an accident. Smith knows she is a good driver; Jones knows she is an accident waiting to happen. What about the insurance company? Unless insurance agents were to follow Smith and Jones around town and interview friends and neighbors, the insurance company cannot differentiate between Smith and Jones. Unable to gather such costly information, the insurance company sells automobile insurance to Smith and Jones at the same rate. Jones, who knows she is a terrible driver, will jump at the chance to buy insurance at the same rate as Smith. If the insurance company knew more about Smith and Jones, Jones would have to pay higher insurance rates to compensate for the higher probability of an accident.

In another example, business firms wish to hire high-quality workers, but it is very costly to find out in advance the true characteristics of workers. O'Neill and O'Leary are alike except that O'Neill is diligent and hardworking while O'Leary is lazy and without ambition. There is no reason for O'Leary to inform a potential employer of his laziness, and O'Neill's claims of diligence are likely to be dismissed as boasting. Because O'Leary and O'Neill appear alike to the firm, they are hired at the same wage rate. O'Leary, aware of his bad work skills, jumps at the chance. Armed with better information, the firm would not have entered into this contract.

Health insurance companies must also face the adverse-selection problem. If insurance companies had perfect information on the health of insurance applicants, they would offer health insurance to healthy 70-year-old people at rates that would reflect their likely health claims. However, because it is impossible for insurance companies to gather extensive health data on individuals, the insurance company will have to rely on available statistical data on general trends for different age groups. The healthy 70-year-old has private information about his or her plans to follow a healthy lifestyle, but the insurance company does not have the same information. For example, whether a person takes a daily walk and eats plenty of fresh fruits and vegetables is information that an insurance company cannot monitor. The healthy 70-year-old must therefore enter into a health insurance contract paying the same premiums as unhealthy 70-year-olds. If the insurance company had access to private information, a more favorable contract would have been written for the healthy 70-year-old.

Markets have developed responses to a variety of information problems. Every effort is made by buyers and sellers to devise contracts that will somehow reveal the true character of the parties involved. For example, to deal with adverse selection and moral hazard, insurance companies include clauses allowing them either to cancel a person's insurance or to raise the rates as experience dictates. Adverse selection can be countered by changing the relative sizes of the basic insurance rate and the penalties, so that drivers will self-select themselves into good-risk or bad-risk categories. A low insurance rate with a high penalty for an accident will attract good drivers. A high insurance rate with a low penalty will attract bad drivers. The same principle applies to different categories of coverage. If you have *liability insurance,* the insurance company pays for the damage you cause to the other party. If you have *collision insurance,* the insurance company pays for part of the damage to your own car. Good drivers might opt for liability insurance instead of collision insurance.

The Role of Intermediaries

Intermediaries specialize in information concerning

1. Exchange opportunities between buyers and sellers
2. The variety and qualities of different products
3. The channels of marketing distribution for produced goods

Intermediaries buy in order to sell again or simply bring together a buyer and a seller.

Real estate brokers, grocery stores, department stores, used-car dealers, auctioneers, stockbrokers, insurance agents, and travel agents are all intermediaries. All these professions "mediate" or stand between ultimate buyers and sellers in return for a profit. Today, many of these same intermediaries are facing competition from online computer services.

For example, it is now possible to buy and sell stocks on a home computer.

Suppose an individual is willing to sell a private airplane for no less than $20 million, and a potential buyer residing in some distant country is willing to pay $25 million for such an airplane. How will they locate one another? Someone with information about the existence of the potential buyer and seller can act as an intermediary and bring the two together. It is possible for the seller to get $20 million, for the buyer to pay $25 million, and for the intermediary to charge as much as $5 million for the service of bringing the two together.

Transactions of this sort occur frequently, although most transactions are less spectacular. The buyers and sellers of residential homes are brought together by realtors who charge a fee for this service. Stockbrokers bring together buyers and sellers of a particular stock. Auction houses bring together sellers of rare works of art and potential buyers, and they charge a fee for this service. Are such intermediaries cheating innocent buyers and sellers, or are they providing a service that is worth the price?

The role of intermediaries in providing information to buyers and sellers is often misunderstood. The export/import agent who brings the airplane buyer and seller together and pockets $5 million may be regarded as criminal by people who think that this "go-between" is trading on the ignorance of others. When food prices rise, many consumers blame the intermediaries. Buyers and sellers of real estate often become upset with the high fees charged by realtors. Implicit in these complaints is the belief that the intermediaries are getting a reward for doing nothing or for doing very little.

The intermediary's share of the price varies substantially from good to good. In real estate, the broker typically receives a 5 to 10 percent fee for bringing together the buyer and seller. This fee depends upon competitive conditions in the market. In stock market transactions the fee varies from about 0.5 percent to about 2 percent of the price of the stock. Supermarkets charge an intermediary fee of perhaps 10 percent to 50 percent of the wholesale price at which they buy.

The fee that intermediaries charge for their services, like other prices, depends on the amount of competition, on the degree of freedom of entry into the business, and on the opportunity costs of bringing goods to the market. If the business is competitive, the fee will reflect a normal profit in the long run. For example, retail grocery stores are in a very competitive business; the typical supermarket earns an accounting profit of about 1 percent on its sales. The markups on supermarket products are almost entirely used for paying rent, stock clerks, checkout clerks, produce specialists, and butchers. The grocery store, for example, must hire employees to prepare produce and meat for display in quantities convenient for inspection and purchase; the store must maintain inventories of products on which it must pay carrying charges. The grocery store must select a location convenient to its customers and pay substantial rents for a good location. In return for the intermediary fee, consumers receive a convenient location, the convenience of inspecting goods before purchase, and the convenience of finding the quantity and quality of goods they want without packing, sorting, and searching for themselves.

Buyers and sellers could, in most situations, avoid paying the intermediary fee. Consumers could drive to farmers' markets and to wholesale distributors of meats and dairy products. They could even drive to canning factories. The intermediary, by specializing in bringing together buyers and sellers, is able to provide the service at a lower cost than if the individuals performed the service themselves.

Another function of intermediaries, such as department stores, is to certify the quality of goods. The consumer is confronted with a vast array of goods, some of which are so complicated that the buyer is at an enormous information disadvantage relative to the producer. In short, the consumer faces the adverse-selection problem. The number of producers is larger than the number of actual stores with which the consumer deals. In such circumstances, the intermediary performs the function of certifying the quality of the good for the buyer. The customer is prepared to pay a price for this valuable service; thus, the intermediary is able to charge a higher markup over costs.

Car dealerships are certifiers of quality. These intermediaries are better informed about the quality of cars (because they can hire skilled mechanics) than the typical car buyer, and they will take advantage of profit opportunities by buying used cars (perhaps from their new-car customers) and reselling them on their used-car lots. They may even provide a guarantee (usually with a time limit) that the used car is not a "lemon." Customers will be willing to pay a fee

EXAMPLE 3

The Lemons Principle: Adverse Selection

The certification of quality helps prevent market breakdown resulting from adverse selection. In the case of used cars, the seller knows the value of the product, but the buyer must guess the quality. Most buyers would probably assume that the car is of average quality. If every used-car dealer operated on a disreputable basis, the only used cars that would sell would be the lemons—those of lowest quality. If there were used cars in the market ranging from $1000 to $6000 in true value (a range known, say, to all potential buyers), but potential buyers could not tell the difference among them, would any rational consumer buy a used car priced at $5000? At a price of $5000, cars worth more than $5000 would not be offered for sale; only those worth $5000 or less would be put on the market—so that the average car offered for sale would be worth $3000. Why pay $5000 for a car that is more than likely worth much less than $5000? At a price of $3000, only cars worth $3000 or less would be placed on the market (so the average car offered would be worth only $2000). Why pay $3000 for a car that is likely worth much less than $3000? Indeed, any price above $1000 would bring forth cars worth less than the price. What type of cars would therefore be sold in this fly-by-night market? Only those lemons that are worth exactly $1000 because buyers paying more could only expect to be ripped off. In these circumstances, only when established dealers serve as certifiers of quality will non-lemons be placed on the market.

Source: Based upon George Akerlof, "The Market for 'Lemons': Quality, Uncertainty, and the Market Mechanism," *Quarterly Journal of Economics* 84 (August 1970): 488–500.

(in the form of a price markup) for this certifier-of-quality service. (See Example 3.)

Manufacturers also certify quality by identifying their products with brand names. If prior to purchase and use consumers could not distinguish the product of one manufacturer from that of all other manufacturers, there would be little incentive for the manufacturer to produce products of reasonable or uniform quality. Brand names such as Sara Lee, Levi's, Maytag, Intel, and Xerox serve as certifiers of product quality.

Speculation and Risk Bearing

Although product information is important to consumers, information about changes in the market conditions for any number of goods and services is important to speculators.

Speculators are those who buy or sell in the hope of profiting from market fluctuations.

The person who stocks up on peanut butter after hearing of a shortage of peanuts, the frozen-orange-juice distributor who buys oranges in response to a late frost in Florida, and the young couple that buys a house now because they fear home prices will rise beyond reach if they wait another year are all speculators. The professional speculator, however, is more maligned than any other economic agent.

Most people, however, do not associate the term *speculator* with the family that stocks up on goods whose prices are expected to increase dramatically or purchases a home as an inflation hedge. Most people associate the term *speculator* with the person who buys up agricultural land and holds it for future shopping-center development or the person who buys and sells foreign currencies or gold in the hopes of buying low and selling high. Such speculators buy or sell commodities in huge quantities hoping to profit from a frost, war scare, bumper crop, bad news, or good news.

The Economic Role of the Speculator

Speculators do, indeed, often profit from the misfortunes of others. They buy from the hard-pressed farmer when prices are low, and they sell later at much higher prices. Has the farm family been robbed by the speculator? Not really. The farmer is not in the business of risk-bearing. Upon hearing of a frost in Florida, speculators buy oranges in large quantities, thereby driving up the prices of orange juice for the consumer. At the first sign of international trouble, speculators may buy gold and sell American dollars, thereby weakening the American dollar. The popular view of speculators is that they do only harm; however, speculators are performing a useful economic function—that is, engaging in arbitrage *through time.*

Arbitrage is buying in a market where a commodity is cheap and reselling in a market where the commodity is more expensive.

The arbitrageur buys wheat in Chicago at $5 per bushel and resells it for $5.10 the next minute in Kansas City. Thus, arbitrageurs serve to keep the prices of wheat in Chicago and Kansas City approximately equal.

Simple arbitrage of this type is not very risky because information about prices in Chicago and Kansas City can be obtained instantly from commodity brokers. Arbitrageurs must act quickly if they are to prosper. Unlike the arbitrageur, who buys in one location and sells in another, the speculator buys goods *at one time* and resells *at another time.* Speculation is a risky business because tomorrow's prices cannot be known with certainty. The speculator is bearing risks that others do not wish to carry.

> The speculator is performing the economic function of sharing in the risky activities of producers and consumers.

Profitable Speculation

The objective of the speculator is to make a profit by buying low and selling high. When the speculator is making a profit—and when there are enough speculators—low prices will be driven up and high prices will be driven down. When speculators buy at low prices, they add to the demand and drive prices up. When speculators sell when prices are high, they drive prices down by adding to the supply.

> Profitable speculation (that is, speculation that succeeds in buying low and selling high) stabilizes prices and consumption over time by reducing fluctuation in prices and consumption over time.

Profitable speculation is illustrated in Figure 2. Panel (*a*) shows that the supply of wheat in the first period (say, 2000) is S_1, or 4 million bushels. Panel (*b*) shows that the supply of wheat in the second period (say, 2001) is S_2, or 2 million bushels. If there were no speculation, the price of wheat would be $3 in period 1 and $5 in period 2 (we assume that demand does not change between the two periods). Thus, without speculation, prices and consumption would vary dramatically between the two periods.

If speculators correctly anticipate that next year's wheat crop will be small, they could make handsome profits by buying at $3 and selling next year at $5. But what happens as speculators begin to buy this year's wheat? When speculators buy wheat, they withdraw it from the market and place it in storage. As a result, the supply of wheat offered on the market is reduced. This trend will continue until the profits of the marginal speculator are driven down to zero. When speculators buy 1 million bushels in the first period, the effective supply shifts (left) to 3 million bushels, and the price rises to $4. When speculators resell this wheat in the second period, the effective supply also shifts (right) to 3 million bushels in year 2. When speculative profits are zero, the price will remain stable at $4 and the quantity of wheat sold on the market will remain stable at 3 million bushels—despite substantial differences in the wheat harvest in the two periods. In this example, we assume that storage costs are zero. Had storage costs been positive, the price of wheat in the second period would have been higher by the cost of storage.

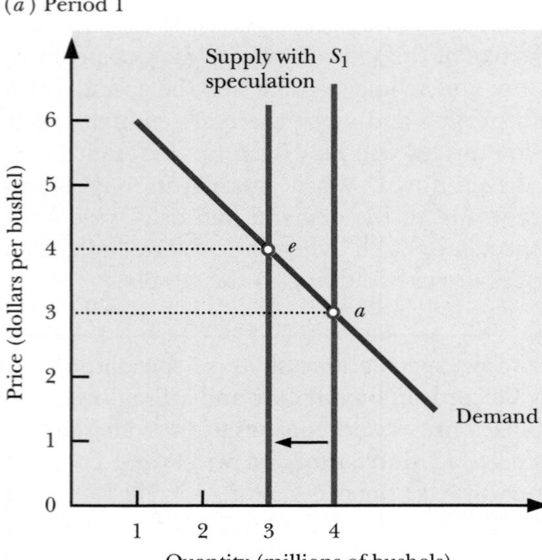

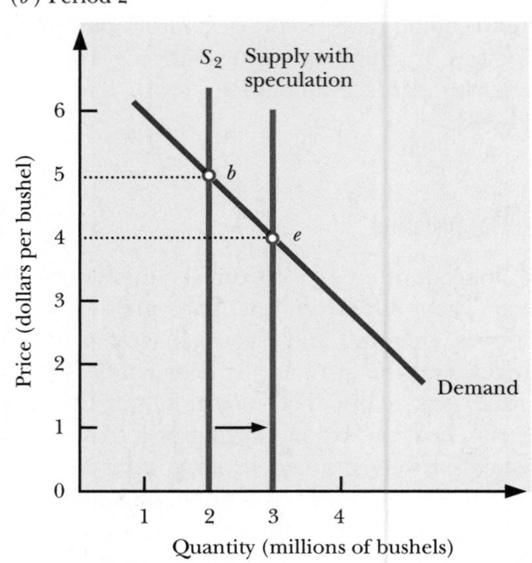

FIGURE 2 Profitable Speculation

Period 1's wheat harvest is 4 million bushels, while period 2's wheat harvest is only 2 million bushels. If there were no speculation, the price would be $3 in period 1 and $5 in period 2. Perfect speculation will cause 1 million bushels of wheat to be purchased and stored by speculators in period 1, to be sold in period 2. As a result, the price is driven up to $4 in period 1 and driven down to $4 in period 2. Both price and consumption are stabilized by the speculation in this case.

> Profitable speculation shifts supplies from periods when supplies are relatively abundant and prices potentially low to periods when supplies are relatively scarce and prices potentially high. In this sense, profitable speculation provides the valuable economic service of stabilizing prices and consumption over time.

The $4 price of wheat reflects all the available information about the future. In this sense, the market is efficient. No one can then make a profit buying wheat and reselling it because the price is the same in both periods. Profits can be made only when information available to some people is not reflected in the current market price. Those individuals can make a profit by exploiting their information advantage.

In the preceding example, speculators accurately predicted the future. Such predictions are not as difficult as we might expect. For example, spring wheat is harvested in September and winter wheat is harvested in June or July. The amount of wheat harvested in other months is negligible. This seasonal pattern of wheat supply is predictable. What if no one were to speculate in this situation? In harvest months, farmers would harvest and sell their wheat, and wheat prices would be driven down to very low levels. In the months when very little wheat is harvested, wheat prices would be astronomical. Such a situation would not be satisfactory.

Because the pattern of wheat harvesting is well known, speculators (who also include the farmers who put their grain into storage rather than sell it immediately) purchase grain at harvest time, put it into storage, and then sell it throughout the rest of the year. This activity assures that we will not lack for wheat during the remainder of the year and that consumers will not have to pay wildly fluctuating prices. Of course, speculators will make some errors in the process; for instance, they may incorrectly predict the size of the coming harvest. However, these mistakes are minor compared to the situation that would exist if there were no speculators. (See Example 4.)

Unprofitable Speculation

Speculation is risky. Speculators cannot always guess correctly. They may buy when they think prices are low only to find that prices sink even lower. They

EXAMPLE 4

SCALPING

One of the small puzzles of the theory of supply and demand is the existence of scalping, where tickets to specific events are apparently priced below what the market will bear (concerts, the Super Bowl, the baseball World Series, NBA finals, etc.). Scalpers purchase these tickets at less than market value and resell them at a profit. Two questions: Is this an economically efficient practice? Why doesn't the owner of the original tickets try to get the market price for himself?

It is certainly economically efficient. Remember, economic efficiency is the transfer of resources from those that have little value to those that have higher value. This increases the amount of economic welfare in society.

Why does scalping happen? We think that the reason it occurs is associated with the economies of information. The scalper may be more attuned to the market than the promoter; it is a question of who has the best information. If the good were priced correctly, that is, at the market price, then scalpers would not exist. The fact that it is not priced correctly arises from the information costs and uncertainty about demand. We can test this by showing that scalping is more prevalent in those situations in which the demand appears less predictable. Scalping is really an example of short-term speculation.

may sell when they think prices are at their peak only to watch the prices rise even further. In such cases, speculation destabilizes prices and consumption over time. When prices would otherwise be high, such speculators are buying and driving prices even higher; when prices would otherwise be low, such speculators are selling and driving prices even lower.

Unprofitable speculation is shown in Figure 3. The supply of corn is 5 million bushels in period 1 and will also be 5 million bushels in period 2. Because demand remains the same in the two periods, the equilibrium price of corn will be $4 in both periods without speculation. Now assume speculators incorrectly guess that the supply of corn will decrease in period 2 because of an anticipated poor harvest. Speculators buy 2 million bushels, which they place in storage for later sale, driving up the price to $6 in period 1 (point *a*). The speculators then wait in vain for a decline in supply that never materializes. They must then sell the 2 million bushels in period 2, and they drive the price down to $2 a bushel (point *b*).

Without speculation, the price and consumption of corn would have been the same in both periods (point *e*). With unprofitable speculation, consumption is 3 million bushels in period 1 and 7 million bushels in period 2. Period 1's price is $6 and period 2's price is $2. Unprofitable speculation is inefficient for the economy as a whole.

> Unprofitable speculation is destabilizing because it creates artificial scarcities in some periods and artificial abundance in other periods. In this sense, speculation can be costly to society.

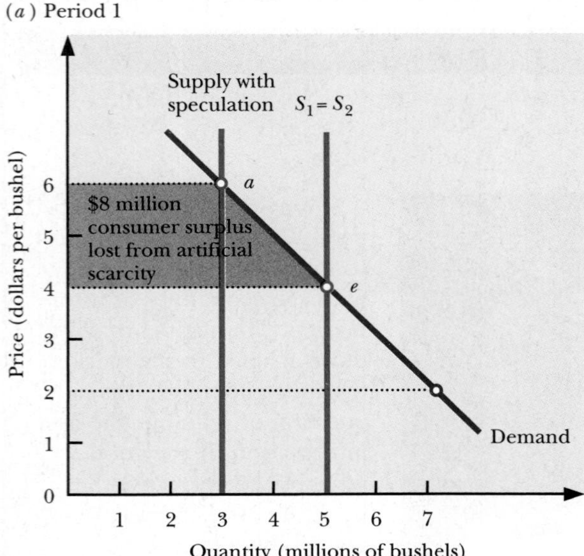

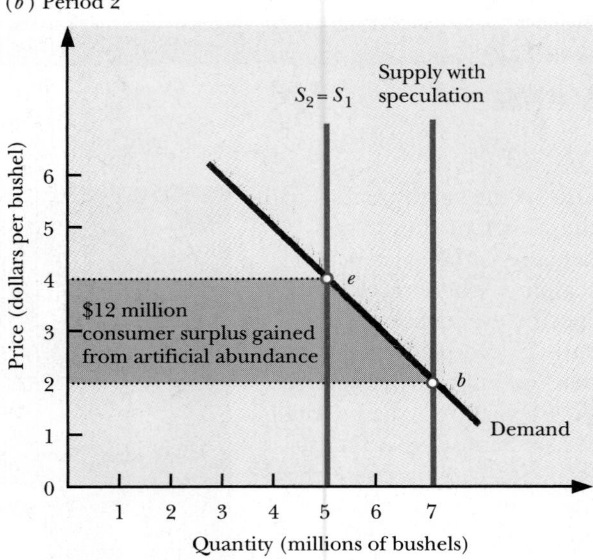

FIGURE 3 Unprofitable Speculation

In this example, period 1 and period 2 have the same demand and supply conditions. Without speculation, the price would be $4 in both periods. Speculators guess incorrectly that the supply of corn in period 2 will be less than in period 1. They buy 2 million bushels in period 1 and drive period 1's price up to $6. When they must resell the 2 million bushels in period 2, they drive the price down to $2. In the case of unprofitable speculation, price and consumption are seriously destabilized.

The Futures Market

Speculation is so highly specialized that markets have developed that separate the business of storing the commodity being bought and sold from the actual business of speculation. The grain speculator does not have to worry about what the purchased grain looks like, where it is stored, and how much to take out of storage. Those who wish only to speculate can buy and sell in a futures market.

A **futures market** is an organized market in which a buyer and seller agree now on the price of a commodity to be delivered at some specified date in the future.

Many of us are familiar with futures markets only through sensational press reports, like those about the oil-rich Hunt family seeking unsuccessfully to corner the silver market, about European and Asian speculators driving the price of gold to dizzying heights, or about the increase in coffee prices that is blamed on speculators following a freeze in Brazil.

The type of market most people know best is one in which there is an actual outlay of cash (or the arrangement of credit) for the immediate delivery of a good. The market in which a good is purchased today for immediate delivery is called a spot (or cash) market.

In a **spot (cash) market**, agreements between buyers and sellers are made now for payment and delivery of the product now.

Most of the goods consumers buy and sell are transacted in spot markets. In the grocery store, consumers pay now for goods that are delivered now. Stocks, foreign exchange, gold, and commodities such as wheat, pork bellies, lumber, and copper are traded in organized spot markets. Unlike the grocery store, however, such commodities are also traded on futures markets.

Futures contracts are bought and sold in futures markets. In a futures contract, the terms (the price and the quantity) of a future transaction are set today. The buyer of a futures contract enters a contract today to purchase a specified quantity of a good at a specified price at some specified date in the future. Both delivery and payment are to be made *in the future*. The seller is obliged to deliver the specified quantity of the good at the specified price at the specified future date. The seller of a futures contract need not even own the commodity at the time of the sale (but will, in many instances).

> The *seller* of a futures contract is in a *short position* because something is being sold that is not owned. The *buyer* of a futures contract is in a *long position* because a claim on a good is being acquired.

When the seller agrees to sell and the buyer agrees to buy at a specified price at a specified date in the future, what guarantees that both parties will fulfill their part of the bargain? The buyer and seller must each put up cash—called a *margin requirement*—equal to a small percentage of the value of the contract.

The Mechanics of Futures Trading

Futures trading is different from the types of transactions with which most people are familiar. Futures trading is a topsy-turvy world. Traders can sell something before they buy it: traders are buying and selling obligations to buy or sell in the future a commodity they will likely never even see.

Most daily newspapers supply futures prices. The futures price is the price agreed upon now for a commodity to be paid for and delivered on some future date; yet at any time between now and the future date, the seller or buyer can *close out* the futures contract by engaging in an offsetting transaction. The seller offsets the transaction by simply buying another futures contract with the same delivery date; a buyer closes out by selling another futures contract with the same delivery date. Two examples of futures trading, illustrating a long position and a short position, follow.

A Long Position. George Bull thinks that oil prices will rise in the future more than other buyers generally expect them to rise. In January, George thinks that the July oil price of $21 is too low; he expects the actual price of oil in July to be well above $21. On January 1, George buys 1000 barrels of July oil, paying the futures price of $21 per barrel. George is now in a long position in oil.

On March 1, the price of July oil rises to $22. George has made a profit because he bought the oil at $21 a barrel and can now sell it for $22 a barrel. If George closes out his long position by selling a contract for 1000 barrels of July oil, he will make a profit of $1000 (or $1 × 1000 barrels). Even if George does not close out his long position, his broker will add $1000 to his account.

A Short Position. In January, Sue Bear thinks that July oil will be lower in price than people currently anticipate. She thinks that if she sells July oil at $21 per barrel, the futures prices will fall and she can make a profit. Thus, Sue Bear sells 1000 barrels of July oil on January 1 at the market futures price of $21 a barrel. Sue is now in a short position in oil (she sold something she doesn't completely own). While this will probably not be the case, it is convenient to think of Sue as the one who sells to George. If the price of July oil rises above $21, Sue loses; if the price falls below $21, Sue wins. As we already indicated, on March 1, the futures price of July oil is $22. If Sue closes out her short position, she loses $1 per barrel, or $1000. Even if Sue does not close out her short position, her broker will deduct $1000 from her account. In the futures market, there are no paper losses or paper gains.

Hedging

The person who "hedges a bet" bets both sides in order to minimize the risks of heavy losses. Such a person might bet $5 it will rain tomorrow and $4 it won't rain. Hedging also takes place in futures markets.

> **Hedging** is the temporary substitution of a futures market transaction for an intended spot transaction.

Futures markets can provide an opportunity to traders of commodities in both spot and futures markets to reduce the risks of price fluctuations over time as well as to increase their profits. A futures market allows those involved in the distribution, processing, or storage of a good to concentrate on their specialized productive activities by taking advantage of the relationship between spot and futures prices.

Suppose, for example, that on July 1, the operator of a grain elevator buys 5000 bushels of wheat from a farmer for $5 a bushel (the spot price on that date). The grain is put into storage for intended sale at some date in the future. What are the risks to the operator? If the price of wheat drops, the operator will incur losses. Through the futures market, the elevator operator hedges by immediately selling a futures contract for 5000 bushels of wheat to be delivered at a price of, say, $5.15 in November.

If the elevator operator holds his wheat until November, the wheat purchased for $5 can be delivered on the futures contract for $5.15. The elevator operator has locked in a profit of $0.15 per bushel to cover carrying charges.

Now suppose the spot price of wheat falls and, one month later, the elevator operator sells this wheat for $4 on the spot market to General Mills. On this spot transaction, he has lost $5000 ($1 per bushel on 5000 bushels). But what about the November futures contract that he previously sold? Because wheat prices are falling, the price of November wheat might fall to $4.10. Because the elevator operator previously sold November wheat for $5.15 per bushel, this operator can close out the position by buying November wheat at $4.10, for a profit per bushel of $1.05. The elevator operator can earn $1.05 × 5000, or $5250, by closing out the position. Through hedging, the elevator operator has not only limited the risks from falling grain prices but has made a profit. The elevator operator lost $5000 from the spot market and gained $5250 in the futures market and, in effect, earned $250—$0.05 per bushel—by holding wheat for 1 month.

Large grain users, such as General Mills, can also hedge against the risks of fluctuating wheat prices by using the futures market. General Mills knows in July that it will require 100,000 bushels of wheat in December. It does not know what the price of wheat will be in December, but it can purchase a December futures contract for 100,000 bushels of wheat at $5 per bushel and thus protect itself against the risk that wheat will be selling well above $5 in December.

Hedgers and speculators play highly complementary roles in the economy. Hedgers are interested primarily in storing commodities or in using these commodities in their business; they are interested in their particular business and in minimizing the risks of price fluctuations. The speculator, on the other hand, does not have to be concerned with the details of storing grain or making flour and grain products. The speculator specializes in information about supply and demand in the future. There is division of labor between the hedger and the speculator.

Information and Speculation in the Futures Market

The futures market provides information concerning the future. This information is not always accurate; sometimes it predicts that prices will rise but instead they fall, and vice versa. Prices in futures markets reveal to the economy what speculators *anticipate* will happen to the prices of different commodities in the future. If the futures price of wheat is well above the current spot price, then speculators believe that wheat prices will rise. These futures prices represent the best information available to the economy on the course of prices in the future.

Economic decisions must be made today concerning actions that must be taken in the future. Farmers must plant crops that will not be harvested for many months; mine operators must plan the expansion of mine capacity. If prices in the future were known with certainty, such planning would be grossly simplified; however, the future is always uncertain. Clearly, having a futures market that establishes effective future prices today is of great benefit in an uncertain world. For those who need to know future prices, a futures market provides a summary indicator of market sentiment—a single price reflects much of what people know today about tomorrow.

This chapter completes our study of product markets. The next section will turn to the bottom half of the circular-flow diagram: factor markets. In the next chapter we shall consider factor markets and how they compare to product markets. In subsequent chapters we shall examine individually the markets for the different kinds of factors—labor, land, capital, entrepreneurship.

SUMMARY

1. Information is costly because of our limited ability to process, store, and retrieve facts and figures about the economy and because real resources are required to gather information. Individuals acquire information to the point where the marginal cost of acquiring more information equals the marginal benefit of more information.

2. Search costs explain the observed dispersion of prices. When the benefits to further search are great, price dispersion will be limited.

3. Two problems encountered by buyers and sellers because of the cost of information are the moral-hazard problem and the adverse-selection problem. The moral-hazard problem refers to postcontractual opportunistic behavior; the adverse-selection problem refers to precontractual opportunistic behavior. Both arise because one party cannot verify the claims of the other party.

4. Intermediaries bring together buyers and sellers; they often buy in order to sell again and sometimes serve as certifiers of quality.

5. Speculators buy at one time in order to sell at another time. If speculators are profitable, they stabilize prices and consumption over time. If they are unprofitable, they destabilize prices and consumption over time.

6. In a futures market, contracts are made now for payment and delivery of commodities in the future. Futures markets provide information about the uncertain future and allow hedging by those who wish to reduce risks.

KEY TERMS

transaction costs 276
information costs 276
optimal-search rule 278
reservation price 279
moral-hazard problem 280
adverse-selection problem 281
intermediaries 282
speculators 284
arbitrage 285
futures market 288
spot (cash) market 288
hedging 289

QUESTIONS AND PROBLEMS

1. Investors can purchase shares of stock through a full-service broker (who provides information and investment advice) or the Internet. The commission charged by the full-service broker is much higher than that charged by the Internet broker. They both provide the service of buying the shares of stock ordered by the buyer. Explain why many investors use the services of the higher-priced brokers.
2. The market for wheat is highly centralized. In fact, one can say there is a world market for wheat. Why is this market centralized while other markets, such as the automobile market, are decentralized?
3. You have learned that prices of $3, $3.50, and $4 are being charged by various pharmacies for the same generic drug. The marginal benefit of further search is $0.15; marginal cost is $0.10. Should you search for a lower price?
4. You have been quoted the prices of $20, $21, $23, and $24 for a wheel alignment on your car. The marginal benefit for further search is $1, and the marginal cost is also $1. What is your reservation price? Should you search further?
5. What are the transaction costs of selling a home? What effect do real estate brokers have on these costs?
6. Explain why more is spent on the advertising of deodorants than on the advertising of farm machinery.
7. If search costs in a market are zero and the market is competitively organized, what predictions can you make about prices in this market?
8. The stock market is highly competitive, with thousands of speculators trying to buy low and sell high. Using the concepts of information and search costs, explain why with a little study and research we all can't get rich by playing the stock market.
9. What is the moral-hazard problem? Give examples.
10. An attendance clause gives a major-league baseball player a season-end bonus if attendance exceeds a target figure. Explain how this is a result from the moral-hazard problem.
11. What is the adverse-selection problem? Give examples.
12. How will the adverse-selection problem be affected by the Internet?
13. Assume that on January 1, July wheat is selling for $4. How could a speculator profit from the expectation that in July spot wheat will sell for $3.50? How could a speculator profit from the expectation that in July spot wheat will sell for $4.50?

14. Indicate whether each of the following examples is a potential moral-hazard problem or a potential adverse-selection problem.
    a. "The chair broke when I sat down," complained the customer to the furniture store.
    b. "This chair will last a lifetime," asserted the furniture salesperson.
    c. "I am a safe, married driver," claimed the student buying car insurance.
    d. "We insure all drivers," claims the ad.

INTERNET CONNECTION

15. Examine the IBM presentation on Internet commerce by following the link on http://www.awl.com/ruffin_gregory.
    a. In what way will the Internet have an effect on the information problems described in this chapter?
    b. Will the Internet change the nature of moral hazard?

PUZZLE ANSWERED: For any business firm, the larger the elasticity of demand facing it, the greater the firm's price markup over cost. Thus, since the Internet provides consumers with a much cheaper and faster way to compare prices across firms, the elasticity of demand facing any particular retail store should be larger because consumers are not locked in by transportation and search costs.

Part III

Factor Markets

Chapter 16

FACTOR MARKETS

Chapter Insight

As a college graduate in the early 2000s you can expect to earn about $2 million over your lifetime. Drop out of college and your lifetime income will fall to slightly less than $1 million. Your cousin who never finished high school will earn only $750,000 over his lifetime. What determines these incomes?

We have completed our examination of the product markets, where the prices of goods and services are determined. It is now time to consider the factor markets, where the prices of land, labor, and capital are determined.

The study of factor markets takes us into a battleground of economics. Almost all of us think we should be earning higher wages on our labor, higher interest on our money, or higher rents on land. The pay people earn often determines whether they like or don't like the economy in which they reside. It is therefore important for us to understand the general principles that govern the determination of factor prices.

LEARNING OBJECTIVES

After completing this chapter, you will be able to:

1. Understand the difference between price makers and price takers in the factor markets.
2. Calculate the marginal contribution of a factor to a firm's revenue.
3. Explain the profit-maximizing rule in the factor market.
4. Understand the least-cost rule for hiring inputs.
5. Describe how the functional distribution of income is determined.

CHAPTER PUZZLE: What does a buying cartel have in common with a selling cartel?

Competition in Factor Markets

A business firm participates both in the product market, where it sells the goods or services it produces, and in the factor market, where it buys the land, labor, and capital it needs to produce this output. In the previous chapters we discussed the four types of markets a firm can face in the product market. In this chapter we will consider the types of markets it faces in the factor market.

Factor markets differ from product markets in one important respect: They tend to be more competitive than product markets. In product markets, firms compete against other sellers of like or similar products. In many cases, there are few enough producers or their products are sufficiently differentiated that they can exercise some control over price—they are price makers.

In factor markets, all business firms tend to compete for the same factor resources. General Motors, Intel, Microsoft, grocery stores, and television stations, while producing quite different goods and services, compete for the general pool of labor, capital, and land. They all need word processing specialists, computers, trucks, drivers, and managers. It is therefore rare that one firm can exercise sufficient control over a particular factor market so as to be able to influence the price of that factor. There are indeed cases where specific firms are price makers in specific factor markets, but most firms are price takers in factor markets.

Price taking means that business firms simply must pay the going rate for the factors of production they hire. If the going wage rate for computer programmers is $40 per hour, this is what they have to pay for one more hour of programming. If retail space rents for $100 per square foot, this is what they have to pay for one more square foot of space.

In this chapter, we examine the behavior of firms that are price takers in the factor market. Price taking means that the extra (marginal) cost of hiring one more unit of the factor is simply its factor price.

Basic Concepts of Factor Demand

The firm's demand for a factor input depends upon the input's physical productivity and the demand for the good the factor is being used to produce. The chapter on productivity and costs defined the production function as the relationship between outputs and inputs. Recall that a factor's marginal physical product (MPP) is the increase in output divided by the increase in the amount of the factor, if all other factors are constant.

As explained earlier, all production functions exhibit the law of diminishing returns, which states that as ever larger quantities of a variable factor are combined with fixed amounts of the firm's other factors, the marginal physical product of the variable factor will eventually decline.

Derived Demand

A consumer buys products because they provide satisfaction. The firm buys factors of production because they produce goods and services that create revenue for the firm. The garment industry buys sewing machines because they help to produce suits, shirts, and dresses that consumers will buy. Automobile workers are hired because they help produce automobiles that people will buy. Farmland is rented because it yields wheat that people will consume. The demand for workers, the demand for farmland, and the demand for tailors are all examples of derived demand.

The demand for a factor of production is a **derived demand** because it results (is derived) from the demand for the goods and services the factor of production helps produce.

The principle of derived demand is essential to understanding the workings of factor markets. (See

EXAMPLE 1

Farmers and Food Markets

The demand for farmers' produce is derived from the demand from retail supermarkets. Farmers continually complain that the prices they receive on their produce are far below the prices in the supermarket. The Western Growers Association, based in California, has a Web site that compares the prices farmers receive for various farm products with supermarket prices. In September 1999, lettuce sold in Atlanta at a price 741 percent higher than the farmer received, and avocados sold in New York for 152 percent of the farmer's price.

Farmers argue that they are forced to sell their products to fewer and fewer chains. The argument sounds plausible, but economists know that it is costly to transport and display produce items. Farm products are also perishable, and someone has to bear that risk. Grocery stores no longer roll out the apples in a barrel but require extra workers and expensive refrigeration equipment. With profit margins of 1 percent to 2 percent, it is difficult to argue that grocery stores are exploiting the farmer.

It is theoretically possible for a handful of buyers to hold down the prices they pay for a product, but it is difficult to do so. In fact, each grocery chain has an incentive to pay slightly more for superior produce, for the gains from doing so are great given the high fixed costs associated with selling produce to the final customer. It is a general rule in competition that the higher fixed costs, the less likely it is for a cartel to be effective.

As much as we might like to side with the farmer, we should remember that here we are dealing not only with large grocery stores, but with extremely large farms as well.

Source: "Growers to Supermarkets: We Want More Green," *Wall Street Journal,* September 15, 1999, California ed.

Example 1.) If consumers reduce their demand for lettuce, the demand for workers employed in lettuce growing, the demand for farmland used for lettuce, and even the demand for water used in farm irrigation will also fall. When the demand for automobiles falls, there is unemployment in Detroit. When world demand for Boeing commercial aircraft is booming, employment rises in Seattle and Wichita, the cities where Boeing is located.

Joint Determination of Factor Demand

The production of a good requires the cooperation of different factors of production. Farmworkers can produce no corn without farmland; farmland without farm labor is useless. Both farmland and farmworkers require farm implements (ranging from hand tools to sophisticated farm machinery) to produce corn.

> In general, the marginal physical product of any factor of production depends upon the quantity and quality of the cooperating factors of production.

The marginal physical product of the farmworker will be higher on 1 acre of farmland than on 1 square yard of land, it will be higher on 1 acre of fertile Iowa land than on 1 acre of rocky New England land, and

TABLE 1 MARGINAL REVENUE PRODUCT

Labor (workers), L (1)	*Output (units), Q* (2)	*Price, P* (3)	*Total Revenue, TR* (4) = (2) × (3)	*Marginal Revenue Product, MRP* (5) = (6) × (7) = Δ(4) ÷ Δ(1)	*Marginal Revenue, MR* (6) = Δ(4) ÷ Δ(2)	*Marginal Physical Product (units), MPP* (7) = Δ(2)
0	0	$24	$ 0			
				$95	$19	5
1	5	19	95			
				40	10	4
2	9	15	135			
				9	3	3
3	12	12	144			

Columns 1 and 2 give the production function (the amount of output produced by 0, 1, 2, and 3 units of labor input). Columns 2 and 3 give the demand schedule facing the firm. MRP is calculated by taking the increase in total revenue associated with one-unit increases in the labor input. It can also be calculated by multiplying MR times MPP. MR in column 6 is calculated by dividing the increase in revenue in column 4 by the difference between rows in column 2. MPP in column 7 is the increase in output for every unit increase in the factor, or the difference between rows in column 2.

it will be higher with the use of modern heavy farm machinery than with hand implements. The interdependence of the marginal physical products of land, labor, and capital does not make the problem of factor pricing in a market setting difficult.

Marginal Revenue Product

The demand for a factor of production—land, labor, or capital—is a derived demand. The factor is valuable because the firm sells the output on the product market. The dollar value of an extra worker, an extra unit of land, or an extra machine is that factor's marginal revenue product (MRP).

The **marginal revenue product (MRP)** of any factor of production is the extra revenue generated per unit increase in the amount of the factor.

We can calculate a factor's marginal revenue product in two ways. Both approaches yield the same value.

Method 1. The first method of calculating marginal revenue product is to simply change the quantity of the factor and observe the change in revenue. According to this direct method, marginal revenue product is the change in total revenue (TR) divided by the change (increase or decrease) in the factor.

$$\text{MRP} = \frac{\Delta\text{TR}}{\Delta\text{Factor}}$$

Table 1 demonstrates this method. The different quantities of labor the firm employs are given in column 1, and the resulting output is given in column 2. Thus, columns 1 and 2 represent the production function. Column 3 shows the market prices that clear the market (equate quantity supplied and demanded) for the various output levels produced. This firm is a price maker in the product market because the price falls with higher output levels. The firm's total revenue (price times quantity of output) is given in column 4. Because marginal revenue (see column 5) is the difference between the revenues generated at consecutive levels of labor input, it is recorded between the rows corresponding to the input levels. The revenue generated when one worker is employed is $95; the revenue when two workers are employed is $135. The marginal revenue product of the second worker therefore is $135 − $95 = $40. In other words, the firm's total revenue increases by $40 if the firm hires a second worker.

Method 2. We can calculate a factor's marginal revenue product indirectly as well. The marginal physical product (MPP) is the increase in output from a one-unit increase in the factor; the marginal revenue (MR) indicates the increase in revenue associated with this increase in output of one unit.[1] Therefore:

$$MRP = MPP \times MR$$

This formula works for the price maker (see Table 1). Because the firm increases its output from five to nine units as a consequence of adding a second unit of labor, marginal physical product equals four units. The four extra units of output add $40 to revenue, or $10 per extra unit ($40/4); therefore, the marginal revenue is $10. The marginal revenue product equals $40 ($10 × 4). Thus, the indirect method of calculating marginal revenue product yields the same answer as the direct method.

> The marginal revenue product of a factor can be calculated directly, by determining the increase in revenue at different input levels, or indirectly, by multiplying marginal physical product by marginal revenue.

PROFIT MAXIMIZATION

In the product market, the firm maximizes profit by producing that output at which marginal revenue and marginal cost are equal. The firm is also guided by profit maximization in the factor market. Profit-maximizing decisions in the factor market are basically the same as profit-maximizing decisions in the product market because deciding on the quantity of inputs determines the level of output.

To understand how firms choose the profit-maximizing level of factor inputs, consider the case of a firm deciding how much unskilled labor to hire. *The firm will hire one more unit of unskilled labor if the extra revenue (the extra benefit) the firm derives from the sale of the output produced by the extra unit exceeds the extra cost of the extra unit of unskilled labor.* If the firm is a price taker, the extra cost will be the market wage. As in any other economic activity, a firm will hire inputs to the point where marginal benefits equal marginal costs.

The firm will continue to hire unskilled labor as long as their marginal revenue product exceeds the market wage. If the marginal revenue product of labor is $40 and its price (the wage) is $30, it pays the firm to hire another unit. By hiring an additional unit of the labor, the firm can increase its profit by $10.

The Demand Curve for a Factor

Figure 1 shows the MRP curve of Factor A. The curve is downward sloping because in the short run, the greater the amount of Factor A used, the lower its marginal physical product (because of the law of diminishing returns). Also, if the firm is a price maker in the product market, higher levels of output will result in a lower marginal revenue. Thus, as the quantity of Factor A increases, both marginal physical product and marginal revenue tend to decline, so that MRP (which is MPP × MR) declines. The firm will hire Factor A until its price equals marginal revenue product.

> The MRP curve is the firm's demand curve for a factor because the firm hires that factor quantity until the marginal revenue product of the factor equals the price of the factor.

In Figure 1, the supply curve of Factor A to the firm is horizontal at the market price of $14. The price-

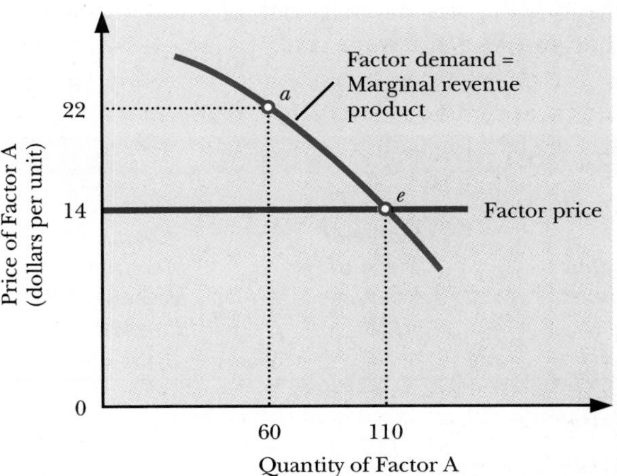

FIGURE 1 Firm Equilibrium: The Hiring of Factor Inputs

The firm's derived demand for Factor A is the MRP curve. The supply schedule of Factor A as seen by the firm is perfectly horizontal at the market price of $14. Equilibrium *e* will be reached at a price of $14 and a quantity of 110 units of Factor A. At this point, MRP = factor price.

---

[1]For a price taker in the product market, $P \times MPP = MR \times MPP$. For a price maker in the product market, $P \times MPP > MR \times MPP$. In intermediate textbooks, the product $P \times MPP$ is called the *value of the marginal product.*

taking firm in the factor market can hire all it wants at \$14. If the firm hired only 60 units of Factor A (point *a*), it would not maximize its profit: At 60 units, A's MRP equals \$22 and A's factor price or cost equals \$14. The firm's incentive to hire additional factors continues as long as MRP exceeds \$14. Thus, the firm will continue to hire to the point where MRP and the factor's price are equal, which occurs at 110 units of Factor A (point *e*). The firm will be in equilibrium (earning a maximum profit or minimizing its losses) when each factor is employed up to the point where the price of the factor equals the marginal revenue product of the factor.

> In equilibrium, $MRP_A = P_A$, $MRP_B = P_B$, and so on, where A and *B* are specific factors and P_A and P_B are their prices.

The Two Sides of the Firm

In the product market, the rule of profit maximization is MR = MC. In the factor market, the rule is MRP = the price of each factor. These rules are logically the same. Recall that marginal cost is the mirror image of marginal physical product. That is:

$$MC = \frac{W}{MPP_L} \tag{1}$$

where MPP_L is the marginal physical product of labor and *W* is the wage rate.

The rule for profit maximization in the product market is:

$$MR = MC \tag{2}$$

Because MC equals W/MPP_L according to equation (1), equation (2) can be rewritten as:

$$MR \times MPP_L = W \tag{3}$$

Because the wage for a factor is equal to its extra cost, and because MR × MPP = MRP, equation (3) can become:

$$MRP = W \tag{4}$$

which is the profit-maximizing rule in the factor market.

Table 2 provides a numerical example of how profit maximization in the product market is equivalent to profit maximization in the factor market. The firm is a price taker in both markets. The product price is \$10 and the wage rate is \$20 per day. The MPP schedule is given in columns 1 and 2 of Table 2. Column 3 shows marginal revenue (which equals price in this case), and column 4 shows the wage rate. Marginal revenue product is simply column 2 multiplied by column 3 and is shown in column 5. Marginal cost is the wage for an additional unit of labor divided by the change in output resulting from the additional unit, or *W* ÷ MPP (see column 6). When *P* = MC (both \$10), it is also true that MRP = *W* (both \$20). When one rule is satisfied, the other rule is also satisfied. (See Example 2.)

TABLE 2 TWO WAYS OF LOOKING AT PROFIT MAXIMIZATION

Labor Hours L (1)	*Units of Marginal Physical Product, MPP (2)*	*Price Equals Marginal Revenue, P = MR (3)*	*Wage, W (4)*	*Marginal Revenue Product, MRP (5) = (2) × (3)*	*Marginal Cost, MC (6) = (4) ÷ (2)*
0					
	5	\$10	\$20	\$50	\$4
1					
	4	10	20	40	5
2					
	2	10	20	20	10
3					

This firm is a price taker on both sides of the market. Column 5 equals column 2 times column 3 because the additional revenue from 1 more unit of labor is simply the marginal product multiplied by the price (or marginal revenue). Column 6 equals column 4 divided by column 2 because marginal cost equals the wage per unit of marginal physical product. This table shows that profits are maximized at 3 units of labor where *W* = MRP and *P* = MC.

EXAMPLE 2

Is the Marginal Productivity Theory True?

Theories are tested by what they imply about the real world. Let's consider the implications of the marginal productivity theory. Over time, we know that in most industries productivity improves because of technological innovations. Since $W = P \times \text{MPP}$, it follows that as productivity rises as a result of technological changes, the ratio of wages to prices must rise in that industry. But the wages paid in a particular industry must be competitive with wages in other industries. Thus, the wages paid in a particular industry should not change as much as productivity growth in that industry. Productivity growth in a particular industry that is in excess of productivity growth in other industries must translate into relatively lower prices. If productivity in general is growing at 2 percent, but productivity is not growing in construction, for example, we would expect that construction prices would be rising relative to other prices. This is exactly what happens. The accompanying figure shows the average annual productivity growth in a number of industries. Productivity growth was high (3 percent) in agriculture, and the relative price of agricultural goods fell. Productivity growth in construction was virtually zero, and the construction prices rose relative to other goods. Productivity growth in mining was closer to the national average, and the prices of mining products barely changed.

Source: The Economic Report of the President, 1994, p. 118.

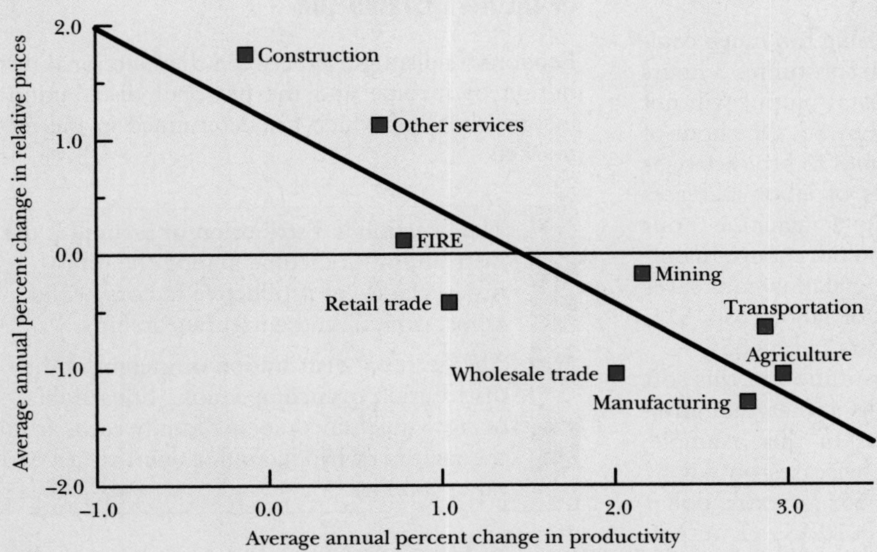

Productivity Growth and Price Reductions, 1950–1990

Productivity growth in an industry leads to lower relative prices.

Note: FIRE = finance, insurance, and real estate.

Source: Department of Commerce.

Cost Minimization

The rules of profit maximization explain the behavior of firms in the factor market. These rules predict that firms will employ that level and combination of inputs that maximize their profit.

To maximize profit, it is necessary to minimize the cost of producing a given quantity of output. Thus far, we have explained how a firm selects the optimal level of *one* factor input. But firms produce output with cooperating factors. How will they know when they are combining *all* their inputs in a least-cost fashion? Suppose a firm has decided to produce 200 units of output and currently uses 15 labor hours and 25 machine hours to produce this output. The wage rate (the price of labor) is $5 per hour, and the rental rate on the machinery is $20 per hour; thus, an extra hour of machine time costs *four* times as much as an extra hour of labor. The marginal physical product of capital is 30 units of output. The marginal physical product of labor is 10 units of output. Thus, an extra hour of machine time produces *three* times as much as an extra hour of labor. Is the firm using the optimal amount of labor and capital?

In this example, the firm is using too much capital and too little labor. If the firm substitutes 3 hours of labor for 1 hour of capital, total output will not change, but costs will be reduced by $5. One hour of capital (at the margin) is three times as productive as 1 hour of labor. Adding 3 units of labor increases output by 30, and subtracting 1 machine hour decreases output by 30; there is no net change in output. However, cutting back on 1 machine hour saves $20, while hiring 3 more hours of labor costs $15. Output remains the same, but costs fall by $5.

To determine whether a substitution of this sort will increase profits, the firm looks at marginal physical product *per dollar of cost.* In this example, because an extra hour of labor increases output by 10 units and increases costs by $5, an extra dollar spent on labor produces 2 units (10/$5) of output. Because an extra machine hour increases output by 30 units and increases costs by $20, an extra dollar spent on capital produces 1.5 units of output. In our example, a dollar spent on more labor is more effective than a dollar spent on more capital.

The marginal physical product per dollar of a factor is its marginal physical product divided by its price. The price-taking firm takes both the wage rate for labor (W) and the rental rate on capital (R) as given. As the preceding example shows, if the marginal physical product per dollar of labor is greater than the marginal physical product per dollar of capital, the firm is not combining inputs in a least-cost fashion. It can produce the same output at lower cost by substituting labor for capital until:

$$\frac{MPP_L}{W} = \frac{MPP_K}{R}$$

where MPP_K is the marginal physical product of capital.

> According to the least-cost rule, the price-taking firm is producing at minimum cost only if the marginal physical products per dollar of the various factors are equal to one another.

The Marginal Productivity Theory of Income Distribution

Economists distinguish between the functional distribution of income and the personal distribution of income, both of which are determined in the factor market.

The **functional distribution of income** is the distribution of income among the four broad classes of productive factors—land, labor, capital, and entrepreneurship.

The **personal distribution of income** is the distribution of income among households, or how much income one family earns from the factors of production it owns relative to other families.

The profit-maximizing and least-cost rules resolve the *how* problem in economics. They show how firms go about combining inputs to produce output. These same rules also resolve the *for whom* problem. Given the prices of the factors of production, what people earn depends on the resources they own. We shall consider the details of the personal distribution of income in a later chapter.

Factors of production, unless they are highly specialized (such as 7-foot basketball players), are demanded by many firms and by many industries. For example, the market demand for truck drivers comes from a wide cross section of American industry: The steel industry, retailers, the moving industry, and the local florist all have a derived demand for truck drivers. The demand for urban land also comes from a broad cross section of American industry: Heavy industry requires land for its plant sites, motel chains require land for their motels, and home builders require land to develop subdivisions. Similarly, the demand for capital goods comes from a cross section of American industry.

How the price (wage) of truck drivers is determined is shown in Figure 2. The wage rate of truck drivers reflects two forces: the derived demand for truck drivers as represented by their marginal revenue product, and the supply of truck drivers. At equilibrium (point *e*), quantity supplied and quantity demanded are equal, and the wage equals the marginal revenue product. In other words, truck drivers will be paid their marginal revenue product. The same is true of the other factors of production, as the marginal productivity theory of income distribution states.

According to the **marginal productivity theory of income distribution**, the functional distribution of income among land, labor, and capital is determined by the relative marginal revenue products of the different factors of production. The price of each factor will equal the marginal revenue product of that factor.

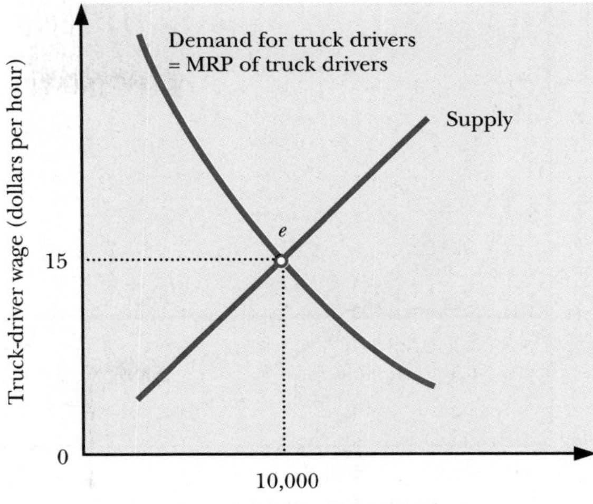

FIGURE 2 Determination of the Market Price (Wage) of Truck Drivers in a Competitive Market

The market supply curve of truck drivers is upward sloping, which indicates that truck drivers are prepared to work more hours at high wages than at low wages. The market demand curve is derived from the MRP curve of truck drivers across several industries. Equilibrium is achieved at point *e,* where the supply of truck drivers equals the quantity demanded. At the equilibrium wage of $15, 10,000 labor hours are used in the various industries employing truck drivers.

Marginal Productivity and Efficiency

In the preceding chapters on product markets we examined the relative efficiency of different market structures, particularly perfect competition and monopoly. We know that monopoly is inefficient because it creates contrived scarcity by failing to expand output to the point where price (the measure of the marginal benefit to society) and marginal cost (the measure of the extra cost to society) are equal.

If a firm has monopoly power in the product market, $P >$ MR. Although the monopolistic firm will pay each input its marginal revenue product, which will equal MR × MPP, the factor is actually worth $P \times$ MPP to society because each unit of MPP is valued at P. Because MR × MPP is less than $P \times$ MPP, the monopolist is paying less for factors than what they are worth to society.

Figure 3 illustrates a monopolist in the product market who is a price taker in the factor market. The curve $P \times$ MPP shows the marginal benefits to society of an additional unit of the factor. The MRP curve shows the marginal benefit to the monopolist of hiring an additional unit of the factor. When the monopolist operates at point *a* rather than at point *b*, the monopolist stops hiring workers short of their marginal worth to society (or pays them less than they are worth to society, as represented by point *c*). Society loses the green area *abc*.

If the firm is perfectly competitive in the product market, the marginal revenue product of a factor equals the marginal benefit of the factor to society.

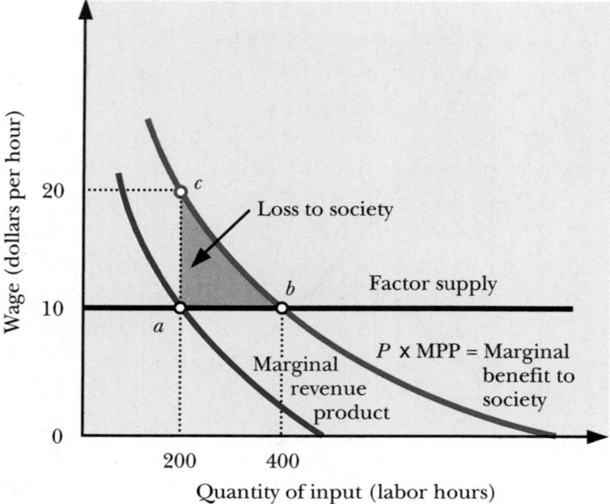

FIGURE 3 The Monopolist Hires Too Few Inputs

The firm is a monopolist in the product market and a price taker in the factor market. The value of the marginal product to society is $P \times$ MPP (the marginal benefit to society), and the marginal benefit to the monopolist is its marginal revenue product. If the wage rate is \$10, the monopolist employs 200 labor hours because at that point marginal revenue product equals the wage.

Because price equals marginal revenue in a competitive firm, the firm will hire factors until the point at which $P \times$ MPP equals the factor's price. Each factor adds a net marginal benefit to society equal to the factor's market price. This market price reflects its opportunity cost to society.

Marginal Productivity and Factor Incomes

The marginal productivity theory of income distribution suggests that a productive factor is usually paid its marginal revenue product. The marginal revenue product of one factor depends upon the quantity and quality of cooperating factors. For example, two textile workers, one in the United States and the other in India, may be equally skilled and diligent, but one works with a \$50 sewing machine while the other works with a \$100,000 advanced knitting machine. The New England farmer may be just as skilled as the Kansas farmer but may have a low MRP because of the low quality of the land. Marginal revenue product also depends upon the supplies of factors. The supply of residential land is limited in Hawaii but abundant in Iowa. The equilibrium MRP of land is, therefore, higher in Hawaii. If women are limited to employment opportunities in only a few professions, they will overcrowd these professions and drive down the MRP and, thus, wages. Finally, marginal revenue product, as stated earlier, depends upon the demand for the product being produced. If product demand falls, so will the factor's MRP.

> The marginal productivity theory of income distribution states that a competitively determined factor price reflects the factor's marginal revenue product. Marginal revenue product is the result of (1) the relative supplies of the different factors, (2) the quantity and quality of cooperating factors, and (3) the market demands for the goods the factors produce.

The Aggregate Production Function

The marginal productivity theory of income distribution has both wide and narrow applications. In its narrow form, the theory can explain why one person earns more than another or why one plot of land rents for more than another. The aggregate economy is the summation of all the participants in the economy; therefore, it is possible to talk about average wages, average land-rental rates, and average interest rates. The relationship between the total inputs used by an economy and the total amount of goods and services produced by an economy can be expressed by an aggregate production function.

> The **aggregate production function** shows the relationship between the total output produced by the economy and the total labor, capital, and land inputs used by the economy.

The aggregate production function is a simplified representation of the economy, but it is a useful tool for investigating the functional distribution of income among the broad factors of production—land, labor, and capital. (See Figure 4.)

To simplify the analysis, assume the economy produces only one product—corn—and that it is perfectly competitive in all markets. The demand curve

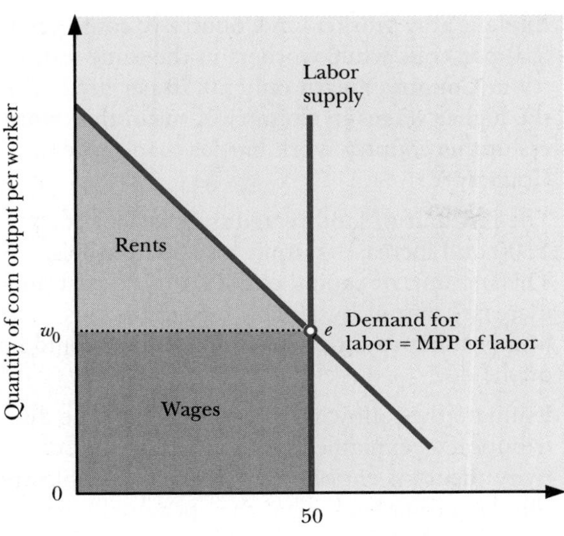

FIGURE 4 The Aggregate Production Function and the Functional Distribution of Income

This figure represents the aggregate production function of an entire economy. The economy produces a generalized physical output at a product price of $1. All markets are assumed to be perfectly competitive. Because the price of a unit of output is $1, the demand curve for labor is the marginal physical product of labor; it declines according to the law of diminishing returns. The vertical supply line represents the supply of labor, which is fixed at 50 million workers. The MPP curve will be the demand for labor, and the market wage will be set at w_0 where the quantity of labor supplied equals the quantity of labor demanded.

How much output has the economy produced and how much will go to labor? Each unit of labor adds to the economy's output. The area under the demand curve is the total output of the economy at that point. The 50 million workers will produce an output equal to the entire red area. Workers will receive their wage, w_0, times the number of workers. Their share of output is the dark red rectangle labeled *Wages*. The cooperating nonlabor factors (land and capital) will get what is left over, or the light red triangle labeled *Rents*.

for labor is the marginal physical product of labor for the entire economy. If we assume that the price of a bushel of corn is $1, the demand curve for labor measures both the marginal physical product and marginal revenue product for the entire economy. The supply of labor is assumed to be fixed at 50 million workers. The equilibrium wage rate is w_0, which brings about a quantity of labor demanded of 50 million workers (the quantity supplied).

The total output of the economy is the area under the demand curve in Figure 4, because each point on the curve shows the additional corn produced by the last worker. (The demand curve shows the MPP at each level of labor input. We add together the MPPs for each successive unit of labor to get total output. For 50 million workers, total output is the entire red area in Figure 4.) Of this total output, labor will receive the area of the dark red rectangle labeled *Wages*. The nonlabor factors, such as capital and land, will receive the area of the light red triangle labeled *Rents*. Each worker is paid the dollar value of the marginal physical product of the 50-millionth unit rather than the dollar value of earlier units that have larger MPPs (as measured by the height of the demand curve).

The marginal productivity theory states that each factor of production will be paid its marginal revenue product. If the world is sufficiently competitive, the theory suggests that each factor of production will be paid the dollar value of its marginal physical product.

In this chapter we have an overview of how factor markets work. We should note, however, that each market has its own unique features. In the labor market, the supply of labor is determined by how individuals choose among market work, work in the home, and leisure. These are choices not faced by the owners of capital and land. Moreover, the labor market is affected by the organization of workers into unions and by the effect of education and training on labor's marginal physical product. In the capital market, buyers of capital receive the benefits of capital over a long period of time; suppliers of capital must choose between consumption today and more consumption tomorrow. The market for land is characterized by the relatively fixed supply of land.

In the next three chapters we shall examine each factor market in detail, building upon the general theoretical framework established in this chapter.

SUMMARY

1. Firms sell their output in the product market, and they buy inputs to produce output in the factor market. Because all firms compete for basically the same inputs, there is more competition in factor markets than in product markets. A price taker in

the input market will usually have a marginal factor cost equal to the price of the input.

2. The firm's demand for a factor of production will depend upon the demand for the product being produced and upon the factor's productivity. The marginal physical product (MPP) of a factor of production is the increase in output that results from increasing the factor by one unit, other things being equal. The demand for a factor of production is a derived demand because it depends on the demand for the goods and services the factor helps produce. Marginal revenue product (MRP) is the increase in revenue brought about by hiring one more unit of the factor of production.

3. Profit-maximizing firms that are price takers will observe the following rule in the factor markets: Factors of production will be hired to the point where MRP = factor price.

4. The least-cost rule for firms is to hire factors of production so that MPP per dollar of one factor equals the MPP per dollar of any other factor.

5. The marginal productivity theory of income distribution helps to explain the functional distribution of income (among the three classes of production factors) and the personal distribution of income (among households).

KEY TERMS

QUESTIONS AND PROBLEMS

1. The MPP of a 100th worker is 33 units of output. The marginal revenue of the firm for the corresponding level of output is $2, the price of the product is $3, and the wage rate is $99.
   a. Is the firm maximizing its profit?
   b. What would the wage rate have to be for 100 workers to maximize profit?

2. Explain how workers in Country X could earn $10 per hour while workers in the same industry in Country Y earn only $0.50 per hour. Do the higher wages in Country X mean that workers in this country work harder than those in Country Y?

3. The last unit of land rented by a farmer costs $100 and increases output by 1000 bushels. The last unit of capital costs $1000 to rent and increases output by 20,000 bushels. Is this farmer minimizing costs? If not, what should he or she do?

4. Evaluate the following statement: "Income distribution as explained by the marginal productivity theory is entirely fair. After all, people are simply getting back what they personally have contributed to society."

5. One type of equipment—such as specialized oil-drilling equipment—can be used only in one particular industry. Another type—such as general-purpose lathes—can be used in a wide variety of industries. How would the elasticity of demand differ for these two types of equipment?

6. Complete Table A by filling in columns 4 and 5. If the wage rate is $55, how many units of labor should the firm hire?

TABLE A

Labor (number of workers), L (1)	*Units of Output, Q (2)*	*Price, P (3)*	*Units of Marginal Physical Product, MPP (4)*	*Marginal Revenue Product, MRP (5)*
0	0	$8		
1	10	8		
2	17	8		
3	23	8		
4	28	8		

7. Assume that the MPP of a first worker is 20 units of output, that the MPP of a second worker is 30 units, that the MPP of a third worker is 20 units, and that the MPP of a fourth worker is 15 units. If four workers are hired, how many units of output are produced?

8. A Ph.D. engineer costs a firm $100,000 a year; an engineer with a B.A. degree costs a firm only

$50,000 a year. What information is required to determine the firm's optimal decision?

9. How does the concept of marginal productivity help explain the functional distribution of income among the four classes of productive factors?
10. State arguments for and against boycotting products produced by sweatshop labor.

INTERNET CONNECTION

11. Using the link from http://www.awl.com/ruffin_gregory, read the Web page created by the U.S. Department of Labor on U.S. Labor Markets."
    a. Has the wage gap between blacks and whites narrowed since 1968?
    b. Does it matter if we correct for income and inequality?

PUZZLE ANSWERED: Both buyer and seller cartels have difficulty enforcing the cartel. In a seller cartel, each seller has an incentive to cut the price in order to gain market share and increase profit; in a buyer cartel, each buyer has an incentive to raise the price because the item being purchased has a higher marginal revenue product than the cartel price.

Chapter 17

LABOR: THE HUMAN FACTOR

Chapter Insight

In 1910, the 7-year-old Ford Motor Company moved into a new plant in Highland Park, Michigan, that boasted the world's first automobile assembly line. This new factory used the "work-in-motion" concept, in which individual workers repeated one or two steps over and over while rope cables towed partly assembled cars from one worker to the next. This method enabled the rate of production to increase from 15 cars per day to one car every 10 seconds. Ford's use of the assembly line spread to other industries, perpetuating the successes of the ongoing Industrial Revolution (a Defining Moment in economics) in the United States, which had become the world's leading industrial power.

On January 5, 1914, Henry Ford announced he would pay his workers the then-incredible sum of $5 per day. Just a few years earlier, autoworkers had been paid only $0.15 per day. Despite paying workers the outrageous daily wage of $5, Ford was able to sell cars to a mass market and achieve the high levels of profits that made him one of the richest men of his day.

Ford understood that if productivity is increased, workers can be paid more. It is profitable for the firm to hire more workers as long as what each worker adds to revenue exceeds what each worker costs. By achieving tremendous gains in productivity from the mass production of a standardized car, not only could Ford pay workers substantially more, but the $5 a day also served to attract higher quality workers.

In this chapter, we shall examine how low wages are determined, why wages and productivity are connected, why some people are paid more than others, and why some jobs pay more than others. We shall show that as with other prices the wage rate is the outcome of the supply and demand for labor. We shall also consider the role of labor unions.

LEARNING OBJECTIVES

After completing this chapter, you will be able to:

1. Understand how labor differs from other factors of production.
2. Use the backward-bending supply curve to explain why the average workweek has become shorter than it was.
3. Understand why more women have entered the workforce.
4. Understand why the nation's share of the labor force has been declining.
5. See how unions deal with the trade-off between higher wages and lower employment.
6. Explain how collective bargaining with the threat of strike raises union wages.
7. Discuss why it is clear that unions raise wages in unionized industries but not clear whether they raise or lower wages in nonunionized industries.

CHAPTER PUZZLE: How does society allocate its labor force so that some people are doing the dirty jobs and other people the fun or pleasant jobs?

THE DIFFERENCE BETWEEN LABOR AND OTHER FACTORS OF PRODUCTION

In the preceding chapter, we considered how factor markets work and reviewed economic principles for the use of land, labor, and capital inputs. Four special features differentiate labor from the two other factors:

1. We cannot be bought like an acre of land or a computer or office phone system; slavery is against the law. As the owners of labor, we can only rent our services. True, we can sell our labor services under short- or long-term contracts, but we cannot legally sell ourselves.

2. We have alternatives to using our time for labor. If land and machines are not put to productive use, they stand idle. When we are not engaged in the labor market, we can spend our time in domestic or leisure activities.

3. Land and capital cannot care about the use to which they are put. However, we have preferences for particular types of work in particular locations. We care whether we work in Alaska or New York and whether we are actors or programmers.

4. Labor unions differentiate labor from the other factors of production. By joining labor unions, we can affect the conditions of work and pay.

Labor Market Trends

To understand the economics of labor, we must be able to explain trends and patterns in labor markets. Some of the most important of these are listed in Table 1.

1. The labor force has expanded substantially in the United States. The number of nonagricultural employees today is more than five times greater than it was 85 years ago.

2. The composition of the labor force has changed dramatically. The share of manufacturing employment has declined since 1950. The gender composition of the labor force has changed. Eighty-five years ago, only one in five women worked in the labor force. Today almost 60 percent of women work in the labor force.

3. The average number of hours worked per week has declined. In 1914, manufacturing workers worked an average of 49.4 hours per week. By 1998, this number had fallen to less than 40 hours per week.

4. Real wages have risen. The real (adjusted for inflation) hourly wage rate of American manufacturing workers increased almost four times between 1914 and the present. An hour of work today buys nearly four times the quantity of goods and services as did an hour of work in 1914.

TABLE 1 FACTS ABOUT THE LABOR MARKET, 1914 TO PRESENT

Year	*Nonagricultural Employees (millions)*	*Manufacturing (percent)*	*Average Hours Worked per Week*	*Hourly Earnings (1998 dollars)*	*Fringe Benefits (1998 dollars per hour)*	*Female Labor Force Participation Rate (percent)*
1914	23.2	8.2	49.4	3.62	—	22.8
1930	29.4	9.6	42.1	5.40	.07	24.8
1940	32.4	11.0	38.1	7.65	.35	27.4
1950	45.2	33.6	40.5	9.75	.52	31.4
1960	54.2	31.6	38.6	12.44	1.06	34.8
1970	70.9	27.3	37.1	14.11	1.57	42.6
1980	90.4	22.3	35.3	14.38	1.65	51.5
1995	111.0	15.8	34.5	13.23	5.30	57.5
1998	125.8	14.8	34.6	13.49	6.00*	59.9

*estimated by authors

Source: Historical Statistics of the U.S., Economic Report of the President (1999).

5. Despite their rising trend, real wages, excluding fringe benefits, have fallen during some periods. Real wages rose by over 400 percent from 1914 to 1980, but then fell by about 6 percent from 1980 to 1998.
6. The composition of compensation has changed. Today, fringe benefits constitute nearly one-third of compensation; the rest, wages. Eighty-five years ago virtually all compensation was from wages.

The Working of the Labor Market

Markets bring together buyers and sellers of a particular good or service for the purpose of making transactions.

A **labor market** brings together buyers and sellers of labor services to determine pay and working conditions.

Labor markets may be local, national, or even international in scope. The services of salesclerks, teenage employees, unskilled workers, and sanitation workers are bought and sold in local markets, whereas there are national and even international labor markets for engineers, academics, airline pilots, and upper-level executives, among others.

Some labor markets are informal. Job announcements are posted at the factory gate, "help wanted" ads are placed in the local newspaper, and jobs are promoted by word of mouth. Other labor markets fill positions according to a well-defined set of rules. Civil service jobs are regulated by detailed legislation and rules, and in unionized industries, rules for hiring and firing are spelled out in considerable detail.

Most labor arrangements are governed by contracts between the employer and employee. Labor contracts, which spell out conditions of work and pay, can be either *explicit* (formal) or *implicit* (informal). An explicit contract such as a union contract specifies the wage rate, the term of employment, working conditions, and the conditions under which the contract can be terminated. Other labor contracts are implicit. An informal understanding may exist that workers receive generous wages when jobs are available but will be laid off when business is slow. There may also be an understanding that laid-off workers will not seek other jobs during short lay-offs in return for being rehired when business improves.

Employers can also use an internal labor market to hire the most qualified persons with a minimum of information costs.

An **internal labor market** works by promoting or transferring workers it already employs.

Workers enter a firm's internal labor market through general entry-level positions such as management trainee, bookkeeper, or apprentice machinist. Rules and established procedures then determine who will be promoted and the manner in which vacancies are filled. Firms that use an internal labor market hire a large number of entry-level people without much testing, interviewing, or screening. A large department store hires a large number of management trainees; a factory hires a large number of general laborers. Once a person is on the job, the firm has the opportunity to observe actual job performance. The firm can learn a great deal about the person being considered for a promotion. Promoting from within is often less costly than hiring from outside. The major cost of using the internal labor market is that the firm passes up the opportunity to hire more-qualified persons from outside by restricting promotions to those it already employs.

Labor markets are differentiated by the ability of hiring firms to affect wage rates. Firms may be price takers or price makers in the labor market.

> If a firm must pay the wage rate dictated by the market regardless of how much labor it hires, the firm is a price taker. If the firm is large enough to raise the wage rate by hiring more, and lower it by hiring less, the firm is a price maker.

As we know from the preceding chapter, competition is more common in the labor market (and other factor markets) than it is in the product market. In this chapter we consider price-taking firms.

Household Production and Leisure

Household production and leisure are alternatives to working in the labor force. These options affect the total supply of labor to the economy.

> **Household production** is work in the home, including such activities as meal preparation, do-it-yourself repair, child-rearing, and cleaning. **Leisure** is time spent in any activity other than work in the labor force or work in the home.

Economists believe that we use rational economic decision making to allocate our time among work in the labor market, household production, and leisure.

The opportunity cost of leisure is the income (or household production) that must be given up. The opportunity cost of leisure rises when the price of market work rises. We would therefore expect leisure to decline as real wages rise. Why, then, have average hours worked per week declined while real wages have increased?

Panel (*a*) of Figure 1 shows a labor supply curve relating wages and hours worked. The curve is backward bending. Let's consider why an increase in wages first raises and then lowers the quantity of labor supplied.

An increase in wages raises the price of leisure and motivates individuals to substitute other things—in this case, market work—for leisure, thereby discouraging leisure. But the increase in wages also raises income, making leisure more affordable.

In Panel 1 (*a*), when the wage is $2 per hour and only 15 hours are worked per week, a dollar increase in the wage rate adds an additional $15 per week to income. This is not enough extra income to afford much more leisure. When wages are $5 per hour and 40 hours are worked per week, a dollar increase in wages is like an extra $40 per week; the increase in income is much larger. When wages are $9 per hour and 45 hours are worked per week, the income effect of another $1 increase in the wage rate is even stronger. In Panel (*a*), the effect of higher income dominates the effect of higher wages after wages reach $9 per hour. Further increases in wages cause hours worked to decline, as shown by the backward-bending section of the labor supply curve. (See Example 1 on page 314.)

Some of us worry about the effects of mechanization on job opportunities. As machines become more and more efficient, will there one day be no jobs left? Mechanization raises labor productivity, which translates into higher real wages. With higher real wages, we can take more leisure and work fewer hours. The ultimate payoff of mechanization is that it gives us more leisure and higher incomes.

Panel (*b*) of Figure 1 shows the impact of greater wealth on the supply of labor. The wealth effect shifts the labor supply curve to the left for the same reason the income effect of a higher wage rate leads to workers' choosing more leisure. Since 1914,

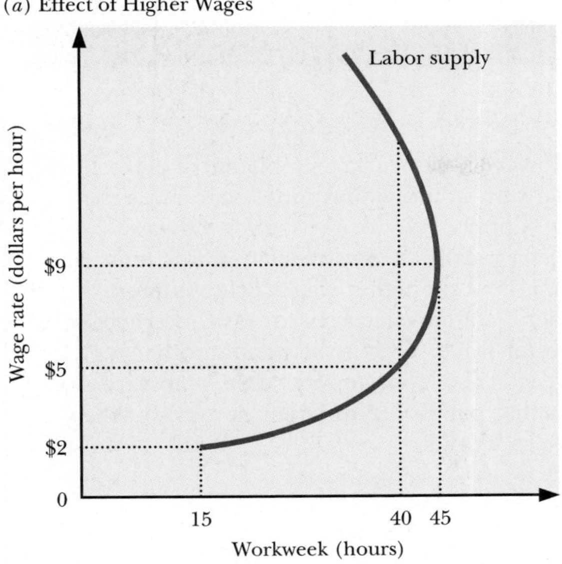

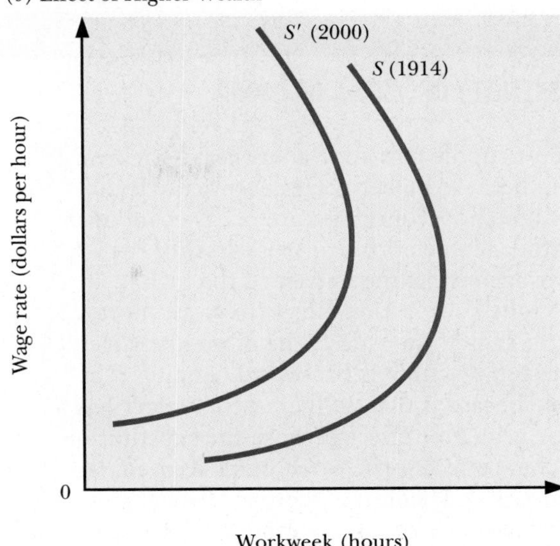

FIGURE 1 The Backward-Bending Labor Supply Curve

Panel (*a*) shows the impact of higher wages on the quantity of labor supplied, holding wealth constant. Panel (*b*) shows the effect of greater wealth on the supply curve of labor, shifting it from *S* to *S*′, helping to explain the decline in workweek.

wealth in the United States has increased substantially; it is probably this factor more than any other that has lowered the average workweek from 49 hours to 39. This effect is difficult to measure directly, but in a study of the impact of inheritances on work incentives, it was found that those who received large bequests reduced their labor force participation rates from 70 to 65 percent as well as lowered their hours per week.[1] Those who worked long hours in factories during the Industrial Revolution (a Defining Moment in economics) could hardly know that one of its results would be an eventual increase in leisure time.

Wages and Household Production

Most people cite social factors such as high divorce rates, one-parent families, and the enforcement of antidiscrimination legislation for the rising female labor-force participation rate reported in Table 1.

Economic theory provides another plausible explanation. Whether we work in the labor force or in household production also depends upon the value of our household production. If my work in the home (child-rearing, cleaning, food preparation) is worth $10 per hour, and my market wage is $8 per hour, I would work at home. If my market wage rises to $15 per hour, I would work at a job. The market wages of women have risen more rapidly than the value of household production and thus caused more and more women to enter the labor force. This principle explains the rise in the female labor force participation rate in Table 1.

The Demand for Labor

The wage rate for a particular type of labor is determined in the market for that type of labor. The wage rate and the quantity of labor are determined by

[1] Douglas Holtz-Eakin, David Joulfain, and Harvey Rosen, "The Carnegie Conjecture: Some Empirical Evidence," *Quarterly Journal of Economics* (1993): 413–435.

EXAMPLE 1

The Elasticity of Supply of Labor

The labor supply curve for a worker is backward bending because higher wages eventually lead workers to choose more leisure or, as economists put it, the income effect (to work less) of the higher wage offsets the impact of the higher wage on the substitution effect (to work more). Thus, the higher the wages, the more likely it is that the supply curve is backward bending. The most likely case is that an increase in wages has a small or negligible effect because the substitution and income effects offset each other. Indeed, the empirical evidence on this score is fairly consistent: the elasticity of labor supply to the wage rate for individual workers is close to zero for both married males and married females.

However, the market supply curve is the horizontal sum of individual supply curves. Is the labor supply curve for the market upward sloping or vertical? The answer is that it is upward sloping because higher wages bring in more workers, and lower wages cause workers to leave the labor force. To put the point another way, the reason the labor supply curve is upward sloping is that people are different in terms of their desire to work.

Source: James Heckman, "What Has Been Learned About Labor Supply in the Past Twenty Years?" *American Economic Review* (May 1993), 116–121.

demand and supply, just as product price and quantity are determined by demand and supply.

We know, from the preceding chapter, that profit-maximizing firms hire factors up to the point where the factor price equals the marginal revenue product (MRP) of the factor. The firm will continue to hire labor as long as the marginal revenue product of the additional worker exceeds that worker's wage. The firm shown in Figure 2, panel (*a*), is perfectly competitive in the computer programmer market (it must take the market wage as given). It can hire all the labor it wants at the prevailing wage rate. Its labor supply schedule is a horizontal line (perfectly elastic) at the market wage.

Table 2 shows the outputs associated with different inputs of labor of a single grade, such as computer programmers. Columns 3 and 4 give the marginal physical product (MPP) and marginal revenue product (MRP) for each level of input. The firm's product sells for $2 per program line, and the capital input is fixed in the short run. With capital fixed, the law of diminishing returns applies to the labor input; MPP and MRP decline as labor inputs rise.

The firm is a price taker in both the product market and the labor market; therefore, its marginal revenue product equals its product price, *P*, times labor's marginal physical product (MPP). The firm will demand the quantity of labor at which $W = \text{MRP}$.

When the market wage is $28, the firm will demand that quantity of labor (2 hours) at which MRP is $28. If the wage falls to $16 per hour, the firm will hire more labor. As the firm increases its labor inputs, the law of diminishing returns causes MRP to fall. At the $16 wage, the firm will use 4 programmer hours because the MRP of the fourth hour is $16. The quantity of labor demanded varies inversely with the wage rate, which is shown by the downward-sloping shape of the demand curve in Figure 2, panel (*a*).

> The individual firm's demand curve for labor is its marginal revenue product curve.

The demand curve for labor is a derived demand curve, reflecting the demand for the product that that particular labor produces. If there is no demand for computer programming, the price of computer programming will be zero and MRP will equal zero. The greater the demand for the product, the higher the price and the higher the MRP.

The market demand is the sum of the demand of all firms hiring that single grade of labor.

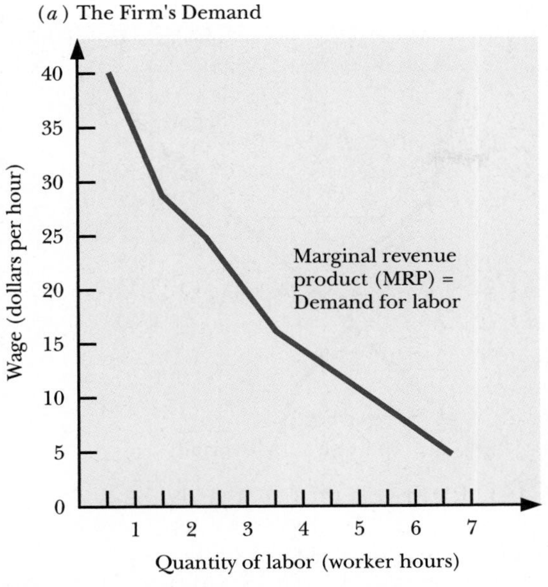

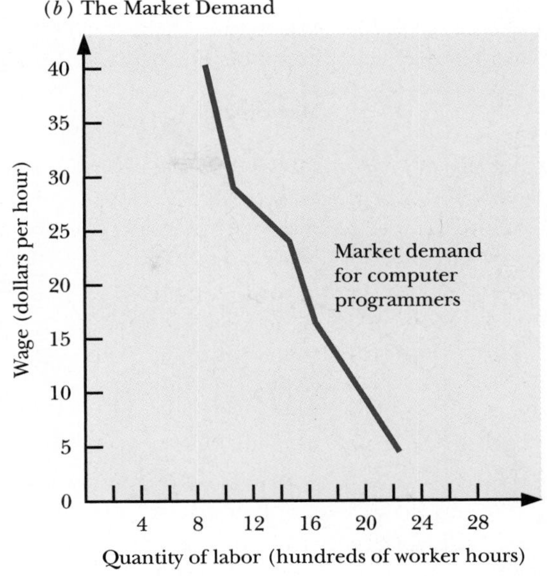

FIGURE 2 Demand for Computer Programmers

In panel (*a*) the price of this firm's output is $2 per line programmed. Its capital input is fixed in the short run. Hence, MRP = MPP × $2. The labor demand curve shows the marginal revenue product of different quantities of labor hours. The firm uses 4 programmer hours when the wage rate is $16 per hour (the MRP of the fourth hour is equal to the $16 wage). If the wage rises to $28, the firm would employ only 2 programmer hours because the MRP of the second hour equals $28.

In panel (*b*), the market labor demand curve for programmers indicates the number of programmer hours that would be demanded by all firms that hire programmers at different wage rates. Because the demand curves of each firm are negatively sloped, the market labor demand curve is also negatively sloped.

> The market demand curve for labor shows how the total quantity of labor demanded varies as the wage changes.

The market demand curve for computer programmers is given in Figure 2, panel (*b*). This curve shows the quantities of a single grade of labor demanded by all 400 potential employers. Because the labor demand curves of individual firms are negatively sloped, the market demand curve will be negatively sloped as well. The market demand curve in panel (*b*) is the sum of 400 firms like the one shown in panel (*a*).

The Supply of Labor

If all other factors are held constant, the amount of labor of a single grade (such as computer programming) supplied depends on the wage rate. We compare the wage we can earn in one occupation with

TABLE 2

Labor Input (hours) (1)	*Quantity of Output (lines programmed)* (2)	*Marginal Physical Product (lines), MPP* (3)	*Marginal Revenue Product, MRP = P × MPP* (4)
0	0		
		20	$40
1	20		
		14	28
2	34		
		12	24
3	46		
		8	16
4	54		
		6	12
5	60		
		4	8
6	64		
		2	4
7	66		

The price of this firm's output is $2 per line. Its capital input is fixed in the short run. Hence, MRP = MPP × $2. The demand schedule is the marginal revenue product schedule in column 4.

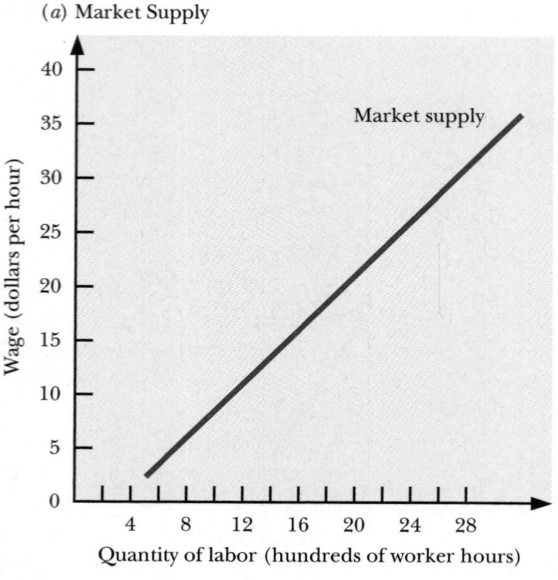

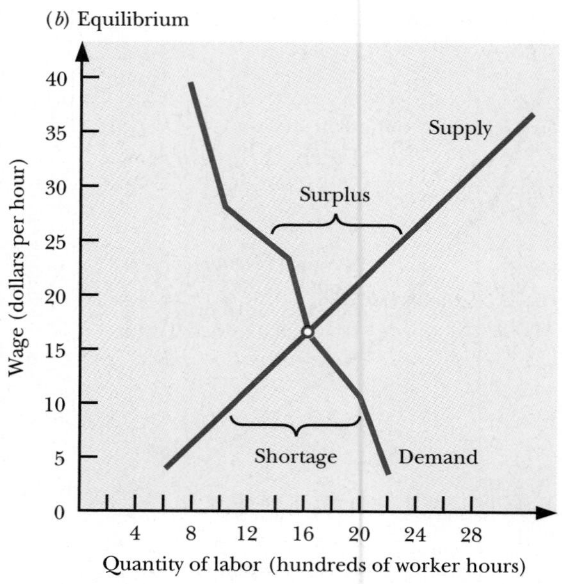

FIGURE 3 Labor Supply, Demand, and Equilibrium Wage

In panel (*a*), the market labor supply curve shows the number of hours programmers are willing to work at different wage rates, all other things remaining the same. The labor supply curve is positively sloped because at higher wages, programmer employment is more attractive relative to other types of employment.

In panel (*b*), the market supply of programmers, from panel (*a*), and the market demand for programmers, from Figure 2, panel (*b*), are brought together in this figure. The equilibrium wage rate is $16 per hour. At the $16 wage, the quantity demanded (1600 hours) equals the quantity supplied. At wage rates above $16, there is a surplus (quantity supplied exceeds quantity demanded); at wage rates below $16, there is a shortage of labor (quantity demanded exceeds quantity supplied).

our opportunity cost—the wage we could receive in another occupation. The higher the wage offered for labor of a particular grade, the more the workers of that grade will offer their services. (The backward-bending supply curve in Figure 1 refers to the supply of all labor relative to the average wage across all occupations. It doesn't apply in this case.)

We receive a wage that is at least equal to the opportunity cost of our next-best alternative. The employer who fails to pay us our opportunity costs will have no workers because we will take a better alternative.

Figure 3, panel (*a*), shows a market supply curve indicating the number of hours computer programmers are willing to work at different wage rates. The supply curve is positively sloped because at higher wages, computer programming becomes more attractive relative to other occupations. Computer programmers will therefore shift hours from other occupations for which they are qualified (e.g., engineering, accounting, mathematics) into programming work. The market labor supply curve is the sum of the individual labor supply curves of computer programmers.

LABOR MARKET EQUILIBRIUM

Wage rates are determined in labor markets by demand and supply. The market demand curve for labor of a single grade is negatively sloped; the market supply curve for labor of a single grade is positively sloped.

The market demand and supply curves for computer programmers are combined in Figure 3, panel (*b*). A $16 wage rate equates the quantity of programmer hours supplied with the quantity demanded, or 1600 hours. At any wage above $16, the number of hours programmers wish to work exceeds the number demanded. At any wage below $16, the number of hours firms wish programmers to work exceeds the number of hours programmers are willing to work.

> The equilibrium wage rate in a labor market is the wage rate at which the quantity of labor demanded equals the quantity of labor supplied.

If there is a *labor surplus,* some workers willing to work at the prevailing wage will be without jobs. Some will offer their services at lower wages and thus drive down the wage rate. If there is a *labor shortage,* some firms wishing to hire workers at the prevailing wage rate will go away empty-handed. Some will offer higher wages to attract employees and thus drive up wages.

When price-taking firms pay the equilibrium wage, workers are paid their marginal revenue products. In equilibrium, $W = \text{MRP}$. In Figure 3, panel (*b*), workers are paid \$16 and their contribution to the firm's marginal revenue is also \$16. (See Example 2.)

Efficiency Wages

If a firm pays above-equilibrium wage rates, the number willing to work at those jobs will exceed the number of jobs available. Employers could still fill jobs and yet offer lower wages. It is for this reason that we expect firms to pay the equilibrium wage. The efficiency wage model explains why firms might want to pay more than the equilibrium wage rate.

> The **efficiency-wage model** states that it is rational for certain firms to pay workers a wage rate above equilibrium to improve worker performance and productivity.

Economists often cite the example of Henry Ford's 1914 policy of paying workers \$5 a day (described in the Chapter Insight). By paying wages in excess of equilibrium, firms create an incentive for workers to work efficiently without careful monitoring. The costs of shirking and getting caught are high when the worker is receiving the bonus of an above-equilibrium wage.

Firms also use above-equilibrium wages to reduce turnover and create a stable workforce. If all wages were finely balanced at equilibrium, workers could move from one job to another at relatively low cost. With wages above equilibrium, workers are less inclined to leave high-paying jobs. With a stable workforce, training and search costs are reduced, and workers become more specialized and skilled the longer they stay on the job. Firms can use higher wages as a screening device to sort out less desirable job candidates. A higher wage attracts more able job candidates, and workers willing to work for less can be screened out as potential labor market "lemons."

EXAMPLE 2
Matching Workers and Employers

The Internet has over 2500 sites that deal with matching workers with potential employers. The biggest such site, www.monster.com receives about 2.5 million visits per month by people interested in every conceivable type of job, whether that of an accountant or a nanotechnologist. Businesses pay for listing on the site, just as they do for newspaper classified ads.

By reducing the cost of information, the Internet will make the labor market work more efficiently: workers will find jobs more quickly at wages that more nearly reflect an equilibrium pattern. For example, the *Wall Street Journal* conducted a search for a pharmaceutical sales job in Houston and found that there were at that time 10 jobs available with big companies.

Source: "The Internet: Find a Job," *Wall Street Journal,* December 6, 1999.

EXAMPLE 3

COMPENSATING DIFFERENTIALS FOR SCIENTISTS

Dangerous jobs, such as putting out oil field fires, command a premium in order to provide a compensating differential for the extra hazard. But some jobs are pleasant, and the people who choose those professions pay the price for the privilege of working in a desirable field. An excellent example is scientific work. A scientist receives considerable personal pleasure from doing research, publishing the results, and receiving the applause of other scientists. It should not be surprising to find out that they are paid less than those who cannot publish their research.

But how do you test for this when scientists as a whole make higher than average incomes? A recent study examines scientists who must and those who need not publish their results. By examining a sample of postdoctoral biologists in science-based research and development organizations, Scott Stern discovered a highly significant compensating differential. Firms that allow their researchers to publish paid, on average, 25 percent less for scientists with the same ability than firms that did not allow their scientists to publish independent research results.

Source: Scott Stern, "Do Scientists Pay to Be Scientists?" *NBER Working Paper No. W7410*, October 1999.

Shifts in Labor Demand and Supply Curves

Four factors affect the demand curve for labor. These factors shift the demand curve for labor when they change.

1. Labor demand increases when the demand increases for the product produced by that labor. The demand increase raises the price of the product, which raises the marginal revenue product of labor and shifts the demand curve to the right.
2. Automated equipment can substitute for bank tellers, skilled labor substitutes for unskilled labor, and chemical fertilizers substitute for farmworkers. If the prices of substitute factors increase, firms will increase their demand for labor.
3. Labor demand increases when the price of a factor complementary to labor decreases. Complementary factors are used in combination with labor. Materials such as steel, aluminum, and plastics are used in combination with labor to make automobiles, for example. If the prices of these materials fall, the demand for labor will rise.
4. When the MPP of labor rises, the MRP (and therefore the demand for) labor rises.

Like the labor demand curve, the labor supply curve shifts in response to changes in other factors. Three factors affect the supply of labor to a particular occupation:

1. The wages that can be earned in other occupations affect labor supply. If engineering wages increase, the supply of computer programmers should fall.
2. The nonmonetary aspects of the occupation affect labor supply. We dislike heavy, unpleasant, or dangerous work or work in harsh climates. An increase in the unpleasantness or danger associated with a particular job will decrease the supply of labor. As the number of robberies at convenience stores increases, the supply of convenience store clerks will fall. (See Example 3.)

3. Labor unions can affect labor supply through collective bargaining and strikes. We shall consider this subject later in the chapter.

We can use the tools of labor demand and supply to explain trends in real wages. Table 1 showed that real wages have increased over the long run but that they fell between the mid-1970s and the late 1990s.

The demand for labor depends on the productivity of labor. If the productivity of labor of a specific grade increases, the demand for that labor will rise. If labor productivity rises throughout the economy, the demand for labor will increase throughout the economy. The general trend for labor productivity is positive. Since the Industrial Revolution (a Defining Moment in economics), economies have experienced technological progress. We seem able to find better ways of doing things, new inventions, and new technologies. These factors cause labor productivity to rise.

The supply of labor to the economy at large depends upon labor/leisure choices. More of us are willing to work in the labor force, and work more hours, if real wages are rising. The supply of labor to the economy also depends upon demographic factors. If a large number of young people are completing their educations and entering the labor force, the supply of labor rises. If the labor force is aging and a large number of people are retiring, the supply of labor declines.

During the period 1914 to the 1970s, the number of individuals in the prime working age population (ages 25–44) fell from almost 30 percent to 24 percent of the total population. In effect, labor became more scarce. From 1970 to 1998, the prime working age population rose from 24 percent to 33 percent of the total population. The percentage increase of the 25–44 population between 1970 and 1998 (a 28-year period) was greater than its percentage increase between 1914 and 1970 (a 56-year period). It is the growth of population that feeds the labor force and its expansion.

The baby boom of the early post–World War II period explains the recent phenomenal growth of the 25–44 population. Born in the late 1940s and 1950s, the baby boomers came into the labor market in force after 1970. As they entered the labor force, the supply of labor exploded.

Figure 4 shows the effects of the baby boom on real wages. Panel (*a*) includes the period 1914 to 1970. The prime age population was not growing rapidly, the supply of labor was not expanding rapidly, and increases in labor productivity caused the demand for labor to outgrow the supply of labor. The result: Real wages rose. Panel (*b*) shows the 1970 to 1998 period. The exceptionally rapid expansion of the prime age population caused the supply of labor to outpace the demand for labor. The result: Real wages fell.

After 1965, birth rates in the United States dropped. Since then, there has been a baby bust instead of a baby boom. As the baby bust cohort matures, employment should grow at slower rates and real wage rates should again rise. In the year 2001, the first baby busters will be in their mid-30s,

(*a*) Rising Real Wages, 1914–1970

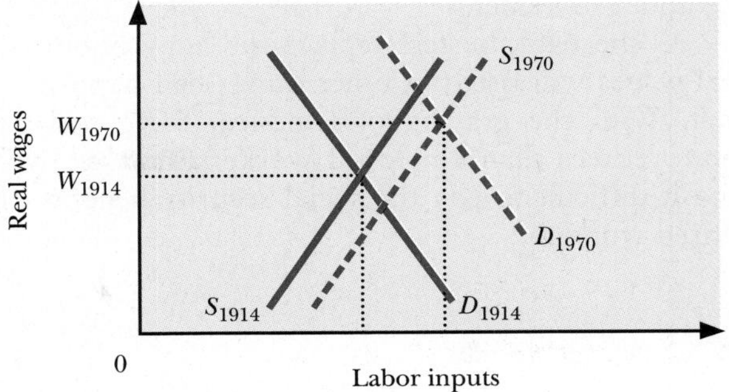

(*b*) Falling Real Wages, 1970–1998

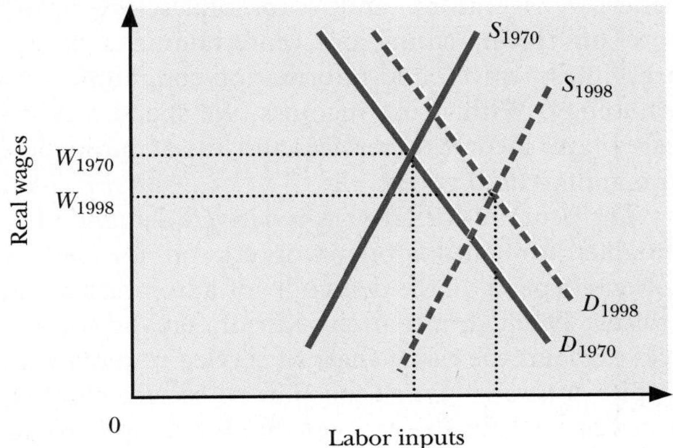

FIGURE 4 Why Real Wages Rise or Fall

During the period 1914 to 1970, in panel (*a*), the growth of the prime age labor force was slow, and the labor supply increased slowly. The increase in the demand for labor due to rising productivity was greater, and real wages rose. During the period from 1970 to 1998, in panel (*b*), the prime labor force grew rapidly, causing the increase in the supply of labor to outpace the increase in the demand for labor. Real wages therefore fell.

and the baby boomers will be 55 years old and thinking about retirement.

As the baby busters replace the baby boomers, real wages will rise, but other things will happen as well. With the graying of America, there will be more retirees than employed workers, and we will find it difficult to pay the social security benefits of retired workers.

Rising Service Employment

As we grow more affluent, we spend our income differently. Instead of spending most of our money on shelter, refrigerators, and automobiles, we spend more on travel, eating out, entertainment, health care, fitness, travel, and information/communication technology. With rising incomes, we spend a rising share of our income on services and less of our income on manufactured goods.

The demand for labor is a derived demand. The demands for automobile workers or for service workers depend on the demands for automobiles and services. The high rate of growth of demand for services explains the rising share of service employment. Despite contrary myths, the shift to service employment does not mean that we will all end up cooking fries at Burger King. The shift has been caused by the fact that employment and earnings opportunities in services have become better than those in manufacturing. The U.S. worker of the twenty-first century will be a software programmer, a financial analyst, an accountant, a technician for sophisticated medical equipment, a specialist in global trading—not an assembly-line worker or a drilling rig operator.

Fringe Benefits

Thirty years ago, virtually all compensation was in the form of money wages. Now nearly one-third of compensation is in the form of benefits.

Benefits are forms of employee compensation such as employer-subsidized health insurance or employer contributions to retirement plans.

The rise in benefits as a form of compensation is explained by government mandates and by tax laws.

Obligations mandated by government regulations—including Social Security, workers' compensation, and unemployment insurance—now comprise nearly one-third of benefit costs. The rise in benefits is also explained by the rapid increase in medical costs, which raise employer contributions to employee health insurance programs.

In addition to higher medical costs and government-mandated contributions, there are several other reasons for the increase in benefits. Employees' demand for nonwage benefits is reinforced by the tax code, which gives tax benefits on retirement contributions and on the employer's portion of health and life insurance premiums. If an employee has to pay an income tax of 25 percent on every extra dollar of wages, that extra dollar is "worth" 75 cents. If the same employee receives an extra dollar of retirement or health-care benefits, which are not taxed, that dollar is worth more to the employee.

The increase in the fringe benefits also accounts for the drop in wages from 1970 to 1998. If a worker is paid $6 an hour in fringe benefits in addition to a $13.50 wage, this arrangement is roughly the same as $19.50 an hour, assuming the worker places the same value on fringe benefits as she does on money income. Whatever the case, the employer must pay the $19.50 rather than the $13.50. Fringe benefits are a compensating wage differential. It is therefore not correct to say that total compensation fell from 1970 to 1998—only paid wages fell.

Labor Unions

Workers in the same industry or occupation may join together to form a labor union.

A **labor union** is a collective organization of workers and employees whose objective is to improve conditions of pay and work.

Unions perform a variety of functions for employee members, the most visible of which is to engage in collective bargaining with employers. Instead of individual negotiation by each employee in regard to wages, fringe benefits, job security, and work conditions, the union represents all employees in collective negotiations.

There are three general types of labor unions: craft unions, such as an electricians' union or a plumbers' union; industrial unions, such as the United Automobile Workers (a union that represents automobile workers of all types) and the United Mine Workers (a union that represents all types of workers engaged in mining); and employee associations, such as the National Education Association, the American Bar Association, the American Medical Association, and state employee associations. Historically, employee associations have primarily been concerned with maintaining professional standards. In the last few decades, however, they have become increasingly involved in the customary union function of improving the pay, benefits, and working conditions of members.

A **craft union** represents workers of a single occupation. An **industrial union** represents employees of an industry regardless of their specific occupation. An **employee association** represents employees in a particular profession in order to both maintain professional standards and improve conditions of pay and work.

A Brief History of American Unionism

Unions were formed to create a more level playing field between workers and employers. Unions were not a powerful force in the American workplace until the late 1930s, even though national conventions of labor unions met as early as 1869. Union membership expanded rapidly after 1886, with the creation of the American Federation of Labor (AFL) under the leadership of Samuel Gompers, the father of the American labor movement.

An antiunion political climate restricted the growth of unionism until the 1930s. Antitrust laws were applied against unions, and companies used private police forces, threats, and intimidation against them. Employees had to sign "yellow dog" contracts, pledging not to join a union.

Industrial unionism blossomed in the 1930s under the leadership of John L. Lewis, who formed the Congress of Industrial Organizations (CIO) in 1936 to organize workers on an industrial rather than a craft basis. In 1955, the AFL and CIO merged to form the AFL-CIO.

Laws passed during the Great Depression promoted the growth of organized labor. The Norris-LaGuardia Act of 1932 gave workers full freedom of association, self-organization, and designation of representatives to negotiate the terms and conditions of their employment. The Norris-LaGuardia Act restricted the use of injunctions and prohibited "yellow dog" contracts. The National Labor Relations Act (the Wagner Act) of 1935 required employers to bargain in good faith with unions, and it became illegal to interfere with employees' rights to organize. The National Labor Relations Board (NLRB) was authorized to investigate unfair labor practices and conduct union elections.

The Taft-Hartley Act of 1947 permitted states to pass right-to-work laws prohibiting the requirement that union membership be a condition for employment. It also allowed major strikes to be delayed by an 80-day cooling-off period if ordered by the U.S. president. The Landrum-Griffin Act of 1959 was designed to protect the rights of union members and to increase union democracy. It included provisions for the periodic reporting of union finances and for regulating union elections.

American Unionism Today

Today, there are about 15 million union members in the United States. Fewer than 15 of every 100 workers belong to a union, down from a peak of 25 percent in the mid-1950s.

There are a number of reasons for the decline in union membership. First, the percentage of women in the labor force has been rapidly increasing, and women have historically not joined unions. The employment share of another group that tends not to join unions, white-collar workers, has risen as well. Increased employment in the service sector (which is only 6 percent unionized) has also retarded unionization. Moreover, there has been a shift in population from the northeast and midwestern states to the southern and southwestern states, where union membership is weakest.

Union Objectives

Unions desire higher wages, better fringe benefits, and safer working conditions for their members. They also want to keep their members employed. Are

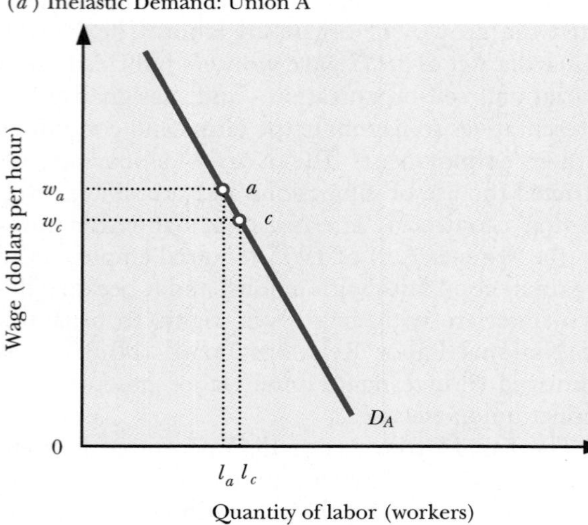

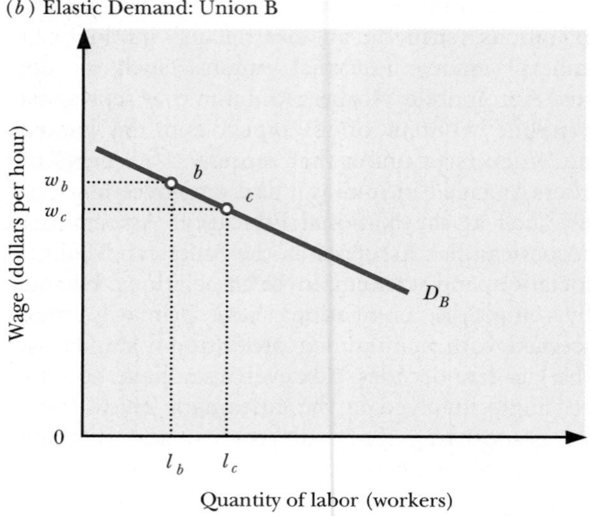

FIGURE 5 The Trade-off between Wages and Employment: The Competitive Case

The demand curve for the members of Union A is relatively inelastic, whereas the demand curve for the members of Union B is relatively elastic. If both unions, in the collective bargaining process, push for the same wage increases, more jobs will be lost by workers in Union B (where demand is elastic) than by workers in Union A.

the two objectives of higher wages and lower unemployment economically compatible?

Let's assume that two unions, A and B, collectively bargain with management to determine wages. For simplicity, we'll assume that the average worker in each union is earning the same wage (w_c) and that the level of employment is the same in each union (at l_c). The demand curve for each union's labor force is graphed in Figure 5. The demand for Union A's labor is inelastic. Thus, a large percentage increase in the wage yields a small percentage reduction in the quantity of labor demanded. The demand for Union B's labor is elastic. Thus, an increase in the wage causes a larger percentage decrease in the quantity of labor demanded than the percentage increase in the wage.

Union B is faced with a dilemma. If it pushes for higher wages, the number of union jobs will decline. Jobs will be traded for higher wages, and those who lose their jobs will be dissatisfied. This wage/employment trade-off is less acute for Union A because the same increase in wages loses fewer jobs.

The **wage/employment trade-off** means that higher wages reduce the number of jobs; lower unemployment requires sacrificing higher wages.

Union Behavior

The wage/employment trade-off explains which types of industries are most easily unionized. Unions are easier to form in industries where the demand for labor is inelastic. Indeed, skilled crafts such as carpentry, printing, glass-blowing, and shoemaking were the first occupations to be unionized.

The demand for skilled labor is relatively inelastic because of the lack of close substitutes. It is not easy to substitute unskilled for skilled labor, or a skilled printer for a skilled glassblower. The last (and presumably most difficult) occupations to organize were the unskilled occupations in which the demand for labor is highly elastic, such as wholesale and retail trade.

Unions seek not only to increase the demand for labor but also to reduce the elasticity of demand. By increasing demand, labor unions can obtain both higher wages and higher employment. By reducing the elasticity of demand, unions can raise wages with a smaller cost in lost employment.

Unions attempt to increase the demand for labor and lower its elasticity of demand in a variety of ways. They lobby for tariffs and quotas on competing foreign products and conduct advertising campaigns telling the public to "look for the union label" or to "buy American." The AFL-CIO has opposed the relaxation of immigration laws and has spoken out against illegal immigration. Unions were strongly opposed to the North American Free Trade Agreement (NAFTA), passed in 1994. Unions support raising the minimum wage to increase wages for unskilled labor relative to the more skilled union workers.

Unions have also pushed for minimum staffing requirements called *featherbedding*, perpetuating jobs that have become redundant (such as fire stokers on diesel-powered locomotives). Unions also bargain for rules that make it difficult to substitute other grades of labor for union labor. In construction contracts, for example, unions specify in detail which jobs can be performed only by electricians or by plumbers.

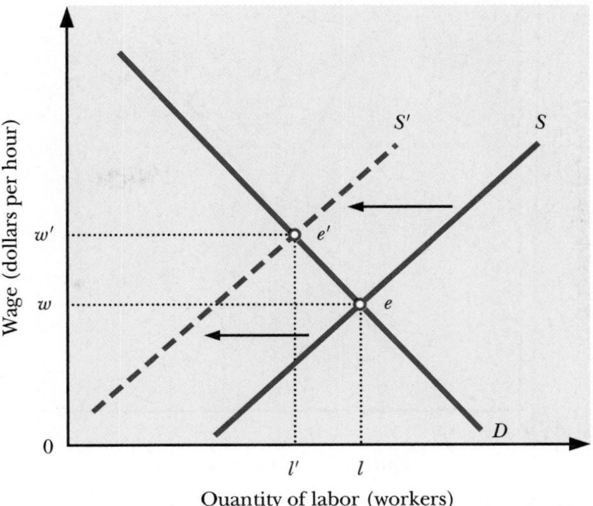

FIGURE 6 Craft Unions and Wages: Limiting Supply

By limiting entry into the profession, a craft union shifts the labor supply curve to the left (from S to S'), and the wage rate of union members is raised above what it would have been without the union.

Limitations of Labor Supply

Another strategy for raising wages is to limit the supply of union labor. Some unions control who will be allowed to work in a particular occupation by means of certification and qualification requirements. In craft unions, the number of union members can be restricted by long apprenticeships, difficult qualifying exams, state licensing, and ceilings on total membership. In the process of limiting labor supply, the union screens out unqualified workers, but it may also exclude some qualified people who are prepared to work in a particular occupation.

Figure 6 shows the effect that limiting the labor supply has on wages. The decrease in supply (from S to S') moves the equilibrium wage/employment combination to higher wages and fewer jobs. If unions are to control wages through limitations on the supply of union labor, it is necessary to prevent employers from substituting nonunion labor. For this reason, craft unions favor rigid certification requirements and rules prohibiting nonunion workers.

Strikes and Collective Bargaining

Industrial unions that represent all of the workers in a particular industry cannot limit the supply of labor. Such unions wield only limited influence on overall labor supply conditions by supporting immigration restrictions, mandatory retirement, shorter workweeks, and laws against teenage employment. Unlike plumbers, electricians, and physicians, industrial unions cannot control the number of union members. Industrial unions, therefore, use collective bargaining to raise the wages of union members.

Collective bargaining is the process whereby a union bargains with management as the representative of all union employees.

Collective bargaining gives workers a stronger voice than if each worker negotiated separately with management.

The threat of a strike is a union's most potent weapon in collective bargaining.

A **strike** occurs when all unionized employees cease to work until management agrees to specific union demands.

The effect of the collective-bargaining process (with threat of strike) is portrayed in Figure 7. The supply curve S represents the supply of labor to the industry if each individual were to bargain separately with management. When a union threatens to strike, it is, in effect, telling management that at wages less than w_c, no labor will be supplied; at the wage of w_c, management can hire as much labor as it wants up to l_c; as wages increase above w_c, management can hire

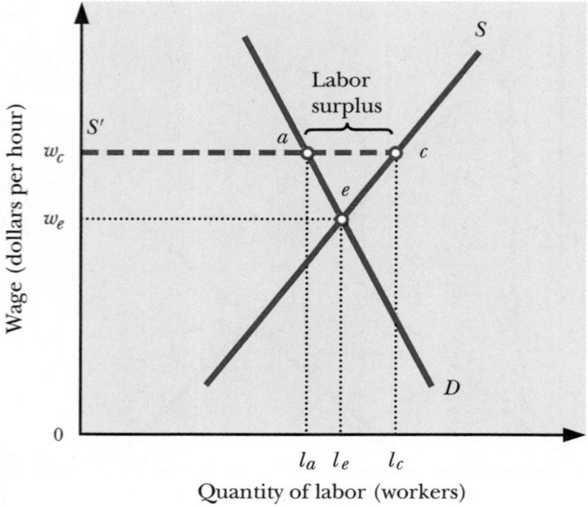

FIGURE 7 Collective Bargaining with the Threat of a Strike

The supply curve S represents the labor supply if each worker were to bargain separately with the employer. The supply curve formed by S' to the left of point c and S above c results from collective bargaining; no union labor will be supplied at a wage below w_c. Point e is the equilibrium wage/employment combination without collective bargaining or the threat of a strike; point a is the equilibrium wage/employment combination with collective bargaining.

increasing amounts of labor beyond l_c. Thus, the new labor supply curve incorporating the threat of a strike is the line S' that connects w_c on the vertical axis with point c and then continues along the original supply curve above point c. Without the threat of a strike, the supply curve would be the original curve S, and point e would be the equilibrium wage/employment combination. With the threat of a strike, the demand curve meets the new supply curve at point a, and the firm hires l_a workers at a wage of w_c.

From the standpoint of union members, collective bargaining has both costs and benefits. The benefits are the higher wages that collective bargaining brings (w_c is higher than w_e). However, if the industry is entirely unionized, some union members who are willing to work at the negotiated wage will not be employed. Although l_c workers are willing to work at w_c, only l_a workers will be hired. The unemployment effects of collective bargaining are regulated by numerous rules within the union governing the order of layoffs. Typically, union members who have seniority (have been in the union the longest time) are laid off last.

The Effects of Unions on Wages and Efficiency

Workers represented by unions earn more than nonunionized workers. In the 1990s, the 18 percent of employed wage and salary workers represented by unions earned 29 percent more than the 82 percent not represented by unions.

The fact that unions raise the wages of their members above nonunionized workers does not prove that unionization results in generally higher wages for the economy as a whole. As discussed above, higher union wages mean less employment in unionized businesses. Those who are left without jobs due to higher union wages spill over into the nonunionized labor force. The fewer the number of union jobs, the greater the supply of labor for other jobs. Accordingly, higher union wages can depress wages elsewhere. (See Example 4.)

Most economists believe that unions have a negative effect on efficiency and labor productivity. If unions use work rules, such as prohibiting carpenters from turning a screw on an electrical fixture, business firms are prevented from combining resources in the most efficient manner. If unions use collective bargaining or control of labor supply to raise union wages above nonunion wages, labor resources will not be used efficiently. If union workers earn $20 per hour and nonunion workers $15 per hour, competitive firms will hire workers until these wage rates equal marginal revenue products. By using collective bargaining or supply restrictions, union workers have a higher productivity. More output could be produced from the same amount of labor by reallocating labor from nonunionized to unionized employment, but labor unions prevent this from happening.

Some economists argue that unions actually raise productivity by improving work conditions, giving workers a voice in the company, and reducing turnover. Unionization could mean that firms have more experienced and dedicated workers.[2] It is unlikely, however, that these positive effects can outweigh the negative effects of unions. In fact, the share prices of

[2]Richard B. Freeman and James L. Medoff, *What Do Unions Do?* (New York: Basic Books, 1982).

EXAMPLE 4

MONOPSONY: HOW LABOR UNIONS CAN INCREASE WAGES AND EMPLOYMENT

There is a special case in which a union not only can improve wages but also can increase employment of its workers. This is the case in which there is a single buyer of labor, called a monopsonist (a buyer monopoly). A single buyer or monopsony faces no competition from other buyers and can pay workers less than their marginal revenue product because the cost of hiring another worker exceeds the wage rate. Why? With a single buyer of labor, the supply curve of workers to the firm is upward sloping. Hiring more workers will drive up the average wage rate the firm must pay. The average/marginal rule tells us that if the average is rising, the margin must exceed the average. Thus, the marginal cost of hiring another factor (called marginal factor cost) exceeds the wage. A profit-maximizing firm will therefore hire workers up to the point where the marginal revenue product of the last worker hired equals its marginal factor cost; accordingly, the marginal revenue product must exceed the wage.

A union can take the advantage of the wedge between marginal revenue and the wage by organizing the workforce to ask for a higher wage. If the union is effective in this regard and if the higher wage is less than the marginal factor cost, not only will the the workers earn more wages, but more will be employed.

A big question in economic research has been, How extensive is monopsony? A recent survey concluded that monopsony power is "probably rare but occasionally large." Well-known examples are U.S. professional players of baseball and other sports, small-town teachers, nurses, and coal miners in company towns. On the whole, the authors conclude that monopsony power is "widespread but small on the average."

Source: William Boal and Michael Ransom, "Monosony in the Labor Market," *Journal of Economic Literature* (March 1997): 86–112.

companies usually fall when they are unionized. Unionization is taken as a sign that the profits of the company will suffer.[3]

Labor Unions: A Brief International Perspective

There are significant differences among the labor union movements in the United States, Europe, and Asia. Although associations of journeymen existed in the form of medieval guilds, labor unions were not organized in Europe until the nineteenth century. The United Kingdom's Trade Union Act of 1871 guaranteed legal recognition for labor unions. On the Continent, unions were organized on industrial rather than craft lines, and they engaged in partisan political activity. In Germany, for example, unions were responsible for much social legislation prior to World War I. The Solidarity labor movement in Poland played a major political role in achieving Polish independence in 1989.

In Europe, labor organizations tend to be either constituted as or affiliated with political parties, usually from the left wing. In England, the labor unions joined forces with the socialists to form the Labour Party in 1893. In Sweden, there is a close alliance between the two major labor unions and the Social Democratic Party. In Italy, Belgium, and the Netherlands, rival Christian and socialist trade union movements are present. The American labor movement avoided forming a political party, although it tends to support the Democratic Party.

[3]Richard Ruback and Martin Zimmerman, "Unionization and Profitability: Evidence from the Capital Market," *Journal of Political Economy,* December 1984, 1134–1157.

The United States is one of the least unionized industrial economies. Membership in Germany, Japan, and the United Kingdom hovers around one-quarter to one-third.

In Germany, unions are organized on an industry basis and are grouped into federations. Collective bargaining takes place at industrywide levels, and compulsory arbitration is used to settle disputes. German enterprise laws require that union representatives sit on management boards in large companies.

Sweden is dominated by a comprehensive labor movement. Virtually all blue-collar workers belong to the Confederation of Trade Unions, and white-collar workers belong to one of two other unions. As close allies of the Social Democratic Party, Swedish unions have developed profit-sharing plans and have pushed for social welfare policies to equalize the distribution of income.

In Japan each company has its own union that cuts across all craft and class boundaries. Japanese union presidents are key workers who are often promoted to the ranks of management. Japanese unions typically foster cooperation between management and workers, and commonly adopt a management perspective. The founding slogan of the Nissan Company labor union, for example, is "Those who truly love their union, love their company."

In this chapter, we have examined how labor markets work and how unions affect wages and economic efficiency. In the next chapter, we shall turn to the nonlabor factors of production: land, capital, and entrepreneurship.

SUMMARY

1. Labor is different from the two other factors of production because workers desire leisure and have preferences concerning different jobs. Laborers cannot be bought and sold. A labor market brings buyers and sellers of labor services together. The buyer who must accept the market wage as given is a price taker in the labor market.

2. When wage rates rise, the opportunity cost of leisure increases, as does income. Whether or not the aggregate labor-supply curve will be backward bending depends upon the relative strengths of the income and substitution effects. Whether people work in household production or in the market labor force depends upon the value of time in the home compared with their market wage.

3. If firms are price takers, they hire labor to the point where $W = \text{MRP}$. The firm's MRP schedule is its labor demand schedule. The labor demand curve will be negatively sloped both for firms and for the market.

4. The labor supply curve for a particular occupation will be positively sloped because workers must be paid their opportunity costs.

5. The labor demand curve will shift if the demand for the firm's final product changes, if the price of either substitute or complementary factors changes, or if the productivity of labor changes. The labor supply curve will shift if job conditions or wages in other industries change.

6. The market wage rate is typically that wage at which the quantity demanded of labor of a single grade equals the quantity supplied. A new equilibrium wage/quantity combination will result when either the market supply or market demand curve shifts. Demand and supply analysis explains the behavior of real wages and rising service employment. The post–World War II baby boom helps explain the recent decline in real wage rates. Government legislation and taxation explain the rising importance of benefits.

7. A union is a collective organization of workers and employees whose objective is to improve pay and work conditions. A craft union represents workers of a particular occupation. An industrial union represents workers of a particular industry.

8. The formation of unions in the United States was aided by prolabor legislation beginning with the Norris-LaGuardia Act of 1932, which facilitated union organizing drives. The National Labor Relations Act of 1935 made it illegal for employers to interfere with the rights of employees to organize. The Taft-Hartley Act of 1947 was a reaction against the prounion legislation of the 1930s.

9. Union membership in the United States is lower than that of most industrialized countries.

10. Unions must weigh the advantages of higher wages against the disadvantages of less employment. Unions respond to the trade-off between jobs and employment by attempting to increase the

demand for union labor and reduce the elasticity of that demand. In collective bargaining, the most potent weapon of the union is the threat of a strike.

11. Unions have raised the wages of their members relative to nonunion wages. Unions can have a negative effect on nonunion wages. When unions raise wages in the union sector, the workers who lose employment spill over into the nonunion sector. This increase in the labor supply lowers nonunion wages. Most economists believe that unions adversely affect labor productivity. Another view argues that unions raise the labor productivity of union workers.

KEY TERMS

labor market 311
internal labor market 311
household production 312
leisure 312
efficiency-wage model 317
benefits 320
labor union 320
craft union 321
industrial union 321
employee association 321
wage/employment trade-off 322
collective bargaining 323
strike 323

QUESTIONS AND PROBLEMS

1. Why do labor's special features cause the labor market to work differently from the other factor markets?

2. What is the information cost strategy of a firm that fills all positions by promoting from within?

3. A price-taking firm in both its product and factor markets is currently employing 25 workers. The twenty-fifth worker's marginal revenue product is $1000 per week, and the worker's wage is $800 per week. Is this firm maximizing its profits? If not, what would you advise the company to do?

4. There is a close positive association between labor productivity and wages. Use the theory presented in this chapter to explain this relationship.

5. State law in New Jersey requires that employees in licensed gambling casinos be residents of New Jersey for a specified period of time. What effect does this legislation have upon the demand for casino employees in New Jersey?

6. During recessions and periods of falling wages, the number of volunteers for the all-volunteer army rises. Use the theory of this chapter to explain why this supply of labor rises.

7. You are a surgeon earning $200,000 per year. When the demand for your services increases, the charge for each operation increases by 25 percent. What effect will this increase have on the number of operations you perform?

8. Rank each of the following jobs according to the difficulty of devising an incentive pay system that is compatible with the overall objectives of the firm. Explain your ranking.
   a. Janitorial work performed at night in an office building
   b. Assembly-line work in a washing-machine factory
   c. Traveling sales work
   d. The creation of hand-carved figures for a crafts company
   e. Professional basketball playing

9. Using the computer programming example in the chapter, explain what would happen to the wage of computer programmers if the number of program lines produced per hour were to double for each level of labor input. Explain what would happen if the price paid per program line fell to $1.

10. Draw hypothetical labor demand and labor supply curves for truck drivers. Shift the curves to show what happens when
    a. Truck driving becomes safer.
    b. Truck drivers become more efficient.
    c. Truck drivers must be licensed by a state agency.
    d. The earning of surgeons increases.
    e. The earning of moving-equipment operators falls.

11. Explain how the efficiency-wage model justifies paying wages that exceed marginal productivity.

12. If you were the president of a major industrial union, what would your attitude be toward free immigration? What would your attitude be toward the minimum-wage law? Explain.
13. Explain why both the automobile unions and the management of the automobile industry favor import restrictions on foreign-made cars.
14. You belong to a union of bank tellers. What would your attitude be toward automated bank tellers? Explain.
15. If unions do succeed in raising productivity, what effect would this increase have on the costs of production of unionized versus nonunionized companies?

INTERNET CONNECTION

16. Using the link from http://www.awl.com/ruffin_gregory, examine Tables 2–4 in "Changes in Hours Worked Since 1950" on the Federal Reserve Bank of Minneapolis Web site.
    a. Using Table 2, plot the number of hours worked per week by men and then by women from 1950–1990. What do you conclude from the data? Do you have an explanation?
    b. In what age bracket do people work the greatest number of hours per week? Has this changed over time?

PUZZLE ANSWERED: Society would allocate its labor force so that some people are doing the dirty jobs and other people the fun or pleasant jobs even if the entire labor force were homogeneous. According to the theory of compensating differentials, people doing the hard jobs would have to be paid more to compensate them for the working conditions or, indeed, training costs; otherwise, with equal wages, all would try to work in the jobs that were easy and required no training. Compensating differentials are the allocation mechanism.

Chapter 18

INTEREST, RENT, AND PROFIT

Chapter Insight

About 73 percent of all the income in the United States is earned from salaries and wages. While we might earn a little bit each year from interest on a savings account or dividends on shares of stock, most of us live on what we earn through the sweat of our labor. Most of us are satisfied with this arrangement—never thinking of starting a business, of saving or borrowing to buy land, or of investing our last penny in a real estate deal.

There are, however, people who live off businesses they have started, from rents they receive for renting their land to a shopping center, from interest they receive from loaning money to shopkeepers, or from profitable investments in the stock market. They do not live off a steady paycheck; they live off what they earn for themselves.

Whether these people earn a lot or a little appears to depend on several factors. Have they taken a safe or risky approach? The most successful businesspeople did not get rich by playing it safe: They took risks. Were they smarter than others? Did they see and take advantage of opportunities that others did not see? Did they have good or bad luck? Maybe others were just as talented or took as many risks, but their luck was bad.

In this chapter, we shall consider the sources of nonlabor income and its relationship to risk, ingenuity, and luck.

LEARNING OBJECTIVES

After completing this chapter, you will be able to:

1. Describe how interest rates are related to productivity and thrift.
2. Understand why interest rates on some assets are higher than on others.
3. Explain the function of economic rent.
4. Identify the sources of economic profit.

CHAPTER PUZZLE: Is there any social reason why some athletes should earn $10 million per year?

INTEREST

Capital goods are required for the production of consumer goods. Capital goods such as trucks, conveyors, buildings, lathes, cranes, hammers, and computers harness the mechanical, electrical, and chemical powers of nature to expand the production possibilities of society far beyond what could otherwise be accomplished by unaided human hands or minds. Productivity increases, for example, when a net is used instead of bare hands to catch fish, or when workers assemble cars on an assembly line with sophisticated equipment rather than in a small garage with hand tools.

Saving is necessary if a society is to invest in capital goods. Through saving, resources are diverted from producing consumption goods to producing capital goods. When people save, they buy stocks and bonds or deposit their funds in various bank accounts. Although some of these funds are used to finance the consumption expenditures of ordinary people, the rest are channeled directly or indirectly into investments in new buildings, plants, machinery, and inventories.

We human beings are impatient. To be convinced of the value of saving a dollar today, we must be rewarded with more than a dollar tomorrow. Because capital is productive, a dollar invested today in capital goods yields more than a dollar tomorrow. Thus, investors are willing to pay the interest that savers demand. Interest coordinates the number of dollars that businesses want to invest with the number that people want to save.

Interest is the price of credit and is determined in credit markets.

The Stock of Capital

Economists distinguish between *tangible capital* and *intangible capital.* Tangible capital differs from the other factors of production in that, in its concrete form (from trucks and computers to fishnets and shovels), it has already been produced. An automatic assembly line is the product of past work and effort.

Intangible capital has two forms. *Research and development (R&D) capital* consists of accumulated investments in technology, productive knowledge, and know-how; *human capital* consists of accumulated investments in human beings—in training, education, and improved health that increase the productive capacities of people. We shall consider human-capital investments, an important determinant of income distribution, in detail in the next chapter. Human-capital theory suggests that the human capital embodied in trained labor is "produced" in the same economic sense as a truck or factory.

The stock of capital that exists in an economy at any given moment depends on (1) the accumulated savings and investment decisions that have been made in the past, and (2) the extent to which old capital goods have undergone depreciation through use or obsolescence.

Depreciation is the decrease in the economic value of capital goods as they are used in the production process.

The new capital goods that are added to the stock of capital during a given period depend on how much consumers are saving and how much firms are investing. Over time, capital goods accumulate and depreciate. If the rate of accumulation exceeds the rate of depreciation, the stock of capital will grow.

> The current stock of capital is determined by past savings and investment decisions. The stock of capital grows if the rate of capital accumulation exceeds the rate of depreciation. The stock of capital declines if the rate of accumulation is less than the rate of depreciation.

Credit Markets

Robinson Crusoe, living alone on a deserted island, did not need a special market to coordinate his saving and investment decisions. When he took three days off from fishing to weave a net, he was both *saving* (giving up some present consumption) and *investing* (increasing his future consumption). Simultaneous saving and investing were also characteristic of early agricultural societies. Farmers saved and invested in the same act of taking time off from current production to drain a swamp or to build an earthen dam in order to produce capital goods. In a modern economy, however, we use financial assets—stocks, bonds, bank credit, and trade credit—to finance the accumulation of capital goods. Investors and savers are usually separate entities, with their actions coordinated by credit, or capital markets.

Credit, or **capital, markets** facilitate the exchange of financial assets in a modern society.

Credit, or capital, markets are necessary because of specialization. Business firms have the ability to take advantage of profitable investment opportunities by expanding production capacities, but, unlike Robinson Crusoe, they must usually find a separate source of funds. Households, meanwhile, specialize in saving because they do not have the information to act on profitable investment opportunities. Therefore, households can trade their savings with businesses who wish to use them for investments. In credit markets, firms wishing to invest in capital goods borrow from households.

The growth of the stock of tangible capital is paralleled by the growth of the financial assets of those who accumulate savings. These financial assets, such as stocks, bonds, and various IOUs, are specific types of claims on the net productivity of real capital. The owners of such capital receive *interest* (or *dividend*) *income* from investors as payment for the use of their capital.

The Rate of Interest

An interest rate is usually expressed as an annual percentage rate.

An **interest rate** measures the yearly cost of borrowing as a percentage of the amount loaned.

For example, if you borrow $1000 on January 1 and repay $1100 ($1000 borrowed plus $100 interest) on December 31 of that same year, the $100 interest represents a 10 percent rate of increase on an annual percentage basis. If the loan is for only 6 months and $1050 is repaid on June 30, the $50 interest still represents a 10 percent annual rate.

The rate of interest is not the "price of money." *Money* is the medium of exchange used by an economy; it is the unit of borrowing, rather than the act itself. The "price of credit" is a better description of the interest rate because the term *credit* incorporates the passage of time between borrowing and repayment.

The rate of interest shows the terms of trade between the present and future. A low interest rate means that future goods are expensive relative to present goods; a high interest rate means future goods are cheap relative to present goods. Suppose you are planning to go to law school in four years, and you know that it will cost $50,000. If the interest rate is 10 percent, you would have to set aside $34,247 now. At 5 percent interest, you would have to set aside $41,152 now. If interest rates are high, you will not have to save as much as you would with low interest rates. In other words, high interest rates make future goods and services (that is, the law degree) cheaper in terms of present sacrifices.

Determining the Rate of Interest

The interest rate is determined in credit markets just as the price of General Motors stock or the price of July wheat is determined by the forces of demand and supply—by the demand and supply for loanable funds.

The Supply of Loanable Funds. Credit markets arrange for the lending and borrowing of loanable funds.

Loanable funds comprise the lending from all households, governments, and businesses, or the bank credit made available to borrowers in credit markets.

The supply of loanable funds comes primarily from the net savings of businesses and households. If we have savings, we have choices concerning how to invest these savings. We must decide among bank savings accounts, government bonds, stock market shares, life insurance, or even precious metals. Whether we lend our savings to borrowers or buy stocks or precious metals depends on the price we are offered. It will simplify matters if we consider the

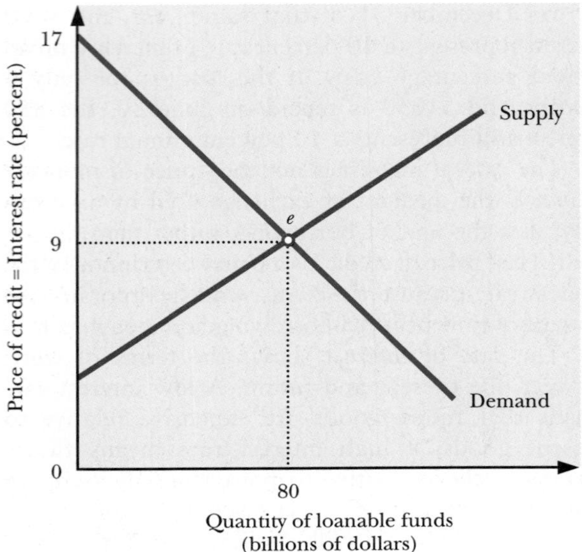

FIGURE 1 The Market for Loanable Funds

The supply curve shows the quantity of loanable funds offered by lenders at different interest rates; lenders will offer more at high interest rates. The demand curve shows the quantity of loanable funds demanded by borrowers at different interest rates; less will be demanded at high interest rates. The market for loanable funds is in equilibrium at an interest rate of 9 percent, where the quantity demanded equals the quantity supplied.

purchase of bonds. The supply curve in Figure 1 shows the quantity of loanable funds savers are willing to save and, thereby, to make available to lenders at each interest rate. This supply curve is positively sloped because a larger quantity of loanable funds will be made available to lenders at high interest rates than at low interest rates, if all other things are equal. The higher the interest rate, the more attractive are bonds and savings accounts and the less attractive are stocks and precious metals.

The Demand for Loanable Funds. The demand for loanable funds is principally the demand for new investments in capital goods of businesses. Although households also demand loanable funds for automobile loans, consumer credit, and home mortgages, here we shall concentrate on business investment.

What determines the demand for capital goods? New capital raises the output and, therefore, the revenue of the firm for a number of years because capital goods are in use for more than 1 year. A machine may be used for 8 years and a plant may be used for 35 years. Capital's *marginal revenue product* (the amount an extra unit of capital will contribute to a firm's revenues) must be estimated over each year of the capital's useful life in order to determine the rate of return of a capital good.

The **rate of return of a capital good** is that rate for which the present value of the stream of marginal revenue products for each year of the good's life is equal to the cost of the capital good.

The law of diminishing returns applies to capital just as it applies to labor. Additional capital investment projects yield successively lower rates of return. In making their investment plans, businesses consider a variety of investment projects. By adding a new wing onto their plant, they may achieve a high rate of return. By acquiring new equipment, they may achieve a substantial but lower rate of return. Successive projects bring lower and lower rates of return due to the law of diminishing returns.

The demand curve for loanable funds in Figure 1 shows the quantity of loanable funds that investors are prepared to borrow at each interest rate. It is negatively sloped because at high interest rates there are fewer investment projects that have a rate of return equal to or greater than the interest rate. At low interest rates, there are more investment projects with rates of return equal to or greater than the interest rate. The demand curve also reflects the rate of return on capital-investment projects; business firms will be willing to add to their capital stock as long as the rate of return of investment projects exceeds the rate of interest.

The rate of return measures the marginal benefit of capital, and the interest rate measures the marginal cost of capital. Business firms will carry out those investment projects in which the rate of return exceeds the interest rate. Firms will not carry out investment projects with returns below the interest rate.

The cost of additional capital is the interest rate that firms must pay for credit. The marginal benefit of capital is its rate of return.

The equilibrium amount of capital for the firm will be that amount at which the rate of interest and the rate of return on the last investment project are equal.

The Equilibrium Interest Rate. Like any other price, the rate of interest established by the credit market is that rate at which the quantity of loanable funds supplied equals the quantity demanded.

In Figure 1, the quantity supplied of loanable funds equals the quantity demanded at point *e*, where the interest rate is 9 percent and there are $80 billion worth of investment projects that yield a rate of return of 9 percent or above. Thus, the equilibrium rate of interest is 9 percent.

> The equilibrium interest rate equates the quantity demanded and quantity supplied for loanable funds. Only those investments yielding the equilibrium (market) interest rate or above are financed.

Productivity and Thrift. The demand for loanable funds reflects the basic productivity of capital.

Firms demand loanable funds for investment as long as rates of return are greater than or equal to the rate of interest. Any occurrence that makes capital more productive will shift the demand curve to the right and cause the interest rate to rise. The supply curve of loanable funds reflects the basic thriftiness of the population. Any occurrence that causes the population to be more thrifty (that is, to save more at each interest rate) will shift the supply curve to the right and cause the interest rate to fall.

If a technological breakthrough (such as new information technologies) raises the productivity of capital, the demand curve will shift to the right, driving up the interest rate, if all other things are equal, as in panel (*a*) of Figure 2. If tax laws are changed to reward those families that save, the supply curve will shift to the right, lowering the market rate of interest, if all other things are equal, as in panel (*b*) of Figure 2.

Real Versus Nominal Interest Rate: The Impact of Inflation

Inflation occurs when the money prices of goods, on the average, rise over time. Supply-and-demand analysis explains how inflation affects interest rates. Anticipated inflation affects both the demand and supply of loanable funds. Inflation causes the dollars to be repaid over the course of the loan to become cheaper. Lenders will become less eager to lend and the borrower more eager to borrow if the rate of

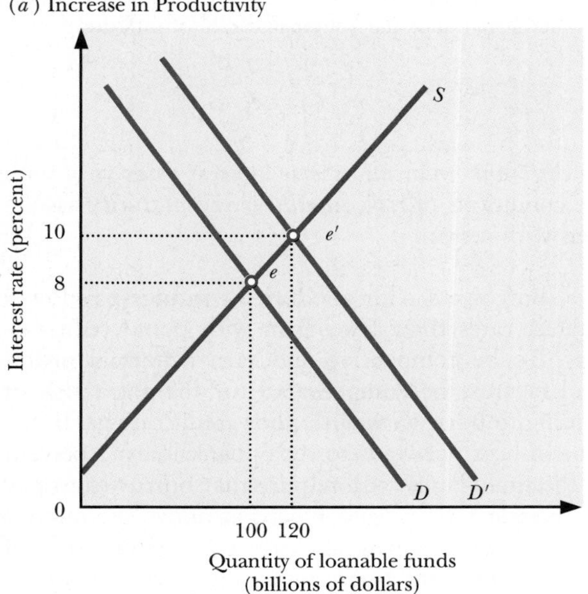

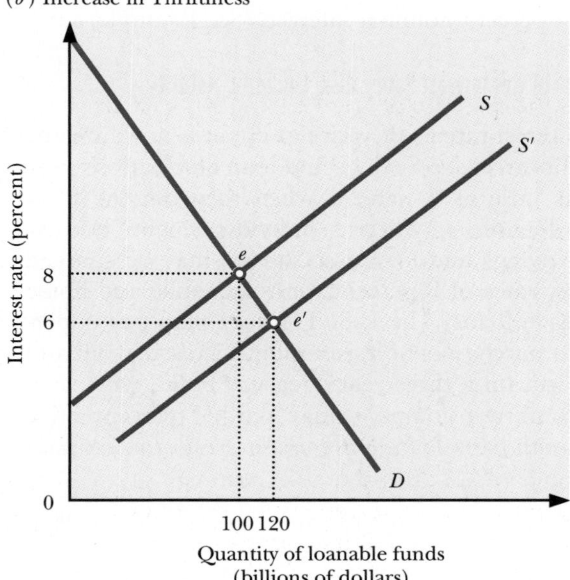

FIGURE 2 Interest Rates, Productivity, and Thriftiness

Panel (*a*) shows that an increase in the productivity of capital raises interest rates, and panel (*b*) shows that an increase in the thriftiness of the population lowers interest rates.

inflation is expected to increase. Clearly, lenders will want to be compensated for the declining value of the dollars in which the loan is repaid, and borrowers will be willing to pay a higher interest rate because they can repay the loan in cheaper dollars.

It is the real interest rate that matters to borrowers and lenders rather than the nominal interest rate.

The **nominal interest rate** is the cost of borrowing expressed in terms of current dollars unadjusted for inflation.

The **real interest rate** equals the nominal interest rate minus the anticipated rate of inflation.[1]

Anticipated inflation causes the demand curve for loanable funds to shift to the right and the supply curve of loanable funds to shift to the left. In Figure 3, the initial equilibrium interest rate is 4 percent when there is 0 percent inflation. If both borrowers and lenders now anticipate a 5 percent rate of inflation, both curves shift upward by the same amount. When a 5 percent inflation is anticipated, borrowers will be willing to pay 5 percent more. Lenders will require 5 percent more to stay even with inflation.

The demand and supply curves for loanable funds at 9 percent nominal interest intersect at the same quantity of loanable funds (in constant dollars) as at 4 percent nominal interest. (See Example 1.)

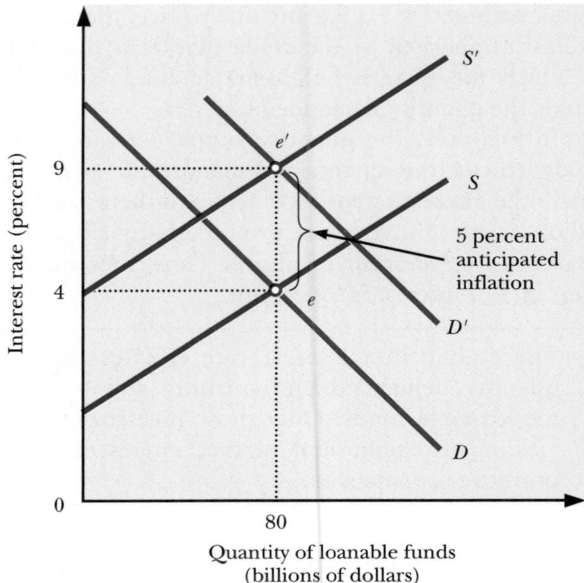

FIGURE 3 Anticipated Inflation and Interest Rates

The original equilibrium at a 0 percent rate of inflation is point *e*. When a 5 percent inflation rate is anticipated, borrowers will be willing to pay an interest rate 5 percent higher than before, and lenders must be paid an interest rate 5 percent higher because repayments are in cheaper dollars. Thus, both *S* and *D* shift upward by 5 percent. The new equilibrium is point *e'*, at a 9 percent nominal interest rate. The real interest rate is still 4 percent (equal to the nominal rate minus the anticipated rate of inflation).

The Structure of Interest Rates: Risk, Liquidity, Maturity

The interest rate as the price of credit is not the same for all borrowers. Savings and loan associations may pay as little as 2 percent when they borrow from their depositors, whereas individuals who borrow from savings and loan associations may be charged interest rates of 9 percent for automobile and home mortgage loans. The U.S. Treasury may pay 5 percent to purchasers of its six-month Treasury bill and 7 percent on a three-year Treasury bond, whereas a near-bankrupt company may pay 21 percent on a six-month bank loan. *Different interest rates are paid on different financial assets.* Interest rates vary with the conditions of *risk, liquidity,* and *maturity* associated with a loan.

Risk. Borrowers with good credit ratings pay lower interest rates than borrowers with poor credit ratings. To be competitive and earn a normal profit, lenders must be compensated for the extra risk of lending to borrowers with poor credit ratings. If one type of borrower fails to repay bank loans 1 percent of the time, banks will require that borrower to pay an interest rate at least 1 percent above the interest rate charged borrowers with a 0 percent risk of default. The extra 1 percent is called a *risk premium.* Lenders who demand 10 percent interest per month of those with poor credit histories are demanding an enormous risk premium because of the high default rate on such loans. (See Example 2.)

[1]This formula holds approximately. The actual formula is

$$r = i - p - rp$$

where r is the real interest rate, p is the inflation rate, and i is the nominal interest rate. When r and p are small, rp is close to zero. If $r = 0.10$ and $p = 0.05$, then $rp = 0.005$.

EXAMPLE 1

The Timeless Real Rate of Interest

The real interest rate balances the thriftiness of the population with the productivity of capital.

Surprisingly, the real rate of interest has remained about the same for centuries. It is possible to trace the course of real interest rates from Roman times to the present by examining newspapers and other records. In ancient Rome, the real interest rate was 4 percent for more than a century. In the United States and the United Kingdom, the real interest rate was around 3 percent from 1867 to 1995.

The long-term stability of real interest rates suggests that the real productivity of capital and thriftiness have been remarkably stable over time.

Source: Julian Simon, "Great and Almost Great Magnitudes in Economics," *Journal of Economic Perspectives* 4 Winter 1990: 151–152.

EXAMPLE 2

The Price of Risk

A good measure of risk is the interest rate "spread" between government bonds and low-grade junk bonds. Since government bonds are assumed to have no default risk, the difference in interest rates measures the risk premium that must be paid to people who buy low-grade or junk bonds in order to compete with government bonds. The accompanying chart shows the risk premium measured over the 46-year period from 1953 to 1999. Note that the periods in which the price of oil increased sharply (the middle and late 1970s and early 1980s) also showed higher than normal risks for business activity. In the early 1980s, the risk premium reached nearly 4 percent. In the vibrant economy of the 1990s, the risk premium was around 2 percent.

Source: http://www.Economagic.com

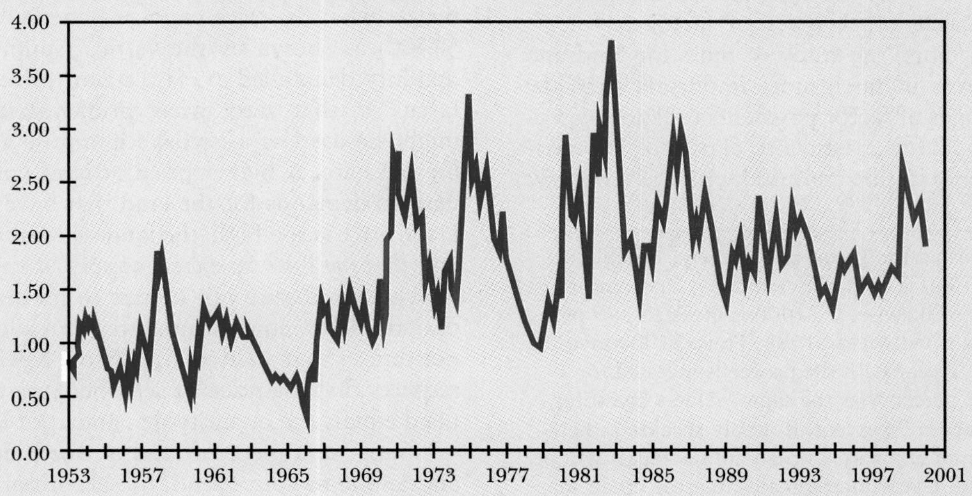

Liquidity. A financial asset that can be turned into cash quickly or with a small penalty is said to be *liquid.* People may be willing to hold savings accounts paying 3 percent interest when six-month certificates of deposit pay 6 percent simply because the former can be turned into cash (the medium of exchange) quickly and without penalty. Interest rates usually vary inversely with liquidity.

Maturity. Interest rates also vary with the term of maturity. A corporation borrowing $1000 for 1 year may pay a lower annual rate of interest than if it borrows the same $1000 for 2 years. If the credit market expects the interest rate on one-year loans to be 6 percent during one year and 12 percent during the next, the interest rate on a two-year loan covering the same period will be 9 percent—the average of the two interest rates.[2]

RENT

The rent on land is a relatively small proportion—about 2 or 3 percent—of the total payments to factors of production. This figure includes payments for the natural fertility of the land and its locational advantages but excludes capital improvements in the land (such as irrigation). The unique feature of land and other natural resources is that they are inelastic in supply. They are nature's bounty, and the quantity supplied is not affected by the price received as a factor payment.

Relative inelasticity of supply can characterize productive factors other than land and natural resources. Because other types of factor payments resemble land rents, the study of rents for land and natural resources is much more important than the small percentages of factor payments to land suggest.

"Rents" paid for apartments, cars, tools, or moving trucks should not be confused with the *economic rents* studied in this section. "Rental payments" for the temporary use of a particular piece of property owned by someone else can be returns to land, labor, or capital. Apartment rent is a payment both to land (for the land on which the apartment building sits) and to capital (for the structure itself). Thus, the common term *rent* is simply a price or rental rate rather than a payment to a specific factor of production.

Pure Economic Rent

The price of a fixed amount of land or some natural resource like a coal deposit or diamond mine—or any other factor in fixed supply—is determined by its demand. The market demand curve is the sum of the demand curves of all firms in that market. The demand curve of each firm is its marginal revenue product curve. The supply curve is completely inelastic; more land is not forthcoming at higher prices. The competitive price paid to land is that price at which the fixed quantity supplied equals the quantity demanded. As such, the equilibrium price rations the fixed supply of land among its various claimants.

Pure economic rent ensures that the factors of production that are fixed in supply are put to their highest and best use.

A **pure economic rent** is the price paid to a productive factor that is completely inelastic in supply. Land is the classic example of such a factor.

Figure 4 illustrates the concept of pure economic rent. The same quantity of land will be supplied, no matter what the price per acre (whether $0, $900, or $1400) as shown by the vertical supply curve. The quantity demanded at, say, a zero price will be very large. At that zero price, prime agricultural land might be used as a garbage dump or as a junkyard for old cars. A higher price of land will cut off the various demands for the land that have a low MRP. If the price is too high, the land will not be fully used, and there will be an excess supply. If the price is too low, the land may not be put to its best use. Prices that are below equilibrium levels can allow land to be put to uses that yield relatively low MRPs. Efficiency requires that the price be set where the quantity supplied equals the quantity demanded of land.

Suppose a piece of land is worth $1000 to you and $2000 to your friend, Jill. If both of you can rent the land for, say, $800, you would both want it, and

[2]If $1000 is invested for 1 year at 6 percent, it will yield $1060; if the $1060 is then reinvested at 12 percent it will yield $1188. Likewise, if $1000 is invested at 9 percent for 2 years, it will yield $1188. Thus, $1000 invested at 6 percent for 1 year with the proceeds invested for 1 more year at 12 percent has the same yield as investing $1000 for 2 years at 9 percent. Roughly speaking, the 2-year interest rate (expressed on an annual basis) will be an average of the 1-year interest rates that the credit market anticipates over the 2 years.

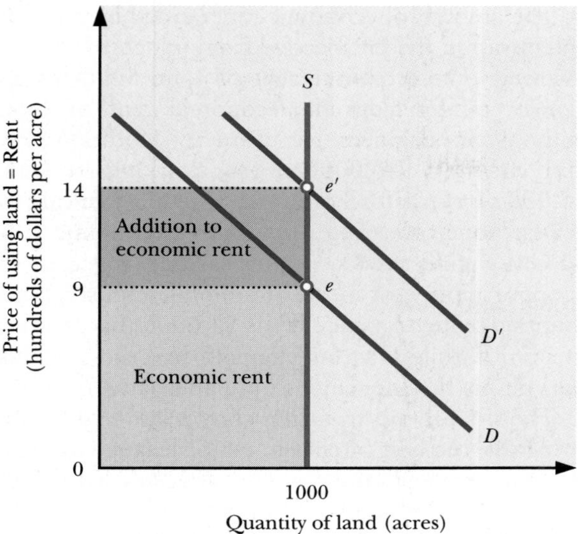

FIGURE 4 Pure Economic Rent

Because the supply of land is fixed at 1000 acres, the supply curve *S* is perfectly inelastic. The equilibrium price of \$900 per acre at point *e* is pure economic rent, since the land has no alternative uses. The entire rental payment is a surplus over opportunity costs. In this case, opportunity costs are zero. If the demand curve for land increases from *D* to *D′*, the economic rent will rise from \$900 to \$1400 per acre at point *e′*. Changes in economic rents are determined by demand because supply is fixed.

you might get it and Jill not. If so, the land is not in its highest and best use. But if the price rises to \$1001, the land will go to Jill and to its highest and best use.

> The pure economic rent that is paid to a productive factor does not increase its supply, which is perfectly inelastic. Pure economic rent in a competitive market ensures efficient resource use by rationing the available supply to the most efficient use.

If pure economic rents were not paid for beachfront properties, they might be used as used car lots or garbage dumps. If pure economic rents were not paid to the owners of underground oil deposits, they might choose to keep their land unspoiled by the sight of drilling rigs.

When something is perfectly inelastic in supply, price incentives cannot lead to an increase in its supply. This feature has made land an attractive target of taxation. The price of a good or factor that is perfectly inelastic in supply is therefore determined by demand. If the demand curve in Figure 4 shifts from *D* to *D′*, competitive economic rents will be bid up.

From the standpoint of the economy as a whole, rent is not a true opportunity cost to society. The land and other resources that are fixed in supply are free gifts of nature; the economy has use of the land whether it pays something or nothing. In the case of pure rent, the payment to the factor of production exceeds the payment required to keep the resource available to the economy by the entire amount of the rental payment. Thus, the opportunity cost is zero. From the standpoint of an individual firm that uses agricultural land, however, economic rent is most certainly a cost of production. In order to bid the land away from other uses, the individual firm must pay the competitive price. In other words, *rents accrue to factor owners, not factor users.*

Quasi Rents

Naturally, productive land and land located in prime urban and manufacturing areas are inelastic in supply in the long run. No matter what is done, no matter what economic rents are paid, such land cannot be increased in supply. Payments for such land are *pure economic rents.* Because the opportunity cost of this land to society is zero in both the short and long runs, the entire factor payment is a payment of economic rent. Many factors that are fixed in supply in the short run, however, are more elastic in supply in the long run.

For example, in a booming Sun Belt city, the amount of space in office buildings is fixed in supply in the short run; when the demand for office space increases, office rental rates rise dramatically. The demand curve shifts upward (or to the right) along a vertical supply curve. In the long run, however, developers will respond to soaring office rents by constructing new office buildings. As the buildings are completed, the supply curve becomes more elastic and office rents are reduced.

The supply of professional soccer players is essentially fixed in the short run, since it takes years of training and practice for a player to attain professional caliber. If the demand for professional soccer players increases because of an increase in the popularity of the sport, the earnings of the fixed number of soccer professionals will increase. In the short run, they will be able to earn extraordinary salaries.

In the long run, however, new professional-caliber players will enter the profession, attracted by the high earnings. The supply becomes more elastic, and the extraordinary earnings of soccer professionals will be bid down.

As these examples show, the owners of a resource that is fixed in supply in the short run will receive economic rent. But such a payment is a quasi rent, not a pure economic rent, because it cannot be maintained in the long run.

A **quasi rent** is a payment in excess of the short-run opportunity cost necessary to induce the owners of the resources to offer their resources for sale or rent in the short run.

In the long run, quasi rents will disappear as the supply curve becomes more elastic. In the long run, the supply curve will become more and more elastic until quasi rents have been dissipated. At this point, the factor of production receives no economic rents.

Economic Rent and Other Factors of Production

Pure economic rents represent an extreme case of factor payment. At the other extreme is payment to a factor that just equals its *opportunity cost* (its earnings in its next-best alternative use). A factor of production that is perfectly elastic in supply earns no economic rent because the factor is paid its opportunity cost. For example, a small farmer must compete with other farmers and potential users of the land. If the farmer does not pay what the land could earn in its next-best use, the land will be used elsewhere.

In between factors of production that are perfectly elastic in supply and those that are perfectly inelastic are numerous factors of production that earn some surplus return over their opportunity costs, or economic rent.

Economic rent is the amount by which the payment to a factor exceeds its opportunity cost.

The major distinction between *economic rent* and *pure economic rent* is that a factor earning pure economic rent has an opportunity cost of zero. A factor earning economic rent has an opportunity cost that is positive but smaller than the payment to the factor.

The amount of economic rent earned by a factor depends upon the perspective from which the factor is viewed. The economic rent of John Smith as an *engineer* differs from the economic rent of John Smith as an engineer *for General Motors Corp.* Smith can earn $40,000 per year working for GM, $35,000 working for Ford, and $25,000 working in his best nonengineering job. Smith's economic rent as a GM engineer is $5,000 (his earnings in excess of his opportunity cost in the automobile industry); his economic rent as an engineer is $15,000 (his greatest potential earnings as an engineer in excess of his salary in his best nonengineering alternative).

The prices paid to a film star, a late-night talk-show host, the best pitcher in major league baseball, for Iowa farmland, and for offices in New York City surprisingly have much in common: a large fraction of each factor's income is economic rent. These factors receive payments in excess of their opportunity cost (their earnings in alternative uses). The factor payment serves the function of ensuring that the factor is employed efficiently in its highest and best use. Basketball great Michael Jordan's million-dollar contracts served the important economic function of promoting an efficient utilization of his assets; the utility of sports fans would have been reduced if he had been employed as a waiter at a local restaurant. Paying one of the world's most talented tenors $50,000 per performance ensures that he will devote himself to opera rather than working as a plumber.

Although we sometimes resent individuals with inherited talents, rare skills, or good looks who earn substantial salaries, we should recognize that oil-drilling rigs, Hawaiian real estate, Iowa corn land, and high-speed computers are earning similar rewards—namely, payments in excess of their opportunity costs. Although land is the most obvious, economic rents are paid to a wide variety of economic factors. Actors, professional athletes, musicians, surgeons, professors, television repair persons, and even nobility can earn economic rents. (See Example 3.)

Profits

Many of us are suspicious of the ethics of those individuals and companies who earn high profits. (In the Middle Ages, high profits were seen as a sure sign that a pact had been made with the devil.)

Profits that are headlined on the business pages are accounting profits. Accounting profits can be misleading because they do not take into account the firm's *opportunity costs,* which include both actual payments to factors of production and the costs of the next-best alternative that the firm has sacrificed. Economists prefer to evaluate a firm's profitability on the basis of normal profits and economic profits.

Accounting profits are revenues minus explicit costs.

Normal profits are the profits required to keep resources in that particular business. Normal profits are earned when revenues equal opportunity costs.

Economic profits are revenues in excess of total opportunity costs (which include both actual payments and sacrificed alternatives). Economic profits are profits in excess of normal profits.

You may own a small business to which you devote all your time and effort. You don't pay yourself a salary. Your company's accounting profit is $40,000, but you could have earned $60,000 in a job. To make a normal profit, your company would have to earn at least $60,000—to cover your opportunity cost.

As we discussed in earlier chapters, economic profits regulate entry into and exit from an industry. When they are positive, firms will enter; when they are negative, firms will exit. If your company's accounting profits continue to fall short of your opportunity cost, eventually you would want to abandon the business.

Entry Barriers, Risk, and Innovation

There are three basic sources of economic profits. The first source is barriers to entry in an industry or business. The economic profits from barriers to entry, called *monopoly profits,* form the basis of popular misgivings about profits. The second source of profits is the dynamic and ever-changing nature of the economy, which renders the success of some activities risky or uncertain. The third source of economic profits is innovation. Economic profits that are the result

EXAMPLE 3

"Happy Birthday" and Economic Rents

There is only one "Happy Birthday" song and, believe it or not, the rights to the song are owned by the copyright holder, Birchtree Ltd. Written by two sisters in 1893, "Happy Birthday" was copyrighted, and for it to be played at official functions a fee must be paid to the current owners of copyright. "Happy Birthday" currently earns about $1 million per year. The copyright will not expire until 2010, at which time it will become part of the public domain. Birchtree Ltd. can sell the rights to "Happy Birthday," and this may earn the present value of all expected fees until the year 2010.

The copyright fees earned on "Happy Birthday" are an economic rent. The supply is fixed, and it is there whether people play it or not. The entire amount of the fee is in excess of what is required to keep the song in existence.

Source: "Yes, You Did Hear It Right: "Happy Birthday Is For Sale," *New York Times,* October 20, 1988.

of risk-taking and innovation are considered a reward for the *entrepreneurship* of individuals.

Entry Restrictions. As you already know, monopolies can earn a profit rate in excess of normal profits.

Unlike the transitory profits of a competitive industry, monopoly profits can persist over a long period of time. Monopoly businesses can earn revenues that exceed the opportunity costs of the factors they employ. In this sense, monopoly profits are like economic rents, and consequently, economists often refer to monopoly profits as *monopoly rents*. Monopoly profits can also be earned in a potentially competitive industry where entry is restricted by government licensing or franchising. So long as monopoly profits cannot be eliminated by the entry of new firms, existing firms can enjoy monopoly rents. Monopoly rents are due to the ceiling placed on supply by entry restrictions.

Examples of monopoly profits due to entry restrictions are plentiful. Cable television franchises are granted by municipal authorities, protecting cable companies by law from the entry of competitors. In most cities, taxicab drivers must be licensed, and entry into the business is controlled by the high cost of the license. Monopoly profits in the prescription-drug industry are protected by patents. Economies of scale similarly limit the entry of competitors into power generation and telecommunications.

Monopoly profits are often not reflected in accounting profits because they are *capitalized* (converted to their present value) when the firm is sold to a new owner. For example, in New York City, when taxicab drivers sell their licenses (called *medallions*) to others, the market price of the license reflects the value of the cab's monopoly profits. The cab driver who purchases the license earns no economic profit because it has gone to the original owner of the license.

Risk. If there were no entry restrictions, if people could predict the future perfectly, and if there were no costs for obtaining information about market opportunities, there would be no economic profits. All businesses would earn normal profits. Any opportunity to earn economic profits would be anticipated and the free entry of new firms would serve to keep profits down to a normal return.

However, no one can predict the future. Industry is unprepared for wars, new inventions, and changes in fashion, preferences, and weather. Even with free entry, at any given time some industries will earn economic profits and others will suffer losses. Unanticipated shifts in demand or costs cause economic profits to rise and fall. The majority of people wish to limit their exposure to the ups and downs of the economy; they want a steady income. Therefore, there must be rewards for those who are willing to risk the ups and downs of economic fortunes. Just as those who lend money to poor credit risks require risk premiums, so those who are willing to take risks must be rewarded with economic profits if they are successful. In his classic book, *Risk, Uncertainty, and Profit,* published in 1921, Frank Knight emphasized that uncertainty and risk-taking are the ultimate source of profit. Knight noted the presence of a large element of luck in the fortunes of different enterprises. Economic profits cannot be assured in an uncertain world; the outcome of the profit game will be, to a large extent, random. Knight's perceptions are as relevant today as they were in 1921.

Uncertainty turns the quest for profits into something resembling a game of chance in which there are winners and losers even in the long run. Entrepreneurs are the ones who bear this risk. The winners earn economic profits; the losers incur losses. As in a game of chance, profits average out to a normal return over all firms, but there is a wide range of profit outcomes. Most business firms deviate little from the average return to risk bearing. Some, though, have good luck and experience large returns; others experience large misfortunes. All is not fair in love, war, . . . and business.

Innovation. Luck cannot explain all economic profits, however. The economy is in a constant state of flux. Consumer tastes are changing, new technologies are being developed, new markets are being discovered, and resource availabilities are being altered. To be an innovator requires ability and foresight in order to take advantage of these changes.

Austrian-born economist Joseph Schumpeter, whom we encountered in Chapter 1, maintained that profits, primarily the return to the entrepreneur and innovator, are temporary. Economic progress requires a succession of new innovations. A successful entre-

EXAMPLE 4

The Entrepreneurship of Fred Smith

Fred Smith, the founder of Federal Express, dreamed of a company that could deliver packages overnight to large and small cities. The air express business already had two giant firms, Emery Air Freight and Flying Tiger, but Smith was convinced he could offer a better product. Smith recognized opportunities that his competitors failed to see. Smith knew that nine out of ten commercial airlines were on the ground between 10:00 P.M. and 8:00 A.M., so the air lanes were wide open during these hours. Second, Smith recognized that the bulk of urgent, small package business was concentrated in the 25 largest cities. Third, Smith realized that it would be more efficient to have a single hub system (which he eventually located in Memphis) through which all packages would flow. A package originating in Los Angeles for San Francisco would be flown to Memphis, processed, and then sent on another plane to San Francisco. Armed with these business insights, Smith risked all his own capital to start up Federal Express. The phenomenal success of the company was due to the entrepreneurial genius of its founder. Smith created the "hub-and-spoke" system used by the largest carriers today, and he created a boom in the overnight mail delivery business. Even the U.S. Postal Service was forced to copy Federal Express.

preneur will earn substantial economic profits only until another entrepreneur with a newer and better idea comes along to take customers and profits away.

Business history is replete with success stories of business geniuses—Henry Ford and the Model T, Edwin Land and the Polaroid camera, Richard Sears and Alvah Roebuck and their mass retailing, and Bill Gates and computer software. (See Example 4.) More was involved than a game of chance with an uncertain outcome; ability and entrepreneurial genius were crucial to the success of each of these companies. Yet even ability does not guarantee success. Many able people are trying to become the next Henry Ford, but few succeed.

Armen Alchian has pointed out that it is not even necessary for the entrepreneur to maximize profits:

> Realized positive profits, not *maximum* profits, are the mark of success and viability. It does not matter through what process of reasoning or motivation such success was achieved. The fact of its accomplishment is sufficient. This is the criterion by which the economic system selects survivors: those who realize *positive profits* are survivors; those who suffer losses disappear.[3]

Sources of Profits

Profits arise from monopoly restrictions and barriers, uncertainty and risk, and entrepreneurial innovation. Does the factual record support these propositions? It is very difficult to test the relationship between economic profits and these three factors because it is difficult to measure economic profits. Business firms report accounting profits, not economic profits, and the theory is about economic profits. Accounting profits can sometimes be misleading. Nevertheless, empirical studies typically assume that accounting profits are indicative of economic profits.

---

[3]Armen A. Alchian, "Uncertainty, Evolution, and Economic Theory," *Journal of Political Economy* 58, 3 (June 1950): pp. 211–221; reprinted in *Economic Forces at Work* (Indianapolis: Liberty Press, 1977), pp. 15–36.

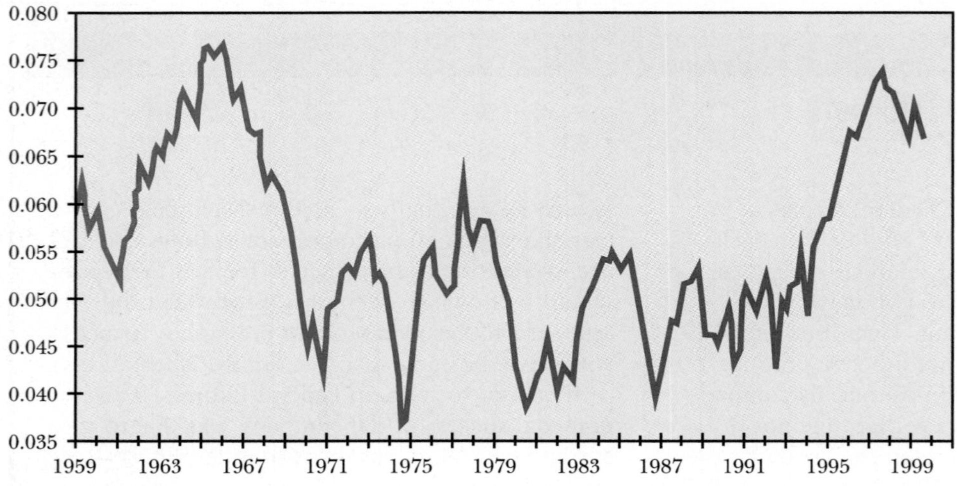

FIGURE 5 Corporate Profits after Tax as Share of GDP
Source: http://www.Economagic.com

Barriers to Entry and Profits. The empirical literature supports the theory that economic profits are strongly associated with monopoly barriers to entry. For example, prescription drugs protected by patents sell at 60 to 100 times average costs, and price-fixing conspiracies have been shown to create extraordinary profits. We have encountered other examples of the correlation between barriers to entry and profit rates in the chapter on oligopoly.

Risks and Profits. Determining the relationship between risk and profit rates is problematic because of the difficulty of measuring risk. In empirical studies, risk is typically measured by the variability of profits. If there are considerable fluctuations in profits over time or among firms in a particular industry, substantial risk is said to be present.

Figure 5 shows corporate profits (after taxes) as the share of gross domestic product (GDP) from 1959 to 1999. The share ranges from less than 4 percent in 1974–1975 to a high of 7.5 percent in 1966–1967. This is highly variable; it is the most volatile element of income in the economy. There is a much greater risk of being dependent upon profits than wages. There must be reward for risk-taking, just as there is for people who purchase low-grade corporate bonds rather than government bonds (refer to Example 2). Thus, on average, those whose incomes depend on profit earn more than those who depend on wages. This volatility of profit also explains the great volatility of the stock market, which sets a present value to future corporate profits.

Variability of profits may not be an accurate guide to risk, however, because serious risk stems from long-run dangers from new technology and new competition that can cause a permanent decline in the profits earned by individual firms.

Economists who have studied the relationship between the rate of profit and risk (as measured by the variability of profits) find that profit rates are indeed higher in risky industries. Firms and industries that are subject to greater risk earn *risk premiums*. Entrepreneurs and stockholders who bear more risk than others are compensated in the form of higher average profits.[4]

Innovation and Profits. As in the case of risk, the difficulty in measuring the trends in entrepreneurial activity precludes establishing an empirical correlation with profit. Nevertheless, history provides ample exam-

[4]The latest studies on profits as measured by stock returns are summarized in Narayana R. Kocherlakota, "The Equity Premium: It's Still a Puzzle," *Journal of Economic Literature,* March 1996, pp. 42–71, which explains the 6 percent premium of the real rate of return on stock investments over the rate of return on Treasury bills by appealing, among other factors, to high risk aversion.

ples of the relationship between innovation and profits. Huge fortunes (such as those of the Rockefeller, DuPont, Carnegie, Mellon, and Ford families) have been amassed by great entrepreneurs. It is new ideas that create profits, and it is the entrepreneur that executes this new idea that receives the profits.

In this chapter and the previous one we have surveyed how the economy determines wages, rents, interest, and profit—the payments to the productive factors of labor, land, capital, and entrepreneurship. In the next chapter, we shall turn from the functional distribution of income to the personal distribution of income, addressing such difficult questions as these: How equally or unequally is income distributed among persons? How has the personal distribution of income changed over time? How does America's income distribution compare with that of other countries? What can be done about poverty and inequality?

SUMMARY

1. Interest is payment for the use of capital. The supply of capital is the result of past saving and investment decisions. Interest rates are determined in credit markets, which are necessitated by the specialization of savings and investment decisions in today's modern economy. Interest rates are determined in the market by the demand and supply of loanable funds. The real rate of interest is the nominal interest rate minus the anticipated rate of inflation. The structure of interest rates depends upon risk, liquidity, and maturity.

2. Pure economic rent is the payment to a factor of production that is completely inelastic in supply and for which the price is determined by demand. A quasi rent is payment to a factor of production in excess of short-run opportunity costs. In the long run, quasi rents tend to disappear. Economic rent is the amount by which the payment to a factor exceeds its opportunity cost.

3. Economic profits are revenues in excess of total opportunity costs. The sources of economic profits are restrictions to entry into an industry, risk, and entrepreneurship and innovation. Empirical evidence, though limited in the cases of risk and entrepreneurship, generally supports the correlation between profits and each of the three sources.

KEY TERMS

interest 330
depreciation 330
credit markets (capital markets) 331
interest rate 331
loanable funds 331
rate of return of a capital good 332
nominal interest rate 334
real interest rate 334
pure economic rent 336
quasi rent 338
economic rent 338
accounting profits 339
normal profits 339
economic profits 339

QUESTIONS AND PROBLEMS

1. Why is it misleading to call interest the price of money?
2. This chapter emphasized that the credit market is another example of specialization in economics. Explain how this specialization works and how it affects economic efficiency.
3. If you borrow $10,000 from the bank and repay the bank $12,000 after 1 year, what is the annual rate of interest?
4. A company is considering four investment projects that yield returns of 20 percent, 15 percent, 10 percent, and 5 percent, respectively. Explain how the company will decide which of these projects to carry out.
5. The interest rate is currently 10 percent and the inflation rate is 5 percent. If people anticipate that the inflation rate will rise to 10 percent, what will happen to interest rates?
6. Distinguish between pure economic rents and quasi rents.
7. Evaluate the validity of the following statement: "Pure economic rents play no useful role in the economy because the supply of the factor in question is fixed. The factor will be supplied no matter what rent is paid."
8. Why should the profit rate be higher for businesses that are risky? How do we measure risk?
9. What is the logic behind taxing economic rents rather than other kinds of factor incomes?
10. Identify the sources of economic profits earned by the following:

a. Steel companies after the government imposed restrictions on competitive steel imports from foreign countries
b. The coal industry after the Organization of Petroleum Exporting Countries quadrupled the price of oil in 1974
c. A firm that developed a surefire method of increasing gas mileage

11. Evaluate the validity of the following statement: "High interest rates make for a better retirement."
12. The great baseball player Babe Ruth earned more than the president of the United States; yet if he had not played baseball, his income might have equaled that of a common laborer. Explain this situation in terms of the concepts of this chapter.

INTERNET CONNECTION

13. Using the links on http://www.awl.com/ruffin_gregory, examine the Federal Reserve's Federal Funds rate, a key interest rate in the economy.
    a. Plot the Federal Funds rate for the past 24 months.
    b. Can you think of a reason for the changes in this rate?

PUZZLE ANSWERED: Paying $10 million to a gifted athlete ensures that his or her skills are used as an athlete rather than in some alternative employment. Presumably, the person's skills are worth at least $10 million to society (or more)—a sum that would be wasted if the person were paid a trifling amount in some other activity. The competition among sports teams for the athlete's services ensures that payment of his or her marginal worth. If an athlete were paid less than marginal worth by a particular team, another team could make a profit by bidding the valuable player away. This competition explains why free agency became such an important issue in sports such as major league baseball. Michael Jordan's value to society was much greater as a great basketball player than what he might have been had a cap been placed on his salary; the price serves as a guarantee that the athlete is used in the best possible way for society.

Chapter 19

Inequality, Income Distribution, and Poverty

Chapter Insight

The prolific historian and essayist Thomas Carlyle (1795–1881) called economics the "dismal science" because he opposed the analytical treatment of social questions. One of the most controversial areas of economics is the study of economic inequality. It is always easy to say that some people are too rich and others too poor. Perhaps no other phrase in economics is as well known as "the rich are getting richer and the poor are getting poorer." Many people think that there is nothing that can be done to alleviate poverty, because of the adverse effects of work incentives of government handouts. What is true about the distribution of income? What can and has been done about poverty? Have antipoverty programs worked? Is the distribution of income becoming more unequal?

LEARNING OBJECTIVES

After completing this chapter, you will be able to:

1. Understand how income is distributed in the United States.
2. Describe the effect of education on income.
3. Understand the Lorenz curve and how it measures the distribution of income.
4. Know the sources of inequality of income distribution.
5. Discuss how to measure poverty and trends in poverty.
6. Describe the negative income tax.

CHAPTER PUZZLE: Does growing income inequality mean that the rich are getting richer at the expense of the poor?

PATTERNS OF INCOME DISTRIBUTION

We earn income from our labor and from the capital and land assets we own. Most of us earn relatively little from dividends, interest, and profits, but some earn a great deal. Some of us receive transfer payments from government programs such as Social Security or Aid to Families with Dependent Children (AFDC) programs. The most important source of income for most of us is what we earn from our labor. We all have the same amount of time—24 hours per day—but we earn different amounts of labor income because people are different and jobs are different. We also earn different amounts because some of us choose to work more hours.

Table 1 shows U.S. personal income per capita—its magnitude and its sources. As a nation, we earn about 68 percent from our labor, 12 percent from transfer payments, 8 percent from businesses we own and operate, and the remainder, or 12 percent, from capital—from rental, dividend, and interest income.

Income is unevenly distributed. Table 2 shows that in 1997 about 11 percent of all households earned less than $10,000 and about 19 percent, less than $15,000. Different ethnic and racial groups have different experiences. For example, over 20 percent of African Americans earn less than $10,000 and over 30 percent, less than $15,000.

Table 2 needs careful study. It measures money income in constant or real dollars in 1970 and 1997. From 1970 to 1997 the median real income of all households increased 8.8 percent, from about $34,000 to about $37,000. But the median income of blacks increased by 16.3 percent, from $21,500 to $25,000. Moreover, from 1970 to 1997, the percentage of households with real incomes less than $10,000 *fell* from 13.4 percent to 11 percent. The percentage of African Americans with incomes less than $15,000 fell from 36.5 percent to 31.9 percent—still too high but going in the right direction. Significantly, the greatest changes took place in the money incomes of about $75,000 (remember, these figures are adjusted for inflation). The percentage of all households above $75,000 more than doubled, from 9 percent to 18.4 percent, and the percentage of African Americans at $75,000 and above increased from a paltry 3 percent to a more respectable 7.9 percent. In other words, in 1997 the percentage of upper-income blacks was only slightly less than the percentage of upper-income whites in 1970. Again, we see that there is movement in the right direction. Above all, what the table tells us is that the rich are

TABLE 1 PERSONAL INCOME IN THE UNITED STATES (1999)

	Personal Income	*Income per Capita*	*Percentage of Total*
Labor income	$5,300 billion	$19,400	67.9%
Proprietor's income	650	2,370	8.3
Capital income (rent, interest, dividends)	950	3,500	12.3
Net transfer payments	900	3,300	11.5
Total	$7,800 billion	$28,570	100.0

Source: Statistical Abstract of the United States.

TABLE 2 MONEY INCOME OF HOUSEHOLDS—PERCENT DISTRIBUTION. BY INCOME LEVEL, RACE, AND HISPANIC ORIGIN, IN CONSTANT (1997) DOLLARS: 1970 AND 1997

Year	Number of Households (1,000)	*Percent Distribution* Under $10,000	$10,000–$14,999	$15,000–$24,999	$25,000–$34,999	$35,000–$49,999	$50,000–$74,999	$75,000 and over	Median Income (dollars)
All Households[a]									
1970	64,778	13.4	7.5	15.1	16.1	21.1	17.7	9.0	33,942
1997	102,528	11.0	8.1	14.9	13.3	16.3	18.1	18.4	37,005
White									
1970	57,575	12.2	7.0	14.5	16.1	21.8	18.6	9.7	35,353
1997	86,106	9.5	7.8	14.6	13.2	16.5	18.8	19.7	38,972
Black									
1970	6,180	24.3	12.2	20.9	15.8	14.5	9.2	3.0	21,518
1997	12,474	21.4	10.5	17.9	14.2	14.9	13.1	7.9	25,050
Hispanic[b]									
1975	2,948	16.5	11.2	21.8	17.2	18.7	10.8	3.8	25,317
1997	8,590	16.8	10.7	19.7	15.0	16.6	12.2	9.1	26,628

[a]Includes other races not shown separately.
[b]Persons of Hispanic origin may be of any race. Income data for Hispanic origin households are not available prior to 1972.
Source: U.S. Census Bureau, *Statistical Abstract of the United States, 1999.*

getting richer, but the poor are *not* getting poorer. The most accurate statement is:

Compared to 1970, today there is a smaller percentage of households, both white and minorities, with low incomes and a higher percentage of households with high incomes.

The fact that both whites and minorities experience improvements in their income suggests considerable income mobility. Indeed, from one year to the next, roughly three-fourths of Americans experience fluctuations in their economic well-being, as measured by their incomes. In 1993–1994 the U.S. Census Bureau carried out some studies of the dynamics of income distribution. An interesting discovery was that whites and African Americans have very similar income dynamics. Over that period 40 percent of whites, African Americans, and Hispanics increased their incomes by at least 5 percent, while about one-third of each group saw their incomes fall by more than 5 percent.[1]

[1]U.S. Census Bureau, "Moving Up and Down the Income Ladder," *Current Population Reports* (P70-65), July 1998.

Sources of Income Inequality

We have discussed some of the causes of income inequality in the chapters on labor and interest, rent, and profit. Here we shall consider the unequal distribution of labor income.

Noncompeting Groups

We have different mental and physical abilities that limit our choice of occupation. Not everyone has the mental skills and dexterity to become a surgeon; few of us have the physical endowments to become professional athletes or highly paid fashion models. By contrast, many of us possess the skills to perform unskilled labor, or to serve as salesclerks and bank tellers.

Because we are different from one another, the labor market segregates us into noncompeting groups that earn different wages. Such wage differentials can persist over a long period of time. The six-figure earnings of surgeons will not cause construction workers to switch to surgery. The prospect of having to lift 100 pounds will keep many of us from seeking

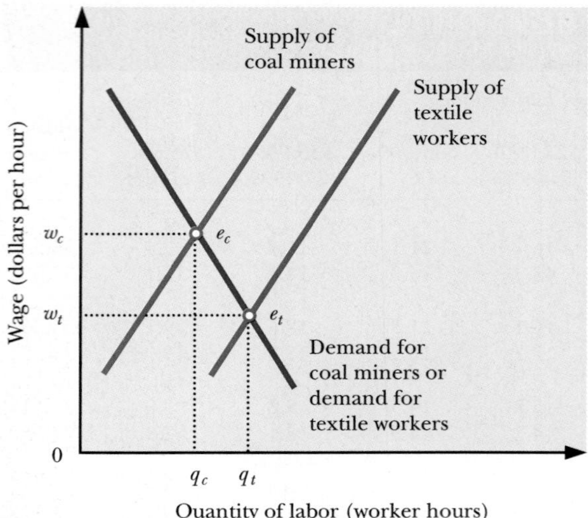

FIGURE 1 Wages in Coal Mining and Textiles

For simplicity, the demand curve for coal miners is assumed to be identical to the demand curve for textile workers. Wages are higher for coal miners because the quantity supplied of coal miners is less than the quantity supplied of textile workers at each wage rate.

employment on offshore drilling rigs despite its high wage rates.

Occupational Differences

Most of us prefer to work in occupations that are safe, offer pleasant surroundings, and do not require heavy or dirty work. The supply of labor to attractive occupations and jobs is greater than that to unattractive ones. Even though garbage collectors earn more than many others with the same skills, labor does not move automatically into these higher-paying jobs to wipe out the wage differential. We demand a reward for working in unpleasant and dangerous jobs.

Figure 1 shows the effect on relative wages of the danger of the occupation. For simplicity, the demand curve for underground coal miners is assumed to be identical to the demand curve for textile workers, but the labor supply curves are quite different. The higher placement of the coal miners' supply curve reflects the fact that workers prefer less dangerous employment, if everything else is equal. To get an equivalent supply of coal miners, coal mine employers must offer higher wages than textile employers.

Compensating wage differentials explain why welders on the Alaskan pipeline have to be paid more (to compensate for the harsh climate and higher living costs) or why sanitation workers are better paid than clerical workers (to compensate for the unpleasantness and social stigma). Loggers must be paid more because of the hazardous nature of logging.

Compensating wage differentials are the higher wages that must be paid to compensate workers for undesirable job characteristics.

Compensating wage differentials imply that some inequality is a matter of choice. This choice may also involve a trade-off between pay and leisure. Some of us value leisure time more than others. You may work a 60-hour week, whereas I (who earn the same hourly wage) work a 30-hour week.

Different occupations have different risks. A small business owner has a more uncertain income than a tenured university professor does. A wheat farmer, whose crops may be destroyed by blights and droughts, has a more uncertain income than a union employee with seniority does. Society comprises risk seekers or risk avoiders who have different attitudes toward risk.

Risk seekers are more willing to incur risks than **risk avoiders**, who are reluctant to take on risks.[2]

The more risk seekers in a society, the more unequal the distribution of income. A few risk seekers strike it rich; most risk seekers fail. The vast majority—the risk avoiders—are in the middle, earning the steadiest incomes.

Human Capital Investment

Just as businesses invest in plant and equipment to increase the firm's productive capacity, so do we

[2]The theory of individual choice of inequality was formulated by Milton Friedman in the article, "Choice, Chance, and the Personal Distribution of Income," *Journal of Political Economy* 61, 4 (August 1953): 277–290.

TABLE 3 MONEY INCOME OF HOUSEHOLDS—DISTRIBUTION, BY INCOME LEVEL AND EDUCATION: 1997

Characteristic	*Number of Households (1,000)*	*Number (1,000)*							*Median Income (dollars)*
		Under $10,000	*$10,000–$14,999*	*$15,000–$24,999*	*$25,000–$34,999*	*$35,000–$49,999*	*$50,000–$74,999*	*$75,000 and over*	
Educational attainment of householder:[a]									
Total	97,093	10,155	7,731	14,021	12,635	15,888	18,070	18,594	38,190
Less than 9th grade	7,369	2,223	1,344	1,664	843	690	375	231	15,541
9th to 12th grade (no diploma)	9,686	2,321	1,402	2,079	1,303	1,240	898	443	19,851
High school graduate	30,739	3,254	2,657	5,245	4,729	5,691	5,755	3,409	33,779
Some college, no degree	17,225	1,227	1,287	2,429	2,591	3,121	3,533	3,038	40,015
Associate degree	7,263	417	389	900	940	1,357	1,742	1,518	45,258
Bachelor's degree or more	24,811	712	652	1,704	2,229	3,789	5,768	9,956	63,292
Bachelor's degree	16,098	529	456	1,276	1,604	2,581	4,020	5,633	59,048
Master's degree	5,735	136	140	323	462	873	1,257	2,544	68,118
Professional degree	1,693	29	27	58	88	213	261	1,017	92,228
Doctorate degree	1,285	19	29	47	76	122	231	762	87,232

[a]Persons 25 years old and over.
Source: U.S. Census Bureau, *Statistical Abstract of the United States,* 1999.

invest in ourselves to raise our own productivity. We invest in education, we move to areas that have better job opportunities, and we invest in medical care to improve our health or appearance.

Human-capital theory teaches that we make rational choices of different lifetime earnings streams when we invest in ourselves.[3]

If human-capital investment translates into higher lifetime earnings, why doesn't everyone acquire equal levels of such investment? Although human-capital investment yields benefits, it also has its costs. Physicians must study and train an extra eight years at a cost of more than $200,000, but they are compensated by higher lifetime earnings. Confronted with the costs and benefits of human-capital investment, we make rational investment decisions. We acquire more human capital as long as the marginal benefit exceeds the marginal cost.

Because we make different human-capital choices, the distribution of income is partly the result of our own decisions. We choose between more money now (going to work after high school) and more money later (going to college with no earnings now). Those of us who place a high value on having money now are less likely to acquire human capital. When we make that choice, we will earn less lifetime income.

Table 3 shows the effects of education on median incomes. In 1997 there were about 25 million householders with a bachelor's degree or more. Their median income was over $63,000; fewer than 6 percent earned less than $15,000, while 40 percent earned $75,000 or more a year. On the other hand, there were about 31 million householders with only a high school diploma; almost 20 percent earned less than $15,000, while only 11 percent earned $75,000 or more a year! Education is a good way to reduce income disparities.

[3]The pioneering articles in human-capital theory are Gary Becker, "Investment in Human Capital: A Theoretical Analysis," *Journal of Political Economy* 70, 5 (October 1962): 9–49; and Theodore W. Schultz, "Capital Formation by Education," *Journal of Political Economy* 68, 6 (December 1960): 571–583.

Discrimination

If we are denied equal access to education and training, our career opportunities will be limited. If we are denied access to jobs in labor unions, we cannot earn higher union wages.

Discrimination occurs when individuals are blocked from entering jobs and occupations or when workers with equal skills and qualifications are treated differently on the grounds of race, sex, or some other characteristic.

Different racial and gender groups earn, on average, different amounts of income. The median income of nonwhite U.S. households currently equals about 64 percent of white household income, up considerably from 50 percent in 1947. Women who work full time currently have an average income about three-quarters that of males, up from 60 percent since the late 1950s.

Are these average differences the result of discrimination? A substantial portion of ethnic and racial differences in earning reflect differences in schooling. Table 3 showed the positive correlation between schooling and earnings. More than twice the percentage of whites complete college as do African Americans or Hispanics. Therefore, the most effective means of reducing earning differentials by race is to provide equal access to quality education.

The female income differential does not result from a disparity in years of schooling. A higher percentage of women than men complete high school, and about the same percentage have at least some college-level education. Women work fewer hours and spend fewer years in the labor force, but these factors cannot explain more than half of the female earning gap.[4]

After completion of schooling, individuals may encounter labor market discrimination. Labor-market discrimination does not normally entail discrimination between two workers (of different race or sex) performing the same job. In fact, federal laws guarantee equal pay for equal or even "comparable" work. Affirmative action programs may even give minority job candidates an advantage in the labor market. More often, discrimination occurs when nonwhites or women are channeled into occupations regarded as "suitable" for them. This channeling may result from an employee's own preferences (a woman may want to be a schoolteacher) or employer discrimination (an employer may not hire women for heavy assembly-line work). The employer may use screening rules (such as not hiring women for manual labor) that exclude women. As a consequence, "suitable" professions—say, nursing and schoolteaching for women or bus driving for African American males—become crowded, and the relative earnings of these professions are driven down. (See Example 1.)

Screening and Inequality

Table 3 indicates that those of us who have more education earn more income. Is this because the better educated we are, the more productive we are? Although that may be true, the statistics present us with a puzzle: A householder with a high school degree (and no further education) earns 70 percent more than a high school dropout. A college graduate earns 48 percent more than someone who has attended college but has not completed college. Can it be true than an extra year or two of college makes you 48 percent more productive, or that dropping out of high school one year prior to graduation makes you 70 percent less productive? (See Example 2 on page 352.)

Economists explain this puzzle by noting that completion of schooling—the act of getting a high school diploma or a college degree—signals to employers that you are likely to possess traits that they are looking for. These traits are tenacity, discipline, and endurance, all of which make you more valuable and productive. There may indeed be others who are more productive than you but lack a college or high school diploma. Employers, however, cannot

---

[4]Henry Aaron and Cameron Loughy, *The Comparable Controversy* (Washington, DC: The Brookings Institution, 1986), 12–13; Ronald Ehrenberg and Robert Smith, *Modern Labor Economics*, 4th ed. (New York: HarperCollins, 1991), chap. 14; James Smith and Michael Ward, *Women's Wages and Work in the Twentieth Century* (New York: Rand Corporation, 1984).

EXAMPLE 1

Comparable Worth and Unintended Consequences

The Supreme Court and the federal courts have ruled that employees have a right to equal pay for "comparable" work. This is a significant extension of the law requiring equal pay for equal work. In Washington State, the courts ordered employers to adjust pay scales so that employees with comparable jobs would receive the same pay. A committee assigned points to each job on the basis of knowledge and skills, mental demands, accountability, and work conditions. Registered nurses won the highest evaluation, well above computer system analysts. Clerical supervisors won a higher rating than chemists; electricians were assigned lower points than beginning secretaries. In all these evaluations, the market had assigned different relative wages than the comparable-worth point system.

Like many policy issues in economics, the comparable-worth ruling had unintended consequences that tended to negate its noble goal. By setting the comparable-worth wages of secretaries and clerical supervisors above their market wages, surpluses of secretaries and clerical supervisors were created in the state of Washington. There were too many applicants and too few positions. A second unintended consequence of the artificial increase in wages in traditionally female-dominated professions such as secretaries and clerical supervisors was to reduce the incentive for women to break into higher-paying traditionally male professions.

take the time and expense to find them. They are content to screen out individuals who lack formal credentials because this is an inexpensive way of selecting employees.

Screening is the requirement that potential employees possess certain characteristics, such as a high school or college diploma, or a B+ or better average.

By using screening, employers know that they will select the right employees on average, although they know they will pass up some good employees who do not have the right credentials. This is simply a cost-effective way to select employees.

Screening indicates that more educated individuals or persons with high grades earn more not necessarily because they are more productive. They earn more because they have the credentials that qualify them for jobs that offer higher lifetime earnings.[5]

[5]The classic studies of screening theory are: Michael Spence, "Job Market Signaling," *Quarterly Journal of Economics* 87, 3 (August 1973): pp. 355–374; Kenneth Arrow, "Higher Education as a Filter," *Journal of Public Economics* 2, 3 (July 1973): pp. 193–216.

EXAMPLE 2

How Important Is Human Capital?

When national income statistics are examined, wages represent about 70 percent of national income. However, a large fraction of these wages consists of a return to investment in human capital—education and training that increase the productivity of a worker. The problem is that anyone from the owner of a business to the janitor, the star football player to the waterboy, or the corporation president to her secretary is included in "wages." This complication raises the question, What percent of national income goes to raw or unproved labor? Alan Krueger of Princeton University and the National Bureau of Economic Research estimated that the share of national income going to raw labor was 13 percent in 1959, but fell to only 5 percent by 1996. In other words, over 90 percent of the income going to workers is a payment for human capital. Krueger came to this conclusion by examining the wages of many individuals, together with their schooling and years of experience. After controlling for just schooling and years of experience, the remaining amount of wages represents the payment to "raw labor."

Source: Alan Krueger, "Measuring Labor's Share," *NBER Working Paper W7006,* March 1999.

Measuring Income Inequality

The Lorenz Curve

The most common measure of equality in the distribution of income is the Lorenz curve.

The **Lorenz curve** shows the percentages of total income earned by households at successive income levels. The cumulative percentage of households (ranked from lowest to highest incomes) is plotted on the horizontal axis, and the cumulative share of income earned by each cumulative percentage of households is plotted on the vertical axis.

Lorenz curves are typically plotted in quintiles, or fifths. A household in the top fifth has greater earnings than at least 80 percent of all households.

A 45-degree-line Lorenz curve shows absolute equality. If income were distributed equally, the bottom 20 percent of households would receive 20 percent of all income, the bottom 40 percent of households would receive 40 percent of all income, and so on. The more the Lorenz curve bows away from the 45-degree line, or the line of perfect equality, the more unequal is the income distribution. Figure 2 provides three U.S. Lorenz curves, for 1929, 1970, and 1998 (see also Table 4).

The Gini Coefficient

Another measure of the inequality of income distribution is the Gini coefficient, a numerical measure of inequality.

The **Gini coefficient** is the area between the 45-degree line and the Lorenz curve, divided by the total area under the 45-degree line.

If there is perfect equality, the Lorenz curve and the 45-degree line coincide, and the Gini coefficient is zero. If there is perfect inequality (one household gets all the income), then the difference between the Lorenz curve and the 45-degree line equals the entire area under the 45-degree line, and the Gini coefficient equals 1. In between these two extremes, the Gini coefficient can measure whether one income distribution is more or less unequal than another. (See Example 3 on page 356.)

Facts and Figures on the U.S. Distribution of Income

Over the past half-century, there has been a distinct trend toward greater equality. The Lorenz curve in Figure 2 gives the U.S. distributions of income in 1929, 1970, and 1998. The top 5 percent of households accounted for 30 percent of all income in 1929 but for 21.4 percent in 1998. The share of the lowest 40 percent of households rose from 12.5 percent in 1929 to 12.6 percent in 1998. The middle-class households in the third and fourth quintiles increased their relative standing most over the past 60 years; from 33.1 percent to 38.2 percent.

Despite the long-term trend toward a more equal distribution of income, considerable inequality still exists. In 1998, the top 5 percent of U.S. households accounted for 21.4 percent of all income, whereas the bottom 20 percent accounted for only 3.6 percent. If we consider only money incomes before taxes, the U.S. income distribution became more unequal between 1970 and 1998. But since 1929 inequality has been reduced.

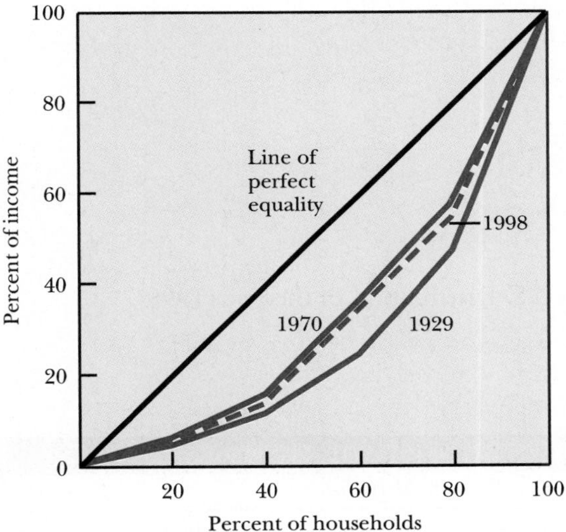

FIGURE 2 Lorenz Curves of the U.S. Income Distribution, 1929, 1970, and 1998

For more than 70 years, there has been a distinct trend toward more equality in the U.S. distribution of income. Since 1970, however, there has been a trend toward greater inequality. *Sources: Statistical Abstract of the United States, Historical Statistics of the United States.*

Government and Income Redistribution

Figure 2 shows the distribution of money income before taxes and before services provided by the government. Government can alter the distribution of income through taxes, money payments, and in-kind income.

In-kind income consists of benefits—such as free public education, school lunch programs, public housing, or food stamps—for which the recipient is not required to pay the full cost.

Figure 3 and Table 5 show the substantial impact of government redistribution programs on the distribution of income. Without government money transfers, the poorest fifth of households would account for only 1 percent of money income. After such transfers, their share is raised to 4.7 percent. Income taxes and payroll taxes do not significantly alter the

TABLE 4 U.S. INCOME DISTRIBUTION—1929, 1970, 1998

	Lowest Fifth	*Second Fifth*	*Third Fifth*	*Fourth Fifth*	*Highest Fifth*	*Top 5%*
1929	3.8%	8.7%	13.8%	19.3%	54.4%	30.0%
1970	5.4%	12.2%	17.6%	23.8%	40.9%	15.6%
1998	3.6%	9.0%	15.0%	23.2%	49.2%	21.4%

Sources: Statistical Abstract of the United States, Historical Statistics of the United States.

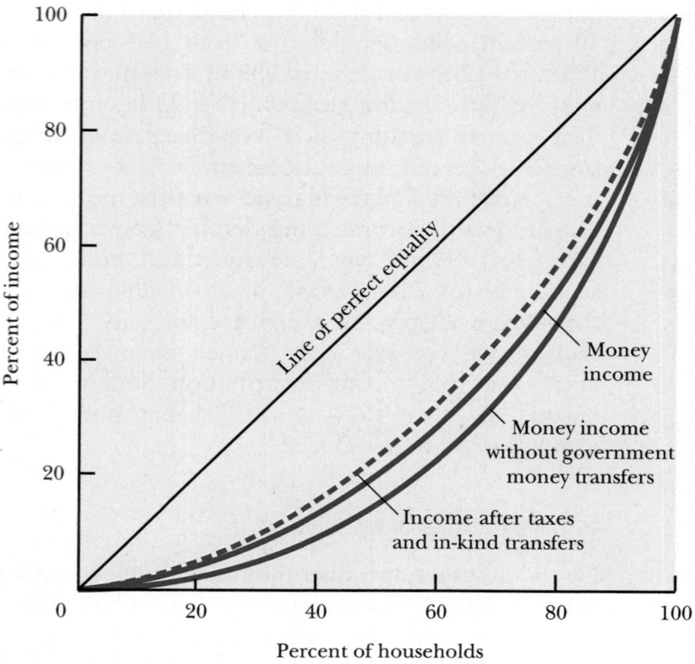

FIGURE 3 The Effect of Government Taxes and Transfers on the U.S. Distribution of Income (1998)
Source: Statistical Abstract of the United States.

TABLE 5 DISTRIBUTION OF INCOME WITH AND WITHOUT GOVERNMENT MONEY TRANSFERS AND TAXES AND IN-KIND TRANSFERS 1998

		Percent of Income				
	Gini	*Lowest fifth*	*2nd fifth*	*3rd fifth*	*4th fifth*	*Highest fifth*
Money income	.446	3.6	9.2	14.9	23.3	49.0
Money income without government money transfers	.509	1.0	7.1	14.2	23.4	54.1
Income after taxes and in-kind transfers	.405	4.7	10.6	16.0	23.0	45.8

distribution of income. The distribution of money incomes before and after taxes are about the same. In-kind income, such as Medicare, school lunches, and other assistance programs, significantly raises the share of the bottom fifth—from 3.6 percent to 4.7 percent of total income. Without this redistribution of income through government programs, the richest fifth would earn 54 times more than the poorest fifth. Government cash and in-kind transfers lowers this figure to 10 times.

A Brief International Perspective

Is the U.S. distribution of income like that of other countries? Does the United States have extremes of wealth and poverty unlike other countries? Figure 4 shows a mix of countries at different levels of economic development, including Hungary, a former communist state. It reveals that at a roughly equivalent level of income, the U.S. distribution of income is more unequal than that of other industrialized

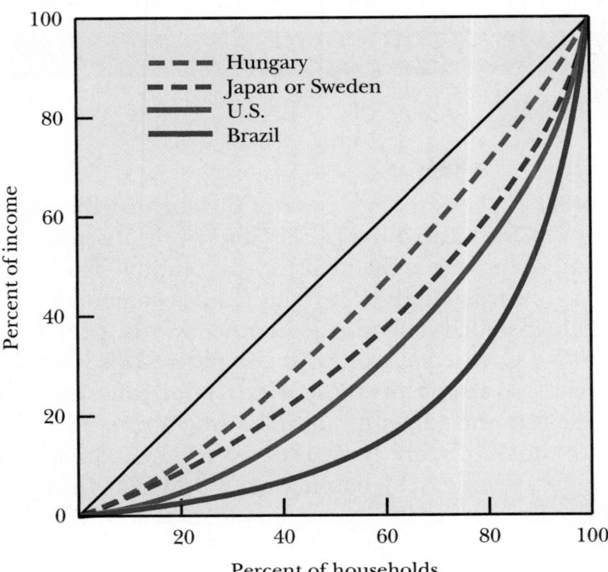

FIGURE 4 Lorenz Curves for the Distribution of Income in the United States and Other Countries

Source: The World Bank, *World Development Report, 1999* (New York: Oxford University Press).

countries, such as Japan and Sweden. Our distribution of income is much more equal than that of developing countries, such as Brazil. In fact, there is a strong relationship between the level of development and a country's income distribution:

> The lower the level of income in a country, the more unequal its distribution of income.

There are exceptions to the rule: Hungary is not an affluent industrialized country, but it has the equal distribution characteristics of a rich country. The United States has a more unequal distribution of income than many other highly industrialized countries because the United States remains a melting pot of different nationalities and races, unlike homogeneous countries like Hungary or Sweden. The more heterogeneity, the more unequal the distribution of income. Also, the U.S. government plays less of a redistributive role than most of the governments in Europe. Although our welfare state appears big to us, the welfare state is more pervasive in Europe.

What Is a Just Distribution of Income?

Philosophers have debated the ethical issue of distributive justice for centuries. Is it fair to have extremes of wealth and poverty? Economists can better describe the economic consequences of different income distributions than judge whether one is better than another. Different philosophies of distributive justice have been formulated over the years.

Natural Law, Marginal Productivity, and the Leaky Bucket

According to the natural-law philosophers of the seventeenth century, we have the right to receive the fruits of our own labor.

> **Natural law** states that individuals should be rewarded according to their contribution to output.

This philosophy is consistent with the marginal productivity theory of income distribution, according to which, the owner of a factor of production receives its marginal revenue product (MRP). Under this arrangement, those who are more productive (those who have high MRPs) will receive more.

The major advantage of distributing income according to marginal productivities is that the owners of factors of production are encouraged to raise marginal productivity. Thus, we are motivated to invest in human capital and to acquire more physical capital; entrepreneurs are spurred to assume risks. If we were not paid in accordance with marginal productivity, we would reduce effort, acquire less human and physical capital, and take fewer risks—and the economy would produce less income.

There is a trade-off between equality and income. If income were redistributed away from those who possess high-priced factors of production, the efficiency of the economy would decline and less income would be produced. The equity/efficiency trade-off can be explained using the analogy of a leaky bucket.[6] Redistributing income is like transferring water from one barrel to another with a leaky bucket. In the process of making the transfer, water (income) is lost forever. If the leak is a slow one, the

[6]Arthur Okun, *Equality and Efficiency: The Big Trade-Off* (Washington, DC: The Brookings Institution, 1975).

EXAMPLE 3

Why Has the Distribution of Income Become More Unequal?

The Gini coefficient shows the percentage by which the distribution of income depicted in a Lorenz curve deviates from perfect equality. It allows us to numerically express how much income inequality has changed over a given period. A Gini ratio of 1 indicates perfect inequality; a Gini ratio of 0, perfect equality. It is a convenient summary measure of income distribution. For example, as measured by the Gini coefficient, the distribution of income is virtually the same for whites, African Americans, and Hispanics. It does not imply that blacks or Hispanics have the same income as whites, but that within each group the distribution of income is about the same.

From 1982 to 1993 there was continuous deterioration in the distribution of income as measured by the Gini coefficient. However, since 1993 there has been no change in income inequality. Moreover, from 1947 to 1982 the Gini measure was virtually unchanged. Here are selected statistics showing the distribution of family income:

1997	.429	1967	.358
1993	.429	1962	.362
1987	.393	1957	.351
1982	.380	1952	.368
1977	.363	1947	.376
1972	.359		

What explains the behavior of income distribution? One basic cause of this shift in the distribution of income is the high-tech revolution. This has rewarded high-skilled individuals compared to low-skilled individuals. In other words, people with a good education with computer skills have benefited relative to those with a poor education. The ratio of skilled to unskilled wages rose by around 50 percent from 1960 to 1993. Another cause was the baby boom after World War II. As the Gini coefficient has stabilized since 1993, so has the ratio of skilled to unskilled wages. Another piece of good news is that the trend may not be inevitable. From 1900 to 1949 the wages of skilled workers did not rise as fast as unskilled wages; thus, the relative wage of skilled to unskilled workers fell by about 33 percent. The trend toward increasing inequality may not be a permanent phenomenon.

Sources: U.S. Census Bureau, March Current Population Survey; U.S. Census Bureau, *Measuring 50 Years of Economic Change,* September 1998, P60-203; Roy Ruffin, "Quasi-Specific Factors: Worker Comparative Advantage in a Two-Sector Production Model," *Journal of International Economics,* 2000.

costs to society of the redistribution are small. If the leak is fast, the losses of total income will be substantial. We must decide whether the costs of greater equality are worth the price.

The Utilitarian Case for Equality

The utilitarian theory holds that a more equal income distribution will maximize the utility of society.

Utilitarian theory argues for an equal distribution of income by saying that equality maximizes welfare.

The law of diminishing marginal utility supplies the rationale of the utilitarian theory. If we are basically alike (if we have the same tastes and the same satisfaction from the same amount of income), the total utility of society will be greatest when income is distributed equally because of the law of diminishing marginal utility. If your friend Jones were rich and you were poor, Jones would be getting much less utility from his last dollar than you. If income were redistributed from Jones to you, your utility would increase more than Jones's would be reduced. Therefore, the reduction in inequality would increase the total utility of society.

We are, in fact, different. Some of us care little for money and worldly goods; others care a great deal. Therefore, it is not at all certain that the rich get less marginal utility from their last dollar. We cannot make interpersonal utility comparisons; we cannot conclude scientifically that the total utility of society is greatest when income is equally distributed. Even if it were, we would have to consider the loss of production caused if everyone earned the same amount.

Poverty

The fact that income is distributed unequally means that there will be rich and poor. As a society, we must decide how to deal with poverty. During the Industrial Revolution (a Defining Moment), poverty was viewed as a problem for which the poor themselves were responsible. Debtors were thrown into debtors' prisons, and youths caught stealing bread were imprisoned. As the welfare state grew in Western Europe, politicians and government officials concluded that the state should do something to eliminate poverty. In the United States, the Great Depression of the 1930s (another Defining Moment) caused federal, state, and local governments to enact poverty programs and unemployment assistance.

Definitions of Poverty

Defining poverty is not an easy task. Some define poverty in terms of the income necessary to provide a family of a certain size with the minimum essentials of food, clothing, shelter, and education. This approach provides an absolute poverty standard.

An **absolute poverty standard** establishes a specific income level for a household of a given size, below which the household is judged to be living in a state of poverty.

But is an absolute measure of poverty appropriate? Poverty can, after all, be relative. If my income is 10 percent of everyone else's, I may feel poor even if my income is sufficient to purchase the minimum essentials. Similarly, our conception of poverty does not necessarily match that of other countries. The American poor might be considered wealthy in the poorest Asian or African nations. A second approach to poverty, therefore, is a measurement in relative terms. A relative poverty standard might classify a household as poor if the household's income is, say, less than 25 percent of the average household's income.

A **relative poverty standard** defines the poor in terms of their income relative to others.

The choice of a poverty definition determines the number of poor and the poverty rate. If an absolute standard is selected, increasing real living standards will push more and more families above the poverty line. According to a relative standard, poverty can be eliminated only by equalizing the distribution of income. If both the rich and the poor experience equal percentage increases in income, the poor will not have improved their relative position.

Trends in Poverty

According to the absolute poverty standards of the U.S. government (Figure 5), the percentage of persons in poverty households declined from 22.4 percent to 12.7 percent between 1959 and 1998. During periods of rising prosperity, such as the 1960s and 1980s, the percentage of poverty households declined. During the recessions of the 1980s, 1980–1981, and 1990–1991, the rate of poverty increased.

Figure 5 refers only to money income, which does not include in-kind services received by the poor but does include government cash transfers, such as welfare payments and unemployment insurance. The government spends $3 in noncash benefits to every $2 in cash payments for its antipoverty programs.

What effects do government antipoverty programs have on the number of persons classified as living below the poverty line? Table 6 shows that the number of persons living below poverty levels in 1997 would have been substantially higher without government antipoverty programs. Without cash or

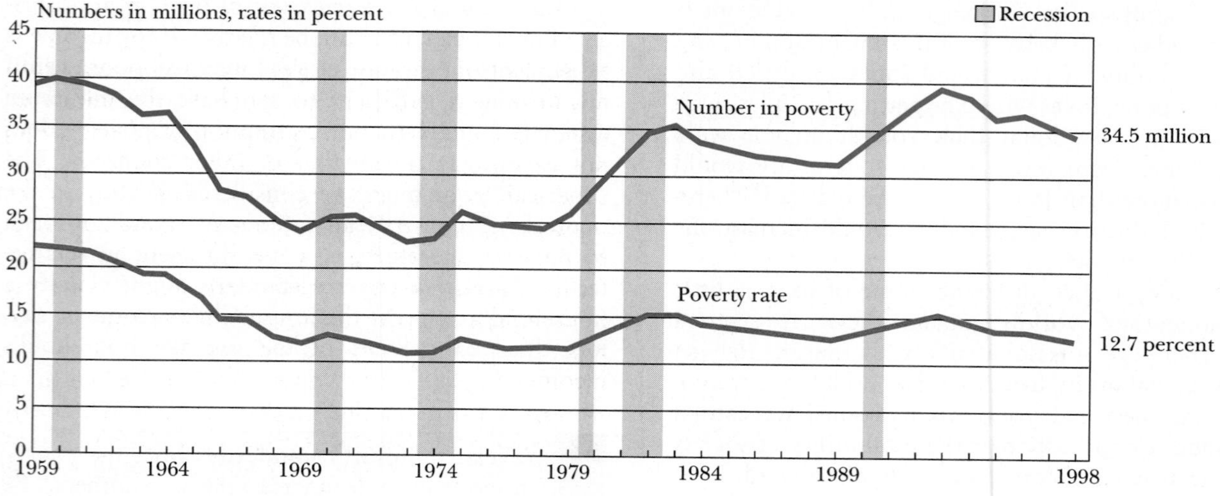

FIGURE 5 Number of Poor and Poverty Rate: 1959–1998 (money income only)

Note: The data points represent the midpoints of the respective years. The latest recession began in July 1990 and ended in March 1991.
Source: The U.S. Census Bureau, March 1960–March 1999 *Current Population Survey.*

TABLE 6 THE PERCENTAGE OF PERSONS BELOW POVERTY BEFORE AND AFTER GOVERNMENT ANTIPOVERTY PROGRAMS (1997)

	Before Taxes and Cash Payments[a]	*After Cash Payments*[b]	*After Cash and In-Kind Payments*[c]
All households	21.0%	13.4%	10%
White	18.9%	10.3%	8.4%
African American	34.9%	27.3%	19.3%
Hispanic	32.3%	25.9%	19.6%

[a]Official Def. 2
[b]Official Def. 9
[c]Official Def. 14
Source: Statistical Abstract of the United States, 1999.

in-kind payments, 21 percent of the U.S. population would have been below the poverty line. When both cash payments and in-kind benefits are included, the poverty percentage fell to 8.4 percent of the white population, 19.3 percent of the African American population, and 19.6 percent of the Hispanic population.

These figures reveal the massive effects of government programs on the incidence of poverty and suggest that a very large percentage of the U.S. population would be below the poverty line were it not for government assistance. Even after government welfare assistance, one in ten whites and nearly two in ten blacks or Hispanics live below the poverty line.

Who Are the Poor?

Table 7 provides a statistical profile of poor families. The poor are disproportionately African Americans

TABLE 7 CHARACTERISTICS OF POVERTY FAMILIES (1997)

Category	*Percentage of Families Below Poverty Levels*
Race	
White	8.4
African American	23.6
Hispanic	24.7
Education of family head	
No high school diploma	24.1
High school, no college	9.9
Some college, no degree	6.6
Bachelor's degree or more	2.0
Age of family head	
15–24 years	31.0
25–34 years	16.2
35–44 years	10.5
45–54 years	5.8
55–64 years	7.0
65 or more years	6.0

Source: Statistical Abstract of the United States.

and Hispanics. The family head has little education and is young. About one-third of the American poor are children under the age of 18. The poor live in central cities and in rural areas. Contrary to popular myth, a majority are working poor. About two-thirds of the poor receive some form of cash assistance from government antipoverty programs.

Government Solutions: The Welfare State

In the United States, poverty was viewed as a problem for religious and private charitable organizations until the Great Depression. Prior to the Depression, private charity seemed sufficient to handle the job. Between 1929 and 1933, hard-working families were left without jobs, whole industries collapsed, and the banking system was in disarray. The economic suffering created by the Great Depression was clearly not the fault of the unemployed workers and was too great to be solved by private charity.

President Franklin Roosevelt and his administration enacted legislation in the 1930s—unemployment insurance, Social Security, jobs programs, and the like—that gave government the role of dealing with poverty. Subsequent administrations, particularly Lyndon Johnson's Great Society programs of the mid-1960s, solidified the government's role as a provider of jobs, training, health, and education for the poorer segments of American society. Today, federal, state, and local governments oversee a vast array of welfare programs such as job training for poor youth, Aid to Families with Dependent Children, school lunch programs, and free immunization programs.

Table 8 shows the magnitude of the U.S. welfare state: By the late 1990s, the government was spending $1.5 trillion—or $15,000 per U.S. household—on social welfare expenditures, and almost $300 billion of government cash and in-kind benefits directly

TABLE 8 MEASURES OF THE U.S. WELFARE STATE (1995)

1. Social welfare expenditures under public programs, federal, state, and local governments		$1,505 billion
2. Total number of U.S. households		98.7 million
3. Social welfare expenditure per household		$15,250
4. Federal, state, and local government cash and noncash benefit programs for persons with limited income		
Public aid	$254 billion	
Health	86	
Veterans	38	
Housing benefits	29	
Education	366	
Other	13	
Total		

Source: Statistical Abstract of the United States.

EXAMPLE 4

Our Modest Negative Income Tax

The Earned Income Tax Credit (EITC) reduces the tax burden for low-income workers. Workers apply directly to the Internal Revenue Service for the EITC and generally receive the credit as part of their tax refund. Only families with a working member are eligible for the EITC, and the amount depends on the family's labor market earnings. For example, in the 1999 tax year, a worker with one child received a credit of 34 cents per dollar of 1998 earnings, up to a maximum of $2,271. The tax credit becomes part of the tax refund when the taxpayer files. A large family could earn a maximum of about $4,000. The tax credit is phased out as earnings increase.

The EITC is targeted to families living in poverty, with the goal of lifting their income above the poverty line. The latest estimate from the Bureau of the Census shows that the EITC lifted 4.3 million persons—workers themselves and their family members—out of poverty in 1997, more than twice as many as in 1993. Just over half (2.2 million) of these were under the age of 18, and 1.8 million were living in families headed by unmarried women.

The EITC is still smaller than the negative income tax that Friedman envisioned. Friedman suggested replacing the entire welfare system by a negative income tax. There is some evidence that the EITC has worked to increase work incentives. According to the *Economic Report of the President,* by 1996 the EITC increased the labor supply by 19.9 million hours and induced an estimated 516,000 families to move from welfare into the workforce.

Source: Economic Report of the President, 1999.

on the poor. The percentage of poverty households has stubbornly remained above 10 percent. Why has this government effort not had a more positive impact? Has it had unintended consequences?

The U.S. welfare system is founded on the principle that public assistance should be granted primarily on the basis of need. The government has established a number of programs—such as Aid to Families with Dependent Children (AFDC), the food stamp program, public housing, and Medicaid—in which the amount of public assistance is based upon family income. Welfare authorities must determine what resources the family has.

The army of welfare workers that is required to document needs and resources makes the system very costly. Dollars that could be devoted to public assistance are diverted to pay the bureaucratic costs of operating the system.

One way to sidestep most of these bureaucratic costs would be to institute a proposal by Milton Friedman, one of the first Nobel Prize winners in economics. Friedman proposed a *negative income tax* that would give an amount of money to people who make less than a certain minimum to increase their money income to some basic level. As income increases, the negative tax payment would be reduced. But the negative income tax has this key feature: As people work more, their money income increases so that the disincentive effects of other welfare programs are reduced. We do have something like this today, called the earned income tax credit, which does substantially the same thing. Example 4 describes how it works.

Unintended Consequences

The intent of government welfare assistance programs is to reduce or even eliminate poverty. Like many government programs, welfare assistance programs have unintended consequences that have created long-term problems.

The granting of government assistance on the basis of demonstrated need reduces the household's incentive to earn income. A welfare mother risks losing assistance if she takes a job or if the children's father lives in the home and earns income. The welfare system, as currently structured, encourages welfare fathers to desert the home. By having assistance rise with the number of children, existing programs encourage pregnancies.

Welfare dependency is passed from one generation to another. Young women grow up in broken homes headed by their mother, who is dependent on welfare assistance. One escape from that broken home is to have children—with the father absent—and to collect welfare payments.

Despite the substantial portion of all government spending devoted to welfare, the incidence of poverty has not declined, and the percentage of poverty families headed by single mothers has risen. In 1970, 11 percent of all births were to unmarried women. In 1997, about one-third of all births were to unmarried women. In 1970, 40 percent of all births of African American children were to unmarried women; by 1997 it was 70 percent. In 1970, 9 percent of white families, 28 percent of African American families, and 15 percent of Hispanic families were headed by females. In 1998, 14 percent of white families and 47 percent of African American families were headed by females.

Many government programs have unintended consequences, confirming that it will be difficult to devise policies that do not have these undesired consequences. The mere recognition of unintended consequences does not necessarily explain how to devise a policy that avoids them. In order to minimize these unintended consequences, recent welfare reforms have limited welfare assistance to five years.

These past mistakes do not suggest, however, that we should not care for the poor and less fortunate. Instead, they make clear that in establishing socioeconomic programs, we must devise policies that achieve the desired result—such as solving the problem of poverty—without perpetuating or accentuating the problem. Such economic policies must provide incentives for the poor to escape poverty, not encourage them to remain poor.

Welfare Reform

The unintended consequences of permanent welfare assistance led, in 1996, to the Personal Responsibility and Work Opportunity Reconciliation Act (PRWORA). This law changed the nation's welfare system substantially. Welfare assistance is now focused on work and is time-limited. Federal welfare assistance is strongly linked to the recipient's efforts to find a job. Adults cannot receive aid for more than a total of five years during their lifetime, and in some states the maximum is even lower. PRWORA also shifted greater responsibility to states and localities. Welfare caseloads have fallen dramatically since PRWORA was enacted. The national welfare caseload peaked in 1994; over the next four years it declined by 42 percent. This reduction was due in part to the unprecedented economic expansion of the U.S. economy during the period when national unemployment rates fell from over 6 percent to, in early 2000, just over 4 percent.

There is also a Welfare-to-Work Grants Program that targets long-term, hard-to-employ welfare recipients, helping them move into lasting, unsubsidized employment. These resources are channeled through localities to private businesses. In addition, employers who hire and retain long-term welfare recipients may receive a welfare-to-work tax credit. The credit for each eligible worker hired is equal to 35 percent of the first $10,000 in wages during the first year of employment and 50 percent of the first 10,000 in the second year.

In this chapter, we have examined the causes of inequality in the distribution of income and directed attention to the role of government in the redistribution of income to the poor. In the next three chapters, we shall focus on the role of government and its impact on the environment, public finance, and public choice.

SUMMARY

1. The sources of income inequality include different abilities, discrimination, occupational differences, different amounts of human-capital investment, and inheritance. Differences in schooling may affect earnings because employers use educational credentials to screen and select job candidates for high-paying careers. Earning differentials, both between whites and nonwhites and between males and females, have been reduced in recent years.

2. The Lorenz curve measures the degree of income inequality. It shows the cumulative percentages of all income earned by households at successive income levels. If the Lorenz curve is a 45-degree line, income distribution is perfectly equal. The

more the Lorenz curve bows away from the 45-degree line, the more unequal is the distribution of income. The government may change the distribution of income through taxes and the distribution of public services. The Gini coefficient is an alternate measure of income inequality.

3. The U.S. distribution of income became more equal from 1929 to 1970. It has become less equal after 1970. It also becomes more equal after it is adjusted for taxes and in-kind services.

4. There are different views on what constitutes distributive justice. Marginal productivity theory calls for a distribution of income according to the marginal productivity of the resources owned by households. The utilitarian school believes that an equal distribution of income maximizes total utility.

5. Poverty can be measured in either absolute or relative terms. The absolute measure is based on a definition of the minimum income necessary to allow a household to buy the minimum essentials. The relative standard measures poverty in terms of the household's location in the income distribution. According to the absolute measures of poverty made by the U.S. government, the number of people living below the poverty line declined between 1960 and 1970 but has not had a distinct trend thereafter. Poor Americans tend to be nonwhite, poorly educated members of households headed by females, and either very young or very old.

6. Income maintenance programs provide only short-run solutions to the problem of poverty. They also have unintended consequences.

7. Currently, the United States provides earned income tax credits and tax credits to employers who hire long-term welfare recipients. There is also a total lifetime federal limitation of five years on welfare assistance.

KEY TERMS

compensating wage differentials 348
risk seekers 348
risk avoiders 348
human-capital theory 349
discrimination 350
screening 351
Lorenz curve 352
Gini coefficient 352
in-kind income 353
natural law 355
utilitarian theory 356
absolute poverty standard 357
relative poverty standard 357

QUESTIONS AND PROBLEMS

1. Draw a Lorenz curve for absolute equality. Draw a Lorenz curve for absolute inequality. Explain the situation illustrated by the absolute inequality Lorenz curve.
2. Evaluate the validity of the following statement: "If all people were the same, the Lorenz curve would be a 45-degree line."
3. Evaluate the validity of the following statement: "The fact that a woman earns, on average, two-thirds of what a man earns proves beyond a shadow of a doubt that there is sexual discrimination."
4. There are two views of the causes of poverty. One school says that the poor are poor through no fault of their own. The other says that the poor are poor through choice. Give arguments for each position.
5. How does screening theory explain the apparently poor correlation between ability and inequality?
6. Explain why measured Lorenz curves that use disposable income before and after taxes may not give an accurate picture of the distribution of real income.
7. Explain some of the unintended consequences of current poverty programs. Explain how we should devise new programs that avoid unintended consequences.
8. Assume that a society consists of eight risk avoiders and two risk seekers. Contrast that society with one that consists of five risk seekers and five risk avoiders. Which society will have a more equal distribution of income?
9. Joe wants goods today; Bill is more willing to wait until tomorrow. Which one is more likely to invest in human capital?
10. The official U.S. poverty income standard is adjusted upward each year to account for the general increase in prices. If a family's income just keeps up with the poverty income over the years, what is happening to its relative poverty position?
11. Education is distributed among the population more equally than income. What does this tell

you about the relationship between education and inequality?

12. What are the main purposes of each of the following:
    a. The earned-income tax credit for poor working families
    b. Credits to employers for hiring long-term welfare recipients
    c. Overall time limits on welfare assistance

INTERNET CONNECTION

13. Using the links from http://www.awl.com/ruffin_gregory, examine the Census Bureau's Web page on inequality.
    a. Plot a graph using the Gini coefficient for total inequality in the United States starting from 1968 to the most current year. What can you conclude from this graph about inequality in the United States?
    b. Do the same thing for African American households. Are there any differences in the trend of African American inequality over time?

PUZZLE ANSWERED: Income is not growing more unequal because the poor are getti ng poorer, but because the rich are getting richer in absolute terms. Inequality is measured by relative differences. In constant dollars, a smaller percentage of households have incomes less than $10,000 among whites and African Americans, and a larger percentage of households have incomes above $75,000, especially among African Americans and Hispanics. Thus, more people are moving up the ladder of success and fewer down the ladder.

part IV

Microeconomic Issues

Chapter 20

Market Failure, the Environment, and Natural Resources

Chapter Insight

Doomsayers warn that unless we change our ways we shall be left with a dying planet. There will be no forests, no drinkable water, no wildernesses. We shall scarcely be able to venture outdoors because of the depleted ozone layer. Global warming will cause the arctic ice caps to melt, thereby flooding much of the earth's land mass. We shall all have to move to higher land; there will not be enough land to feed us all. Even if we escape skin cancer or malnutrition, we shall face the prospect of running out of resources. We will not be able to sustain our standard of living, as we now know it; we will be forced to return to a more primitive style of life.

Optimists, on the other hand, characterize such dire predictions of doom as hogwash—as the rantings and ravings of radical ecologists, who use scare tactics to gain public support. Optimists point out that there is no firm scientific evidence of greenhouse effects, of global warming, or of other impending ecological disasters. The greatest environmental damage, they argue, has occurred in the developing countries, not in the highly industrialized world. The radical ecologists simply do not like capitalism and the high standard of living it has created. They wish to spoil the party.

Who is right? Who is wrong? That is the subject of this chapter. Does Adam Smith's invisible hand somehow protect us from pollution and resource exhaustion? Can we rely on private incentives, or must government intervene?

LEARNING OBJECTIVES

After completing this chapter, you will be able to:

1. Define externalities.
2. Define the social optimum.
3. List the three approaches to internalizing externalities.
4. Determine optimal abatement expenditures.
5. Differentiate between the regulatory approach and the incentive approach to environmental protection.

CHAPTER PUZZLE: How can private behavior take into account the possibility that some resources are finite and are used up by modern production techniques?

Why Does the Market Fail?

In earlier chapters we have discussed a number of instances where the market economy may not satisfactorily solve the economic problem of *what, how,* and *for whom.* In a monopoly industry, consumers pay prices that are higher than necessary for a quantity of output that has been artificially restrained by the producer. The market economy may distribute income so unevenly among households that there is general dissatisfaction with the result. In both cases, the government can take action to correct the errors made by the market. The government might use antitrust laws to break up the monopoly; it can use progressive taxes to redistribute income from the rich to the poor.

In this chapter, we deal with market failures in which the invisible hand has not worked properly.

Market failure occurs when the price system fails to yield the socially optimal quantity of a good.

Market failures can take the form of environmental pollution, in which enterprises pollute water, air, the earth's surface, and even outer space. They can also take the form of public goods—such as national defense or a legal system—that may not be produced at all or are underproduced because the decision has been left to the market. In this chapter we shall examine environmental pollution and nonrenewable resources. Can a market economy deal with pollution or with a finite resource? We shall discuss public goods in the next chapter.

Market failures have a number of causes. They occur when private costs and benefits diverge from social costs and benefits. They occur when nonpayers for goods cannot be kept from enjoying their benefits and when your use of a good does not detract from my use.

Market failures raise the question of whether government action is required to correct the failure of the market economy.

Externalities: Private Versus Social Costs

Externalities plague all economies. They are present whenever the actions of one agent have direct economic effects on other agents. Simple examples are the negative external effects of smoking, or noisy neighbors, or the positive effects of a neighbor's beautiful rosebushes.

Externalities exist when producers or consumers do not bear the full marginal cost or enjoy the full marginal benefit of their actions.

When externalities are present, market transactions between two parties will have harmful or beneficial effects on third parties. The effects are "external" to the price system and are not the outcome of mutual agreement among all the interested parties.

Let's take the case of a factory that pollutes the air, thereby imposing cleaning or health care costs on the surrounding community. These external costs are paid not by the factory, but by others; external costs do not appear in the factory's cost accounting.

Externalities can be positive as well as negative. The person who pays for an education is not the only one who benefits: Society benefits when education creates a trained workforce and scientific and technological progress.

Social Efficiency

When external costs or benefits are present, we determine social efficiency by comparing social costs and social benefits.

Social costs equal private costs plus external costs. **Social benefits** equal private benefits plus external benefits.

We considered private costs in earlier chapters on costs, competition, and monopoly. Private costs are the enterprise's opportunity costs. The firm's marginal private cost is its opportunity cost of increasing its output by one unit. When external costs are present, the marginal cost to society of producing one more unit of output equals this marginal private cost plus the marginal external cost. External costs create a market failure by inducing the private firm to produce too much output (see Figure 1).

External costs cause the competitive firm to produce too much output. The firm produces that level of output at which marginal private costs and marginal private benefits are equal. If a firm ignores the external costs of its actions, its marginal social costs will exceed its marginal social benefits at the profit-maximizing level of output. Society as a whole would be better off if the competitive firm reduced its output to where marginal social costs and marginal social benefits are equal. Figure 1 shows that the socially optimal level of output is less than the competitive output when external costs are present. (See Example 1).

Social efficiency requires that marginal social benefits and marginal social costs be equal, but private participants equate only marginal private benefits with marginal private costs.

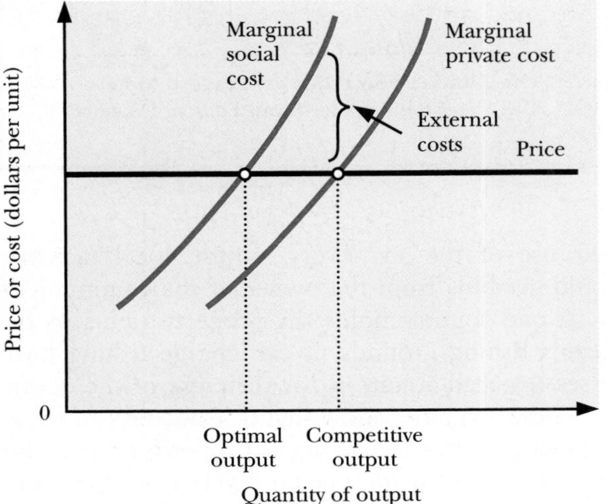

FIGURE 1 Perfect Competition with External Costs

When external costs are present, competitive firms produce too much output because they produce at the level where marginal private costs equal price, not where marginal social costs equal price.

Pollution by industry and by private cars are externalities that can impose substantial external costs on the community. Commercial fishers deplete fishing waters by not considering the external costs of overfishing. Modern reflective-glass skyscrapers raise the air-conditioning costs of neighboring buildings. A family that allows its house and lawn to deteriorate reduces the pleasure neighbors obtain from their own houses and lawns as well as real estate values.

The failure of even competitive firms to produce the socially optimal level of output represents a market failure.

What to Do About Externalities

In order to eliminate an externality problem, a firm must include external costs or benefits in its calculations of private gain. The solution is to internalize, or put a private price tag on, externalities. This price must be paid by those who impose costs on others.

An externality undergoes **internalization** when private price tags are placed on external costs (or benefits) so that private and social costs (or benefits) coincide.

If we pay for the costs we impose on others or receive a payment for the benefits that others receive from our actions, we incorporate such costs and benefits into our private cost-benefit calculations. An example of internalization is the merger of two factories located on a river. Prior to the merger, the downstream factory has to pay water purification costs because the upstream factory is polluting the water. After the merger, the external costs of the downstream factory become internal costs that the merged firms consider in private cost/benefit calculations.

Internalization can be accomplished by the redefinition of property rights, by voluntary agreements, or by government action.

Redefinition of Property Rights

An externality can be internalized by the redefinition of property rights.

Property rights specify who owns a resource and who has the right to use it.

Poor definition of property rights is a prominent source of externalities. If we do not know who owns

EXAMPLE 1

How to Deal with Trash

In a vibrant economy, an enormous amount of trash is generated by the bulging consumption habits of a rich economy. If trash represents a negative externality on the long-run health of the environment, reducing trash will be a benefit. The problems with controlling trash in the state of Oregon are typical. Oregonians pride themselves as national leaders in recycling; the first state to pass a bottle bill, Oregon established a five-cent deposit on all soft-drink and beer bottles. But the state is fighting a losing battle with trash. Although Oregonians recycle 37 percent of their trash compared to 28 percent for the country, the amount of trash is piling up. In 1998 the average Oregonian threw away 7.2 pounds of garbage each day, up from 5.7 pounds five years earlier. The state is trying to figure out what can be done, since their goal is to have 100 percent recycling and completely empty trash cans.

The problem with some programs to control recycling is that they rely on the voluntary efforts of each citizen. Citizens can be harried and hectored as much as the government wants, but the amount of trash will continue to grow because each person has an incentive to use the lowest cost method of trash disposal. This currently represents just tossing the garbage in the trash can and letting the garbage truck take it. But if trash is an externality—raising the cost of other goods by raising production costs—then the best way to handle the problem is through a tax. Voluntary recycling efforts run into the prisoner's dilemma: It is in the interest of all to recycle, but without financial encouragement it is in the interests of each to throw the garbage in the trash. The evidence is that most people do just that. The five-cent deposit on bottles is the type of incentive that works. Fines are difficult to implement.

Source: "Ore. Officials Fear Prosperity Leads to More Trash," *Wall Street Journal,* Northwest Edition, December 8, 1999.

the property rights to the air in a domed stadium or in an airplane, to the whales in the seas, or the rights to scenic views, these resources will likely be exploited and abused. Fishing businesses will overfish ocean waters, factories will pollute the air, and scenery will be destroyed by unsightly signs.

When no one knows who the owner of a resource is, there is no one to limit its use. However, if private property rights can be clearly defined, the private owner will make sure that the resource is efficiently used. The owner of hunting land can set fees high enough to prevent game from being depleted. If the city council is somehow given ownership of the community's air, it can charge polluting factories for their use of the air. Every month, local factories would get bills from the owner of the community's air. If one country holds the property rights to the ocean's fishing grounds, it can charge fishing businesses from all countries for their use of the ocean.

These examples show that it is not easy to eliminate externalities by changing property rights. This strategy will not work when it is very costly to define or enforce property rights. Let's consider, for example, the overkilling of whales. How do we determine who owns the whales and how do we protect the owner's property rights? The ownership rights to clean air are so vague that those harmed by air pollution have difficulty suing polluters. In both cases, we have too little information to enforce property rights. If we do not know how many whales there are and how many each whaler has killed, or how much pollution each car has emitted, how can we know the real marginal cost to society of each whale killed or of the pollution from each car?

Voluntary Agreements

Voluntary agreements are a second means of internalizing externalities. The merger of the two factories on a river mentioned above is an example of such a voluntary agreement. When property rights are well defined, voluntary agreements can internalize external costs.

The proposition that voluntary agreements can solve externality problems is called the Coase theorem, after 1991 Nobel laureate Ronald H. Coase. Coase argues that external costs and benefits can be internalized by negotiations among affected parties. He uses the example of a rancher whose cattle stray onto a neighboring farm and damage the neighbor's crops. If the rancher were legally liable for the crop damage, private bargaining would result in a deal in which the farmer would be paid by the rancher for the increased cost caused by the straying cattle. These extra costs would induce the rancher either to reduce the size of the herd or to build better fences.

The same result would be achieved even if the rancher's cattle had the legal right to stray onto the farmer's land. The farmer could agree to pay the rancher to reduce the size of the herd or build a fence. Again, when a price tag is placed on the externality, it disappears. Although the social effect—the amount of crops and cattle produced—is the same, the distribution of income depends upon who has the property rights. In the first case, the rancher transfers income to the farmer. In the second case, the farmer transfers income to the rancher.

Some externalities can indeed be resolved by voluntary agreements. Washington State apple growers actually pay beekeepers a fee for pollination. Ships pay lighthouses for their guidance during nighttime travel near the coast. Large industrial enterprises agree to buy and sell pollution rights. Like the redefinition of property rights, voluntary agreements work only in selected cases. The number of parties has to be small; the costs of bargaining must be small.

Consider the case of hayfever sufferers who would be willing to pay farmers to reduce the amount of ragweed. There are too many hayfever sufferers, dispersed over a large territory, and there are too many potential sources of ragweed. In this case, the externality cannot be internalized by voluntary agreement between hayfever sufferers and farmers.

> The Coase theorem states that if small numbers are involved and bargaining costs are small, voluntary agreements can internalize an externality. When large numbers are involved and the costs are widely dispersed, voluntary agreements will be difficult to reach.

Government Taxes and Subsidies

A third way for an externality to be internalized is for the government to impose corrective taxes or subsidies. When private activities result in external costs, the volume of transactions will exceed what is efficient because private agents ignore external costs. An appropriate tax on the externality will force the business firm to take into account the costs imposed on others and will, accordingly, reduce the amount of production to the efficient level where marginal social costs equal marginal social benefits.

Figure 2 shows how taxation can be used to internalize an external cost. If a tax equal to the external cost per unit of output is imposed on the factory, the supply curve will shift automatically to the left. With the new supply curve, the firm will produce the optimal level of output at which marginal social costs and benefits are equal.

Government action to correct externalities is most appropriate when they cannot be internalized through redefinition of property rights or by voluntary agreements. Government internalization, like private solutions to externalities, requires considerable information. To levy the right tax, the government must know who is imposing external costs. The government must also be able to measure these external costs. The government must be careful not to enact measures that result in negative unintended consequences. (See Example 2.)

Pollution, Externalities, and Government Action

Pollution illustrates the difficulties of internalizing externalities. Pollution can be the consequence of both production and consumption. Factories discharge their wastes into the atmosphere and water. Nuclear power plants must dispose of their nuclear

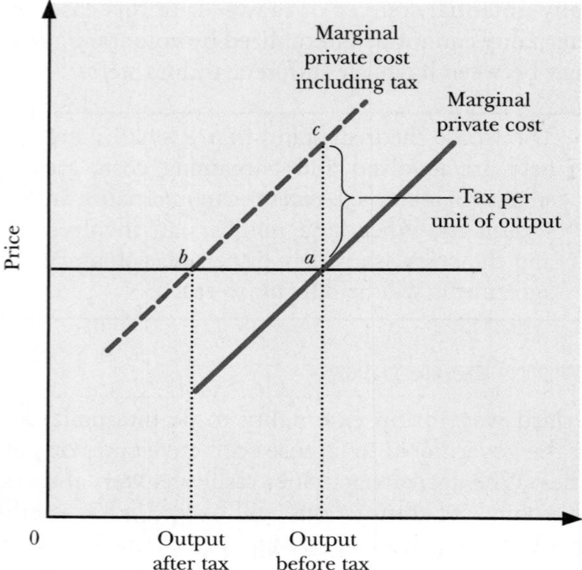

FIGURE 2 Use of Taxes to Correct Externalities

Competitive firms in this industry operate at point *a*, which is too much output because each unit of output creates an external cost equal to *ac*. If the government levies a tax on procedures equal to this external cost, it will be internalized and firms will produce the optimal level of output at *b*.

wastes. Households produce sewage and garbage, and pollute the air with their automobiles. The polluting factory and the polluting household both create external costs. The private costs of their activities are less than the social costs.

Pollution can be local, regional, or even global. Local pollution affects the immediate surroundings of the site of emission. The damage from regional pollution is realized at a distance from its source. Global pollution occurs when pollutants are released into the earth's upper atmosphere, from which it is broadly dispersed.

Environmental pollution is an externality that often requires government intervention. Other means of internalization—redefinition of property rights and voluntary agreements—are usually not effective. It is difficult if not impossible to assign property rights to a river, a lake, air, or outer space. Even if property rights can be established, the legal costs of suing another party for violating a property right can be high. Because pollutants cross political boundaries and many parties are affected, effective action is rarely taken. It is difficult to enforce those private contracts that are negotiated when polluters are numerous or when monitoring costs are high.

EXAMPLE 2

Unintended Consequences: The Electric Car

The Clean Air Act set tough standards for ozone emissions from automobiles to contain urban smog. To meet the standards in the Clean Air Act, several states set the goal of having "zero emissions vehicles" constitute 10 percent of all vehicles on the road by the year 2003. The only zero emissions vehicles that are close to mass production are powered by electric lead-acid batteries.

The law of unintended consequences warns that policy makers must be careful to anticipate unforeseen secondary effects. Scientific evidence now suggests that switching from conventional gasoline engines to lead battery–powered engines would trade off one form of pollution for another. An available-technology electric car generates about 2000 milligrams of lead emissions for every mile, about six times as much as a tiny Geo Metro burning gasoline with the lead additives that were eliminated in the 1980s. Exposure to low levels of lead can cause brain damage in young children, and severe exposure can cause convulsions and death.

To devise the correct environmental policy, we must be able to measure the benefits from reducing ozone emissions versus the costs of more lead emissions. There are few if any free lunches!

Source: "Electric Car Batteries Called a Toxic Peril," *New York Times,* May 9, 1995.

Some pollutants can be returned naturally to the environment. Carbon dioxide, for example, is absorbed by plant life and by the oceans. Other pollutants, such as nonbiodegradable bottles or lead, cannot be absorbed naturally. When the emission of pollutants exceeds the environment's absorptive capacity, pollutants accumulate and cause environmental damage. Environmental waste must be disposed of, whether in the ground, in water, or in the air.

Waste disposal costs are real opportunity costs. Resources devoted to pollution prevention, such as scrubbers on smokestacks, are not available for other uses. There is an opportunity cost to you when you purchase bottled water or air filters to prevent health damage. Diseases from toxic-waste dumps represent costs to individuals and the community, be they cash outlays or less visible opportunity costs.

Optimal Pollution

Pollution can be reduced (abated) either by reducing the activity of the polluting agent or by paying the costs of pollution abatement. Air pollution can be reduced through cutbacks in factory production or in the use of cars that produce air pollutants, or through installation of scrubbers on smokestacks and antipollution devices on automobiles. In all these cases, the reduction of pollution has abatement costs.

What is the optimal level of pollution abatement? How much of society's resources should be devoted to pollution abatement? Optimal abatement is achieved at that level where the marginal social costs of further abatement equal the marginal social benefits. It may be surprising to someone who is not an economist, but the optimal level is not achieved at zero pollution. How much pollution society should tolerate is determined by weighing costs and benefits at the margin.

Figure 3 shows the marginal social costs and marginal social benefits of different amounts of pollution abatement—in this case, the number of gallons of water purified through filtration. The marginal social cost of each successive unit of abatement increases as more and more water is purified. Marginal social benefits decline as abatement intensifies because we value the first unit of abatement more highly than subsequent units.

The **optimal level of abatement** occurs when the marginal social cost of an extra unit of abatement equals its marginal social benefit.

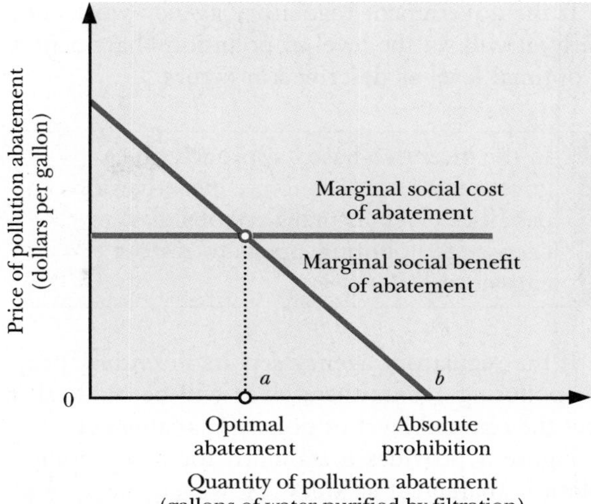

FIGURE 3 Optimal Pollution Abatement

This figure shows how the optimal amount of pollution abatement is determined. The marginal social benefit curve is downward sloping (people place a higher value on the first units of abatement). The marginal social cost of pollution abatement is assumed constant. The optimal amount of abatement is quantity *a* (where marginal social cost equals marginal social benefit). Point *b*, the total prohibition of pollution, is not optimal because the marginal social benefit (zero) is less than the marginal social cost.

If abatement is undertaken beyond this optimal level, the extra benefits fall short of the extra opportunity costs. We should not aim for the total elimination of pollution. To do so, we would have to devote more and more scarce resources to abatement, until the marginal social benefits are zero. The last dollar spent on pollution abatement will yield zero benefits and will have a high marginal cost. It may cost $5 million to have the last drop of water purified, but the benefit may be worth only $5.

Pollution and Government Considerations

Figure 3 provides a guide to government action concerning pollution abatement. If the government can indeed calculate the marginal costs and marginal benefits of pollution abatement, it can establish either regulations or incentives to achieve the optimal level of pollution abatement.

With the **regulatory approach**, the government requires polluting agents to limit emissions to a prescribed level.

If the government regulatory agency works efficiently, it will set the level of pollution abatement at the optimal level as described in Figure 3.

In the **incentive-based approach**, the government uses economic incentives or penalties (such as taxes or subsidies) to encourage polluting agents to restrict emissions.

If the regulatory agency sets its incentives properly, polluting agents themselves will be induced to select the optimal level of pollution abatement.

Figure 3 provides a standard for determining a pollution abatement strategy. However, the application of such a cost/benefit analysis presents practical problems. First, it is difficult to calculate the marginal costs and benefits of various pollution abatement activities. Some costs and benefits are apparent only over time. Pollution affects large numbers of people and different areas. Second, waste disposal involves complicated physical, biological, and chemical interactions. One abatement procedure that increases water purity may have the unintended consequence of shifting discharges to the atmosphere. Third, we must decide who should receive the benefits and who should bear the costs of pollution abatement. Should private firms pay? Should only affected individuals pay? These decisions affect the distribution of income.

If the regulatory approach is properly applied, the government would require the polluting agent to limit emissions to the optimal level as shown in Figure 3. Each factory, for example, would have a limit on the amount of pollutants that it is allowed to discharge. Automobile manufacturers would be required to place catalytic converters on their cars and trucks; oil refiners would be required to eliminate lead from gasoline.

An incentive-based approach, on the other hand, uses economic incentives or penalties to induce polluting agents to restrict their emissions to the efficient level. Factories, for example, are charged a fee for every ton of pollutant emitted into the atmosphere.

U.S. Environmental Policy

In the United States, various state, local, and federal agencies are responsible for pollution control. Since 1970, the Environmental Protection Agency (EPA), acting through the states and on its own, has been charged with regulating pollution activities. The EPA derives its legislative authority from a number of congressional acts, including the Clean Air Act, the Water Pollution Control Act, the National Environmental Policy Act, and the Toxic Substances Control Act.

In enforcing federal environmental laws, the EPA has usually followed the regulatory approach. It specifies standards for waste discharge with respect to air, water, and noise pollution. It issues permits setting ceilings on the amounts of pollutants that can be discharged and requiring that the discharger meet these ceilings by a specified date using the most practical or best available technology.

It is difficult to devise regulatory controls that produce optimal abatement. The EPA usually sets discharge limits without reference to marginal costs or benefits, yet environmental policies require a balancing of costs and benefits. For this reason, the EPA has also experimented with incentive-based approaches.

Indeed, U.S. practice has demonstrated that government agencies are ineffective at devising optimal pollution abatement. The regulatory approach has been increasingly criticized for its rigidity and its high costs. Accordingly, there has been a distinct trend toward incentive-based programs, which place price tags on pollution externalities. Incentive-based programs, however, do not necessarily yield optimal abatement because of the complexity of the pollution problem and the consequent difficulty of setting appropriate price tags.

In an ideal incentive-based policy, the government controls pollutants by imposing fees—called effluent charges—that should be equal to the marginal external cost of the pollutant. Such effluent charges cause the polluting firm to consider external costs in its private economic calculations. The EPA has experimented with a number of "market solutions" to establish optimal effluent charges. Under its emissions trading program, companies are allowed to trade, or even buy and sell, pollution rights from one another. Under its bubble program, the EPA permits new pollution sources to operate if they are able to buy an equivalent reduction in pollution discharges from existing firms.

Incentive schemes reduce the costs of pollution abatement because dischargers are allowed to make their own decisions. Firms that can reduce discharges cheaply will sell their pollution rights to firms that can reduce emissions only at high costs. Even if the

EXAMPLE 3

TRADING POLLUTION RIGHTS

In December 1990, in an unprecedented arrangement, Metallized Paper Corporation of America bought pollution rights from USX's Clairton Works and from Papercraft Corporation in Allegheny County, Pennsylvania. Metallized Paper paid USX $75,000 for the right to emit 75 tons of pollution per year, purchased 32 tons from Papercraft, and received an additional 500-ton donation from USX. The sale of pollution rights was legal under the Federal Clean Air Act. Both USX and Papercraft Corporation possessed rights to emit a certain number of tons of pollutants into the environment up to a limit determined by the Environmental Protection Agency. By selling these rights, both agreed to cut back on their pollution emissions by the number of tons sold.

Since this initial trade in 1990, trading in pollution rights has grown into a market managed by the Chicago Board of Trade, which auctions billions of dollars of air pollution credits. Notably, the prices paid for pollution rights fell in mid-1996 to half of what they were only a year earlier. This fall in prices means that firms have learned to reduce pollution at a much lower cost. In 1996 the per ton cleanup cost was $750, down from almost $1500 a year earlier.

end result is not optimal, at least the costs of pollution control are reduced. (See Example 3.)

> Incentive-based programs allow pollution reduction standards to be achieved at a lower cost of society's resources.

Although the EPA may not have been able to achieve an optimal level of pollution abatement, nevertheless achievements have been notable. For example, according to the EPA, toxic emissions into the atmosphere were reduced by more than 25 percent during the 1990s, arising for the most part from cleaner gasoline. However, the financial costs have been large but not substantial. The EPA's budget for fiscal year 2000 was about $7.5 billion for all of its programs (out of a total government budget of about $1800 billion).

EXHAUSTIBLE RESOURCES

Externalities can cause market failure and require government action. Exhaustible resources represent another potential market failure. Government action may also be necessary to prevent the exhaustion of our nonrenewable resources.

> An **exhaustible** (or **nonrenewable**) **resource** is any resource of which there is a finite amount in the long run because the stock is fixed by nature.

Examples of exhaustible resources are oil, gas, coal, titanium, gold, and other mineral resources.

Rational Allocation of Exhaustible Resources

Consider a firm that owns an exhaustible resource. It must decide how to allocate its fixed stock of the resource over time. A firm that extracts crude oil from a reservoir must decide how much to supply to the market this year, next year, 5 years from now, and 20 years from now. Will economic incentives cause it automatically to conserve on the use of this resource?

A firm extracting nonrenewable resources faces a different type of opportunity cost. In the case of renewable resources (such as trees), the decision to supply x units this year does not limit the future supply (trees can be planted). In the case of nonrenewable resources, every unit supplied this year is 1 unit not available for future years. Accordingly, suppliers of nonrenewable resources must make an *intertemporal* (across time) comparison of the costs and benefits of supplying the resource today versus supplying it tomorrow.

Let's suppose a firm can extract crude oil from a 1000-barrel reservoir at a zero marginal extraction cost (the oil simply rises by itself to the surface). For simplicity, let's also suppose that the firm must sell its entire stock of 1000 barrels within a 2-year period. The market rate of interest is 10 percent. How will this firm allocate its supply of crude oil between the 2 years? If the price of crude oil today is \$20 per barrel and the price expected next year is \$21.50, the firm should produce all 1000 barrels this year. By selling now, the firm gets \$20 per barrel that can be invested at 10 percent interest; next year, the firm will receive \$22 per barrel (\$20 × 1.1), a greater return than next year's selling price of \$21.50. If next year's price is more than \$22, the firm should wait until next year to sell all 1000 barrels. If the price rises at the same rate as the market interest rate (in this case, by 10 percent per annum), the firm will be indifferent as to whether it sells its stock of the nonrenewable resource this year or next year. It earns the same amount of revenues.

The Market for Exhaustible Resources

We have looked at how a firm decides to use its exhaustible resources over time. Let's now consider a perfectly competitive market consisting of a large number of competitive firms (see Figure 4). The stock of the exhaustible resource owned by all the firms together is fixed at 30 units, and firms must sell their entire stock within a 2-year period (either in period 0 or in period 1). The market rate of interest is 10 percent.

In Figure 4, the horizontal axis is 30 units long because only 30 units of the resource are available; the resource that is extracted in period 0 will not be available for period 1. The period 0 demand curve is

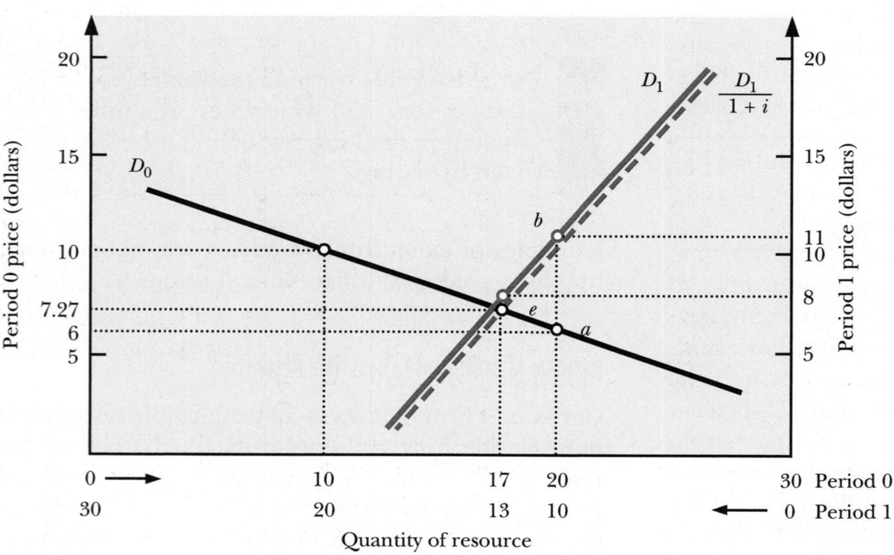

FIGURE 4 Market Equilibrium for an Exhaustible Resource in Two Periods

This figure represents a competitive market composed of a large number of perfectly competitive firms. The firms in the market together have a fixed supply of 30 units of the nonrenewable resource, and these 30 units must be used either in period 0 or period 1. The market demand curves are D_0 for period 0 and D_1 for period 1. (Period 1 quantity increases from right to left rather than from left to right.) Firms will contrast the price received in period 0 with the present discounted value of the price received in period 1. If the interest rate is 10 percent, $D_1 \div 1.1$ is the present discounted value of the period 1 demand curve. When the available supply is allocated between periods 0 and 1, the prices in the two periods are established. As long as the period 0 price is less than the present value of the period 1 price (as it is when the period 0 quantity is 20 and the period 1 quantity is 10), firms will reallocate supplies from period 0 to period 1. Equilibrium is attained when quantity is 17 in period 0 and 13 in period 1 and when price is \$8 in period 1 and \$7.27 in period 0. In equilibrium, the ratio of the price in period 1 to the price in period 0 will be 1 plus the interest rate, or 1.1.

a standard demand curve read from left to right, but the period 1 demand curve must be read from right to left. Both demand curves show what quantities are demanded in each period at various prices. Because only 30 units are available, the quantity available in period 1 is the amount left over after period 0.

The price in each period depends upon how many units are sold. If 20 units are sold in period 0 and 10 units are sold in period 1, period 0's price is $6 per unit (point *a*) and period 1's price is $11 per unit (point *b*). The individual firms will not be content with this outcome. Each unit sold in period 0 and invested at 10 percent interest is worth only $6.60 in period 1, whereas each unit sold in period 1 yields $11. Clearly, firms will want to supply fewer than 20 units in period 0 and more than 10 units in period 1.

An equilibrium is attained when the period 0 price equals the present discounted value of the period 1 price (when the period 0 price equals the period 1 price divided by 1.1). At this point, there is no longer an incentive to switch production from one period to the other. The dashed demand curve in Figure 4 shows the period 1 prices divided by 1.1 and represents the present discounted values of the period 1 prices. The quantity where the dashed curve intersects the period 0 demand curve (at point *e*) is the equilibrium quantity. The quantity corresponding to point *e* is 17 units in period 0 and 13 units in period 1. The period 0 price for 17 units is $7.27, and the period 1 price for 13 units is $8. These prices reflect the fact that the present discounted value of $8 is $7.27 in period 0 at a 10 percent rate of interest. At these prices, firms no longer have an incentive to shift supplies from one period to the other. Note that the price increases by 10 percent between period 0 and period 1 in this example.

> When marginal extraction costs are zero and the market is perfectly competitive, the price of an exhaustible resource will rise at the same rate as the interest rate.

The Technology of Resource Extraction

Figure 4 delivers a reassuring message: Competitive markets deal automatically with the rising scarcity of exhaustible resources. The annual growth rate of the prices of exhaustible resources should equal the market rate of interest. In other words, the natural rise in the prices of nonrenewable resources should discourage their present consumption and make supplies available for the future.

We can see the trend in the real price of a barrel of oil in Figure 5, which graphs the real price of oil from 1985 to 2000. The real price is falling.

The real prices of other exhaustible resources conform even less to the theory. Since the early nineteenth century there has been a distinct *downward* trend in the real price of other exhaustible resources, such as copper, aluminum, and pig iron. Why have the real prices of exhaustible resources not risen steadily as the theory predicts? If extraction costs are falling, the price of an exhaustible resource should rise more slowly than the rate of interest.

Technological Advances. If technological advances allow producers of exhaustible resources to increase their recovery rates, prices would not rise at the rate of interest. In fact, if technological advances are rapid, exhaustible resource prices can even fall.

Consider a resource firm that develops a new technology enabling it to recover more of the exhaustible resource in period 1 than in period 0. For example, suppose an oil company has a total of 200 barrels underground and, with existing technology, can recover one out of every two barrels extracted in period 0. A new technology that permits the recovery of 1.5 barrels from every 2 barrels underground is scheduled to be implemented in period 1. Thus, for every barrel sold in period 0, the firm passes up the opportunity to sell 1.5 barrels (with the new technology) in period 1. The anticipation of technological advances will shift more supplies to period 1, thereby lowering the period 1 price and raising the period 0 price.

> Technological advances that are expected to take place in the future cause supplies of exhaustible resources to be shifted to the future, thereby raising current prices and lowering future prices.

Backstop Resources. A *backstop resource* is a close substitute for an exhaustible resource, available in virtually unlimited supply but at a higher cost. Solar energy is a backstop for conventional energy, and shale oil and tar sands are backstops for conventional crude oil.

What effect does the availability of a backstop fuel, such as shale oil, have on the allocation of crude oil and oil prices over time? Let's assume that shale oil is available in virtually unlimited supply at a price

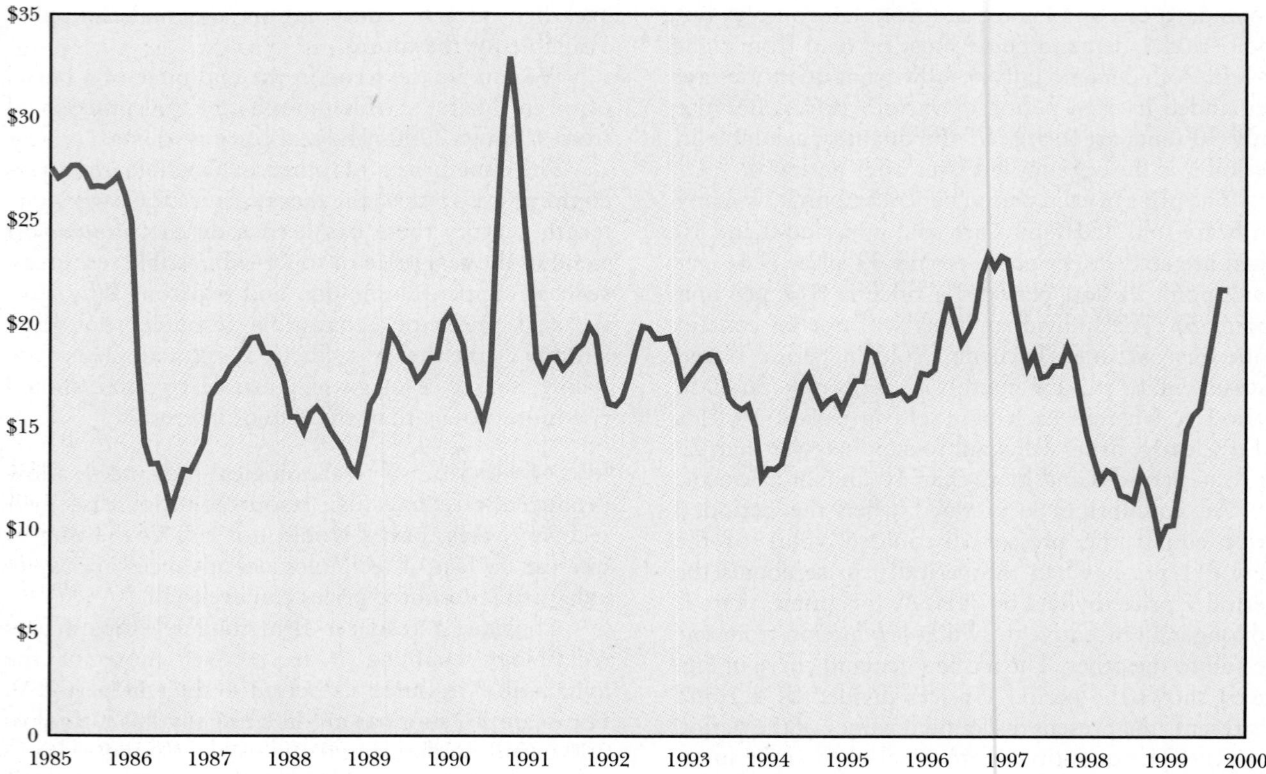

FIGURE 5 Price of Crude Oil, 1982–1984 Dollars (Monthly)

Source: http://www.Economagic.com

of $40 a barrel. The backstop fuel sets a price limit of $40 per barrel on conventional crude oil because consumers will switch to shale oil if the crude oil price rises above $40. With no technological advances, the price should increase by the rate of interest until the $40 backstop price is reached. After that point, the price will remain constant.

The existence of a backstop resource allows greater current consumption of the nonrenewable resource at lower current prices. Supplies of the nonrenewable resource need cover demands only up to the backstop price. As a result, more of the resource can be consumed now with the knowledge that needs in the distant future can be met by the alternative resource.

The Price System and Exhaustible Resources

Market forces cause nonrenewable resources to be allocated efficiently over time. As nonrenewable resources become more scarce, their price rises, and they are used more economically.

Suppliers weigh the returns from exploiting the resource now against waiting for the resource to become more scarce (and, thus, to sell for a higher price) tomorrow. Unless technological progress increases the supply of nonrenewable resources, their prices will tend to rise at the rate of interest. The fact that there is no clear trend in the relative prices of nonrenewable resources is a tribute to technological progress. As technology has improved recovery rates, we have been able to postpone the rising scarcity of nonrenewable resources.

The major threat to the rational use of nonrenewable resources is interference in the pricing of resources. If prices are controlled—for example, if price ceilings are placed on oil or natural gas—firms producing these resources will have to make resource allocation decisions on the basis of prices that do not correctly reflect scarcities today and tomorrow. In other words, price controls distort the natural balance between present and future consumption that is achieved by the price system.

Recycling of Exhaustible Resources

The price system encourages producers of exhaustible resources to sell less today in anticipation of more scarcity tomorrow. Recycling offers yet another opportunity for owners and users of exhaustible resources to be assured of a supply of the resource both now and in the future.

Recycling reintroduces used exhaustible resources (such as iron, metals, and petrochemicals) into the system, providing an alternative to current production.

Recycling of exhaustible resources can occur automatically through the price system or it can be stimulated by government intervention.

Let's consider the case of mercury, an exhaustible resource in which there is an active market for recycling. Mercury is a resource that is limited in supply but is used in many products, including industrial and control instruments, batteries, and dental amalgams. It has high disposal costs because of its toxic characteristics. Currently, about 47 percent of the annual usage of industrial mercury is obtained from recycled mercury. The percentage of recycled mercury depends upon its price and disposal cost. If mercury prices rise, more mercury is recycled.

Recycling proceeds at an economically efficient level when the marginal cost of recycling equals the marginal social cost of disposal. If it costs society $200 per ton to dispose of aluminum cans and $100 per ton to recycle aluminum, too little is being recycled. Whenever the marginal private cost of disposal is less than the marginal social cost, the amount of recycling falls short of the optimum. If people do not have to bear the full marginal costs of throwing away aluminum cans, tires, used cars, or old car batteries, recycling levels will be insufficient. It is for this reason that many states and communities have passed mandatory recycling laws.

Doomsday Predictions

Can market failures, such as those discussed in this chapter, become so severe as to threaten life itself? Various doomsday models have indeed suggested that industrialization and rising living standards will one day result in worldwide disaster. We are threatened with nuclear winters, greenhouse effects, depletion of the ozone layer, and exhaustion of our natural resources.

What evidence do we have for such predictions?

First, there is no evidence that the world is running out of natural resources. (See Example 4.) Technological advances continue to improve recovery rates of exhaustible resources, and we have backstop resources. If the world begins to run out of a particular exhaustible resource, its relative price will rise and its consumption will be reduced.

Second, environmental pollution appears to be lessening in the advanced industrialized countries.

EXAMPLE 4

Doomster Versus Boomster: Are We Running Out of Natural Resources?

Doomsday forecasters ("doomsters") predict that the world will run out of natural resources within the lifetime of our children or grandchildren. More optimistic economists ("boomsters") argue that markets naturally conserve exhaustible resources, as explained in the text.

In 1980, a prominent boomster, economist Julian Simon, and a prominent doomster, biologist Paul Ehrlich, entered into a $1000 bet. Simon allowed Ehrlich to select five natural resources that he thought were being exhausted. Demand-and-supply analysis suggests that if a resource is disappearing, its price will increase. Accordingly, the two decided that Ehrlich would win if the prices of the five natural resources had increased faster than inflation at the end of 10 years.

In 1990, Simon received a $1000 check from Ehrlich confirming that he had won the bet. The prices of all five natural resources declined between 1980 and 1990. More surprisingly, the prices had declined in absolute terms. Their money prices were lower in 1990 than in 1980!

Affluence has allowed these countries to devote scarce resources to environmental programs. In the industrialized world, air and water quality is improving, not deteriorating.

Third, scientists have little reliable data on the publicized major ecological threats to life on this earth. They cannot agree about whether the world is getting warmer or colder. They do not know whether long-term changes in the ozone layer are occurring or even whether such changes occurred before the advent of the chemical reactions (from aerosol sprays and freon, for example) that are purported to be their cause. They do not know whether radon is harmless or something to be feared. (See Example 5.)

Successful economic policy cannot be formulated without hard facts and figures. If we cannot measure costs and benefits, we are not in a position to make policy judgments.

In this chapter, we have discussed some possible arguments for government intervention. Externalities, particularly the environmental problem of waste disposal, represent legitimate cases of market failure. We also discussed how the price system handles the problem of exhaustible resources. In the next chapter, we shall examine the patterns of government spending and taxation.

SUMMARY

1. Market failure occurs when the price system fails to produce the socially optimal quantity of a good. Externalities occur when marginal social costs (or benefits) do not equal marginal private costs (or benefits). Social efficiency requires that marginal social benefits and marginal social costs be equal, but pri-

EXAMPLE 5

Global Warming—The Great Debate

The debate over global warming shows that no matter how much contrary evidence is presented, it does not matter. The popular sentiment by politicians, the press, and educators makes three disputable claims: (1) global warming is occurring, (2) global warming is caused by our consumption of fossil fuels, and (3) global warming is bad for our future. But every single one of these claims is disputed by reputable scientists. For example, the earth has gotten warmer over the past 300 years, but it is still on a cooling trend over the past several thousand years. A warm 1999–2000 winter is hardly conclusive scientific proof. Indeed, when a "scientific consensus" for global warming is presented in the press, that consensus is based on a group consisting largely of social scientists and educators who have no direct knowledge of climate science. There are in fact very few climatologists in the United States, and the majority of them are skeptical of global warming.

Most of the evidence for global warming is really based not so much on measurements but on models of global warming that predict it will occur. These predictions, however, have been systematically biased upward; each year the models have to be revised downward. When a model makes a false prediction, it should be rejected rather than used as a basis for policy. Actual measurements of atmospheric temperatures show no alarming trend.

It has been argued by some economists that even if global warming takes place, it may prove to be beneficial to society. Agricultural production may be stimulated, it will cost less to heat our homes, and we may spend more time fishing, swimming, and golfing.

But the biggest risk of doing something about global warming is that the costs of cutting carbon emissions will fall on the poorest members of our planet—the developing countries. Since economic development is energy intensive, raising the cost of using carbon resources will cut the economic growth rates of countries such as India and Mexico more than that of more advanced countries.

Source: http://www.cato.org/speeches/sp-jt011698.html.

vate agents equate marginal private benefits with marginal private costs. Externalities can be internalized by redefinition of property rights, by voluntary agreements, or by government taxes or subsidies.

2. Waste disposal costs arise because modern production and consumption require disposing of residual wastes such as air pollutants, toxic chemicals, and solid wastes. Pollution problems cannot easily be solved by redefining property rights or by voluntary agreement; government intervention is typically required. In the United States, the Environmental Protection Agency (EPA) is charged with environmental protection. The EPA regulates pollution standards but in recent years, after increasing criticism of high cost, has been experimenting with incentive-based market solutions.

3. Firms that produce nonrenewable (exhaustible) resources must determine how to allocate the available fixed supply over time. When marginal extraction costs are zero, the industry is perfectly competitive, and there is no technological progress, firms will allocate the resource so that the present discounted values of the prices in each period are the same. Prices will rise at the rate of interest.

4. The prices of nonrenewable resources in general have not risen in real terms because of declining marginal extraction costs and rapid technological progress. Natural market forces should cause the efficient allocation of nonrenewable resources over time. Recycling is another means of expanding the supply of exhaustible resources.

KEY TERMS

market failure 368
externalities 368
social costs 368
social benefits 368
internalization 369
property rights 369
optimal level of abatement 373
regulatory approach 373
incentive-based approach 374
exhaustible (or nonrenewable) resource 375
recycling 379

QUESTIONS AND PROBLEMS

1. Factory A produces 1000 tons of sulfuric acid at a cost of $10,000 to produce 1000 tons. For the people in the community, the production of every 1000 tons of sulfuric acid causes an increase of $5000 in medical payments, a loss of $4000 in wages by being sick, and an increase of $1000 in dry-cleaning bills. What are the private and social costs of the 1000 tons of sulfuric acid?
2. Explain how the external costs calculated in the previous example might be internalized. Will this internalization be handled differently when there are three people harmed by the factory than when 300,000 people are harmed? In which case is government action more likely?
3. An oil producer has 100 barrels of oil that must be sold within a 2-year period. The interest rate is 10 percent, and the price of crude oil expected next year is $25 per barrel. At which prices will the oil producer sell all the oil this year? At which prices will the oil producer sell all the oil next year? What will happen if the oil producer expects an improvement in technology to increase the recovery rate (the amount of the resource that can be produced) by 10 percent next year?
4. If new cost-efficient technologies that reduce the marginal costs of pollution abatement are developed, what will happen to the optimal level of pollution abatement?
5. Does the pollution-trading concept used in recent years by the EPA solve the problem of determining the optimal level of pollution?
6. Explain why economists do not favor the total elimination of pollution.
7. It has been proposed that a worldwide tax be placed on aerosol sprays to protect the world's ozone layer. What methods would be used to determine at what rate the tax should be set?
8. In which of these three cases would it be easiest to establish property rights? First, I wish to keep stray cattle off my farm. Second, I wish to prevent the commercial jets landing at a nearby airport from disturbing my egg-laying chickens. Third, I wish to keep my neighbor from depleting the stock of fish in a lake that is shared by the two of us.
9. Many agricultural crops are harmed by beetles and other insects. These harmful insects are prey for the praying mantis, a large insect. The praying mantis is not an endangered species, but several agricultural states still impose a fine on anyone caught killing a praying mantis. Is

there a good economic reason for such a fine? Explain.

10. For about 4000 years, mariners have been dumping wastes into the ocean. In many places, the ocean floor is covered with plastics, bottles, and other refuse. Explain why the market mechanism does not correct for this waste disposal problem. How might the problem be solved by internalization?

INTERNET CONNECTION

11. Using the links on http://www.awl.com/ruffin_gregory, read the Brookings Institute Policy Brief on Environmental Policy.
    a. What do the authors identify as the problems with the first generation of environmental policy?
    b. What solutions do they recommend?
12. Using the links on http://www.awl.com/ruffin_gregory, read "Emissions Trading for Global Warming" on the Cato Institute's Web page.
    a. How does the author suggest that emissions trading can be used to deal with global warming?
    b. What is the RECLAIM program, and what is its significance?

PUZZLE ANSWERED: The answer to this is puzzling to noneconomists. But the private behavior that follows self-interest will take into account the possibility of running out of resources; it does so because the cost of using a finite resource is the price at which it can be sold in the future. As a resource runs out, prices will rise. Private behavior can do too much of a good thing if it imposes costs that are paid by others—the essence of an external cost—but running out of finite resources is not an externality because the opportunity cost of selling a finite resource is not having it available to sell in the future at a possible higher price!

Chapter 21

Government Spending, Taxation, and the Economy

Chapter Insight

In 1999 the federal government collected $1.8 trillion in taxes, and state and local governments took in some $1.2 trillion in taxes and fees in an economy whose total income was $9.5 trillion. In the last year of the twentieth century, governments collected more than $11,000 from every man, woman, and child and took about one out of every three dollars earned. Are these amounts too much, too little, or just right? We have debated the proper size of government since the founding of our country.

Liberals want more government, conservatives want less government. Everyone agrees that there are some things that a government must do. There are some kinds of goods, called *public goods,* that private markets cannot supply. If the government must provide some goods and services, it must have the power to raise revenues through taxation.

Government affects our economic lives in a number of ways. We are particularly reminded of government on April 15 when we must file our federal income taxes. We are reminded of government when we receive our property tax statements from local government. We may be less reminded of government when we receive government services—when we drive on state or federal highways, when we enroll our children in public schools, when we see our troops in a peacekeeping mission on foreign soil, or when we file a suit in a small claims court.

We all ask: Are we getting good value out of our taxes? Does the government intrude too much on our private economic lives? Are we spending our limited public resources on the right things?

LEARNING OBJECTIVES

After completing this chapter, you will be able to:

1. Understand public goods and rival versus nonrival consumption.
2. Use the concept of exclusion costs to explain free-riding.
3. Know the major trends in spending by the federal government and by state and local governments.
4. Distinguish between the ability-to-pay principle and the benefit principle of taxation and define the incidence of taxation.
5. Relate taxes and efficiency to neutral taxes and to marginal tax rates.
6. Understand the basics of the U.S. tax system.
7. Know the various proposals for tax reform.

CHAPTER PUZZLE: Two suburban neighborhoods—one large, the other small—are dissatisfied with police protection and decide to form neighborhood watch programs in which neighbors alternate patrolling their neighborhood after dark. After one year, the watch program in the small subdivision is working well, but the program in the large neighborhood has already been abandoned. Explain the likely reasons for this result.

Public Goods

In the last chapter we considered market failures. Market failures occur when private costs and benefits diverge. The market failures described in the previous chapter were externalities, environmental pollution, and exhaustible resources. Public goods represent another and different form of market failure.

Because competitive markets undersupply or fail to supply them, public goods—such as public schools, public parks, public roads and bridges, national defense, police protection, or public health services—are generally supplied by government at no charge and are financed by taxes.

A **public good** is a good or service whose use by one person does not reduce its use to others and whose use by nonpayers cannot be prevented.

The first characteristic of public goods is referred to as nonrival consumption. Their second characteristic is referred to as nonexclusion.

Nonrival Consumption

If a dam is built to prevent flooding, everyone who lives in the protected flood zone benefits. Moreover, the fact that your house is protected by the dam does not reduce the protection of other homeowners. You can watch a television program without reducing the viewing of other viewers. Both are cases of nonrival consumption.

A good is characterized by **nonrival consumption** if its consumption by one person does not reduce its consumption by others.

A classic example of nonrival consumption is national defense. If the government builds an antimissile system that reduces the likelihood of nuclear attack, everyone in the protected area benefits. The protection of one person's life and property does not reduce the protection of others.

Most goods and services are characterized by rival consumption.

A good is characterized by **rival consumption** if its consumption by one person lowers its consumption by others.

Food and drink, cars, houses, shoes, dresses, and medical services are rival in consumption. The hamburger that you eat cannot be eaten by someone else; the house that you live in cannot be occupied by another. Some goods can be either rival or nonrival, depending on the circumstances. An uncrowded movie is nonrival; you can enjoy it without reducing any other person's consumption. A sold-out movie, however, is rival because your presence would displace another viewer. Rival goods are rationed by charging prices; only those who are willing to pay the market price can use it.

Nonexclusion

The second characteristic of public goods is nonexclusion, which results when it is very costly to exclude nonpayers.

A good is characterized by **nonexclusion** if extreme costs eliminate the possibility (or practicality) of excluding some people from using it.

Flood control illustrates nonexclusion. It is impossible to exclude nonpayers in the area protected by flood control from being protected. It would be too costly to devise a flood-control system that excludes nonpayers.

Exclusion costs are the costs of preventing those who do not pay from enjoying a good.

Most goods are rival and have low exclusion costs. Goods that are rival in consumption and have low exclusion costs can be produced by private markets. Goods that are nonrival and have high exclusion costs cannot be produced by private firms. Nonpayers cannot be prevented from using the good. Figure 1 shows that goods with high exclusion costs, whether rival or nonrival, are normally provided through the government.

Free Riders Versus Cooperation

A person who enjoys the benefits of a good without paying is a free rider.

A **free rider** enjoys the benefits of a good or service without paying the cost.

Why should free riders pay for a public good if they cannot be excluded from its use? If we understand that we cannot have the good (flood control, roads, etc.) unless we cooperate, we may be able to

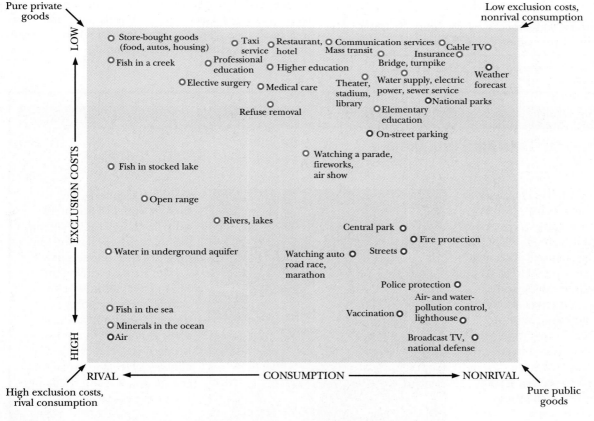

FIGURE 1 Classifying Selected Goods as Private Goods or Public Goods

Pure private goods, in the upper left corner, are characterized by low exclusion costs (free riders can be excluded easily) and by rival consumption. Pure public goods, in the lower right corner, are characterized by high exclusion costs (free riding can't be prevented) and by nonrival consumption (one person's consumption of a good does not detract from another's consumption of it). Goods in the other two corners meet only one of the two characteristics of a public good. In the lower left corner, goods are characterized by high exclusion costs but rival consumption. In the upper right corner, goods are characterized by nonrival consumption but low exclusion costs. *Source:* E.S. Savas, *Privatizing the Public Sector* (Chatham, NJ: Chatham House Publishers, Inc., 1982), p. 34.

finance the good through voluntary contributions. If there is too much free-riding, such goods will not be produced. Consider a dam that costs $2000 to build and protects a community consisting of 10 people. That flood protection is worth $400 to each person. The dam is therefore worth $4000 to the 10 people, and it is worth building by charging each person $200 because its benefits ($400) are double costs ($200).

Voluntary agreement to build the dam may be difficult to reach. There is a strong temptation to be a free rider. Each person realizes that if the other nine build the dam without his or her contribution, the person can still enjoy the benefits. In this example, if six people behave as free riders, the dam will not be built by voluntary agreement; they can raise only $1600. If only four people behave as free riders, the dam will be built.

> Voluntary agreements work only if the amount of free riding is not excessive.

Despite the existence of free-riding, we are able to cooperate in many cases. We make voluntary contributions to civic associations for extra police protection, most of us obey the law, and we do volunteer community work. However, if the group is large, if collective decisions are made infrequently, and if individual gains to cooperation are small, free-riding will prevent cooperative behavior. If there is too much free-riding, either the public good will not be produced privately or it must be produced by government.

Private markets and new technology can provide ingenious solutions for public goods. TV signals can be blocked for nonsubscribers. Toll highways can charge motorists electronically through electronic sensors. (See Example 1.)

There is no simple formula for dealing with public goods. Different societies have come up with different solutions. Let's consider television. Some countries have state television monopolies, where the state provides all television programming at taxpayer

EXAMPLE 1

Technological Change and Public Goods

Public goods are characterized by nonexclusion. It is simply too costly to exclude free riders from enjoying the good. Technological change has made it possible to exclude free riders from enjoying a number of goods. In the old days, championship fights or special concerts were viewed in movie theaters, which were equipped to receive special cable feeds. Such events could not be carried on regular television because there was no way to exclude free riders. With the development of cable television, scrambling technologies made it possible to exclude viewers who do not call up a special number to pay for viewing the event. In the near future, most households will be able to receive a television signal via their telephone line, so that viewers can automatically be charged for viewing just as they are charged for long distance phone service.

In the past, drivers on toll highways could be charged only by going through toll booths that often slowed traffic flow. Modern electronics now allows electronic scanners to charge users of toll roads by activating electronic receivers in the users' automobiles.

As technology develops, more and more goods will have low exclusion costs. One day we may all have electronic monitors on our cars, television sets, phone lines, and even on our bodies so we can be electronically charged for the use and enjoyment of services.

expense. The rationale for this approach is that it doesn't cost us anything to add one more viewer (nonrivalry). Therefore, it is not socially optimal to exclude nonpaying viewers. But is it fair for general taxpayers who do not like television to pay for those who do? An alternative approach is pay television, made possible by technologies that allow broadcasters to block signals to nonpaying customers. With pay television, only those who watch programming pay; it excludes nonpayers even though they could watch without affecting the viewing of paying customers.

Some countries, such as the United States, have a mix of "free" network and local programming, public television, and pay television (cable, pay-per-view, and satellite dishes). Network programming is paid for by advertisers, who pay programming costs to gain access to customers. With advertising, there is no problem of forcing nonviewers to pay or excluding nonrival viewers who are not prepared to pay. Pay television excludes viewers not willing to pay even though they do not diminish the enjoyment of payers. Public television is funded largely by government to permit "quality" TV programming that does not have to attract large audiences for advertisers and to accommodate for the fact that free-riding limits voluntary contributions.

Government Spending

Government spending is carried out by the 87,000 federal, state, and local governments in the United States. Government provides not only public goods but also goods that could have been provided by the private sector. Governments spend their money differently. The federal government focuses on national and international matters such as defense, international diplomacy, and a national highway system. State governments spend their funds on state universities, state highways, and the state court system. Local governments spend their funds on local schools, roads, and police protection.

Government expenditures are either exhaustive expenditures or transfer payments.

Exhaustive expenditures are government purchases that divert resources from the private sector, making them no longer available for private use. **Transfer payments** transfer income from one individual or organization to another.

In 1998, the government purchased 17.5 percent of all goods and services. In an economy that produced $8.5 trillion worth of goods and services, government purchases totaled almost $1.5 trillion. Exhaustive expenditures accounted for 56 percent of total government spending (see Figure 2). The remaining 44 percent of government expenditures were transfer payments. Most transfers are made by the federal government; state and local governments make more exhaustive expenditures on goods and services than the federal government.

Transfer payments affect the distribution of income among families but do not change the amount of goods and services that are exhausted (consumed) by government. For example, the Social Security program transfers income from currently employed workers to retired or disabled workers. The federal government transfers funds to state and local governments.

Total government expenditures in 1998 accounted for 30 percent of the total output of the U.S. economy. The ratio of total government expenditures to total output is a common measure of the economic scope of government.

Table 1 tells us what we get from government spending. The federal government spends almost $7000 annually for every man, woman, and child. State and local governments provide most of the government services that are so important to our daily lives, like education, police, sewage and sanitation, parks and recreation, and fire protection. The federal government provides a significant portion of government spending on education, welfare, and hospitals, but its most significant spending items are for defense, interest on the national debt, and social security. The federal government spends more on welfare assistance and subsidies than do state and local governments.

Federal, state, and local governments all spend for social infrastructure—buildings, highways, equipment, laboratories, and so forth. Table 2 shows that federal government expenditures on human and infrastructure capital equal $246 per capita, or less than 5 percent of federal government spending.

Trends in Government Spending

Government expenditures have increased at a rapid pace over the past 70 years. In 1929, government purchases of goods and services were $112 billion; in 1998, they were $973 billion (both figures in constant 1987 prices). In 1929, the government purchased

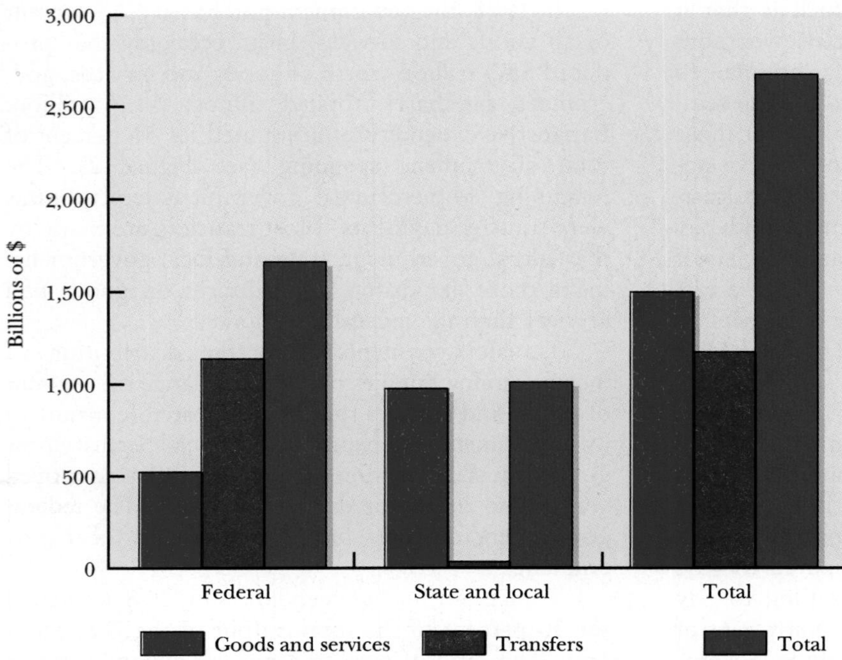

FIGURE 2 Government Spending 1998 Exhaustive and Transfer Payments
Government spending is for goods and services or for transfer payments.
Source: Statistical Abstract of the United States.

TABLE 1 HOW THE GOVERNMENT SPENDS MONEY (PER CAPITA EXPENDITURES, 1998)

	Federal	*State and Local*
By Function		
Defense	$1303	0
Education	$121	$1535
Public welfare	$218	$724
Health and hospitals	$140	$414
Highways	$4	$313
Police protection	$30	$162
Fire protection	0	$66
Corrections	$9	$134
Natural resources	$234	$58
Sewerage and sanitation	0	$152
Housing and community development	$73	$80
Government administration	$76	$236
Parks and recreation	$8	$74
Interest on general debt	$910	$259
Insurance trust expenditure	$2073	$424
Intergovernmental	$848	$17
Utility and liquor store expenditures	$892	$396
Total	$6939	$5044

Source: Statistical Abstract of the United States. Updated by authors.

TABLE 2 FEDERAL GOVERNMENT HUMAN AND CAPITAL INVESTMENT. PER CAPITA (PER CAPITA DOLLARS, 1998)

Human investments	
Young children	$35
Education	$40
Work force investments	$28
Subtotal	$103
Infrastructure	
Transportation	$124
Water treatment	$12
Water resources	$7
Subtotal	$143
Total	$246

Source: Statistical Abstract of the United States. Updated by authors.

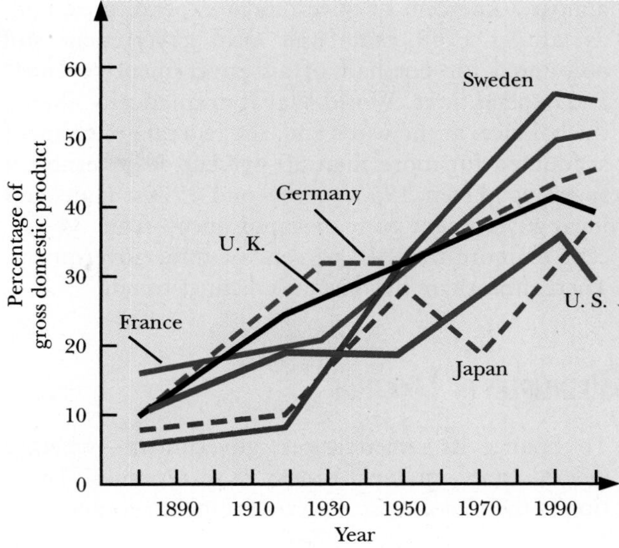

FIGURE 3 Total Government Spending as a Percentage of GDP, U.S. and Other Countries, 1890–2000

The ratio of total government expenditures to total economic activity (or GDP) is a better measure of the changing role of government than measures of government spending alone. *Source:* http://www.oecd.org.

$924 worth of goods and services per capita. By 1998, this figure had risen to $3918 per capita (in 1987 prices). Government expenditures rise with population growth and with the growth of the economy. The most relevant yardstick is the ratio of total government spending to total output (see Figure 3). In 1890, government expenditures accounted for 6.5 percent of total output, but by 1998 this ratio had risen to 30 percent. An increase in the government share has characterized other industrialized countries, as Figure 3 shows as well.

The economic role of government, especially of the federal government, has increased because government has increasingly taken responsibility for health, education, and welfare. The Industrial Revolution (a Defining Moment in economics) created a need for more government services. A modern and complex economy requires more government services than rural societies—sanitation, police protection, traffic control, water supplies, legal systems.

Government's claim on resources has also increased because government is less efficient than the private sector. It has proven easier to increase productivity in the private sector than in the public sector. Hence, price increases have been more rapid in the public sector. Since 1950, prices paid by government to purchase goods and services have increased at roughly double the rate of private goods. Whereas private businesses must earn a profit to survive, the public sector is financed by taxpayer dollars. There is therefore less incentive to provide the public service efficiently.

The growing power of special-interest groups and lobbyists also increases government spending. Special interests have made it increasingly difficult to control government spending.

Spending by Federal, State, and Local Governments

Government economic activities are distributed among federal, state, and local governments. Each society must determine at what level of government public services—roads and public education, for example—should be provided. There has been intense debate over these issues since the founding of this country. Many citizens think that the federal government is too remote and too powerful and that the states and localities have too little power.

In 1998, the federal government (not including spending from grants in aid to state and local governments) accounted for 62 percent of all government expenditures, while state and local government accounted for the remainder. The dominance by federal government is a fairly new phenomenon. In 1932, state and local government accounted for almost 70 percent of government expenditures, and, as late as 1940, state and local government still accounted for one-half of all government revenues and expenditures. World War II dramatically altered the balance; at the war's end, the federal government accounted for more than 80 percent of government spending. From 1955 to the mid-1970s, state and local government grew in importance—from 34 percent to more than 45 percent of total government. Thereafter, there has been no distinct trend.

Principles of Taxation

To finance its expenditures, government—whether federal, state, or local—must raise revenues. Taxation is the major source of government revenue.

Taxes and Fairness

There has always been debate over what constitutes a fair tax system. If we believe that our taxes are unfair, we will seek to evade them and join taxpayer revolts. In some countries, tax evasion is an accepted social practice; in other countries, it is considered immoral. Whether the public voluntarily pays taxes depends upon whether it perceives the tax system as fair.

The Benefit Principle. The benefit principle is one approach to fairness.

The **benefit principle** of taxation states that those who benefit from a public expenditure should pay the tax that finances it.

According to this principle, those who benefit from a new state highway, an airport, or a flood-control project—all financed from tax revenues—should pay for it. If community members are not willing to pay for a public project (if citizens vote against a local flood-control project), they demonstrate that the project's benefits do not outweigh its costs. If all taxes were levied on the benefit principle (and if the beneficiaries voted on each public expenditure), benefits of voter-approved projects would exceed costs.

Examples of benefit taxes are a tax on gasoline used to finance highway construction, and special taxes assessed for specific road repairs, street lighting, and sidewalks.

To apply the benefit principle, we must be able to identify who benefits and by how much—and this is often difficult to do. Motorists benefit from public highways, and residents of New York City benefit from the New York subway system; however, it is often difficult to determine who benefits from national defense, police protection, or the legal system. When we cannot determine benefits, we cannot use the benefit principle.

The Ability-to-Pay Principle. The second approach to fairness is the ability-to-pay principle.

The **ability-to-pay principle** states that those better able to pay should bear the greater burden of taxes, whether or not they benefit more.

According to this principle, the rich benefit less from public education and public hospitals because they use private facilities; however, because they are better able to pay than the poor, they should bear a heavier burden.

A tax system that follows the ability-to-pay principle should have both vertical equity and horizontal equity.

Vertical equity exists when those with a greater ability to pay bear a heavier tax burden.

Horizontal equity exists when those with equal abilities to pay do pay the same amount of tax.

Without vertical equity, taxes are not being paid on an ability-to-pay basis. Without horizontal equity, the ability-to-pay principle is violated because taxpayers with equal abilities to pay are being treated differently.

Incidence of Taxation. Once society has decided who should bear the burden of taxes, tax authorities must devise a tax system that fulfills its goals. At first glance, this plan seems simple. If society wants the rich to pay 40 percent of their income and the poor to pay 10 percent, income tax rates need only be set at 40 percent and 10 percent for these two groups. Or, if we decide that cigarette manufacturers and big oil companies should pay a heavy share of taxes, we simply levy a tax on each carton of cigarettes and on each barrel of oil.

In reality, the individual or company that is being taxed does not necessarily bear the burden of the tax. In many cases, the incidence of a tax can be shifted to someone else.

The **incidence of a tax** is the actual distribution of the burden of tax payments.

Let's consider what happens when a $1 tax is levied on each carton of cigarettes. The tax causes cigarette manufacturers to supply fewer cigarettes at each price, thereby raising the market price. As the price of cigarettes rises, the manufacturer shifts the tax forward so that smokers pay a part of the tax in the form of a higher price. If the price rises by $0.80 as a consequence of the $1 tax, 80 percent of the tax has been shifted forward to the consumer. In this example, most of the tax burden is borne not by the manufacturer, but by the final consumer.

A tax is shifted forward to the consumer when the consumer pays a portion of the tax by paying a higher price for the product.

Virtually any tax can be shifted. An increase in income tax rates may motivate physicians to reduce their patient load. If physicians reduce their supply of labor, they will raise their fees. Who has paid the tax? The patient pays a portion of the tax in the form of higher doctors' bills. If the government places a tax on imported cars, car buyers pay in the form of higher prices on imported cars because of the reduced supply of imports.

Taxes and Efficiency

The fairness of a tax system is only one measure of how "good" it is. We can also judge tax systems by how they affect economic efficiency. If an economy operates on its production possibilities frontier and taxes reduce output, they have reduced the efficiency of the economy.

Taxes cause us to change our economic behavior. Increases in income tax rates cause high-income earners to reduce their supply of effort. Property taxes affect where businesses locate. Tax breaks on historic restoration costs cause historic buildings to be preserved. Sales taxes cause prices to rise. All taxes except neutral taxes affect private economic decisions.

A **neutral tax** cannot be altered by a change in private production, consumption, or investment decisions.

It is very difficult, if not impossible, to devise a neutral tax. Any tax that we can alter as a consequence of our actions is not neutral. A $1000 tax on each adult male between the ages of 20 and 55 is neutral because there is nothing the targeted taxpayer can do to avoid or reduce the tax (outside of a sex-change operation). But such a tax violates both the benefit principle and the ability-to-pay principle. A tax that takes 20 percent of income is not neutral because we can reduce the tax by earning less income.

Marginal Tax Rates and Work Effort. Labor-supply decisions are affected by taxes. When deciding whether to work overtime, whether both husband and wife should work, or whether to play golf one or two days a week, we consider our marginal tax rate.

The **marginal tax rate** is the increase in tax payments divided by the increase in income. The marginal tax rate shows how much extra taxes must be paid per dollar of extra earnings.

The marginal tax rate is different from the average tax rate.

The **average tax rate** is the ratio of the tax payment to taxable income.

The distinction between average and marginal tax rates is important. Suppose Ann Smith is a physician who earns $150,000 annually and who pays $60,000 a year in income taxes for an average tax rate of 40 percent. If working a few more hours per week would increase her taxable income by $50,000 (from $150,000 to $200,000), Smith's taxes rise to $90,000 for an average tax rate of 45 percent. The $50,000 increase in taxable income causes her taxes to rise by $30,000. Her marginal tax rate is the ratio of the increase in taxes ($30,000) to the increase in earnings ($50,000), or 60 percent. The marginal tax rate (60 percent) is higher than the average tax rate (45 percent).

We base our economic decisions on marginal tax rates. Faced with a marginal tax rate of 60 percent,

Ann Smith may decide it is not worth the extra effort to earn an additional $50,000 of income if she can keep only $20,000 of it. If she decides not to work the extra hours, economic efficiency has been reduced because fewer goods and services are being produced than without the tax.

Many tax reformers favor lowering marginal tax rates to encourage greater work effort. Lower marginal tax rates raise the output of goods and services, thereby improving economic efficiency.

Taxes and Social Goals

Many people believe that the tax system should be an instrument of social policy. Because we respond to marginal tax rates, the tax system can be used to cause us to engage in desirable behavior. If we wish to promote private home ownership, we offer tax incentives to buy homes. If we wish to encourage marriage, we tax married couples at lower rates. If we wish to encourage risk taking or innovation, we give tax breaks to those who earn income through innovation and risk taking.

Taxes affect economic decision making. The challenge to politicians and tax authorities is to devise a tax system that minimizes the efficiency losses of taxes while moving society in the direction of desirable social goals.

Taxes can have many unintended consequences. Taxes intended to raise government revenues may actually lower them. Taxes intended to "soak the rich" may be paid by the poor. Taxes on employers end up being paid by employees.

The U.S. Tax System

The U.S. tax system consists of a variety of federal, state, and local taxes. The federal government obtains most of its revenues from individual income taxes and Social Security contributions (see Figure 4). Corporate income taxes and sales taxes (excises, customs, and duties) account for a small percentage of the total. Since 1955, the structure of federal revenues has changed substantially. The revenue share of the personal income tax has remained fairly constant, near 45 percent, but the shares of corporate income taxes and of sales taxes have dropped considerably. The share of Social Security contributions has risen considerably (from about 12 percent in 1955 to more than 33 percent today).

The financing of state and local governments has also changed over the past 40 years (see Figure 4). The share of sales taxes has declined but there has been a notable drop in the share of property taxes and a notable rise in the share of state income taxes. Local and state governments have become more dependent upon transfers from the federal government.

The Federal Individual Income Tax

As Figure 4 shows, the personal income tax is the single most important source of revenue for the federal government. The current federal income tax system is the result of countless changes, reforms, and revisions. (See Example 2 on page 392.)

The U.S. federal income tax is administered by the Internal Revenue Service. The personal income tax is levied on taxable income according to tax rates set by Congress. In 1999, taxable income was taxed at five rates: 15 percent, 28 percent, 31 percent, 36 percent, and 39.6 percent.

Taxable income is the income that remains after all deductions and exemptions are subtracted. Taxes are levied on taxable income.

We are allowed to take itemized deductions (medical and dental expenses, state and local taxes, mortgage interest, and charitable contributions), standard deductions for each family member, and deductions for contributions to retirement accounts. Because of these various deductions, our taxable income averages only 65 percent of our gross income.

Since 1970, various tax reforms (particularly the 1986 tax reform) lowered marginal tax rates. In 1970, the marginal tax rate for a family earning $75,000 per year was 56 percent. In 1993, the marginal tax rate for that same family was 34 percent. The trend toward lower marginal rates was reversed in 1993 when marginal tax rates were raised.

The federal income tax serves as an instrument of social policy. By allowing charitable contribution deductions, the tax system encourages families to give to charities. By allowing interest deductions on home mortgages, it encourages home ownership. By allowing deductions for contributions to retirement programs, it induces workers to save for retirement. Deductions for education expenses encourage education.

Federal Government Revenues
(billions of $)

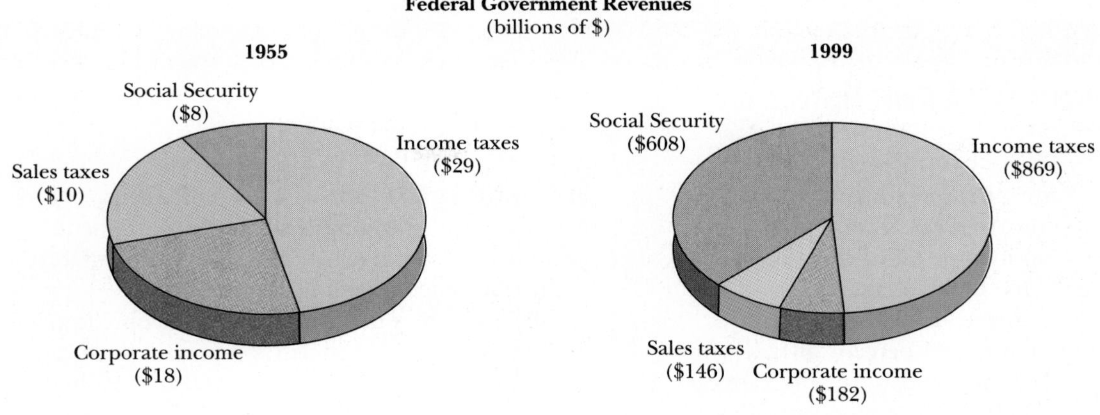

State and Local Government Revenues
(billions of $)

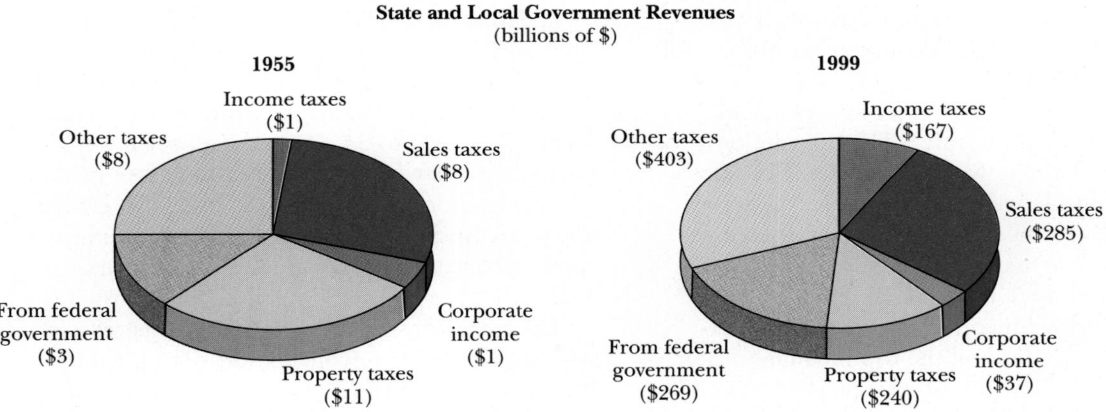

FIGURE 4 Sources of Government Revenue: Federal and State and Local Governments, 1955 and 1999

The federal government's two main sources of revenue are income taxes and contributions to Social Security. The major increase in federal government revenues since 1955 has been in Social Security contributions. State and local governments get their revenues from sales taxes, other taxes, property taxes, and from the federal government. The major change since 1955 has been the reduction in the share of property taxes and the rise in the share of federal transfers. *Source: Statistical Abstract of the United States.*

The Federal Corporate Income Tax

U.S. corporations are subject to a federal tax on their profits, called the federal corporate income tax. As Figure 4 shows, the share of the corporate income tax of total federal tax revenues has been declining over the years, accounting for 10 percent in the late 1990s.

Critics of corporate income taxes argue that corporations pass corporate taxes forward to consumers. Although voters may think that the tax burden of corporations is rising, this opinion may be purely illusory. We are all paying in the form of higher prices.

Corporate profits that are distributed to stockholders as dividends are taxed twice: once as corporate income and again when stockholders pay taxes on their dividends. Many tax specialists have argued against the double taxation of corporate profits, and some propose only one tax on dividends.

Social Security and Payroll Taxes

Founded in 1935 during the Great Depression (a Defining Moment), the Social Security Program is financed by a payroll tax. Unlike the individual income tax, under which families below a certain

EXAMPLE 2

The U.S. Income Tax: A Brief History

In 1913, the Sixteenth Amendment to the U.S. Constitution authorized the federal government to levy a personal income tax. Prior to World War II, the personal income tax was not a major source of federal government revenue. In the 1930s, it accounted for 14 percent of federal revenues. In the 1920s and 1930s, the tax rate on an income of $100,000 (the equivalent of more than $1 million today) was 25 percent. During World War II, tax rates were raised. By 1948, the personal income tax accounted for 40 percent of all federal revenue.

The United States entered the postwar era with high personal tax rates. The tax rate on $200,000 and above was 91 percent. Tax rates of this magnitude were unacceptable; therefore, various tax reforms were passed that altered the personal income tax system in three directions. First, tax rates were reduced. By 1970, the tax rate on the lowest income bracket was 20 percent, and the tax rate on the top income bracket was 75 percent. The tax reform of 1981 lowered rates to a range of 11 to 50 percent.

The second direction of tax change established numerous deductions and exemptions from taxable income—interest earned on bonds of state and local governments (so-called *tax-exempt bonds*), contributions to retirement programs (such as Keogh accounts), taxes paid to state and local governments, medical expenditures, and charitable contributions.

The third direction of tax change was to use the personal income tax to promote economic or social goals. Tax credits for investments in equipment (the investment tax credit) were used to encourage capital formation. The deduction of certain forms of savings (such as in retirement accounts) encouraged savings. Mortgage-interest deductions encouraged home ownership.

These changes made the federal income tax extremely complex. Its critics argued it gave too many tax loopholes to the rich and that its high marginal tax rates discouraged hard work and risk taking.

In September 1986, Congress passed, and President Reagan signed, the Tax Reform Act of 1986. The number of tax rates was reduced from fourteen to three. The top tax rate was lowered from 50 percent to 34 percent. Tax rates were partially adjusted for inflation. Many low-income families were removed from the tax rolls. Deductions, exemptions, and exclusions from income were restricted to make up for the lower tax rates.

The trend toward lower tax rates was reversed with the Omnibus Reconciliation Act signed by President Clinton in 1993, which raised to 36 percent the tax rate for individuals earning $115,000 or married couples earning $140,000 or more. A fifth tax rate of 39.6 percent was placed on families earning $250,000 or more.

With the election of a Republican Congress in 1994, sentiment grew for tax reductions, more favorable treatment of capital gains, and the eventual introduction of a flat tax. The Taxpayer Relief Act of 1997, passed by a Republican Congress and signed by President Bill Clinton, provided new child-care tax credits and credits for higher educational expenses and for Roth IRAs.

income level are not taxed, Social Security and Medicare payroll taxes are paid starting with the first dollar of earnings. In 1998, the payroll tax was 15.3 percent of the first $68,000 of earnings, of which the employer and the employee each paid half. A worker earning $15,000 per year pays $1,148 in payroll taxes (and the employer also pays $1,148). Because the tax is imposed only on the first $68,000, a person earning $500,000 pays the same tax as one earning $68,000.

Social Security payroll taxes finance the Social Security retirement, health, and disability programs. The Medicare program that subsidizes medical care for the elderly is also part of the Social Security system.

Current recipients of Social Security can look forward to receiving more in benefits than they contributed to government taxes. Young people, however, do not face such a bright prospect. With the graying of America, there will be fewer and fewer working-age people to support the retirement income of older Americans. It is for this reason that changes in the Social Security system must be made in the near future. In fact, most young Americans do not believe that they will eventually get back what they put into their Social Security taxes or get back anything at all! Although it is politically difficult to reduce Social Security benefits, experts tell us that, within a decade, payments into the system will not be sufficient to pay benefits, as they currently exist.

State and Local Government Revenue Sources

State and local governments rely on revenues different from those utilized by the federal government. They earn revenues primarily from sales taxes and property taxes. State and local governments also operate utilities, sanitation departments, and liquor stores, from which they earn fees. The major change in state and local revenues over the past 40 years has been the growing importance of state income taxes and the declining importance of property taxes. As of 1999, only seven states—Alaska, Florida, Nevada, South Dakota, Texas, Washington, and Wyoming—did not have a state income tax. The decline in the share of property tax is explained by the tax revolt against property taxes in the 1970s and 1980s.

Is the U.S. Tax System Progressive?

The fraction of income paid by taxpayers who earn different amounts of income determines whether the tax system redistributes income. A tax can be either proportional, progressive, or regressive.

With a **proportional tax**, each taxpayer pays the same percentage of income as taxes.

With a **progressive tax**, the percentage of income paid as taxes increases as income increases.

With a **regressive tax**, the percentage of income paid as taxes decreases as income increases.

The federal income tax is progressive. Families with higher incomes pay higher tax rates. Sales taxes are regressive because wealthy families spend a smaller portion of their income than do poor families. Suppose a family with $40,000 of taxable income spends $20,000 and saves the rest, while a family with $10,000 taxable income spends the full $10,000. Each pays a 5 percent sales tax; the higher-income ($40,000) family pays sales taxes of $1000, or 1/40 of its income, while the lower-income ($10,000) family pays sales taxes of $500, or 1/20 of its income. Although the poor family spends fewer dollars on sales taxes, it pays a larger percentage of its income.

When progressive income taxes are combined with regressive sales taxes, is the overall U.S. tax system regressive, proportional, or progressive? The answer depends on the measurements of the incidence of taxation. Experts have fundamental disagreement on how the burden of taxes is distributed among different income groups because, to answer this question, we must know the extent to which taxes are shifted.[1]

Proposals for Federal Tax Reform

Our system of federal taxation has evolved over the years through a series of tax reforms, legislative amendments, and court interpretations.

Specialists have recommended a number of reforms of the tax system to make it more efficient or equitable.

Tax Consumption

Personal taxes are normally levied on personal income. The higher the earnings, the higher the income tax payments. Numerous distinguished economists and social thinkers have favored the taxing of

[1]For classic studies of the progressivity of the U.S. tax system see Joseph Pechman and Benjamin Okner, *Who Bears the Tax Burden?* (Washington, DC: The Brookings Institution, 1974); Joseph A. Pechman, *Who Paid the Taxes, 1966–85?* (Washington, DC: The Brookings Institution, 1985); Edgar K. Browning and William R. Johnson, *The Distribution of the Tax Burden* (Washington, DC: American Enterprise Institute, 1979); Edgar K. Browning, "Pechman's Tax Incidence Study: A Note on the Data," *American Economic Review* 76 (December 1986): 1214–1218.

consumption rather than income for two reasons. First, if we are taxed according to what we take out of production (consumption) rather than according to what we put in (saving), we would gain a larger stock of capital. We could reduce our taxes by saving more; hence, savings and capital formation would rise. Second, expenditures are a more accurate measure of a household's permanent spending power or ability to pay taxes than is current income.

Consumption taxes are typically collected as sales taxes. The value-added tax (or VAT) that is widely used in Europe is a consumption tax. Although sales taxes are regressive, consumption taxes can be made progressive. For example, by using progressive tax rates, taxpayers could be taxed on their income minus savings (which would equal their consumption).

Eliminate Corporate Income Taxes

The earlier chapter on business organization showed that corporations are useful devices for raising capital. Many economists argue that taxing corporate income reduces the social gains of the corporation. Currently, corporate profits are taxed twice, once as corporate income taxes and then as dividends in personal income taxes. Corporations can avoid the second tax by reinvesting their profits in the corporation. The double taxation of dividends thus dams up billions of dollars of investment funds inside corporate treasuries and encourages reinvestment in the corporation itself. Eliminating the tax on corporate dividends would allow these funds to be used for other purposes.

Impose a Flat Tax

Advocates of a flat tax call for everyone earning above an agreed-upon poverty level to pay the same tax rate (say, 20 percent). No deductions or exemptions from income would be allowed. Wealthy taxpayers would pay the same tax rate as middle-income taxpayers, but they would lose their tax loopholes. Because we would all pay the same tax rate (which would be kept low), there would be less unproductive tax-avoidance, and we would go about the business of earning money, not avoiding taxes.

Tax "Real" Capital Gains

When we sell stocks, bonds, or other assets for more than their purchase price, we earn a capital gain.

A **capital gain** occurs whenever assets such as stocks, bonds, or real estate increase in market value over the price paid to acquire the asset.

The capital gain is "realized" when the asset that has risen in value is actually sold, thereby creating the gain. Prior to the 1986 tax reform, capital gains were taxed at considerably lower rates than ordinary income to encourage risk taking and innovation. Between 1986 and the early 1990s, capital gains were taxed at about the same rate as other forms of income. By 1998, the tax rate on capital gains had been lowered so that most people paid between 10 percent and 20 percent in income from capital gains. In 2001 the 10 percent rate is scheduled to be reduced to 8 percent.

When a capital gain is realized on the sale of an asset that has been held for a period of time, much of the gain may have been eaten up by inflation. If a stock that has been held for 10 years is sold at a price 50 percent higher than the purchase price but inflation over that same period has also been 50 percent, there is no real profit after inflation. For this reason, experts favor taxing only real capital gains—capital gains in excess of the inflation that has occurred over the period during which the asset has been held.

Index for Inflation

When individuals whose earnings have been raised by inflation are pushed into higher tax brackets, their real income after taxes can be reduced. Indexing prevents inflation from pushing taxpayers into higher tax brackets.

Indexing is the tying of tax rates to the rate of inflation.

With indexing, tax rates are lowered with inflation to prevent the taxpayer's real income after taxes from falling. (Real income is income after adjustment for inflation.) Let's say that the Jones family pays $5,000 in income taxes on its income of $25,000 (a tax rate of 20 percent) and has $20,000 after taxes. A 10 percent inflation raises the Jones family income to $27,500. At $27,500, however, the tax rate is 22.5 percent, and the Jones family pays $6,188 in income taxes and has $21,312 after taxes. After adjustment for inflation, the Jones's $21,312 is worth less than the original $20,000. With indexing, tax rates would automatically fall to ensure that inflation does not lower after-tax income.

Government Surpluses and Deficits

Governments collect revenue primarily through taxes; they purchase goods and services and make transfer payments. Like households and businesses, governments can spend more or less than their income. The government budget surplus or deficit shows the relationship between government revenue and outlays.

A **government budget surplus** is the excess of government revenues over government outlays.

A **government budget deficit** is the excess of government outlays over government revenues.

Governments that run deficits typically use deficit financing.

Deficit financing is government borrowing in credit markets to finance a government deficit.

If a government borrows over a number of years to finance its deficits, it accumulates a government debt.

The **government debt** is the cumulated sum of outstanding IOUs that a government owes its creditors.

Government debt is reduced by running a surplus. If the government debt is $100 billion and government runs a $10 billion surplus, its debt would be reduced to $90 billion.

Government finances differ from household and business finances in one important respect: Governments can make up the difference between expenditures and revenues by printing money. The financing of deficits through the printing press has been used by governments to pay for wars and for costly government programs.

Figure 5 shows federal, state, and local budgets, surpluses, and deficits. The total government deficit is less than the federal deficit because state and local governments tend to have surpluses. Since 1950, the federal government has run surpluses in only 6 years, the latest being in 1999. In 1950, the federal debt was $257 billion—only 3 percent of today's debt. Today, the federal debt is more than $5 trillion.

How Big Should Government Be?

Many of us think that the government is too large. How do we determine what is "too large" or "too small"? One way is to look at the government's role in our economy in international perspective. Compared to other affluent countries, is our government relatively large or small?

Figure 6 shows that the role of government in our economy is actually smaller than that in other affluent countries. Its role is particularly small when compared with states like Sweden or Germany that have very large social welfare expenditures. Our tax burden is relatively low; the percent of output we spend on government is relatively low. (See Example 3 on page 398.)

How big a role government should play is a decision that must be made by democratic societies at the ballot box. Once a country decides that it has allowed government to play too large a role, voters can reverse this process. In recent elections, for example, Swedish voters reacted against the overwhelming role of government. For almost 15 years, voters in the United Kingdom have supported policies of a conservative government designed to reduce the role of government through privatization of public enterprises and reductions in tax rates. The Republican victory in the 1994 congressional elections was a reaction against "big government."

Voters decide on the scope of government. We must decide whether education, health, postal services, sanitation services, electricity, and other goods and services are to be provided by government or by private enterprise. We must decide whether our children should be educated by private or public schools, whether we should entrust government or private health providers with our health problems, or whether prisons should be operated by private or public providers.

Irrespective of the market in which they operate, private firms are motivated to produce at minimum costs, and they produce goods and services whose benefits outweigh their costs. If a company spends $20 to produce a good that buyers are willing to purchase only for $15, it cannot stay in business. It will fail the market test. Private goods must pass a market test that their benefits (as measured by the price customers are prepared to pay) exceed their costs.

Government does not have to pass this market test. In fact, in the next chapter we shall discuss why government goods are often produced at costs that outweigh benefits. This is no accident. If the federal government runs the postal service, there is no requirement that it make a profit. Losses will automatically be covered by taxpayers. Postal employees can be paid high salaries. If the city education department runs the public schools, there is no requirement that public education be provided at a reasonable cost or at an acceptable quality. In fact, the actual providers of the service (administrators and teachers) decide on standards, services, and costs. If a state health department supplies the community with medical care, it will determine how and in what form medical services are to be provided.

Government provision of goods and services is very different from private provision. With private provision, "the customer is king." The customer can simply put a company out of business by not buying the product. With public provision, such safeguards do not prevail. The parent dissatisfied with local public schools cannot put them out of business. The customer of the federal post office cannot put it out

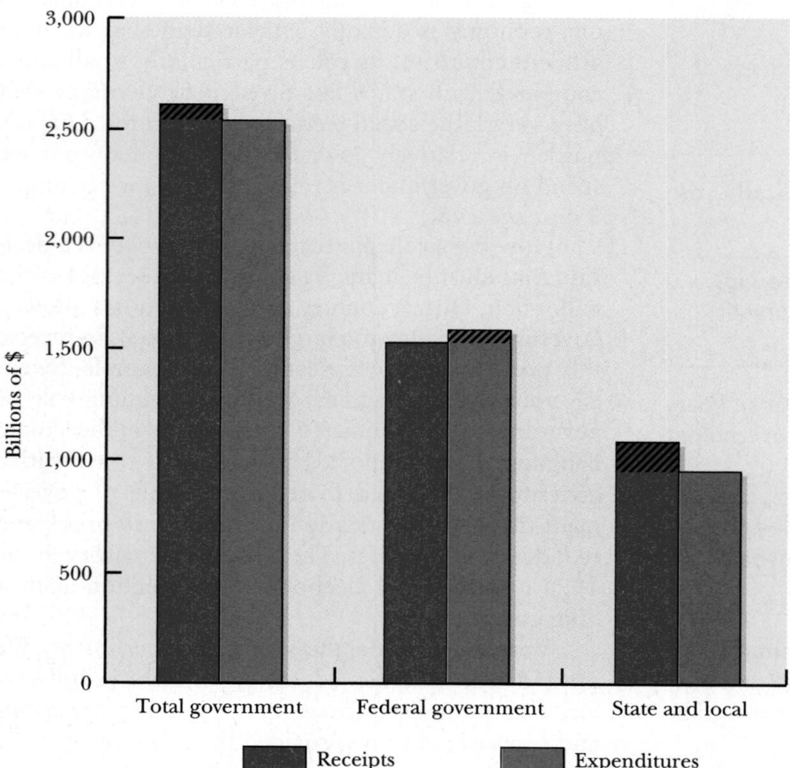

FIGURE 5 U.S. Government Budgets, 1994–1999 Average

Federal government expenditures exceeds revenues by the amount of the rectangle in hatch marks, which represents the federal deficit. The fact that state and local revenues exceed expenditures shows that they ran a surplus. The deficit of total government is therefore less than the federal deficit by the amount of the state and local surplus. For the five-year period 1994–1999, total government ran a small surplus.

Note: The hatch-marked areas are government deficits and surpluses.

Source: Statistical Abstract of the United States.

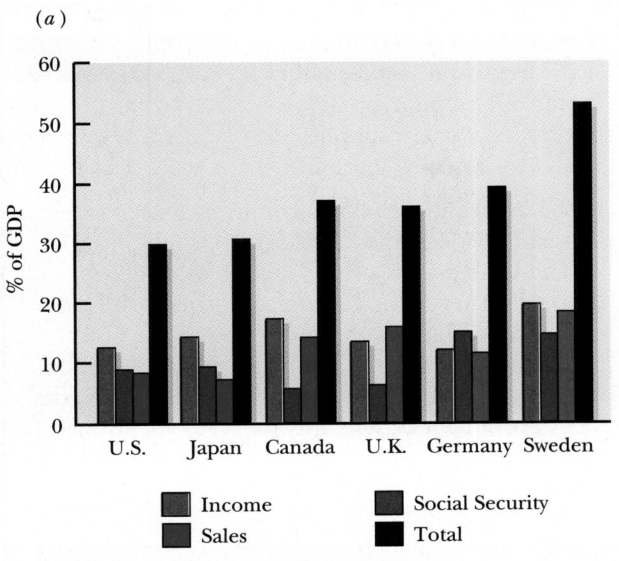

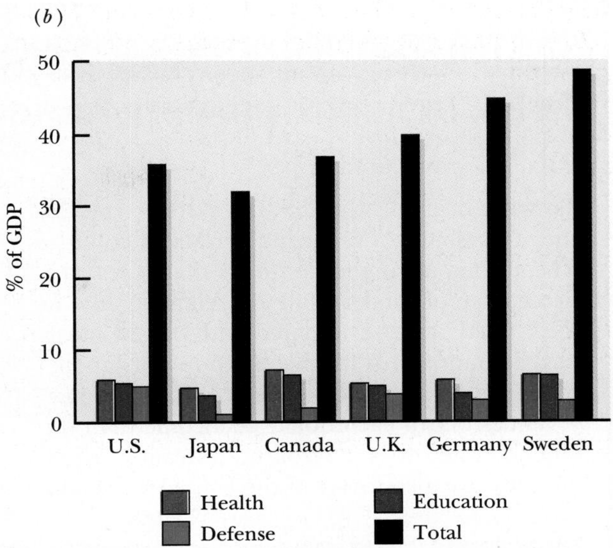

FIGURE 6 Relative Size of Government

Panel (*a*) shows that the relative share of taxes as a percent of GDP is smaller in the United States than in other highly industrialized countries. Panel (*b*) shows that the relative share of government expenditures as a percent of GDP in the United States is also small relative to other highly industrialized countries. Both tables show the different distributions of tax revenues and of expenditures. *Source: Revenue Statistics, 1965–1997,* OECD, Paris, 1998.

of business by not sending mail, although we can increase its deficit by using Federal Express. Only in our roles as voters can we exercise control over publicly provided goods.

The particular danger of government deficits is that they allow government to pass the costs of government programs to future generations. Balanced government budgets at least create pressure to limit spending to programs whose benefits at least equal costs. Politicians know that taxes are unpopular. Having to balance the budget would also pressure government to provide goods and services at a reasonable cost. Being able to pay for government by deficit financing allows politicians to place the burden of payment on future generations.

In the next chapter we shall assess how well we voters are able to exercise control over the goods and services provided by government.

SUMMARY

1. Public goods have two characteristics: First, the consumption of the good by one user does not reduce its consumption by others (nonrival consumption), and second, no one can in practice be prevented from using the good (nonexclusion).

2. Government expenditures are either exhaustive expenditures or transfer payments. Exhaustive expenditures divert resources to the public sector. Transfer payments affect the distribution of income. Government spending rose from 10 percent of GDP in the late 1920s to one-third percent in the late 1990s. Expenditures shifted away from local government and toward state and federal government.

3. There are two competing principles of fairness in taxation. One is that taxes should be levied according to benefits. The other is that taxes should be allocated on the basis of ability to pay. If the ability-to-pay principle is used, the tax system should have both vertical and horizontal equity.

4. A neutral tax system does not influence production, consumption, and investment decisions. Neutral taxes are almost impossible to devise. Other taxes do affect economic efficiency. The challenge is how to devise a tax system that moves the economy in a socially desired direction without severe losses

EXAMPLE 3

The U.S. Tax System in International Perspective

To what degree is the U.S. tax system typical of the tax systems of other industrialized countries? The accompanying table shows that taxes as a percentage of total output are relatively low in the United States, compared with other industrialized countries. With the exception of Japan, other industrialized countries collect more tax revenues out of each dollar of income than the United States does. Payroll tax rates for Social Security are also lower in the United States than in the other industrialized countries (except the United Kingdom and Canada).

The United States relies less on sales taxes than the other industrialized countries (with the exception of Japan) and more on income and profit taxes. The other countries rely on a combination of social security taxes and sales taxes, the most prominent of which is the VAT mentioned in the text.

The U.S. Tax System in International Perspective, 1996

	Tax Revenues as a Percentage of Total Output (1)	*Percentage Distribution of Tax Receipts (2)*			*Highest Rate of Income Tax (3)*
		Income Tax (a)	*Social Security (b)*	*Sales Taxes (c)*	
United States	28.5	37.6	23.5	17.2	46.6
Canada	36.8	37.7	16.0	24.9	72.3
France	45.7	14.1	39.6	27.3	71.9
Italy	43.2	25.1	40.5	25.9	71.0
Japan	28.4	20.2	32.8	15.4	60.7
Netherlands	43.3	17.5	31.8	28.6	65.5
Sweden	52.0	35.3	29.4	22.8	74.8
United Kingdom	36.0	25.9	16.8	35.2	57.7
Germany	38.1	24.7	38.1	27.9	53.0

Source: http://www.oecd.org.

of efficiency. Taxpayers are presumed to base their economic behavior on marginal tax rates.

5. The U.S. tax system blends personal income taxes, corporate income taxes, sales and property taxes, and payroll taxes collected by the federal, state, and local governments. The federal tax system has changed over the years from high tax rates combined with liberal exemptions, deductions, and credits to lower tax rates for both individual and corporate income taxes. The tax reform of 1986 lowered tax rates for both persons and corporations and eliminated many tax loopholes that had previously eroded the tax base. The tax reform of 1993 raised tax rates for higher-income families. There is disagreement as to whether the overall U.S. tax system is progressive or proportional.

6. Suggestions to change the current tax system include taxing consumption instead of income, eliminating the corporate income tax, taxing real capital gains, indexing for inflation, and levying a flat tax.

7. Publicly provided goods are not subject to a market test. Deficit financing allows government to pass the burden of payment for government programs to future generations.

KEY TERMS

public goods 384
nonrival consumption 384
rival consumption 384
nonexclusion 384
exclusion costs 385
free rider 385
exhaustive expenditures 387
transfer payments 387
benefit principle 390
ability-to-pay principle 390
vertical equity 390
horizontal equity 390
incidence of a tax 391
neutral tax 391
marginal tax rate 391
average tax rate 391
taxable income 392
proportional tax 395
progressive tax 395
regressive tax 395
capital gain 396
indexing 396
government budget surplus 397
government budget deficit 397
deficit financing 397
government debt 397

QUESTIONS AND PROBLEMS

1. Explain why a tax on Japanese cars (to be paid by Japanese manufacturers) may end up being paid by someone else.
2. Explain the different principles of fairness in taxation. Why can't the benefit principle simply be applied to all taxes?
3. What is meant by vertical and horizontal equity in a tax system?
4. Mr. Jones has a taxable income of $25,000. He pays a tax of $5,000. Ms. Smith has a taxable income of $50,000. How much tax would Ms. Smith have to pay for the tax system to be
   a. Proportional?
   b. Progressive?
   c. Regressive?
5. Evaluate the validity of the following statement: "A tax on shoe sales that requires the dealer to pay a $2 tax on every pair of shoes sold should not be of concern to consumers because the dealer has to pay the tax."
6. Define the marginal tax rate.
7. Explain double taxation of corporations.
8. Why is there a trade-off between equity and efficiency in any tax system?
9. When Jones's taxable income increases by $1000, Jones's income tax increases by $200. What is Jones's marginal tax rate?
10. Explain why adding a consumption tax would be more likely to result in a higher national saving rate than raising the income tax would.
11. Proponents of flat taxes maintain that flat taxes are more fair than the existing tax system. How can they make this argument when both high-income and low-income taxpayers would pay the same rate under a flat tax?
12. The state of Michigan hires an assistant professor to teach at one of its state universities. The state of Michigan pays an unemployed automobile worker $500 in unemployment compensation out of state funds. Which transaction is an exhaustive expenditure? How will the two transactions differ in their effect on resource allocation?
13. Which of the following taxes satisfies the benefit principle? Which satisfies the ability-to-pay principle?
    a. A gasoline tax
    b. A progressive income tax
    c. A general sales tax
    d. A special levy on a community to build a dam
14. Is the Social Security payroll tax progressive or regressive? Explain your answer.

INTERNET CONNECTION

15. Using the links from http://www.awl.com/ruffin_gregory, examine the federal tax administration information.
    a. Which states do not have an income tax?
    b. Which state has the highest percentage tax on high-income earners?

16. Using links from http://www.awl.com/ruffin_gregory, examine the Congressional Budget Office Web page.
    a. In the most recent year available, what percentage of total outlays was net interest payments? What percentage of total outlays was discretionary spending?
    b. Plot a graph of total outlays from 1962 to the present.

PUZZLE ANSWERED: It is easier to reach voluntary agreements and to limit free-riding when a small number of families are involved. In the large neighborhood, it is harder to reach voluntary agreements and there would be more free-riding.

Chapter 22

PUBLIC CHOICE

Chapter Insight

A distinguished politician once said that democracy is a flawed system, but society has yet to invent anything better to replace it. Television and the press provide endless accounts of corruption, of costly programs that benefit narrow special interest groups, of vote trading in smoke-filled rooms. These instances lead us to question whether public choices are indeed being made in the best interest of the majority. Consider the following example:

Every year, the Commodity Credit Corporation (CCC) of the federal government buys from 5 to 10 percent of the milk produced in the United States to remove it from the market. The CCC buys enough milk to keep its price from falling below limits set by Congress. Expert testimony shows that the government's dairy price supports cost consumers an extra 50 cents a gallon plus their share of the annual quarter billion dollar cost of the program to taxpayers. Insofar as millions of dairy consumers are hurt by the program and only 200,000 dairy farmers are helped, we would expect elected representatives to vote against the dairy subsidy. In fact, the dairy subsidy has always passed Congress with a substantial vote majority.

The congressional victories of the dairy farmers show how a small group of persons who stand to gain a great deal from a government program can muster more votes than a much larger, diverse group who each stand to lose a relatively small sum as consumers or taxpayers. The dairy cooperatives collect substantial political contributions by withholding contributions from the checks sent to farmers for selling their milk. The cooperatives then make sizable contributions to congressional candidates, including those running in big cities who have no dairy producers in their districts. One congressman from a large city had the distinction of being the fifteenth-highest recipient of dairy money. Statistical evidence shows a strong correlation between dairy money and voting for the dairy subsidy program.

In this chapter we shall discuss how elected officials make public spending decisions. We shall see that majority-rule voting can result in inefficient public choices.

LEARNING OBJECTIVES

After completing this chapter, you will be able to:

1. State the condition for efficiency in the provision of public goods.
2. Understand why efficiency is difficult to achieve in practice.
3. Evaluate pork-barrel politics.
4. Explain how government can be reformed using public choice theory.

CHAPTER PUZZLE: How can majority rule lead to minority rule?

Cost/Benefit Analysis of Government Activity

The rule that guides the private sector's economic decision making has been repeated throughout this book: *Any economic activity should be carried out as long as its marginal benefit exceeds or equals its marginal cost.* The profit-maximizing firm expands its production to the point where marginal costs and marginal revenues are equal. It carries out investment projects as long as the rate of return exceeds the interest rate. We established in an earlier chapter that such decisions are economically efficient if carried out in a competitive market with no externalities.

The efficiency rule for the public sector would be the same as that for the private sector, except that it compares the marginal benefits and marginal costs to those of *society.* A government project that yields $10 million in benefits while costing $5 million is worth undertaking. A project that yields $50 million in benefits while costing $200 million should not be undertaken.

> The optimal amount of government spending is that amount at which the marginal social costs and marginal social benefits of the last public expenditure program are equal.

Even if public officials agree to base all public expenditure decisions on such cost/benefit analysis, they would find it difficult to assess social costs and benefits. Consider a proposed dam that will benefit downriver communities with better flood control and cheaper electricity but will displace longtime residents or threaten an endangered species of fish with extinction: What cost/benefit price tags should we use? In society at large, there are substantial differences of opinion on costs and benefits.

The benefits may go to one group, and costs to another group. Unless the people who pay the costs are somehow compensated—which seldom occurs—the government program entails a redistribution of income.

In the private sector, the market provides safeguards to prevent costs from exceeding benefits. If private firms produce a product whose benefit (as reflected in its market price) is less than its cost, the firm will incur losses. In the long run, it will either go out of business or switch to products that yield a benefit equal to or greater than cost.

> The market test ensures that private goods and services yield a benefit equal to or greater than their cost.

EXAMPLE 1

Why Zero-Tolerance Drug Programs Don't Work

The U.S. government follows "zero-tolerance" drug enforcement, which means that arrests are authorized for possession of even very small quantities of illegal drugs. Under this program, a number of boats have been seized in which a fraction of an ounce of marijuana or cocaine was found. Enforcement rules in effect prior to 1988 set minimum possession limits for arrests and impoundment of property.

Law enforcement officials complain that zero-tolerance programs are economically inefficient. Law enforcement resources are limited; they cannot be stretched to apprehend all drug abusers and dealers. Minimum possession rules encourage law enforcement officials to pursue only drug dealers or large users. The marginal social benefits to a big drug bust are much larger than those of apprehending a small consumer of illegal drugs. The marginal social costs of arresting small drug users far exceed the social benefits. Without rules setting minimum possession limits, law enforcement resources will not be efficiently allocated.

Zero-tolerance programs present yet another example of unintended consequences. The intent of zero-tolerance is a drug-free society. The reality, however, has been to divert law enforcement resources away from major suppliers.

In 1969 the Nixon administration spent $65 million on drug enforcement. In 1988 the Clinton administration requested $17 billion. Thus, at the federal level expenditures have increased by more than an annual rate of about 20 percent without a great deal to show for it. If you had invested $1000 at such a rate of return your money would have grown to about $250,000 over that time period! The drug problem is a very serious social problem; indiscriminate spending on programs that violate basic economic principles simply results in social waste.

Goods provided by government are not subject to this market test. There is no guarantee that public expenditures will yield benefits equal to or greater than cost. In the rest of this chapter, we shall consider how public expenditure decisions are made. Cost/benefit analysis provides an alternative framework for evaluating the efficiency of public choices in the absence of a market test. (See Example 1.)

Unanimity: The Ideal World

In an ideal world, government would work so well that everyone would unanimously approve its actions. A perfectly working price system also achieves a type of unanimity. The price system is *efficient* when it is impossible to make anyone better off without hurting someone else. An efficient economic system makes as large a pie as possible; to give one person a larger piece is to give someone else a smaller piece. An *inefficient* economic system is one in which the pie could be made larger without hurting anyone. Unanimity characterizes a good price system. When two people engage in voluntary exchange, they are unanimous in agreeing to the deal because it makes them both better off.

A turn-of-the-century Swedish economist, Knut Wicksell, suggested that the public analogue to the private market is unanimity.

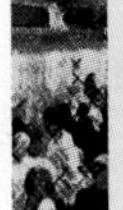

Unanimity exists when all voters agree on or consent to a particular government action.

Under certain circumstances, government action can reflect the voluntary and unanimous actions of each individual. Let's use the example of a community where everyone knows everything about everyone else. In such a community, unanimous collective decisions are not difficult. The community is considering a flood-control project, a pure public good because it is nonrival and no community member can be excluded from its benefits. The market will fail to provide it; the community must therefore decide how much flood control to produce.

In the community, each person's demand schedule for flood control is known to everyone else. Suppose the community consists of individuals A, B, and C. Figure 1 shows their three demand schedules. The demand curve D_A shows A's marginal valuation of flood control at different amounts. (The quantity of flood control is measured by the height of a dam. A higher dam provides a larger "quantity" of flood control.) In Figure 1, the hundredth foot of a dam is worth $1 to A. Because flood control is characterized by nonrival consumption, the same amount of flood control is available to A as to B or C irrespective of the height of the dam. According to the three demand schedules, A's marginal valuation is $1, B's is $5, and C's valuation is $6 at one hundred feet. The vertical height of each person's demand curve at each quantity of flood control is his or her marginal valuation at that quantity. The community's *total* marginal valuation of the hundredth foot of a dam is thus $12 ($1 + $5 + $6). When consumption is nonrival, the total demand curve is the *vertical sum* of each of the individual demand curves.

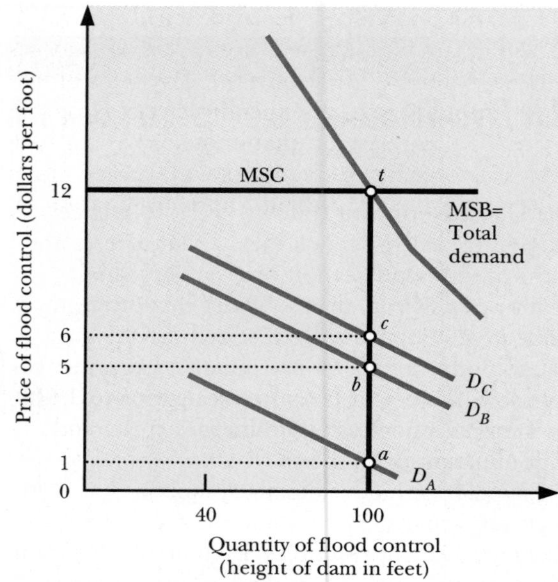

FIGURE 1 Unanimity: Benefit Taxes in a Three-Person Community

This graph shows a three-person community where the demand curves of persons A, B, and C for a nonrival good—flood control—are known to all. The total demand for flood control is the vertical sum of the three individual demand curves because, with a nonrival good, providing one person with flood control provides all with flood control. The marginal social cost (MSC) of flood control is $12; the height of the demand curve measures the marginal social benefit (MSB) of flood control. The marginal social cost is constant at $12. The optimal amount of flood control is a 100-foot dam because marginal social cost equals marginal social benefit at 100 units. With the individual demand curves known to all, benefit taxes of $1 (per unit of flood control) on A, $5 per unit on B, and $6 per unit on C would lead to the unanimous choice of 100 units of flood control.

> The market demand curve for a nonrival (public) good is the *vertical sum* of each individual's demand curve. (Recall for contrast that the market demand curve for a rival good is the *horizontal sum* of all the individual demand curves.)

The optimal quantity of flood control in Figure 1 is a 100-foot dam because the $12 marginal social cost (MSC) of this quantity of flood control (which, for simplicity, we assume to be constant) equals marginal social benefits.

In this three-person community, an optimal result (unanimity) can easily be attained. The government knows the demand schedules of all three citizens and simply taxes them according to their marginal valuations. Thus A is required to pay $1 per unit of flood control; B and C pay $5 and $6 per unit, respectively. The tax paid by each exactly matches the benefits they receive. If such taxes were imposed, citizens would vote unanimously for a 100-foot dam's worth of flood control. Each is getting his or her money's worth.

In the real world, governments do not have enough information to operate on the basis of unanimity. If the individual demand schedules for a public good are not known, some voting process other than unanimity must be used. The costs of discovering the government expenditure/tax program that would bring about unanimous approval are prohibitive; hence it is necessary to accept some principle of collective action short of unanimity, such as majority rule.

Majority Rule

The most popular method of making political decisions is majority rule. In the three-person community, any proposal for flood control would require two *yes* votes in a majority rule system.

Majority rule is a system of voting in which a government decision is approved if more than 50 percent of the voters approve.

For simplicity, let's assume that the $12 marginal cost per unit of flood control is divided equally among the three persons. The "tax price" would then be $4 per person per unit of flood control. The tax liability of each individual would depend on the number of units the community chooses.

Figure 2 illustrates majority voting. With a tax price of $4 per person per foot, A prefers a 40-foot dam, B prefers a 120-foot dam, and C prefers a 140-foot dam. If any dam lower than 40 feet is put to a vote (the dam height of the person who desires the least flood control), all three would favor flood control, but B and C would not be happy. At a tax price of $4 per foot, B and C want a 120-foot and a 140-foot dam, respectively. To them, a 40-foot dam is far too small. If a 100-foot dam (the optimal height under unanimity) is proposed, A (who wants only a 40-foot dam) would vote against the proposal, but B and C would favor it over a 40-foot dam. However, B and C would still conclude that a 100-foot dam is not enough flood control for the price. The median voter, B, wants a 120-foot dam.

The **median voter** on a public expenditure program wants more expenditure than half the remaining voters and less expenditure than the other half.

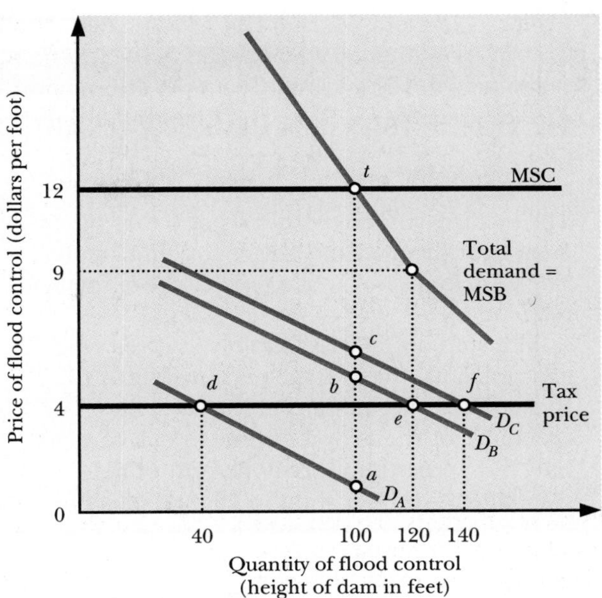

FIGURE 2 Majority Rule in a Three-Person Community

For the same three-person community as in Figure 1, majority rule now reigns and the individual demand curves are not known to all. For simplicity, let's suppose that the $12-per-unit cost of flood control is shared equally by all so that the tax price is $4 per unit per person. At this price, A will want 40 units, B will want 120 units, and C will want 140 units of flood control. Voter B, the median voter, determines the outcome under majority rule. Thus, 120 units of flood control will be provided. This quantity is inefficient because the marginal social benefit of the 120th unit is only $9 (compared with the marginal social cost of $12).

B and C will press for higher levels of flood control until the median voter is satisfied. If a 120-foot dam is proposed, A will vote against it, but both B and C will vote for it and it will pass. If a dam higher than 120 feet is proposed, A and B will vote against it and it will fail. Thus the median voter (B) gets his or her wish: a 120-foot dam. Under majority rule, the proposal to provide a 120-foot dam costing a total of $1440 (= $12 × 120 feet) will defeat all other proposals. Each voter will be assessed $480 to pay for flood control.

Under majority rule, the median voter determines the outcome because precisely half of the

EXAMPLE 2

THE MEDIAN-VOTER RULE AND SCHOOL DISTRICT BUDGETS

The median-voter hypothesis states that the preferences of the median voter will dominate in single-issue elections, like public school financing referenda.

In a study of 2001 randomly selected Michigan residents, the average person wanted to spend $2225 per pupil. But the actual level of spending for the period of time in question was only $1814 per pupil. Fifty percent of the respondents did not want to change spending, 11 percent wanted less spending, and the remaining 39 percent wanted more spending. But the median voter—the one that split the sample exactly in half—wanted less spending. Thus, the results show that the median voter rules, even if this results in an amount of spending that is less than is optimal.

Source: Patricia Ann Nold, "Public Choice and Allocation of Public Goods," *American Economic Review* 82 (1992).

remaining voters prefer less of the public good and half prefer more.

Three conclusions follow from the decisive role of the median voter in simple, direct voting under majority rule. (See Example 2.)

1. *Social choices need not respond to individual wants.* Many people are dissatisfied with government, because the votes of those in the minority (up to 49 percent of the voters on some issues) do not count. The most disgruntled members of society are those whose preferences are almost always in the minority.
2. *Majority voting rules do not reflect the relative intensity of preferences.* Because the median voter determines the outcome, a change in the intensity of anyone else's preferences has no impact. Shifting the demand curve of A downward and C upward in Figure 2 has no impact on the outcome. The intensity of A's and C's preferences is irrelevant. Only the intensity of the median voter's preference counts. This system contrasts sharply with the market for private goods, where dollar votes for goods duly register the intensity of each person's preferences.
3. *Majority voting need not be optimal.* In Figure 2, majority rule led to a 120-foot dam, which is higher than the 100-foot dam an efficient economy would provide. Although the intensity of preferences of nonmedian voters is irrelevant, the intensity of their preferences affects marginal social benefits. In Figure 2, too much of the public good is produced. Whether too much or too little is produced depends on the distribution of demands around the median voter.

VOTING PROBLEMS

In our example, the flood-control program that was adopted had the support of the majority of voters. In this sense, it was the "right" decision. When more than one issue is voted on, however, logrolling, or "pork-barrel politics," can result in the approval of policies that are actually opposed by a majority.

Logrolling

Logrolling is the trading of votes to secure a favorable outcome on decisions of more intense interest to that voter.

On a single issue (such as voting for flood control) the vote of a person who is passionately against some measure and the vote of one who is only marginally in favor have equal weight in determining the final outcome. Politics, however, involves not just one decision but a combination of decisions. One

TABLE 1 BUILDING ACCESS ROADS FOR FARMERS B AND C: BENEFITS EXCEED COSTS

Beneficiaries	*Net Benefit (+) or Cost (−) of Access Road for B (dollars)*	*Net Benefit (+) or Cost (−) of Access Road for C (dollars)*
A	−2	−2
B	+5	−2
C	−2	+5
Society	+1	+1

In this example, access roads cost $6; these costs are shared equally by each farmer ($2 each). But each access road is worth $7 to the affected farmer. Building both roads is socially efficient in this case because total benefits ($14) exceed cost ($12). Under simple majority rule without logrolling, and voting on each road separately, neither road is built, because the *number* of voters benefiting does not exceed the number of voters who do not benefit. However, if farmers B and C link their votes (if both vote for both roads), then both roads can be built and society benefits.

TABLE 2 BUILDING ACCESS ROADS FOR FARMERS B AND C: COSTS EXCEED BENEFITS

Beneficiaries	*Net Benefit (+) or Cost (−) of Access Road for B (dollars)*	*Net Benefit (+) or Cost (−) of Access Road for C (dollars)*
A	−2	−2
B	+3	−2
C	−2	+3
Society	−1	−1

In this case, access roads still cost $6 each, and cost is still shared equally by all three farmers. But each access road is worth only $5 to the affected farmer. Building the roads is socially inefficient in this case. Under simple majority rule without logrolling, neither road is built; but when farmers B and C link their votes, both roads are built even though the benefits to the two farmers do not exceed the costs to society.

politician who is only mildly in favor of one proposal might trade his or her vote with another politician strongly against the proposal in exchange for a similar trade when their positions are reversed.

Consider three farmers—A, B, and C—who by voting must decide about building access roads. Suppose B and C could each use a separate access road from their farm to the main highway. Farmer B would gain $7 from his access road, and Farmer C would gain $7 from her access road; each access road would cost the community $6. The cost of each access road would be equally shared by all three farmers ($2 each). Table 1 describes the net benefits (+) or costs (−) to each farmer from building these access roads at the public expense.

Because the $6 cost is shared equally, building each road has a $2 cost per farmer. Roads built for B or C do not benefit A at all. But a road built for B gives B a net benefit of $5, as the gains from the road are worth $7 and B's share of the cost is only $2. If a road is built for C, B and A do not benefit, but C gains a net benefit of $5.

According to majority rule, if an access road for B is proposed, farmers A and C will vote against it; similarly, an access road for C will be defeated by A and B. Majority rule without logrolling causes the defeat of such special interest legislation.

But farmers B and C each perceive that they can gain by voting for the other's access road. If farmers B and C link their votes, both roads will be built, and farmer A will have to shell out $4 in taxes for the two roads for which he gains no benefits. Farmers B and C each receive a net gain of $3 (= $7 − $4) from building both roads.

Logrolling's effect on economic efficiency depends on the circumstances. In this example, building both roads yields a social benefit of $14 at a cost of $12, for a net social benefit of $2; each road brings benefits of $7. Without logrolling, the roads would not have been built.

But logrolling can also result in inefficiencies (see Table 2). Suppose each road yields benefits of only $5 each to farmers B and C instead of $7. If farmers B and C link their votes, each must pay out $4 ($2 for each access road). Because the benefit to B and C ($5 each) exceeds their cost ($4 each), it is still worthwhile to them to logroll. Two roads are approved for a benefit of $10 but at a cost of $12, for a net social cost of $2.

Table 2 demonstrates that majority rule with logrolling can reduce the size of the total economic pie in that the majority shift the cost of the public good to the minority. As a voter you can get what you want and have someone else pay. Thus, it is highly likely that majority-rule voting will result in more government spending than is optimal. As Nobel laureate James Buchanan and coauthor Gordon Tullock stated,

> There is nothing inherent in the operation of [a majority voting] rule that will produce "desirable" collective decisions. . . . Instead, majority rule will result in an overinvestment in the public sector when the investment projects provide differential benefits or are financed from differential taxation.[1]

The Paradox of Voting

Majority rule can cause policy inconsistencies. Governments pass minimum-wage laws that create unemployment, and then create job-training programs to put people to work. Governments raise the cost of food to the poor through farm price supports and then give them food stamps. Governments fight inflation and then put a tax on imports that raises the prices of foreign goods.

We can better understand these inconsistencies by analyzing an example. Let's suppose that three voters (A, B, and C) must vote on three policies (Alpha, Beta, and Gamma). The Alpha policy redistributes income to voter A, Beta redistributes income to voter B, and Gamma redistributes income to voter C. Table 3 describes how voters A, B, and C rank these policies. Naturally, the first choice of each voter is the policy that benefits him or her. But each voter also has preferences for the other policies as well. Voter A, for instance, might like voter B more than voter C. Hence, the Beta policy is A's second choice, and Gamma policy is A's third choice. Table 3 shows that voter B prefers Gamma to Alpha and that voter C prefers Alpha to Beta.

Every policy in this example is one person's first choice, another's second choice, and a third person's third choice. The table is perfectly symmetrical in this respect. Only two issues are voted on at a time. In a contest between policies Alpha and Beta, voter C determines the outcome because A and B vote for their own policies. Because voter C prefers Alpha to Beta, the Alpha policy wins.

TABLE 3 POLICY RANKINGS

Policy	*Voter A*	*Voter B*	*Voter C*
Alpha	First Choice	Third Choice	Second Choice
Beta	Second Choice	First Choice	Third Choice
Gamma	Third Choice	Second Choice	First Choice

TABLE 4 POSSIBLE CONTESTS AND OUTCOMES

Contest	*Winning Policy*
Alpha versus Beta	Alpha
Beta versus Gamma	Beta
Alpha versus Gamma	Gamma

Table 4 shows the three possible contests and outcomes. In each contest, a different policy wins. No one policy wins more than one contest. If someone witnessed only the first two contests and realized that Alpha was preferred to Beta and Beta to Gamma, logic would suggest that Alpha should be preferred to Gamma. However, the third row of Table 4 shows that Gamma is preferred to Alpha. Majority rule has resulted in an inconsistent outcome. If the second and third choices of just one of the voters are reversed, however, the paradox disappears.

The **paradox of voting** is that majority rule can yield inconsistent social choices. Even if each voter is perfectly rational, the majority of voters can choose *a* over *b*, *b* over *c*, and then choose *c* over *a*.

The Political Market

The political market consists of voters, special interest groups, politicians, political parties, and government bureaucracy. How does each group affect the public choices made by democratic governments?

Voters

After an election, journalists and television commentators frequently bemoan the difficulty of motivating people to vote. The decline in voter turnout in the

---

[1]James Buchanan and Gordon Tullock, *The Calculus of Consent* (Ann Arbor: University of Michigan Press, 1962), p. 169.

U.S. presidential elections from 1960 to 1996 has led observers to conclude that there is considerable voter apathy.

What motivates us to vote? Objectively, there is a marginal cost (in time and effort) of voting. The probability that any single person's vote would decide an election is close to zero. According to one study,[2] most people vote out of a sense of obligation and duty, but important determinants of voter turnout are the cost of going to the polls and the closeness of the election. If we expect a close election, the chances of our voting are larger. We make a cost/benefit calculation when we decide whether to vote. The benefit is the knowledge that we have performed our civic duty; this benefit increases with closer elections.

Do we make informed decisions when we go to the polls? Anthony Downs called the lack of information-gathering on the part of the voting public rational ignorance.[3]

Rational ignorance is a decision not to acquire information because the marginal cost exceeds the marginal benefit of gathering the information.

In an earlier chapter on information costs we concluded that we gather information as long as the marginal benefits exceed the marginal cost. The cost of acquiring information is greater for public choices than for private choices because public programs are more complicated and the link between voting and the benefits received is very uncertain. Hence, most people know much more about private choices than public ones. This public ignorance is a rational response to the costs of information.

Special Interest Groups

The major implication of rational ignorance is that voters know much more about legislation that affects them than about legislation that affects someone else. Special interest groups can take advantage of rational ignorance (See Example 3.)

Special interest groups are minority groups with intense, narrowly defined preferences about specific government policies.

In this type of situation, vote trading among politicians can result in special-interest legislation that is economically inefficient.

Politicians and Political Parties

President John F. Kennedy was fond of quoting the mother who wanted her offspring to grow up to be president but did not want a politician in the family. We somehow expect politicians to behave on a higher or more altruistic level than we do. When politicians act just like anyone else or worse, we are disappointed in their low moral character.

The successful politician is a political entrepreneur who determines government policies by voting and logrolling. Like a private entrepreneur who stays in business by offering consumers what they want, the political entrepreneur can stay in office only by offering a record that will attract enough votes at election time. The rewards of reelection are many: popularity, power, prestige, and increased income opportunities. Politicians may be more interested in getting votes than in serving the public interest. Even if they are completely unselfish, politicians cannot serve society unless they are reelected.

Given that most voters are rationally ignorant about the complex policies a particular politician supports, a vote-maximizing politician can put together a package of policies in support of special-interest legislation that benefits a minority but hurts the majority. Each member of each minority will benefit enormously while each member of the majority will be hurt only a small amount. The politician can thereby attract enough support from a coalition of minority groups to win. The politician who opposes all the special-interest legislation would probably be looking for a job after the next election.

The central problem of public choice is that the benefits of government policies are highly concentrated while the costs are highly diffused.

[2]O. Ashenfelter and S. Kelly, Jr., "Determinants of Participation in Presidential Elections," *Journal of Law and Economics* 18 (December 1975): 695–733.

[3]Anthony Downs, *An Economic Theory of Democracy* (New York: Harper and Row, 1957).

EXAMPLE 3

Special Interest Legislation: Ethanol

Archer Daniels Midland (ADM) is an agricultural conglomerate that processes and sells agricultural commodities, producing, among other products, oil, seeds, flour, biochemical animal foods, ethanol, and pasta. ADM is headed by a hard-charging chief executive officer, well known as a Washington insider and major campaign contributor to both political parties.

ADM is the major producer of ethanol, a clean-burning fuel made from corn. Under current federal regulations, automobile gasoline must contain a certain percentage of ethanol. This single regulation boosts the demand for ADM's ethanol, thereby raising its price and allowing ADM to make monopoly-like profits from its ethanol division.

The public argument for the ethanol additive sounds convincing—to create a cleaner-burning fuel. The unstated argument for ethanol is that it is good for ethanol producers. ADM every year mounts a massive lobbying campaign to promote its interests. The result of this lobbying, the requirement for an ethanol additive in gasoline, raises gas prices to the consumer less than one cent, but it creates enormous benefits for one company.

Restricting Japanese car imports makes the American automobile manufacturer and automobile worker better off. The costs of import restrictions, however, are distributed over the entire population in such a subtle fashion that we cannot distinguish between the increase in the price caused by import restrictions and that caused by other factors. The French economist Frederick Bastiat referred to *what is seen* and *what is unseen.* What is seen is the fact that auto firms and workers are better off with import restrictions; what is unseen is that the price of automobiles is higher for everyone.

Bureaucrats

Besides assorted lobbyists and pressure groups, another actor on the political stage is the much-maligned bureaucrat.

A **bureaucrat** is a nonelected government official responsible for carrying out a specific, narrowly defined task.

A bureaucracy is needed to run the government programs enacted by politicians. Bureaucrats tend to be the experts (e.g., social scientists, lawyers, and accountants) who execute the programs.

Bureaucracies tend to produce budgets that are too large. In private firms, profit seeking provides the incentive to minimize costs. If the firm's resources are not allocated efficiently, profits will disappear and the firm will go out of business. In bureaucracies, there are few incentives to minimize costs; instead, bureaucrats may maximize "personal profits" in the form of plush offices, large staffs, or unnecessary "inspection" trips.

Because of their rational ignorance, taxpayers do not even know which bureaucrats run their offices efficiently. Because of *their* rational ignorance, elected politicians cannot monitor the large budgets they must approve. Legislators, who must be concerned with thousands of different programs, get their information from bureaucrats. The bureaucrat has an enormous information advantage over the typical legislator. Because bureaucrats are interested in expanding their budget, government budgets tend to be larger than necessary.

Proposals for Government Reform

Most economists and voters believe that government has grown too large. The 1986 Nobel Prize–winner James Buchanan has argued that constitutional limits must be imposed to constrain the inherent tendency of government to overexpand:

> Modern America confronts a crisis of major proportions in the last decades of the 20th century. In the seven decades from 1900 to 1970, total government spending in real terms increased 40 times over. . . . The point of emphasis is that this growth has occurred, almost exclusively, within the predictable workings of orderly democratic procedures.[4]

We now understand those forces—special interests, vote trading, and rational ignorance—that increase the size of government. Public spending in support of particular groups or industries such as agriculture or steel is in the public interest, these groups argue.

Not everyone thinks government has grown too large. Anthony Downs has pointed out that the voter will usually underestimate the *benefits* (not just the costs) of fully justifiable government expenditures because they are remote and uncertain. In Downs's view, a fully informed voter would vote for larger budgets.

Modern public choice theory suggests that, regardless of the size of government, substantial failures exist in the way public choices are made. The preferences of everyone, from the on-line worker to the captain of industry, should be duly registered when public choices are made. Currently, however, the median voter dominates, logrolling allows the passage of special-interest legislation, and voters are rationally ignorant about the costs and benefits of government programs. Thus, as Buchanan has argued, there is constant pressure for the government to engage in economically inefficient activities. (See Example 4.) Experts have proposed a variety of reforms to make government more responsive to individual preferences, including the following:[5]

1. Elected officials should be subject to term limits so they can devote themselves to making the right decisions rather than worrying about reelection. Term limits also motivate them to think like private citizens and not professional politicians.
2. A three-fourths majority should be required for some types of legislation (particularly obvious special-interest legislation, such as tariffs, price supports, minimum-wage laws, and loans to bankruptcy-prone firms).
3. Decisions on major spending or taxation proposals should be made by direct majority voting by the general public.
4. Whenever possible, public expenditures should be replaced by market-type allocation. Prisons, schools, libraries, and garbage collection should be handled by private companies that are able to provide the service more efficiently.
5. All new expenditure programs should be linked to a visible tax increase.
6. Members of Congress should be determined by a process of random selection from the general public.
7. More public expenditures should be handled locally where there is competition among communities. As economist Charles Tiebout pointed out, voters can "vote with their feet as well as the

---

[4]James M. Buchanan, *The Limits of Liberty* (Chicago: The University of Chicago Press, 1975), p. 162. Chapter 9 of Buchanan's book contains compelling reasons why governments can get too large.

[5]The proposals are given in E. Browning and J. Browning, *Public Finance and the Price System,* 3d ed. (New York: Macmillan Publishing Co., 1987).

EXAMPLE 4

THE 2000 ELECTIONS

In the 2000 elections, there was a great deal of debate over campaign finance reform. But the debate centered on restricting contributions to political parties or making contributions public knowledge. Public choice theory suggests that these debates are a waste of time. Politicians follow their own self-interest. Their principal source of influence is the tax system; without the tax system, contributions to political parties and candidates would be much smaller. It is not likely that politicians will change the system in a way that is against their interests. Indeed, if they do so, the "fix" won't last long. As an example, in the 1830s Congress voted to move to a uniform tariff rate of 20 percent. By 1842 this goal was reached. But a uniform tariff rate removed the gains to politicians from fiddling with individual tariff rates. Public choice theory predicts that such a change cannot last; and, indeed, it lasted no more than two months! The Tariff Act of 1842 raised some tariffs and lowered others. By 1860 the uniform tariff of 20 percent was a distant memory.

This 1842 lesson applies to campaign finance reform in the year 2000 or any future year. As long as politicians have an interest in receiving campaign contributions, they will find a way to collect them. If method A of collecting money is declared illegal, some bright lawyer will figure out method B that is legal. One law that might work would be to allow complete freedom but also complete disclosure, so that the only illegal act would be to keep a contribution secret.

Source: Authors.

ballot box." Households, Tiebout observes, are not frozen in particular localities but can instead shop around for the bundle of public goods and taxes that most closely approximates their demands for local public goods, such as parks, police protection, roads, zoos, and schools.[6] Consumers thus have some discretion over their consumption of public services. The competitive aspects of the provision of public services may stimulate local officials to try to minimize costs and respond to consumer tastes.

8. There should be increased public information on legislation including electronic bulletin boards to inform the electorate.

These reforms attempt to address the problems of rational ignorance, logrolling, and the overrepresentation of special interests.

[6]Wallace E. Oates, "On Local Finance and the Tiebout Model," *American Economic Review* 71 (May 1981): 93–98.

DEMOCRACIES AND ECONOMIC EFFICIENCY

Democracy is the best political system we have. Compared to its alternatives—dictatorships of the right or the left—majority rule looks good, despite the problems we have discussed in this chapter.

The previous section identified a number of reforms, which, if enacted, would improve public choice in democratic societies. If increased public understanding of the abuses were combined with the desire of elected officials to be reelected, public officials would shun their support of special-interest legislation. If all democratic decision making were to take place in the full light of day, elected officials would be less likely to vote for special-interest legislation.

SUMMARY

1. Cost/benefit analysis suggests that government spending should be carried to the point where marginal social benefits and marginal social costs are

equal. Cost/benefit analysis could serve as a substitute for the market test that private goods must pass.

2. The government must make resource allocations because the market fails to allocate public goods efficiently. In an ideal world, all government actions would have the unanimous support of all citizens. Unanimous collective decisions, however, require perfect information. Governments would have to price public goods according to each individual's marginal valuation of the good. Unanimity is virtually impossible in the real world.

3. The most popular alternative in democratic societies is majority rule. Under majority rule, the median voter decides on public goods. Social choices therefore do not reflect the relative intensities of preference of different voters. Majority rule does not guarantee that the socially optimal amount of the public good will be produced.

4. Majority rule creates "paradoxes of voting" in situations involving more than one decision. By forming vote-trading coalitions, beneficiaries of public goods can create majorities that would not have been possible otherwise.

5. The political market consists of voters, special interest groups, politicians, political parties, and the government bureaucracy. Voters use personal cost/benefit analysis in their voting decisions; they vote when the perceived costs are low and the perceived benefits are high. Voting decisions are characterized by *rational ignorance.* The costs to most voters of acquiring information on complex public issues are high, and the benefits are low. For special interest groups, however, the benefits are high relative to the costs of acquiring information. Politicians must adopt policies that will improve their chances of reelection. The fact that voters are rationally ignorant and do not understand the effects of many government policies encourages special-interest legislation.

6. Economic analysis indicates that government undertakes many programs for which the marginal social benefits do not exceed the marginal social costs, or that government fails to undertake many programs for which the marginal social benefits exceed the marginal social costs. Suggestions to improve public choices include term limits, supermajority voting on special-interest legislation, direct voting on major issues, privatization, and a shift toward local spending and taxation.

KEY TERMS

unanimity 405
majority rule 407
median voter 407
logrolling 408
paradox of voting 410
rational ignorance 411
special interest groups 411
bureaucrat 412

QUESTIONS AND PROBLEMS

1. What factors limit unanimity on political decisions?
2. In the course of political contests (for example, between the primary and the general election), some politicians switch their positions. Is this fact consistent with the theory of the role of the median voter in majority-rule elections? Why or why not?
3. If people are rational, how can public choice result in government actions with benefits that are less than the costs?
4. Explain why government bureaucrats would be less interested in cost minimization than would managers of private firms.
5. Do you think government is more or less efficient than a competitive enterprise? Is it more or less efficient than private monopoly? Explain.
6. Do you think lobbying promotes or reduces the general welfare? Explain.
7. How would you reform the political process to make majority rule work better?
8. Evaluate the validity of the following statement: "The more localized are public goods, the more likely it is that unanimity about them can be achieved in public choices."
9. A balanced-budget amendment narrowly missed being passed by Congress in 1994. How would you justify such an amendment in terms of the concepts used in this chapter?

10. How can majority rule be inefficient? Does inefficiency mean majority rule should not be used?
11. Must logrolling result in economic inefficiency? Explain.
12. Bob prefers apples over bananas and bananas over oranges. Maria prefers oranges to apples and apples to bananas. Sam prefers bananas to apples and apples to oranges. If majority rule is used to choose among these goods, does a voting paradox arise?
13. Would a world with zero information costs have economic inefficiency in the provision of government services?
14. Art, Bob, and Charlie own a lake in Wisconsin that they use for recreational purposes. A proposed mosquito abatement program will benefit all. Art places a value of $1, Bob places a value of $19, and Charlie places a value of $100 on a mosquito-free environment. If approved, the program would cost each owner $35.
    a. What decision would be reached under majority rule? Would the result be efficient?
    b. What decision would be reached if Art, Bob, and Charlie would engage in costless negotiation? Could unanimity be achieved?

INTERNET CONNECTION

15. Public choice theory is developed at the following Web site: http://www.magnolia.net/~leonf/sd/pub-choice.html. How is it that self-interest works with private goods but not with public goods?

PUZZLE ANSWERED: The benefits and costs of government policies are not spread uniformly over the population. The gains from a particular policy may be small in the aggregate, but spread over a small number of people; the costs may be large, but spread over a large number of people. As a consequence, the gainers have an incentive to fight hard for the policy, while the losers—greater in number—have so little at stake on an individual level that the minority, through logrolling, gets the policy through the legislature.

The World Economy

part VIII

Chapter 35

International Trade

Chapter Insight

One of the defining moments in the evolution of an economy is its realization that faster economic growth requires full participation in the world economy. This awareness occurs at different times for different countries. It occurred in Great Britain during the 1840s, the United States during the Great Depression, Asia during the 1970s, Latin America during the 1980s, and China in the 1990s.

International trade has always changed the way people live. Traders throughout history have helped transmit knowledge and inventions. Today, foreign products from Sony, BMW, Mitsubishi, and Chanel are as familiar to us as U.S. products from General Electric, Chevrolet, and IBM. We continue to debate, however, whether or not trade is beneficial. In the early 1990s, a television newscast showed an angry American worker destroying a Japanese car with a sledgehammer because of the fear that imports were taking away American jobs. In late 1999, protesters in Seattle shut down meetings of the World Trade Organization on the grounds that trade hurts national autonomy, labor, children, and the environment. Similar protests occurred in 2000 in Washington, D.C., over even broader issues.

It is easy to fall prey to the fallacy that imports eliminate domestic jobs. People often fail to realize that in the long run exports pay for imports. Indeed, it was conventional wisdom in the sixteenth and seventeenth centuries that a country should encourage exports and discourage imports. In 1817, however, David Ricardo developed the law of comparative advantage, which demonstrates the benefits of international trade. In this chapter, we shall explain the workings of the law of comparative advantage and how it applies to the United States and the world economy.

LEARNING OBJECTIVES

After completing this chapter, you will be able to:

1. Explain why exports are not better than imports.
2. Understand the basic causes for international trade.
3. Explain the law of comparative advantage.
4. Show why high wages are not a barrier to trade.
5. Show why low wage countries do not undercut the United States in world markets.

CHAPTER PUZZLE: How is it that the American textile industry can be the most productive in the world and yet the United States does not have a comparative advantage in textiles?

THE GLOBAL ECONOMY

The production of goods and services throughout the world has become truly global. Many Japanese cars are built in America. Nike running shoes—an American product—are produced in Malaysia. International production has obscured the dividing line between "American" goods and "foreign" goods. Electronic components are shipped to Asian countries and return as completed computers or calculators. American companies form alliances with foreign companies: DaimlerChrysler has an alliance with Mitsubishi, General Motors with Fiat, and International Business Machines (IBM) with Toshiba. Almost all large companies have foreign branches. For example, the Ford Escort is produced in Europe, and Ford owns Jaguar.

Since the end of World War II, world trade has increased faster than world output, because of low trade barriers, smaller transportation costs, and dramatic reductions in the costs of international communication achieved through the use of space satellites.

How extensive is world trade? About one-fifth of world GDP is made up of exports (or imports) from one country to the next. In the 1990s, world trade was larger than the German and Japanese economies combined. Indeed, trade has grown about twice as fast as GDP for the simple reason that trade barriers of all sorts have come down.

Mercantilism

Understanding the nature of international trade was one of the first accomplishments of economics as a science. In the sixteenth and seventeenth centuries, journalists and politicians promoted a set of policies called *mercantilism*. These writers held that a nation was like a business. To make a profit, a country had to sell more than it bought from foreign countries. Thus, according to mercantilist writers, the best policies would promote exports to the rest of the world and discourage imports from foreign competitors.

According to the mercantilists, domestic producers must be protected from foreign competition through various kinds of subsidies. These would increase exports and lower imports. It was the mercantilists who coined the phrase "favorable trade balance," still in use today. A favorable trade balance is one in which exports exceed imports.

What can be wrong with this philosophy? The answer: The mercantilists confused what is good for particular industries with what is good for the economy as a whole. In other words, they committed the fallacy of composition, which we discussed in Chapter 1: What is true for a part is not necessarily true for the whole. If a country subsidizes one industry, it can actually hurt other "unseen" industries, because the subsidy will cause resources to shift from relatively efficient industries (those competing without the subsidy) to those that are relatively inefficient.

From the standpoint of the whole economy, the total supply of goods and services that are available within the country equals domestic production *plus* imports *minus* exports. When the United States imports Japanese cars, we have more cars; when the United States exports wheat, we have less wheat. The import of cars brings about a reduction in the car industry; the export of wheat brings about an expansion of the wheat industry. However, by exporting wheat and importing cars, the country can actually have more of both! To understand this point we must once again consider the law of comparative advantage.

Reasons for International Trade

A major tenet of market economics is that people benefit from specialization. People increase their incomes by specializing in those tasks for which they are particularly suited. Different jobs have different intellectual, physical, and personality requirements. Because people are different from one another and because each person has the capacity to learn, it pays to specialize. As Adam Smith stated, "It is the maxim of every prudent master of a family never to attempt to make at home what it will cost him more to make than to buy." People trade with each other primarily because each individual is endowed with a mix of traits that are different from those of most other people. Some of these traits are an inherent part of the individual that cannot be shared with other individuals.

Trade between individuals has much in common with international trade between countries. Each country is endowed with certain characteristics: a particular climate, a certain amount of fertile farmland, a certain amount of desert, a given number of lakes and rivers, and the kinds of people that compose its population. Over the years, some countries have accumulated large quantities of physical and human capital, whereas other countries are poor in capital. In short, each country is defined in part by the endowments of productive factors (land, labor, and capital) inside its borders. Just as one person cannot transfer intelligence, strength, personality, or health to another person, one country cannot transfer its land and other natural resources to another country. Similarly, the labor force that resides within a country is not easily moved; people have friends and family in their native land and share a common language and culture. Even if they wish to leave, immigration laws may render the labor force internationally immobile.

It is easier to transfer to another country the goods and services produced by land, labor, and capital than to transfer the land, labor, and capital themselves. Thus, to some degree various countries possess land, labor, and capital in different proportions. A country like Australia has very little labor compared with land and, hence, devotes itself to land-intensive products, such as sheep farming and wheat production. A country like Great Britain tends to produce goods that use comparatively little land but much labor and capital. Therefore, each country specializes in those goods for which its mix of resources are most suited; international trade in goods and services substitutes for movements of the various productive factors.

> The fundamental fact upon which international trade rests is that goods and services are much more mobile internationally than are the resources used in their production. Each country will tend to export those goods and services for which its resource base is most suited.

International trade allows a country to specialize in the goods and services that it can produce at a relatively low cost, and to export those goods in return for imports whose domestic production is relatively costly. Through international trade, as John Stuart Mill (1806–1873) said, "A country obtains things which it either could not have produced at all, or which it must have produced at a greater expense of capital and labor than the cost of the things which it exports to pay for them." As a consequence of obtaining goods more cheaply, international trade enables a country—and the world—to consume and produce more than would be possible without trade. We shall later see that a country can benefit from trade even when it is more efficient (uses fewer resources) in the production of *all* goods than any other country.

Trade has intangible benefits in addition to the tangible benefits of providing the potential for greater totals of all the goods and services the world consumes. The major tangible benefit is the diversity that trade offers to the way people live and work. The advantages of particular climates and lands are shared by the rest of the world. The United States imports oil from the hot desert of Saudi Arabia so that Americans can drive cars in cool comfort. We can enjoy coffee, bananas, and spices without living in the tropics. We can take advantage of the economy and durability of Japanese cars without driving in hectic Tokyo. Thus, international (and interregional) trade enables us to enjoy a more diverse menu of goods and services than we could without trade. World trade also encourages the diffusion of knowledge and culture because trade serves as a point of contact between people of different lands.

The Law of Comparative Advantage

In Chapter 3 we used the law of comparative advantage to explain the benefits people enjoy from specialization. Individuals are made better off by specializing and engaging in trade with other people. The law of comparative advantage can also help explain the gains from international specialization. In 1817, David Ricardo proved that international specialization pays if each country devotes its resources to those activities in which it has a comparative advantage.

The **law of comparative advantage** states that people or countries specialize in those activities in which they have the greatest advantage or the least disadvantage compared with other people or countries.

Profound truths are sometimes difficult to discover; the real world is so complex that it can hide the working of these truths. Ricardo's genius was that he was able to provide a simplified model of trade without the thousands of irrelevant details that would cloud our vision. He considered a hypothetical world with only two countries and only two goods. The two "countries" could be America and Europe; the two goods could be food and clothing. For the sake of simplicity, let us also assume the following.

1. Labor is the only productive factor, and there is only one type of labor.
2. Labor cannot move between the two countries (this assumption reflects the relative international immobility of productive factors compared with goods).
3. The output from a unit of labor is constant (in other words, productivity is constant no matter how many units of output are produced).
4. Laborers are indifferent about whether they work in the food or clothing industries, provided that wages are the same.

Table 1 shows the hypothetical output of food or clothing from 1 unit of labor in each of the two countries. America can produce 6 units of food with 1 unit of labor, and 2 units of clothing with 1 unit of labor. Europe can produce either 1 unit of food or 1 unit of clothing with 1 unit of labor. America is 6 times more efficient than Europe in food production (it produces 6 times as much with the same labor); America is only twice as efficient in clothing production (it produces twice as much with the same labor).

We have deliberately constructed a case in which America has an absolute advantage over Europe in all lines of production.

A country has an **absolute advantage** in the production of a good if it uses fewer resources to produce a unit of the good than any other country.

Even under these circumstances, however, both countries stand to benefit from specialization and trade according to comparative advantage, as we shall see.

The Case of Self-Sufficiency

Let's suppose that each country in our hypothetical world is initially self-sufficient and must consume only what it produces at home.

America. A self-sufficient America must produce both food and clothing. American workers can produce 6 units of food or 2 units of clothing from 1 unit of labor (see Table 1). Since money is just a unit of account, to understand the benefits of international trade it is best that we concentrate on what goods are worth in terms of each other. Under conditions of self-sufficiency, the American price of a unit of cloth-

TABLE 1 HYPOTHETICAL FOOD AND CLOTHING OUTPUT FROM 1 UNIT OF LABOR

Country	*Units of Food Output from 1 Unit of Labor*	*Units of Clothing Output from 1 Unit of Labor*
America	6	2
Europe	1	1

Trade patterns depend on comparative advantages, not on absolute advantages. In our hypothetical example, America is 6 times more efficient than Europe in food production and twice as efficient in clothing production. America has an absolute advantage in both food and clothing but has a comparative advantage only in food production. Europe has an absolute disadvantage in the production of both goods but has a comparative advantage in clothing-production. Europe will export clothing to America in return for food, and both will gain by this pattern of trade. Each country exports the good in which it has the greatest efficiency advantage (in the case of America) or the smallest inefficiency disadvantage (in the case of Europe).

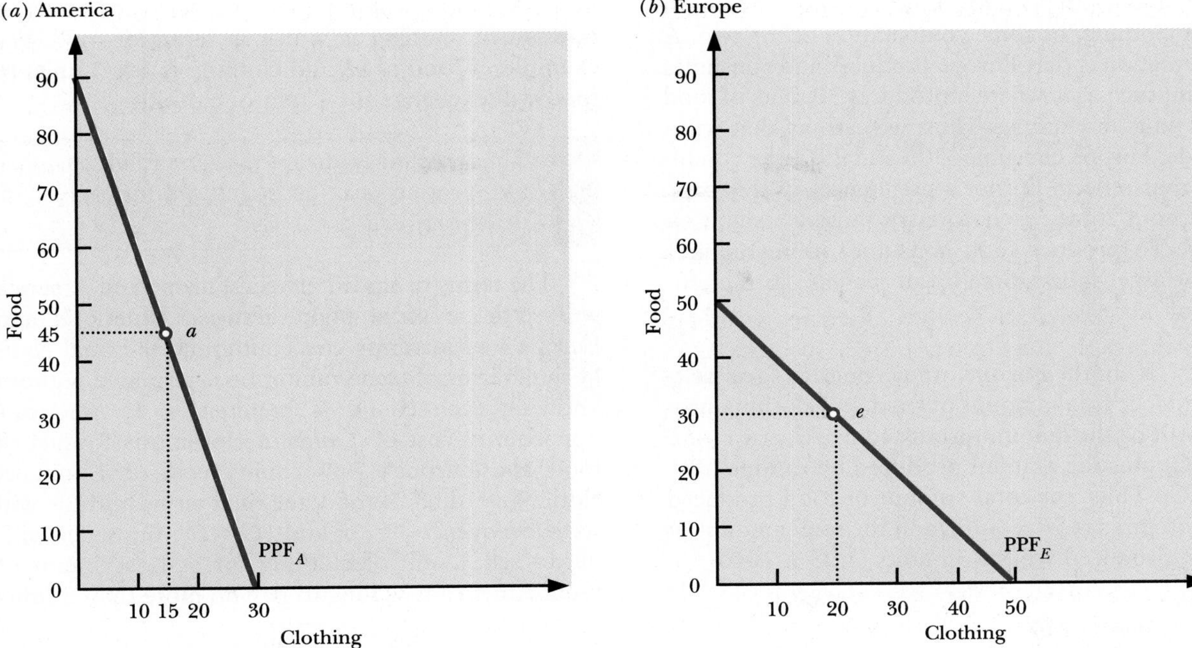

FIGURE 1 Hypothetical American and European Production Possibilities Frontiers

Panel (*a*) shows a hypothetical production possibilities frontier for America. Based on the labor productivity rates in Table 1, if 15 units of labor are available and labor is the only factor of production, America could produce either 30 units of clothing, 90 units of food, or some mixture of the two—such as the combination represented by point *a*, where 45 units of food and 15 units of clothing are produced. Panel (*b*) shows a hypothetical PPF for Europe, where 50 units of labor are available. Again, based on the labor productivity rates in Table 1, Europe could produce 50 units of clothing, 50 units of food, or a combination—such as that represented by point *e*, where 30 units of food and 20 units of clothing are produced.

ing will be three times the price of a unit of food. Why? In the marketplace, 6 units of food will have the same value as 2 units of clothing, or, to simplify, 3 units of food (F) will have the same value as 1 unit of clothing (C) because they use the same amount of labor. To produce more clothing, food must be sacrificed because labor must be moved out of food production. Thus, America's opportunity cost of 1 unit of clothing is 3 units of food:

$$3F = 1C$$

These same facts are shown in panel (*a*) of Figure 1, which graphs America's production possibilities frontier (PPF). Labor is the only factor of production, and we assume for simplicity that a total of 15 units of labor are available to the American economy. America's PPF is a straight line because opportunity costs are constant in our example. If everyone works in clothing production, 30 (= 15 × 2) units of clothing can be produced. If everyone works in food production, 90 (= 15 × 6) units of food can be produced. The economy will likely produce a mix of food and clothing to meet domestic consumption. Such a combination might be point *a*, where 45 units of food and 15 units of clothing are produced and consumed. Thus, we can say that without trade, America consumes $45F$ and $15C$, the combination that reflects America's preferences in this case.

Europe. In a self-sufficient Europe, workers can produce 1 unit of food or 1 unit of clothing with 1 unit of labor (see Table 1). A unit of clothing and a unit of food have the same costs, and hence, the same price. In other words, Europeans must give up 1 unit of food to get 1 unit of clothing. Thus, Europe's opportunity cost of 1 unit of clothing is 1 unit of food.

$$1F = 1C$$

Panel (*b*) of Figure 1 shows Europe's PPF. In our example, we assume Europe is more populous than the United States; it has 50 units of labor available. Europe also has a straight-line production possibilities frontier, and it can produce either 50 units of food, 50 units of clothing, or some combination of the two. A likely situation is that Europe produces and consumes at a point such as *e,* where it produces 30 units of food and 20 units of clothing. Thus, we can say that without trade, Europe consumes 30*F* and 20*C*, the combination that reflects Europe's preferences in this case.

Without trade, each country must consume on its PPF. To produce (and consume) more requires either a larger labor force or an increase in the efficiency of labor.

The World. If both Europe and America are self-sufficient, the total amount of food and clothing produced will be the amount produced by America (45*F* and 15*C*) plus the amount produced by Europe (30*F* and 20*C*). Thus, the total amount of food produced will be 75 units (45*F* + 30*F*), and the total amount of clothing produced will be 35 units (15*C* + 20*C*).

The Case of International Trade

Before trade opens between Europe and America (as described in Table 1), a potential trader would find that 1 unit of clothing sells for 1 unit of food in Europe but sells for 3 units of food in America. If the trader then applies 1 unit of labor in American food production and ships the resulting 6 units of food to Europe, he or she can obtain 6 units of clothing instead of the 2 obtained by producing it in America! It makes no difference that clothing production is half as efficient in Europe. What matters is that in Europe, a unit of food and a unit of clothing have the same market value; thus, before trade, food and clothing sell for the same price in Europe.

As Americans discover that clothing can be bought more cheaply in Europe than at home, the law of supply and demand will then do its work. Americans will stop producing clothing in order to concentrate on food production, and they will begin to demand European clothing. This increased demand will drive up the price of European clothing. Europe will shift from food production to clothing production, and eventually the pressure of American demand will lead Europe to produce only clothing. In the long run, Americans will get clothing more cheaply (at less than 3*F* for 1*C*) than before trade, and Europeans will receive a higher price for their clothing (at more than 1*F* for 1*C*).

In making decisions about trading, people in each country need to know the prices of goods on the international market. The prices of food and clothing in this example will determine the terms of trade, or how much clothing is worth in terms of food. For example, if food is $2 and clothing is $4, 2 units of food will exchange for 1 unit of clothing.

The **terms of trade** are the rate at which two products can be exchanged for each other between countries.

The terms of trade between Europe and America will settle at some point between America's and Europe's opportunity costs, although the final equilibrium terms of trade cannot be determined without knowing each country's preferences. If America's opportunity cost of 1 unit of clothing is 3 units of food and Europe's opportunity cost of 1 unit of clothing is 1 unit of food, the final terms of trade will settle between 1*C* = 3*F* and 1*C* = 1*F*. Europe is willing to sell 1 unit of clothing for at least 1 unit of food; America is willing to pay no more than 3 units of food for 1 unit of clothing.

The cheap imports of clothing from Europe will drive down the price of clothing in America. When Europe exports clothing to America, the price of clothing in Europe will rise. If the world terms of trade at which both Europe and America can trade are set by the market at 2*F* = 1*C*, Americans will no longer get only 2 units of clothing for 1 unit of labor; instead, they can produce 6 units of food, and trade that food for 3 units of clothing (because 2*F* = 1*C*) in Europe. Europeans will no longer have to work so hard to get 1 unit of food. They can produce 1 unit of clothing and trade that clothing for 2 units of food instead of getting only 1 unit of food per unit of clothing.

When the terms of trade in the world are 2*F* = 1*C*, Americans will devote all their labor to food production and Europeans will devote all their labor to clothing production. (If increasing, rather than constant, opportunity costs had been assumed, the two countries need not have been driven to such complete specialization.)

The Gains from Trade

When American workers specialize in food production, and European workers specialize in clothing production, the gains to each can be measured by comparing their sacrifices before and after trade. Americans, before trade, sacrificed 3 units of food for 1 unit of clothing. After trade, Americans need sacrifice only 2 units of food for 1 unit of clothing (with terms of trade at $2F = 1C$). Europeans, before trade, sacrificed 1 unit of clothing for 1 unit of food. After trade, Europeans need sacrifice only half a unit of clothing per unit of food (because clothing sells for twice as much as food after trade).

The gains from trade are shown dramatically in Figure 2. Before trade, America is at point *a* in panel (*a*), and Europe is at point *e* in panel (*b*). When trade opens at the terms of trade $2F = 1C$, America moves its production to point x_A (specialization in food production), as the arrow shows. Thus, America increases its food production from 45 units to 90 units. America can now trade each unit of food for half a unit of clothing. If America trades 40 units of food for 20 units of clothing, America can consume at point c_A, with consumption at 50 units of food and 20 units of clothing. Trade enables America to consume above its production possibilities frontier. In this example, trade shifts consumption from *a* to c_A. The dotted line shows the consumption possibilities available to Americans when $2F = 1C$ in the work market.

As column 1 of Table 2 shows, America produces 45*F* and 15*C* before trade. The opening of trade shifts American labor entirely out of clothing production. As column 2 shows, America produces only food (90*F*) after trade opens. Columns 3 and 4 describe America's trade; America keeps 50*F* for domestic consumption and sells 40*F* for 20*C*. Column 5 shows consumption after trade, and column 6 shows America's benefits from trade. As a result of trade, America increases its consumption of each product by 5 units.

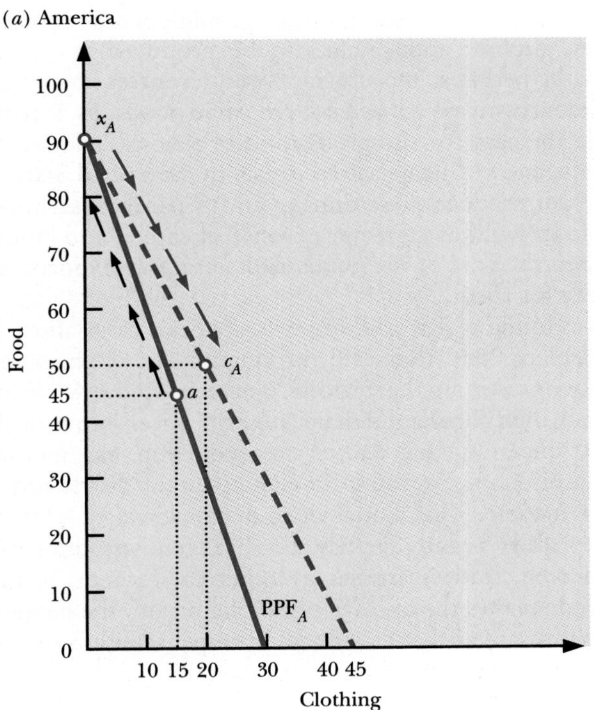

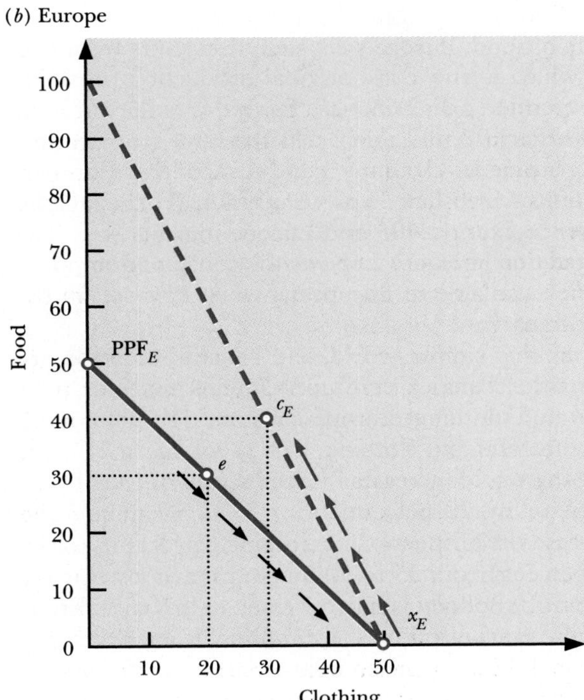

FIGURE 2 The Effects of Trade

As shown in panel (*a*), before trade, America produces and consumes at point *a*. When trade opens at the terms of $2F = 1C$ (where F = units of food and C = units of clothing), America produces at x_A, specializing in food production, and trades 40 units of food for 20 units of clothing. America, therefore, consumes at point c_A, where it consumes 50 units of food and 20 units of clothing. Trade shifts American consumption from *a* to c_A. As shown in panel (*b*), before trade, Europe produces and consumes at point *e*. When trade opens, Europe shifts production to x_E, specializing in clothing production, and trades 20 units of clothing for 40 units of food. Europe, therefore, shifts consumption from *e* to point c_E, where 30 units of clothing and 40 units of food are consumed. In both panels, the black arrows show the effects of trade on domestic production, and the red arrows show the effects of trade on domestic consumption. Both countries consume somewhere on the dashed line above their original production possibilities frontiers.

TABLE 2 THE EFFECTS OF INTERNATIONAL TRADE

	Consumption and Production Before Trade (1)	*Production After Trade* (2)	*Exports* (3)	*Imports* (4)	*Consumption After Trade* (5)	*Gains* (6)
(*a*) America	45*F*	90*F*	40*F*	0*F*	50*F*	5*F*
	15*C*	0*C*	0*C*	20*C*	20*C*	5*C*
(*b*) Europe	30*F*	0*F*	0*F*	40*F*	40*F*	10*F*
	20*C*	50*C*	20*C*	0*C*	30*C*	10*C*
(*c*) World	75*F*	90*F*	—	—	90*F*	15*F*
	35*C*	50*C*	—	—	50*C*	15*C*

F = units of food
C = units of clothing

Europe's story is told in panel (*b*) of Figure 2. Europe shifts production from *e*, where 30*F* and 20*C* are produced, to point x_E, where 50 units of clothing are produced. With the terms of trade being 2*F* = 1*C*, Europe can trade 20 units of clothing for 40 units of food. Europe's consumption shifts from *e* to c_E, which is above the original production possibilities frontier. Like America, Europe is better off with trade. Part (*b*) of Table 2 tells the same story in simple arithmetic. Columns 3 and 4 show that Europe's trade is consistent with America's. For example, America exports 40*F* and Europe imports 40*F*. The dotted line in Figure 2 shows the consumption possibilities available to Europeans when 2*F* = 1*C* in the world market.

In this simple world, the benefits of trade are dramatic. America consumes 5 units more of both food and clothing; Europe consumes 10 units more of both food and clothing. Part (*c*) of Table 2 shows that the world increases its production of food by 15 units, or by 20 percent (from 75 to 90 units), and increases its production of clothing by 15 units, or by 43 percent (from 35 to 50 units). Everybody is made better off; nobody is hurt by trade in this case. Trade has the same effect on consumption as an increase in national resources or an improvement in efficiency of resource use. As a consequence of trade, countries are able to consume beyond their original production possibilities frontiers. (See Example 1.)

The advantages of international trade are sometimes obvious and sometimes subtle. They are obvious when trade enables a country to acquire some good that it cannot produce (such as tin or nickel or manganese in the United States) or that would have an exorbitant production cost (such as bananas, coffee, or tea in the United States). As Adam Smith pointed out, "By means of glasses, hotbeds, and hotwalls, very good grapes can be raised in Scotland, and very good wine can be made of them at about thirty times the expense for which at least equally good can be bought from foreign countries."

The advantages of trade are subtle when a country imports goods that can be produced at home with, perhaps, the use of fewer resources than the resources used abroad for the same goods, as would be the case for the production of textiles, television sets, and videocassette recorders in the United States. It can produce these things, but (to paraphrase John Stuart Mill) at a greater expense of capital and labor than the cost of the goods and services it exports to pay for them.

In the real world, imports of goods from abroad displace the domestic production of competing goods, and in the process, some people may find that their income falls. Because the Ricardian model assumes only one factor of production, the model simply cannot account for changes in the distribution of income. The model does demonstrate that in a world with many factors and shifts in distribution of income, trade increases average real income. Since trade makes the average person better off, the people who are made better off could compensate those who are made worse off.

Low-Wage and High-Wage Countries

Hourly wages in the United States are about ten times higher than Mexican hourly wages. Japanese hourly wages are three times higher than Korean hourly wages. Yet the United States and Japan are two of the world's largest exporting countries; Korea and Mexico are comparatively small exporting countries. The law of comparative advantage explains

EXAMPLE 1

Does Free Trade Pay?

Does free trade really pay? As evidenced by the unilateral adoption of free or freer trade by countries throughout the world, there is a widespread belief that free trade pays. Since 1817, the theory of comparative advantage has suggested that this is the case. Mercantilism, the sixteenth- and seventeenth-century doctrine that exports were good and imports were bad, suggested that home merchants must be protected from foreign competition. Economists did not really have extensive evidence for the benefits of free trade compared with protectionism until the half-century following World War II, by which time they had collected enough data on the growth rates of a large number of countries experiencing different degrees of protectionism.

The following table gives some evidence for the proposition that free trade pays. It shows the per capita rates of growth of countries that have the highest amounts of protection versus those with the lowest amounts of protection. The measures are based on a combination of different measures. The growth rates are measured over about three decades. The countries that had the lowest amount of protection grew at the average rate of 3.8 percent per year while those with the highest protection grew at the rate of only 1.3 percent per year. This evidence has constituted the thrust behind the worldwide movement toward freer trade. Some countries in the highest protection group (e.g., Egypt and Gabon) grew faster than the average rate of growth in the lowest protection group—because trade is only one factor behind economic growth. Studies show that when all the other factors are held constant, trade does add from 1 to 2 percent per year to economic growth. the average rate of growth across countries actually tells the tale.

Highest Protection		*Lowest Protection*	
Country	*Growth*	*Country*	*Growth*
Angola	−2.7	South Africa	1.6
Zambia	−1.4	New Zealand	1.8
Ghana	−0.5	United States	1.9
Senegal	−0.2	United Kingdom	2.2
Uganda	−0.2	Luxembourg	2.3
Sudan	0.1	Ireland	2.7
Zaire	0.2	Ecuador	2.8
Somalia	0.2	Denmark	2.9
Guinea	0.5	Belgium	2.9
Nigeria	0.7	Netherlands	3.0
India	0.8	France	3.4
Ethiopia	0.8	Finland	3.6
Bolivia	1.0	Spain	3.6
Chile	1.0	Italy	4.0
Argentina	1.1	Portugal	4.5
Ivory Coast	1.3	Malta	5.4
Zimbabwe	1.6	Korea	5.6
Burundi	1.7	Taiwan	6.0
Pakistan	1.9	Hong Kong	6.1
Rwanda	2.0	Japan	6.1
Tanzania	2.3	Singapore	6.6
Burma	2.6		
Gambia	2.9		
Iran	3.1		
Panama	3.5		
Cameroon	3.6		
Egypt	4.3		
Gabon	5.2		
Average	1.3	Average	3.8

Source: Research Department, Federal Reserve Bank of Dallas.

Source: David Gould and Roy Ruffin, "Human Capital, Trade, and Economic Growth," *Weltwirtschaftliches Archiv* 131 (1995), 425–445.

how high-wage countries can compete with low-wage countries.

Table 1 assumed that America is six times as productive in food and two times as productive in clothing production as Europe. Since wages reflect productivity, American wages should be between six and two times as high as European wages. When the world terms of trade are $2F = 1C$, the price of clothing is twice that of food. In our example, the price of food can be \$3 per unit and the price of clothing can be \$6 per unit. If Americans specialize in food production, food is \$3 per unit, and 1 unit of labor produces 6 units of food, wages must be \$18 (= \$3 × 6 units) per unit of labor in America.

Europeans specialize in clothing production. Because the price of clothing is \$6 per unit and 1 unit of European labor produces 1 unit of clothing, wages must be \$6 (= \$6 × 1 unit) per unit of labor in Europe. (Prices are measured in dollars to avoid currency differences.) Thus, with the given terms of trade, American wages are three times European wages.

Assertions that high-wage countries like the United States cannot possibly compete with low-wage countries like Taiwan or Korea are economically unsound. Wages are higher in the United States because productivity is higher. Claims that people who live in low-wage countries cannot compete with high-productivity countries like the United States are also unsound. When comparative advantage directs the allocation of resources, both high-wage and low-wage countries share in the benefits of trade. The high-productivity country's wage rate will not be high enough to completely wipe out the productivity advantage nor be low enough to undercut the low-productivity country's comparative advantage. Likewise, the low-productivity country's wage will not be high enough to make it impossible to sell goods to the rich country nor low enough to undercut the rich country's comparative advantage. (See Example 2.)

Given the hypothetical case in Table 1, American wages will be somewhere between six and two times as high as European wages (depending on the terms of trade). If American money wages are seven times higher than European money wages, American money prices will be higher than European money prices for both food and clothing because America's labor-productivity advantage cannot offset such a high wage disadvantage. This situation cannot persist. The demand for American labor will dry up, while the demand for European labor will rise. With American wages seven times European wages, forces will be set into operation to reduce American wages and raise European wages until the ratio of American to European wages returns to a level between six and two. With market-determined wages, all countries can compete successfully.

Intraindustry Trade

Differences in comparative advantage constitute one reason for international trade. Another reason is decreasing costs, or economies of scale, which explain the simultaneous export and import of goods in the same industry.

Our discussion example thus far assumes that food and clothing are produced under constant returns to scale. If America and Europe can produce food and clothing with the same labor costs but with decreasing costs as production increases (economies of scale), advantages of large-scale specialization will be gained if each product is produced by only one country.

Decreasing costs are present when the cost of production per unit decreases as the number of units produced increases.

Decreasing costs play a vital role in what is called *intraindustry trade*. Many products—such as cars, television sets, clothing, watches, and furniture—come in different varieties. Germany exports ultraluxury sports cars, whereas Japan traditionally exported economy cars but is now successfully invading Germany's territory. The same generic products, such as cars or furniture, can be both exported and imported. There is two-way trade. This intraindustry trade often involves decreasing costs: When many varieties of a good are produced, an increase in the production of any one variety spreads fixed overhead costs (such as rent, machinery, and administration) over more units. As a result, each country can specialize in a particular variety of some generic production. (See Example 3 on page 694.)

Trading Blocs and Free Trade

The European Union

The best example of free trade within a group of nations, called a trading bloc or a common market, is the European Union (EU). The EU formally began as the European Communities (EC), with the 1957

EXAMPLE 2

North American Free Trade Agreement (NAFTA)

On January 1, 1994, the North American Free Trade Agreement (NAFTA) among the United States, Canada, and Mexico went into force. Prior to NAFTA, Mexico had trade barriers that were 2.5 times higher than those in the United States. The United States had a preexisting agreement with Canada. This is what NAFTA achieved:

1. A phaseout of most tariffs and nontariff barriers over 10 years on industrial products and over 15 years on agricultural products.
2. Investment rules ensuring national treatment of U.S. investors in Mexico and Canada as well as reduced barriers to investment in Mexican petrochemicals and financial services.
3. Protection of intellectual property rights (patents, copyrights, and trademarks).
4. Funds for environmental cleanup and community adjustment along the border between the United States and Mexico.

Domestic opponents of NAFTA argued that terrible things would happen if it was adopted. Ross Perot, the main opponent of NAFTA, argued that there would be a "giant sucking sound," as jobs in America would be lost to Mexico. He argued that America could not compete with Mexican workers because their daily wages were less than American hourly wages.

These fears, of course, were not realized. The fact of the matter is that advanced countries can compete with poorer countries because of the law of comparative advantage. They can because workers in each country compete with other workers in the same country, not with workers in other countries. An American company must pay wages competitive with wages elsewhere in the U.S. economy, not in Mexico. The same is true in Mexico. Thus, the successful companies in the United States are those whose productivity is relatively higher than the average productivity (wages) in the United States. These are the industries in which the United States has a comparative advantage.

Treaty of Rome among six nations—Belgium, West Germany, France, Italy, Luxembourg, and the Netherlands. The purpose of the EC was to create a region of free trade. By 1968 all tariffs among the member states were eliminated. From 1958 to 1972 the EC's total real GDP grew at about 5 percent per year while intra-European trade expanded at about 13 percent per year. The success of the EC attracted more nations. Between 1972 and 1985 six more countries joined—Denmark, Ireland, Britain, Greece, Spain, and Portugal.

But from 1972 to 1985, the member states did not do nearly as well as the original six. The oil price shocks in the 1970s, a slowdown in European economic growth, and rising European unemployment reversed the trend toward integration. Member states began to impose new barriers to trade with the outside world as well as with other EC countries. The growth rate in real GDP fell by about one-half.

Europeans became convinced that rising trade barriers were partially responsible for their economic ills. Thus, in 1986, the 12 nations of the European Communities signed the Single European Act. In 1992, the EC member countries became the European Union (EU), and a single market for goods, financial services, capital, and labor movements.

The EU eliminates many types of barriers to trade. First, countries must share the same set of standards for safety and consumer protection. Second, the large differences in tax rates must be reduced. Third, border controls must be minimized. For example, in the past truck drivers had to show border officials up to 100 documents—invoices, forms for import statistics, and tax reports. Now truck drivers can go through customs showing only a single document.

In addition to eliminating these barriers, the EU creates a single market for financial services. For example, a bank established in one EU country can operate a branch in another EU country, and EU firms in one country can borrow in another. European Union citizens can keep bank accounts in any member nation. Thus, financial capital will flow freely throughout the bloc.

North American Free-Trade Bloc

The United States has responded to the EU by forming its own trading bloc. (See Example 2 once again.) The United States signed a free-trade agreement with Canada in 1989 and signed an agreement with Mexico in 1994. The Canada–United States agreement generated little debate in the United States, but much in Canada. The free-trade agreement among Mexico, the United States, and Canada was opposed by some labor and farm groups.

Labor groups have expressed the fear that a pact with Mexico will lower U.S. wages because Mexican wages are only about one-seventh as high. Yet, even though more international trade can lower some wages, the principle of comparative advantage tells us that average U.S. wages will rise. As a country specializes in the goods in which it has a comparative advantage, its average real income—and wages—will rise, not fall. In fact, the United States is more productive than Mexico. Only lower wages enable Mexico to compete in spite of the absolute advantages of the United States. Moreover, much of the impact of freer trade with Mexico has already taken place. Beginning in 1986 Mexico unilaterally opened its markets to foreign goods. In 1999 the United States exported almost $90 billion worth of goods to Mexico.

EXAMPLE 3

The Importance of Intraindustry Trade

The top U.S. imports and exports, as well as those of most industrial countries, are actually similar items; they are roughly the same industries. For example, in 1998 the United States exported $77 billion worth of office machinery, but the country also imported $41 billion worth of office machinery.We imported $79 billion in electrical equipment at the same time we exported $65 billion worth. We exported $28.6 billion worth of power-generating machinery and imported almost the same amount. Indeed, about 50–60 percent of all U.S. trade is intraindustry. Even a larger percentage of U.S. trade with Mexico and Canada is intraindustry, as we share a North American automobile industry.

The significance of intraindustry trade arises form its basic character: It is based on decreasing costs and locational advantages rather than comparative advantage. The more sport utility vehicles Ford makes, the lower the unit cost; the more Mercedes-Benz convertibles produced, the lower the unit cost. Thus, even though there are no comparative advantages, it pays to produce some cars in the United States and some in Germany. This strategy saves on the fixed costs of setting up particular production lines. Another advantage of intraindustry trade is that it is more suggestive of industrial innovation. When Japan began exporting more reliable cars to America, U.S. manufacturers took notice and copied Japanese quality control and production techniques. It is easier to improve upon existing products if they are similar to imports rather than dissimilar—petroleum imports do not suggest how to produce better airplanes.

Source: Roy Ruffin, "The Nature and Significance of Intraindustry Trade," *Federal Reserve Bank of Dallas, Economic and Financial Review*, Spring 2000.

The U.S. Comparative Advantage

According to Swedish economist Bertil Ohlin, a country tends to export those goods that intensively use the abundant productive factors with which that country is blessed. The Ohlin theory is based on the relative abundance of different productive factors. For instance, if a country has a large quantity of labor relative to land or capital, its wages will tend to be lower than wages in countries with abundant land or capital. Even if technical know-how were the same across countries, countries with cheap labor would have a comparative advantage in the production of labor-intensive goods. Whereas the Ricardian theory assumes only one factor and takes technology differences as given, the Ohlin theory explains comparative advantage as the consequence of differences in the relative abundance of different factors.

Compared with other countries, the United States is rich in agricultural land. This abundance lowers the cost of agricultural goods compared with other countries. Despite protection abroad, the United States exports large quantities of goods such as wheat, soybeans, corn, cotton, and tobacco.

The United States also has an abundance of highly skilled technical labor. The United States tends to export goods that use highly skilled labor. Thus, the United States has a comparative advantage in manufactured goods that require intensive investment in research and development (R&D); industries with relatively high R&D expenditures contribute most to American export sales. Computers, semiconductors, software, chemicals, nonelectrical and electrical machinery, aircraft, and professional and scientific instruments are the major R&D-intensive industries. These industries generate a trade surplus, with exports exceeding imports. The manufacturing industries that are not in this category—such as textiles, paper products, and food manufactures—generate a trade deficit (a surplus of imports over exports).

The products of R&D industries tend to be new products, which are nonstandardized and not well suited to simple, repetitive, mass-production techniques. As time passes, the production processes for these products, such as personal computers, become more standardized. The longer a given product has been on the market, the easier it is for the good to become standardized and the lesser the need for highly trained workers. When new goods become old goods, other countries can gain a comparative advantage over the United States in these goods. In order to fulfill its comparative advantage, the United States then moves on to the next new product generated by its giant research establishment and abundant supply of engineers, scientists, and skilled labor. The U.S. comparative advantage in manufacturing is in new products and processes.

In this chapter, we have considered the global economy, the law of comparative advantage, the gains from trade, how high-wage countries compete with low-wage countries, regional trading blocs, and the pattern of U.S. trade.

SUMMARY

1. Just as trade and specialization can increase the economic well-being of individuals, so specialization and trade between countries can increase the economic well-being of the residents of the trading countries. The basic reason for trade is that countries cannot readily transfer their endowments of productive factors to other countries. Trade in goods and services acts as a substitute for the transfer of productive resources among countries. In 1817, David Ricardo formulated the law of comparative advantage, which demonstrates that countries export according to comparative—not absolute—advantage.

2. In a simple two-country, two-good world, even if one country has an absolute advantage in both goods, both countries can still gain from specialization and trade. If the two countries were denied the opportunity to trade, they would have to use domestic production to meet domestic consumption. With trade, specialization allows each to consume beyond its domestic production possibilities frontier by producing at home and then trading the product in which it has a comparative advantage. Countries will specialize in those products whose domestic opportunity costs are low relative to their opportunity costs in the other countries. Through trade, countries are able to exchange goods at more favorable terms than those dictated by domestic opportunity costs.

3. Money wages are set to reflect the average productivity of labor in each country. Higher average labor productivity is reflected in higher wages. Money wages are not set in such a manner as to undercut each country's comparative advantage. Economies of scale help account for intraindustry trade among countries.

4. Regional trading blocs abolish trade barriers among member nations. The most important blocs are the European Union and the North American free-trade pact among Canada, Mexico, and the United States.

5. The United States is rich in agricultural land and highly skilled technical labor. This advantage gives the United States a comparative advantage in agricultural goods and high-technology research and development products.

KEY TERMS

law of comparative advantage 686
absolute advantage 686
terms of trade 688
decreasing costs 692

QUESTIONS AND PROBLEMS

1. Adam Smith noted: "What is prudence in the conduct of every private family can scarce be folly in that of a great kingdom. If a foreign country can supply us with a commodity cheaper than we ourselves can make it, better buy it from them with some part of the produce of our own industry." Strictly speaking, a fallacy of composition is involved in Smith's famous remark. But when applied to international trade, what is true of the family is also true of the kingdom. Why is it true that the fallacy of composition does not apply?

2. Suppose that 1 unit of labor in Asia can be used to produce 10 units of food or 5 units of clothing. Also suppose that 1 unit of labor in South America can be used to produce 4 units of food or 1 unit of clothing.
   a. Which country has an absolute advantage in food? In clothing?
   b. What is the relative cost of producing food in Asia? In South America?
   c. Which country will export food? Clothing?
   d. Draw the production possibilities frontier for each country if Asia has 10 units of labor and South America has 20 units of labor.
   e. What is the range for the final terms of trade between the two countries?
   f. If the final terms of trade are 3 units of food for 1 unit of clothing, compute the wage in Asia and the wage in South America, assuming that a unit of food costs $40 and a unit of clothing costs $120.

3. What happens to the answers to parts *a, b,* and *c* of question 2 when the South American productivity figures are changed so that 1 unit of labor is used to produce either 40 units of food or 10 units of clothing?

4. In congressional hearings, American producers of such goods as gloves and shoes claim that they are the most efficient in the world but have been injured by domestic wages that are too high compared to foreign wages. Without disputing the facts of their case, how would you evaluate their plight?

5. Most advanced countries both export and import automobiles. How do you explain this fact?

INTERNET CONNECTION

6. Using the links from http://www.awl.com/ruffin_gregory examine the U.S. International Trade Administration's Web page.
   a. Draw a graph of the U.S. trade balance for the last 20 years. What has been the general pattern?
   b. Now draw separate graphs for goods and for services showing the trade balance for each of these items. What can you conclude from these data?

PUZZLE ANSWERED: The United States does not have a comparative advantage in textiles because the country is even more productive in other goods, such as airplanes and high-tech products. The textile industry must pay wages that are competitive with wages in other U.S. industries; the high productivity of these other industries is the true competition to the American textile industry, not the low-wage countries.

GLOSSARY

ability-to-pay principle states that those better able to pay should bear the greater burden of taxes, whether or not they benefit more. (21)

absolute advantage in the production of a good exists for a country if it uses fewer resources to produce a unit of the good than any other country. (35)

absolute poverty standard establishes a specific income level for a household of a given size, below which the household is judged to be living in a state of poverty. (19)

accounting profits are revenues minus explicit costs. (18)

adverse-selection problem occurs when a buyer or seller enters a disadvantageous contract on the basis of incomplete or inaccurate information because the cost of obtaining the relevant information makes it difficult to determine whether the deal is a good one or a bad one. (15)

agent is a party that acts for, on behalf of, or as a representative of a principal. (8)

aggregate production function shows the relationship between the total output produced by the economy and the total labor, capital, and land inputs used by the economy. (16)

allocation is the apportionment of scarce resources to specific productive uses or to particular persons or groups. (2)

arbitrage is buying in a market where a commodity is cheap and reselling in a market where the commodity is more expensive. (15)

average fixed cost (AFC) is fixed cost divided by output:

$$AFC = FC \div Q \qquad (9)$$

average revenue (AR) equals total revenue (TR) divided by output. (11)

average tax rate is the ratio of the tax payment to taxable income. (21)

average total cost (ATC) is total cost divided by output, or the sum of average variable cost and average fixed cost:

$$ATC = TC \div Q = AVC + AFC \qquad (9)$$

average variable cost (AVC) is variable cost divided by output:

$$AVC = VC \div Q \qquad (9)$$

barter is a system of exchange where products are traded for other products rather than for money. (3)

benefit principle of taxation states that those who benefit from a public expenditure should pay the tax that finances it. (21)

benefits are forms of employee compensation such as employer-subsidized health insurance or employer contributions to retirement plans. (17)

bond market is a market in which bonds of different types are traded. Bond markets buy and sell corporate bonds and bonds of governmental organizations. (8)

bonds are obligations to repay the principal at maturity and to make annual interest payments until the maturity date. (8)

budget line represents all the combinations of goods the consumer is able to buy, given a certain income and set prices. The budget line shows the consumption possibilities available to the consumer. (7A)

bureaucrat is a nonelected government official responsible for carrying out a specific, narrowly defined task. (22)

capital includes equipment, buildings, plants, and inventories created by the factors of production; that is, capital is used to produce goods both now and in the future. (2)

capital gain occurs whenever assets such as stocks, bonds, or real estate increase in market value over the price paid to acquire the asset. (21)

cartel is an organization of producers whose goal is to operate the industry as a monopoly. (13)

***ceteris paribus* problem** occurs when the effect of one factor on another is masked by changes in other factors. (1)

change in demand is a change in the quantity demanded because of a change in a factor other than the good's price. It is depicted as a shift in the entire demand curve. (4)

change in quantity demanded is a movement along the demand curve because of a change in the good's price. (4)

change in quantity supplied is a movement along the supply curve because of a change in the good's price. (4)

change in supply is a change in the quantity supplied because of a change in a factor other than the good's price. It is depicted as a shift in the entire supply curve. (4)

circular-flow diagram summarizes the flows of goods and services from producers to households and the flow of the factors of production from households to business firms. (3)

collective bargaining is the process whereby a union bargains with management as the representative of all union employees. (17)

common stock confers voting privileges and the right to receive dividends only if they are declared by the board of directors. (8)

compensating wage differentials are the higher wages that must be paid to compensate workers for undesirable job characteristics. (19)

competing ends are the different purposes for which resources can be used. (2)

complements are two goods related such that the demand for one falls when the price of the other increases. (4)

concentration ratio calculates the percentage of industry sales accounted for by the (four, eight) largest firms in an industry. (5)

conglomerate merger is a merger of companies in different lines of business. (14)

constant returns to scale are present when an increase in output does not change long-run average costs of production. (9)

consumer equilibrium or **optimum** requires that (1) all income be spent and (2) the marginal utilities per dollar for each good purchased are equal. Thus, if goods A, B, C, . . . and so forth are being purchased, it must be that

$$MU_A/P_A = MU_B/P_B = MU_C/P_C = \ldots \text{ for all goods.} \qquad (7)$$

consumers' surplus represents the consumer benefits (the dollar value of total utility) from consuming a good in excess of the dollar expenditure on the good. (7, 10)

contrived scarcity is the production of less than the economically efficient quantity of a good by a monopoly. (12)

convertible stock pays the owner fixed interest payments and gives the privilege of converting the convertible stock into common stock at a fixed rate of exchange. (8)

corporation is a business enterprise that has the status of a legal person and is authorized by federal and state law to act as a single person. The corporation is owned by stockholders who possess shares of stock in the corporation. The stockholders elect a board of directors that appoints the management of the corporation. (8)

Cournot oligopoly exists when (1) the product is homogeneous, (2) each firm supposes that its rivals will continue to produce their current outputs independently of that firm's choice of outputs, and (3) there is a fixed number of firms. (13)

craft union represents workers of a single occupation. (17)

credible threat is the commitment of significant resources by existing firms to convince potential entrants to the industry that entry would result in severe losses for the entrant. (13)

credit, or **capital, markets** facilitate the exchange of financial assets in a modern society. (18)

cross-price elasticity of demand (E_{xy}) is the percentage change in demand of the first product (x) divided by the percentage change in the price of the related product (y). (6)

deadweight loss is a loss to society of consumer or surplus that is not offset by anyone else's gain. (12)

decreasing costs are present when the cost of production per unit decreases as the number of units produced increases. (35)

deficit financing is government borrowing in credit markets to finance a government deficit. (21)

Defining Moment of economics is an event or idea, or a set of related events or ideas over time, that has changed in a fundamental way the manner in which we conduct our everyday lives and the way in which we think about the economy. (1)

demand for a good or service is the amount people are prepared to buy under specific circumstances such as the products price. (4)

demand curve or **demand schedule** shows the negative (or inverse) relationship between quantity demanded and price. (4)

depreciation is the decrease in the economic value of capital goods as they are used in the production process. (18)

derived demand is the demand for a factor of production that results (is derived) from the demand for the goods and services the factor of production helps produce. (16)

discrimination occurs when individuals are blocked from entering jobs and occupations or when workers with equal skills and qualifications are treated differently on the grounds of race, sex, or some other characteristic. (19)

diseconomies of scale are present when an increase in output causes long-run average costs to increase. (9)

disequilibrium price is one at which the quantity demanded does not equal the quantity supplied. (5)

economic efficiency means that the economy is producing the maximum output of useful things with its given resources and technology. (12)

economic growth occurs when a economy expands its outputs of goods and services. (2)

economic profits are revenues in excess of total opportunity costs (which include both actual payments and sacrificed alternatives). Economic profits are profits in excess of normal profits. (18); represent the amount by which revenues exceed total opportunity costs. (10)

economic rent is the amount by which the payment to a factor exceeds its opportunity cost. (18)

economic system is the property rights, resource allocation arrangements, and incentives that a society uses to solve the economic problem. (2)

economics is the study of how people choose to use their limited resources (land, labor, and capital) to produce, exchange, and consume goods and services. It explains how these scarce resources are allocated among competing ends by the economic system. (1)

economies of scale are present when large output volumes can be produced at a lower cost per unit than small output volumes. (8); are present when an increase in output causes long-run average costs to fall. (9)

efficiency occurs when an economy is using its resources so well that producing more of one good results in less of other goods. No resources are being wasted. (2)

efficiency-wage model states that it is rational for certain firms to pay workers a wage rate above equilibrium to improve worker performance and productivity. (17)

employee association represents employees in a particular profession in order to both maintain professional standards and improve conditions of pay and work. (17)

entrepreneurs organize the factors of production to produce output, seek out and exploit new business opportunities, and introduce new technologies and inventions. The entrepreneur takes the risk and bears the responsibility if the venture fails. (2, 8)

equilibrium (market-clearing) price is the price at which the quantity demanded by consumers equals the quantity supplied by producers. (4); of a good or service is that price at which the amount of the good people are prepared to buy (demand) equals the amount offered for sale (supply). (3, 5)

exchange complements specialization by permitting individuals to trade the goods in which they specialize for those that others produce. (3)

exclusion costs are the costs of preventing those who do not pay from enjoying a good. (21)

exhaustible (or **nonrenewable**) **resource** is any resource of which there is a finite amount in the long run because the stock is fixed by nature. (20)

exhaustive expenditures are government purchases that divert resources from the private sector, making them no longer available for private use. (21)

externalities exist when an economic activity of one party results in direct economic costs or benefits for someone else who does not control that economic activity. (12); exist when producers or consumers do not bear the full marginal cost or enjoy the full marginal benefit of their actions. (20)

factors of production or **resources** are the inputs used to produce goods and services. (2)

fallacy of composition is the assumption that what is true for each part taken separately is also true for the whole or, in reverse, that what is true for the whole is true for each part considered separately. (1)

false-cause fallacy is the assumption that because two events occur together, or one event precedes the other, one event has caused the other. (1)

fixed costs (FC) are those costs that do not vary with output. (9)

free good is an item for which there exists an amount available that is greater than the amount people would want at a zero price. (2)

free rider enjoys the benefits of a good or service without paying the cost. (21)

functional distribution of income is the distribution of income among the four broad classes of productive factors—land, labor, capital, and entrepreneurship. (16)

futures market is an organized market in which a buyer and seller agree now on the price of a commodity to be delivered at some specified date in the future. (15)

game theory is the study of how we interact with others in our economic and social behavior. (5)

Gini coefficient is the area between the 45-degree line and the Lorenz curve, divided by the total area under the 45-degree line. (19)

globalization refers to the degree to which national economic markets and international businesses are integrated and interrelated into a world economy. (1)

government budget deficit is the excess of government outlays over government revenues. (21)

government budget surplus is the excess of government revenues over government outlays. (21)

government debt is the cumulated sum of outstanding IOUs that a government owes its creditors. (21)

Great Depression was a sustained period of high unemployment and falling output that occurred in Europe and North America in the 1920s and 1930s. (1)

growth distortion is the measurement of changes in a variable over time that does not reflect the concurrent change in other relevant variables with which the variable should be compared, such as population size or the size of the economy. (1A)

halfway rule states that when the demand curve can be represented by a straight line, the marginal revenue curve bisects the horizontal distance between the demand curve and the vertical axis. (11)

hedging is the temporary substitution of a futures market transaction for an intended spot transaction. (15)

horizontal equity exists when those with equal abilities to pay do pay the same amount of tax. (21)

horizontal merger is a merger of two firms in the same line of business (such as two insurance companies or two shoe manufacturers). (14)

household production is work in the home, including such activities as meal preparation, do-it-yourself repair, child-rearing, and cleaning. (17)

human capital is the accumulation of past investments in schooling, training, and health that raise the productive capacity of people. (2); theory teaches that we make rational choices of different lifetime earnings streams when we invest in ourselves. (19)

immediate run is a period of time so short that the quantity supplied cannot be changed at all. In the immediate run—sometimes called the *momentary period* or *market period*—supply curves are perfectly inelastic. (6)

incentive-based approach is when the government uses economic incentives or penalties (such as taxes or subsidies) to encourage polluting agents to restrict emissions. (20)

incidence of a tax is the actual distribution of the burden of tax payments. (21)

income effect occurs when the price of a good falls and we buy more of it because (1) the price reduction is like an increase in income that in itself normally results in larger demands for all goods and services; and (2) we tend to substitute that good for other, relatively more expensive goods (the **substitution effect**). (7)

income elasticity of demand (E_i) is the percentage change in the demand for a product divided by the percentage change in income, holding all prices fixed. (6)

indexing is the tying of tax rates to the rate of inflation. (21)

indifference curve shows all the alternative combinations of two goods that yield the same total satisfaction to a particular consumer and among which the consumer is indifferent. (7A)

Industrial Revolution occurred as a result of extensive mechanization of production systems that shifted manufacturing from the home to large-scale factories. This combination of scientific and technological advances and the expansion of free-market institutions created, for the first time, sustained economic growth. (1)

industrial union represents employees of an industry regardless of their specific occupation. (17)

industry or **market supply curve** is, in the short run, horizontal summation of the supply curves of each firm, which in turn are those portions of the firms' MC curve located above minimum AVC. (10)

inferior good is one for which demand falls as income increases, holding all prices constant. (4)

inflation is a general increase in money prices. (3)

inflation distortion is the measurement of the dollar value of a variable over time without adjustment for inflation over that period. (1A)

information costs are the costs of acquiring information on prices, product qualities, and product performance. (15)

information revolution is the term describing the staggering improvements in our ability to create, use, and exchange information that have accompanied the vast improvements in information technology (computerization, the Internet, wireless telephones, and so forth). (1)

in-kind income consists of benefits—such as free public education, school lunch programs, public housing, or food stamps—for which the recipient is not required to pay. (19)

interest is the price of credit and is determined in credit markets. (18)

interest rate is the price of credit that is paid to savers who supply credit. (3); measures the yearly cost of borrowing as a percentage of the amount loaned. (18)

intermediaries buy in order to sell again or simply bring together a buyer and a seller. (15)

internal labor market works by promoting or transferring workers it already employs. (17)

internalization of an externality involves placing private price tags on external costs (or benefits) so that private and social costs (or benefits) coincide. (20)

isocost line shows all the combinations of labor and capital that have the same total costs. (9A)

isoquant shows the various combinations of two inputs (such as labor and capital) that produce the same quantity of output. (9A)

labor is the combination of physical and mental talents that human beings contribute to production. (2)

labor market is an arrangement that brings together buyers and sellers of labor services to determine pay and working conditions. (17)

labor union is a collective organization of workers and employees whose objective is to improve conditions of pay and work. (17)

land is a catchall term that covers all of nature's bounty—minerals, forests, land, and water resources. (2)

law of comparative advantage is the principle that people should engage in those activities for which their advantages over others are the largest or their disadvantages are the smallest. (3); states that people or countries specialize in those activities in which they have the greatest advantage or the least disadvantage compared with other people or countries. (35)

law of demand states that there is a negative (or inverse) relationship between the price of a good or service and the quantity demanded, if other factors are constant. (4)

law of diminishing marginal rate of substitution states that as more of one good *(A)* is consumed, the amount of another good *(B)* that the consumer is willing to sacrifice for one more unit of good *A* declines. (7A)

law of diminishing marginal utility states that as more of a good or service is consumed during any given time period, its marginal utility eventually declines, if the consumption of everything else is held constant. (7)

law of diminishing returns states that when the amount of one input is increased in equal increments, holding all other inputs constant, the result is ever-smaller increases in output. (2)

law of increasing costs states that as more of a particular commodity is produced, its opportunity cost per unit increases. (2)

least-cost rule is that the least-cost combination of two factors can be found at the point where a given isoquant is tangent to the lowest isocost line. In other words, the least-cost combination of two factors can be found where

$$\frac{P_L}{\text{MPP}_L} = \frac{P_C}{\text{MPP}_C}$$

leisure is time spent in any activity other than work in the labor force or work in the home. (17)

loanable funds comprise the lending from all households, governments, and businesses, or the bank credit made available to borrowers in credit markets. (18)

logrolling is the trading of votes to secure a favorable outcome on decisions of more intense interest to that voter. (22)

long run is a period of time long enough for new firms to enter the market, for old firms to disappear, and for existing plants to be expanded. In the long run, firms have more flexibility in adjusting to price changes. (6); is a period of time long enough to vary all inputs. (9)

long-run average cost (LRAC) consists of the minimum average cost for each level of output when all factor inputs are variable (and when factor prices and the state of technology are fixed). (9)

Lorenz curve shows the percentages of total income earned by households at successive income levels. The cumulative percentage of households (ranked from lowest to highest incomes) is plotted on the horizontal axis, and the cumulative share of income earned by each cumulative percentage of households is plotted on the vertical axis. (19)

luxuries are those products that have an income elasticity of demand greater than 1. (6)

macroeconomics is the study of the economy as a whole, rather than individual markets, consumers, and producers. It concerns the *general* price level (rather than individual prices), the national employment rate, government spending, government deficits, trade deficits, interest rates, and the nation's money supply. (2)

majority rule is a system of voting in which a government decision is approved if more than 50 percent of the voters approve. (22)

managerial coordination is the disposition of the firm's resources according to the directives of the firm's manager(s). (8)

marginal analysis examines the costs and benefits of making small changes from the current state of affairs. (5)

marginal cost (MC) is the change in total cost (or equivalently in variable cost) divided by the increase in output or, alternatively, the increase in costs per unit of increase in output.

$$\text{MC} = \frac{\Delta \text{TC}}{\Delta Q} = \frac{\Delta \text{VC}}{\Delta Q}$$

marginal physical product (MPP) of a factor of production is the change in output divided by the change in the quantity of the input, if all other inputs are constant. (9)

marginal productivity theory of income distribution states that the functional distribution of income among land, labor, and capital is determined by the relative marginal revenue products of the different factors of production. The price of each factor will equal the marginal revenue product of that factor. (16)

marginal rate of substitution (MRS) is how much of one good a person is just willing to give up to acquire one unit of another good. (7A)

marginal revenue (MR) is the additional revenue raised per unit increase in quantity sold; that is, MR = ΔTR/ΔQ, where TR is total revenue. (11); is the increase in total revenue (TR) that results from each 1-unit increase in the amount of output:

$$\text{MR} = \frac{\Delta \text{TR}}{\Delta Q}$$

marginal revenue product (MRP) of any factor of production is the extra revenue generated per unit increase in the amount of the factor. (16)

marginal tax rate is the increase in tax payments divided by the increase in income. The marginal tax rate shows how much extra taxes must be paid per dollar of extra earnings. (21)

marginal utility (MU) of any good or service is the increase in utility that a consumer experiences when its consumption of that good or service (and that good or service alone) is increased by 1 unit. In general,

$$\text{MU} = \frac{\Delta \text{TU}}{\Delta Q}$$

where TU is total utility and Q is the quantity of the good. (7)

marginal utility per dollar for any good or service is the ratio of its marginal utility to its price (MU/P). (7)

market is an established arrangement that brings buyers and sellers together to exchange particular goods or services. (2, 4)

market demand curve is the demand of all buyers in the market for a particular product. (4); shows the total quantities demanded by all consumers in the market at each price. It is the horizontal summation of all individual demand curves in that market. (7)

market failure occurs when the price system fails to yield the socially optimal quantity of a good. (20)

median voter on a public expenditure program wants more expenditure than half the remaining voters and less expenditure than the other half. (22)

microeconomics studies the economic decision making of firms and individuals in a market setting; it is the study of individual decision making and its impact on resource allocation. (2)

midpoint elasticity formula for determining the elasticity of demand (E_d) for a given segment of the demand curve is

$$E_d = \frac{\text{Percent change in quantity demanded}}{\text{Percent change in price}}$$

$$= \frac{\text{Change in quantity demanded}}{\text{Average of two quantities}}$$

$$\div \frac{\text{Change in price}}{\text{Average of two prices}}$$

minimum efficient scale (MES) is the lowest level of output at which average costs are minimized. (9)

money is anything that is widely accepted in exchange for goods and services. (3)

money price is a price expressed in monetary units (such as dollars, francs, etc.). (3)

monopolistic competition has four essential characteristics: (1) the number of sellers is large enough to enable each seller to act independently of the others; (2) the product is differentiated from seller to seller; (3) there is free entry into and exit from the industry; (4) sellers are price makers. (11)

monopoly rent-seeking behavior is the use of scarce resources on lobbying and influence—buying to acquire monopoly rights from government. (12)

moral-hazard problem exists when one of the parties to a contract has an incentive to alter his or her behavior after the contract is made at the expense of the second party. It arises because it is too costly for the second party to obtain information about the first party's postcontractual behavior. (15)

multinational corporation engages in foreign markets through its own affiliates located abroad, and pursues business strategies that transcend national boundaries. (8)

mutual interdependence exists when a firm recognizes that its decisions are likely to invite reactions by rivals. (13)

Nash equilibrium of a game is the point at which each player is doing the best he or she can given what the other players are doing. (13)

natural law states that individuals should be rewarded according to their contribution to output. (19)

natural monopoly prevails when industry output is cheaper to produce with one firm than two or more firms. (11)

natural selection theory states that if business firms do not maximize profits, they will be unable to compete with other firms and will be driven out of the market or taken over by outsiders. (8)

necessities are those products that have an income elasticity of demand less than 1. (6)

negative (inverse) relationship exists between two variables if an increase in the value of one variable is associated with a *reduction* in the value of the other variable. (1A)

neutral tax cannot be altered by a change in private production, consumption, or investment decisions. (21)

nominal interest rate is the cost of borrowing expressed in terms of current dollars unadjusted for inflation. (18)

nonexclusion characterizes a good if extreme costs eliminate the possibility (or practicality) of excluding some people from using it. (21)

nonprice competition is the attempt to attract customers through improvements in product quality or service, thereby shifting the firm's demand curve to the right. (11)

nonrival consumption characterizes a good if its consumption by one person does not reduce its consumption by others. (21)

normal good is one for which demand increases when income increases, holding all prices constant. (4)

normal profit is the return that the time and capital of an entrepreneur would earn in the best alternative employment. It also is the return that is earned when total revenues equal total opportunity costs. (10); is the profit required to keep resources in that particular business. Normal profits are earned when revenues equal opportunity costs. (18)

normative economics is the study of what ought to be in the economy; it is value-based and cannot be tested by the scientific method. (1)

oligopoly is an industry (1) that is dominated by a few firms, (2) whose individual firms must consider the policies of their rivals in making their decisions, and (3) whose firms are price makers. (13)

opportunity cost of a particular action is the loss of the next-best alternative. (2, 9)

optimal level of abatement occurs when the marginal social cost of an extra unit of abatement equals its marginal social benefit. (20)

optimal-search rule states that people will continue to acquire economic information as long as the marginal benefits of gathering information exceed the marginal costs. (15)

paradox of voting is that majority rule can yield inconsistent social choices. Even if each voter is perfectly rational, the majority of voters can choose *a* over *b*, *b* over *c*, and then choose *c* over *a*. (22)

partnership is owned by two or more people called partners, who make all the business decisions, share the profits, and bear the financial responsibility for any losses. (8)

patent is an exclusive right granted to an inventor to make, use, or sell an invention for a term of 20 years in the United States. (12)

perfect competition prevails in an industry when each individual seller faces so much competition from other sellers that the market price is taken as given. (10)

perfectly elastic demand ($E_d = \infty$) is illustrated by a horizontal demand curve; quantity demanded is most responsive to price. (6)

perfectly elastic supply ($E_s = \infty$) is illustrated by a horizontal supply curve; quantity supplied is most responsive to price. (6)

perfectly inelastic demand ($E_d = 0$) is illustrated by a vertical demand curve; quantity demanded is least responsive to price. (6)

perfectly inelastic supply ($E_s = 0$) is illustrated by a vertical supply curve; quantity supplied is least responsive to price. (6)

personal distribution of income is the distribution of income among households, or how much income one family earns from the factors of production it owns relative to other families. (16)

positive (direct) relationship exists between two variables if an increase in the value of one variable is associated with an *increase* in the value of the other variable. (1A)

positive economics is the study of how the economy works; it explains the economy in measurable terms. (1)

preferred stock does not give voting privileges, but corporations must pay dividends on preferred stock before paying those on common stock. (8)

present value (PV) is the most anyone would pay today to receive the money in the future. (8)

price discrimination exists when the same product or service is sold at different prices to different buyers. (11)

price/earnings (P/E) ratio is the price of a share of stock divided by the earnings per share. (8)

price elasticity of demand (E_d) is the percentage change in the quantity demanded divided by the percentage change in price. (6)

price elasticity of supply (E_s) is the percentage change in the quantity supplied divided by the percentage change in price. (6)

price maker is a firm with some degree of control over the price of the good or service it sells. (11)

price system coordinates economic decisions by allowing resource owners to trade freely, buying and selling at whatever relative prices emerge in the marketplace. (3)

price taker is a firm that considers the market price as something over which it has no control. (10)

principal is a party that has controlling authority and engages an agent to act subject to the principal's control and instruction. (8)

principle of substitution states that practically no good is irreplaceable. Users are able to substitute one product for another when relative prices change. (3)

principle of unintended consequences holds that economic policies may have ultimate or actual effects that differ from the intended or apparent effects. (5)

prisoner's dilemma is a game with two players in which both players benefit from cooperating, but in which each player has an incentive to cheat on the agreement. (5, 13)

privatization is the conversion of publicly owned assets—such as land, buildings, companies—to private ownership. (14, 38)

producers' surplus represents the amount that producers receive in excess of the minimum value the producers would have been willing to accept. (10)

production function summarizes the relationship among labor, capital, and land inputs and the maximum output these inputs can produce for a given state of knowledge. (9)

production possibilities frontier (PPF) shows the combinations of goods that can be produced when the factors of production are used to their full potential. (2)

profit maximization is the search by firms for the product quality, output, and price that give the firm the highest possible profits. (8)

profit-maximization rule states that a firm will maximize profits by producing that level of output at which marginal revenue (MR) equals marginal cost (MC). (10)

progressive tax is one where each the percentage of income paid as taxes increases as income increases. (21)

property rights are the rights of an owner to buy, sell, or use and exchange property (that is goods, services, and assets). (2); specify who owns a resource and who has the right to use it. (20)

proportional tax is one where each taxpayer pays the same percentage of income as taxes. (21)

public good is a good or service whose use by one person does not reduce its use to others and whose use by nonpayers cannot be prevented. (21)

pure economic rent is the price paid to a productive factor that is completely inelastic in supply. Land is the classic example of such a factor. (18)

pure monopoly exists when (1) there is one seller in the market for some good or service that has no close substitutes; (2) barriers to entry protect the seller from competition. (11)

quantity demanded is the amount of a good or service consumers are prepared to buy at a given price (during a specified time period), if other factors are held constant. (4)

quantity supplied of a good or service is the amount offered for sale at a given price, holding other factors constant. (4)

quasi rent is a payment in excess of the short-run opportunity cost necessary to induce the owners of the resources to offer their resources for sale or rent in the short run. (18)

rate of return of a capital good is that rate for which the present value of the stream of marginal revenue products for each year of the good's life is equal to the cost of the capital good. (18)

rational ignorance is a decision not to acquire information because the marginal cost exceeds the marginal benefit of gathering the information. (22)

real interest rate equals the nominal interest rate minus the anticipated rate of inflation. (18)

recycling reintroduces used exhaustible resources (such as iron, metals, and petrochemicals) into the system, providing an alternative to current production. (20)

regressive tax is one where the percentage of income paid as taxes decreases as income increases. (21)

regulation is government control of firms, exercised by regulatory agencies through rules and regulations concerning prices and service. (14)

regulatory approach is when the government requires polluting agents to limit emissions to a prescribed level. (20)

relative poverty standard defines the poor in terms of their income relative to others. (19)

relative price is a price expressed in terms of other goods. (3)

reservation price is the highest price at which the consumer will buy a good. Although the consumer will buy any good with a price lower than the reservation price, he or she will continue to search for a lower price only if the lowest price found exceeds the reservation price. (15)

resources See *factors of production.*

risk seekers are more willing to incur risks than **risk avoiders,** who are reluctant to take on risks. (19)

rival consumption characterizes a good if its consumption by one person lowers its consumption by others. (21)

rule of reason stated that monopolies were in violation of the Sherman Act if they used unfair or illegal business practices. Being a monopoly in and of itself was not a violation of the Sherman Act. (14)

scarce good is a good for which the amount available is less than the amount people would want if it were given away free of charge. (2)

scatter diagram consists of a number of separate points, each plotting the value of one variable against a value of another variable for a specific time interval. (1A)

scientific method is the process of formulating theories, collecting data, testing theories, and revising theories. (1)

screening is the requirement that potential employees possess certain characteristics, such as a high school or college diploma, or a B+ or better average. (19)

short run is a period of time long enough for existing firms to produce more goods but not long enough for existing firms to expand their capacity or for new firms to enter the market. Thus output can be varied, but only within the limits of existing plant capacity. (6); is a period of time so short that the existing plant and equipment cannot be varied; such inputs are fixed in supply. (9)

shortage results if at the current price the quantity demanded exceeds the quantity supplied; the price is too low to equate the quantity demanded with the quantity supplied. (4)

shutdown rule states that if a firm's revenues at all output levels are less than variable costs, it can minimize its losses by shutting down. If there is at least one output level at which revenues exceed variable costs, the firm should not shut down. (10)

slope of a curve reflects the response of one variable to changes in another. (1A)

slope of a curvilinear relationship at a particular point is the slope of the tangent to the curve at that point. (1A)

slope of a straight line is the ratio of the rise (or fall) in *Y* over the run in *X*. (1A)

social benefits are private benefits plus external benefits. (12)

social costs equal private costs plus external costs. (12, 20)

sole proprietorship is owned by one individual who makes all the business decisions, receives the profits that the business earns, and bears the financial responsibility for losses. (8)

special interest groups are minority groups with intense, narrowly defined preferences about specific government policies. (22)

specialization is the tendency of participants in the economy (people, businesses, and countries) to focus their activity on tasks to which they are particularly suited. (3)

speculators are those who buy or sell in the hope of profiting from market fluctuations. (15)

spot (cash) market is a market where agreements between buyers and sellers are made now for payment and delivery of the product now. (15)

stock exchange is a market in which shares of stock of corporations are bought and sold and in which the prices of shares of stock are determined. (8)

strike occurs when all unionized employees cease to work until management agrees to specific union demands. (17)

substitutes are two goods related such that the demand for one rises when the price of the other rises (or if the demand for one falls when the price of the other falls). (4)

supply of a good or service is the amount that firms are prepared to sell under specified circumstances. (4)

surplus results if at the current price the quantity supplied exceeds the quantity demanded: The price is too high to equate the quantity demanded with quantity supplied. (4)

tangent is a straight line that touches the curve at only one point. (1A)

taxable income is the income that remains after all deductions and exemptions are subtracted. Taxes are levied on taxable income. (21)

terms of trade are the rate at which two products can be exchanged for each other between countries. (35)

theory is a simplified and coherent explanation of the relationship among certain facts. (1)

total costs (TC) are variable costs plus fixed costs:

$$TC = VC + FC$$

total revenue (TR) of sellers in a market is the price of the commodity times the quantity sold:

$$TR = P \times Q$$

total revenue test uses the following criteria to determine elasticity:

1. If price and total revenue move in different directions, $E_d > 1$ (demand is elastic).
2. If price and total revenue move in the same direction, $E_d < 1$ (demand is inelastic).
3. If total revenue does not change when price changes, $E_d = 1$ (demand is unitary elastic). (6)

transaction costs are the costs associated with bringing buyers and sellers together. (15)

transfer payments transfer income from one individual or organization to another. (21)

trust is a combination of firms that sets common prices, agrees to restrict output, and punishes member firms who fail to live up to the agreement. (14)

unanimity is when all voters agree on or consent to a particular government action. (22)

utilitarian theory argues for an equal distribution of income by saying that equality maximizes welfare. (19)

utility is a numerical ranking of a consumer's preferences among different commodity bundles. (7)

variable costs (VC) are those costs that do vary with output. (9)

vertical equity exists when those with a greater ability to pay bear a heavier tax burden. (21)

vertical merger is a merger of two firms that are part of the same materials, production, or distribution network (such as a personal computer manufacturer and a retail computer distributor). (14)

wage/employment trade-off means that higher wages reduce the number of jobs; lower unemployment requires sacrificing higher wages. (17)

welfare state provides substantial benefits to the less fortunate—unemployment insurance, poverty assistance, old-age pensions—to protect them from further economic misfortune. (1)

Name Index

Subject Index